Financing Micro Health Insurance

Theory, Methods and Evidence

World Scientific Series in Health Investment and Financing

ISSN: 2591-7315

Series Editor: Alexander S. Preker *(Columbia University, USA and Health Investment & Financing Corp, USA)*

Most western developed countries offer universal access to healthcare through mechanisms that provide financial protection against its high cost, either through insurance or government subsidy programs.

In most middle- and low-income countries, financing is often at the center of reforms in the healthcare sector. Success or failure of these reforms can have major impact on the political survival of governments that get involved, and major implications for the dynamics of the healthcare industry and overall economy.

With this series, World Scientific will contribute knowledge about a policy area which is still poorly-understood. The series merges policy and practice, exploring the economic underpinnings of real trends in health investment and financing.

The series will appeal and be accessible to investors, the health insurance industry, healthcare actuaries, business schools with healthcare tracts, healthcare management programs, researchers, graduate students, policy makers and practitioners working in the health sector worldwide.

Vol. 2 *Financing Micro Health Insurance: Theory, Methods and Evidence*
by David M. Dror

Vol. 1 *Financing Universal Access to Healthcare: A Comparative Review of Landmark Legislative Health Reforms in the OECD*
by Alexander S. Preker

Forthcoming

Financing Universal Access to Healthcare: A Comparative Review of Incremental Health Insurance Reforms in the OECD
Alexander S. Preker

Role of Private Financing in the Education of Health Workers: Gaining the Competitive Edge
Alexander S. Preker, Hortenzia Beciu and Eric Keuffel

Capital Finance in the Health Industry: A User Manual for Investors and Companies
Alexander S. Preker and Les Funtleyder

Handbook on Health System Financing and Organization
Dov Chernichovsky

World Scientific Series in Health Investment and Financing – Vol. 2

Financing Micro Health Insurance

Theory, Methods and Evidence

David Mark Dror
Micro Insurance Academy (New Delhi), India

World Scientific
NEW JERSEY • LONDON • SINGAPORE • BEIJING • SHANGHAI • HONG KONG • TAIPEI • CHENNAI • TOKYO

Published by

World Scientific Publishing Co. Pte. Ltd.

5 Toh Tuck Link, Singapore 596224

USA office: 27 Warren Street, Suite 401-402, Hackensack, NJ 07601

UK office: 57 Shelton Street, Covent Garden, London WC2H 9HE

Library of Congress Cataloging-in-Publication Data
Names: Dror, David M., author.
Title: Financing micro health insurance : theory, methods and evidence / by
David Mark Dror (Micro Insurance Academy, New Delhi, India).
Other titles: World Scientific series in health investment and financing ; v. 2.
Description: New Jersey : World Scientific, 2018. | Series: World Scientific series in
health investment and financing ; volume 2 | Includes bibliographical references and index.
Identifiers: LCCN 2018012719 | ISBN 9789813238473 (hc : alk. paper)
Subjects: | MESH: Insurance, Health--economics | Insurance, Health--organization &
administration | Poverty | Rural Population | Developing Countries
Classification: LCC HG9383 | NLM W 250.1 | DDC 368.38/2--dc23
LC record available at https://lccn.loc.gov/2018012719

British Library Cataloguing-in-Publication Data
A catalogue record for this book is available from the British Library.

For any available supplementary material, please visit
https://www.worldscientific.com/worldscibooks/10.1142/10944#t=suppl

Desk Editors: Herbert Moses/Shreya Gopi

Typeset by Stallion Press
Email: enquiries@stallionpress.com

About the Author

Dr. David M. Dror is an acclaimed international expert in microinsurance with over 35 years' experience in social protection and health financing. He served as a Senior Social Security Specialist for the International Labour Organization (UN-ILO) from 1982 to 2003, advising on social and health insurance systems worldwide. Dr. Dror has been Hon. Professor of health insurance at Erasmus University Rotterdam (2004–2014). He has been working in India since 2005 and has professional experience in numerous countries across Asia and Africa, including Bangladesh, Nepal, Philippines, Rwanda, South Africa, and Vietnam. In 2007, he established the *Micro Insurance Academy* (MIA) in New Delhi. Under his direction, MIA has conducted research into key pain points of catalyzing demand for microinsurance, providing technical assistance toward implementation of microinsurance projects in the informal economy in India (multiple states), Nepal, Tanzania, and Vietnam, covering several risk categories — health, crop, livestock, and climate change. MIA also provides insurance education, as well as consultancy services in microinsurance. Prof. Dror was named "Personality of the Year" in 2009 by the Asia Insurance Industry for "groundbreaking research and study which has helped boost understanding of how the world's poorest communities can benefit from microinsurance". In 2011 and in 2014, he received the "Global Citizen Lifetime Achievement 'Karmaveer Puraskaar' Award" for Social

Justice and Citizen Action, from the Indian Confederation of NGOs. Prof. Dror holds a Ph.D. (Summa cum Laude) from Université Claude Bernard Lyon 1, France, and DBA (Magna cum Laude) in International Health Services. He published over 90 peer-reviewed publications. His book *Financing Micro Health Insurance: Theory, Methods, and Evidence* is part of the World Scientific Publications' series on *Financing and Investing in Health*.

About the Contributors

John Armstrong is an actuary and health economist with over 20 years of experience working in the field of health care worldwide. He is currently Global Chief Actuary/Head of Actuarial for Allianz Worldwide Partners, Health, and Life, the dedicated global health insurance business of Allianz SE. His previous roles have included acting as Chief Underwriting Officer and Chief Actuary for two large well-known health insurers. His work has concentrated on health financing including national health insurance and micro-health insurance. He has advised governments, in over 20 countries in diverse parts of the world, and worked on a range of health reform topics with international organizations including the World Bank, European Commission, and Inter-American Development Bank. He also advised a number of leading non-governmental and philanthropic organizations on micro-health insurance. He has continuously, and successively, combined and accommodated applied actuarial and health economics work with academic and research interests in related areas. He currently contributes as a researcher on health policy matters at the Institute of Health Policy and Management at Erasmus University Rotterdam, the Netherlands, and serves as an associate lecturer in health economics at the Institute of Public Administration in Ireland.

Rosebelle May Azcuna holds an M.Sc. degree in Epidemiology from the University of the Philippines Manila. She has worked in the area of health information and statistics for over 10 years. In collaboration with WHO and ADB, she helped develop regional monitoring tools for universal health coverage and the broader health-related sustainable development goals and is now assisting countries adopt these tools. She also works in the area of service availability and readiness assessment of health facilities, and on malaria elimination through health systems strengthening. Prior to this work, Ms. Azcuna was a WHO staff at the Regional Office for the Western Pacific working on health statistics, MDG monitoring, and health information systems strengthening.

Arjun Singh Bedi holds a Ph.D. and is Professor of Development Economics at the International Institute of Social Studies (ISS) of Erasmus University Rotterdam, The Netherlands. Prior to joining ISS in 1999, he held positions at the University of Bonn (1998–1999) and Columbia University (1996–1998). In 2013–2014, he was visiting a professor at Georgetown University's campus in Doha. His research focuses on labor and human resource economics in developing countries. His work has been published in several international economics and development studies journals.

Erika Binnendijk holds a Ph.D. and has a Master's degree in Health Economics, Policy, and Law and a Ph.D. (thesis on the design of community-based health insurance among rural poor in India). Dr. Binnendijk has published papers in peer-reviewed journals such as *Social Science and Medicine* and *BMC Health Services Research.* She has presented research results at several conferences of the International Health Economics Association (iHEA). Currently, she is working as a policy advisor for a consortium of nursing homes in The Netherlands.

Arpita Chakraborty has an M.Phil. in Economics from Jawaharlal Nehru University, New Delhi, and is a Ph.D. candidate at the same university. She has some 13 years' experience in development-sector research using both quantitative and qualitative methods. Her core area of research is public health (especially health finance), nutrition, child health, fertility decisions and health promotion. Additionally, Arpita has also worked in the areas of elementary education, public finance, and poverty. Presently she is working as a Consultant with the National Institute of Public Finance and Policies. She has had professional involvement with independent think tanks (Public Health Foundation of India, Micro Insurance Academy, and Collaborative Research and Development), multilateral donor agencies (The World Bank), development consultancy agencies (ICRA Management Consultancy Services Limited), and academic bodies (Indian Statistical Institute).

Marion Danis is a physician and health policy expert. She serves as Head of the Section on Ethics and Health Policy in the Department of Bioethics at the Clinical Center of the National Institutes of Health. She also serves as Chief of the Ethics Consultation Service at the Clinical Center. She has chaired the International Society on Priorities in Health Care. She has studied patients' treatment preferences at the end of life and the effectiveness of advance directives in promoting their preferences. She has studied strategies for fair rationing of limited health care resources by the involvement of the public and strategies to address the social determinants of health to reduce health disparities. She designed the CHAT exercise with Susan Dorr Goold, the decision tool that was used in several studies in collaboration with Professor Dror. She has been the lead editor of several books published by Oxford University Press including *Ethical Dimensions of Health Policy* and *Fair Resource Allocation* and *Rationing at the Bedside*.

Lucy A. Firth holds a Ph.D. and is an Economist with an international career in health, innovation, ICT, and strategic management to drive and exploit innovation, particularly in service delivery. Having led projects for the UN, various governments, corporations, NGOs, and universities globally, Dr. Firth's passion remains the promotion of innovation to improve outcomes for individuals, communities, and organizations. In semi-retirement, Dr. Firth is focusing on challenging projects that promote the broader good.

Meenakshi Gautham holds a Ph.D. in public health and policy from the London School of Hygiene and Tropical Medicine. Meenakshi is a health system and policy researcher with broad and crosscutting research interests in the private health sector, informal health care providers, rural health services, maternal and child health, equity and quality of health care, mobile health applications for low-resource settings, and a growing interest in antimicrobial resistance. She was a post-doctoral fellow with the Institute of Health Policy and Management, Erasmus University Rotterdam, Netherlands, and the Micro Insurance Academy in New Delhi, working on health services research to support the development of micro-health insurance schemes in low-income communities. She has been a Research Fellow with the London School of Hygiene and Tropical Medicine and India Country Coordinator of the IDEAS project, a Gates Foundation-funded measurement, learning, and evaluation project in maternal, newborn and child health. She is also the Principal Investigator of a study on antibiotic use by informal private health care providers in the state of West Bengal in India. She has also worked with various other national and international health organizations.

Eric Gerelle holds a Ph.D. and is a Physicist and Mathematician by training. He is an international consultant on the management and application of information technology to sustainable development. During his career in academia and the private sector, he worked as a designer, developer, and manager of robotics, data acquisition, database and workflow management systems. He has organized international conferences and workshops on knowledge management, project financing, and sustainable development. His published works include a book on Computer Integrated Manufacturing and papers in the areas of robotics, industrial automation, database integration, knowledge management, and microinsurance. He is currently developing mathematical models of sustainable development and applying them to decision support and scenario planning in health, insurance, technology, and education.

Christina (May) Gollan holds an M.A. degree in Latin American Studies from the University of Cologne, Germany. She has extensive experience in the evaluation of international cooperation projects and programs in the fields of civil society development, gender, energy, rural development, health care and health care financing, microfinance and cooperative organizations in Latin America, Asia, and Africa. Currently, she is a Research Associate at the Center for Evaluation (Germany). Before that, she worked at the Department for Cooperative Studies (University of Cologne) with a focus on the impact of community-based micro-health insurance in India.

François-Xavier Hay is a Certified Actuary and Chartered Enterprise Risk Analyst (ERM). He is currently Chief Risk Officer of a French life insurance company. He started his career in reinsurance and motor insurance sectors, then worked as a microfinance program manager launching and developing microfinance institutions in India, since 2000. In 2002, he founded UpLift Mutuals, a mutual microinsurance model providing health, accident and death cover to members of several MFIs. François-Xavier acted as a consultant on microinsurance to various state health ministries in India, as well as to various public/private international organizations in Asia. He keeps supervising actuarial and technical support to various microinsurance and micropension projects.

Shahed Hossain holds MBBS, M.Sc, and Ph.D. degrees. He is a physician trained in public health with 30 years of experience in working with the health systems in Bangladesh, with WHO Bangladesh and as a research scientist with the International Centre for Diarrheal Disease Research, Bangladesh. He has conducted community-based interventions, monitoring, and evaluation of interventions, operational, implementation, and health systems research. Dr. Hossain is also engaged in the teaching of implementation science at the James P. Grant School of Public Health, BRAC University, Dhaka (Bangladesh). He is trained in systematic review processes with Cochrane "Effective Practice and organization of Care" (EPOC) group and participated in conducting systematic reviews in the issues of public health importance. He has also organized capacity building workshops on systematic review processes in Bangladesh, India, Nepal, and Sri Lanka.

Denny John holds an MPH from the University of Auckland and an MBA in Health Care Management from Indian Institute of Health Management Research, Jaipur. Denny is a public health specialist with experience across various domains: managing hospitals and community programs, implementation research, economic evaluations, systematic reviews and epidemiological forecasting studies. He is currently engaged as Evidence Synthesis Specialist, Campbell Collaboration at its New Delhi office. He is also an Adjunct Scientist with the National Institute of Medical Statistics, Indian Council of Medical Research, providing technical and research support in the field of evidence synthesis, economic evaluation, and health technology assessment. Denny is a Fellow of the Royal Society of Public Health and Royal Society of Tropical Medicine and Health in the UK. At the Micro Insurance Academy (MIA), Denny worked as Deputy Director, Implementation and was responsible for implementation activities across 14 states in India and 2 districts in Nepal.

Shrikant B. Khadilkar holds a degree in Ayurveda (B.A.M.S.) from Nagpur University, with over 28 years of experience in the research & community development sector (focusing on health). Currently, he is based in Pune as Sr. Program Director, anchoring the section of Reproductive, Maternal, Newborn and Child Health (RMNCH) at International Center of Equity & Inclusion for Transformation (IC EQUI-T) of the All India Institute of Local Self-Government. His experience in the health sector has a strong base of community-based initiatives. In the past, he headed Community Health Research Center of BAIF and set up a community insurance scheme. He also served the society as an ayurvedic physician for some time.

Tracey Lynn Pérez Koehlmoos holds Ph.D. and MHA degrees and is a health system and policy researcher who has spent more than 20 years on the frontline in the war against poverty and disease — generating, synthesizing, and translating knowledge into action in global communities. She is presently serving as Associate Professor of Preventive Medicine & Biostatistics and Director of the Health Services Administration Division at the Uniformed Services University of the Health Sciences, USA. Previously she served as Special Assistant to the Assistant Commandant of the US Marine Corps, and prior to that as Director of the Health Systems and Family Planning Programme at ICDDR, B in Dhaka, Bangladesh.

Ruth Koren obtained her Ph.D. from the Hebrew University of Jerusalem and completed her post-doctoral studies at Cornell University. She worked for many years as the Director of a research laboratory in the Felsenstein Medical Research Center, Tel Aviv University at Beilinson Hospital, Israel. Ruth also served as Professor of medical sciences at the Tel Aviv Sackler School of Medicine. She has extensive research experience in Community-based Health Insurance schemes in LMICs and has co-authored several research papers on microinsurance.

Fely Marilyn E. Lorenzo is a policy analyst and researcher with a DrPH degree specializing in Health Policy and Management from UC Berkeley. She was a Professor at the University of the Philippines, Manila, College of Public Health, where she was the founding chair of the MA Health Policy Studies (MAHPS) program committee and taught MAHPS, MHA and MPH students there for 28 years. Dr. Lorenzo does extensive policy and health services research. Her research policy research areas cover the broad spectrum of health systems strengthening including health financing and human resources for health. She was also founding Director of the Institute of Health Policy and Development Studies of the National Institutes of Health and directed the research and policy development work there from 1999–2006. She is presently the chair of the Technical Committee on Nursing Education at the Commission on Higher Education (CHED) and Project Director of the HRH2030Philippines, a USAID funded project.

Atanu Majumdar holds an M. Stat degree in Statistics from the Indian Statistical Institute (Kolkata) with over 30 years of experience in commercial and development sectors (particularly in the area of health). He is currently Director of the Micro Insurance Academy, New Delhi. His experience in the health sector includes a wide range of topics, from HIV/AIDS to reproductive and child health, improving health care delivery system and microplanning. Previously he has worked for EPOS Health Consultants (in the Basic Health Project, Govt. of West Bengal, India), UNICEF (as a Consultant) and renowned NGOs like Child In Need Institute and Bhoruka Public Welfare Trust.

Shirin Nosratnejad holds a Ph.D. in health economics from the Tehran University of Medical Sciences (Tehran, Iran) with over 9 years of experience in management and health economics. She is currently Director of the department of Health Services Management of Tabriz University of Medical Sciences, Assistant Professor, and Economics Consultant of Vice Chancellor of Health. She has contributed as a researcher at the Iranian Center of Excellence in Health Services Management, as well as at the Tabriz Health Services Management Research Center. Her research interests include economic evaluation and health care financing.

Pradeep K. Panda holds a Ph.D. and is a Health Economist and a Demographer by training. Dr. Panda is a Professor of Health Economics and Dean (Research) at IIHMR Delhi. He has worked in reputed national and international organizations in various capacities — Director of

Research and Implementation (Micro Insurance Academy), Health Economist (Population Council), and Associate Professor (Centre for Development Studies). He has acted as Principal Investigator/Project Director, published several research papers in peer-reviewed journals, co-edited a book, and guided thesis/dissertation of seven researchers. He was engaged as a research advisor/consultant to National Commission for Enterprises in the Unorganized Sector, UNDP, Centre for Studies in Ethics and Rights, and Population Council. He was a visiting research fellow at the International Institute of Social Studies, Erasmus University, The Netherlands and at International Centre for Research on Women, Washington DC. Dr. Panda is a Visiting Professor at the Institute for Human Development, and a Visiting Faculty at XIMB, Xavier University Bhubaneswar.

Ralf Radermacher is an Economist who has worked on various issues around microinsurance, health system strengthening, and social protection. He currently heads the Sector Initiative on social protection in Deutsche Gesellschaft für Internationale Zusammenarbeit (GIZ). Prior to this, he was the team leader of the GIZ Social Protection Programme in Malawi. At the Micro Insurance Academy, where he worked before GIZ, he served first as Director of Research & Training and then coordinated international work as Deputy Chairman.

Arash Rashidian has an M.D. degree from the Tehran University of Medical Sciences, a Ph.D. from the University of York, and completed a research fellowship at the London School of Hygiene and Tropical Medicine. Arash is the Director, Information, Evidence, and Research of the WHO regional office in Cairo. Prior to joining WHO, Dr. Rashidian worked as Professor of Health Policy and Management at the School of Public Health, Tehran University of Medical Sciences, and was its Vice Chancellor for Public Health and Primary Care. He has experience in conducting consultancies in Europe, Central Asia, Middle East, Africa and South-east Asia. His main interests are evidence-based health policy, health systems reform and financing, quality improvement and changing professionals' behavior. His expertise is in understanding health systems in high-income and low- and middle-income countries, and applying different quantitative, qualitative and review research methodologies to answer health policy and health services questions.

Jesus N. Sarol Jr. is an Epidemiologist and Biostatistician with a B.S. from the Philippines, an M.S. and a Ph.D. from the USA, and a post-doctoral degree from Germany. He has taught courses on epidemiology, biostatistics, research methods and health professions education at the University of the Philippines Manila for more than 25 years. He gained extensive research experience from involvement in various capacities as principal investigator, co-investigator, epidemiologist, biostatistician, data manager and computer programmer in several large-scale health surveys, epidemiologic and clinical studies and program evaluations in the Philippines. He provided consultancies to the Philippine Department of Health, Philippine Council for Health Research and Development, Philippine Business for Social Progress, World Health Organization and German Technical Cooperation, among others. His international work experience includes serving as Migration Health Studies Manager for the International Organization for Migration in Geneva, a Consultant for Health Information Systems in American Samoa, Professor in Health Professions Education in Cambodia and Research Scientist in Humboldt University Berlin. He is a recipient of research excellence awards from the Philippine National Academy of Science and Technology and the University of the Philippines System.

Petra Schout holds a Master's degree in Health Economics, Policy, and Law from Erasmus University Rotterdam. As a student researcher, she was engaged in the project 'Strengthening Micro Health Insurance for the Poor in India'. She was Director of long-term care at the Dutch Patient Federation. She is currently working as a policy advisor at the Dutch Nurses Association.

Arbind Singh is Executive Director, Nidan Microfinance, Patna, Bihar. He holds a Bachelor's and Master's degrees in Sociology from Delhi University. He heads Nidan and is also the National Coordinator of NASVI (the National Association of Street Vendors of India). He played a pioneering role in getting a Street Vendors Act in India which empowers millions of street vendors against eviction and harassment. Arbind is also the Secretary of StreetNet International (a Durban-based Global Federation of Street Vendors). An activist and a social entrepreneur, he was elected as Ashoka and Eisenhower Fellow in 2007. He was awarded the Social Entrepreneur of the Year 2008 by the Schwab

Foundation at World Economic Forum. He was also awarded at the first innovation forum set up by the Govt of Bihar in 2007. In 2012, Skoll Foundation awarded him with Skoll Award for Social Entrepreneurship. He has won many other recognitions. He is on the board of many government and non-government committees at national and state level, lobbying for new laws, policies, and programs, and by securing for informal workers across India access to markets, financial services, and technology.

Elmer S. Soriano holds an M.D. from the Philippines and an M.P.A. from the Harvard Kennedy School of Government. Elmer has over 20 years' experience in health systems development. He started as a manager of a cooperative health microinsurance scheme and then scaled up the model through social franchising in the Philippines. He has done consulting and action-research projects in health care financing, policy, governance, and knowledge management and designed health leadership courses for mayors and governors. He has held teaching positions at the Asian Institute of Management and the Ateneo University and currently heads the Social Impact Bond Lab and the City Futures Lab at the Civika Asian Development Academy.

David M. Steinberg holds a Ph.D. and is a Professor of Statistics in the Department of Statistics and Operations Research at Tel Aviv University. His field of research specialization is research design, including factorial experiments, Latin hypercubes, computer experiments, robust parameter design experiments, and seismic networks. He has collaborated with researchers in a variety of fields, such as medicine, biology, social science, and seismology. In 2013, he received the George Box Medal from the European Network for Business and Industrial Statistics (ENBIS). In 2017, he was awarded the Walter Shewhart Medal from the American Society for Quality.

Sukumar Vellakkal completed his Ph.D. in Economics at ISEC, Bangalore, on Health Insurance, followed by a Ph.D. internship at the University of Calgary Canada and a post-doctoral fellowship at the University of Oxford. He also holds an M.Sc. in Health Economics, Policy and Law from Erasmus University Rotterdam, the Netherlands, and M.A.

in Economics from Calicut University. Sukumar is an Assistant Professor of Economics at BITS Pilani Goa Campus. His research and teaching expertise include health insurance, health financing, chronic diseases, economic evaluation, and health econometrics. Prior to joining BITS Pilani, he worked as a faculty member at a number of organizations for nearly 10 years: Azim Premji University, Bangalore; Public Health Foundation of India (PHFI), New Delhi; Indian Council for Research on International Economic Relations (ICRIER), New Delhi; Government College Kasaragod.

Acknowledgments

This book gives voice to my work over many years in teamwork with mentors, students, and colleagues. This collaborative approach has enabled me to fashion an argument from many pieces that together are stronger and more compelling than any one of them standing alone.

I thank World Scientific Publishing and Alexander S. Preker, Editor-in-Chief of the World Scientific Series in Health Investment and Financing, for accepting my manuscript for publication. I am also grateful to the original publishers and journals of the articles in this volume for granting their permission to reproduce them here. I would also like to acknowledge my 30 co-authors whose industry, ingenuity and creativity influenced the formulation of insights from the evidence. Finally, I am grateful to Kathleen A. Lynch for the editorial assistance, to the team of the Micro Insurance Academy (New Delhi), and in particular to Jacquiline Roberts Singh, for the research assistance.

Contents

Chapter 1

Synthesis*

"If you think you are too small to be effective, you have never been in bed with a mosquito." (*Betty Reese*)

"In order to change, we must be sick and tired of being sick and tired." (*Anonymous*)

All people spend money on their health care. What triggers their decisions to spend, how much to spend, when to spend it, and how to obtain that money, can make all the difference.

Governments of most high-income industrial countries promote Universal Health Coverage (UHC)[1] in an attempt to limit individuals' out-of-pocket spending (OOPS). UHC is the "code name" for each country's particular blend of taxes, dedicated contributions, regulations obliging individuals to be insured, and other price and market controls, for ex-ante health care financing.[2] These measures are designed to propel and control the supply of health insurance (HI) and the supply of inputs for health care delivery (staff, perishables, medicines, buildings, equipment, hospitality, and other services). Most low- and middle-income countries (LMIC) generally follow the early models but with their more limited resources,

*For supplementary material containing comprehension questions for all chapters, please visit https://www.worldscientific.com/worldscibooks/10.1142/10944#t=suppl

[1] http://www.who.int/universal_health_coverage/un_resolution/en/

[2] WHO, http://www.who.int/universal_health_coverage/en/

smaller subsidies and limits on individual mandating in order to reach formally employed groups. These limits leave most of the population unprotected, especially rural dwellers and unsalaried self-employed workers whose activities outside the formal sector are subject to weaker governmental supervisory, regulatory, and organizational control (Schanz and Wang, 2014). Attempts to provide health care have been least effective in rural and informal settings where most of the world's poorest people live and work.

The shortage of public health care facilities, especially in rural areas, has prompted the rural poor to seek care from nearby private practitioners (most often non-degree allopathic practitioners), paying high — and increasing — health OOPS at the time and place of receiving care (Jayakrishnan *et al.*, 2016; Binnendijk *et al.*, 2012a). This is the default solution of people in the informal sector in LMICs (Gautham *et al.*, 2011). As most persons are uninsured and do not have sufficient current income or liquid savings to pay their health care costs in full, they borrow money (and/or sell assets) not just for inpatient care, but also for outpatient and maternity care. To already unaffordable health costs, this widespread practice adds a big surcharge (for interest on loans or lost value on suboptimal asset sales — "hardship financing") (Binnendijk *et al.*, 2012b). Individual attempts to reduce hardship financing can be uglier: postpone care, seek cheaper care from untrained practitioners, or forgo care altogether (Escobar *et al.*, 2010).

Collective attempts to offer people a structured local approach and "locally best available" safeguards to reduce members' solvency risks, liquidity pressures, and external uncertainties of politics, the global economy, and poor corporate governance include "Community-Based Health Insurance" (CBHI),[3] "Health Microinsurance" and "Micro Health Insurance" (MHI). Generically, we refer to these as MHI or simply as "micro insurance units" (MIUs).[4]

---

[3]In Asia, the word "scheme" is commonly used to describe what in the United States is commonly referred to as "plan". In this book, we prefer to use unit, or Micro Insurance Unit (MIU).

[4]In the book, we use the terms "Micro Health Insurance (MHI)", "Micro Insurance Unit (MIU)" and "Community Based Health Insurance (CBHI)" interchangeably to refer to a microinsurance model that is managed by the community members. The term "Health Insurance (HI)" may refer to a commercial insurance or microinsurance model depending on the context in which the author(s) refers to the term.

The economy is sometimes described as a "wealth pyramid", with a broad base of poor persons. The "base of the pyramid" (BOP) is the context of the poor, where neither demand for HI nor supply is ample. HI is barely known or understood, and not even the rare buyers of insurance can detect potential misrepresentation by their agents or defend themselves against unfair practices. Thus, market equilibrium cannot occur at BOP without some corrective intervention. Nor can the MIU model be confused with (Uber-like) "on-demand economy", which matches ample existing demand to ample supply for some well-known services.

This book deals with the voluntary uptake of HI in low-income settings in LMICs (where governments cannot apply a mandate to insure) and where local micro insurance units secure their income mainly or only from premiums (without subsidies). This paradigm differs fundamentally from the discussion of financing HI as a state-sponsored activity or variants sponsored by such intergovernmental agencies as the World Health Organization or the World Bank, and from the issues associated with purely commercial insurance or from provider-owned or employment-linked HI that serve other objectives.

What is Micro Health Insurance?

MHI is health insurance designed to fit the willingness to pay, needs and priorities of people in the informal sector who are excluded from other forms of HI. The entities offering it (microinsurance units, MIUs) are voluntary, with premiums suited to people with low incomes. Although health MIUs are not defined by their size, the scope of the risk covered, or the delivery channel, the MIUs must be designed to benefit the insured. For all practical intents and purposes, this definition implies a central role for the community in at least package design and possibly in its operation and governance (Dror, 2014). Three essential characteristics of this definition set MIUs apart from other health financing systems:

- Enrollment is voluntary.
- The regime is contributory without *a priori* reliance on external sources of income (such as subsidies).
- Evaluation of its results must extend to total welfare gains of its members and not be limited to financial results.

These characteristics invite a discussion of the theory of demand for voluntary and contributory HI in the informal sector of LMICs before examining another fundamental question of how to determine premiums suitable for people with low incomes.

Demand for MHI

Classical economic theories of voluntary demand for HI posit the assumption that humans are consistently rational and narrowly self-interested, usually pursuing their subjectively defined ends optimally (*homo economicus*, economic man). In light of HI's dismally low penetration rates in the informal sector, the first question to be answered is: If the benefits of HI are positively provable, how can theory explain the conditions that would induce the 3 billion uninsureds in LMICs' informal sector to seek voluntary HI? This question suggests two possible replies: first, that the benefits of HI are NOT positively provable, and second, that a new theory of demand for HI is needed because the conventional economic theories do not adequately explain behavioral practices in the informal sector and in the context of poverty and informality (Dror and Firth, 2014). We explore the second issue now and will discuss the first one later.

In the informal sector, people seek welfare gains through affiliation with family, friends, peers, and groups, rather than through isolated transactions with agents they do not know and with whom they have little transactional experience (Mani *et al.*, 2013). This common practice has been studied in behavioral economics literature (based on actual economic behavior, rules-in-use in the informal sector, and societal "cognitive" biases). Beyond the doubts on the validity of conventional assumptions related to the independence of individual choices in the informal sector, or the conventional assumption of perfect market conditions, alternative notions have been developed that point to collective, cooperative, and reciprocal behavior (also known as *homo reciprocans*, cooperating/reciprocating man) (Kahan, 2002; Dohmen *et al.*, 2009). Most assumptions of conventional economic theories of demand for HI related to expected utility, attitudes toward risk, and moral hazard are violated in the informal sector context and have not found full and satisfactory replies in other theoretical frameworks, notably the Prospect Theory (Kahneman and

Tversky, 1979) which also looks at individual choices. Therefore, an alternative theory of demand is proposed, based on relevant and workable assumptions of the role of groups in financial decisions in the informal sector. The postulated theory of demand covers not only purchase decisions but also the influence of local governance arrangements on enhancing trust in the system, which is a necessary but insufficient condition for the establishment of an HI market.

Since an HI market is unlikely to emerge without demand for HI (either true demand, based on voluntary decisions, or mandated purchasing), let's look briefly at some preconditions for the emergence of such voluntary demand. Two key issues underlie the manifestation of demand in the informal sector: First, people must understand and accept the rules governing the MHI. This would put to rest members' concerns about their inability to enforce the contract should the MIU refuse to respect its end of the deal. The presence of a "bottom-up governance structure" is a simple way of reassuring prospective members that they are dealing with trusted locals rather than with unknown parties controlling the local MIU and that the trusted persons are in positions to ensure that the agreement will be kept. The second key issue is that voluntary and contributory demand for HI in the informal sector makes sense when the community recognizes that purchasing HI enhances their welfare. In the informal sector, the understanding of welfare gains might not be limited only to the benefits specified in the package. For one thing, because people are well aware of the surcharge they incur due to "hardship financing" when they pay out of pocket, they expect a useful HI to reduce both their OOPS on health care and their hardship financing load. Moreover, high reliance on reciprocal arrangements makes people eager to participate in and conform to group decisions on enrollment. Furthermore, when families pool resources to manage family expenses out of the common fund, they may see the payout by the MHI to one member as ample return for the cost of enrolling several persons. The salient point is that catalyzing demand at the local, community level is the prerequisite to the establishment of an MIU and a likely indicator that a market for HI in the informal sector is emerging.

Panda *et al.* (2014) identified factors that drive enrollment in CBHI schemes launched in three rural locations in Uttar Pradesh and Bihar.

The analysis used two data sources: a baseline survey covering 1,294 households and 7,659 individuals for which valid data could be collected, and information on actual enrollments, premium payments and claims, extracted from the schemes' management information system. It was observed that a household's socioeconomic status such as education and occupational status did not substantially influence uptake. Rather, households with greater financial liabilities and households classified as scheduled caste/scheduled tribe found insurance more attractive and were more likely to enroll. Other households with access to formal insurance within their family network were less likely to enroll. However, access to the national hospital insurance scheme Rashtriya Swasthya Bima Yojana (RSBY) did not dampen CBHI uptake, suggesting that the potential for greater development of insurance markets and products beyond existing ones would respond to a need. Recent episodes of illness and self-assessed health status did not influence uptake. Another noteworthy insight was that insurance coverage was prioritized within households, with the household head, the spouse of the household head and both male and female children of the household head, more likely to be insured compared to other relatives.

A systematic review and meta-analysis of the literature on factors affecting CBHI uptake in LMICs stated that education, age, female household heads, and the socioeconomic status of households positively affect enrollment (Dror *et al.*, 2016b). Furthermore, when individuals understand how their CBHI functions they are more likely to enroll, and when people have a positive claims experience, they are more likely to renew. Other factors enhancing enrollment include higher prevalence of chronic conditions or the perception that health care is of good quality and available nearby. On the same note, the perception that services are distant or deficient leads to lower enrollments. On the supply side, the authors observed that trust in the scheme enables enrollment. Clarity about the legal or policy framework also influences enrollments. And the 18 qualitative studies included in that systematic review identified nine major factors as enablers for enrollment: knowledge and understanding of insurance principles and CBHI, quality of health care, trust, benefits package, CBHI scheme rules, cultural beliefs, affordability, distance to health facility, and legal and policy framework. Among deterrents to renewal reported were:

stringent rules of some CBHI schemes, inadequate legal and policy frameworks to support CBHI, and inappropriate benefits package. Decisions regarding renewal or dropout were influenced most by the factor of trust in the insurer, followed by the male head of household and household head's education.

Once the MHI framework is manifest, the members can discuss the desired benefits package. Why decisions to include certain benefits in the package have consequences on the premium payable is self-explanatory as is why the intensity of willingness to pay (WTP) can determine the scope of these benefits. The question is: *does price determine the package or does the package determine the price?* When HI is sold by commercial insurance that aims to generate a profit, the answer is clear: coverage determines price (and customers cannot review the prices). That is why clients paying subsidized premiums (under many mandated HI systems) have no say over the composition of their coverage, which may include several benefits that they would not choose that do not reflect any notion of solidarity with other insured persons. The subsidies are applied to adjust the price to levels people can pay, based on other parameters, for example, taxable (i.e., declared) income.

Not so in the context of MHI: here, as prospective members have experience with OOPS, they know the overall amount they pay for health care and local practitioners' prices. Moreover, they can also validate the results of data used to propose packages reflecting local priorities (based on the frequency and severity of health care events). With that information, people discuss and explore options for benefits package options and premiums presented to them. They also probe how the different options present "welfare for the insured" (when "insured" refers to many people, not just one person). Ultimately, price choice determines the composition of the package. Because WTP defines the MIU's estimated income and the financial boundaries of package design, a reliable estimate of WTP is essential before MHI can be launched.

Estimating Willingness to Pay

Whenever health financing specialists, policymakers, and HI providers contemplate charging for services, they need to know how much clients

Box 1: Demand for MHI

- **An alternative theory of demand for MHI:** Classical theories of demand for HI do not hold up when applied in poor communities where many people are self-employed. To help develop demand for MHI among these groups, an alternative theory of demand is proposed, based on recognizing the importance of groups in financial decisions in this environment.
- **Creating demand for MHI using a "bottom-up governance structure":** To see value in participating in MHI, people must understand the ground rules and believe they will have the power to enforce the contract. This would assuage their concerns about being left holding the bag. A "bottom-up governance structure" allows prospective members to deal with trusted locals, a reassuring pledge that people they know — and who know them — will keep to the agreement.
- **Welfare enhancing traits of purchasing MHI:** Voluntary and contributory demand for HI in the informal sector can work, once a community recognizes HI enhances their general welfare, beyond the health benefits specified in the package. Specifically, HI can reduce their OOPS on health care and their hardship-financing load.
- **Factors affecting MHI uptake:** Factors favoring enrollment include education, age, female household heads, and household socioeconomic status. So do knowledge and understanding of insurance principles, health care quality, trust in the organizers, the desirability of the benefits package, HI scheme rules, cultural beliefs, affordability, distance to health facility, and legal and policy framework. Deterrents to renewal included too stringent rules of some HI schemes, inadequate legal and policy frameworks to support HI, and inappropriate benefits package.
- **Prospective members decide on the contents and value of the package:** Prospective members, through experience with OOPS, know what they pay for health care and what local practitioners charge. This information shapes their WTP and choice of package contents.

think the benefits in question are worth paying for. This estimate can be achieved through one of two pathways of choice modeling, namely revealed preferences (RP) or stated preferences (SP) (Scott *et al.*, 2003; Ryan *et al.*, 2008). The RP method, first introduced by Samuelson (1938), is a predictive modeling approach based on studying actual purchasing behavior of a related product to estimate the WTP for a product for which no purchasing information exists. Economists prefer this method as it is based on observation of actual behavior. However, such observations may be difficult to find when the market is imperfect or when the option being investigated is not yet available. Not surprisingly, we have been unable to find any published study that uses this method to estimate the WTP for MHI.

When RP cannot be observed, surveys have often been considered as the way forward; in other words, just ask (SP). Such investigations usually unfold by applying a method called contingent valuation (CV) (Diamond and Hausman, 1994; Venkatachalam, 2004; Whitehead and Blomquist, 2006), developed by S.V. Ciriacy–Wantrup (1947) for environmental goods that were not yet on the market. It is "contingent" because the valuation infers hypothetical options for which respondents' preferences and WTP are elicited. CV studies have been popular for several decades (e.g., Acton, 1976) and since the 1990s, have been used often in the context of health services or insurance (Blumenschein *et al.*, 2001; Klose, 1999; Olsen and Smith, 2001).

Three CV techniques have been used most often to elicit WTP: Open-Ended question (OE) (Ahmed *et al.*, 2016); Take-It-or-Leave-It (TIOLI) (Carson, 2012); and Double-Bounded Dichotomous Choice (DBDC) (Boyle, 2017). In the OE elicitation technique, consumers state the maximum amount they would be willing to pay for a good or a service presented in a scenario. Experience with OE suggests that respondents find it easy to respond (Klose, 1999) but that such estimates of WTP for HI have not been very conclusive in LMICs (Nosratnejad *et al.*, 2016). In TIOLI, respondents can accept or reject an offered bid price. This approach is easy for respondents and considered more suitable for telephonic and postal interviews. However, its disadvantage lies in that it elicits only discrete choices. The DBDC technique consists of presenting respondents with an initial bid and follow-up bids: in the follow-up phase, respondents that accepted the initial bid are offered a higher bid, and those that rejected the first bid are offered a cheaper bid. This approach is now used frequently in WTP studies (not just relating to health), notwithstanding its main limitation, which is that the initial bid serves as an anchor influencing the final reply (Donfouet *et al.*, 2014).

WTP by definition is the maximum amount people are willing to spend to acquire a service. While it is recognized that a successful launch of MHI in the informal sector requires an estimate of WTP, the experience with CV studies raise three particular concerns:

- How reliable are the WTP estimates obtained by those methods in the informal sector (declared versus actual WTP)?
- Which variable(s) explain(s) differences in WTP across households in the same locations, and across different locations and points in time?
- Are there better (cheaper) ways of obtaining WTP estimates, for example, expending less time and money?

A review of 20 papers describing 14 experimental field studies on eliciting WTP for HI among low-income persons in developing countries revealed that the same CV methods were used but with notable differences in the definition of parameters and techniques for eliciting WTP (Dror and Koren, 2012). This diversity makes a comparison of quantitative results across studies difficult. The common ground found was a convergence of WTP estimates in a relatively narrow range of around 2% of income. Also, WTP levels appeared sensitive to benefits package design, suggesting that, when the target population is involved in package design, estimated WTP levels could increase. And, no "one-size-fits-all" option emerged for determining the expected WTP in different settings, necessitating local exploration of this issue.

Time and the high cost of conducting household surveys make them impractical for generalized implementation of MHI. Is there an alternative solution? This was the topic of a study of rural poor households in six locations in India (total 7,874 households) (Binnendijk *et al.*, 2013). Basing the analysis on previous findings that showed a positive relationship between nominal increase in income and WTP but a negative relationship when WTP is expressed as a percentage of income (Dror *et al.*, 2006a), the authors of the 2013 study examined whether the same relationships between income and WTP as reported in 2006 recurred in other locations they studied. The relationships between WTP and income were indeed positive everywhere, but not consistent across income groups within locations, or across the locations. This characteristic of the relationships calls to mind Engel's Law (describing the relationship between food expenditures and income (Engel, 1957; Perthel, 1975). Therefore, it was examined whether the relationship between income and WTP for HI could be replicated when WTP was expressed as a percentage of food expenditures. The detailed calculations revealed that the WTP for CBHI was approximately 4.5% of food expenditure in the six locations and gave a better estimation of WTP than either overall income or discretionary income. Now, if that method of estimating WTP could be confirmed as generally valid, it could replace household surveys, because the only information required is average food expenditures, which are well-known in every community and can be obtained through cheaper and faster research methods, such as focus group discussions.

More recently, Nosratnejad *et al.* (2016) attempted to express WTP estimates as a percentage of another parameter that is available in most countries, namely GDP per capita. With a similar aim, to obtain estimates of WTP by reference to an available dataset rather than conducting household surveys, this systematic review of the literature and meta-analysis (of 16 studies — 21 articles from 10 countries) suggested that WTP amounted to just below 2% of GDP per capita per household per year, with a lower figure obtained for individuals' WTP.[5]

These studies offer replies to the three questions posited earlier.

First, progress has been made in estimating WTP by methods other than CV. One method based the estimates of WTP for HI on food expenditure. The other used GDP per capita. These studies have also shown that, in estimating WTP for HI, rigidly following the classical theoretical precepts on demand for HI is not very helpful, since only a limited set of empirical variables corresponding to the theory-driven factors consistently affected the WTP for HI. Poor predictors in the context of MHI include insurance price, risk aversion, household ability to pay and income, the magnitude of expected loss from illness (i.e., user fees), the probability of illness, service coverage and the insurer's payoff amount

[5]Given that many of the studies included in the meta-analysis reported data originating from rural areas in low-income countries, and considering the cumulative effect of a limited understanding of insurance and a lower socioeconomic status among rural populations, we can treat the result as a minimal expression of WTP.

(Nosratnejad *et al.*, 2016). This finding upholds the arguments of Dror and Firth (2014) on the theory of demand for HI in the informal sector of LMICs, which pointed to other factors affecting the level of WTP for HI such as group consensus, general economic financial exposure to health care costs, availability of health care facilities locally, all of which are independent of the socio-demographic status of respondents. Moreover, some of the classical variables that significantly explained WTP in one study were not significant in other studies (Dror and Koren, 2012).

Second, we have confirmation that the factors that were consistently correlated with higher WTP for HI included family size, educational level, income, past hospitalization and perceived poor health status. It was observed that the elderly were correlated with reduced WTP, which is probably due to lower ability to pay rather than the lower perception of risk. Low awareness of the value proposition of insurance was also associated with a lower WTP.

Third, we include in this book a reference to a method called "Illness Mapping" (Binnendijk *et al.*, 2012), a quick and cheap intervention for estimating morbidity and health care utilization locally. Another reference, in the chapter on "Implementation of Microinsurance" in this book, elaborates the method for obtaining (or estimating) local cost of health care. And finally, we have discussed in detail several non-survey, low-cost methods to estimate WTP for HI.

Thresholds and Caps

Every HI unit must ensure that payouts do not exceed income in the long-term. In the case of CBHI units, which collect low premiums and usually cannot obtain income from other sources like subsidies or investments, this constraint is an integral part of benefits package design. Limiting payouts is possible by applying *thresholds* (predetermined amounts payable by the insured before the insurance reimburses that insured's additional costs) and/or *caps* (predetermined maximum payout on an insured person's claims relating to specific benefit types, events, or bills (e.g., hospitalization), above which costs are not reimbursable). Thresholds are sometimes used to limit administrative costs associated with processing many small claims ("nuisance claims"), and caps are applied to protect the

Box 2: Estimating Willingness to Pay

- **Issues with CV techniques of eliciting WTP:** Differences in defining parameters and techniques to estimate the WTP complicated the comparison of quantitative results across studies. Moreover, the time and money needed to conduct household surveys make them impractical for the study of MHI implementation. These difficulties impelled the quest for faster and cheaper ways of obtaining WTP estimates.
- **WTP as a percentage of food expenditures:** A nominal increase in income increases WTP, but when WTP is expressed as a percentage of its value decreases. When the relationship between income and WTP for HI was replicated with WTP expressed as a percentage of food expenditures, the WTP was about 4.5% of food expenditure.
- **WTP as a percentage of GDP per capita:** Another attempt was made to obtain estimates of WTP from available data rather than collect any data. The study, using GDP per capita, suggested that WTP amounted to just below 2% of GDP per capita per household per year, and a bit lower figure for individuals.
- **Estimating WTP using other low-cost and time-saving methods:** A method called "Illness Mapping" was used as a quick and cheap intervention for estimating morbidity and health care utilization locally. This method was intended to estimate the local cost of health care, which is essential information to match to WTP for HI.
- **Issues with using classical theoretical precepts on HI demand to estimate WTP:** Rigidly following the classical theoretical precepts on demand for HI is not very helpful, since only a limited set of empirical variables corresponding to the theory-driven factors consistently affected the WTP for HI. Poor predictors in the context of MHI include insurance price, risk aversion, household ability to pay and income, the magnitude of expected loss from illness (i.e., user fees), the probability of illness, service coverage, and the insurer's payoff amount.
- **Factors correlated with high/low WTP:** Factors consistently correlated with higher WTP for HI include family size, educational level, income, past hospitalization, and perceived poor health status. The elderly and people with a low awareness of the potential value of insurance were associated with a lower WTP.

MIU from high outlier costs. The consequences of applying thresholds and/or caps on the expected average payout of insurance, and thus on the premium, can be calculated only when the distribution of health care costs is known.

The distribution of location-specific health care costs is obtained from actual claims data, available after MIUs begin operations. For an MIU that is being launched, we seek cheaper and faster solutions than sourcing data from household surveys (the concerns about the time and cost of surveys have been mentioned). A theoretical model was developed to project the distribution of health care costs and to demonstrate the quantitative impact of thresholds and/or caps on claim reimbursements, with the view to obviating the need to collect data (Binnendijk *et al.*, 2014). The model simulates the expected performance of the CBHI in the local context considering the optimal level of thresholds and caps that would best meet the assumed WTP levels when the benefits package is designed. The model was tested using data from 11 household surveys, conducted in nine Indian and two Nepalese rural locations, on the cost distributions of two benefits: hospitalization and diagnostic tests. The shape of the distribution was determined by the relative frequency of small bills versus high/outlier bills. The shape of the distribution was also found to be very similar in all locations for both benefits and could be represented by the lognormal distribution model. The information obtained from the model can be used to refine premium calculations of MIUs, and predict expected client satisfaction with locally relevant HI packages.

Application of the model could inform better package design at the local level, without prior data collection. To the best of our knowledge, this has never before been done in development projects aiming to develop CBHI with suitable HI coverage under severe rationing rules.

Applying thresholds and caps would have two effects:

- These measures could influence the premium amount
- They would define the uninsured amounts of costs that insured persons must bear (OOPS).

These are defining considerations in package design, especially when the MHI aims to reduce hardship financing of the poor. All MIUs apply caps but without suitable estimates of the effect on both premiums and benefits. The proposed model offers a way to refine and professionalize the rationing exercise by projecting the impact of the measures taken, using the proposed model.

While low benefit caps and loss ratios are applied to maintain financial sustainability of MIUs, sometimes such limits may reduce a scheme's ability to extend coverage, offer financial protection, and retain members. A study of three microinsurance schemes operating in two Indian states revealed that low caps and loss ratios are counterproductive in extending insurance coverage, financial protection, and high renewal rates among the poor in India (Dror *et al.*, 2009). The study was based on household survey data, obtained in areas covered by the three microinsurance schemes: BAIF, Uplift Health, and Nidan. The three schemes differ in target membership, benefits, and claims management practices. Around 350 insured and 350 uninsured households were surveyed in each location, and the scheme managers were also interviewed regarding some details about the microinsurance units (for example, claims ratios). The two cohorts and respondents across locations were compared.

It was observed that low benefit caps and a low share of premiums paid as benefits limited these schemes' ability to extend coverage, offer financial protection, and retain members. On a more positive note, it was evident that although the microinsurance units received less funding and professional resources than commercial insurers, they provided their insured populations no less, and maybe more, protection through mobilization of context-relevant social processes.

In all three schemes, the low caps protected the insurance scheme rather than the resource-poor insured. As a result, microinsurance with too low a cap was associated with inequity, whereas its aim should be to reduce inequity. To ensure continuity of operations, the three schemes adopted different methods. The study identified the strengths and shortcomings of the different approaches as judged by their impact on financial protection and equitable access to expensive health care. BAIF followed a "relative benefit" plan which ensured that its microinsurance unit will never pay out more than its premium income. UpLift constituted a reserve fund and vested the authority to control expenses with members acting as a committee and using local information, notably through case-by-case benefit curtailment. Of the three schemes, Nidan was most at risk of

Box 3: Thresholds and Caps

- **Budgeting for MIU sustainability:** Projecting health care cost distribution is a basic part of budgeting and estimating the consequences of applying thresholds and caps on insurance payouts — and premiums. To circumvent data collection for these projections, a theoretical model was developed that tested the effects of thresholds and/or caps on claim reimbursements. With this information, premium calculations can be refined and client satisfaction with benefits packages can be predicted.
- **Effects of thresholds and caps:** These measures could define the insured person's uncovered, out-of-pocket costs and also influence premiums.
- **Impact of thresholds and caps:** Low caps and loss ratios can be counterproductive in extending insurance coverage, financial protection, and high renewal rates among the poor in India. Low benefit caps and low payout rates limit the scheme's ability to extend coverage, offer financial protection — and retain members.

insurance discontinuity as it depended on the commercial underwriter's decisions to (dis)continue business with this group, while Nidan had no say.

Hardship Financing

Definitions of catastrophic health care costs are relatively recent. Two definitions have been proposed.

- The first defines health expenditure as catastrophic if a household's financial contributions to the health system exceed 40% of income remaining after subsistence needs have been met (Xu *et al.*, 2003).
- The second definition stipulates that catastrophic health care expenditure occurs when the OOP paid by a household exceeds 10% of its income (O'Donnell *et al.*, 2008).

Neither definition considers the cost of having to finance OOPS through interest-bearing borrowing or through the urgent (suboptimal) selling off of assets. OOPS are high in most LMICs' informal sector (for instance, in India, OOPS represent 69.5% of total health care expenditure (Ministry of Health and Family Welfare India, 2009). Ignoring this portion of the costs when defining "catastrophic health costs" constitutes a major flaw that must be rectified. The term "hardship financing" has been coined to describe the additional costs/losses incurred when OOPS is financed by borrowing with interest or selling assets. The hardship associated with these costs extends well beyond the duration of the health event. Hardship financing includes losses when assets are sold at less than optimal price, or the loss of future income when income-generating assets (like land or livestock) are sold.

How big is the problem? Binnendijk *et al.* (2012a) gave a quantified expression of the problem and identified factors influencing the risk of hardship financing, using logistic regression with data of 5,383 low-income households in three districts of Odisha (India). Financing health care by selling assets or borrowing money with interest from a bank, microfinance or moneylender was categorized as hardship financing. Households that reported at least one of these financing sources were categorized as having experienced hardship financing. Households that reported using only current income and/or savings and/or borrowing from relatives or friends/neighbors were defined as having had no hardship financing. Overall, about 25% of all households that incurred any health care cost reported hardship financing during the year preceding the survey. And hardship financing affected nearly 40% of households that experienced a hospitalization. The additional costs due to illness-related interest costs were estimated at 24% of the health expenditure, a cost equal to nearly 5% of the households' annual overall expenditure. The loss due to selling assets, though also aggravating household hardship, was hard to quantify for lack of all monetary information on fair market value.

Hardship financing is neither rare, nor quantitatively negligible, nor a mere short-term mishap. It is a trade-off between welfare gains (procured from the treatment of an ill person) and welfare loss (emanating from interest payments on health-related loans or future income forgone due to hardship sale of assets). This trade-off is skewed toward welfare loss because its effects can extend over a much longer period of time, and adversely affect several significant other persons. Moreover, the poorest are likely to be hardest hit by hardship financing because they are least likely to get a bank loan, least likely to have high current income or rich relatives providing interest-free loans, and most likely to borrow at higher interest rates from moneylenders. Another highly exposed group is the chronically ill, whose hardship financing risk can be expressed as a function of its frequency, severity, and duration. The understanding of indirect and longer-term effects of OOPS due to changing epidemiological patterns paves the way for a policy solution that would limit hardship financing in the informal sector.

Box 4: Hardship Financing

- **Defining hardship financing:** This is a member's additional costs/losses incurred when OOPS is financed by selling assets or borrowing with interest from a bank, microfinance institute, or moneylender. The hardship associated with these costs extends well beyond the duration of the health event. Hardship financing includes losses when assets are sold at less than optimal price or the loss of future income when income-generating assets (like land or livestock) are sold.
- **Estimating hardship financing:** About 25% of households that incur any health care cost report hardship financing in the year before the survey. And hardship financing affected nearly 40% of households that experienced a hospitalization. The additional costs due to illness-related interest costs were estimated at 24% of the health expenditure, a cost equal to nearly 5% of the households' annual overall expenditure.
- **Interpreting hardship financing:** Hardship financing is a trade-off between welfare gains (from the treatment of an ill person) and welfare loss (from interest payments on health-related loans or future income forgone due to hardship sale of assets). This trade-off is skewed toward welfare loss because its effects can extend over a much longer period of time, and adversely affect several significant other persons. Moreover, the poorest and the chronically ill are likely to be worst hit by hardship financing because they are unlikely to receive interest-free loans from rich relatives, have access to bank loans (at lower interest rates), and have to borrow at higher interest rates from moneylenders.

Financial Sustainability of Microinsurance Units

Any discussion of MHI financing would be incomplete without proving their path to financial sustainability. MHI units persistently face the challenge of keeping premiums low enough to be perceived as affordable by the target population, and high enough to ensure sufficient income to keep the MIU solvent. The premium must reflect the aggregate risk borne by insurers, which is much more than the cost of the pure risk. Other costs that underwriters must load on the pure risk premium include the possible error in calculating the risks, regulatory surplus requirements ("capital loading") and transaction costs associated with product design, client acquisition and premium collection, and claims processing ("administration loading"). Commercial insurers also load the cost of reinsurance and profits.

A detailed analysis of the impact of group size on capital needs of MIUs was conducted using the 2001 dataset of a large health insurer in Ireland, containing more than 1.3 million insured (Dror and Armstrong, 2006). The analysis used an empirical distribution of health care expenditure of the Irish health insurer and split the large data source into many small "virtual MIUs", each treated as a stand-alone entity. The simulation exercise indicated that an increase in portfolio size increases diversification of risk and that an insufficient capital loading exposes the MIUs to an unacceptable risk of insolvency and bankruptcy. The most salient insight from that simulation was that with an identical risk exposure and an identical premium, MIUs — by definition with few members — may go bankrupt when larger groups would not. This creates a "premium bias" that could disadvantage MIU clients. Moreover, the market cannot offer an automatic corrective measure for this bias, which necessitates regulatory intervention (in the nature of risk equalization across all health insurers) to ensure fair pricing.

Governments have many options for correcting premium bias caused by the higher capital requirement imposed on small group MIUs. Governments can subsidize the difference in capital loading that is directly related to small group size, by applying the capital loading rate that would apply to a large (national) group rather than the higher rate applicable to smaller MIUs. Governments could also create a facility that would allow MIUs to draw loans to meet their capitalization requirements in bad years. The third option available to governments is to link MIUs to reinsurance and to subsidize a part of the reinsurance premium. This is the safest available solution to tackle the issue of premium bias, which would release governments from having to carry any risk related to MIUs and level the playing field for MIUs relative to any commercial insurer. Opting for reinsurance coverage is also a cheaper substitute for holding solvency capital directly. In fact, if the barriers to ceding risks to reinsurance that MIUs face today were removed, MIUs could prove relevant and sustainable vehicles for extending insurance coverage to low-income persons in LMICs' informal sector.

Adding capital loading to premiums could create an enrollment disincentive for clients, however, if they consider the premiums unaffordable or unfairly high. However, insolvency is the bigger of the two risks, because defaulting on benefits payment is a killer of trust. Without trust, voluntary and contributory insurance cannot exist, particularly in the informal sector. Therefore, insurers need surplus capital as a buffer against insolvency when they encounter outlier costs.

Absent a state-sponsored mechanism for equalization of risk or access to capital, MIUs may secure their capital needs by borrowing at reasonable interest rates and repaying over the long-term as part of operational costs. MIUs stand a chance of obtaining commercial capital sourcing only if they can demonstrate a business case that they can pay at least the cost of claims and administration while they are becoming established as well as, when they reach maturity and scale, repay principal and interest on start-up loans.

To evaluate the business case of MHI, a prototype scheme was devised, based on empirical data collected from two CBHI schemes operating in Bihar (India) and Banke (Nepal) with 6 and 3 years of operations, respectively. It was assumed that operating costs of prototype schemes follow the standard costing methodology. Studying the impact of various factors on the sustainability and scalability of the prototype scheme showed that operational sustainability can be reached with multiple combinations of five sustainability parameters. These include the number of insured households, average number of insured persons in each household, renewal rates, claims ratio and premiums per person per year. Progress on all five parameters implies that MIUs can reach full sustainability even while defraying high operating costs in the early years, possibly exceeding premium income (Dror *et al.*, 2018).

During the first 4 years of the prototype scheme, additional capital was needed to cover operating costs; premium income met only yearly claims. The scheme became operationally sustainable from the fifth year, and by the end of the fifteenth year was debt-free and had achieved full sustainability. The pace towards full sustainability depends on both the size of the loan and the interest rate applied. The study demonstrates that a compelling business case can be made for operating voluntary and contributory MHI even without any premium subsidies, when the MIUs could meet investors' legitimate expectations (loan repayment with interest) as well as those of members (full payment of their claims every year and growth of their organization's capital assets). As for the members' expectation of welfare gains (beyond claims payment), the simulation showed that, for every US$1 of capital borrowed at inception, each prototype scheme could mobilize US$52 as premium income over 15 years, and US$85 over 20 years. This revenue is generated by attracting more members who are currently uninsured. As those surpluses belong to the MIU and assuming that these are mutual schemes, the surpluses belong to the members. Thus, by generating considerable additional resources MIUs could add value that could be used for whatever social benefits the members decide on, including an increase in health care benefits.

Some MIUs have been relying on philanthropic support to fulfill their capital requirements, but such support is not sustainable. They need to shift away from survival based on donations, and toward survival based on operational returns that enable schemes to guarantee financial returns to investors and to their members at competitive rates. Such a shift of funding sourcing is justified also by its social ramifications, of extending HI coverage to previously uninsured rural populations in schemes that are voluntary, contributory, and unsubsidized. Governments that are keen to achieve higher uptake of HI among rural and informal sector groups should encourage the expansion of MHI. Governments can do that, even without financial support, by putting in place an enabling regulatory framework that facilitates investment of private funds in MIUs.

Box 5: Financial Sustainability of Microinsurance Units

- **Balancing affordability and solvency:** MHI units persistently face the challenge of keeping premiums low enough to be perceived as affordable by the target population, and high enough to ensure sufficient income to keep the MIU solvent. The premium must reflect aggregate risk borne by insurers, which is much more than the cost of the pure risk.
- **"Premium bias" faced by MIU members:** According to a study of the impact of group size on MIUs capital needs, an increase in portfolio size increases diversification of risk and insufficient capital loading exposes MIUs to an unacceptable risk of insolvency and bankruptcy. The most salient insight from that study was that with an identical risk exposure and an identical premium, MIUs may go bankrupt when larger groups would not. This creates a "premium bias" that could disadvantage MIU clients. This necessitates regulatory intervention (in the nature of risk equalization across all health insurers) to ensure fair pricing.
- **Proposed government intervention:** Governments can subsidize the difference in capital loading that is directly related to small group size, by applying the capital loading rate that would apply to a large (national) group rather than the higher rate applicable to smaller MIUs. Governments could also create a lending facility from which MIUs could borrow in lean years to meet their capitalization requirement. Governments could also link MIUs to reinsurance and to subsidize part of the reinsurance premium.
- **Impact of capital loading on MIU enrollment:** Adding capital loading to premiums could create an enrollment disincentive for clients if they then find the premiums too high. However, insolvency is the bigger of the two risks, because defaulting on benefit payments kills trust. Therefore, insurers need surplus capital as a buffer against insolvency when they encounter outlier costs.
- **The business case of MHI:** MIUs stand a chance of sourcing commercial capital only if they can demonstrate a business case in which they can pay at least the cost of claims and administration while they are becoming established and, once they reach maturity and scale, can repay principal and interest on start-up loans. A prototype scheme suggested that operational sustainability can be reached with multiple combinations of five sustainability parameters. These include the number of insured households, average number of insured persons in each household,

(*Continued*)

Box 5: ***(Continued)***

renewal rates, claims ratio and premiums per person per year. Progress on all five parameters implies that MIUs can reach full sustainability even while defraying high operating costs in the early years, including borrowing to bridge income deficits.

- **Business case without premium subsidies:** A compelling business case can be made for operating voluntary and contributory MHI even without any premium subsidies, when the MIUs could meet investors' legitimate expectations (loan repayment with interest) as well as those of members (full payment of their claims every year and growth of their organization's capital assets). The simulation showed that, for every US$1 of capital borrowed at inception, each prototype scheme could mobilize US$52 as premium income over 15 years, and US$85 over 20 years.

Financial Aspects of Implementation

The definition of MHI draws attention to *a central role for the community at least in the design of the MHI, and possibly its operation and governance.* This central role has implications for financials and operations and, for MHIs that are legally constituted along the lines of a mutual society, on ownership as well.

Community participation in the design of the MHI translates into tangible steps to enable people to choose benefits packages based on their risk perceptions. Field evidence shows that even the most innumerate and illiterate segments of the population can reach decisions on trade-offs between the risks they would like to cover through insurance and how much they are willing to pay. The desire to be a part of the group that reaches such decisions through consensus, rather than remaining apart from the consensus, is a strong motivator to join the scheme.[6]

[6] CHAT or Choosing All Together is a consensus-building exercise used by the rural poor for selecting a benefits-package for an MIU. CHAT is conducted in three rounds CHAT 1, CHAT 2, and CHAT 3. The findings of a baseline study form the basis for designing the benefits packages by community members. A detailed description of this method can be found in Dror *et al.* (2014a).

Such trade-offs in package design do not require subsidies and mandates. It is fallacious to assume that (resource-poor) people always want a discount or low-cost products. A study based on four sources of data, showed that despite the lack of HI experience among the target community, when the poor had access to a game-like way of selecting the benefits package, without compromising actuarial accuracy, they could select the health package within their WTP and their perceived priorities for health care coverage (Dror *et al.*, 2014a). Thus, group consensus can be harnessed to enhance demand for MHI in the informal economy. The four sources of data were a baseline study, CHAT (Choosing All Together) exercises (Dror *et al.*, 2007), in-depth interviews, and evaluation interviews. The baseline study of a 5-year project (2009–2014), funded by the European Commission (FP7) and implemented by the Micro Insurance Academy (New Delhi), conducted in three locations in rural India, provided the source data for actuarial calculations of premiums of different benefits. The communities surveyed were willing to pay because they trust that they have control over the fairness and enforcement of contracts. This is achieved through an independent governance structure of MIUs by locals (Dror *et al.*, 2014b), trained to execute specific "key actor" roles in community mobilization, claims adjudication and scheme oversight (Dror and Jambhekar, 2017). The rules are set by the broader group of members, and implementation is administered by skilled locals, subject to easy access to a grievance redressal procedure, which assures an equitable application of rules to all participants — a key function often overlooked in commercial HI. Local governance is not synonymous with laissez-faire management. Roles, responsibilities, timelines and reporting lines are defined for each key activist, and an in-house customized management information system (MIA-MIS) helps manage data for operation and managerial oversight (Dror and Majumdar, 2018, forthcoming).

Many advantages are gained from the shift from external ("top-down") to local ("bottom-up") command-and-control through community participation and local key activists. Reduced staff costs, better job opportunities for local staff, enhanced trust in the scheme, reduction of transaction costs, lower incidence of fraudulent claims (gossip is free-of-charge and feeds important information to everybody, for example, on hospital admissions, illness episodes). These contribute to MIU financial sustainability.

Sustainability depends on many factors. A common belief is that financial sustainability means that premium income is higher than claims costs. In fact, the sustainability equations are not so simple or linear. Indisputably, income from premiums should be adequate to pay all eligible claims, cover operational costs, help create reserves for lean years, and earn a profit for insurers. These loadings on pure risk premium push up total premiums. At the same time, when people are convinced that the proposition offers value for money, they are keen to participate. And when more people join, a small virtuous cycle kicks in, because applying a *community rating* policy encourages its twin rule of *en bloc affiliation* of all members of one household, which together lead to higher income, lower acquisition costs, lower risk of moral hazard, and lower claims ratios. These four implementation factors reduce the expenditure side and thus enhance sustainability.

Finally, we consider the ownership issue. Members of a mutual society are its owners, although they do not purchase shares upon joining, as they do in a cooperative. Scheme ownership confers both rights and responsibilities, most notably the ultimate responsibility for the scheme's financial self-reliance. Mutuals cannot raise capital by selling equity shares to investors because such equity holding could create conflicts of interest between the equity shareholders and the other member-owners, who manage the MHI for their own benefit. The mutual can utilize the funds collected only for purposes for which the mutual is formed; the contributions paid by its participants are the sole source of funding/financing, and the benefits assured by the mutual (and administration) are the sole legitimate uses of funds. In the case of MHI, the funds of the mutual can be used only to reimburse eligible claims and to cover the scheme's operational costs. Any surplus retained in any financial year is carried forward to the next period, with the concurrence of all participants, rather than distributed as a dividend to shareholders.

Box 6: Financial Aspects of Implementation

- **Community participation in MHI design:** Even the most innumerate and illiterate segments of the population can reach decisions on trade-offs between the risks they would like to cover through insurance and how much they are willing to pay, according to field evidence. Such trade-offs in package design do not require subsidies and mandates. When the poor have access to a game-like way of selecting the benefits package, without compromising actuarial accuracy, they select the health package within their WTP and their perceived priorities for health care coverage. Thus, group consensus can be harnessed to enhance demand for MHI in the informal economy.
- **Independent governance structure:** Locals are trained to execute specific "key actor" roles in community mobilization, claims adjudication and scheme oversight. The rules are set by the broader group of members, and implementation is administered by skilled locals, easily accessible for grievance redressal procedure. This assures equitable application of rules to all participants. Roles, responsibilities, timelines and reporting lines are defined for each key activist, and an in-house customized management information system (MIA-MIS) helps manage data for operation and managerial oversight.
- **Gains from "bottom-up" governance structure:** Advantages include reduced staff costs, better job opportunities for local staff, enhanced trust in the scheme, reduction of transaction costs, and lower incidence of fraudulent claims. These contribute to MIU financial sustainability.
- **Implementation factors reducing the expenditure side:** Income from premiums should cover all eligible claims, operational costs, contributions to reserves for lean years, and profits for insurers. People are keen to participate when convinced the premium is worth the price. As membership grows, a small virtuous cycle kicks in. A *community rating* policy encourages *en bloc affiliation* of all household members, which together lead to higher income, lower acquisition costs, lower moral hazard risk, and lower claims ratios. These four implementation factors reduce expenditures, thus enhancing sustainability.
- **Ownership rights:** Mutual society members are its owners and hold the ultimate responsibility for the scheme's financial self-reliance. Mutuals cannot raise capital by selling equity shares to investors because such equity holding could create conflicts of interest between the equity shareholders and the other member-owners, who manage the MHI for their own benefit. MHI funds can be used only to reimburse eligible claims and to cover operational costs. A surplus in any financial year is carried forward to the next period, with the concurrence of all participants.

Evidence of Positive Externalities of MHI

Empirical evidence on a gamut of issues related to health care financing and microinsurance provide the necessary thrust for future research and policy development in LMICs.

CBHI encourages early health care intervention

There exists evidence that access to low-cost HI among the rural poor population encourages early health care intervention, leading to lower health care costs and lower wage loss. Dror *et al.* (2005) analyzed field data collected in six MIUs in the Philippines through a household survey encompassing 890 insured and 1,063 uninsured households, in order to establish evidence that affiliation with these schemes increases health care utilization. The two cohorts did not differ in demographic parameters and differed only marginally in income and educational levels, both higher among the insured.

A comparison of the two cohorts revealed that while the socioeconomic differences between the two cohorts are small, insured persons reported higher hospitalization rates, higher rates of professionally attended deliveries, lower rates of delivery at home, a higher frequency of primary-care physician encounters, a higher rate of diagnosed chronic diseases, and better drug compliance among chronically ill. This increased utilization by the insured is not due to adverse selection, judging by two facts: morbidity of the two cohorts, as assessed by a proxy indicator (the reported number of episodes of illness) did not differ; and rates of deliveries were even slightly higher among the uninsured. Thus, it is evident that persons insured by MIUs reported higher health care utilization than uninsured persons.

CBHI schemes promote preventive health care measures

One of the positive externalities of CBHI schemes is the regular interaction and dissemination of information on diseases and preventive practices (Panda *et al.*, 2015). The authors evaluated the effectiveness of preventive care awareness campaigns in increasing knowledge about airborne, vector-borne and waterborne diseases, as well as enhancing preventive practices among rural communities. The CBHI model gave ample opportunities for regular gatherings and knowledge exchanges between the members. The study was conducted in three rural communities in

Pratapgarh and Kanpur-Dehat districts in Uttar Pradesh, and Vaishali district in Bihar. Data for this analysis were collected from two surveys, one done before, the other after, the campaign.

The findings suggest that well-crafted health educational campaigns can be effective in raising awareness and promoting health-enhancing practices in resource-poor settings. The campaigns were effective in encouraging the application of preventive practices (based on self-reported preventive practices), indicating that better awareness of the risks was a necessary first step to the adoption of preventive practices. Another implication is that repeating the campaigns may lead to increased adoption of preventive practices.

CBHI awareness campaigns enhance understanding of health insurance

Part of the explanation for the low insurance penetration in India is that the target population is predominantly illiterate, innumerate and lacks insurance experience. The low awareness of the benefits of insurance emphasizes that considerable insurance education and capacity development are pivotal for the successful launch of CBHI, for sustainable operations and for scaling. Panda *et al.* (2015a) assess the awareness campaign conducted prior to the launch of three CBHI schemes in rural northern India. The research focused on three questions: Has the awareness campaign enhanced participants' understanding of health insurance? What awareness tools were most useful from the participants' point of view? Has enhanced awareness resulted in higher enrollment in the CBHI schemes? Data for this analysis was sourced from a baseline survey (2010) and a follow-up survey (2011) of more than 800 households in the pre- and post-campaign periods.

Empirical evidence provided by this study suggested that the awareness campaigns enhanced understanding of HI among treatment groups. The most popular awareness tool among the participants, the interactive sessions, were perceived as enjoyable and most useful by respondents, independent of the target group's educational level found the awareness tools useful. The authors found no published previous analysis of awareness campaigns associated with CBHI or microinsurance, and thus this study fills a gap in the in-depth empirical analysis of the effect of insurance education campaign on enrollment.

Box 7: Evidence of Positive Externalities of MHI

- **CBHI encourages early health care intervention:** Access to low-cost HI among the rural poor population encourages early health care intervention and improves physical and economic health, in the long run, leading to lower health care costs and lower risk of wage loss. Insured persons reported higher hospitalization rates, higher rates of professionally attended deliveries, lower rates of delivery at home, a higher frequency of primary care physician encounters, a higher rate of diagnosed chronic diseases, and better drug compliance among chronically ill. This increased utilization by the insured is not due to adverse selection, judging by two facts: morbidity of the two cohorts, as assessed by a proxy indicator, did not differ; and rates of deliveries were even slightly higher among the uninsured.
- **CBHI schemes promote preventive health care measures:** Regular interaction and dissemination of information on diseases and preventive practices through the records-keeping systems enables proactive health planning and targeted health care campaigns that can raise awareness and promote health-enhancing practices in resource-poor settings.
- **CBHI awareness campaigns enhance understanding of HI:** Awareness campaigns before launching a scheme enhance understanding of HI among treatment groups. The interactive sessions are the most popular awareness tool among the participants.

Impact of MHI

Earlier in this synthesis, in the section dealing with demand for MHI, the question was raised of how the theory could explain the conditions under which most people in the informal sector of an LMIC would seek voluntary HI when the benefits of HI are positively provable. We now are ready to deal with the conditional question of whether the benefits of HI are positively provable. In other words, what evidence is there that MHI has a positive impact, or positive welfare gains, for insured persons?

The interest in the impact of MHI in a book about financing emanates from the simple logic that its visibly positive impact on members attracts and impels others to enroll. So in this section, we present this evidence.

Studies on the impact of CBHI on insured households are necessary to understand the benefits of enrollment, and new avenues in this field of research need to be explored for further propagation of CBHI in LMICs. Dror *et al.* (2016a) investigated the impact of community-based health insurance (CBHI) on access to health care and financial protection within a large-scale, randomized, controlled field experiment in three rural locations in India. The selected MIUs were BAIF Development Research Foundation (Uttar Pradesh), Shramik Bharti (Uttar Pradesh), and Nidan (Bihar). The analysis was based on data from two sources: household surveys and MIS maintained for each CBHI by the MIA. A baseline survey of 3,685 households was conducted in March–May 2010, and an endline survey was conducted 3 years later when 3,307 households of the households included in the baseline were revisited. The authors hypothesized that CBHI improves insured households' (1) access to health care, by reducing self-medication and (2) financial protection, by reducing hardship financing and enhancing economic mobility.

The key to identifying the impact of CBHI was the accurate identification of the treatment and control groups to ensure that the analysis was not flawed due to self-selection enrollment bias. The treatment group was composed only of people that were "offered and joined" the insurance, and the control group was composed of all the other uninsured persons (including "offered not joined" and "not offered"). Reduction in self-medication, namely consumption of unprescribed medicines, was used as an indicator of improved access to health care, on the assumption that insured people would reduce self-medication when insured. Moreover, this indicator can be examined independently of the question of whether all studied locations applied a uniform benefits package. Furthermore, self-medication is recognized globally as a major health risk that can lead to misdiagnosis and health complications. The study revealed that post-intervention, households reduced their self-medication even though the morbidity patterns of the insured population did not change over the study period. The reduction in self-medication seemed to be a result of insurance status because the reduction was more pronounced among the insured population, and because this effect increased the longer people were insured. Being insured made people feel more positive about seeking medical help.

To measure the impact of CBHI on financial protection, two measures of financial protection were applied. First, the proportion of households that borrowed with interest to pay health care costs (hardship financing) was analyzed, since borrowing-with-interest is a strong indicator of the risk of falling into poverty. The study observed a reduction in health-related household borrowing among the insured, but not among the uninsured. The second measure was the effect of insurance on economic mobility measured by consumption spending on nonhealth items. This measures a participant's capacity to improve (or reduce) his/her economic status.

For the sample population, after 2 years of being insured, the probability of an insured household's benefiting from quintile upgrade increased, and the risk of quintile downgrade decreased. This association between being insured and economic mobility could be a direct effect related to money saved during financing of ambulatory care or the increased likelihood of an insured household's investing in productive assets or education that could increase income.

The authors (Dror *et al.*, 2016a) conclude that HI creates welfare gains in the form of better access to health care, reduced financial risks, and improved economic mobility. This has holistic implications for theoretical, ethical, policy, and practice considerations.

Having seen the welfare gains flowing from CBHI enrollment, the next step is to assess the impact of CBHI on equality of access to health care among groups with inequitable income distribution. A study based on a household survey conducted in five MIUs in the Philippines examined whether membership in the MIUs was accompanied by equality of access with respect to income, alongside the increase in overall access to health care (Dror *et al.*, 2006). The findings confirmed that insurance status with MIUs improved the income-related equality of access to two major health benefits: hospitalization (which can generate catastrophic costs) and medical consultation (which includes referral encounters that lead to hospitalization). However, there was no increase in equality of access to professional attendance in deliveries. A comparison with unequal access recorded among the uninsured cohorts reinforces the observation that insurance by MIUs contributes to income-related equality of access. The inverse correlation between relative income and relative utilization found among the uninsured is absent among the insured cohorts. In none of the cases were the insured cohorts worse off than the uninsured from the point of view of income-related equality. This indicates that there is better income-related equality of access among MIU affiliates regardless of their income.

Box 8: Impact of MHI

- **Impact of CBHI on access to health care and financial protection:** CBHI improves insured households' access to health care by reducing self-medication, and improves financial protection by reducing hardship financing and enhancing economic mobility.
- **Impact of CBHI on financial protection:** CBHI reduces health-related household borrowing among the insured but not among the uninsured. The effect of insurance on economic mobility is reflected in consumption spending on non-health items. In the case of a sample population, after 2 years insured, the probability of a household's benefiting from quintile upgrade increased, and the risk of a quintile downgrade decreased. This association between being insured and economic mobility could be a direct effect related to money saved during financing of ambulatory care or the increased likelihood of an insured household's investing in productive assets or education that could increase income.
- **Impact of CBHI on equality of access to health care:** A household's insurance by MIUs contributes to income-related equality of access to two major health benefits: hospitalization (which can generate catastrophic costs) and medical consultations (including referrals leading to hospitalization).
- **Impact of CBHI on inter-group equality:** The findings showed that rich uninsured households have a clear advantage in accessing health care services over poor uninsured households. However, in the insured cohort, there was almost perfect equality of access between the richer and poorer households despite the marked differences in household income. There was an improvement in the condition of the poor after they joined MIUs, and this improvement of access among low-income groups was not at the cost of other income groups.
- Without a state-sponsored arrangement to equalize risk or access to capital, MIUs can borrow at reasonable rates to meet their capital needs, repay over many years, and book this expenditure as one of many operational costs.

To understand inter-group equality, the insured cohorts in all locations were compared with groups of uninsured households residing in the same communities. The findings showed that rich uninsured households have a clear advantage in accessing health care services compared to poor uninsured households. However, in the insured cohort, there was almost perfect equality of access between the richer and poorer households despite the marked differences in household income.

The authors infer that there was an improvement in the condition of the poor after they joined MIUs, and this improvement of access among low-income groups was not at the cost of other income groups. This study offers health policymakers the evidence that displays equality of access within MIUs and justifies the promotion of MIUs as successful suppliers of HI.

Conclusions

This synthesis attempts to convey *all you must know* regarding financing micro health insurance.

The first, overriding, message is that neither the invisible hand of the market nor the visible hand of the state can explain economic choices of persons at the base-of-the-pyramid and the informal sector in LMIC. The visible hand of the state, exemplified for HI mainly through mandating and subsidies, cannot be applied effectively in the informal sector because most LMIC lack the political will, information, and resources. And the invisible hand of the market is ineffective in the informal sector because there is practically no demand for commercial HI. Buying health insurance, an unknown product, from a stranger would not rank anywhere among the first choices of people at BOP. These people seek welfare gains through affiliation with family, friends, peers, and groups rather than through isolated transactions with agents they do not know and with whom they have little transactional experience. Based on relevant and workable assumptions of the role of groups in financial decisions in the informal sector, an alternative to the classical theory of demand is proposed. It covers not only purchase decisions but also the influence of local governance arrangements on enhancing trust in the system, which is a necessary but insufficient condition for the establishment of HI market.

Second, modern industrial societies have accepted a condition whereby the most important resource, capital, is accumulated and controlled by a minority of natural or legal persons that devise rules for using their property mainly to maximize their own wealth. Everyone else has to work under those rules, like it or not. In times when trade unions were powerful, they were instrumental in mitigating the command of capital. This paradigm is considerably weakened in the informal sector, both because much less private capital reaches it and because collective action at the local level is at the heart of many decisions, with a view to maximizing local welfare gains. Such collective action is all the more effective at the local level as it is absent at the national level. It offers an alternative to external rule setting at BOP when the business process is adapted to mobilize group dynamics, establish a dialog with the group, and enhance group buy-in by other means. If the objective is to demonstrate that HI can create welfare gains for members of the insured group, this alternative business process can be applied at scale, and sustainably. The business case and the business process are described in this book, and evidence that they work is shared. The open issue is that the MIUs require loan capital at inception, which they can repay over time.

The third key issue is that the price of insurance does not alone determine its value proposition. The uninsured risks of insured benefit-types (determined by thresholds and caps) plus the benefit-types that are not included in the package will determine insured persons' true risk exposure to OOPS. And, as most uninsured persons are ill-prepared to pay large OOPS, they often resort to borrowing with interest or selling assets, which add "hardship financing" costs. The uninsured in BOP are familiar with OOPS and hardship financing, but curiously, most health financing specialists ignore this aspect when planning the HI. Scaling of HI among BOP populations has to include ways of reducing both hardship financing and OOPS. This book includes detailed discussions of how to measure, and by implication how to decrease hardship financing.

A fourth insight is that price determines the HI package, not vice versa. This is the opposite of take-it-or-leave-it (TIOLI) marketing of a standard benefits package with a standard premium, which could include payments for benefits that locals may never be able to enjoy, or which may be calculated with data that do not reflect local frequency and severity of risk exposure. As WTP defines the group's financial boundaries for package design, a reliable estimate of WTP is essential before a package can be designed. It is self-explanatory that when conditions differ across locations (both risk exposure and the quantity, quality, and price of health care services), people prefer different benefits. With regard to customization, therefore, context is king. Customization can be applied when local data are available, and when a dialog is nurtured with the local client-base. Price adjustment and package customization are also an expression that the clients and the insurer are much closer in terms of power disparity than in commercial health insurance plans or in national (social) health protection schemes.

Finally, we recall the essential and compelling evidence that MHI makes a positive impact on welfare gains of the insured households. MHI has been demonstrated to improve insured households' access to health care (by reducing self-medication); to enhance financial protection (by reducing hardship financing and increasing economic mobility); and to establish equality of access between richer and poorer households despite the marked differences in household income (when the results showed that among the uninsured, rich households had a clear advantage in accessing health care services compared to poor households).

When both theory and evidence converge, the conclusion is irrefutable: MIUs that are founded on mutual aid and community governance can

- deliver better access to health care
- provide better financial protection
- bring about more equitable access to health care
- practice unconditional enrollment (regardless of age, gender, income, prior condition, etc.)
- raise considerable additional resources for health care, and
- raise additional resources for other welfare gains.

The message is clear: MIUs can be successful suppliers of HI, even among the very poor. This message has holistic implications for theoretical, ethical, policy, and practical considerations.

References

Acton, J. (1973). '*Evaluating Public Programs to Save Lives: The Case of Heart Attacks*', RAND Corporation, Santa Monica.

Ahmed, S., Hoque, M. E., Sarker, A. R., Sultana, M., Islam, Z. and Gazi, R. (2016). 'Willingness-to-pay for community-based health insurance among informal workers in Urban Bangladesh', *PLoS one*, **11**(2), p. e0148211.

Binnendijk, E., Gautham, M., Koren, R. and Dror, D. M. (2012). 'Illness Mapping: a time and cost effective method to estimate healthcare data needed to establish community-based health insurance', *BMC Medical Research Methodology*, **12**(1), p. 153.

Binnendijk, E., Koren, R. and Dror, D. M. (2012a). 'Can the rural poor in India afford to treat non-communicable diseases', *Tropical Medicine & International Health*, **17**(11), pp. 1376–1385. doi:10.1111/j.1365-3156.2012.03070.x.

Binnendijk, E., Koren, R. and Dror, D. M. (2012b). 'Hardship financing of healthcare among rural poor in Orissa, India', *BMC Health Services Research*, **12**(1), p. 23. doi:10.1186/1472-6963-12-23.

Binnendijk, E., Dror, D. M., Gerelle, E. and Koren, R. (2013). 'Estimating Willingness-to-Pay for health insurance among rural poor in India by reference to Engel's law', *Social Science and Medicine*, **76**, pp. 67–73.

Binnendijk, E., Koren, R. and Dror, D. M. (2014). 'A model to estimate the impact of thresholds and caps on coverage levels in community-based health insurance schemes in low-income countries', *Health*, **06**(9), pp. 822–835.

Blumenschein, K., Johannesson, M., Yokoyama, K. K. and Freeman, P. R. (2001). 'Hypothetical versus real willingness to pay in the health care sector: Results from a field experiment', *Journal of Health Economics*, **20**(3), pp. 441–457. doi:10.1016/S0167-6296(01)00075-3.

Boyle, K. J. (2017) 'Contingent Valuation in Practice', Chapter 5 in Champ, P. Boyle, K. J. and Brown, T. C. (eds.), *A Primer on Nonmarket Valuation*, Springer, pp. 83–131.

Carson, R. T. (2012). 'Contingent valuation: A practical alternative when prices aren't available', *Journal of Economic Perspectives*, **26**(4), pp. 27–42.

Ciriacy-Wantrup, S. V. (1947). 'Capital returns from soil-conservation practices', *American Journal of Agricultural Economics*, **29**(4) Part_II, pp. 1181–1196.

Diamond, P. A. and Hausman, J. A. (1994). 'Contingent valuation: Is some number better than no number?', *The Journal of Economic Perspectives*, **8**, pp. 45–64.

Dohmen, T., Falk, A., Huffman, D. and Sunde, U. (2009). 'Homo reciprocans: Survey evidence on behavioural outcomes', *The Economic Journal*, **119**, pp. 592–612. doi:10.1111/j.1468-0297.2008.02242.x.

Donfouet, H. P. P., Jeanty, P. W. and Mahieu, P.-A. (2014). 'Dealing with internal inconsistency in double-bounded dichotomous choice: An application to community-based health insurance', *Empirical Economics*, **46**(1), pp. 317–328.

Dror, D. M., Soriano, E. S., Lorenzo, M. E., Sarol, J. N., Azcuna, R. S. and Koren, R. (2005). 'Field based evidence of enhanced healthcare utilization among persons insured by micro health insurance units in Philippines', *Health Policy*, **73**(3), pp. 263–271. doi:10.1016/j.healthpol.2004.11.018.

Dror, D. M. and Armstrong, J. (2006). 'Do micro health insurance units need capital or reinsurance? A simulated exercise to examine different alternatives', *The Geneva Papers on Risk and Insurance — Issues and Practice*, **31**(4), pp. 739–761. https://doi.org/10.1057/palgrave.gpp.2510107.

Dror, D. M., Koren, R. and Steinberg, D. M. (2006). 'The impact of Filipino micro health-insurance units on income-related equality of access to healthcare', *Health Policy*, **77**(3), pp. 304–317.

Dror, D. M., Radermacher, R. and Koren, R. (2006a). 'Willingness to pay for health insurance among rural and poor persons: Field evidence from seven micro health insurance units in India', *Health Policy*, **82**(1), pp. 12– 27.

Dror, D. M., Koren, R., Ost, A., Binnendijk, E., Vellakkal, S. and Danis, M. (2007). Health insurance benefit packages prioritized by low-income clients in India: Three criteria to estimate effectiveness of choice, *Social Science and Medicine*, **64**, pp. 884–896.

Dror, D. M., Radermacher, R., Khadilkar, S. B., Schout, P., Hay, F.-X., Singh, A. and Koren, R. (2009). 'Microinsurance: Innovations in low-cost health insurance', *Health Affairs*, **28**(6), pp. 1788–1798. doi:10.1377/hlthaff.28.6.1788.

Dror, D. M. and Koren, R. (2012). 'The Elusive Quest for Estimates of Willingness to Pay for Health Micro Insurance among the Poor in Low-Income Countries', in Churchill, C. and Matul, M. (eds.) *Micro Insurance Compendium II*. Geneva: ILO, pp. 156–173.

Dror, D. M. (2014). 'Health Microinsurance Programs in Developing Countries', in Culyer A. J. (ed.) *Encyclopedia of Health Economics*, Vol. 1, San Diego: Elsevier, pp. 412–421.

Dror, D. M. and Firth, L. A. (2014). 'The demand for (micro) health insurance in the informal sector', *The Geneva Papers on Risk and Insurance Issues and Practice*, **39**(4), pp. 693–711.

Dror, D. M., Panda, P., May, C., Majumdar, A. and Koren, R. (2014a). '"One for all and all for one": consensus-building within communities in rural India on their health microinsurance package'. *Risk Management and Healthcare Policy*, **7**, pp. 139–153. http://doi.org/10.2147/RMHP.S66011.

Dror, D. M., Majumdar, A., Panda, P., Denny John, P. D. and Koren, R. (2014b). 'Implementing a participatory model of micro health insurance among rural poor with evidence from Nepal', *The Geneva Papers on Risk and Insurance Issues and Practice*, **39**(2), pp. 280–303.

Dror, D. M., Chakraborty, A., Majumdar, A., Panda, P. and Koren, R. (2016a). 'Impact of community-based health insurance in rural India on self-medication and financial protection of the insured', *Indian Journal of Medical Research*, **143**(6), pp. 809–820.

Dror, D. M., Hossain, S. A. S., Majumdar, A., Pérez Koehlmoos, T. L., John, D. and Panda, P. K. (2016b). 'What factors affect voluntary uptake of community-based health insurance schemes in low- and middle-income countries? A systematic review and meta-analysis', *PLoS One*, **11**(8), p. e0160479. doi:10.1371/ journal.pone.0160479.

Dror, D. M. and Jambhekar, S. (2017). '*Microinsurance Implementation Training Manual*', Micro Insurance Academy, New Delhi.

Dror, D. M., Majumdar, A. and Jangle, N. (2018). 'Estimating capital requirements to scale health microinsurance serving rural poor populations' (forthcoming).

Dror, D. M. and Majumdar, A. (2018). 'Collection, interpretation, and utilization of data in microinsurance' (forthcoming).

Engel, E. (1957). Die Productions- und Consumtionsverhaltnisse des Konigreichs Sachsen. *Zeitschrift Des Statistischen Bureaus Des Koniglich Sachsischen Ministeriums Des Inner*, 8 and 9, 1–5454, It was reprinted as an appendix to Die Lebenskosten Belgischer Arbeiter Familien fruher und jetzt. Bulletin de l'Institut International de Statistique (1895), 9, premiere livraison.

Escobar, M.-L., Griffin, C. C. and Shaw, R. P. (eds.) (2010). 'The Impact of Health Insurance In Low- And Middle-Income Countries', The Brookings Institution, Washington, DC. ISBN 978-0-8157-0546-8. Page 180. Accessed on 19 Aug 2017 at https://www.brookings.edu/wp-content/uploads/2016/07/theimpactofhealthinsurance_fulltext.pdf.

Gautham, M., Koren, R., Binnendijk, E. and Dror, D. M. (2011). 'First we go to the small doctor: First contact for curative health care sought by rural communities in Andhra Pradesh & Orissa, India', *The Indian Journal of Medical Research*, **134**(5), p. 627.

Jayakrishnan, T., Jeeja, M. C., Kuniyil, V. and Paramasivam, S. (2016). 'Increasing out-of-pocket health care expenditure in India due to supply or demand?', *Pharmacoeconomics*, **1**, p. 105. doi: 10.4172/2472-1042.1000105.

Kahan, D. M. (2002). 'The Logic of Reciprocity: Trust, Collective Action, and Law', John M. Olin Center for Studies in Law, Economics, and Public Policy Working Papers, Paper 281. Accessed online on 20 Aug 2017 at http://digitalcommons.law.yale.edu/lepp_papers/281.

Kahneman, D. and Tversky, A. (1979). 'Prospect theory: An analysis of decisions under risk', *Econometrica*, **47**(2), pp. 263–291.

Klose, T. (1999). 'The contingent valuation method in health care', *Health Policy*, **47**(2), pp. 97–123.

Mani, A., Rahwan, I. and Pentland, A. (2013). 'Inducing Peer Pressure to Promote Cooperation', Scientific Reports 3, Article number: 1735. doi:10.1038/srep01735.

Ministry of Health and Family Welfare India: National Health Accounts, India — 2004/2005. National Health Accounts Cell, Ministry of Health and Family Welfare, Government of India, New Delhi; 2009.

Nosratnejad, S., Rashidian, A. and Dror, D. M. (2016). 'Systematic review of willingness to pay for health insurance in low and middle-income countries', *PLoS One*, **11**(6), p. e0157470.

O'Donnell, O., van Doorslaer, E., Wagstaff, A. and Lindelow, M. (2008). 'Analyzing health equity using household survey data: A guide to techniques and their implementation', World Bank Publications, pp. 203–212.

Olsen, J. A. and Smith, R. D. (2001). 'Theory versus practice: A review of "willingness-to-pay" in health and health care', *Health Economics*, **10**(1): pp. 39–52.

Panda, P., Chakraborty, A., Dror, D. M. and Bedi. A. (2014). 'Enrolment in community-based health insurance schemes in rural Bihar and Uttar Pradesh, India', *Health Policy and Planning*, **29**, pp. 960–974.

Panda, P., Chakraborty, A. and Dror, D. M. (2015). 'Mobilizing community-based health insurance to enhance awareness & prevention of airborne, vector-borne & waterborne diseases in rural India', *Indian Journal of Medical Research*, **142**(2), pp. 151–164. doi: 10.4103/0971-5916.164235.

Panda, P., Chakraborty, A. and Dror, D. M. (2015a). 'Building awareness to health insurance among the target population of community-based health insurance schemes in rural India', *Tropical Medicine and International Health*, **20**(8), pp. 1093–1107.

Perthel, D. (1975). 'Engel's law revisited', *Revue Internationale De Statistique* (*International Statistical Review*), **43**(2), pp. 211– 218.

Ryan, M., Gerard, K. and Amaya-Amaya, M. (2008). '*Using Discrete Choice Experiments to Value Health and Health Care*', Dordrecht: Springer.

Samuelson, P. (1938). 'A note on the pure theory of consumer's behaviour', *Economica*, **5**, pp. 61–71.

Schanz, K.-U. and Wang, S. (eds.) (2014). 'The Global Insurance Protection Gap: Assessment and Recommendations', A Geneva Association Research Report', Geneva. Accessed online on 19 Aug 2017 at https://www.genevaassociation.org/sites/default/files/research-topics-document-type/pdf_public/ga2014-the_global_insurance_protection_gap_1.pdf.

Scott, A., Maynard, A. and Elliott, R. (eds.) (2003). '*Advances in Health Economics*', Wiley Online Library.

Venkatachalam, L. (2004). 'The contingent valuation method: A review', *Environmental Impact Assessment Review*, **24**, pp. 89–124.

Whitehead, J. C. and Blomquist, G. C. (2006). 'The Use of Contingent Valuation in Benefit-Cost Analysis', in Alberini, A. and Kahn, J. R. (eds.) *Handbook on Contingent Valuation,* Northampton: Edward Elgar, pp. 92–115.

Xu, K., Evans, D. B., Kawabata, K., Zeramdini, R., Klavus, J. and Murray, C. J. L. (2003). 'Household catastrophic health expenditure: A multicountry analysis', *The Lancet*, **362**, pp. 111–117.

Part 1

Theory

Chapter 2

The Demand for (Micro) Health Insurance in the Informal Sector*

Main Messages

- Conventional theories of health insurance are ill-suited to the context of poverty in the informal sector.
- Eight conditions are identified, which a relevant theory of demand for health insurance must recognize and accommodate.
- A total of 3 billion people in the informal sector of LMIC would seek voluntary health insurance only when local awareness about the welfare gains of health insurance is widespread, supported by local governance.

Focus Points

- Low insurance penetration rates in the informal sector raise an underlying question: If the benefits of health insurance are positively provable, how can theory explain the conditions under which the 3 billion or so in the informal sector of LMIC would seek voluntary health insurance?

---

*This chapter is reproduced from *The Geneva Papers on Risk and Insurance — Issues and Practice* (2014), **39**(4), 693–711, Open Access, available at https://www.researchgate.net/publication/263734080_The_Demand_for_Micro_Health_Insurance_in_the_Informal_Sector.

- Standard economic theories of demand for health insurance are based on assumptions that are largely inconsistent with the context of poverty and informality.
- In the informal sector, demand for health insurance is not an individual's decision, instead, it is contingent on groups of people agreeing that most of their members can enhance their welfare by buying insurance.
- Perfect market conditions cannot be assumed in the informal sector as it is only when community-based governance is manifest that member households express WTP for health insurance and thereby create solvent demand on which viable supply can be based.
- In the informal sector, WTP for health insurance reflects group consensus on its value to all members of the community, and therefore subsequent increases in WTP would depend on increases in the community's perception of the welfare gains, rather than on higher input prices of providers, or additional services in the benefits package that most people neither need nor are likely to claim.
- The proposed theory is structured by eight conditions that together provide a contextualized explanation of the demand for health insurance in the informal sector of LMICs.
- Demand for health insurance in the informal sector can be generated by strengthening the ground-up governance consistent with group-based decision making under local conditions.

Structured Abstract

Introduction

The low health insurance penetration rates in the informal sector raise an underlying question: If the benefits of health insurance are positively provable, how can theory explain the conditions under which the 3 billion or so in the informal sector of LMIC would seek voluntary health insurance? The conventional economic theories of demand do not provide a convincing answer to this question, and the authors of this study attempt to fill the gap in understanding the demand for health insurance in the context of informality and poverty by proposing a new theory.

Box 1: Conventional Theories of Demand for Health Insurance

The theories of demand for health insurance can be grouped into two families: those that deal with risk aversion and loss aversion; and those that elaborate moral hazard.

Conventional assumptions relating to expected utility

- The decision to buy (health) insurance is taken by individuals expecting a payoff in return.
- People have no cover other than formally contracted insurance.
- Individuals have access to adequate information and knowledge to understand the value proposition of health insurance.
- Willingness to pay is a monetized expression of marginal utility, which is expressed as demand.
- Exchange occurs in an environment of predictable certainty.

Conventional assumptions relating to attitudes to risk

- The demand for (health) insurance is demand for certain outcomes over uncertain ones of equal value.

Assumptions relating to moral hazard

- Individuals purchase health insurance in order to take advantage of prices below marginal cost, and they can access the information to do so.
- There is ample supply of health care to meet demand.
- The demand for health insurance is the demand to obtain "income effect" benefits, that is, transfer from healthy insured to sick insured.

Method

The authors draw on the literature and on evidence from the field to study the applicability of the core assumptions of conventional economic theories of demand for health insurance to the context of poverty and informality. The assumptions are categorized into three groups for the analysis, those relating to expected utility, attitudes to risk and moral hazard.

Findings

On analyzing the assumptions of conventional economic theories of demand for health insurance, the authors recorded three key insights.

The first insight is that in the informal sector, individuals seek welfare enhancements through affiliation with groups rather than through isolated transactions with unfamiliar partners with whom they have little experience transacting. Thus the demand for health insurance is contingent on groups agreeing that most of their members can benefit by buying insurance.

Secondly, perfect market conditions are not met in the informal sector of LMIC. Instead, governance constitutes the necessary but not sufficient driver for the establishment of the health insurance market. It is suggested that only when community-based governance is manifest, will its member households express WTP for health insurance and so create solvent demand on which viable supply can be based.

The third insight is that WTP reflects group consensus on the value of the good/service to all members of the community. As a result, health insurance covering only very rare events are less likely to be perceived as welfare enhancing by most. Furthermore, increases in WTP for health insurance over time would depend on increases in the community's perception of the welfare gains, rather than on higher input prices of providers, or additional services in the benefits package that most people find redundant.

In the backdrop of various theoretical inadequacies in explaining the conditions under which the 3 billion or so in the informal sector of LMIC would seek voluntary health insurance, the authors posit that a new theory of the demand for health insurance in the informal sector, based on relevant, workable assumptions is required. The study lays down the conditions that the proposed theory must recognize.

Conclusion

The policy implication of the analysis showing the incompatibility of conventional theories of demand in the informal sector and the proposed alternative theory of demand is that demand for voluntary and contributory health insurance can be enhanced by supporting the propagation of:

(i) bottom-up governance structures among communities in the informal sector, and
(ii) the perception that health insurance enhances welfare to the entire community, rather than to single individuals.

The Geneva Papers, **2014**, **00**, (1–19)

www.genevaassociation.org

Open

The Demand for (Micro) Health Insurance in the Informal Sector

David M. Dror[a,b] and Lucy A. Firth[a]
[a]Micro Insurance Academy, 52-B, Okhla Industrial Estate phase III, New Delhi 110020, India.
E-mails: daviddror@socialre.org; Lucy.firth1@gmail.com
[b]Erasmus University Rotterdam (Institute of health policy and management), PoBox 1738, Rotterdam 3000DR, The Netherlands.

We identify the need for a theory of demand for health insurance suited to the informal sector in low- and middle income countries (LMIC) where some 3 billion people lack health cover. Excluded from formal governance structures, they rely on informal arrangements by which rules-in-use shape choices, behaviours and decisions. We explore the fundamental assumptions of standard economic theories of demand for health insurance in the light of arguments from the literature and field evidence. We show that the assumptions are largely inconsistent with the context of poverty and informality. And we propose a new theory based on assumptions better suited to the context of informality and poverty. Our major conclusion is that, in order to grow the demand for health insurance in the informal sector in LMIC, it is first necessary to strengthen ground-up governance consistent with group-based decision-making under local conditions.
The Geneva Papers (2014) **0,** 1–19. doi:10.1057/gpp.2014.24

Keywords: theory of demand; low- and middle income countries; informal sector; micro insurance; health insurance; governance; community-based health insurance

Article submitted 17 June 2013; accepted 27 May 2014; advance online publication, 16 July 2014

The online version of this article is available Open Access

Introduction

Most of the world's population in low- and middle income countries (LMIC) lives and works in the informal sector.[1] In the developing world, the informal sector means small-scale, self-employed activities (with or without hired workers), typically unrecorded, unregistered and conducted without proper integration with the administrative machinery responsible for enforcing laws and regulations, usually escaping both the attention of and recognition from the authorities.[2]

The strong incentive to be in this informal context is that people are outside the framework through which most countries collect taxes or dedicated contributions. The down sides are numerous, notably being de facto excluded from the practical engagements of governments to recognise a universal "right to health" for all citizens[3] through constitutions or engagements under international conventions and recommendations[4] notably, the WHO

[1] Pratap and Quintin (2006); Bacchetta *et al.* (2009).
[2] ILO (2000).
[3] Dror (2001).
[4] Backman *et al.* (2008).

decision on universal health coverage (UHC).[5] Health insurance is a favoured road towards achieving UHC in most LMIC.[6] While health insurance has the potential to reduce out-of-pocket payments (that the poor in the informal sector of developing nations make for health care) and improve access to necessary health care (that is often foregone when unaffordable),[7] health insurance penetration rates in the informal sector are very low.[8] This low penetration raises an underlying question: If the benefits of health insurance are positively provable, *how can theory explain the conditions under which the 3 billion or so in the informal sector of LMIC would seek voluntary health insurance?*

While governments of LMIC have a central role in delivering health services to population segments in the informal sector, their ability to fund such services through taxation is severely limited when the untaxed informal sector is larger than the taxed formal sector,[9] and their ability to expand service delivery through insurance is compromised by lack of capacity to enforce mandated affiliation,[10] which is aggravated further when the mandate entails premium payments.[11] This combined constraint suggests that affiliation to health insurance in the informal sector would probably have to be voluntary and contributory.[12] Thus, the question *how can theory explain the conditions under which the 3 billion or so in the informal sector of LMIC would seek voluntary and contributory health insurance?* begs a convincing answer that, we submit, the theories on health insurance do not yet provide.

The plan of this paper is that: in the next section, we draw on the literature and on evidence from the field to analyse the applicability of the core assumptions of conventional economic theories of demand for health insurance to the context of poverty and informality. In the subsequent section, we propose a theory structured by eight conditions that together provide a contextualised explanation of the demand for health insurance in the informal sector of LMIC. The last section contains our conclusions and policy recommendations on how to establish conditions under which the population in the informal sector of LMIC would seek voluntary and contributory health insurance.

Review of conventional theories of the demand for health insurance

In this section, we review the main assumptions that form the tenets of conventional economic theories of the demand for insurance generally and health insurance particularly. Starting from common historic origins, based on marginal values, and posited on "perfect knowledge", conventional theories differ from one another on various issues. Here, we focus on differing treatments of attitude to risk (i.e. Friedman and Savage vs Kahneman and Tversky) and of moral hazard (i.e. Pauly vs Nyman) to show that the conventional economic theoretic approach is, in general, ill-suited to the context of poverty in informal sectors. We have organised our

---

[5] WHO (2005).
[6] Faden *et al.* (2011).
[7] Mielck *et al.* (2009).
[8] Roth *et al.* (2007); De Bock and Gelade (2012).
[9] Narayan *et al.* (2000a, b); Backman *et al.* (2008).
[10] Navarro (1989); Narayan *et al.* (2000a, b).
[11] Gumber (2002).
[12] Dror (2007).

investigation of the relevance of conventional theories in this section under three groups of assumptions, those relating to expected utility, attitudes to risk and moral hazard.

Assumptions relating to expected utility

The conventional treatment of the demand for health insurance has its genesis in the theories of diminishing marginal utility and expected utility, both of which were developed in relation to gambles, and are attributed to Bernoulli 1738.[13] The law of diminishing marginal utility states that the first unit of consumption of a good or service (or income or wealth) yields more utility than the second and subsequent units, with a continuing reduction of utility for greater amounts. The expected utility hypothesis states that the utility from the expected value of a gamble will depend on the gamblers' risk appetite and exposure. The method to measure utility in terms of income or wealth for the rational decision-maker under conditions of uncertainty was developed by von Neumann and Morgenstern[14] as a function of probability and attitude to risk. Marginal and expected utility theory has been extensively discussed in the literature (e.g. the 2007 commemorative edition of von Neumann and Morgenstern has been cited 16,000 times by May 2013) and analysed in microeconomic courses,[15] but the relevance of its embedded assumptions and their application to the demand for health insurance in the informal sector have not been systematically explored. Here we do so for a selection of assumptions.

Conventional assumption: the decision to buy (health) insurance is taken by individuals in return for an expected payoff to them

Three issues are at the core here: individual decision-making, individual payoff and specific monetised sums. The independence of individual choice must be nuanced in the context of the informal sector.[16] Based on historically seated de facto attributes of governance structures (with norms, protocols and local rules-in-use), communities create consensus and influence decisions adopted by single community members.[17] The group priorities uphold decisions that are commonly considered to be welfare-enhancing.[18] In traditional and informal sectors, this creates a powerful pressure on individual members that determines what economic activity they can/must/must not enter into, who can/cannot do so, and how the benefits will be distributed.[19] Applying to health insurance the insight that communities prioritise welfare-enhancing choices, it follows that the consensus would uphold the decision to buy health insurance only when the contracted benefits of the insurance can be expected to flow to community members. This is consistent with the seminal micro health insurance work of Dror and Jacquier[20] that proposed that the basis for decision-making in micro health insurance was group consensus, and supported by recent evidence from rural India.[21]

[13] Arrow (1963).
[14] von Neumann and Morgenstern (1947).
[15] For example, Varian (1990).
[16] Platteau (1997).
[17] Granovetter (1973); Ostrom (2010).
[18] Sen (1970, 1999a, b).
[19] Crawford and Ostrom (2005).
[20] Dror and Jacquier (1999).
[21] Dror *et al.* (2014a).

Compliance by community members with consensus flows from their reliance on the community's patterns of reciprocity.[22] Moreover, non-conformity with the consensus could be understood by other group members as a form of not meeting expectations of reciprocity, which can lead to punishment in the form of partial or total exclusion from the group.[23] The need to belong to the group, implying access to benefits that are generated by the members but not otherwise available widely as public goods, reinforces the norms and networks that enable individuals to act collectively, also known as "social capital".[24] Informal communities may have stronger and more pervasive impacts on their members than do formal communities[25] because the threat of exclusion for noncompliance may not be as significant with formal groups. This is consistent with the findings of Zhang *et al.*[26] and Donfouet *et al.*[27] for China and Cameroon, respectively. We posit that these arguments and findings challenge the fundamentally different assumption about the direct association between paying a premium in expectation of a specific payoff from an insurance contract.

Conventional assumption: people have no cover other than formally contracted insurance
Although not formally stated, conventional theory rests on the simplifying assumption that either people have bought insurance or they do not have insurance, suggesting that there is no cover for those who are not "formally" insured. Von Neumann and Morgenstern's axiom of independence of preferences, which relies on the separation of risks, may not be widely applicable in the context in which there is informal cover of many risks from birth through the community's systems of reciprocity that are typical within the informal sector,[28] and which are akin to informal mutual insurance.[29] Works by Graham,[30] Stiglitz[31] and Linnerooth-Bayer and Mechler[32] have investigated pre-existing informal cover in developing contexts and found that although such arrangements were intended for times of need, in practice they were sometimes vague, unpredictable, incomplete and unstable due to constraints associated with covariance of risk across the group. While the separation of risks is apparently violated in the informal context, others have investigated the complementarity between private and public insurance, but have done so in the formal context of developed countries.[33] Morduch,[34] in a review of informal health and other insurances, provides evidence suggesting that the limitations of arrangements that prevail in the informal sector generate a desire to

[22] Granovetter (1973, 2005).
[23] Henrich *et al.* (2001).
[24] Woolcock and Narayan (2000).
[25] Granovetter (1985).
[26] Zhang *et al.* (2006).
[27] Donfouet *et al.* (2011).
[28] Narayan *et al.* (2000a).
[29] Coate and Ravallion (1993).
[30] Graham (1994).
[31] Stiglitz (2004).
[32] Linnerooth-Bayer and Mechler (2007).
[33] For example, Nyman (2003); Preker and Bassett (2013).
[34] Morduch (1999).

systematise and strengthen the imperfect dependence between risk and pre-existing informal mutual-aid through formal health insurance.

Conventional assumption: individuals have access to adequate information and knowledge to understand the value proposition of health insurance

Fundamental to making an informed choice to buy health insurance based on the expected utility is the ability to understand the value-proposition of the payoff. There are at least three issues here. The first is that levels of technical knowledge and awareness of health insurance may be very low in the informal sector[35] making it difficult for individuals to perceive the value proposition. The paradigm of transacting under information asymmetry or imperfect knowledge is known.[36] Secondly, qualities of health insurance as a credence good[37] might exacerbate difficulties in understanding its value proposition. Moreover, the value proposition of health insurance may be less clear when related to group-based interests, and to the need that health insurance should be complementary to pre-existing informal cover and/or to services that can be accessed free-of-charge. The third issue is that, contrary to excellent intra-community information-flows (e.g. gossip), flows of information between external parties and informal sector interlocutors are typically highly constrained,[38] subject to deliberate misleading[39] and extensively misinterpreted.[35] Occasional mis-selling, deliberate over-simplification or obfuscation on the part of the insurer and the insured has made (health) insurance the butt of endless jokes and court cases; they also challenge the assumption that adequate information and knowledge to understand the value proposition of health insurance is a given. This assumption is challenged not just by intentional lack of transparency that is often part of the business model of commercial companies in developing countries (von Pischke), but also by the fact that the poor in the informal sector have no inkling of what they need to know or how to access the information they seek because of their lack of experience in making such contracts.[40] In the words of Donald Rumsfeld in a totally different context they face "unknown unknowns".[41]

Moreover, in the informal sector, many people's only experience of insurance is the mandatory credit life insurance required when borrowing money, which is a further financial burden at a time of need and, as such, builds antagonism towards insurance.[42] Whether negative perceptions of insurance are gained directly or vicariously, local information sources[38] ensure that all within the community know the perils of insurance, which impacts the community's consensus on the benefits of health insurance and knowledge of its value proposition.

---

[35] Platteau and Ontiveros (2013).

[36] Akerlof (1970); Simon (1972); Stiglitz (2001).

[37] Credence goods are goods and services for which the value can only be ascertained when characteristics are tested sometime after the transaction is complete (Baron, 2011).

[38] Granovetter (1973).

[39] von Pischke (2008); Narayan *et al.* (2000a, b).

[40] von Pischke (2008); Gandhi (1959).

[41] Donald Rumsfeld, American Secretary of State 2002 (on the issue of Iraq's supposed weapons of mass destruction), "There are known knowns; there are things we know we know. We also know there are known unknowns; that is to say, we know there are some things we do not know. But there are also unknown unknowns – the ones we don't know we don't know".

[42] Roth *et al.* (2007).

Conventional assumption: willingness to pay is a monetised expression of marginal utility, which is expressed as demand

Another basic premise of neoclassical economics is that demand, as manifest in willingness to pay (WTP), is equivalent to marginal utility,[15] which suggests the utility maximising framing of "what do I want/need and how much am I prepared to pay for it?"[40] Does this also apply in the informal sector? A review of 14 evidence-based studies of WTP for health insurance among the poor in low-income countries in Asia and in Africa demonstrated that evaluation of WTP was influenced by socioeconomic parameters (e.g. income, education, morbidity patterns, availability of health care). Furthermore, marked differences in these parameters across locations and over time made it very difficult to associate estimated WTP with the actuarial pure premium or the price of benefits on offer. In fact, when WTP was measured as a per cent of their income, the poorer sub-groups within resource-poor population segments expressed higher WTP than the richer sub-groups for identical packages.[43] A more general model of WTP in rural settings (based on data from India) found that, in all locations, WTP expressed as percentage of income decreases with household income. This reminds of Engel's law on food expenditures; and WTP as percentage of food expenditures had the most consistent relationship with WTP (other anchors examined included WTP as per cent of overall income and discretionary income).[44] That WTP is influenced by other things than income is perhaps not surprising, but that it is negatively associated with income is counterintuitive and important to stress. These findings indicate that like food, health insurance is considered a necessity good even by people with very low income and no prior experience with health insurance. This may echo von Pischke's explanation of a different logic among poor people in the informal sector (demonstrated in the context of borrowing money) whereby the poor do not consider whether the price (interest rate) is reasonable and whether they can gain on the deal overall, but whether they can meet the repayment schedule and whether it will enable them to meet a need or an obligation. This suggests that the decision to purchase insurance in the informal context might be framed as "*how much can I afford not to participate in this transaction*?" Therefore, in the informal sector there is no certainty that the assumption holds that WTP for health insurance is the monetised value of the marginal utility of the expected benefits.

Conventional assumption: that exchange occurs in an environment of predictable certainty

Two important, often unstated premises are that consumers are able to enter into insurance contracts at will, and can assume that the insurer will fulfil the contract or that such fulfilment can be enforced. Neither of these premises may hold in the informal sector: the individual's capacity to enter into contracts may be curtailed in contexts where group-based institutions can "prescribe, permit or advise" individual actions (p. 583)[19]; and there is constrained access to external rules of law.[45] Although expected value theory has been applied elsewhere to cover the possibility of contract failure,[46] this probability-based extension of theory may not be relevant in the informal sector where

[43] Dror and Koren (2011).

[44] Binnendijk *et al.* (2013).

[45] Narayan *et al.* (2000a, b); Straub (2005).

[46] Doherty and Schlesinger (1991).

there are fundamental difficulties in establishing and enforcing contracts. The capacity of low-income countries to provide governance of transactions is limited[47,48] both within the informal sector and between informal and formal segments of the economy. Exclusion from the governance arrangements of the formal sector exposes people in the informal sector to greater transaction costs related to contract enforceability.[49] The efforts, costs and risks of transaction failure "have particularly damaging effects, as they undermine the very processes of exchange and specialization".[50] Therefore, we assert that in the informal sector, the environment of predictable certainty cannot be assumed to exist, or is severely hampered.

Assumptions relating to attitudes to risk

Friedman and Savage[51] specified insurance as a gamble in which the risk-averse individual will prefer a certain gain to an uncertain gain of equivalent expected value. Applying the law of diminishing marginal utility, because utility increases with wealth at a decreasing rate, risk-averse people prefer a certain gain to an uncertain gain of the equivalent value, therefore insurance is rational. It also shows that poorer people benefit more from insurance of a given monetary sum. Kahneman and Tversky[52] argued that insurance relates to potential loss (rather than a gain) and showed that as the rational individual will prefer an uncertain loss over a certain loss of equivalent expected value, purchasing insurance in order to avoid risk is not rational.

We now examine whether the assumptions associated with these arguments hold.

Conventional assumption: the demand for (health) insurance is demand for certain outcomes over uncertain ones of equal value

Evidence from LMIC indicates that people seeking insurance seek certainty of payment rather than certainty of expected value. The informal sector is characterised by a general deficit of formal governance and predictability, which relates not merely to extremely rare events. In fact, Platteau[16] explained that the norms of balanced reciprocity require that all should be able to receive payoffs in a reasonable period, which could be met better when insurance covers higher frequency events with fairly certain occurrences. The quest for that kind of certainty among rural poor was reported in studies that recorded the choices when asked to compose the health insurance package; rural poor people in the informal sector in India devised composite packages with low per-event maximum cover above which the insurance does not pay anything ("caps") plus outpatient care and maternity, rather than a

---

[47] Knack (2003).

[48] Governance consists of the traditions and institutions by which authority is exercised. This includes the capacity of the government to effectively formulate and implement sound policies; and the respect of citizens and the state for the institutions that govern economic and social interactions among them. The Rule of Law "captures perceptions of the extent to which agents have confidence in and abide by the rules of society, and in particular the quality of contract enforcement, property rights, the police, and the courts, as well as the likelihood of crime and violence" *www.info.worldbank.org/governance/wgi/index.asp*, (World Bank (yearly) and World Bank (year unknown))

[49] Williamson (1981, 1989, 1985 and 2003).

[50] Kydd and Dorward (2003, pp. 5–6).

[51] Friedman and Savage (1948).

[52] Kahneman and Tversky (1979).

package of only hospitalisation with higher coverage.[53] Moreover, where communities organise their community-based health insurance (CBHI) schemes in which members participate in package design, the poor in the informal sector in India seek to avoid uncertainty in health-care costs by including high frequency events the costs of which they perceive as less predictable (e.g. tests or imaging) and leave out services for which the price is both lower and predictable (e.g. consultation).[54] These packages offered many members a higher likelihood to draw some benefit. Such packages are not usually offered by commercial insurers in India.

An additional element of uncertainty is the cost of financing the payment to health-care providers, called "hardship financing".[55,56] Hardship financing can represent as much as 5 per cent of households' annual income in the informal sector of rural India, and is associated not only with hospitalisations but also with cases of maternity and even outpatient care (some 25 per cent of the households reported hardship financing in outpatient cases). Therefore, the "*demand for fairly certain outcomes*" should include the fairly certain reduction of the risk of hardship financing, which occurs in most types of health-seeking, and thus it follows logically that its reduction would take precedence over reducing only rarer risks, for example, hospitalisations. However, health insurance never compensates for the interest paid to moneylenders for loans to pay for uninsured health costs ("hardship financing"). Commercially available insurance packages that neither reduce health-related borrowing by covering frequent events, nor cover hardship financing are unlikely to be viewed by most people in the informal sector as a mechanism enhancing certain outcomes. Therefore, we posit that conventional assumptions of attitude to risk are irrelevant not only because of their reliance on marginal utility but also because they are ill suited to application to the risks faced in the informal context.

Assumptions relating to moral hazard

The trade-off between risk sharing and incentives to change behaviour was identified by Arrow[13] who argued that doctors' mediation of access to medical services could control any tendency to moral hazard.[57] Pauly[58] assumed a stronger role for the patient/consumer in moral hazard. He reasoned that the value of health insurance to the consumer (price pay-off insurance contracts only, not lump sum contracts[59]) originates from his/her ability to consume health care at a price below the efficient marginal cost price which results in demand for a quantity of health care above the efficient level. Pauly argued that moral hazard is inefficient because the price the insured consumer pays is below the efficient market price, which she/he would pay if uninsured. When that cost difference is greater than the gain from

[53] Danis *et al.* (2007); Dror *et al.* (2007b).
[54] Dror (2007a); Panda *et al.* (2013, Table 1); Dror *et al.* (2014b, Tables 2 and 3).
[55] Hardship financing refers to selling assets or borrowing at interest to pay for health care, which is the single greatest cause of families falling into poverty in low and middle income countries.
[56] Binnendijk *et al.* (2012).
[57] "Moral hazard" refers to changes in behaviour due to being insured.
[58] Pauly (1968).
[59] Price payoff insurance contracts pay an agreed amount of a health-care cost (e.g. $50 towards the cost of a physician consultation) thus reducing the price paid for health care by the insured party. Contingent contracts pay an agreed amount upon diagnosis (e.g. $500 if diagnosed with appendicitis).

the avoidance of risk (Friedman and Savage), there is a net overall welfare loss to all insured.[60] Zeckhauser[61] and others have shown that co-payments, exclusions and discrimination on the basis of medical condition reduce demand-driven moral hazard and lessen inefficiencies. This led to the introduction of deductibles and co-payments into insurance policies, on the assumption that it was an effective way to remedy the welfare loss due to moral hazard. Shifting some of the cost to the policyholders meant a net increase in the cost of health insurance (or lower payout for the risk premium). Pauly *et al.*[62] argued that risk-averse customers would agree to pay even higher premiums (than actuarially fair) as long as they are cheaper than their expected expenses for the same basket of services without insurance, and therefore consistent with rational behaviour. However, Pauly recognised that demand for health insurance would weaken when the variance of the medical costs covered by the insurance is low.

Wagstaff and Lindelow[63] reported that in China, being insured increased the risk of high and catastrophic spending rather than lowering it, because of insurer-induced moral hazard and encouragement to seek care from higher-level providers. Such a situation could mean that uninsured are required to pay lower prices than insured persons, which would lower the potential gain from insurance. This invalidates the assumption that the demand for health insurance would always increase due to expected moral hazard. In most discussions with grassroots groups (and in many professional meetings as well) the common perception is that providers of care charge the insured higher prices than from uninsured.[64] In the informal sector in countries like India, such pricing practices would lead to higher rather than lower costs when insured, because the standard practice of health insurance is not to charge a deductible or co-pay, but to impose low caps (maximum cover above which the insurer does not pay anything). Therefore, the only opportunity to benefit from moral hazard would be for low-cost procedures, the prices of which are known, competition higher and price variance low. These conditions indicate that, in the informal sector, the assumption that the demand for health insurance is enhanced by moral hazard does not hold.

Nyman[65] recognised that the sick have health-care costs that reduce their disposable income, a situation that is inexistent among healthy insured. This is an application to health insurance of Arrow's assertion that "medical services, apart from preventive services, afford satisfaction only in the event of illness, a departure from the normal state of affairs" (p. 948).[13] In other words, moral hazard happens when price elasticity for demand is significantly different from zero, which is the case for non-catastrophic illness treatments, but not necessarily for catastrophic treatments (e.g. amputations or cancer treatments). Nyman argues that lower prices paid by the insured for health care lead not only to a price effect, but also to an income effect that is comparable with a redistribution of income from the insured well to the insured sick.[66] By enabling the sick to buy needed health care that they could otherwise not afford, insurance leads to a welfare gain for the insured sick

[60] Pauly (1986).
[61] Zeckhauser (1970).
[62] Pauly *et al.* (2009).
[63] Wagstaff and Lindelow (2008).
[64] Aikins and Okang (2006).
[65] Nyman (2003, 2008).
[66] Nyman (2006).

(efficient moral hazard). Nyman's work complements and extends Pauly's work by identifying that while the price elasticity of demand may or may not be significantly different from zero for any individual, price and income elasticities of the sick will vary greatly from those of the well. Nyman explains the demand for health insurance thus: "consumers demand health insurance mostly to obtain a welfare gain from moral hazard. Consumer preferences regarding risk are largely irrelevant and, if anything, inhibit the purchase of health insurance. Under the new theory, the voluntary purchase of insurance makes consumers better off" (p. xiv).[65] Typically, in the informal sector, the population under-utilises necessary health care[67]; thus an increase in utilisation following insurance is welfare-enhancing rather than welfare-decreasing moral hazard, and this is true not only for the seriously sick.

Conventional assumption: individuals purchase health insurance in order to take advantage of prices below marginal cost; and they can access the information to do so

Pauly's assumption that consumers have the information and capacities to assess the cost they would face for a particular health treatment when insured vs uninsured has been questioned.[68] And Knowles[69] stated that the assumptions of marginal cost pricing and of access to the necessary information by consumers are at odds with the reality prevailing in the health sector (not only in the informal sector). In addition, not only is there a general lack of competitive supply of health care in the informal sector, providers of health services (e.g. government, non-profit health organisations or informal providers) do not compete with each other on prices or even know their marginal costs.[70] The prospect of price-effect moral hazard is further reduced in community-based health insurance schemes that can detect, stop or punish members that abuse the CBHI.[71] Moreover, as many health insurance schemes offer very limited coverage, the likelihood is greatly diminished to take advantage through insurance of prices below marginal costs, simply because expensive health care (including for life-threatening conditions) depends on the patients' ability to pay out-of-pocket (regardless of insurance status). This suggests that as most costs are excluded from coverage (either not insured at all, or above the cap of insurance) the demand for health insurance in the informal sector cannot be attributed to the desire to capture price reductions that may or may not be below marginal costs through insurance. It would seem that demand reflects a desire to access care affordably.

Conventional assumption: there is ample supply of health care to meet demand

Though rarely stated by conventional arguments, they rely on an implied assumption that ample and competitive supply of health care exists to satisfy the extra demand generated by the price effect of insurance. As already stated, there is no reason to assume that the fragmented supply of health care in the informal sector is either ample to satisfy the demand or competitive, as Kupferman and Ron[72] showed in the Philippines, or that it is price sensitive.[73] Therefore, the assumption must be treated with reserve.

[67] Acharya *et al.* (2013).
[68] Boone (2013).
[69] Knowles (1995).
[70] Dror (2014).
[71] Lahkar and Sundaram-Stukel (2010); Biener and Eling (2012).
[72] Kupferman and Ron (2002).
[73] Donaldson *et al.* (2004).

Conventional assumption: the demand for health insurance is the demand to obtain "income effect" benefits, that is, transfer from healthy insured to sick insured
Nyman[65] explains the income effect (i.e. flows of funds from healthy insured to sick insured) in the context of catastrophic expenses of serious illness (e.g. cancer), but as already mentioned, high-cost events are not normally insurable under health insurance that can be accessed in the informal sector. It could be claimed that the income effect kicks in even with smaller quantum transfers associated with low to medium health-care costs that are relevant to insurance in the informal sector. However, the empirical evidence of the income effect is yet to be shown; in the informal sector, this assertion would apply only when the enrollees have certainty that the contract (which means redistribution from healthy insured to unhealthy insured) is applied fairly and fully, a condition that is neither explicit in policies nor guaranteed. Moreover, as most of the health insurance in the informal sector has been reported to be in the form of mutual-aid or CBHI schemes in India and Africa, the additional question which needs addressing is whether this income effect applies in the same manner when benefits from insurance are sought at the community rather than individual level.

Towards a theory of demand for health insurance in the informal sector

The discussion in the previous section raised several issues pointing to theoretical inadequacies to explain *the conditions under which the 3 billion or so in the informal sector of LMIC would seek voluntary health insurance,* when at present most people in the informal sector of developing countries do not join health insurance, even though they pay for health care. Our analysis of the conventional theoretic assumptions leads us to posit that a new theory of the demand for health insurance in the informal sector, based on relevant, workable assumptions is required. As a starting point, a relevant theory must recognise and accommodate the following conditions:

1. The demand is a collective decision of a specific group to formalise and expand pre-existing informal arrangements for financial support of its members when ill;
2. A necessary (but not sufficient) condition for the formulation of demand for health insurance in the informal sector is that practical arrangements in place ensure clients that their contract will be enforced;
3. The demand reflects an intention to reduce financial risks from frequent low to medium health-care costs rather than rare health-care costs;
4. The formulation of demand can occur when a consensus is apparent on the value of health insurance within the context, even though the relevant value may differ from the monetised marginal value to each individual;
5. The demand can be expected to increase when moral hazard is welfare enhancing (i.e. when more sick people that did not utilise health care without insurance are getting more needed care when insured);
6. The demand reflects the intention to reduce the risk of hardship financing associated with fairly certain events;
7. The demand can occur either under profit-sharing mutual aid or under profit-taking commercial insurance, either of which can formulate even without competition;
8. The demand for health insurance can be combined with other community activities (i.e. may not be limited to health insurance).

In this context, a theory of demand must cover not only purchase decisions (which include both decisions of rationing and of priority-setting) but also governance arrangements and relationships with supply. Therefore, we offer this explanation of the demand for health insurance in informal contexts of poverty in LMIC as a more relevant and useful theory. Health insurance is a mechanism through which communities seek to enhance the welfare of members. Demand can be manifested only when the community, applying its rules-in-use, recognises that purchasing health insurance is welfare enhancing and consistent with "what responsible adults should do" to increase the likelihood of benefits to most of the members. Owing to information problems, demand decisions occur through affiliation with groups, rather than through isolated transactions of individuals with partners they do not know and with whom they have little experience transacting. Appropriate, local governance constitutes the necessary but not sufficient driver for the establishment of the health insurance market. Supply, wherever sourced, can capture local demand only when it is trusted, and trust is enhanced when the local rules of governance apply. As demand is the only condition that can drive the creation of a health insurance market, and can only do so with locally trusted governance, the establishment of markets for health insurance must begin with establishing demand at the community level.

This presentation of an alternative explanation of demand in the informal sector is at variance with conventional theories, which have been analysed in the previous section and are summarised below.

One can group the theories of demand for health insurance into two families: those that deal with risk aversion and loss aversion; and those that elaborate moral hazard.

Conventional EU theory of demand is based firstly on the axiom that events are independent from each other. The informal sector with its rural or urban-slum settings offers many challenges to that assumption, and supports a more plausible assumption that the covariant component of health risks predominates. Think of well-documented conditions such as lack of access to safe drinking water; dearth of hygiene or open defecation near or into water sources; malnutrition or under-nutrition; higher likelihood of contracting illnesses from other humans due to communal living of many people in small and enclosed spaces that frequently enforce contact with ill persons even as they do not offer protection from too much heat or cold or air pollution due to indoor cooking; or higher likelihood of contracting illnesses from animals—both domestic and wild—due to close and frequent contact with animals. This leads us to submit that in the informal sector, the violation of the axiom of independence of health events seems undeniable, weakening any argument based on it.

Secondly, the expected marginal utility theory assumes that risk-averse *individuals* accept a reduction in *their wealth* if such reduction (i.e. the payment of a premium) could *guarantee* to escape the *risky situation*. The four italicised terms are all seriously compromised in the informal sector. The detailed analysis in the previous section shows why most economic decisions are not taken by single individuals or motivated only by personal interests; rather, decisions are taken by a larger human collectivity (the family, the extended family and even the reference group or the "community") of which each person is part. Even if formally a decision could be traced to a single individual, that person's group of significant others influences the decision how much money to spend, when, and for what. The trade-offs of an individual considering only his/her needs often differ fundamentally from those of the group of which she/he is part (e.g. buy something only for my personal use vs pay for health care for a sick relative, or to feed the family, or for a child's school, or for seeds for the next agricultural season, or save up to pay for a wedding or a festival). The group decision reflects not only ROI but social priorities and rules-in-use. Moreover, the call to pay a premium to reduce an intangible risk that has not yet occurred (against a promise by an external party that may not be trusted to keep its part of the bargain, or that may legitimately not be required to pay) competes directly with the call to pay for apparent needs against unconditional delivery of good or service. All previous theories have remained silent on the question whether voluntary purchase of a credence good differed from purchasing a normal good even among resource-poor groups; we submit that (at least) in the informal sector, such assumption is invalid, as in fact there is a circumstantial (and theoretical) hierarchy of priorities, which the group shares and its members most often follow. The other assumption, that one person's wealth commands priority over the wealth or well-being of the entire household or community, is also devoid of evidence in the informal sector; in fact, we have provided many references that the collective good often has priority over individual choices because the common good is inclusive and distributive while the individual utility is exclusive and proprietary.

Moreover, the assumption that payment of a premium can guarantee the reduction of risk to wealth subsumes that contracts can be enforced with acceptable costs, risk or time-loss, which is anything but proven in the informal sector. Based on the field evidence cited, we submit that in the informal sector of LMIC, social contracts within community members are backstopped by community pressure to abide by rules-in-use, mostly reciprocity that requires entire families to step in to meet obligations undertaken by their members. Legal contracts with external parties are handled by external arbitrators with a different logic, cost and time frame, and therefore often not accessed at all by informal sector persons.

Finally, we examine the assumption about the risky situation: in addition to the covariate characteristics of risks themselves (explained above), attitudes to risk (risk appetite or aversion) exhibit a covariate component originating from the influence of the majority of the reference community on attitudes held by single individuals. When most people prefer uncertain losses (as postulated by the Prospect theory) that leads them to logically refrain from premium payments that represent a certain loss, most individuals in that community are less likely to opt for a certain loss just to demonstrate their completely independent choice.

Many of the auxiliary assumptions about the conditions under which health insurance operates subsume perfect market conditions (e.g. that insurance is the only or most economical option to pool risks; or that individuals can make informed choices; or that individuals can estimate the monetised value of their marginal utility from health insurance and are willing to pay that amount for any level of risk exposure in isolation of all alternative utility gains that can be availed by other uses of the same amount; or that the transaction occurs in a market obeying predictable rules). All have been shown to be compromised in the informal sector. The cumulative effect of these imperfections weighs heavily on the validity of those theories of demand for health insurance, at least in the conditions prevailing in the informal sector of LMIC.

A different order of theoretical arguments is that voluntary demand for insurance occurs among risk-averse customers to reduce both the risk of high out-of-pocket payments and the variance of such payments. The underlying logic here is that demand for health insurance is the demand of premium payers to tacitly transfer the excessive cost[74] to

[74] Excessive costs in this context means the difference between the cost that an uninsured would have to pay minus the cost that the insured has to pay, including the premium and any co-pay or deductible amount.

others ("others" means society at large according to Pauly, and the group of healthy insured according to Nyman). That demand can exist when health-care costs are high and variable. This form of demand for insurance is the demand to engage in a win-lose paradigm (the gain of each insured that is paid a claim is the loss of other non-claimants). This expression of the transaction ignores several fundamental situations that are important in the informal sector: (i) members of CBHI often select high-frequency and low cost events for their insurance but leave out high cost benefits because the premium would be too high. As this demand for coverage of lower costs (and probably low variance of OOPS) is not explained by this theory, we must assume it is incomplete; (ii) the theory ignores the possibility that poorer people would avoid OOPS by foregoing care. This is not a rare phenomenon, which is more prevalent in low-income groups (which are of course more prevalent in the informal sector of LMIC). However, people foregoing unaffordable care may still seek assistance from others in their reference community; could this form of pooling and reciprocity explain the demand to be part of a welfare-enhancing group? (iii) In LMIC generally, and in the informal sector and CBHI specifically, even insured persons must pay the cost of health care above the cap, which can be considerable. In such cases, the demand for health insurance cannot be the expectation to avoid catastrophic costs (and the definition of "catastrophic" is secondary). A more likely explanation is that the demand reflects an expectation to participate in the network through which people can borrow easily to cover above-cap costs (which, as shown earlier, occasion hardship financing). Maintaining a good standing with potential lenders is very valuable in this case, even if it does not allow transferring either health-care costs or the cost of hardship financing to others. (iv) Finally, it has been proposed that the demand for health insurance is explained by an expectation that insurance would reduce the variance of high out-of-pocket payments. This expectation subsumes that providers fix prices freely and that there is ample supply to allow price competition. And, that the effective way to reduce variance in the costs is to increase the size of the pool (in application of the Law of Large Numbers). Two observations challenge this line of argumentation in the informal sector: first, in the informal sector the most effective social context is the community, which can be effective for as long as it remains relatively homogeneous and small. Several communities can federate if they wish to capture the benefits of larger size, but the basic unit must remain small. Secondly, there is ample evidence that supply of health care and supply of health insurance is extremely limited in the informal and rural sectors of LMIC, obviating the assumption that price competition can be countered by a large pool of insured clients.

Conclusion and policy implications

This article set out to answer the question *how can theory explain the conditions under which the 3 billion or so in the informal sector of LMIC would seek voluntary health insurance?*

The first insight from this analysis is that people in the informal sector seek welfare enhancements through affiliation with groups, rather than through isolated transactions with partners they do not know and with whom they have little experience transacting. Therefore, the demand for health insurance is contingent on groups agreeing that most of their members can gain welfare from engaging in this transaction.

The second important insight is that perfect market conditions,[75] which are assumed by conventional theories of health insurance in rich countries, are not met in the informal sector of LMIC. Rather, governance constitutes the necessary but not sufficient driver for the establishment of the health insurance market. Supply, wherever sourced, can capture local demand only when it is trusted, and trust is enhanced when the local rules of governance apply. Demand is the necessary and sufficient condition for the creation of a health insurance market. However, the demand can be manifested only when the community, applying its rules-in-use, recognises that purchasing health insurance is welfare enhancing and consistent with "what responsible adults should do". The community could create such consensus only when the health insurance scheme is governed by rules people understand and accept, which local governance can ensure well. Only when community-based governance is manifest, will its member households express WTP for health insurance and so create solvent demand on which viable supply can be based.

Thirdly, WTP reflects group consensus on the value of the good/service to all members of the community, which means that very rare events are less likely to be perceived as welfare enhancing by most. Therefore, health insurance covering only rare events, even when provided at discounted cost (as some countries do with "below poverty line" populations segments), does not per se guarantee that most people will see it as adding welfare to the community, since the measure is different from price only. Health insurance is perceived as a necessity good, not a normal good, and WTP determined heuristically notably by consensus on the amount that all or most can pay, rather than the actuarial value of out-of-pocket payments that the insurance is supposed to replace. Therefore, increases in WTP for health insurance over time would depend on increases in the community's perception of the welfare gains, rather than on higher input prices of providers, or additional services in the benefit package that most people neither need nor are likely to claim.

The policy implication of our analysis why most assumptions of conventional theories of demand are violated, and our alternative theory of demand in the informal sector is that governments and all those wishing to see more demand for voluntary and contributory health insurance in the informal sector of LMIC can assist the process by supporting the propagation of (i) bottom-up governance structures among communities in the informal sector; and (ii) the perception that health insurance enhances welfare to the entire community, rather than to single individuals. Only when communities are comfortable about the governance of their health insurance are the conditions ripe for expression of WTP, which in turn determines the supply of health insurance. Therefore *the 3 billion or so in the informal sector of LMIC would seek voluntary health insurance* only when local awareness about the welfare gains of health insurance is widespread, supported by local governance. As these are the drivers for the development of the market for (micro) health insurance in the informal sector, they should be facilitated and enhanced by institutions of state and by the business community.

---

[75] Including free and full information on transactions, ample comparable supply which enables free competition based on price and quality of services; ample demand that is keen to buy; and governance structures ensuring that contracts can be enforced and that are known and trusted by most clients. There is not one LMIC that can boast ample supply either of health services or of health insurance in its informal sector, or that has efficient governance that ensures contract enforcement in matters of credence goods like insurance and that the majority of the population trusts.

Acknowledgements

The authors acknowledge the support of the Micro Insurance Academy in providing the opportunity for this work. We also acknowledge the useful comments by Ruth Koren on an earlier draft, as well as those by two peer reviewers. David M. Dror gratefully acknowledges funding support provided by the European Commission 7th Framework Program (grant ID HEALTH-F2-2009-223518 – Community-based Health Insurance in India).

References

Acharya, A., Vellakkal, S., Taylor, F., Masset, E., Satija, A., Burke, M. and Ebrahim, S. (2013) *The impact of health insurance schemes for the informal sector in low- and middle-income countries: a systematic review*, World Bank Research Paper 6324.

Aikins, M. and Okang, G. (2006) *Utilization and Cost of Health Care Under the District Health Insurance Schemes: A Case Study of Brong-Ahafo and Eastern Regions*, Accra: JSA Consultants.

Akerlof, G.A. (1970) 'The market for "lemons": Quality uncertainty and the market mechanism', *Quarterly Journal of Economics* 84(3): 488–500.

Arrow, Ken. J. (1963) 'Uncertainty and the welfare economics of medical care', *American Economic Review* 53(5): 941–973.

Bacchetta, M., Ekkehard, E. and Bustamante, J. (2009) *Globalization and Informal Jobs in Developing Countries*, Geneva: International Labour Organization.

Backman, G., Hunt, P., Khosla, R., Jaramillo-Strouss, C., Mekuria Fikre, B., Rumble, C., Pevalin, D., Acurio Páez, D., Armijos Pineda, M., Frisancho, A., Tarco, D., Motlagh, M., Farcasanu, D. and Vladescu, C. (2008) 'Health systems and the right to health: An assessment of 194 countries', *The Lancet* 372(9655): 2047–2085.

Baron, D.P. (2011) 'Credence attributes, voluntary organizations, and social pressure', *Journal of Public Economics* 95(11/12): 1331–1338.

Biener, C. and Eling, M. (2012) 'Insurability in microinsurance markets: An analysis of problems and potential solutions', *The Geneva Papers on Risk and Insurance—Issues and Practice* 37(1): 77–107.

Binnendijk, E., Dror, D., Gerelle, E. and Koren, R. (2013) 'Estimating willingness-to-pay for health insurance among rural poor in India, by reference to Engel's law', *Social Science and Medicine* 76(1): 67–73.

Binnendijk, E., Koren, R. and Dror, D.M. (2012) 'Hardship financing of healthcare among rural poor in Orissa, India', *BMC Health Services Research* 12: 23.

Boone, J. (2013) *Does the market choose optimal health insurance coverage?* TILEC Discussion Paper No. 2013-008, from *www.papers.ssrn.com/sol3/papers.cfm?abstract_id=2240172*, accessed June 2014.

Coate, S. and Ravallion, M. (1993) 'Reciprocity without commitment: Characterization and performance of informal insurance arrangements', *Journal of Development Economics* 40(1): 1–24.

Crawford, S. and Ostrom, E. (2005) 'A grammar of institutions', in E. Ostrom (ed.) *Understanding Institutional Diversity*, Princeton, NJ: Princeton University Press, pp. 137–174.

Danis, M., Binnendijk, E., Vellakkal, S., Ost, A., Koren, R. and Dror, D.M. (2007) 'Eliciting health insurance benefit choices of low income groups', *Economic and Political Weekly* 42(32): 3331–3339.

De Bock, O. and Gelade, W. (2012) *The Demand for Micro-Insurance: A Literature Review*, Geneva: International Labour Office (ILO).

Doherty, N.A. and Schlesinger, H. (1991) 'Rational insurance purchasing: Consideration of contract non-performance', in J.D. Cummins and R.A. Derring (eds.) *Managing the Insolvency Risk of Insurance Companies*, the Netherlands: Springer, pp. 283–294.

Donaldson, C., Gerard, K., Mitton, C., Jan, S. and Wiseman, V. (2004) *Economics of Health Care Financing: The Visible Hand*, Basingstoke, UK: Palgrave Macmillan, pp. 298–464.

Donfouet, H.P., Essombè Edimo, J.-R., Mahieu, P.-A. and Malin, E. (2011) 'Social capital and willingness-to-pay for community-based health insurance in rural cameroon', *Global Journal of Health Science* 3(1): 142–149.

Dror, D. (2007) 'Why "one-size-fits-all" health insurance products are unsuitable for low-income persons in the informal economy in India', *Asian Economic Review* 49(1): 47–56.

Dror, D.M. (2001) 'Reinsurance of health insurance for the informal sector', *Bulletin of the World Health Organization* 79(7): 672–678.

Dror, D.M. (2014) 'Health microinsurance programs in developing countries', in A.J. Culyer (ed.) *Encyclopedia of Health Economics*. Vol. 1, San Diego: Elsevier, pp. 412–421.

Dror, D.M. and Jacquier, E. (1999) 'Micro-insurance: Extending health insurance to the excluded', *International Social Security Review* 52(1): 71–97.

Dror, D.M. and Koren, R. (2011) 'The elusive quest for estimates of willingness to pay for health micro insurance among the poor in low-income countries', in C. Churchill and M. Matul (eds.) *Micro Insurance Compendium II*. 2012, Chapter 7. Geneva: ILO, pp. 156–173.

Dror, D.M., Radermacher, R. and Koren, R. (2007a) 'Willingness to pay for health insurance among rural and poor persons: Field evidence from seven micro health insurance units in India', *Health Policy* 82(1): 12–27.

Dror, D.M., Koren, R., Ost, A., Binnendijk, E., Vellakkal, S. and Danis, M. (2007b) 'Health insurance benefit packages prioritized by low-income clients in India: Three criteria to estimate effectiveness of choice', *Social Science & Medicine*. 2007 64(4): 884–896.

Dror, D.M., Panda, P., May, C., Majumdar, A. and Koren, R. (2014a) '"One for all and all for one"; Consensus-building within communities in rural India on their health microinsurance package', *Risk Management and Healthcare Policy*. June 2014, Vol 2014;1 doi: http://dx.doi.org/10.2147/RMHP.S66011.

Dror, D.M., Majumdar, A., Panda, P.K., John, D. and Koren, R. (2014b) 'Implementing a participatory model of micro health insurance among rural poor, with evidence from Nepal', *The Geneva Papers on Risk and Insurance—Issues and Practice* 39(April): 280–303.

Faden, L., Vialle-Valentin, C., Ross-Degnan, D. and Wagner, A. (2011) *The role of health insurance in the cost-effective use of medicines*, Working Paper 2, Drug Policy Research Group and WHO Collaborating Center in Pharmaceutical Policy, from *www.haiweb.org/medicineprices/24072012/HealthinsurancefinalMay2011.pdf*, accessed June 2014.

Friedman, M. and Savage, L.J. (1948) 'The utility analysis of choices involving risk', *Journal of Political Economy* 56(4): 279–304.

Gandhi, M. (1959) *India of My Dreams*, Delhi: Rajpal and Sons.

Graham, C. (1994) *Safety Nets, Politics, and the Poor: Transitions to Market Economies*, Washington: Brookings Inst Press.

Granovetter, M. (1973) 'The strength of weak ties', *American Journal of Sociology* 78(6): 1360–1380.

Granovetter, M. (1985) 'Economic action and social structure: The problem of embeddedness', *American Journal of Sociology* 91(3): 481–510.

Granovetter, M. (2005) 'The impact of social structure on economic outcomes', *Journal of Economic Perspectives* 19(1): 33–50.

Gumber, A. (2002) *Health insurance for the informal sector: Problems and prospects*, Working Paper No. 90, Indian Council for Research on International Economic Relations, from *www.icrier.org/pdf/WP-90.pdf*, accessed June 2014.

Henrich, J., Boyd, R., Bowles, S., Camerer, C., Fehr, E., Gintis, H. and McElreath, R. (2001) 'Cooperation, reciprocity and punishment in fifteen small-scale societies', *American Economic Review* 91(2): 73–78.

ILO (International Labour Organisation) (2000) The informal sector UN, Bangkok 2000, from *www.ilo.org/public/english/region/asro/bangkok/feature/inf_sect.htm*, accessed May 2013.

Kahneman, D. and Tversky, A. (1979) 'Prospect theory: An analysis of decisions under risk', *Econometrica* 47(2): 263–291.

Knack, S.F. (2003) *Democracy, Governance, and Growth*, Michigan: University of Michigan Press.

Knowles, J.C. (1995) 'Research note: Price uncertainty and the demand for health care', *Health Policy Plan* 10(3): 301–303.

Kupferman, A. and Ron, A. (2002) *Structuring Demand and Supply in Community Health in Philippine Insurance, in Social Reinsurance: A New Approach to Sustainable Community Health Financing*, Washington: World Bank and International Labour Organisation.

Kydd, J. and Dorward, A. (2003) *Implications of market and coordination failures for rural development in least developed countries*, Paper presented at the Development Studies Association Annual Conference, Strathclyde University, Glasgow, 10–12 September.

Lahkar, R. and Sundaram-Stukel, R. (2010) 'Protecting the poor through community based health insurance', in *6th Annual Conference on Economic Growth and Development*, Indian Statistical Institute, New Delhi, 17 December.

Linnerooth-Bayer, J. and Mechler, R. (2007) 'Disaster safety nets for developing countries: Extending public-private partnerships', *Environmental Hazards* 7(1): 54–61.
Mielck, A., Kiess, R., von dem Knesebeck, O., Stirbu, I. and Kunst, A.E. (2009) 'Association between forgone care and household income among the elderly in five Western European countries—analyses based on survey data from the SHARE-study', *BMC Health Services Research* 9: 52.
Morduch, J. (1999) 'Between the state and the market: Can informal insurance patch the safety net?' *The World Bank Research Observer* 14(2): 187–207.
Narayan, D., Patel, R., Schafft, K., Rademacher, A. and Koch-Schulte, S. (2000a) *Voices of the Poor: Can Anyone Hear Us?*, Washington, DC: World Bank and Oxford University Press.
Narayan, D., Chambers, R., Shah, M.K. and Petesch, P. (2000b) *Voices of the Poor: Crying out for Change*, Washington, DC: World Bank and Oxford University Press.
Navarro, V. (1989) 'Why some countries have national health insurance, others have national health services, and the United States has neither', *International Journal of Health Services* 19(3): 383–404.
Nyman, J.A. (2003) *The Theory of Demand for Health Insurance*, Stanford: Stanford University Press.
Nyman, J.A. (2006) 'Evaluating health insurance: A review of the theoretical foundations', *The Geneva Papers* 31(4): 720–738.
Nyman, J.A. (2008) 'Health insurance theory: The case of the missing welfare gain', *European Journal of Health Economics* 9(4): 369–380.
Ostrom, E. (2010) 'Beyond markets and states: Polycentric governance of complex economic systems', *American Economic Review* 100(3): 641–672.
Panda, P., Chakraborty, A., Dror, D.M. and Bedi, A. (2013) 'Enrolment in community-based health insurance schemes in rural Bihar and Uttar Pradesh, India', *Health Policy and Planning*. doi:10.1093/heapol/czt077.
Preker, A. and Bassett, M. (2013) *From Cradle to Grave in the United Kingdom, Canada, Australia, and Elsewhere, in Scaling Up Affordable Health Insurance*, New York: World Bank.
Pauly, M.V. (1968) 'The economics of moral hazard: Comment', *American Economic Review* 58(3): 531.
Pauly, M.V. (1986) 'Taxation, health insurance, and market failure in the medical economy', *Journal of Economic Literature* XXIV(2): 629–675.
Pauly, M.V., Blavin, F.E. and Meghan, S. (2009) 'How private, voluntary health insurance can work in developing countries', *Health Affairs* 28(6): 1778–1787.
Platteau, J.-P. (1997) 'Mutual insurance as an elusive concept in traditional rural communities', *The Journal of Development Studies* 33(6): 764–796.
Platteau, J.-P. and Ontiveros, D.U. (2013) *Understanding and information failures: Lessons from a health microinsurance program in India*, ILO Research Paper, (29) Geneva.
Pratap, S. and Quintin, E. (2006) *The informal sector in developing countries: Output, assets and employment* (No. 2006/130), Research paper, UNU-WIDER, United Nations University (UNU).
Roth, J., McCord, M. and Liber, D. (2007) 'The landscape of microinsurance in the world's 100 poorest countries', MicroInsurance Centre, from *www.microinsurancecentre.org/resources/documents/doc_details/634-the-landscape-of-microinsurance-in-the-worlds-100-poorest-countries-in-english.html*, accessed June 2014.
Sen, A. (1970) *Collective Choice and Social Welfare*, San Francisco: Holden-Day.
Sen, A. (1999a) 'The possibility of social choice', *The American Economic Review* 89(3): 349–378.
Sen, A. (1999b) *Reason before Identity (The Romanes Lecture for 1998)*, Oxford: Oxford University Press.
Simon, H. (1972) 'Theories of bounded rationality', in C. McGuire and R. Radner (eds.) *Decision and Organization*, Amsterdam: North-Holland Publishing Company, pp. 161–176.
Stiglitz, J. (2001) 'Information and the change in the paradigm in economics', Nobel Lecture at Colombia Business School, from *www.nobelprize.org/nobel_prizes/economics/laureates/2001/stiglitz-lecture.pdf*, accessed June 2014.
Stiglitz, J.E. (2004) 'Globalization and growth in emerging markets', *Journal of Policy Modeling* 26(4): 465–484.
Straub, S. (2005) 'Informal sector: The credit market channel', *Journal of Development Economics* 78(2): 299–321.
Varian, H.R. (1990) *Intermediate Microeconomics: A Modern Approach*, New York: W.W. Norton.
von Neumann, J. and Morgenstern, O. (1947) *Theory of Games and Economic Behavior*, Princeton: Princeton University Press.
von Pischke, J.D. (2008) 'Gandhi vs gauss: Ethical issues in micro and small business finance', *Savings and Development* 32(3): 127–152.

Wagstaff, A. and Lindelow, M. (2008) 'Can insurance increase financial risk?: The curious case of health insurance in China', *Journal of Health Economics* 27(4): 990–1005.
WHO (2005) 'WHA58.33 Sustainable Health Financing, Universal Coverage and Social Health Insurance', from *www.apps.who.int/iris/bitstream/10665/20383/1/WHA58_33-en.pdf May 2013*, accessed June 2014.
Williamson, O.E. (1981) 'The economics of organization: The transaction cost approach', *American Journal of Sociology* 87(3): 548–577.
Williamson, O.E. (1985) *The Economic Institutions of Capitalism*, New York: The Free Press.
Williamson, O.E. (1989) 'Transaction cost economics', in R. Schmalensee and R.D. Willig (eds.) *Handbook of Industrial Organization*. Vol. 1, Handbook in Economics, Amsterdam: North Holland, pp. 135–182.
Williamson, O.E. (2003) 'Examining economic organization through the lens of contract', *Industrial and Corporate Change* 12(4): 917–942.
Woolcock, M. and Narayan, D. (2000) 'Social capital: Implications for development theory, research, and policy', *The World Bank Research Observer* 15(2): 225–249.
World Bank (yearly) 'World Wide Governance Indicators', from *www.info.worldbank.org/governance/wgi/index .asp*.
World Bank (year unknown) 'Definition of Rule of Law' (title unknown), March 2013, from *www.info.worldbank .org/governance/wgi/pdf/rl.pdf*), accessed June 2014.
Zeckhauser, R. (1970) 'Medical insurance: A case study of the tradeoff between risk spreading and appropriate incentives', *Journal of Economic Theory* 2(1): 10–26.
Zhang, L., Wang, H., Wang, L. and Hsiao, W. (2006) 'Social capital and farmer's willingness-to-join a newly established community-based health insurance in rural China', *Social Science & Medicine* 67(7): 1173–1182.

Chapter 3

The Effect of Consensus on Demand for Voluntary Micro Health Insurance in Rural India*

Main Messages

- Consensus on various issues related to the reasons for joining/not-joining varied across the target population.
- Individuals in the informal sector sought voluntary health insurance when they could participate with their peers in formulating collective perceptions of qualitative welfare gains.
- The factors which influenced the groups' decisions to join the insurance were mainly qualitative, about the likelihood to experience certain cost-generating health events, and about the collective perception of the quality of care.

Focus Points

- Exogenous household characteristics alone cannot explain the probability of joining health insurance.

*This chapter is reproduced from *Risk Management and Healthcare Policy* (2018), **11**, 139–158, Open Access, available at https://www.dovepress.com/the-effect-of-consensus-on-demand-for-voluntary-micro-health-insurance-peer-reviewed-article-RMHP.

- Collective perceptions are context-dependent, and cannot be isolated from the specific conditions applying in each location such as the local evaluation of service quality of health care providers.
- Success in catalyzing voluntary and contributory demand for health insurance in the informal sector depends on facilitating group dialog within targeted communities.
- Consensus in the groups on several critical issues like price of the insurance, perception of the households to experience adverse health events, and perceptions of quality of service of health care providers deliver in the local areas, were important determinants of demand for insurance.

Testimonials/Real-life Experience

- One respondent in Pratapgarh said that "*I used to sit in the meetings but I was unable to say anything. I could not form an opinion at the time as I could not understand it. I thought to myself when all the group members will join this scheme, I will also join it.*"
- One participant stated that "*there were two or three members of our group who were not willing to join. So we explained everything to them. Finally, they also joined.*"
- In Vaishali, one lady said: "*my husband told me that the villagers would do everything, outsiders will not decide anything. When the villagers are in charge of the decisions, go ahead and enroll in it.*"

Structured Abstract

Introduction

The success of voluntary and contributory microinsurance schemes depends to a large extent on their enrolment rates, as these schemes are voluntary and contributory. While there has been a perpetual interest in understanding the factors affecting enrollment in these schemes, there is almost no theoretical examination of the influence of peers on decisions to join CBHI. The authors hypothesize that demand for health insurance is a collective decision in the context of informality and poverty, thus challenging the classical theory of demand which posits individual expected diminishing utility.

Method

Data for this study was collated from four sources. (1) A household survey was conducted prior to the implementation of three community-based micro health insurance schemes through SHGs in rural India in the states of Uttar Pradesh and Bihar; (2) Information on actual enrollment was collected from the MIS system maintained by the schemes; (3) Qualitative data was obtained from 35 FGDs conducted with both the enrolled and non-enrolled members of the SHGs; (4) Village level socio-demographic and infrastructural indicators were collected from the Village Directory of Census of India, 2011.

The authors first applied logistic regression to estimate the probability of a household joining the scheme and compared it with the actual uptake. Following this, ordinary least square regressions were applied to analyze the role of groups' consensus on demand for health insurance.

Findings

The logistic regression suggested that exogenous household characteristics alone could not explain the probability of joining health insurance. Following Manski (1993),[1] the authors attributed the household decision to influences of the group and to local characteristics, which they termed as the "social effect". This led to studying other influences on individual decision making reached when the process is undertaken by groups rather than in isolation from peers.

A model was built to explain the phenomenon with variables which remain constant at the group level, such as access to health care facilities, the average socio-demographic profile of the groups, and other village level characteristics. Although "better access to health care facilities" stood out as the only factor that strengthens the propensity to join, it failed to indicate a major improvement of the results when its adjusted R-square values were considered. The study then focused on qualitative variables capturing opinions and views of the respondents on various aspects of the insurance scheme.

---

[1] Manski, C. F. (1993). 'Identification of endogenous social effects: The reflection problem', *The Review of Economic Studies*, **60,** pp. 531–542. doi:10.2307/2298123.

Box 1: Consensus in the Groups

- Consensus on perceptions about the pricing of the product emerged significantly in two of the three locations separately and in combined data for the three locations.
- Consensus on the likelihood that the household would experience adverse health events was significant in all three locations separately, and combined.
- Consensus on the parameters for choosing an inpatient health care facility emerged significantly in one location and also in the three locations combined.
- Consensus on the perceptions about the quality of service at the nearest in-patient health care facility emerged significantly for one location.
- Consensus on the perceptions about the quality and availability of medical supplies in the nearest out-patient health care facility emerged significantly for combined data.
- Consensus on the perceptions about the quality and availability of medical supplies received from the nearest pharmacy emerged significantly for one location and for all three locations combined.

A Consensus Coefficient was constructed to be used as an independent variable of the linear regression model estimating proportion of members who joined the schemes. This helped in assessing the effect of the perception about pricing, trust in the institutions, the likelihood of adverse health events occurring in the household etc.

There are two main takeaways from the findings of the study. Firstly, the process of achieving consensus among the groups reduced information asymmetry by supplementing perceptions based only on individual experience with the experiences and perceptions of other trusted peers.

Secondly, the factors which influenced the groups' decisions to join the insurance were mainly qualitative, about the likelihood to experience certain cost-generating health events, and about the collective perception of the quality of care. It is not possible for an individual alone to be informed about the collective qualitative evaluations of exposure to risk or the quality of care to expect when seeking care. Such information cannot be provided by an insurance agent or any other person outside the group, who is neither informed about these things nor motivated to seek and share such information at village level.

Conclusion

The findings of the study lead to rejection of the null hypothesis that demand is an individual decision. The analysis upholds the assumption that demand is created through a process of consensus-building on perceptions of risk exposure, welfare gains from the insurance, and quality of local health care provision. Since demand for microinsurance is a collective decision, success in catalyzing demand for health insurance in the informal sector depends on encouraging group dialogue.

The effect of consensus on demand for voluntary micro health insurance in rural India

David Mark Dror[1,2]
Atanu Majumdar[1]
Arpita Chakraborty[3]

[1]Research Department, Micro Insurance Academy, Garhi, East of Kailash, New Delhi, India; [2]School of Health Policy and Management, Erasmus University Rotterdam, Rotterdam, the Netherlands; [3]Centre for Economic Studies and Planning, School of Social Sciences, Jawaharlal Nehru University, New Delhi, India

Introduction: This study deals with examining factors that catalyze demand for community-based micro health insurance (MHI) schemes. We hypothesize that demand for health insurance is a collective decision in the context of informality and poverty. Our hypothesis challenges the classical theory of demand which posits individual expected diminishing utility. We examine factors beyond the traditional exogenous variables.

Methods: This study uses data collected through a household survey conducted among self-help groups in rural India in the states of Uttar Pradesh and Bihar before the implementation of three community-based MHI schemes. Additional information was extracted from the management information system maintained by the schemes. At the first step, we compared the estimated probability of a household joining the scheme (obtained by applying logistic regression) to the actual uptake. In the next step, we analyzed the role of consensus within groups on demand for health insurance (by applying ordinary least square regressions).

Results: The results of the logistic regressions indicated that exogenous household characteristics could not explain the probability of joining health insurance. We observed that group consensus on several critical issues, such as the price of the insurance, perceptions about exposure to adverse health events, and perceptions of the quality of service of local health care providers, was the important determinant of demand for insurance.

Conclusion: Based on the analysis, we reject the null hypothesis that demand is an individual decision at the household level. The analysis upholds the assumption that demand is created through a process of consensus building on perceptions of risk exposure, welfare gains from the insurance, and quality of local health care provision. Success in catalyzing demand for health insurance in the informal sector depends on encouraging group dialog.

Keywords: Community-based Health Insurance, micro insurance, consensus coefficient, consensus building, demand for micro insurance, collective decision

Introduction

The United Nations (UN) and the World Health Organization (WHO) promote the universalization of health insurance coverage to provide financial protection from health shocks (a policy called Universal Health Coverage [UHC]).[1] However, in many low- and middle-income countries (LMIC), the efforts of government to implement UHC are unsuccessful because much of the population is in the "informal sector", ie, outside the reach of most governmental social programs and ill-informed about the advantages of being included.[2] India is a case in point: notwithstanding health insurance schemes in some 30 states (also known as social health insurance [SHI] schemes) in 2017,[3] uptake was limited in 2015–2016 to ~29% of the population.[4] Uninsured households had to pay

Correspondence: David Mark Dror
Micro Insurance Academy, A-153
(Ground Floor), DDA Double Storey
Flats, Garhi, East of Kailash, New Delhi
110065, India
Tel +41 78 790 6789
Email daviddror@socialre.org

a large share of health care costs out of pocket.[5] Moreover, as loans often fund out of pocket spending (OOPS), the welfare losses extended beyond the cost of care to include the cost of interest (called "hardship financing").[6] Estimates from India of the outright impoverishment due to these cumulative costs vary from 2.2%[7] to 3.3%[8] and to 3.5% of the total population annually.[9] Even in the face of these severe consequences and the fact that there are no effective alternatives to health insurance (HI) to deal with OOPS in the informal and rural sector,[10,11] most people do not join on a voluntary basis. This situation begs an answer to the question: "If the benefits of HI are positively provable, how can theory explain the conditions under which the 3 billion or so in the informal sector of LMIC would seek voluntary health insurance?"[12]

Classical theories of demand for HI posit the hypothesis that the decision to purchase HI is individual and based on the expected payoffs relative to individual risk perception.[13,14] Dror and Firth[12] developed an alternative theory of demand, stating that in the environment of poverty and informality in LMICs, group consensus influences personal decisions to join and pay and that groups reach consensus when they are comfortable that the local governance of the scheme will uphold the priorities that each group sets for its plan. This approach reflects a departure from the classical top-down delivery model of HI, in which the promoters (often the government) decide both the package design and governance issues. This study sets out to provide the proof that the effect of group consensus on demand for voluntary enrollment of households in health insurance is determinant.

Since the late 1990s, there has been a gradual increase in piloting of a bottom-up approach to extending health insurance under the name micro health insurance (MHI).[15–17] One form of MHI is mutual aid of a local community, which also owns and operates the plan on a not-for-profit basis, often called Community-based Health Insurance (CBHI). In this study, we examine the null hypothesis that individuals decide independently to join CBHI. If that hypothesis is rejected, we aim to determine the influence of consensus on the decision of individuals belonging to the same community to enroll in CBHI ("the social effect"). If we can prove the existence of a social effect, we will aim to identify the factors that affect the formation of a consensus on enrollment into the CBHI by the members of the group.

The study of the effect of consensus on demand for voluntary MHI uses data from rural India. However, the relevance of this study extends much beyond India, considering that several other developing countries, notably Burkina Faso, China, Ethiopia, Ghana, Philippines, Rwanda, Senegal, Tanzania, and Vietnam, have implemented CBHI schemes.[18] We reviewed the literature on CBHI schemes, with the view to exploring that the research question we pose in this article is not yet resolved. Early reviews confirmed, albeit with substantial variation across schemes, that CBHI schemes were able to mobilize resources to finance health care.[19,20] Ekman[21] confirmed that such schemes could reach low-income groups, although rarely the poorest. Acharya et al[22] confirmed that some of these schemes had provided significant protection from high OOPS, though the impact on the poor was limited. Beiseitov et al[23] confirmed that social networks and "word-of-mouth" played a more decisive role than formal sources of information, and Chatterjee et al[24] confirmed in particular that word-of-mouth dissemination of information resulted in higher scheme utilization. Several publications provided evidence that solidarity, trust, community networks, civil–society links, and state–society links at the local level (all of which are components of social capital) positively affected the uptake of CBHI[25] and that the willingness of farmers to join CBHI in China was significantly and positively associated with community-level and individual-level social capital.[26] Trust and peer effects emerged as the key determinants of demand in a review of 41 articles published between 2000 and early 2013,[27] as well as in the analysis of the uptake of index-based drought insurance among coffee farmers in eastern Kenya.[28] In Senegal, information received from family and friends was trusted and positively associated with uptake in a scheme.[29] A systematic review of 54 studies concluded that the uptake of CBHI in LMICs depends on the socio-economic characteristics of the household (income, education, and age of head), recent episodes of chronic illness in the family, knowledge, and understanding of insurance and the scheme, access to and quality of the health facilities, and trust in the scheme management.[18] Finally, another study about the uptake of the New Cooperative Medical Scheme in rural China pointed to the significant role of social learning.[30] While several previous studies mentioned the important role of peers in affecting the demand for CBHI in the informal sector, none of the previous studies has addressed the theoretical framing of the influence of peers on decisions to join CBHI. We aim to provide such theoretical analysis in this study.

Data, ethical clearance, locations, and methods

Data

The following four sources provided the data for this analysis:

(1) Household survey: A total of 3,685 households (21,373 individuals) were surveyed in March–May 2010 as a part of the cluster randomized controlled trial (CRCT) study design,[31] where at least one female member of the household was a member of a self-help group (SHG) affiliated to selected partner non-governmental organizations (NGOs). The survey questionnaire covered issues related to the socio-demographic and economic profile of the household, self-reported incidence of acute and chronic illness, hospitalization events, the cost of health events, and sources of financing it. A year later, in 2011, 1,335 households (from these 3,685) were offered to join CBHI by paying a premium, of which 525 joined. In 2012, these 1,335 households, during a repeat survey, were asked to confirm their reasons for joining/not joining.

The study population was characterized by low education (44%–48% of the household heads of the combined sample were illiterate) and low economic background (average monthly per capita expenditure (MPCE) was around purchasing power parity $ (PPP$) 75) (Tables S1 and S2). Nearest inpatient facility was located around 0.5–2 hours away, and the nearest outpatient facility was located around 20–40 minutes away. The study locations were around 75 km away from the nearest urban areas.[32]

(2) Management information system (MIS): Information on actual enrollment was collected from the MIS system maintained for the CBHI schemes under this study.

(3) Census, 2011: Village-level socio-demographic and infrastructural indicators were collected from the Village Directory of Census of India, 2011.[33]

(4) Qualitative data: Qualitative data were obtained from 35 focus group discussions (FGDs) (10 in Pratapgarh, 12 in Kanpur Dehat, and 13 in Vaishali) conducted with both the enrolled and non-enrolled members of the SHGs during July–August 2011, after the enrollment process was completed. The qualitative surveys were deductive. The objective of conducting FGDs was to gain an in-depth understanding of the key factors that motivated the households to join/not to join the CBHI. The FGDs were moderated by a team of two highly qualified (at least post-graduate) researchers trained in qualitative methods and techniques, who were proficient in the local language (Hindi). The qualitative data were audio recorded, along with notes taken by the researchers. The data were then first transcribed (verbatim) in Hindi by local researchers and then cleaned and translated into English by the qualitative researchers. The qualitative data were then coded as per thematic responses (such as household decision, group decision, trust, and so on) and analyzed theme-wise.

The FGD participants were all females whose average age was ~40 years (Table S2). Average years of formal education of the participants were ~3–4 years with the majority being illiterate (50%–70%). Approximately 60%–70% of the respondents were engaged in domestic duties.

Ethical clearance

This project obtained ethical clearance first from the ethics committee of the University of Cologne, Germany (knowledge partner in the project) in February 2010. A follow-up approval of changes introduced to the questionnaires after the baseline study was issued by the same committee in February 2012. A third approval was issued by the ethics committee of the Micro Insurance Academy (New Delhi) in August 2015 to confirm that the survey tools, data collection, and analysis methodologies complied with the ethical requirements as practiced in India, in addition to the clearance already obtained earlier.[33]

Study locations

The data relate to three CBHI schemes implemented in rural Pratapgarh and Kanpur Dehat districts of Uttar Pradesh state and in Vaishali district of Bihar state, India. The schemes were implemented through three grassroots NGOs, with technical assistance and facilitation from the Micro Insurance Academy, New Delhi.

Methods

Quantitative methods

Ceteris paribus, when the household decides to join CBHI independently of its reference group, the choice is expected to be dependent on the socio-economic characteristics, financial profile, access to health facilities, and recent health events of that household[34] (see Table S1 for details of the variables). The model can be presented as:

$$CBHI_h = \alpha\, SES_h + \beta FIRP_h + \gamma\, SS_h + \delta\, HE_h + \varepsilon_h \quad (1)$$

Where $CBHI_h$ is a binary variable with a value of 1 if household h has joined CBHI, else 0.

SES_h consists of the socio-economic characteristics of the household that include caste, MPCE quintile in which the household is, age, gender, educational attainment, and employment status of the household head.

The financial profile of the household is represented by the vector $FIRP_h$ (formal insurance and informal risk pooling mechanism), consisting of subscription status to Rashtriya Swasthya Bima Yojna (RSBY, government hospital insurance) household type (joint or nuclear), household size, whether the household shares the income of the earning members for day-to-day activities, and sources of borrowing for non-health purpose in recent past.

The supply side of health characteristics is captured by the vector SS_h (travel time to the nearest inpatient and outpatient facility).

HE_h represents the health profile of the household (number of long-term, short-term illnesses and hospitalization events).

ε_h is the error term that captures the unobservable characteristics, which may affect $CBHI_h$.

To address the first research question, the predicted probability of each household ($CBHI_h$) is estimated using equation 1. In the next step, the expected proportion of members joining CBHI from each SHG is estimated using $CBHI_h$ and then compared with the actual proportion of members that joined from each SHG, followed by a binomial testing of the difference to assess the significance of difference.

Method to determine consensus on enrollment decision

To answer the second research question on the role of consensus in enrollment decision, we define consensus as a "general agreement/resolution arrived at by most of those concerned, after everyone's opinions are heard and understood, and a solution that everyone agrees to is reached" by following the studies by Sultana and Thompson[35] and Mohammed and Ringseis.[36]

To measure consensus, we first estimated the coefficient of unalikeability (CUA), which measures the variability of the binary outcome (yes or no) – in our context the decision to join CBHI within a group of households affiliated with an SHG. In other words, CUA measures how often the decisions of households differ from one another.[37] The CUA can be explained as:

$$CUA = \frac{\sum_{i \neq j} C(x_i, x_j)}{n2 - n}, \text{where } C(x_i, x_j) = \begin{cases} 1, x_i \neq x_j \\ 0, x_i = x_j \end{cases} \quad (2)$$

Here, x_i and x_j are the possible outcomes (decision to join or not join), and $C(x_i, x_j)$ is the number of events where the decision is different. The denominator, n^2–n, represents the total number of possible combinations of outcomes.[38]

Next, we estimated the coefficient of consensus (CC) using the following formula:

$$CC = 1 - CUA \ (3)$$

A value of 1 means that all group members made an identical choice; a value of zero means that no two members held the same position. The higher the value, the stronger is the group consensus.

We calculated CC for the enrollment decision to join CBHI at the group level using equation 3. The explanatory variables mentioned in equation 1 were recalculated at the group level (see Table S2 for the details of the variables). In addition to that, we also included several village-level characteristics as explanatory variables. Hence, the model specification changes to:

$$CC_g = a\,SES_g + \beta FIRP_g + \gamma\,SS_g + \alpha HE_g + \mu SHG_g + \nu VILL_v + \varepsilon_g \ (4)$$

Here, CC_g is a continuous variable representing the level of consensus for SHG *g* on the decision to join CBHI (CC-CBHI).

The explanatory variables are grouped under six categories: (i) socio-economic characteristics of the household (SES), (ii) variables reflecting access to formal insurance and informal risk pooling mechanism within the household (FIRP), (iii) variables related to access to health facilities (SS), (iv) variables reflecting perception about the health status of the household members (HE), (v) variables reflecting the level of consensus with an SHG on the decision to join CBHI and other SHG level characteristics such as average education level within the group, proportion of working members, proportion of members engaged in domestic duties etc. (SHG) and finally, (vi) variables representing the characteristics of the village the household belongs to (VILL).

The vector also includes a variable to indicate the group's (above average) empowerment score; this score represents the average level of empowerment of the members of each SHG in taking vital decisions in their household, calculated based on the average score of answers to five questions that the respondents were asked about their role in day-to-day household operations. The questions were whether the woman SHG member of the household decides 1) what food to buy, 2) what major goods to buy, 3) how much schooling to give children, 4) what to do when a child is sick, and 5) whether she needs permission from her husband/in-laws/other adults in the household to visit the local market. If the answer was "yes, the SHG member takes the decision (or does not need permission to go to local market)", a score of 1 was assigned to each response, else 0. The average score for each household was used at the group level to calculate the average empowerment score for the group (summation of empowerment score of the households in that SHG/total number of group members). A dummy variable was created to indicate if the group has an above average score of all the SHGs in that locality.

VILL_v includes the village-level indicators (number of secondary schools and family welfare centers, whether there is mobile and newspaper coverage in the village).

An ordinary least square (OLS) regression was applied to estimate the determinants of CC_g.

In the following step, we used only the variables that were significant, after having checked the R-square value (that represents the goodness of fit, which is how close the actual observations are to that of the estimated observation).

We modify equation 4 in the next step by adding other variables that represent the degree of consensus among the group members on why they decided to join/not to join CBHI, the households' perceptions of the health facilities they normally visit for inpatient services, outpatient services, and to buy medicines (see Table S2 for details). The model specification changes to:

$$CC_g = a\,SS_g + \beta SHG_g + \gamma VILL_g + \alpha CC\text{-}RSN_g + \mu CC\text{-}HSS_g + \varepsilon_g \quad (5)$$

In equation 5, we add the CC (vector CC-RSN) for each group to express the reasons the households specified to explain their decision to join or not join CBHI (responses related to the price of insurance, the decision of household head, trust that the NGOs will implement as promised, trust that group members can operate the scheme, insurance understanding, and health events in households).

In addition, in this model we used as explanatory variable the households' consensus on existing health services, represented by the vector CC-HSS, which captures the CC of the households' opinion (reason to choose that facility, perception on services provided by the staff, availability of medical supplies, and overall satisfaction) on the health facility they normally visit (inpatient, outpatient, and pharmacy).

We added the consensus vectors in a phased manner to capture the changes in R-square value and assess the importance of each vector on the group consensus on joining CBHI using an OLS framework.

Qualitative methods

Once the enrollment process was over in 2011, the 141 SHGs that were offered to join CBHI were sub-divided into the following two broad categories in all three locations: 1) enrolled (86 SHGs with at least one member enrolled) and 2) no-one enrolled (55 SHGs from which no one enrolled). For the FGDs, 35 out of the 141 SHGs (25%) were randomly selected from each cohort (20 from enrolled and 15 from non-enrolled). The FGDs were conducted during June–July 2011 with ~90%–100% (~8–10 members) participation rate from each sample group. The discussions focused on the reasons that influenced the groups' and the households' decision to join or not-to-join CBHI. All the FGDs were conducted in Hindi (the local language), qualitative data were then transcribed into English and fitted into the software package Atlas-Ti for coding and analysis.

Results

Quantitative results

Social effect

The results from the regression analysis of equation 1 are given in Table 1. The households classified as scheduled caste or scheduled tribe (SC/ST) were more likely to enroll in CBHI in Pratapgarh. Poorest-quintile households had a lower probability of enrolling than the middle expenditure-quintile households in Pratapgarh and Kanpur Dehat, and in Pratapgarh, the rich-quintiles had a higher probability of joining insurance compared to the middle quintile. Households in which family members share their income to meet daily expenses were less likely to enroll in Pratapgarh and Kanpur Dehat. Presence of children in the family positively influenced uptake in Pratapgarh and Vaishali, and the presence of adults had a negative association in Kanpur Dehat. Formal education of the household head increased the likelihood of enrolling in Vaishali.

Table 2 contains the predicted proportion of group members who would join CBHI, estimated using only the characteristics of household h using equation 1 under the hypothesis that each household decides independently. The result was different from the observed proportion of members who had joined CBHI for all the groups in the study locations. For 73 groups, the actual proportion was less than the predicted proportion (the lowest difference was –0.46), whereas in the other 68 groups the actual proportion was higher than predicted (the highest difference was 0.69). The difference between the observed and the predicted proportions of joining CBHI was significant for 86 out of 141 groups (61%). The high number of groups for which the difference between the predicted and observed proportion was significant indicates that the decision of households to join CBHI is not explainable solely by the household indicators, which leads to the conclusion that the null hypothesis (that the probabilities of household participation in CBHI are independent of each other) does not hold for most groups. It also indicates a possible role of the group (ie, beyond the household level) and geographic influence on the decision-making process. We term this influence 'the social effect'.

Table 1 Logit regression of marginal effect estimates (standard errors) at the household level with household-level characteristics

Indicators	Pratapgarh	Kanpur Dehat	Vaishali
Household socio-economic status			
Caste			
Scheduled caste/scheduled tribe	0.111*	−0.0256	0.0769
	(0.0575)	(0.0543)	(0.0508)
Economic status (quintile 3 middle as base)			
Poorest by MPCE (quintile 1)	−0.158**	−0.153**	0.0871
	(0.0713)	(0.0622)	(0.0729)
Poor by MPCE (quintile 2)	−0.0275	0.0433	0.0295
	(0.0760)	(0.0770)	(0.0739)
Rich by MPCE (quintile 4)	−0.129*	0.0688	0.106
	(0.0718)	(0.0787)	(0.0729)
Richest by MPCE (quintile 5)	−0.117	−0.0523	0.0587
	(0.0746)	(0.0709)	(0.0820)
Formal insurance and risk pooling			
Joint family	−0.0228	−0.00474	0.0562
	(0.0612)	(0.0588)	(0.0625)
Shares income of all members	−0.237***	−0.169**	−0.0690
	(0.0793)	(0.0781)	(0.0510)
Household size	0.00527	0.000805	−0.00221
	(0.0130)	(0.0152)	(0.0156)
HH borrowed money from SHG (non-health)	−0.0413	0.103	0.0982
	(0.0653)	(0.0684)	(0.0950)
HH borrowed money from friends (non-health)	−0.0579	0.0555	0.104
	(0.0588)	(0.0649)	(0.0780)
Household enrolled in RSBY	0.0170	0.0400	0.00304
	(0.0655)	(0.0718)	(0.0487)
Supply-side indicators			
Average travel time for inpatient service	0.000800	2.06e−05	0.00162
	(0.000752)	(0.000288)	(0.00108)
Average travel time for outpatient service	0.000570	0.000760	−0.00120
	(0.00228)	(0.000752)	(0.00143)
Household's health events			
Number of long-term illness events	0.0198	0.0210	0.0176
	(0.0267)	(0.0291)	(0.0285)
Number of short-term illness events	0.0213	−0.0170	0.0212
	(0.0256)	(0.0234)	(0.0240)
Number of hospitalization cases	−0.0306	0.0709	−0.0410
	(0.0640)	(0.0482)	(0.0555)
The age profile of households			
Presence of children <12 years	0.119*	−0.0736	0.195***
	(0.0638)	(0.0690)	(0.0699)
Presence of adult >65 years	−0.0699	−0.106*	−0.0300
	(0.0679)	(0.0612)	(0.0692)
Household head characteristics			
Age	0.00209	5.67e−05	−0.000237
	(0.00251)	(0.00235)	(0.00232)
Male	−0.0351	−0.0884	−0.0498
	(0.0842)	(0.113)	(0.0739)
Employment			
Self-employed in agriculture	0.0668	0.0444	−0.0532
	(0.0862)	(0.0895)	(0.0796)
Self-employed in non-agriculture	0.0354	0.0187	−0.181**
	(0.100)	(0.142)	(0.0782)
Other work (mainly casual wage work)	0.0829	0.0620	−0.104
	(0.0817)	(0.121)	(0.0748)

(Continued)

Table 1 *(Continued)*

Indicators	Pratapgarh	Kanpur Dehat	Vaishali
Education level			
Primary	0.0982	0.0705	0.119*
	(0.0828)	(0.0895)	(0.0691)
Middle	0.0855	–0.0638	0.0391
	(0.0853)	(0.0721)	(0.0727)
Secondary and above	0.0889	–0.00478	0.0201
	(0.0804)	(0.0637)	(0.0664)
Observations	433	378	524
Pseudo *R*-square	0.0645	0.0731	0.0487

Note: Robust standard errors in parentheses; ***P<0.01, **P<0.05, and *P<0.1.
Abbreviations: HH, household; MPCE, monthly per capita expenditure; RSBY, Rashtriya Swasthya Bima Yojna government hospital insurance; SHG, Self-Help Group.

When asked about the reasons for joining/not joining CBHI, 16% of the households said that the price of the insurance was affordable, 23% said that it was too expensive, and the remaining 61% were indifferent to price. Most respondents reported that their household head's decision to join CBHI, their trust in the NGO, and the group members' ability to administer the schemes were not deciding factors to enroll in CBHI. However, their self-assessed understanding of the effects of being insured was quite varied: 21% mentioned that insurance could protect them when health needs arise, 29% reported that they did not understand the benefits of health insurance, and the remaining 50% were indifferent to insurance understanding. This result indicates that consensus on various issues related to the reasons for joining/not joining varied across the target population.

Consensus on enrollment decision

Table 3 contains the results of the OLS regression with the consensus of joining CBHI (CC-CBHI) at the group level. We explored both types of consensus: toward joining and toward not joining. There was a negative association in the pooled sample between the average travel time to the nearest hospital and CC-CBHI, ie, the longer the average travel time, the lower the degree of consensus on joining/not joining CBHI. In two locations, the CBHI reimbursed hospital fees and transportation costs for inpatient care, and all three schemes covered wage loss (up to a cap) in cases of hospitalization. Considering the low level of hospitalization benefits covered by the CBHI schemes, possibly the group members could not agree on joining. CC-CBHI was inversely linked to the proportion of working members in Kanpur Dehat. Hence, the larger the number of members working as self-employed/casual labor/salaried, the lower the consensus on joining the CBHI. This could suggest that as contacts between group members weaken, they may be less likely to participate in group deliberations and thus obviously less likely to share the same reasoning. Also, access to newspapers was negatively associated with CC-CBHI for the pooled data. On the flip side, in Vaishali and the combined sample, the presence of family welfare centers (these are places where village females meet regularly to discuss various family planning issues) was positively correlated with consensus on joining CBHI.

When CC-CBHI was regressed using only the significant variables in the previous step (estimation of equation 4), the trends of a negative association with access to inpatient care, proportion of working members in the SHG with access to a newspaper in the village and positive link with the family welfare centers, remained largely unchanged (Table 4, columns 1, 4, 7, and 10).

In the next step, we included the consensus relating to the reasons of households for joining/not joining CBHI (refer to columns 2, 5, 8, and 11 of Table 4). Consensus on the price of health insurance was positively correlated with the consensus of joining CBHI in Kanpur Dehat, Vaishali, and the whole sample. With a one-unit change in the consensus coefficient on price, CC-CBHI increased by 25% (P=0.051) in Kanpur Dehat, 53% in Vaishali (P=0.006), and 28% (P=0.002) for the combined data. Similarly, the consensus for the existing health events at household as a reason for joining/not joining CBHI was positively associated with CC-CBHI in all three locations. A one-unit change in the consensus coefficient on the member households' vulnerability toward health events increased CC-CBHI by 44% in Pratapgarh (P=0.009), 59% in Kanpur Dehat (P=0.022), 43% in Vaishali (P=0.052), and 34% for all locations together (P=0.001).

In the next step, we included in the model as explanatory variables the consensus indicators of the households'

Table 2 Difference between predicted (using only household characteristics) and actual proportion of total members from an SHG to join CBHI

Group ID	Pratapgarh				Kanpur Dehat				Vaishali			
	Actual proportion of members joined	Predicted proportion of members joined	The difference (actual-predicted)	*P*-value of difference	Actual proportion of members joined	Predicted proportion of members joined	The difference (actual-predicted)	*P*-value of difference	Actual proportion of members joined	Predicted proportion of members joined	The difference (actual-predicted)	*P*-value of difference
Group 1	0.00	0.29	–0.29	0.095	0.89	0.28	0.61	0.000	0.86	0.47	0.39	0.003
Group 2	0.78	0.35	0.43	0.011	0.00	0.20	–0.20	0.256	0.85	0.62	0.22	0.079
Group 3	0.00	0.32	–0.32	0.032	0.00	0.23	–0.23	0.077	0.67	0.44	0.23	0.094
Group 4	0.86	0.50	0.36	0.064	0.00	0.28	–0.28	0.101	0.00	0.46	–0.46	0.001
Group 5	0.00	0.39	–0.39	0.012	0.56	0.31	0.25	0.111	0.69	0.49	0.20	0.120
Group 6	0.00	0.33	–0.33	0.029	0.80	0.30	0.50	0.002	0.20	0.35	–0.15	0.436
Group 7	0.08	0.46	–0.38	0.007	0.00	0.26	–0.26	0.046	0.29	0.39	–0.10	0.446
Group 8	1.00	0.55	0.45	0.005	0.00	0.19	–0.19	0.125	0.50	0.49	0.01	0.606
Group 9	0.86	0.43	0.42	0.029	0.00	0.25	–0.25	0.042	0.80	0.37	0.43	0.007
Group 10	0.86	0.50	0.36	0.061	1.00	0.31	0.69	0.000	0.45	0.49	–0.04	0.519
Group 11	0.50	0.39	0.11	0.301	0.00	0.22	–0.22	0.081	0.67	0.45	0.22	0.167
Group 12	0.75	0.46	0.29	0.103	0.00	0.23	–0.23	0.056	0.00	0.48	–0.48	0.001
Group 13	0.00	0.43	–0.43	0.004	0.00	0.21	–0.21	0.080	0.00	0.40	–0.40	0.011
Group 14	0.67	0.38	0.29	0.151	0.18	0.26	–0.08	0.419	0.00	0.44	–0.44	0.005
Group 15	0.00	0.35	–0.35	0.013	0.82	0.33	0.48	0.001	0.73	0.50	0.23	0.109
Group 16	0.00	0.32	–0.32	0.014	0.57	0.38	0.19	0.258	0.00	0.45	–0.45	0.003
Group 17	0.14	0.47	–0.32	0.088	0.00	0.22	–0.22	0.085	0.00	0.44	–0.44	0.002
Group 18	0.63	0.45	0.17	0.266	0.00	0.29	–0.29	0.177	0.29	0.47	–0.19	0.272
Group 19	0.83	0.42	0.41	0.052	0.00	0.32	–0.32	0.095	0.78	0.46	0.31	0.059
Group 20	0.67	0.40	0.27	0.097	0.43	0.35	0.08	0.463	0.00	0.49	–0.49	0.002
Group 21	0.69	0.41	0.29	0.036	0.67	0.35	0.31	0.027	0.80	0.57	0.23	0.126
Group 22	0.40	0.34	0.06	0.555	0.00	0.27	–0.27	0.077	0.58	0.44	0.14	0.240
Group 23	0.43	0.41	0.02	0.600	0.00	0.32	–0.32	0.030	0.60	0.48	0.12	0.325
Group 24	0.00	0.32	–0.32	0.096	0.00	0.33	–0.33	0.028	1.00	0.46	0.54	0.000
Group 25	0.00	0.36	–0.36	0.046	0.00	0.22	–0.22	0.107	0.00	0.38	–0.38	0.008
Group 26	0.63	0.39	0.23	0.163	1.00	0.36	0.64	0.006	0.00	0.45	–0.45	0.002
Group 27	0.18	0.37	–0.19	0.168	0.00	0.32	–0.32	0.315	0.80	0.49	0.31	0.049
Group 28	0.00	0.31	–0.31	0.054	0.00	0.24	–0.24	0.148	0.55	0.51	0.03	0.534
Group 29	0.88	0.39	0.48	0.007	1.00	0.30	0.70	0.000	0.65	0.51	0.14	0.177
Group 30	0.00	0.36	–0.36	0.637	1.00	0.38	0.62	0.000	0.82	0.49	0.33	0.028
Group 31	0.63	0.41	0.21	0.197	0.85	0.34	0.50	0.000	0.00	0.40	–0.40	0.006
Group 32	0.07	0.33	–0.26	0.030	0.00	0.25	–0.25	0.044	0.59	0.41	0.18	0.105
Group 33	0.29	0.36	–0.08	0.504	0.00	0.31	–0.31	0.153	0.00	0.41	–0.41	0.003
Group 34	0.55	0.38	0.17	0.202	0.00	0.31	–0.31	0.012	0.62	0.52	0.09	0.347
Group 35	0.17	0.31	–0.15	0.226	0.00	0.24	–0.24	0.049	0.00	0.43	–0.43	0.000
Group 36	0.31	0.47	–0.17	0.179	0.00	0.36	–0.36	0.028	0.00	0.45	–0.45	0.002

(Continued)

Table 2 (*Continued*)

Group ID	Pratapgarh				Kanpur Dehat				Vaishali			
	Actual proportion of members joined	Predicted proportion of members joined	The difference (actual-predicted)	*P*-value of difference	Actual proportion of members joined	Predicted proportion of members joined	The difference (actual-predicted)	*P*-value of difference	Actual proportion of members joined	Predicted proportion of members joined	The difference (actual-predicted)	*P*-value of difference
Group 37	0.70	0.35	0.35	0.024	0.00	0.26	−0.26	0.051	0.40	0.45	−0.05	0.508
Group 38	0.60	0.48	0.12	0.333	0.00	0.28	−0.28	0.137	0.22	0.42	−0.19	0.202
Group 39	0.00	0.30	−0.30	0.345	0.00	0.31	−0.31	0.054	0.67	0.38	0.28	0.045
Group 40	0.43	0.49	−0.06	0.522	0.00	0.30	−0.30	0.010	0.00	0.44	−0.44	0.006
Group 41	0.88	0.49	0.39	0.030	1.00	0.39	0.61	0.001	0.67	0.40	0.27	0.100
Group 42	0.18	0.31	−0.13	0.284	0.80	0.36	0.44	0.006	0.60	0.51	0.09	0.411
Group 43	0.00	0.41	−0.41	0.009					0.70	0.44	0.26	0.096
Group 44	0.90	0.49	0.41	0.010					0.63	0.45	0.18	0.256
Group 45	0.00	0.37	−0.37	0.007					0.91	0.47	0.44	0.003
Group 46	0.60	0.48	0.12	0.470					0.67	0.52	0.15	0.287
Group 47	0.70	0.42	0.28	0.067					0.08	0.36	−0.28	0.036
Group 48	0.70	0.57	0.13	0.305					0.85	0.54	0.31	0.021
Group 49	0.40	0.43	−0.03	0.546					0.82	0.55	0.26	0.068
Group 50	0.38	0.37	0.01	0.613								

Abbreviations: CBHI, Community-based Health Insurance; SHG, self-help groups.

perspective on the existing health services (the reason to choose the facility [cheapest/closest/best/other], opinion about the quality of treatment by the medical staff [very well/other], availability of medical supplies [always/usually/other], and overall satisfaction level with inpatient care, outpatient care, and pharmacy [very satisfied/satisfied/other] [columns 3, 6, 9, and 12 of Table 4]). The consensus indicators relating to the price of insurance and health events remained largely unchanged. Consensus on joining CBHI was positively associated with consensus on the reasons to choose the hospital (cheapest/closest/best/other) in Pratapgarh (coefficient =0.414, P=0.044) and overall (coefficient =0.159, P=0.096). Also, consensus on respondents' satisfaction with the treatment provided by the medical staff at the inpatient facility (very well/well/other) was positively associated with CC-CBHI in Vaishali (coefficient =0.696, P=0.032).

Overall, the availability of medical supplies at the outpatient facility had a positive influence on consensus, but the availability of a pharmacy had a negative influence in Kanpur Dehat and the full sample.

Additionally, the inclusion of consensus variables substantially improved the adjusted R-square values, which indicate the percentage of variation explained only by the independent variables that affect the dependent variable of the regression models (adjusted R-square improved from 0.016–0.211 to 0.194–0.386, Table 4).

Qualitative results

Findings from the enrolled groups

When participants of the FGDs from the enrolled groups were asked about the reason for their decision to enroll in CBHI, the highest score was given to "group decision" in Pratapgarh (34%) and Vaishali (31%) (Table 5); in Kanpur Dehat it was also an important reason (25%), second only to affordability and coverage of outpatient services by local practitioners (both at 29%).

Initially, many respondents said that they could not understand the benefits and how the scheme operated. However, it seems that they were doubters or "fence-sitters" rather than opponents because once the group head decided to join, other members followed. One respondent in Pratapgarh said that: "I used to sit in the meetings, but I was unable to say anything. I could not form an opinion at the time as I could not understand it. I thought to myself when all the group members would join this scheme, I will also join it." An SHG leader from Vaishali reported that: "when I decided to join, two other members followed immediately, and a bit later-on,

Table 3 OLS regression with coefficient of consensus of joining CBHI within a group as dependent variable

Indicators	Pratapgarh	Kanpur Dehat	Vaishali	All locations
Socio-economic profile of member households				
Proportion of SC/ST households in SHG	0.0143	0.190	–0.268	0.0343
	(0.159)	(0.186)	(0.212)	(0.0674)
Average monthly per capita consumption expenditure (non-health, PPP$)	0.00189	–0.000170	0.000491	0.000682
	(0.00287)	(0.00226)	(0.00313)	(0.00102)
Financial profile of member households				
Proportion of joint families in SHG	0.192	0.162	–0.460	0.0368
	(0.348)	(0.299)	(0.430)	(0.147)
Proportion of HHs in SHG that pools income of all members for daily expenses	0.251	0.172	0.338	0.148
	(0.298)	(0.309)	(0.257)	(0.115)
Average household size	0.0310	–0.0837	–0.0369	0.0309
	(0.0587)	(0.0675)	(0.0956)	(0.0275)
Proportion of HHs that have borrowed for non-health events from SHG	–0.0404	–0.104	–0.379	–0.128
	(0.247)	(0.429)	(0.459)	(0.125)
Proportion of HHs that have borrowed for non-health events from friends	0.357	–0.0408	–0.0588	–0.000390
	(0.277)	(0.325)	(0.481)	(0.134)
Proportion of HHs that have borrowed for non-health events from money lenders	0.417	0.0165	0.0390	–0.0902
	(0.423)	(0.334)	(0.230)	(0.125)
Proportion of HHs with RSBY coverage	–0.185	–0.356	0.181	–0.0741
	(0.337)	(0.308)	(0.264)	(0.104)
Access to health facilities				
Average travel time to nearest IP facility (in minutes)	–0.000804	–0.00160	–8.11e–05	–0.00140*
	(0.00315)	(0.00135)	(0.00480)	(0.000833)
Average travel time to nearest OP facility (in minutes)	–0.00808	–0.00146	–0.00371	–0.00199
	(0.00973)	(0.00417)	(0.00800)	(0.00256)
Health profile of member households				
Average number of chronic illnesses in SHG	–0.00576	–0.00667	0.0672	0.00920
	(0.137)	(0.159)	(0.151)	(0.0565)
Average number of acute illnesses in SHG	–0.0704	0.0469	–0.0547	0.00566
	(0.0945)	(0.0903)	(0.138)	(0.0464)
Average number of hospitalization events in SHG	–0.103	–0.0806	–0.125	–0.113
	(0.280)	(0.268)	(0.410)	(0.128)
Demographic profile of member households				
Proportion of HHs with children <12 years of age	–0.372	–0.301	0.394	–0.242
	(0.370)	(0.478)	(0.615)	(0.175)
Proportion of HHs with adults >65 years of age	–0.0108	0.625	–0.0410	0.137
	(0.295)	(0.377)	(0.442)	(0.145)
Socio-demographic characteristics of the SHG				
Average age of the group members	–0.00129	–0.0426	–0.164	–0.0374
	(0.00930)	(0.0932)	(0.123)	(0.0415)
SHGs with above average education level (D)	0.0287	0.0524	0.0378	–0.00292
	(0.112)	(0.134)	(0.213)	(0.0588)
SHGs with above average proportion of members working (D)	0.0218	–0.0291*	–0.000796	–0.000745
	(0.121)	(0.0145)	(0.0188)	(0.00504)
SHGs with above average proportion of members engaged in domestic work (D)	–0.0510	0.201	0.0637	0.0415
	(0.137)	(0.127)	(0.218)	(0.0617)
SHGs with above average empowerment score	0.0731	0.0180	0.164	0.0303
	(0.0881)	(0.113)	(0.126)	(0.0432)
Village characteristics				
Number of secondary schools in village	0.176	0.0769	0.0498	0.0630
	(0.199)	(0.0946)	(0.0984)	(0.0446)
Number of family welfare centers in village	0	0.287	0.506**	0.355***
	(0)	(0.263)	(0.216)	(0.108)
Village has mobile phone coverage	–0.0150	0.124	–0.0166	0.0612
	(0.215)	(0.101)	(0.140)	(0.0460)

(Continued)

Table 3 (*Continued*)

	Pratapgarh	Kanpur Dehat	Vaishali	All locations
Village has newspaper coverage	−0.125	−0.0606	−0.234	−0.102*
	(0.240)	(0.118)	(0.168)	(0.0552)
Location dummies[#]				
Pratapgarh				−0.365***
				(0.100)
Vaishali				−0.259**
				(0.109)
Constant	0.603	2.507*	0.740	0.962**
	(0.897)	(1.379)	(1.008)	(0.403)
Observations	50	42	49	141
Adjusted *R*-square	0.116	0.073	0.234	0.199

Notes: Standard errors in parentheses; ***P<0.01, **P<0.05, and *P<0.1. (D) indicates the dummy variable, with value of 1 if SHGs with above average value, else 0. [#]Values of the locational dummies equals 1 if the SHG is in that district, else 0.
Abbreviations: CBHI, Community-based Health Insurance; HH, households; IP, inpatient; MPCE, monthly per capita expenditure; OLS, ordinary least square; OP, outpatient; PPP$, purchasing power parity $; SC, scheduled caste; SHG, self-help groups; ST, scheduled tribe.

everybody joined." The early-joiner members played a vital role in convincing others to enroll by explaining the benefits payable by the CBHI scheme. One participant stated that "there were two or three members of our group who were not willing to join. So, we explained everything to them. Finally, they also joined."

While further probing the discussions that preceded the decision to join CBHI, it was revealed that the participants thought that being part of the group was worthwhile and might lead to added benefits (more likely to get loans). In Kanpur Dehat, one female participant said that: "these groups are like support. We can withdraw our money or take a loan from the group. That is why we have taken everyone's opinion and then decided to join."

Participants also emphasized that one of the deciding factors in favor of enrollment was their trust in the scheme management. In Vaishali, one lady said that: "my husband told me that the villagers would do everything, outsiders will not decide anything. When the villagers are in charge of the decisions, go ahead and enroll in it." Trust in the administrative structure, which included the villagers and the implementing NGOs, was the second highest cited factor for uptake in Pratapgarh (25%) (Table 5).

Findings from the non-enrolled groups

Inability to pay the premium was cited most frequently by SHGs as the reason for not enrolling: 37%–38% of replies in the three locations (Table 5). One participant in Kanpur Dehat stated that: "We have financial problems, as we must feed eight-nine people at home. How can we also pay for the insurance?" The timing of the enrollment (March–April), which coincided with the season when farmers had to invest in farming, was also mentioned by many as a reason. One SHG member in Vaishali pointed that: "a farmer can pay the premium only during the harvest season. I have a family of 6, so my total premium amounts to about Indian rupees (INR) 1,000. Should I spend that to buy seeds or to buy insurance?"

The consensus among the groups not to join was noted with one group in Pratapgarh, following discussions during which the members understood that CBHI, unlike SHGs, would not lend money from the premium amounts collected; everyone from that SHG decided not to enroll as most preferred savings with loans over health insurance. Further probing revealed that many of the group members believed that health was a personal issue which should be taken care of at the household level, without involving the entire group. Not surprisingly, when most group members decided not to join the scheme, the remaining few that initially wanted to join also opted out.

In Vaishali, one member said that: "Our money will be deposited in the bank account of the president of the group. This is problematic. We do not trust her." In this case, some members were reluctant to trust the CBHI administrator because of previous financial irregularities. In addition to lack of trust, some participants also doubted the quality of care they could expect from the scheme.

Discussion

This study sets out to provide a theoretical explanation, verified by evidence, about whether the decision of each member to enroll in CBHI can be considered to be taken purely based on individual utility considerations or whether it is impacted by consensus among peers. The null hypothesis we probed

Table 4 OLS regression with coefficient of consensus of joining CBHI within a group as dependent variable

Indicators	Pratapgarh			Kanpur Dehat			Vaishali			All locations		
	(1)	(2)	(3)	(4)	(5)	(6)	(7)	(8)	(9)	(10)	(11)	(12)
Access to health facilities												
Average travel time to nearest IP facility (in minutes)	−0.003	−0.0026	0.00182	−0.0016**	−0.0014*	−0.00106	1.62e−1	0.00199	0.00449	−0.0017**	−0.0013**	−0.00070
	(0.002)	(0.0021)	(0.0031)	(0.00076)	(0.00071)	(0.00081)	(0.0028)	(0.0028)	(0.0046)	(0.00066)	(0.00062)	(0.00067)
Socio-demographic characteristics of the SHG												
Above average proportion of members working (D)#	−0.0011	0.0473	−0.0321	−0.0229	−0.0126	−0.0303	−0.0477	−0.112*	−0.0723	−0.0160	−7.21e−1	−0.00467
	(0.067)	(0.066)	(0.092)	(0.0588)	(0.0531)	(0.0616)	(0.061)	(0.063)	(0.083)	(0.0348)	(0.0321)	(0.0339)
Village characteristics												
Number of family welfare centers in village	0	0	0	0.273**	0.385**	0.292	0.36***	0.283**	0.267*	0.317***	0.301***	0.252**
	(0)	(0)	(0)	(0.157)	(0.162)	(0.209)	(0.126)	(0.120)	(0.148)	(0.0991)	(0.0938)	(0.0984)
Village has newspaper coverage	0.0068	0.0701	0.0751	−0.0729	−0.0730	−0.0211	−0.107*	−0.0601	−0.0427	−0.0631	−0.0284	−0.0210
	(0.08)	(0.079)	(0.091)	(0.0705)	(0.0635)	(0.0793)	(0.064)	(0.062)	(0.085)	(0.0389)	(0.0366)	(0.0381)
Coefficient of consensus – reasons for joining/not joining												
Price of insurance		0.249	0.310		0.246*	0.279*		0.53***	0.568**		0.278***	0.287***
		(0.205)	(0.232)		(0.127)	(0.142)		(0.183)	(0.240)		(0.0878)	(0.0894)
Head of HH decision		0.0851	0.200		−0.122	−0.144		−0.0934	−0.306		−0.0140	−0.0212
		(0.149)	(0.189)		(0.124)	(0.143)		(0.165)	(0.198)		(0.0801)	(0.0829)
Trust on NGOs to run CBHI		−0.0286	−0.0487		0.172	−0.0103		0.218	0.265		0.132	0.0814
		(0.181)	(0.198)		(0.230)	(0.270)		(0.175)	(0.226)		(0.0996)	(0.103)
Health events in HH		0.44***	0.338*		0.592**	0.437		0.427*	0.381		0.342***	0.278***
		(0.159)	(0.166)		(0.245)	(0.282)		(0.213)	(0.276)		(0.0968)	(0.0968)
Insurance understanding		0.0355	0.179		−0.0629	−0.00951		0.267	0.123		0.00716	0.00739
		(0.182)	(0.209)		(0.134)	(0.160)		(0.180)	(0.245)		(0.0846)	(0.0904)
Trust us to run CBHI		0.109	0.140		−0.0948	−0.138		0.279	0.248		0.0522	0.0474
		(0.149)	(0.171)		(0.145)	(0.204)		(0.223)	(0.259)		(0.0893)	(0.0899)
Coefficient of consensus – perspective on available IP care												
Reason to choose the facility			0.414**			−0.171			0.300			0.159*
			(0.196)			(0.265)			(0.476)			(0.0950)
Perspective on treatment received			−0.318			0.205			0.696**			0.208
			(0.370)			(0.179)			(0.308)			(0.132)
Perspective on medical supply			−0.434			−0.445			−0.185			−0.235
			(0.275)			(0.320)			(0.363)			(0.145)
Overall satisfaction			0.147			−0.344			−0.0920			−0.216
			(0.387)			(0.261)			(0.296)			(0.140)
Coefficient of consensus – perspective on available OP care												
Reason to choose the facility			−0.0875			0.104			0.104			0.0579
			(0.213)			(0.193)			(0.303)			(0.0922)

(*Continued*)

Table 4 (*Continued*)

Indicators	Pratapgarh			Kanpur Dehat			Vaishali			All locations		
	(1)	(2)	(3)	(4)	(5)	(6)	(7)	(8)	(9)	(10)	(11)	(12)
Perspective on treatment received			0.411			0.0635			−0.150			0.0856
			(0.403)			(0.246)			(0.355)			(0.143)
Perspective on medical supply			0.341			0.436			0.271			0.295**
			(0.298)			(0.285)			(0.324)			(0.127)
Overall satisfaction			−0.0183			0.0567			0.0479			0.0328
			(0.456)			(0.266)			(0.314)			(0.143)
Coefficient of consensus – perspective on available pharmacy												
Reason to choose the facility			−0.126			0.0875			−0.0879			−0.0259
			(0.201)			(0.159)			(0.343)			(0.101)
Perspective on treatment received			−0.0950			0.0360			0.212			−0.0460
			(0.280)			(0.192)			(0.315)			(0.118)
Perspective on medical supply			−0.404			−0.445*			−0.346			−0.283**
			(0.268)			(0.232)			(0.372)			(0.127)
Overall satisfaction			−0.101			0.125			−0.0487			0.00732
			(0.322)			(0.215)			(0.328)			(0.126)
Location dummies[#]												
Pratapgarh										−0.31***	−0.170**	−0.196**
										(0.0735)	(0.0731)	(0.0754)
Vaishali										−0.36***	−0.25***	−0.191**
										(0.0817)	(0.0787)	(0.0837)
Constant	0.84***	0.160	0.0687	1.134***	0.388	0.710	0.77***	−0.342	−0.453	1.139***	0.409**	0.482**
	(0.108)	(0.259)	(0.310)	(0.118)	(0.234)	(0.539)	(0.101)	(0.365)	(0.523)	(0.0966)	(0.170)	(0.188)
Observations	50	50	50	42	42	42	49	49	49	141	141	141
R-square	0.016	0.130	0.194	0.037	0.318	0.348	0.119	0.299	0.265	0.211	0.352	0.386

Notes: Standard errors in parentheses; ***$P<0.01$, **$P<0.05$, and *$P<0.1$. (D) indicates the dummy variable, with value of 1 if SHGs with above average value, else 0. [#]Values of the locational dummies equals 1 if the SHG is in that district, else 0.

Abbreviations: CBHI, Community-based Health Insurance; HH, household; IP, inpatient; NGOs, non-governmental organizations; OLS, ordinary least square; OP, outpatient; SHG, self-help groups.

Table 5 Reason to enroll/not-enroll in CBHI – percentage distribution of responses by broad categories during FGDs

Categories	Pratapgarh	Kanpur Dehat	Vaishali
Enrolled			
Group decision	34.4	25.0	30.7
Trust factor/NGO suggested	25.0	10.7	12.0
Ability to pay	15.6	28.6	17.3
Benefit package understanding	0.0	0.0	5.3
Financial protection	18.8	7.1	20.0
Benefit of local doctors and medicine (low cost high frequency)	6.3	28.6	14.7
Non-enrolled			
Ability to pay	38.1	36.8	37.5
Financial liquidity	0.0	0.0	6.3
Group decision	38.1	21.1	25.0
Trust factor	4.8	0.0	16.7
Household decision	9.5	10.5	6.3
Quality of care	9.5	31.6	8.3

Abbreviations: CBHI, Community-based Health Insurance; FGDs, focus group discussions; NGO, non-governmental organization.

was that households decide whether to join CBHI independently from each other.

The findings of the study revealed that the household's decision to join the scheme[34] is significantly influenced by factors such as the caste of the household, its income (proxy MPCE quintile it belongs to), resource-pooling practices within the household, and to a lesser extent age distribution in the household and education status of the household head. However, these factors cannot fully explain the probabilities of a household joining the scheme as the predicted proportion of SHG members joining, calculated based on household characteristics, was significantly different from the observed proportion for most groups. This indicated that the decision whether or not to join CBHI was influenced by factors other than household level characteristics. Therefore, we reject the null hypothesis. Based on the study by Manski,[39] we ascribe the household decision to influences of the group and to local characteristics, which we term as the "social effect".

Dror and Firth[12] identified several theoretical inadequacies to the explanations of demand for health insurance based on individual exogenous variables (such as age, gender, education, occupation, and other socioeconomic characteristics) when these are applied to the informal sector. They contended that the expected utility theory does not take account of the effect of information asymmetry. Furthermore, they argued in their seminal paper that the demand for insurance in the informal sector is a collective decision of informal groups to which people belong. Indeed, it is not very difficult to see that for an intricate product as insurance, most people would tend to seek an opinion from their peers either when they have no information (when insurance is not sold at all) or to lend more credibility to information when obtained from peers than when disseminated by commissioned insurance agents (in the rare cases that agents come to villages to sell health insurance). This is all the more relevant in the case of CBHI, where the community plays a major role in designing the benefits package and in governing the scheme. Peer influence on information dissemination and demand generation has been studied by several other authors,[24,39–41] who concluded that peer effects (including information sharing within peer groups) positively and significantly influence program participation and scheme utilization. These analyses support the assertion of Dror and Firth.[12] Furthermore, Dror et al[42] have shown that voluntary and contributory CBHI for members of SHGs relied on an engaging experience of the members with peers to validate perceived priorities of the target group and that, moreover, the strongest motive for choice (more than price or package-composition) was the wish to join a consensus and the intention that many members should benefit. As they also showed that the degree of consensus improved with iterative discussions among the members, we now seek to explain what issues influence the level of consensus within a group on joining an insurance scheme.

To that effect, we built a model to explain other influences on individual decision-making when the process is undertaken by groups rather than by individuals in isolation from peers. We examined variables that remain constant at the group level, such as access to health care facilities, the average socio-demographic profile of the groups, and other village-level characteristics (Table 3). That model identified only one factor that strengthens the propensity to join – better access to health care facilities – but when its adjusted *R*-square values are considered, this factor did not infer a major improvement.

We then examined qualitative variables capturing opinions and views of the respondents on various aspects of the insurance scheme. As explained in the "Methods" section, we constructed a consensus coefficient (a tweak of the CUA)[37,38] in which 1 signifies full consensus and 0 no consensus at all (full variance). We added the consensus coefficient as an independent variable of the linear regression model estimating the proportion of members who joined the schemes so that we could assess the effect of the perception about pricing, trust in the institutions, the likelihood of adverse health events occurring in the household, and so on. We now observed a substantial increase in the adjusted *R*-square values of the model (Table 4), indicating improved goodness-of-fit in each of the three locations separately and in the data for all three schemes combined. The findings included the following:

1. Consensus on "perceptions about the pricing" of the product emerged significant in two of the three locations separately and in combined data for the three locations (CC-CBHI increases by 25% in Kanpur Dehat [*P*=0.051], 53% in Vaishali [*P*=0.006], and 28% overall [*P*=0.002] for one-unit change in consensus on the price of insurance).
2. Consensus on the "likelihood that the household would experience adverse health events" was significant in all three locations separately and in the combined dataset (increase in CC-CBHI is 44% [*P*=0.009], 59% [*P*=0.022], 43% [*P*=0.052], and 34% [*P*=0.001] for Pratapgarh, Kanpur Dehat, Vaishali, and pooled sample, respectively).
3. Consensus on the "parameters for choosing an inpatient health care facility" emerged significantly in one location (increase in CC-CBHI is 41%, *P*=0.044) and also in the three locations combined (increase in CC-CBHI is 16%, *P*=0.096).
4. Consensus on the "perceptions about the quality of service at the nearest inpatient" health care facility emerged significantly for one location (increase in CC-CBHI=70%, *P*=0.032).
5. Consensus on the "perceptions about the quality and availability of medical supplies" in the "nearest outpatient health care" facility emerged significantly for the combined dataset (increase in CC-CBHI=30%, *P*=0.022).
6. Consensus on the "perceptions about the quality and availability of medical supplies received" from the "nearest pharmacy" was significant for one location (decrease in CC-CBHI=45%, *P*=0.070) and the combined dataset (decrease in CC-CBHI=28%, *P*=0.028).

These results bring to the fore two aspects of the effect of consensus on catalyzing demand for health insurance. First, the process through which the groups reached consensus reduced information asymmetry by supplementing perceptions based only on individual experience with the experiences and perceptions of other trusted peers. The focus was to reach a collective decision, based on the collective perception of welfare gains to many members of the group. Second, the topics that influenced the groups' decisions to join the insurance were mainly qualitative about the likelihood to experience certain cost-generating health events and about the collective perception of the quality of care.

It is self-explanatory why an individual in isolation from other people deciding whether or not to join cannot be informed about the collective qualitative evaluations of exposure to risk or the quality of care she/he might expect when seeking care. Nor can a single individual deciding in isolation get a sense of the considerations that the entire reference group shares in defending the interests of the group. A solo decision-maker is thus deprived of information on the issues that were most instrumental in catalyzing demand for insurance. Such information cannot be provided by an insurance agent or any other person outside the group, who is neither informed about these things nor motivated to seek and share such information at the village level.

Limitation

For the quantitative methods, the small sample size that was used for the consensus analysis (total of 141), particularly at the locational level, limits the generalizability of these findings. At the same time, one of the team members who facilitated the FGDs was from the implementing NGOs and thus very familiar with the participants. This familiarity with the group was an advantage as it sets the participants at ease to share their experiences. We recognize that the familiarity could also have been a barrier to get the non-enrolled participants to participate fully.

Conclusion

The redeeming message of these insights is that persons in the informal sector, in settings of poverty and informality, would seek voluntary health insurance when they could participate with their peers in formulating collective perceptions of (qualitative) welfare gains. These collective perceptions are context-dependent and cannot be divorced from the specific conditions applying in each location, such as the local evaluation of service quality of health care providers. These conditions are fundamentally different from an individual measure of utility gains. The postulate proposed by Dror and Firth[12] is thus upheld.

The policy ramifications of this new evidence are that success in catalyzing voluntary and contributory demand for health insurance in the informal sector is contingent on facilitating group dialog within targeted communities, with the view to reaching consensus on collective perceptions of their exposure to risks, perceptions of the quality of care they might expect, the fairness of the price, and more generally a collective assessment of the welfare gains that the group can expect from being insured.

Acknowledgments

The authors gratefully acknowledge funding to collect the data used provided by European Commission seventh Framework Program; grant ID HEALTH-F2-2009-223518 – Community-based Health Insurance in India. The authors thank Dr Nihar Jangle for his inputs in conceptualizing the analysis methods for this study and Chandan Kumar for his inputs in data analysis at the initial stage. The authors gratefully acknowledge the extensive and substantive contribution of the Micro Insurance Academy and its staff in data collection and cleaning, as well as in analytical inputs, and the implementing partners (BAIF, Shramik Bharti, and Nidan) as well as the respondents for their willingness to share information.

Author contributions

All authors contributed toward data analysis, drafting and critically revising the paper and agree to be accountable for all aspects of the work.

Disclosure

The authors report no conflicts of interest in this work.

References

1. WHO [webpage on the Internet]. *Health Systems Financing: The Path to Universal Coverage – The World Health Report 2010*. Geneva, Switzerland: World Health Organization; 2010. Available from: http://www.who.int/whr/2010/en/. Accessed August 2, 2018.
2. Prinja S, Kaur M, Kumar R. Universal health insurance in India: ensuring equity, efficiency, and quality. *Indian J Community Med*. 2012;37(3):142–149.
3. Jain N. *Role of Government-Funded and Community-Based Health Insurance Schemes in Moving toward Universal Health Coverage in India*. Bethesda, MD: Abt Associates Inc; 2017.
4. International Institute of Population Studies. *National Family Health Survey 4: India Fact Sheet*; 2017. Available from: http://rchiips.org/nfhs/pdf/NFHS4/India.pdf. Accessed April 24, 2017.
5. WHO. *Global Health Expenditure Database*; 2016. Available from: http://apps.who.int/nha/database/Country_Profile/Index/en. Accessed April 24, 2017.
6. Binnendijk E, Koren R, Dror DM. Hardship financing of healthcare among rural poor in Orissa, India. *BMC Health Serv Res*. 2012;12(1):23.
7. Bhandari L, Berman P, Ahuja R. The Impoverishing Effect of Healthcare Payments in India: New Methodology and Findings. *Econ Polit Wkly*. 2010;45(16):65–71.
8. Garg CC, Karan AK. Reducing out-of-pocket expenditures to reduce poverty: a disaggregated analysis at rural-urban and state level in India. *Health Policy Plan*. 2009;24(2):116–128.
9. Hooda SK. Out-of-pocket Payments for Healthcare in India: Who Have Affected the Most and Why? *J Health Manag*. 2017;19(1):1–15.
10. Dhanaraj S. Economic vulnerability to health shocks and coping strategies: evidence from Andhra Pradesh, India. *Health Policy Plan*. 2016;31(6):czv127–758.
11. Philip N, Srinivasan K. Utilization of comprehensive health insurance scheme, Kerala: a comparative study of insured and uninsured BPL households. *BMC Proc*. 2012;6(Suppl 5):P10.
12. Dror DM, Firth LA. The demand for (micro) health insurance in the informal sector. *Geneva Pap Risk Insur – Issues Pract*. 2014;39(4):693–711.
13. Friedman M, Savage LJ. The utility analysis of choices involving risk. *J Polit Econ*. 1948;56(4):279–304.
14. Kahneman D, Tversky A. Prospect theory: an analysis of decision under risk. *Econometrica*. 1979;47(2):263–291.
15. Dror DM, Jacquier C. Micro-insurance: extending health insurance to the excluded. *Int Soc Secur Rev*. 1999;52(1):71–97.
16. ILO/STEP-GIZ. The Role of Micro-Insurance as a Tool to Face Risks in the Context of Social Protection. Geneva, Switzerland: International Labour Organization. Available from: http://www.ilo.org/wcmsp5/groups/public/---ed_protect/---soc_sec/documents/instructionalmaterial/wcms_secsoc_93.pdf. Accessed on December 24, 2017.
17. UNDP. *Building Security for the Poor: Potential and Prospects for Microinsurance in India*. Colombo, Sri Lanka: United Nations Development Programme; 2009. Available from: http://www.asia-pacific.undp.org/content/rbap/en/home/library/human_development/building-security-for-the-poor-2nd-edition.html. Accessed December 24, 2017.
18. Dror DM, Hossain SA, Majumdar A, Pérez Koehlmoos TL, John D, Panda PK. What factors affect voluntary uptake of community-based health insurance schemes in low- and middle-income countries? A systematic review and meta-analysis. *PLoS One*. 2016;11(8):e0160479.
19. Jakab M, Krishnan C. *Community Involvement in Health Care Financing: A Survey of the Literature on the Impact, Strengths and Weaknesses*; 2001. Available from: https://openknowledge.worldbank.org/handle/10986/13706. Accessed April 26, 2017.
20. Preker AS, Carrin G, Dror D, Jakab M, Hsiao W, Arhin-Tenkorang D. Effectiveness of community health financing in meeting the cost of illness. *Bull World Health Organ*. 2002;80(2):143–150.
21. Ekman B. Community-based health insurance in low-income countries: a systematic review of the evidence. *Health Policy Plan*. 2004;19(5):249–270.
22. Acharya A, Vellakkal S, Taylor F, et al. The Impact of Health Insurance Schemes for the Informal Sector in Low- and Middle-Income Countries: A Systematic Review. *World Bank Res Obs*. 2013;28(2):236–266.
23. Beiseitov E, Kubik JD, Moran JR. *Social Interactions and the Health Insurance Choices of the Elderly: Evidence from the Health and Retirement Study*. Rochester, NY: Social Science Research Network; 2004. Available from: https://papers.ssrn.com/abstract=1809901. Accessed January 11, 2018.
24. Chatterjee C, Joshi R, Sood N, Boregowda P. Government health insurance and spatial peer effects: New evidence from India. *Soc Sci Med*. 2018;196(Suppl C):131–141.
25. Mladovsky P, Mossialos E. A conceptual framework for community-based health insurance in low-income countries: social capital and economic development. *World Dev*. 2008;36(4):590–607.

26. Zhang L, Wang H, Wang L, Hsiao W. Social capital and farmer's willingness-to-join a newly established community-based health insurance in rural China. *Health Policy*. 2006;76(2):233–242.
27. Eling M, Pradhan S, Schmit JT. The determinants of microinsurance demand. *Geneva Pap Risk Insur – Issues Pract*. 2014;39(2):224–263.
28. Gine X, Karlan D, Ngatia M. Social networks, financial literacy and index insurance. *World Bank Work Pap*. 2013;(95393):1–17.
29. Mladovsky P. Why do people drop out of community-based health insurance? Findings from an exploratory household survey in Senegal. *Soc Sci Med*. 2014;107:78–88.
30. Liu H, Sun Q, Zhao Z. Social learning and health insurance enrollment: Evidence from China's New Cooperative Medical Scheme. *J Econ Behav Organ*. 2014;97:84–102.
31. Doyle C, Panda P, van de Poel E, Radermacher R, Dror DM. Reconciling research and implementation in micro health insurance experiments in India: study protocol for a randomized controlled trial. *Trials*. 2011;12(1):224.
32. Panda P, Chakraborty A, Dror DM, Bedi AS. Enrolment in community-based health insurance schemes in rural Bihar and Uttar Pradesh, India. *Health Policy Plan*. 2014;29(8):960–974.
33. Census of India. *Village Directory, District Census Handbook; Office of the Registrar General & Census Commissioner, India*. 2011. Available from: http://www.censusindia.gov.in/2011census/dchb/DCHB.html. Accessed May 23, 2017.
34. Panda P, Chakraborty A, Dror DM, Bedi AS. Enrolment in community-based health insurance schemes in rural Bihar and Uttar Pradesh, India. *Health Policy Plan*. 2014;29(8):960–974.
35. Sultana P, Thompson P. Methods of consensus building for community-based fisheries management in Bangladesh and the Mekong Delta. *Agric Syst*. 2004;82(3):327–353.
36. Mohammed S, Ringseis E. Cognitive diversity and consensus in group decision making: the role of inputs, processes, and outcomes. *Organ Behav Hum Decis Process*. 2001;85(2):310–335.
37. Kader GD, Perry M. Variability for categorical variables. *J Stat Educ*. 2007;15(2):1–16.
38. Perry M, Kader G. Variation as unalikeability. *Teach Stat*. 2005;27(2): 58–60.
39. Manski CF. Identification of endogenous social effects: the reflection problem. *Rev Econ Stud*. 1993;60(3):531–542.
40. Dahl GB, Løken KV, Mogstad M. Peer effects in program participation. *Am Econ Rev*. 2014;104(7):2049–2074.
41. Duflo E, Saez E. Participation and investment decisions in a retirement plan: the influence of colleagues' choices. *J Public Econ*. 2002;85(1): 121–148.
42. Dror DM, Panda P, May C, Majumdar A, Koren R. "One for all and all for one": consensus-building within communities in rural India on their health microinsurance package. *Risk Manag Healthc Policy*. 2014; 7:139.

Supplementary materials

Table S1 Descriptive statistics of key variables for household level analysis – mean±SD

Indicators	Pratapgarh		Kanpur Dehat		Vaishali	
	Non-enrolled	Enrolled	Non-enrolled	Enrolled	Non-enrolled	Enrolled
Household socio-economic status						
Caste – scheduled caste/scheduled tribe (D)	0.32±0.47	0.41±0.49	0.27±0.45	0.25±0.43	0.38±0.49	0.44±0.50
Economic status – poorest by MPCE (quintile 1) (D)	0.21±0.41	0.17±0.38	0.23±0.42	0.11±0.31	0.20±0.40	0.26±0.44
Economic status – poor by MPCE (quintile 2) (D)	0.18±0.38	0.25±0.43	0.19±0.40	0.22±0.42	0.20±0.40	0.18±0.39
Economic status – middle by MPCE (quintile 3) (D) (base)	0.16±0.37	0.25±0.44	0.20±0.40	0.23±0.42	0.22±0.42	0.18±0.38
Economic status – rich by MPCE (quintile 4) (D)	0.21±0.41	0.16±0.37	0.17±0.37	0.26±0.44	0.19±0.39	0.21±0.41
Economic status – richest by MPCE (quintile 5) (D)	0.24±0.43	0.17±0.37	0.20±0.40	0.18±0.39	0.18±0.39	0.17±0.38
Formal insurance and risk pooling						
Joint family (D)	0.53±0.50	0.52±0.50	0.46±0.50	0.39±0.49	0.35±0.48	0.40±0.49
Shares income of all members (D)	0.91±0.29	0.83±0.37	0.87±0.33	0.78±0.42	0.70±0.46	0.66±0.47
Household size (C)	5.80±2.79	6.28±2.62	6.09±2.35	5.75±1.91	5.38±2.24	5.57±1.92
HH borrowed money from SHG (non-health) (D)	0.19±0.40	0.19±0.39	0.16±0.37	0.24±0.43	0.06±0.24	0.07±0.25
HH borrowed money from friends (non-health) (D)	0.25±0.44	0.24±0.43	0.19±0.39	0.23±0.42	0.08±0.27	0.12±0.32
HH borrowed money from money lenders (non-health) (D) (base)	0.05±0.22	0.09±0.28	0.14±0.35	0.10±0.30	0.29±0.45	0.43±0.50
Household enrolled in RSBY (D)	0.17±0.37	0.20±0.40	0.14±0.35	0.18±0.39	0.49±0.50	0.48±0.50
Supply-side indicators						
Average travel time for inpatient service (C)	41.7±33.8	47.6±34.2	127. ±84.9	133. ±87.3	28.3±21.4	30.4±22.2
Average travel time for outpatient service (C)	18.8±11.2	19.9±12.0	32.7±30.1	37.6±32.9	17.9±15.8	16.7±17.6
Household's health events						
Number of long-term illness events (C)	1.40±0.89	1.51±1.16	0.70±0.85	0.76±0.88	0.71±0.82	0.76±0.87
Number of short-term illness events (C)	1.12±1.09	1.29±1.15	1.33±1.06	1.32±1.07	1.04±0.94	1.13±1.04
Number of hospitalization cases (C)	0.14±0.42	0.14±0.37	0.16±0.48	0.25±0.49	0.18±0.42	0.18±0.44
Age profile of household						
Presence of children <12 years (D)	0.74±0.44	0.84±0.36	0.78±0.41	0.69±0.47	0.81±0.39	0.90±0.30
Presence of adult >65 years (D)	0.28±0.45	0.22±0.42	0.21±0.41	0.14±0.35	0.20±0.40	0.19±0.39
Household head characteristics						
Age (C)	46.3±12.7	45.9±13.1	44.8±12.6	45.0±11.5	42.6±13.0	41.2±12.0
Male (D)	0.73±0.45	0.77±0.42	0.90±0.30	0.87±0.34	0.78±0.41	0.72±0.45
Employment – self-employed in agriculture (D)	0.21±0.41	0.21±0.41	0.67±0.47	0.68±0.47	0.18±0.39	0.19±0.39
Employment – self-employed in non-agriculture (D)	0.14±0.35	0.14±0.35	0.06±0.24	0.06±0.23	0.21±0.41	0.15±0.36
Employment – other work (mainly casual wage) (D)	0.37±0.48	0.43±0.50	0.14±0.35	0.13±0.34	0.42±0.49	0.39±0.49
Employment – not working (D) (base)	0.27±0.44	0.22±0.41	0.13±0.34	0.14±0.35	0.19±0.39	0.27±0.44
Education level – illiterate (D)	0.37±0.48	0.28±0.45	0.30±0.46	0.28±0.45	0.48±0.50	0.44±0.50
Education level – primary (D)	0.16±0.37	0.20±0.40	0.11±0.31	0.14±0.35	0.13±0.34	0.19±0.40
Education level – middle (D)	0.18±0.38	0.21±0.41	0.16±0.37	0.12±0.33	0.14±0.35	0.15±0.36
Education level – secondary and above (D)	0.29±0.45	0.31±0.46	0.43±0.50	0.46±0.50	0.25±0.43	0.22±0.41
SHG level characteristics						
SHG – average empowerment score (C)	0.39±0.49	0.51±0.50	0.57±0.50	0.66±0.48	0.65±0.48	0.74±0.44
SHG – highest years of formal education (C)	0.39±0.49	0.48±0.50	0.58±0.50	0.55±0.50	0.40±0.49	0.49±0.50
SHG – average age (C)	40.8±5.65	40.6±5.92	38.6±3.72	38.8±3.47	36.5±3.98	36.3±4.16
SHG – proportion of working members (C)	0.66±0.47	0.58±0.49	0.45±0.50	0.57±0.50	0.55±0.50	0.38±0.49
SHG – proportion of domestic workers (C)	0.55±0.50	0.53±0.50	0.27±0.45	0.17±0.38	0.36±0.48	0.49±0.50
Village-level indicators						
Number of secondary schools in village (C)	0.66±0.48	0.73±0.45	0.10±0.54	0.00±0.00	0.53±0.76	0.49±0.61
Number of family welfare centers in village (C)	0.00±0.00	0.00±0.00	0.04±0.19	0.00±0.00	0.10±0.30	0.00±0.00
Mobile coverage in village (D)	0.86±0.35	0.94±0.23	0.58±0.49	0.43±0.50	0.35±0.48	0.50±0.50
Newspaper coverage in village (D)	0.71±0.45	0.81±0.39	0.26±0.44	0.14±0.35	0.61±0.49	0.66±0.47
Sample size	259	174	269	109	282	242

Note: (D) represents dummy (binary) variables, and (C) represents continuous variables.

Abbreviations: HH, household; MPCE, monthly per capita expenditure; RSBY, Rashtriya Swasthya Bima Yojna government hospital insurance; SHG, Self-Help Group.

Table S2 Descriptive statistics of key variables for SHG-level analysis – mean±SD

Indicators	Pratapgarh	Kanpur Dehat	Vaishali	All locations
Coefficient of consensus – joining decision at the group level (dependent variable)				
Coefficient of consensus – joining decision at group level (dependent variable)	0.70±0.23	0.90±0.19	0.70±0.22	0.76±0.23
Socio-economic profile of member households				
Proportion of SC/ST households in SHG	0.33±0.37	0.26±0.24	0.40±0.36	0.33±0.34
Average monthly per capita consumption expenditure (non-health, PPP$)	60.5±19.9	94.9±25.3	73.3±22.3	75.2±26.3
Financial profile of member households				
Proportion of joint families in SHG	0.53±0.23	0.46±0.20	0.36±0.16	0.45±0.21
Proportion of HHs in SHG that pools income of all members for daily expenses	0.88±0.16	0.84±0.18	0.68±0.20	0.80±0.20
Average household size	6.14±1.31	6.05±0.85	5.43±0.72	5.86±1.05
Proportion of HHs that have borrowed for non-health events from SHG	0.19±0.22	0.19±0.14	0.06±0.10	0.15±0.17
Proportion of HHs that have borrowed for non-health events from friends	0.24±0.19	0.20±0.15	0.10±0.10	0.18±0.16
Proportion of HHs that have borrowed for non-health events from money lenders	0.07±0.12	0.13±0.14	0.37±0.21	0.19±0.21
Proportion of HHs with RSBY cards	0.18±0.16	0.16±0.17	0.48±0.25	0.28±0.25
Access to health facilities				
Average travel time to nearest IP facility (in minutes)	44.1±15.5	132.0±46.4	29.6±11.1	65.4±52.2
Average travel time to nearest OP facility (in minutes)	19.1±5.85	35.8±12.8	17.6±7.00	23.6±11.8
Health profile of member households				
Average number of chronic illnesses in SHG	1.44±0.39	0.70±0.31	0.73±0.41	0.97±0.51
Average number of acute illnesses in SHG	1.17±0.55	1.31±0.41	1.08±0.41	1.18±0.47
Average number of hospitalization events in SHG	0.13±0.16	0.18±0.18	0.18±0.13	0.16±0.16
Demographic profile of member households				
Proportion of HHs with children <12 years of age	0.80±0.14	0.76±0.14	0.84±0.12	0.80±0.14
Proportion of HHs with adults >65 years of age	0.25±0.18	0.19±0.16	0.19±0.12	0.21±0.15
Socio-demographic characteristics of the SHG				
Average age of the group members	40.6±5.91	38.4±4.20	36.2±4.05	38.5±5.14
SHGs with above average education level (D)	0.44±0.50	0.60±0.50	0.67±0.47	0.57±0.50
SHGs with above average proportion of members working (D)	0.44±0.50	0.55±0.50	0.47±0.50	0.48±0.50
SHGs with above average proportion of members engaged in domestic work (D)	0.60±0.49	0.52±0.51	0.47±0.50	0.53±0.50
SHGs with above average empowerment score	0.50±0.51	0.24±0.43	0.39±0.49	0.38±0.49
Village characteristics				
Number of secondary schools in village	0.68±0.47	0.07±0.46	0.49±0.68	0.43±0.60
Number of family welfare centers in village	0.00±0.00	0.05±0.22	0.06±0.24	0.04±0.19
Village has mobile phone coverage	0.88±0.33	0.52±0.51	0.41±0.50	0.61±0.49
Village has newspaper coverage	0.74±0.44	0.21±0.42	0.63±0.49	0.55±0.50
Coefficient of consensus – reasons for joining/not joining				
Price of insurance (low, expensive, indifferent)	0.49±0.19	0.70±0.24	0.54±0.18	0.57±0.22
Head of HH decision (yes, no, indifferent)	0.71±0.22	0.75±0.22	0.80±0.19	0.75±0.21
Trust in NGOs to run CBHI (yes, no, indifferent)	0.84±0.18	0.90±0.15	0.84±0.19	0.86±0.18
Health events in HH (too many, very few, not a factor)	0.79±0.22	0.93±0.13	0.86±0.16	0.86±0.18
Insurance understanding (understands insurance, do not understand, not a factor)	0.57±0.21	0.57±0.20	0.52±0.16	0.55±0.19
Trust on us to run CBHI (yes, no, indifferent)	0.60±0.21	0.50±0.18	0.55±0.14	0.55±0.18
Coefficient of consensus – perspective on available IP facility				
Reason to choose the facility (cheapest, closest, best, others)	0.37±0.26	0.16±0.13	0.14±0.11	0.23±0.21
Perspective on treatment received (very well, well, others)	0.68±0.21	0.50±0.19	0.49±0.15	0.56±0.20
Perspective on medical supply (always, usually, others)	0.51±0.16	0.43±0.12	0.46±0.11	0.47±0.14
Overall satisfaction (very satisfied, satisfied, others)	0.71±0.22	0.54±0.16	0.55±0.15	0.61±0.19
Coefficient of consensus – perspective on available OP facility				
Reason to choose the facility (cheapest, closest, best, others)	0.62±0.25	0.52±0.21	0.42±0.17	0.52±0.23
Perspective on treatment received (very well, well, others)	0.73±0.23	0.50±0.17	0.50±0.15	0.58±0.21
Perspective on medical supply (always, usually, others)	0.52±0.18	0.42±0.11	0.50±0.19	0.48±0.17
Overall satisfaction (very satisfied, satisfied, others)	0.76±0.20	0.58±0.17	0.61±0.18	0.66±0.20

(Continued)

Table S2 (*Continued*)

Indicators	Pratapgarh	Kanpur Dehat	Vaishali	All locations
Coefficient of consensus – perspective on available pharmacy				
Reason to choose the facility (cheapest, closest, best, others)	0.67±0.25	0.50±0.18	0.46±0.16	0.55±0.22
Perspective on treatment received (very well, well, others)	0.71±0.21	0.55±0.17	0.55±0.15	0.60±0.20
Perspective on medical supply (always, usually, others)	0.50±0.16	0.47±0.14	0.51±0.16	0.49±0.15
Overall satisfaction (very satisfied, satisfied, others)	0.70±0.22	0.63±0.19	0.58±0.13	0.64±0.19
Sample size	50	42	49	141

Abbreviations: CBHI, Community-based Health Insurance; HH, household; IP, inpatient; NGOs, non-governmental organizations; OP, outpatient; PPP$, purchasing power parity $; Rashtriya Swasthya Bima Yojna (RSBY) government hospital insurance; SC, scheduled caste; SHG, Self-Help Group; ST, scheduled tribe.

Chapter 4

"One for All and All for One": Consensus-building Within Communities in Rural India on Their Health Microinsurance Package*

Main Messages

- Group consensus can be harnessed to enhance demand for health microinsurance in the informal economy.
- It is possible to express consensus quantitatively rather than just categorically (as a binomial Yes/No).
- Mixed-methods methodology was followed using four sources of data: baseline study, CHAT[1] exercises, in-depth interviews, and evaluation questionnaires.

---

*This chapter is reproduced from *Risk Management and Healthcare Policy* (2014), **7**, 139–153, Open Access, available at https://www.researchgate.net/publication/264435730_One_for_all_and_all_for_one_Consensus-building_within_communities_in_rural_India_on_their_health_microinsurance_package.

[1]CHAT is a consensus-building exercise used by the rural poor for selecting a benefits-package for an insurance scheme. CHAT is conducted in three rounds (CHAT 1, CHAT 2, and CHAT 3) using pictorial boards showing different benefit packages and the related premium. The findings of a baseline study form the basis for designing the benefits packages by community members.

Focus Points

- The study provides empirical evidence that the rural poor (some of whom are illiterate and innumerate and with no prior experience with health insurance), can reach consensus on the choice of their health insurance benefits package, rather than simply being told to buy cheap insurance.
- When the poor have access to a game-like way to selecting the benefits-package, without compromising on the actuarial accuracy, they can select the health package within their willingness to pay and their perceived priorities for health care coverage.
- The study describes the process of involving rural poor in benefit-package design and assesses the underlying reasons for choices they made and their ability to reach group consensus.
- The coefficient of unalikeability decreased consistently over consecutive CHAT rounds in all locations, thereby confirming gradual adoption of consensus on one package.
- Harnessing group consensus does not occur spontaneously but requires catalytic intervention by devoted and knowledgeable persons who guide the process from inception at the village level.

Testimonials/Real-life Experience

People enjoyed the participatory nature of the CHAT exercises, liked the deliberations, and liked to make their own decisions.

Facilitator 2, Pratapgarh: "*The best thing in the CHAT was that the women were free to choose any package that they liked. It was not imposed on them, and there were no restrictions or obligations to choose a particular package.*"

While discussing the price, the participants were concerned not merely about their ability to pay, but of other members as well.

Facilitator 2, Kanpur-Dehat: "*Everyone selected packages for themselves keeping in mind their own benefits [...] But when they met among themselves and were informed that a single package is applicable for the whole group they realized that [...] they all should select a package that is affordable for all.*"

Structured Abstract

Introduction

India is facing a dearth of health microinsurance products suitable for the rural poor, with most products either being unaffordable for the community or failing to provide sufficient coverage to meet their health care needs. Against this backdrop, we expect more acceptability from the rural poor community for a health insurance benefits package that is designed and priced through the active participation of its own members. This chapter seeks to describe the process of involving rural poor in benefit-package design, explaining the underlying reasons for choices they made, and assessing their ability to reach group consensus regarding package composition.

Method

The authors used mixed methods and four sources of data: baseline study (conducted in three locations in rural India), CHAT (Choosing Healthplans All Together) exercises, in-depth interviews, and evaluation questionnaires.

The benefits-package selection process entailed four steps: narrowing down the options by community representatives during the "Benefits-package selection workshops", followed by three CHAT rounds conducted among female members of self-help groups.

The term "consensus" is defined here as a community resolution reached by discussion, considering all opinions, and to which everyone agrees. The authors use a "coefficient of unalikeability" to express consensus quantitatively (as variability of categorical variables) rather than just categorically (as a binomial Yes/No).

Findings

The target population was offered four to six health packages for selection through the CHAT exercise. It was observed that the coefficient of unalikeability decreased consistently over consecutive CHAT rounds in all locations, thereby confirming gradual adoption of consensus on one package.

Box 1: Procedure Followed for Benefits-package Design

Benefit-package election workshop to identify benefits-package options

- Representatives of the field partners and of the communities (the SHG federation, SHG members, and community leaders, e.g., teachers, panchayat members, and community health workers) reviewed all the pertinent information about morbidity, costs of care, health-seeking behavior, and availability of health care facilities (obtained through the baseline study).
- The output of each workshop was four to six packages that would be presented to the entire target population for selection in the different CHAT rounds.

CHAT Round 1

- Identified female participants from the SHGs were asked to select the benefits package that met their and their families' priorities (using colored stickers to denote their first and second priority).
- At the end of this individual round, each participant could take home a personal copy of the CHAT board to discuss the choices with family members.

CHAT Round 2

- The next day, a facilitated group discussion was convened, in which each female SHG discussed the consequences of the choices, and the entire group was requested to select the one option that reflected the group's first choice, and an alternative second choice.
- The facilitators kept a record (on a predesigned "CHAT Data Capturing Form") of both individual and consensus choices made in CHATs 1 and 2.

CHAT Round 3

- This round was held about 15 days later, and its purpose was to select a single package that would be offered by the community-based health insurance (CBHI) to all its potential members.
- The decision rule was that each female SHG selected one package (similar to what was done in CHAT 2), and the package that was chosen by most groups was retained in each location.

The evaluation interviews revealed that they wish to be part of a consensus was the dominant motive for the choice of the benefits package and overruled the price or the composition of the package. The in-depth interviews suggested that people enjoyed the participatory deliberations, were satisfied with the selection and that group decisions reflected a consensus rather than the majority.

A key insight of this study is that there is no contradiction in saying that each community can agree on the application of one and only one package to everybody in that community, while also saying that communities living in different conditions choose different packages. The study shows that in arriving at a consensus, although the three communities selected a package that reflected different morbidity patterns, socioeconomic statuses or available health care services, the process of consensus building they followed was the same.

Conclusion

This study offers clear empirical evidence that people living in rural informal settings, some of whom are illiterate and innumerate and with no prior experience with health insurance, can reach consensus on the choice of their health insurance benefit package through a game-like tool called CHAT. The packages that were chosen by the three groups were eventually implemented in the three locations in the form of CBHIs that captured solvent demand and created the supply of health insurance, neither of which existed previously.

Open Access Full Text Article
ORIGINAL RESEARCH

"One for all and all for one": consensus-building within communities in rural India on their health microinsurance package

This article was published in the following Dove Press journal:
Risk Management and Healthcare Policy
4 August 2014
Number of times this article has been viewed

David M Dror[1,2]
Pradeep Panda[1]
Christina May[3]
Atanu Majumdar[1]
Ruth Koren[4]

[1]Micro Insurance Academy, New Delhi, India; [2]Erasmus University, Rotterdam, the Netherlands; [3]University of Cologne, Cologne, Germany; [4]Tel Aviv University, Ramat Aviv, Israel

Introduction: This study deals with consensus by poor persons in the informal sector in rural India on the benefit-package of their community-based health insurance (CBHI). In this article we describe the process of involving rural poor in benefit-package design and assess the underlying reasons for choices they made and their ability to reach group consensus.

Methods: The benefit-package selection process entailed four steps: narrowing down the options by community representatives, plus three Choosing Healthplans All Together (CHAT) rounds conducted among female members of self-help groups. We use mixed-methods and four sources of data: baseline study, CHAT exercises, in-depth interviews, and evaluation questionnaires. We define consensus as a community resolution reached by discussion, considering all opinions, and to which everyone agrees. We use the coefficient of unalikeability to express consensus quantitatively (as variability of categorical variables) rather than just categorically (as a binomial Yes/No).

Findings: The coefficient of unalikeability decreased consistently over consecutive CHAT rounds, reaching zero (ie, 100% consensus) in two locations, and confirmed gradual adoption of consensus. Evaluation interviews revealed that the wish to be part of a consensus was dominant in all locations. The in-depth interviews indicated that people enjoyed the participatory deliberations, were satisfied with the selection, and that group decisions reflected a consensus rather than majority. Moreover, evidence suggests that pre-selectors and communities aimed to enhance the likelihood that many households would benefit from CBHI.

Conclusion: The voluntary and contributory CBHI relies on an engaging experience with others to validate perceived priorities of the target group. The strongest motive for choice was the wish to join a consensus (more than price or package-composition) and the intention that many members should benefit. The degree of consensus improved with iterative CHAT rounds. Harnessing group consensus requires catalytic intervention, as the process is not spontaneous.

Keywords: benefit-package design, micro health insurance, community-based health insurance, CBHI

Video abstract

Point your SmartPhone at the code above. If you have a QR code reader the video abstract will appear. Or use:
http://dvpr.es/1pHeOCs

Correspondence: Pradeep Panda
Micro Insurance Academy, 52-B, Okhla Industrial Estate, Phase III, New Delhi – 110020, Delhi, India
Tel +91 11 4379 9100
Fax +91 11 4379 9117
Email pradeep@mia.org.in

Introduction

In India, as in other low- and middle-income countries, most of the rural population lives and works in the informal sector.[1,2] The implied consequence of being "informal" is that people are often engaged in small-scale, self-employed activities (with or without hired workers), typically unrecorded, unregistered and conducted without proper integration with the administrative machinery responsible for enforcing laws and regulations, usually escaping both the attention of and recognition from the authorities.[3] Thus, they are excluded from market or social arrangements through which they might benefit from health insurance.[4] Under these conditions, several development projects have been launched aimed at implementing health microinsurance at village or local level.[5–11] Health microinsurance has originally been defined as a voluntary, contributory, community-based health insurance (CBHI) scheme for which the group designs the benefits, premiums, and/or governance structure, to be relevant and affordable to the local population.[12,13] Different authors have used other names for the generic "microinsurance", eg, Micro Health Insurance (MHI), Mutual Health Organizations (MHO) (in French Mutuelles de santé), CBHI, Community-based Health Funds (CBHF), Community Owned and Operated Plans (COOP) etc. The difference between these names is not discussed in detail in this paper, and we use the generic "microinsurance" for all kinds of systems versus CBHI to refer to a people-centered mutual aid scheme. This definition departs from classical demand theory, which views the individual as formulating demand; here, the group defines the demand and ideally pools both risks and resources to provide protection to all members.[14] This formulation of demand relies on mobilization of collective action.

The questions that beg empirical evidence are whether and how rural poor without prior experience with health insurance can be engaged in a complex process of selecting a coherent benefit-package that will reflect their communal needs and priorities, rather than simply being told to buy cheap insurance. Involving the rural community means empowering them to define the benefit types that would be payable to insured persons, as well as all the rules on deductibles, co-payments, cost-sharing amounts (thresholds), or maxima (caps), and other conditions and limitations which may determine the share of health-care cost that will be borne by the insurance (and in our context, by the microinsurance or CBHI scheme). The working assumption underlying this research question is that when rural groups are involved, they can reach consensus on the composition and price of the benefit-package that reflects local notions of value-for-money, leading to stronger motivation to enroll.

Literature on consumers' preferences for health insurance plans has so far concentrated on rich countries.[15–21] Only few publications deal with the health insurance benefit choices of low-income persons in low-income countries.[22–24] Dror et al[25] and Danis et al[26] described simulation exercises (called "CHAT" – Choosing Healthplans All Together) in which rural poor in India were asked to compose health insurance packages by selecting benefit types that should be included within a severe budgetary limitation. The main lessons from those experiments were that rural poor were interested in broad coverage rather than coverage of only rare events.

Following on from those experiments, a 5-year EC-FP7 project (2009–2014) on implementation of CBHI was launched by the Micro Insurance Academy (MIA), New Delhi[27] (http://www.microinsuranceacademy.org) in three locations in rural India (Pratapgarh and Kanpur-Dehat districts, Uttar Pradesh, and Vaishali district, Bihar).[28] The MIA implementation model enables prospective members to be involved in decisions on the benefit-package that the CBHI schemes offer.[29] The prospective members selected pre-composed packages (rather than composing packages from a selection of benefit types, as was done under the earlier CHAT exercises) as well as premium levels that such packages commanded. The project unfolded in cooperation with field-partner non-governmental organizations (NGOs): BAIF (Bharatiya Agro Industries Foundation) in Pratapgarh; Shramik Bharti in Kanpur-Dehat; and Nidan in Vaishali, and the implementation aimed at enrolling rural women that participate in self-help groups (groups of 10–15 women saving together and giving each other loans from their common fund) (SHGs) facilitated by these field partners. These SHGs aim at economic and social empowerment and capacity building for women through micro-credit and other activities, with the intention to ultimately benefit the whole community.[30] Both CHAT and the CBHI schemes also possess empowering features, as they allow local communities to exercise more control over decisions relating to health insurance.[31] Additionally, by targeting women in CHAT activities, the implementing partners aim at enhanced participation of women in economic and social spheres. In this context, MIA understands its role as both a catalytic actor and facilitator of the process through which the CBHI is introduced to the communities with the help of field partners, and aiding the establishment of the local schemes.[32]

The setting of the present study was the implementation of these three CBHI schemes. The purpose of this article is to describe the process of involving rural poor in benefit-package design, explaining the underlying reasons for choices they made, and assessing their ability to reach group consensus regarding package composition, against the background of the research question formulated earlier.

The article includes a section describing the data and methods, followed by a section presenting the results from three choice exercises. We then discuss the ramifications of those insurance choices. Finally, we formulate conclusions and policy recommendations.

Data and methods

Data

The study is based on four sources of data: a dataset obtained through a baseline study, CHAT exercises, in-depth interviews, and evaluation interviews. In accordance with the guidelines issued by the Indian Council of Medical Research, the overall study as well as the specific data collection tools used were checked and approved by the ethics committee of the University of Cologne, Germany.[33]

Baseline study

The source data for actuarial calculations of premiums of different benefits originates from a baseline survey of the 5-year project, conducted March–May 2010 in three locations in rural India. The selection criterion of households for inclusion in the sample was that at least one female member was enrolled in an SHG, affiliated with the field partner NGO in March 2010. The calculation of incidence of illness and premiums for each location was based on the entire sample at that site. Table 1 contains the detailed information on the sample, by location. More information on the context of the study is provided in Table S1.

CHAT exercises data

Group choice exercises were conducted in which female SHG groups were invited to "play CHAT" with the help of pictorial boards showing different benefit-packages and the related premium (a picture of a CHAT board is reproduced in Figure S1). CHAT involved different benefit-packages in each of our three study sites, developed in benefit-package selection workshops that are described in detail in the Findings section. The premiums for each of the benefit options were calculated by using the baseline data. The group discussions were led by 6–8 facilitators in each location (some chosen from the SHG members and some from the field partner organization). These facilitators received training from the MIA. The CHAT games were conducted in three rounds: during the first round (CHAT 1) female participants from the SHGs were asked to select the benefit-package that met their and their families' needs (using colored stickers to denote their first and second priority). At the end of this individual round, each participant could take home a personal copy of the CHAT board to discuss the choices with family members. The next day, during the second round (CHAT 2), a facilitated group discussion was convened, in which each female SHG discussed the consequences of the choices, and the entire group was requested to select the one option that reflected the group's first choice, and an alternative second choice. The facilitators kept a record (on a predesigned "CHAT Data Capturing Form") of both individual and consensus choices made in CHAT 1 and 2. The third round (CHAT 3) took place about 15 days later, and its purpose was to select a single package that would be offered by the CBHI to all its potential members; the decision-rule was that each female SHG selected one package (similar to what was done in CHAT 2), and the package that was chosen by most groups was retained in each location. All the community members that facilitated the CHAT rounds did not get any pay or incentive for participating; and the facilitators from the field partner NGOs conducted the sessions as part of their normal work duty. Table 2 provides the number of groups and individuals who participated in CHAT exercises in each site.

Individual in-depth interviews

With the view to understanding the motivations underlying CHAT choices, we followed a mixed-methods methodology using both qualitative, open-ended in-depth interviews, and quantitative, closed-ended evaluation questionnaires. By doing that, we not only got a better picture on the reasons for the choices made, but also an understanding of the underlying processes. In-depth interviews were conducted with six female SHG members (in their households) in each of the three sites (Pratapgarh in November 2010, Vaishali in December 2010, and Kanpur-Dehat in

Table 1 Treatment and control households by location (2011)

Location	Treatment	Control	Total households
Pratapgarh (Uttar Pradesh)	433	850	1,283
Kanpur-Dehat (Uttar Pradesh)	378	661	1,039
Vaishali (Bihar)	524	839	1,363
Total households	1,335	2,350	3,685

Notes: Treatment households are the SHG households that were offered the option to join the CBHI in 2011, and control households are the remaining SHG households who were not offered the option to join at that point in time.
Abbreviations: CBHI, community-based health insurance; SHG, self-help group.

Table 2 Number of groups and individuals that participated in the CHAT exercises

	Pratapgarh	Kanpur-Dehat	Vaishali
CHAT 1			
Individual	383	272	436
CHAT 2			
Group	47	29	49
CHAT 3			
Group	47	29	49

Abbreviation: CHAT, Choosing Healthplans All Together.

March 2011). At each site, we chose three SHGs which had been selected to be offered insurance and to participate in CHAT, and interviewed two members from each group. We decided to use individual interviews instead of group interviews to enable the women to openly voice negative impressions related to the group's decision-making process. Additionally, we conducted interviews with two CHAT facilitators per site to understand the facilitators' perspectives on the CHAT process and decision-making in the groups. In total, we conducted 24 interviews ([6 + 2] ×3). All interviews were conducted in the local language (Hindi), tape-recorded, and later transcribed and translated into English. The interviewers were trained in using two different sets of semi-structured questionnaires (one for SHG members and one for CHAT facilitators) that contained both exploratory and targeted questions inquiring, among other things, about experiences with and perception of CHAT, problems encountered during CHAT, decision-making processes in group and household, and reasons for particular choices. Answers to these questions were then compared using NVivo® (QSR International, Melbourne, Australia) software, version 8. We followed the method for directed qualitative content analysis described by Hsieh and Shannon,[34] combining deductive and inductive coding of data.

Evaluation questionnaires

We additionally conducted structured, closed-ended evaluation interviews with about 20% of the households that participated in CHAT. The main purpose of these interviews was to evaluate the awareness campaign wherein CHAT was one component.[35]

Identification of benefit-package options

The first step in the process of benefit-package design entailed preparing a limited set of options which would be presented to the groups for selection through the CHAT exercise. This was done through an interactive exercise (called "Benefit-package selection workshop") facilitated by MIA, in which representatives of the field partners and of the communities (the SHG federation, SHG members, and community leaders, eg, teachers, panchayat members, and community health workers) reviewed all the pertinent information about morbidity, costs of care, health-seeking behavior, and availability of health-care facilities (obtained through the baseline study). The discussions revolved around several benefit-package options and the premium (the premium [per person per year] is calculated using the basic formula: Pure risk premium = [average expenditures per episode] *[incidence rate] assuming a Poisson distribution of incidence and truncating frequency distributions of expenditures to take account of including thresholds and caps in the insurance coverage) that each package would command (community rated per person per year). The output of each workshop was four to six packages that would be presented to the entire target population for selection.

Method of measuring consensus: coefficient of unalikeability

We define consensus as "general agreement/resolution arrived at by most of those concerned, after everyone's opinions are heard and understood, and a solution is created that everyone agrees to". This definition is in line with the approach used by Sultana and Thompson[36] and Mohammed and Ringseis.[37] We apply "unalikeability", meaning "how often observations differ from one another" to measure the consensus reached within each location.[38] Unalikeability is expressed as a coefficient that measures variability of the categorical variable "the package that people chose". Each package was numbered (see package numbers in Table 3). The choices of every participant were noted in each session and compared with those of other individuals in the same location; individuals were matched to others through a random process of pairing. For each pair, we noted whether the choices were identical (denoted 0) or not (1). By using the techniques of combinatorics we counted all the observations that differed (by Excel® 2010 [Microsoft Corporation, Redmond, WA, USA]). The value of the coefficient lies between 0 and 1, where 0 indicates that all observations within the set are identical and 1 means that all observations differ from each other. If the coefficient of unalikeability decreased over consecutive sessions, we concluded that the differences within the cohort were decreasing, and the zero value of the coefficient of unalikeability meant that complete convergence was reached on a particular package. We preferred this method over Kappa statistics, which is used for measuring reliability of judgment (especially useful when agreement is sought on something rare). Kappa statistics usually involves agreement or disagreement of observers on one event, which is different from the CHAT exercises, where many persons need to select one item from a set of multiple items. Table S2 shows the computation of the coefficients with first and second choices in the three locations.

Kader and Perry[38] did not discuss any statistical properties of the coefficient of unalikeability, but since the coefficient is calculated from the frequency distribution of choices, we calculated the significance of differences of the coefficients by estimating

Table 3 Options retained at the benefit-package selection workshops, and the package selected during CHAT (in INR unless a different unit is stated)

Benefit type/ package	Pratapgarh				Kanpur-Dehat						Vaishali					
	1	2	3	4	1	2	3	4	5	6[a]	1	2	3	4	5	6
Lab test (PPPY)	–	–	–	–	–	–	–	–	–	–	200	200	100	200	200	100
Imaging (PPPY)	–	–	–	–	–	–	–	–	–	–	300	300	200	300	300	200
Wage loss (per day)	100	100		100	75	100	75	100	75	100	0	100	100	0	100	100
From day (numbers represent days)	3	3		3	4	4	4	4	4	4		4	4		4	4
To day (numbers represent days)	8	8		8	13	13	13	13	13	13		9	9		9	9
Consultation with medicine	–	–	–	–	Yes	Yes	Yes	Yes	Yes	Yes	Yes	Yes	Yes	Yes	Yes	Yes
Hospitalization																
PPPY	5,000	5,000	6,800	6,000	3,000	4,000	5,000	6,000	7,000	4,500			2,000			2,000
Per family per year										25,000						
Hospitalization for C-section	3,000	3,000	3,000	5,000												
Deduct (payable by govt)	1,400	1,400	1,400	1,400												
Transportation	–	200		100	100	100	150	150	200	100						
Life																
Natural death														30,000	30,000	30,000
Accidental death														75,000	75,000	75,000
Disability due to accident														37,500	37,500	37,500
Premium per person per year (in INR)																
PPPY – family up to 5	157	162	176	176	192	221	243	270	290	192	187	197	236	1,287	197	236
PPPY – family 6–8	157	162	176	176	192	221	243	270	290	192	178	188	225	1,278	188	225
PPPY – family 9+	157	162	176	176	192	221	243	270	290	192	160	169	203	160	169	203
Life premiums																
PPPY 1 person														100	100	100
PPPY 2 persons														50	50	50
PPPY 3 persons														67	67	67
PPPY 4 persons														50	50	50
PPPY 5 persons														40	40	40
PPPY 6 persons														33	33	33
PPPY 7 persons														29	29	29
PPPY 8 persons														25	25	25
PPPY 9 persons														22	22	22
PPPY 10 persons														20	20	19
Package chosen				***						***		***				

Notes: [a]Package number 6 in Kanpur-Dehat district was not designed in the original workshop; instead, it was created after feedback from the community, which wanted a higher cap for individual hospitalizations. Based on the package originally chosen by the groups in CHAT – package 1 – a new package entailing basically the same benefits and the same price but a family floater instead of an individual cap was designed and then agreed to by the community. ***Indicates the package that was chosen in the respective locations from among the options considered.

Abbreviations: CHAT, Choosing Healthplans All Together; govt, government; PPPY, per person per year; INR, Indian Rupee.

the significance of difference between the distributions under different settings, by employing the chi-square test.

Findings

The benefit-package options considered

The options that were retained in the benefit-package selection workshops were presented to the target population in the different CHAT rounds and drawn as "CHAT boards" (Figure S1). The data are shown in Table 3.

We used the coefficient of unalikeability to measure the variability of choices made. We observed that the coefficient of unalikeability decreased over consecutive CHAT rounds in all locations, indicating that groups gradually adopted a consensus on one package. Incidentally, groups in all three locations converged towards consensus also on their second priority package (data not shown). The differences in the values of the coefficients of unalikeability were significant ($P<0.000$).

The data in Figure 1 clearly shows that consensus was higher in CHAT 2 than in CHAT 1, and increased further in CHAT 3. CHAT 3, like CHAT 2, was a group choice, which took place 15 days after CHAT 2, and following

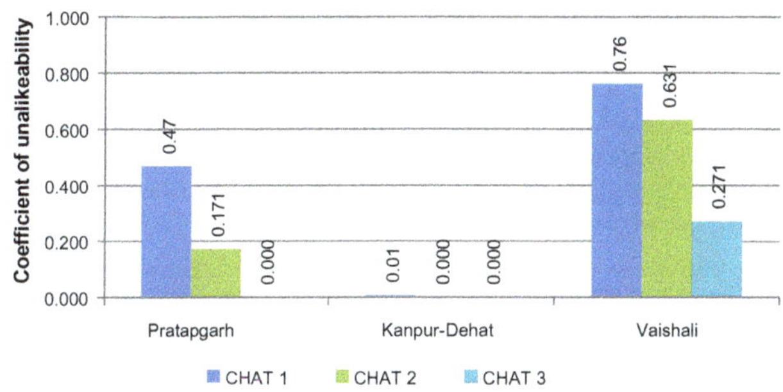

Figure 1 Coefficient of unalikeability in three CHAT rounds and three locations.
Abbreviation: CHAT, Choosing Healthplans All Together.

discussions that each individual had with others in her household and community. One might have expected that external influences from people that did not participate in the deliberations in the SHGs would reduce consensus; however, the coefficient of unalikeability decreased, implying that consensus had actually increased after interactions with outsiders. This finding clearly indicates that the consensual choice was not limited only to persons that participated in the CHAT exercises, but reflects the views of the entire target population in each location on the desirable benefit-package for them.

After the CHAT rounds, we conducted structured closed-ended evaluation interviews with about 20% of the participants, who were asked about the main reason for their choice in CHAT 2 and in CHAT 3. The results are shown in Table 4. Interestingly, at the CHAT 2, about one-quarter of the respondents in all locations said that they wanted to be part of a group choice and therefore chose the package that "other SHG members liked". The three other reasons (cheapest, best, or most benefits) had different weights across the locations. But in CHAT 3, the consensus was dominant in all locations. When all three cohorts were aggregated, increase in the preference for consensus choice was significant (P=0.037, chi-squared test).

Table 4 Why people chose the package they did

	Pratapgarh	Kanpur-Dehat	Vaishali
No of respondents	115	72	104
CHAT 2			
Participated in CHAT 2[a]	80.9	72.2	72.1
Reasons for choosing the final package (among participants)[b]			
Other SHG members liked it	25.8	25.0	24.0
Cheapest	20.4	32.7	26.7
Best	21.5	21.2	25.3
Most benefits	22.6	3.8	14.7
Other	9.7	17.3	9.3
CHAT 3			
Participated in CHAT 3[a]	73.9	62.5	62.5
Reasons for choosing the final package (among participants)[b]			
Other SHG members liked it	35.3	33.3	33.9
Cheapest	24.7	28.9	27.7
Best	12.9	24.4	21.5
Most benefits	25.9	8.9	12.3
Other	1.2	4.4	4.6

Notes: [a]Percentage of the respondents; [b]percentages of those that participated in CHAT 2 or 3, respectively.
Abbreviations: CHAT, Choosing Healthplans All Together; SHG, self-help group.

We conducted in-depth interviews with female SHG members that participated in CHAT and with a few facilitators and cite here their testimonials, as addition to the quantitative information.

In general, respondents expressed their satisfaction with the benefit-package selection process:

> I like that type of game. Everything in that game was to be praised. [SHG member 5, Kanpur-Dehat]
>
> We liked the method, we liked pasting the stickers. [SHG member 2, Vaishali]
>
> [The CHAT exercise] was very good and we all liked it very much. [SHG member 2, Pratapgarh]

According to one facilitator, CHAT encouraged the participation of all SHG members and their families in the decision-making process:

> Usually in our group meetings [...], people listen to these things silently and nod their heads, but in this CHAT game, there was participation from all women. [...] The family members also joined, so this is indeed a good method. [Facilitator 1, Vaishali]

People enjoyed the participatory nature of the CHAT exercises, liked the deliberations, and liked to make their own decisions:

> The best thing in the CHAT was that the women were free to choose any package that they liked. It was not imposed on them, and there were no restrictions or obligations to choose a particular package. [Facilitator 2, Pratapgarh]

The data from our in-depth interviews also confirm that group decisions reflected a consensus rather than majority decision. Respondents described the discussions that occurred and how their opinions were considered:

> [The choice] was a consensus and our opinions were entertained. [SHG member 2, Vaishali]
>
> We all discussed and everyone agreed to it. [SHG member 3, Vaishali]
>
> It was a collective decision. [SHG member 5, Vaishali]
>
> They [the other SHG members] were discussing [...] which package should be chosen and which one is better for us. Every person decided that there would be one insurance for all. [SHG member 2, Kanpur-Dehat]
>
> There was discussion in which some said that package number 4 is best. Then we all favored it as well. [...] After the discussion [...] we all agreed. [SHG member 1, Pratapgarh]

Corresponding to the evaluation interviews, which showed that respondents chose packages other SHG members liked, we found qualitative evidence in all locations that people often looked up to trusted peers in their groups and considered their choices. For instance, in Pratapgarh, one member said:

> Knowledgeable people know their benefits; what is right or what is wrong. Everyone selected the same package. [SHG member 4, Pratapgarh]

And in Vaishali, one facilitator explained:

> Everybody believes in the secretary of the group. Whatever the decision the secretary will take, that will be important. Anyhow everybody gives her opinion but the chairman's opinion is most important. [Facilitator 2, Vaishali]

However, respondents did not simply copy the decisions or opinions of administrative officers. Everyone's opinion was entertained and considered as important, as explained in the following testimonial:

> Everyone's suggestion has equal importance in the groups. This is all about the groups, that everyone has to go together and [has to take] care of each other's interest. [Facilitator 2, Kanpur-Dehat]

It is recalled that as part of the decision-making process, participants in the CHAT 1 took home a copy of the CHAT boards in order to validate choices and obtain support from family and friends. Several interviewees mentioned the value of these consultations:

> After CHAT 1, we gave everybody the CHAT board to discuss all the possibilities with family members. [...] They showed the board to the male members of the family. After that, heads of different families discussed how to deal with it. As the women cannot do all the work, they rely on the head of the family or those who they consider the head of the locality like the teacher or the doctor. [...] When they approve the same, then the women can pursue the matter. [Facilitator 2, Kanpur-Dehat]

Nevertheless, this interaction was not always easy and sometimes necessitated additional explanations from other SHG members or NGO staff to convince family members:

> [During CHAT in the group] everything was good, [...] but when they shared with their respective homes, they were criticized by some family members. [...] It was resolved when the person who criticized was convinced by others, so they understood everything about it. [SHG member 1, Kanpur-Dehat]

Clearly, even though the women were empowered to make choices in the CHAT exercises, it was essential to also secure the agreement of the men in order to enable the women to actually confirm the choice and later actually enroll and pay:

> [...] [T]he decision is taken by the male guardian or the husband in the family, since it is a matter of money. Unless [they] were not told by the family guardian [women] cannot pay the instalments. They said that the way in which they are conducting the meetings with the women of the group, in the same way there should be meeting with other family members, guardians and head of the family, to convince them. [Facilitator 2, Pratapgarh]

In summary, our evidence shows that in all locations, the target population was keen to converge towards consensus. Local leaders, knowledgeable persons, and male household heads influenced the discussion and the decision-making process, and wanted to be involved in more detail.

The benefit-packages chosen

The pre-selectors in the three locations seemed to have different perceptions of the main issues that the population was facing. In Vaishali, the pre-selectors suggested three patterns: one that included hospitalization and outpatient care, another which focused mainly on outpatient care, and the third which included these health packages plus life insurance. The community rejected the life insurance option, and of the two health options, it favored the outpatient model but included wage-loss compensation in case of hospitalization, and chose the option commanding higher premiums. This community could take advantage of government-provided hospitalization insurance for people below the poverty line (RSBY, Rashtriya Swasthya Bima Yojana), which probably explains why they did not retain hospitalization benefits.

In Pratapgarh, the pre-selectors retained benefit-packages covering hospital-related care: hospitalizations, wage-loss during hospitalizations, and transportation to hospital, as well as coverage of delivery with C-section. In this region, RSBY was almost nonexistent when the CBHI was implemented. This group enhanced the likelihood of claims by many members when it added a benefit related to maternity which is not otherwise available free of charge.

In Kanpur-Dehat, the pre-selectors proposed a combined set of benefits covering both hospitalizations and outpatient consultations; the target population reached consensus on the premium level, but wanted a different set of benefits that would enhance intra-household cross-subsidization.

The intention to choose a package that will benefit many members

We observed that both the pre-selectors and the community employed different strategies to enhance the likelihood that many households would benefit from CBHI.

In Vaishali, the pre-selectors proposed a decreasing premium per person as household size increases. This arrangement was a de-facto cross-subsidy from smaller households to larger ones, and the groups in Vaishali confirmed their agreement to this intra-group subsidy. Indeed, 14% of the enrolled families, which actually comprised 24% of the total enrolled individuals, benefited from this discount in Vaishali. Of the families with family sizes between six and eight (average 6.35), 13% got a discount of 5%, and 1% of the families with family size nine and above (average 9.33) paid 15% less than the base premium. As for package composition, this community chose mainly outpatient care benefits that are more likely to be claimed by many members.

In Kanpur-Dehat, the group accepted the benefit types proposed by the pre-selectors, but requested a change in the terms applying to hospital benefits, so that the cap would apply to a household rather than to each individual separately. This was labelled "family floater", which means that within a cap per family and per event (rather than a cap per person per year), one household member can claim more than one event per year. This arrangement institutionalizes intra-household cross subsidization and adds welfare to the most vulnerable members, as well as to the non-claiming household members (that are released from the obligation to pay for repeat hospitalization of close relatives). In addition, the combination of inpatient and outpatient benefits increased the likelihood of claiming a benefit by many insured members.

As already mentioned, some respondents chose a particular package because it was "cheapest" or had "most benefits" (Table 4). We bring a few testimonials to shed more light on the considerations that influenced the choices made, especially in Kanpur-Dehat and Pratapgarh:

> I was going for [the more expensive package] but which may be difficult for other members. Hence I joined the collective decision to accommodate others, as all the others have to benefit. [SHG member 4, Kanpur-Dehat]

This indicates that when discussing the price, the participants were concerned not merely about their ability to pay, but of other members as well. The two facilitators in Kanpur-Dehat observed the same behavior pattern:

> Everyone selected packages for themselves keeping in mind their own benefits [...] But when they met among themselves and were informed that a single package is applicable for the whole group they realized that [...] they all should select a package that is affordable for all. [Facilitator 2, Kanpur-Dehat]

Additionally, SHG members in Kanpur-Dehat chose to go for the cheapest option to "test" CBHI, which was a new concept for the community, as explained by a facilitator:

> Wherever we visited, everyone used to say that they want to opt for the minimum one for the first year. If we benefit then we may look for the better one next year. [Facilitator 2, Kanpur-Dehat]

In Pratapgarh, our in-depth interviews revealed that CHAT participants often set benefits in relation to price and opted for package 4 after realizing that it cost only slightly more but offered more benefits than other packages. It was especially important for them that packages 4 and 2 (their first and second choice) were "broader" than the other packages (ie, offered a higher variety of benefits). This shows that they did not simply assume that the most expensive package would provide the most benefits. Otherwise, they would have chosen package 3 over 2. Instead, they preferred a package with most benefit types with lower caps over few benefit types with higher caps.

In Kanpur-Dehat, the selection emphasized insuring minor illnesses and outpatient care. A facilitator in Kanpur-Dehat described how households which had experienced hospitalization in the past first favored expensive packages with more hospital coverage. However, the community chose cheaper packages, reflecting that most would not need to be hospitalized but would need coverage of outpatient care for minor but frequent illnesses:

> The people selected the packages keeping in mind their own experience. [...] Though there were some people who wanted to get more benefits with the large packages, most people wanted to start with the small package, keeping in mind that very few people do visit the hospitals and most of the people prefer to visit the local doctors. [Facilitator 1, Kanpur-Dehat]

In Pratapgarh, where outpatient care was not included in any of the packages offered, some interviewees criticized the choice of the pre-selectors to include only inpatient coverage:

> There are several issues here [...] they have not included minor ailments and the benefits in case of Caesarian section only. If one is delivering normally, then nothing will be paid. [SHG member 2, Pratapgarh]

Generally, respondents in all three sites expressed their satisfaction with the final package chosen:

> We are fully satisfied with [our choice]. [SHG member 2, Pratapgarh]
>
> Everybody is satisfied [with the package we have chosen]. [SHG member 1, Vaishali]
>
> We are very satisfied with [the package we have chosen]. [SHG member 5, Kanpur]

Discussion

This article deals with benefit-package design for CBHI in rural and informal settings in India. The CBHI model discussed here is characterized by voluntary and contributory affiliation, in which the entire group is encouraged to join en bloc. These new conditions of introducing health insurance include a more meaningful and engaging experience of customers directly with the design of the benefit-package, based on exchanges with others, rather than deciding in isolation, and emphasis on a group solution which addresses perceived priorities of the target group that the community is best placed to validate collectively rather than any individual alone. This process is much more sophisticated than expecting a decision merely on the merit of an unverifiable claim that premiums are low, and the relationship with the insurance to end, not begin, once people pay the premium.

The implementation model relies on collective action to select the benefit-package, which determines the share of health-care costs borne by the CBHI. We explored previous studies of how collective action was mobilized effectively. Ostrom[39] pointed to extensive fieldwork that established that individuals voluntarily organize to provide, inter alia, mutual protection against risk. She added that typically when people engage in direct communications with each other, they can generate cooperative behavior or create a social norm that has a certain staying power in encouraging the growth of cooperative behavior over time. Cooperative behavior thrives on a process that leads to implementation of changes (which in our study entailed a decision on a benefit-package that would be implemented by the CBHI schemes). Consensus magnifies the buy-in of decisions, but there is some debate on whether consensus means unanimity of opinions or involving everybody in the same process (with possibly a large majority of identical opinions). We have shown that consensus can be expressed quantitatively rather than just categorically (as a binomial Yes/No), and that the degree of consensus improved through an iterative process of decision-making. The salient lesson from this study is that the wish to be part of the consensus was the most important motive for choice of benefit-package (Table 4), more than the price or the composition of the package. Another important insight is that there is no contradiction in saying that each community can agree on the application of one and only one package to everybody in that community, while also saying that communities living in different conditions choose different packages. The three communities reached consensus, which was to select a package that reflected different morbidity patterns, socioeconomic statuses or available health-care services. The similarity was the process of consensus building, and the difference was the actual package. This finding corroborates previous claims that one size cannot fit all locations but a similar decision process can.[40] The similarity was in a descending value of the coefficient of unalikeability over subsequent iterations of the facilitated choice exercise (Figure 1) and in the motivation mentioned by many to join a consensus (Table 4).

The finding that individuals chose packages that can enhance benefits to their community is interesting from a perspective of theory of demand. Conventional insurance demand theory posits that demand decisions are made by individuals on the basis of their perceived marginal utility from the purchase of insurance.[41,42] In the CBHI model described, the balance between self and community interests was achieved by starting the process with a phase of individual choice of package, followed by face-to-face exchanges with other community members in small groups. The consensus of small groups (composed of women that participate in SHGs) was then shared with their family members, and the facilitation given to women to discuss their choices with family and community members created an opportunity to discuss why other participants preferred different choices, recognize the legitimacy of other opinions, and seek a way to devise a compromise consensus. The discussions were then repeated with members of other groups in the same community who also elaborated their consensus in a similar process, and the follow-up discussions led to higher consensus. Our evidence corroborates the results of Mohammed and Ringseis[37] that consensus building is gradual and requires multiple iterations with frequent face-to-face informal exchanges between community members. Our participatory process generated high satisfaction with the process and with the resultant benefit-package, as attested by the testimonials. More importantly, participation in the CHAT process was instrumental in enhancing understanding of the insurance process in the context of CBHI, which was positively associated with higher enrolment.[35] As such, the process can serve to scale penetration of insurance in rural settings in India, by creating more awareness, leading to more trust, which in turn leads to higher enrolment.

An important common denominator of the choice process in all three locations was its inclusive nature and the intention to enhance the likelihood that many members of the community should benefit from the CBHI. Additionally, community leaders who participated in the benefit-package selection workshop enhanced the probability that households will be able to cope with multiple episodes within the household (Vaishali) and ensured that poorer households would be able to participate in CBHI by offering discounts for large households (Vaishali) or by choosing cheaper packages affordable to everyone, with the "family floater" cap (Kanpur-Dehat). Some of these novel provisions have been either initiated or confirmed by consensus of the large grassroots groups, so that there can be no doubt that they were able to understand the welfare-enhancing potential of these arrangements. We therefore conclude that the demand for CBHI in the informal sector in rural India is based in large part on collective priorities, and on the general understanding that if most people did not like the package on offer, there would be no CBHI at all for anybody.

The CHAT process specifically involved women organized in SHGs. In CHAT 1, they made their choices independently from other family members. Although it was reported that men would finally decide whether to join CBHI, our data also show that when male household heads provided feedback on choices women made in CHAT 1, most men generally agreed. On the other hand, when women had difficulty explaining their CHAT choices to their family or getting agreement, they were supported by the NGO staff to convince family members. Clearly, each woman commanded a different degree of authority and empowerment within their household. Baily[43] reported that women needed male guardian consent to participate in SHG activities, and the expectation of male villagers that such participation would benefit both the women themselves and their families and communities.

Within SHGs, there are issues of power relations. Although our groups are usually quite homogeneous, some differences may exist in education and socioeconomic status. Each group elected a president, secretary, and treasurer. It was reported in our interviews that the opinion of these women was often followed because they were trusted. At the same time, CHAT facilitators and participants stressed that the opinion of all women was considered when reaching consensus. A similar process was observed by Seshagiri et al[44] when small groups were asked to solve specific tasks (in a village in the Indian Karnataka state): the more educated members and those that were more articulate had more influence solving the tasks, who nonetheless tried to actively engage "weaker" members in the activity. We conclude that although more educated SHG members had an influence on the group's decisions in our study, they did not hijack the decision-making process, as decisions were taken with consent of all group members. On the whole, interactive and continuous engagement in three rounds of CHAT exercise and exposure to insurance education have provided the SHG women an opportunity to be socially empowered.

Limitations of the study

The small number of in-depth interviews conducted does not allow the claim that they were generally representative; we therefore also triangulated this source with the findings from the CHAT exercises and exit questionnaires. The interviews were conducted by researchers employed by the partner NGOs; this might have affected respondents' comments on the CHAT process facilitated by these NGOs. On the other hand, respondents might have been more responsive during the interviews because they were familiar with the local researchers and the NGO.

Most of the SHGs in which we conducted CHAT have been operating for years and are used to collaborate and make decisions in group settings. This could have facilitated the CHAT process.

Conclusion and policy ramifications

This study offers clear empirical evidence that people living in rural informal settings, some of whom are illiterate and innumerate and with no prior experience with health insurance, can reach consensus on the choice of their health insurance benefit-package. The subject matter is quite complex, but when presented in a game-like way, without compromising the actuarial accuracy, people can select packages within their willingness to pay and their perceived priorities for health-care coverage. The evidence suggests that group consensus can be harnessed to enhance demand for health microinsurance in the informal economy. Moreover, the people chose the benefit-packages with a clear intention that as many members of their community as possible should benefit. This suggests that people are sensitive to enhancing equity within the group and that CHAT enables them to make inclusive choices. The packages that were chosen by the three groups were in fact implemented in the three locations in the form of CBHIs that captured solvent demand, and created the supply of health insurance, neither of which existed previously.

The question might be raised whether it is necessary to conduct CHAT exercises and consensus building in each village separately. The evidence from our field experiments points that when a population group is introduced to the concept of CBHI for the first time, following this process is important as it creates the basic sense of empowerment and relevance that cannot be achieved in another way. However, in a region where CBHI has been introduced and is perceived as successful, neighboring villages may well wish to join the same scheme without elaborate preparations. Such villages would be involved in the entire process, along with others, when major changes in the benefit-package are contemplated.

It is noted that harnessing the collective action in a manner described in this article did not occur spontaneously. It required catalytic facilitation by devoted and knowledgeable persons who guide the process at village level from inception, who first collected relevant information in the field, translated it to actuarial estimates of premiums for different benefits, and then guided the community discussions. This process can be replicated anywhere in the informal sector, provided that the similar catalytic actor/change-maker can lead communities to assume the role of market-makers of their own health insurance.

Acknowledgments

David M Dror, Pradeep Panda, and Christina May gratefully acknowledge funding provided by the European Commission 7th Framework Program, grant ID HEALTH-F2-2009-223518 – Community-based Health Insurance in India. The authors gratefully acknowledge the extensive substantive contribution of the MIA and its staff in data collection and cleaning as well as in analytical inputs; the useful involvement of Ralf Radermacher in the early stages of the baseline study and pre-implementing preparations; the contribution of Katja Roth to the development of the qualitative tools; the contribution of Manish Kumar in providing essential explanations on how the preparation of the CHAT process actually unfolded in the field; the contribution of Lucy Firth to reviewing the analysis in this article and offering many useful suggestions and comments; and the implementing partners (BAIF, Shramik Bharti, and Nidan) as well as the respondents, for their ongoing willingness to share information on the implementation.

Author contributions

DD conceptualized the study and drafted the manuscript. PP and DD prepared the tools for quantitative surveys, and CM and PP prepared the qualitative tools. PP managed the data collection and provided oversight for study implementation. AM, PP, and CM conducted the data analyses. RK contributed to interpretation of data. DD, PP, RK, and CM critically reviewed the manuscript. All authors provided comments (including write-up) and approved the final manuscript.

Disclosure

The authors report no conflicts of interest in this work.

References

1. Bacchetta M, Ekkehard E, Bustamante J. Globalization and Informal Jobs in Developing Countries. International Labour Organization. 2009. Available from: http://www.rynekpracy.pl/pliki/pdf/34.pdf. Accessed July 21, 2014.
2. Pratap S, Quintin E. The informal sector in developing countries: Output, assets and employment (No. 2006/130). Research Paper, UNU-WIDER, United Nations University (UNU). 2006. Available from: http://www.wider.unu.edu/publications/working-papers/research-papers/2006/en_GB/rp2006-130/_files/78091818591914218/default/rp2006-130.pdf. Accessed July 21, 2014.
3. International Labour Organisation. *The Informal Sector UN*. Bangkok 2000. Available at http://www.ilo.org/public/english/region/asro/bangkok/feature/inf_sect.htm May 2013. Accessed July 21, 2014.

4. International Labour Organization [homepage on the Internet]. World Labour Report 2000: income security and social protection in a changing world. Geneva: International Labour Organization; 2000. Available from: http://www.ilo.org/public/english/protection/socsec/wlrblurb.htm. Accessed July 7, 2014.
5. Biener C, Eling M. Insurability in microinsurance markets: an analysis of problems and potential solutions. *Geneva Papers*. 2012;37(1):77–107.
6. Borghi J, Maluka S, Kuwawenaruwa A, et al. Promoting universal financial protection: a case study of new management of community health insurance in Tanzania. *Health Res Policy Syst*. 2013;11(1):21.
7. Mahal A, Krishnaswamy K, Ruchismita R, Babu BG. What is a health card worth? A randomised controlled trial of an outpatient health insurance product in rural India. *Lancet*. 2013;381:S87.
8. McCord MJ, Steinmann R, Tatin-Jaleran C, Ingram M, Mateo M. *The Landscape of Microinsurance in Africa 2012*. Munich Re Foundation and GIZ-Program Promoting Financial Sector Dialogue in Africa; 2012. Available from: http://www.microinsurancenetwork.org/publication/fichier/The_Landscape_of_MI_in_Africa_2012_full_study_web.pdf. Accessed July 7, 2014.
9. McCord MJ, Tatin-Jaleran C, Ingram M. The landscape of microinsurance in Latin America and the Caribbean. Multilateral Investment Fund; Citi Foundation; Microinsurance Centre; Munich Re Foundation; 2012. Available from: http://www.microinsurancecentre.org/resources/documents/market-development/the-landscape-of-microinsurance-in-latin-america-and-the-caribbean.html. Accessed July 16, 2014.
10. Roth J, McCord MJ, Liber D. *The Landscape of Microinsurance in the World's Poorest 100 Countries*. Appleton: The Microinsurance Centre; 2007. Available from: http://www.microfinancegateway.org/gm/document-1.9.29195/40285_file_15.pdf. Accessed April 10, 2014.
11. Tabor SR. *Community-Based Health Insurance and Social Protection Policy*. Washington DC: The World Bank; 2005. Available from: http://siteresources.worldbank.org/SOCIALPROTECTION/Resources/0503.pdf. Accessed April 10, 2014.
12. Dror DM, Jacquier C. Micro-insurance: extending health insurance to the excluded. *Int Soc Secur Rev*. 1999;52(1):71–97.
13. Dror DM. Health microinsurance in developing countries. In: Culyer AJ, editor. *Encyclopedia of Health Economics*. Vol 1. San Diego: Elsevier; 2014:412–421.
14. Dror DM, Firth L. The demand for (micro) health insurance in the informal sector. Geneva Papers. In press 2014.
15. Booske BC, Sainfort F, Hundt AS. Eliciting consumer preferences for health plans. *Health Serv Res*. 1999;34(4):839–854.
16. Chakraborty G, Ettenson R, Gaeth G. How consumers choose health insurance. *J Health Care Mark*. 1994;14(1):21–33.
17. Harris KM, Keane MP. A model of health plan choice: inferring preferences and perceptions from a combination of revealed preference and attitudinal data. *J Econom*. 1998;89(1–2):131–157.
18. Kerssens JJ, Groenewegen PP. Consumer preferences in social health insurance. *Eur J Health Econ*. 2005;6(1):8–15.
19. Mechanic D. Consumer choice among health insurance options. *Health Aff (Millwood)*. 1989;8(1):138–148.
20. Van den Berg B, Van Dommelen P, Stam P, Laske-AldershofT, Buchmueller T, Schut FT. Preferences and choices for care and health insurance. *Soc Sci Med*. 2008;66(12):2448–2459.
21. Scanlon DP, Chernew M, Lave JR. Consumer health plan choice: current knowledge and future directions. *Annu Rev Public Health*. 1997;18(1):507–528.
22. De Allegri M, Sanon M, Bridges J, Sauerborn R. Understanding consumers' preferences and decision to enrol in community-based health insurance in rural West Africa. *Health Policy*. 2006;76(1):58–71.
23. Harms J. *Microinsurance Product Design: consumer preferences in Kenya*. Geneva: ILO and Microinsurance Innovation Facility; 2011. Available from: http://www.ilo.org/public/english/employment/mifacility/download/repaper4.pdf. Accessed July 7, 2014.
24. Onwujekwe O, Onoka C, Uguru N, et al. Preferences for benefit-packages for community-based health insurance: an exploratory study in Nigeria. *BMC Health Serv Res*. 2010;10:162–162.
25. Dror DM, Koren R, Ost A, Binnendijk E, Vellakkal S, Danis M. Health insurance benefit-packages prioritized by low-income clients in India: three criteria to estimate effectiveness of choice. *Soc Sci Med*. 2007;64(4):884–896.
26. Danis M, Binnendijk E, Vellakkal S, Ost A, Koren R, Dror DM. Eliciting health insurance benefit choices of low income groups. *Econ Polit Wkly*. 2007;42(32):3331–3339.
27. Micro Insurance Academy. Developing Efficient and Responsive Community-Based Health Insurance in India. Available from: http://www.microinsuranceacademy.org/project/uttar-pradesh-and-bihar-india/. Accessed July 21, 2014.
28. Doyle C, Panda P, Poel EV de, Radermacher R, Dror DM. Reconciling research and implementation in micro health insurance experiments in India: study protocol for a randomized controlled trial. *Trials*. 2011;12(1):224.
29. Panda P, Chakraborty A, Dror DM, Bedi AS. Enrolment in community-based health insurance schemes in rural Bihar and Uttar Pradesh, India. *Health Policy Plan*. Epub October 26, 2013.
30. Tesoriero F. Strengthening communities through women's self help groups in South India. *Community Dev J*. 2006;41(3):321–333.
31. Craig G. Towards the Measurement of Empowerment: the Evaluation of Community Development. *Community Dev Soc J*. 2002;33(1):124–146.
32. Toomey AH. Empowerment and disempowerment in community development practice: eight roles practitioners play. *Community Dev J*. 2011;46(2):181–195.
33. Indian Council of Medical Research. *Ethical Guidelines for Biomedical Research on Human Participants*. New Delhi: Indian Council of Medical Research; 2006. Available from: http://icmr.nic.in/ethical_guidelines.pdf. Accessed July 7, 2014.
34. Hsieh H-F, Shannon SE. Three approaches to qualitative content analysis. *Qual Health Res*. 2005;15(9):1277–1288.
35. Panda P, Chakraborty A, Dror DM. Building awareness to health insurance among the target population of community-based health insurance schemes in rural India. *Social Science and Medicine*. In press 2014.
36. Sultana P, Thompson P. Methods of consensus building for community-based fisheries management in Bangladesh and in the Mekong Delta. *Agricultural Systems*. 2004;82:327–353.
37. Mohammed S, Ringseis E. Cognitive diversity and consensus in group decision making: the role of inputs, processes, and outcomes. *Organ Behav Hum Decis Process*. 2001;85(2):310–335.
38. Kader GD, Perry M. Variability for categorical variables. *J Stat Educ*. 2007;15(2).
39. Ostrom E. Collective action and the evolution of social norms. *J Econ Perspect*. 2000;14(3):137–158.
40. Dror DM. Why "one-size-fits-all" health insurance products are unsuitable for low-income persons in the informal economy in India. *Asian Econ Rev*. 2007;49(1):47–56.
41. Nyman JA. *The Theory of Demand for Health Insurance*. Stanford Univ Press 2003. Available from http://www.sup.org/search/blogthis.cgi?search=0804744882. Accessed July 16, 2014.
42. Pauly MV, Blavin FE, Meghan S. How private health insurance can work in developing countries. *Health Affairs*. 2009;28(6):1778–1787.
43. Baily S. Deconstructing gatekeepers discourses in the establishment of self-help groups for women in rural India. *Community Dev J*. Epub November 28, 2013.
44. Seshagiri S, Kaduskar MV, Bhaskaran P. Understanding group communication in rural India. In: *Proceedings of the 7th Nordic Conference on Human-Computer Interaction: Making Sense through Design. NordiCHI '12*. New York: ACM; 2012:617–626.

Supplementary materials

Table S1 Socioeconomic and demographic profile of the CHAT participants

	Pratapgarh	Kanpur-Dehat	Vaishali	All combined
Average age, years (SEM)	41 (0.59)	39 (0.65)	36 (0.50)	39 (0.33)
Married, %	88.0	86.4	94.1	90.0
Hindu, %	86.6	92.9	97.9	92.8
Scheduled caste and scheduled tribe, %	41.5	26.0	41.8	37.5
Average years of education (SEM)	2.2 (0.19)	3.5 (0.22)	2.3 (0.16)	2.6 (0.11)
Self-employed, %	15.5	19.0	13.9	15.8
Wage employment, %	19.0	6.0	14.1	13.5
Average monthly per capita expenditure, INR (SEM)	1,147 (30.45)	1,776 (71.02)	1,377 (43.47)	1,408 (28.53)
N	432	352	525	1,309

Abbreviations: CHAT, Choosing Healthplans All Together; INR, Indian Rupee; SEM, standard error of the mean.

Figure S1 CHAT board used in Kanpur-Dehat.
Abbreviation: CHAT, Choosing Healthplans All Together.

Table S2 Computation of coefficient of unalikeability

Location	1st choice					2nd choice				
	Session	Number of Participants played CHAT	Total number of possible pairs	Number of pairs in which observations differed	Coefficient of unalikeability	Session	Number of Participants played CHAT	Total number of possible pairs	Number of pairs in which observations differed	Coefficient of unalikeability
Pratapgarh	CHAT 1	383	73,153	34,238	0.468	CHAT 1	383	73,153	49,688	0.679
	CHAT 2	510	129,795	22,157	0.171	CHAT 2	510	129,795	40,581	0.313
	CHAT 3	510	129,795	0	0.000	CHAT 3	510	129,795	5,976	0.046
Kanpur-Dehat	CHAT 1	298	44,253	297	0.007	CHAT 1	298	44,253	5,925	0.134
	CHAT 2	332	54,946	0	0.000	CHAT 2	332	54,946	9,807	0.178
	CHAT 3	332	54,946	0	0.000	CHAT 3	332	54,946	0	0.000
Vaishali	CHAT 1	536	143,380	109,176	0.761	CHAT 1	536	143,380	103,817	0.724
	CHAT 2	659	216,811	136,723	0.631	CHAT 2	659	216,811	158,852	0.733
	CHAT 3	659	216,811	58,824	0.271	CHAT 3	659	216,811	134,506	0.620

Chapter 5

Willingness to Pay for Health Insurance

Main Messages

Following are the consolidated main messages from Chapters 5.1–5.3:

- Estimating Willingness to Pay (WTP) for health insurance (HI) coverage is the only way to estimate the expected income of voluntary and contributory HI schemes. This estimate is needed to ensure that the cost of benefits packages remain within available resources, so as to minimize the risk of bankruptcy.
- Data on WTP are necessary to inform the design of customized HI benefits packages by consumers, notably by groups or communities.
- One approach to estimate individual WTP is the Revealed Preferences method (RP), introduced first by Samuelson, which involves studying actual purchasing behavior of products which are related to the product we are interested in. The assumption is that revealed preferences can identify the value people place on a product for which purchasing information does not exist.
- Another approach to estimate WTP is the Stated Preferences method (SP), which involves asking people what they would be willing to pay for insurance coverage that they do not yet have, and that may

not be available in the market. SP has been refined into several techniques, and the one used most often to value non-market goods is called Contingent Valuation (CV). It consists of asking respondents the maximum amount they would be willing to pay for an intervention under evaluation (e.g. insurance).

- Most of the rural population in low-income countries is not familiar with the concept of insurance. Hence, it is challenged to reveal the price they are willing to pay for (insurance coverage) a product they have never before been offered or purchased.
- Field evidence of experiments with choice of package and price by groups of rural poor people in India points that they tend to converge toward consensus on the components of the benefit package and the price per person per year (PPPY), namely on the generally accepted *declared* WTP.
- It must be recognized that the *actual* level of their WTP could differ from the *declared* level. A first estimate of the gap between declared and actual WTP in community-based health insurance (CBHI) has been obtained from the evidence that households modulate WTP levels not by negotiating a different price, but by limiting the number of household members enrolled (at the agreed price PPPY) to reduce the total cost per household for HI. Initial evidence suggests that households enrolled only half their members in the first and second year. Longitudinal studies could verify whether the gap between the declared and actual WTP would diminish over time.
- Dror and Koren (2012) conducted a review of 14 experimental field studies eliciting WTP for health insurance among low-income persons in developing countries. They observed that the large methodological diversity reported in these studies made it impossible to identify a single "gold standard" method to elicit and estimate WTP.
- However, there was implied consensus that WTP must be explored locally, because there is no single "one-size-fits-all" option to determine the income side of different HMI schemes operating in different settings. Thus, estimates of WTP were based on household surveys. Collecting data with such surveys is both time-consuming and expensive.
- Several studies explored faster and cheaper methods to estimate WTP than surveys.

- Binnendijk *et al.* (2013) examined whether the relation between WTP for HI and income might be similar to Engel's Law, an observation in economics stating that the proportion of income spent on food decreases as income increases, even if actual expenditure on food rises. These authors used data from six locations in India to check WTP expressed as a percentage of three anchors: overall income, discretionary income, and food expenditures, by calculating the Coefficient of Variation (for inter-community variation) and Concentration indices (for intra-community variation). They found that food expenditures had the most consistent relationship with WTP within each location, and across the six locations. This suggests that, just like food, HI is considered a necessity good even for people with very low income and no prior experience with health insurance. Thus, it is possible to estimate the WTP level based on each community's food expenditures.
- On an average, WTP for CBHI was around 4.5% of food expenditures in the studied locations. Food expenditure information can be obtained through cheap and fast research methods, such as focus group discussions with target communities or from data published routinely and in the public domain.
- Nosratnejad *et al.* (2016) estimated WTP for HI on the basis of readily available data pertaining to GDP per capita, by using vote counting to identify factors which were consistently correlated with higher WTP for insurance: family size, education level, income, past hospitalization, and perceived poor health status. Their meta-analysis revealed that the WTP for HI among rural households in low and middle-income countries (LMICs) was just below 2% of the GDP per capita per household per year.

Focus Points

- WTP levels are sensitive to benefits package design. Therefore, involving the target population in the design phase is expected to increase WTP levels.
- The main issues with estimating WTP include the following:

  1. difficulties associated with predicting WTP when the investigation is performed before the respondents are experienced with, or can actually buy HMI;

2. identifying the variables that explain differences in WTP across households in the same locations, and across different locations and points in time;
3. obtaining reliable WTP estimates with minimal investment of time and money.

Chapter 5.1

The Elusive Quest for Estimates of Willingness to Pay for Health Microinsurance*

Main Messages

- Review of 14 experimental field studies eliciting willingness to pay (WTP) for health insurance among low-income persons in developing countries, based on 20 papers.
- "We had to work backward taking into consideration what the community could pay while creating a long-term, self-sustaining scheme" — Testimony of an HMI practitioner in India.
- Estimating WTP for health insurance (HI) in LICs is a challenge given that people have to reveal what they are willing to pay for insurance coverage that they do not yet have and may not even be on the market.

Focus Points

- All researchers agree that WTP must be explored "locally" because there is no "one-size-fits-all" option to determine the income side of different HMI schemes operating in different settings.

---

*This chapter is reproduced from *Health Insurance* (2012), 39–61, Open Access, available at https://www.researchgate.net/publication/255726049_The_Elusive_Quest_for_Estimates_of_Willingness_to_Pay_for_Health_Microinsurance.

- WTP levels are sensitive to benefits package design; involving the target population in the design phase is expected to increase WTP levels.
- Several factors can affect the WTP decision, including socio-economic, demographic and geographic characteristics, and the respondents' experience with health care services and expenses.
- For the time being, it is impossible to devise a simple standard model to predict WTP everywhere because of the methodological diversity in eliciting and estimating WTP in the studies reviewed in this chapter.

Structured Abstract

Introduction

WTP by definition is the maximum amount people are willing to spend to acquire a service. While designing insurance products for the low-income population, an attempt needs to be made to understand the parameters that affect WTP for HI among the target population. The three questions of utmost relevance in this context are as follows:

1. What are the difficulties associated with predicting WTP when the investigation has to be performed before the respondents can actually buy HI?
2. Which variable explains the difference in WTP across households in the same locations, and across different locations and points in time?
3. How can reliable and comparable WTP estimates be obtained with minimal investment of time and money?

Method

The chapter is based on a systematic review of the literature on WTP from a number of countries in Asia and Africa. To identify literature relevant to "willingness to pay for health insurance in low-income countries", the authors first conducted several searches of articles, including a search of MEDLINE database. The key search terms included "WTP", "willingness to pay", "health insurance" and many similar words. After scanning through the available literature, the authors reviewed 14 experimental field studies eliciting WTP for health insurance among low-income persons in developing countries, based on 20 papers.

Findings

The empirical review of WTP studies emphasized the large variety of methods used to estimate WTP. While the methodological diversity was very evident, there were also socio-economic differences, and differences related to researchers' choice to measure WTP of a household rather than a willingness to pay of individuals.

The findings from the identified studies on the association of WTP for HMI with various parameters are summarized in Table 1.

Table 1: Association between WTP and specific parameters.

Parameter	Relation with respect to WTP
Income	WTP as a share of income decreases dramatically as income increases; nominal WTP levels increase when HH incomes grow.
Socio-demographic variables	
Gender	Males were willing to pay more than females.
Education	Positive explanatory variable of WTP in most cases.
HH size	No intuitive explanation for larger households' willingness to pay more.
Age	No intuitive explanation for younger people's willingness to pay more.
Healthcare availability	Better availability and quality of health services would encourage higher WTP for insurance.
Financial consequences of illness	Recent personal experience with the financial consequences of illness is an important explanatory factor for the variation in WTP.
Package composition	Available information on the impact of package composition on WTP is inconclusive.
Location of residence	Impact of location as an explanatory variable needs to be explored more thoroughly.

Conclusion

From this review of field experiments, it is evident that all researchers agree that WTP must be explored "locally" because there is no "one-size-fits-all" option to determine the income side of different HMI schemes operating in different settings. Given the difficulties associated with obtaining WTP estimates that would be relevant locally, new methods have been explored. So for instance, if the income of the target population is known, it could serve as an anchor for initial estimation of WTP.

Besides income, various other parameters also influence WTP levels. It may be possible to extrapolate WTP levels known in one location to other comparable locations using knowledge of these parameters.

From this review, it was also suggested that WTP levels are sensitive to benefits package design. Therefore, involving the target population in the design phase is expected to increase WTP levels. The authors conclude that it is impossible to devise a simple standard model to predict WTP everywhere, as there is a large diversity of methods used to elicit and estimate WTP in the various studies reviewed in this chapter.

7 The elusive quest for estimates of willingness to pay for health microinsurance

David Dror and Ruth Koren[1]

Focusing on poor people in low-income countries (LICs) entails a price constraint for those planning to supply health insurance. The challenge is to price health insurance at a level that ensures a balance between expenditure and income, at least in the long-term, and remains affordable and attractive to poor people. This balance can be achieved either by limiting expenditure to available premium income where membership is usually voluntary – even though the affiliation unit can include more than one individual, e.g. entire households or entire communities, as is typical for mutual and community-based health insurance – or by defining first the benefit package, and then the premiums needed to cover the cost, which is typical for mandatory and commercial schemes.

This chapter focuses on the issue of voluntary membership in health insurance. We should first explain why persons with low income would wish to buy insurance in the first place, as this can shed light on how much people would be willing to pay. One well known explanation linked to the expected utility (EU) theory is that insurance is a trade-off between an uncertain but potentially huge loss (occurring if the uninsured has to pay for the risk) and a certain but small loss (incurred by paying a premium that eliminates the unaffordable risk). The implied assumption is that all people are risk-averse. However, in low-income settings, this assumption does not hold true in all cases; for one, the premium might be considered a high-risk cost rather than a risk-reducing cost, particularly when people who have paid the premium receive no benefit in return (even when they have incurred some healthcare costs). Furthermore, this theory does not explain how much people would be willing to pay for certainty as to their risk exposure. For example, is it worthwhile paying INR 100 or 150 (US$2.25 or US$3.40) for hospitalization cover up to INR 5000 (US $115)? The theory also fails to address what relationship there might be between willingness to pay (WTP) and income levels (e.g. are richer people prepared to pay a different share of their income from poorer people for the same insurance?), risk exposure levels (e.g. does previous exposure to the insured risk affect the amount people are willing to pay as premium?) or other relevant parameters (e.g. does education influence WTP?). A better understanding of the parameters that are likely to affect WTP can be very helpful to practitioners and policy-makers in designing an insurance product that suits the target population.

One way to estimate WTP is by following the Revealed Preferences (RP) method introduced first by Samuelson (1938). RP is a predictive modelling

1 The authors gratefully acknowledge useful comments and suggestions from four peer reviewers: Aparna Dalal (ILO), Denis Garand (DGA) Michael J. McCord (Microinsurance Centre) and Lisa Morgan (Milliman). The authors alone are responsible for errors, omissions and views expressed.

approach to WTP that is based on studying actual purchasing behaviour, not of the product we are interested in, but of other, related products from which we wish to identify the value people place on – or would be willing to pay for – a product for which no purchasing information exists. The first applications of the RP approach were made in the 1940s to predict the amount that could be charged for entry to National Parks in the US; at that time, there was no pricing information because National Parks were new, and this is the case for microinsurance today. People's travel-costs were used to infer the WTP. In the context of our investigation, we could not find any published study reporting estimation of WTP for micro (health) insurance using the revealed preferences method, which leaves open the key question of what a suitable inference or anchor to estimate WTP for health insurance would be.

The alternative option, called Stated Preferences (SP), is to ask people what they would be willing to pay for insurance cover that they do not yet have and that is perhaps not even on the market. There are several ways to value non-market goods. One of the most frequently used, called Contingent Valuation (CV), consists of using survey methods to present respondents with hypothetical scenarios about an intervention under evaluation (or insurance product in this case). Respondents are required to think about the contingency of an actual market for the benefits, and indicate the maximum amount they would be willing to pay for them.

WTP is presumably mediated by ability to pay and by individual and cultural aspects that determine the perceived benefit. We wanted to examine the evidence for this, and embarked on a systematic review of the literature. When this had been completed (in 2010), we found several studies that were reported from a number of countries in Asia and in Africa on WTP for health insurance among the poor in LICs (the target population for microinsurance). This chapter contains a comparison of the findings of these studies, notably the features that emerged as explanatory variables for WTP, some of which are dependent on time and context, while others seem to describe major determinants of WTP for health insurance among the poor in LICs. The paper ends with a synthesis of the findings that point to the way estimates of WTP could be obtained, whilst at the same time highlighting the limitations inherent to methods used to elicit WTP.

7.1 Methods of eliciting WTP

A crucial methodological question in CV is how WTP information can be elicited. For one, replies could be influenced by the product in question and by characteristics of the target population. However, Smith pointed out that the process of elicitation can affect the results of CV surveys, in areas such as 1) how the information is obtained and presented; is it clear and complete? Can people imagine the situation? 2) How would people pay for the health event (e.g. out-of-pocket, by taxation or private health insurance?) 3) Over what time period is the product valued? This provides the respondent's budget and cash-flow constraints. 4) How is the survey administered? (e.g. individual or group responses?).

There is considerable debate on the precise format in which the questions should be asked, because each possible format appears prone to some bias.

7.1.1 Open-ended format

CV applications started with the use of open-ended formats, in which respondents were asked to state the amount that best matched their valuation of the hypothetical insurance package presented. Respondents find it difficult to answer these questions, leading to low response rates and a high degree of variation. Because of the disappointing results, alternative closed-end elicitation formats were developed.

7.1.2 Closed-end formats

The 'bidding game' (BG) is an example of a closed-end elicitation format, in which the respondent is asked whether he or she is willing to pay a specific amount. Depending on the answer, the bid is lowered or raised and the individual is asked about this new bid ("bi-directional BG"). This process continues until the maximum WTP amount is found. Alternatively, an "unidirectional" BG could be either ascending, in which case the initial bid is very low and is increased until respondents reject the offer; or descending, in which the initial bid is very high and is lowered until respondents accept the bid. The descending BG is assumed to yield a higher WTP. A problem with the BG is that the maximum in the auction process can be influenced by the amount of the first bid is; a higher first bid was reported to result in a higher WTP. This is called 'starting-point bias'.

Another method, called the 'Dichotomous Choice technique' (DC) involves asking subjects to answer the question as to whether they would pay a specified amount for a given commodity with "yes" or "no". The demand curve is estimated by varying the bid amount across respondents and the area under this demand curve represents mean WTP.

A variation of the DC technique is "dichotomous choice with follow-up question" (proposed originally by Hanemann). In the first step, respondents state whether they are willing to pay a specified amount; in the second step, those who said "yes" get a higher bid and those who said "no" a lower bid. According to Asfaw and Braun, the problems with the starting point bias can be partially toned down by the presence of the second bid.

Another variant of the DC is the "take it or leave it" approach (TIOLI), in which each respondent is asked one question during surveys of large numbers of persons. The data are then analysed using econometric techniques to identify the shape of the distribution. The difficulties with this approach are in identifying the relevant range of sample bids needed for precise estimation.

Another similar method is called the "payment card" (PC). Each subject is invited to select his or her maximum WTP from the same specified list of possible values, which provides the respondent with a clear context for making the valuation. The PC method achieved a higher completion rate and generated higher valuations than the open-ended format. It is not exposed to starting-point bias (like the bidding game) or to "yes-saying" (as with dichotomous choice) but the potential bias when using the PC method is "mid-point bias": respondents tend to state their maximum WTP in the middle of the card. According to Bayoumi, using the PC method with a follow-up bidding process can define the value more precisely.

Table 7.1 **Advantages and disadvantages of different elicitation methods**

Elicitation format	*Pros*	*Cons*
Open-ended formats (OE)	simple and easy method	– difficult to answer – low response rate – results are sensitive to outliers – compliance bias
Closed-end formats		
Bidding game (BG)	– easy and simple to answer – easy for people who are used to bidding for their daily utility goods	– starting-point bias
Dichotomous choice (DC)	– simple and easy method; the respondent only has to make one or two choices	– results in higher WTP estimates compared to OE and PC – starting point bias – yes-saying bias
TIOLI	– simple method; the respondent only has to make one choice	– yes-saying bias
Payment card (PC)	– comprehensible context for making the valuation – can be self-administered – amenable to data collection (unsupervised or postal questionnaire)	– range bias – anchor-point bias – mid-point bias – hypothetical bias – warm glow effect/social desirability bias

7.2 Search of relevant WTP experiments

To achieve a successful launch of micro health insurance, it is important to understand WTP relative to the stakeholders' context. The three issues that are of particular concern are: 1) what are the difficulties associated with predicting WTP when the investigation has to be performed before the respondents can actually buy micro health insurance? 2) Which variables explain the differences in WTP across households in the same location, and across different locations and points in time? And 3) how can reliable and comparable WTP estimates be obtained with minimal investment of time and money?

With the purpose of reviewing what has been done in this regard, we conducted several searches of literature in 2010, including a search of MEDLINE database; search terms included: "WTP" or "willingness to pay" AND "health insurance": 179 hits came up; a refined search was based on crossing the keyword "willingness to pay" with "health insurance" or "prepayment-health" and one of the following key-words: "developing countries"; "Asia"; "Africa"; "Latin America"; "low income"; "poor"; "microinsurance"; or "CBHI (community-based health insurance)". 18 articles that were relevant for the topic "WTP for health insurance in low-income countries" were retained. We also scanned the references of the above-mentioned articles to identify additional papers that did not come up in the online searches; two articles were identified (one on a study conducted in Pakistan and the other in Cameroon) bringing the total to 20 articles. Finally, we searched the "recent publications" "and "publications" sections of the Microinsurance Network website; this search yielded no hits.

A detailed screening of the articles revealed that three experiments were reported by more than one article, and thus this chapter is based on 14 experimental field studies eliciting WTP for health insurance among low-income persons in developing countries, but on 20 papers. The countries included Burkina Faso (five articles), Cameroon, China (two articles), Ethiopia (two articles), Ghana, India (two articles), Iran, Namibia, Nigeria (two articles), Pakistan, Tanzania and Vietnam.

7.2.1 Elicitation of WTP

We present a summary of elicitation methods used in the field studies. All researchers used the CV approach, but with notable differences in the method to elicit the WTP and the definitions of various parameters.

Table 7.2: **Overview of the data, locations and method of elicitation of WTP used**[2]

Authors	*Date*	*Sample*	*Country*	*Objective*[3]	*Unit of inquiry*	*Method*[4]
Walraven G	1996	821 indiv + 1500 HH	Tanzania	WTP for local health insurance scheme	I+HH	OQ
Asenso-Okyere et al.	1997	164 urban + 142 rural	Ghana	WTP for health insurance	HH	BG
Mathiyazhagan	1998	1000	India	WTP for a rural CBHI	HH	OQ
Masud TI, Farooq N, Ghaffar A.	2003	600	Pakistan	WTP for health insurance primary care	HH	OQ
Dong et al	2003	2414 indiv +705 HHH	Burkina Faso	WTP for CBHI	I+HH	TIOLI + BG
Binam J, Nkama A, Nkenda R	2004	471 rural	Cameroon	WTP for CBHI	HH	BG
Asgary, et al.	2004	2139	Iran	WTP for a rural health insurance	HH	BG
Asfaw A, Braun J	2005	550	Ethiopia	Assess prospects for rural CBHI	HH	DC+F
Bärnighausen et al.	2007	621	China	WTP for basic health insurance	I	PC
Ying XH et al.	2007	2671	China	WTP for private health insurance (urban informal sector)	I	BG+OQ
Dror et al.	2007	3024	India	WTP for CBHI	HH	BG
Lofgren et al.	2008	2070	Vietnam	WTP for health insurance	HH	TIOLI+ OQ
Gustafsson-Wright et al.	2009	1700	Namibia	WTP for low-cost health insurance	HH	DC+F
Onwujekwe et al.	2010	3070	Nigeria	WTP for CBHI	I+HH	BG + OQ

A few researchers used open-ended direct questions such as *"how much would you pay for health insurance?"* (with a detailed explanation of the health insurance product in question). Walraven elicited WTP by asking *"How much are you willing to pay per year for each member of your household (to be covered by services in the hospital)"*? Masud et al. also use a direct question, which was: *"Would you be willing to pay [prepay] for healthcare at the government health facility? … And what is the maximum amount you would be willing to pay?"* Mathiyazhagan and Lofgren et al. first introduced an anchor price by asking respondents whether they would agree to pay a certain amount. The query was of the TIOLI type, and regardless of the reply, all respondents were then asked what would be their maximum WTP; that last amount was retained as the respondents' WTP. Onwujekwe et al. used the DC-with-follow-up method, followed by a direct question: *"What really*

2 About 90 per cent of the target population of 1 million chose to remain uninsured during the first year of operation of CBHI.

3 I = individual, HH = Household

4 OQ = Open question, BG = Bidding game, DC +F = Dichotomous choice with follow-up question, PC = Payment card

is the maximum amount you are willing to pay for CBHI?". This last number was retained as the WTP.

Binam et al. followed a bi-directional bidding game to elicit WTP and they used four initial bids as anchors. Ying et al. used a composite method which consisted of a bi-directional bidding game followed by an open question, which was, however, presented only to respondents that either refused the lowest bid or accepted the highest bid. The open question was *"what is the highest amount that you [the respondent] would be willing to pay?"* It is recalled that respondents knew the last bid, which was their anchor. Ying et al. explained that they used the open question (in addition to the bi-directional bidding game) in order to avoid truncation of the data. Ying et al. used a uniform initial bid for all respondents. Other researchers who conducted a bi-directional bidding game chose different initial bids for different groups of respondents. Dong et al. used 13 different initial bids, randomly assigned to respondents. This multiplicity of initial bids could introduce the starting-point bias, because respondents may think that the initial bid represents the value, or very close to the value, of the good or service in question. Dror et al. used a unidirectional and descending bidding game, the purpose of which was to obtain a more accurate maximum WTP, which is the most relevant for policy decisions. They used an initial bid which they assumed was too high, with a view to examining the quantitative expression of "*maximum WTP for health insurance*"; in fact, 18.4 per cent of their respondents accepted the initial bid, which could suggest that if the intention was simply that it should serve as anchor, it might not have been high enough. Asenso-Okyere et al. also followed a unidirectional and descending bidding game. As 40.1 per cent of their respondents accepted the initial bid, one might think that it was not the best anchor to elicit maximal WTP. It is noted that Dong et al. and Binam et al. could not find significant evidence for a starting point bias in their datasets. However, they used bi-directional bidding games with multiple initial bids. It is assumed that a unidirectional BG with the same anchor for all respondents could neutralize the starting-point bias and improve comparability of results across sampled households.

In the articles reviewed, there was also an experiment that applied an ascending unidirectional bidding game. Asgary et al. applied it in rural Iran to estimate demand and WTP for health insurance. These researchers used three initial bids as anchors, each presented to one third of their sample. A negative response to the initial bid was recorded as zero WTP; otherwise, the highest accepted bid was recorded. Bärnighausen et al. used a modified ascending trajectory in their study among informal sector workers in Wuhan China. They elicited responses by using a *"payment card"* eliciting method.

Asfaw & Braun and Gustafsson-Wright et al. used the DC with follow-up (which they call *"double-bounded contingent valuation – DBCV"*), whereby respondents are given two bids, an initial bid and a second bid. Respondents that rejected the initial bid were presented with a lower second bid, and those that accepted the initial bid got a higher second bid. After these two bids, the game is over; respondents are then classified into four groups: those that said 'yes' + 'yes', 'yes' + 'no', 'no' + 'yes', and 'no' + 'no'. Mean WTP values must then be estimated by maximizing a log likelihood function.[5]

The most striking insight gained from this review of empirical WTP studies is the large variety in the methods used. This diversity makes it difficult to compare quantitative estimates of WTP across the studies as they use different metrics. It is possible to present qualitative explanations for variations in WTP within each group of respondents, but there are no clear "translation rules" for comparing unidirectional and bi-directional bidding games, ascending and descending trajectories, or those using an open question, those who offer a single bid (TIOLI) and those who estimate WTP after multiple bids. In addition to the methodological diversity, there are socio-economic differences (inherent to different locations, which is covered in the next few sections), and differences related to researchers' choice to measure WTP of a household rather than WTP of individuals, whilst in other studies the decision was taken to include both units. The diversity of elicitation methods used highlights the difficulty in comparing quantitative results across several studies.

7.3 Income/socio-economic status/demography and WTP

Most studies presume an intuitive expectation that WTP for health insurance will be positively associated with income, because households would be able to afford a higher prepayment as their income increases. We seek to verify this important assumption, by juxtaposing WTP and income (or its proxies) in the studies described above (summarized in Table 7.3).

Table 7.3 **Association between income and WTP**

Authors	*Income proxy used*	*WTP (per cent of income proxy)*	*Trend*[6]
Walraven G	Weekly expenditure per adult equivalent	3.20 per cent	NS
Asenso-Okyere et al.	Self-reported income (HH survey)	1.9 per cent rural and 2.5 per cent urban	Up
Mathiyazhagan	3 categories: low, middle and high (unspecified criteria)	N/A	Up
Masud TI, Farooq N, Ghaffar A.	Socio-economic score & income	3.0 per cent (only those where WTP>0)	Up
Dong et al.	Consumption/expenditure	2.15 per cent (calculated)	Up

5 Under this method, WTP values (or the distribution of these values) are not observed directly from respondents' replies.

6 Up = WTP increases with income, NS = Not significant

Binam J, Nkama A, Nkenda R	Income of respondent	2.54 per cent (assumed avg. income)	Up
Ali Asgary, et al	"Wealth and income variable" based on assets	1.4 per cent (assumed avg. income)	NS
Asfaw A, Braun J	Annual farm and non-farm income	1.4 per cent (calculated)	Up
Bärnighausen et al	Self-reported income (HH survey)	4.6 per cent, 7.8 per cent, 6.8 per cent, 6.9 per cent (4 packages)	Up
Ying XH	Self-reported income (HH survey)	1.4 per cent, 2.0 per cent, 2.2 per cent (3 packages)	Up
Dror et al	Self-reported income (HH survey)	1.35 per cent income, 1.8 per cent expenditure (median)	Up
Lofgren et al	2 categories: poor/rich households (determined by local leaders).	N/A	Up
Gustafsson-Wright et al	Consumption/expenditure	2.25 per cent	Up
Obinna Onwujekwe et al	SES index, based on assets	N/A	Up

It must be emphasized at the outset that estimation of income in our context is rendered very complex and unreliable by the cumulative effect of 1) there being only partial records (or none at all) of income for households working in the informal economy, which represent the majority of the poor in low-income countries, 2) an endemic and persistent irregularity in income-flows due to seasonal fluctuations and the erratic employment patterns of day-labourers and self-employed people in agriculture or family businesses, and 3) widespread inaccuracy in self-reported income, due to confusion regarding the monetary value of non-monetary income.

As could be expected, different researchers used different methods to obtain income proxy. A commonly used method is self-reported income, obtained through a survey. Since there could be many sources of income at household level, it is unlikely to obtain a reliable estimate in answer to a direct question such as "what is the income of the household?". Therefore, most surveyors use a series of questions, but there is no uniform standard for them.

Asenso-Okyere et al., Asfaw and Braun, Bärnighausen et al., Ying et al., Masud et al., and Dror et al. reported that they had obtained household or personal income information through surveys.

Expenditure/consumption information is often used because it is considered more reliable than income information in developing countries. WHO uses this data, and many low- and middle-income governments, in official surveys, collect information on consumption/expenditure rather than on income (e.g. the Indian National Sample Survey Organization). Masud et al., in addition to income, created a "socio-economic score" based on assets. Asgary, et al. and Onwujekwe et al. constructed slightly different "wealth and income variables" based on assets. Dror et al. also posed questions on the expenditure of respondent households in addition to income, and found a highly significant correlation between both variables. Other researchers of WTP for CBHI used only consumption/expenditure data, e.g. Dong et al. (in yet another paper based on the same dataset), Walraven G, and Gustafsson-Wright et al., and Mathiyazhagan and Lofgren et al. started by dividing the sample into categories; the first scholar divided it into low, middle and high income (but did not specify the classification method), and the second scholar divided it into "poor" and "rich" as determined by local leaders.

Despite the huge differences in methods of measuring a proxy for income, 12 of the 14 studies reported a significant and positive association between nominal WTP for micro health insurance and the economic situation of households (Table 7.3). The remaining three studies reported no significant trend, or did not investigate this issue. This finding validates the initial assumption that a higher income leads to a higher WTP.

In the light of this finding, one might query whether people would be willing to pay a relatively constant share of their income for health insurance? This information is also shown in Table 7.3 either as reported by the authors themselves, or calculated by us, using the original published data. The results are quite similar, not only when comparing WTP relative to income, but also relative to consumption/expenditure. Furthermore, with the exception of one outlier estimate (4.6 per cent to 6.9 per cent for four different packages, reported by Bärnighausen et al.), all WTP values were in the range of 1.35 per cent to 3.2 per cent, with a mean value of 2.2 per cent of the relevant income proxy. This rather narrow range for the estimates strengthens the credibility of the results, even though they have been obtained using very different modes of calculation and with very different populations.

However, could the expression of mean WTP as a share of income obscure a different reality in which different income sub-groups actually differ in the portion of their income that they are willing to pay for health insurance? Some of the articles reviewed offer clues to the answer. Bärnighausen et al. reported that for an increase of one per cent in income, WTP increased by about half a percent. Dong et al. measured this aspect by calculating the measure of inequity (Gini coefficient)[7] in income and in WTP. Dong et al. show that the inequity in income is much higher than in WTP (Gini value of 0.68 in individual expenditure and 0.63 in household expenditure compared to a Gini value of 0.15 for individuals' and 0.08 for households' WTP). These findings indicate that WTP increases at a lower rate than income, i.e. richer households would be willing to pay a smaller share of their income than poorer households.

This assumption was tested further with the data from three studies reviewed. Gustafson-Wright et al. showed that WTP expressed as percentage of consumption/expenditure was 11.4 per cent among the poorest quintile, but only 1.2 per cent among the richest quintile. Dror et al. reported that the median value of

7 The Gini coefficient (developed by Corrado Gini 1912) is a measure of the inequality of a distribution; a value of 0 expresses total equality and a value of 1 maximal inequality.

WTP as a percentage of income decreased from 1.79 per cent among the poorest quintile to 0.84 per cent among the richest quintile, and this negative correlation was significant. Dong et al. provided the value of WTP for five income quintiles and the average income proxy (consumption) for these quintiles, which enables us to calculate WTP relative to income/expenditure; his results show that WTP was 18.9 per cent among the poorest quintile, and only 0.9 per cent among the richest quintile. We therefore conclude that, while nominal WTP levels increase when household incomes grow, they decrease dramatically as income increases when WTP is measured as a share of income.

Most studies also examined the association between WTP and other socio-demographic variables. Table 7.4 contains the summary results.

Table 7.4 **Association of WTP with socio-economic parameters**

Authors	*ind/HH*	*Gender*	*Education*	*HH[8] size*	*Age*	*Insurance experience*
Walraven G	HH+IND	ND	ND	ND	ND	ND
Asenso-Okyere et al.	HH	m>f	+	ND	NS	NS
Mathiyazhagan	HH	ND	+	+	NS	ND
Masud TI, Farooq N, Ghaffar A.	HH	ND	ND	ND	ND	ND
Dong et al.	HH	NS	+	NS	NS	ND
	IND	m>f	+	ND	–	ND
Binam J, Nkama A, Nkenda R	HH	m>f	NS	ND	NS	ND
Ali Asgary, et al.	HH	ND	+	NS	+	NS
Asfaw A, Braun J	HH	NS	+	ND	ND	ND
Bärnighausen et al.	IND	f>m	+	ND	–	ND
Ying XH et al.	IND	m>f	+	ND	–	ND
Dror et al.	HH	m>f	+ (>11y)	+,– (PP[9])	–	+
Lofgren et al.	HH	NS	+	ND	–	NS
Gustafsson-Wright et al.	HH	m>f	+	NS	–	ND
Obinna Onwujekwe et al.	HH	m>f	+	- (PP)	NS	ND
	IND	m>f	+	NS	+	+

As is often assumed, education is a positive explanatory variable of WTP in most cases.

The results (shown in Table 7.4) also suggest that in most cases, males were willing to pay more than females.[10]

As for age, five studies showed no significant effect of age on WTP, and six reported a negative correlation. There is no intuitive explanation for younger people's willingness to pay more, and it cannot be explained by income or education, as the effect of age is independent of these parameters in the analysis.

8 HH = Household; ND = not determined, NS = not significant
9 PP = Persons in household
10 The article by Dong et al. mentioned in Table 7.4 is referenced here.

7.4 Healthcare availability and WTP

It is self-explanatory that paying the premium is relevant only when the insured can access healthcare in case of need. Therefore, the association between WTP and supply-side parameters (including availability, distance, and satisfaction with care) should be examined. Interestingly, only a minority of WTP/CBHI researchers reported the results of associations between WTP for micro health insurance and supply of healthcare. Table 7.4 contains a summary of the findings.

Table 7.5 **Association of WTP with socio-economic parameters**

Authors	*Parameter used*	*Effect*
Walraven G		N/A
Asenso-Okyere et al	Distance travelled to attend clinic	NS
Masud TI, Farooq N, Ghaffar A.		N/A
Dong et al (2003 H Econ)	Distance to health facility (individual WTP)	
	Individual WTP	–
	HH WTP	NS
Binam J, Nkama A, Nkenda R	Categorical variable (yes/no) rapidity in the reception at healthcare centre	NS
	Categorical variable (yes/no) representing the cleanliness of the healthcare centre	NS
	Categorical variable representing the attendance of physician at healthcare centre	+
	Categorical variable representing the availability of basic drugs at healthcare centre	–
	Categorical variable representing confidence in healthcare services	+
Asgary, et al	Drugs available at health service centre	+
	Existence of full time physician in the village	+
	Existence of pharmacy in the village	NS
	Satisfaction with healthcare facilities in the nearest city	+
Asfaw A, Braun J		N/A
Bärnighausen et al		N/A
Ying XH et al		N/A
Dror et al	Distance to preferred primary health facility	NS
	Distance to preferred hospital	–
Lofgren et al		N/A
Gustafsson-Wright et al		N/A
Obinna Onwujekwe et al		N/A

The distance from home to the healthcare point of service is an often-examined parameter considered to represent the accessibility of healthcare. One might expect that the shorter the distance, the higher the WTP would be. This assumption has been confirmed in two studies. Dong et al. obtained significant negative association for individual WTP but no significant association for household WTP levels, and Dror et al. reported a significantly negative correlation for the distance to the preferred hospital, but not to the preferred primary health facility.

Asenso Okiyere et al. did not discover a significant correlation between distance from clinic and WTP for health microinsurance. The other studies did not examine the association between WTP and this proxy.

Association between perceived quality of healthcare and WTP for micro health insurance was examined through several proxies. The correlation with the rapidity with which clients were treated, examined by Binam, was not significant. Binam et al. and Asgary et al. reported significant and positive association between WTP and the presence of physicians at the healthcare centre. The availability of drugs in the health centre was also found to be positively correlated with WTP in one case (Asgary et al.), but negatively correlated in another case (Binam et al.). This apparent contradiction could reflect differences in the terms of the policy regarding reimbursement of medicine costs, but the full information was not reported in those papers. Asgary et al. also investigated satisfaction with healthcare facilities in the nearest city and found the positive association with WTP that one would expect, and Binam et al. also demonstrated a positive association between WTP and a categorical variable representing confidence in healthcare services.

In summary, the results uphold the assumption that better availability and quality of health services would encourage higher WTP for health insurance. However, this assumption should be examined more frequently and in greater detail in the future to provide an up-to-date indication of the specific features of the supply of healthcare that influence WTP most positively.

7.5 Exposure to ill health, financial consequences of illness and WTP

As we have seen, WTP for micro health insurance reflects an understanding that the intrinsic value of health insurance is that it should protect the household from financial shocks by paying costs related to illness and improve access to adequate healthcare. It therefore follows that households with recent experience of costly healthcare would be more willing to spend money to insure against the consequences of such events. As seen in Table 7.5, quite a few of the studies attempted to address this point by searching for an association between WTP values and recent experience with costly illness. It is interesting to note the large variability of the proxies used in the different studies to assess this association, including annual healthcare expenditure, episodes of hospitalization, frequency of illness, experience with chronic illness, payment for healthcare, borrowing money to pay for healthcare and loss of income due to illness. Nine of the reviewed studies found a positive association between WTP and at least one of the proxies for exposure to costly ill health. It seems that recent personal experience with the financial consequences of ill health is an important explanatory factor for the variation in WTP.

Table 7.6 **Effect of health expenditure on WTP**

Authors	*What was measured*	*Association with WTP*
Walraven G		ND
Asenso-Okyere et al	Expenditure on healthcare last month	+
Mathiyazhagan	Illness of respondent	+
	Number of hospital episodes	+
	Working days lost due to illness	+
	Number of consultations with doctor	NS
Masud TI, Farooq N, Ghaffar A.		ND
Dong et al*	HH expenditure on Western Medicine last month	+
Binam J, Nkama A, Nkenda R	Percentage of individuals in the HH ill 6-12 months prior to survey	+
Ali Asgary, et al		ND
Asfaw A, Braun J		
1st bid	HH head reported illness	+
2nd bid		NS
1st bid	Number of HH members reported illness	+
2nd bid		NS
1st bid	borrowed money for healthcare	+
2nd bid		NS
Bärnighausen et al	Average monthly health expenditure in the past year	+
Ying XH et al	Respondent suffered from chronic disease	
	MCDI	NS
	IEI	NS
	OEI	+
Dror et al	Hospitalization in HH in last 2 years	+
Lofgren et al	One or more persons in HH has a chronic disease	+
Gustafsson-Wright et al	Number of HHs members sick	
	WTP the first bid	-
	WTP the second bid	NS
Obinna Onwujekwe et al	Paid OOP for healthcare	-
	Paid with own money	+
	Borrowed money to pay for care	NS

7.6 Package composition and WTP

In our context, the price of different insurance packages might vary due to levels of co-pay, caps and exclusions, but also due to the benefit types included. While one could argue that co-pay and caps reflect economic considerations, the inclusion/exclusion of benefit types could well reflect normative choices. For example, should maternity be included in the package or not? Therefore, it is necessary to examine whether WTP for micro health insurance is influenced by the design of the insurance product, and if so to what extent. Unfortunately, only very few studies examined this issue in detail. Bäringhausen et al. asked respondents about their maximum WTP for a basic health insurance (BHI) and, separately, for three variations: 1) without the ceiling of the basic option (which was four times the average annual formal sector worker's salary); 2) without deductible (which, under the BHI was nine per cent of the average annual salary), and 3) without coinsurance (that ranged from 10 per cent for in-patient care to 20 per cent for special services and 30 per cent for outpatient care). In this experiment, the options examined represented different levels of financial protection within the same set of benefits covered. In comparison to the BHI, respondents were willing to pay 70 per cent more for BHI without a ceiling, 43 per cent more for the BHI without a deductible and 56 per cent more for the BHI without coinsurance. This increase in WTP was not only nominal but also relative to the respondents' income (respectively 4.6 per cent for the BHI, 7.8 per cent for BHI without ceiling, 6.8 per cent for BHI without deductible and 6.9 per cent for BHI without coinsurance).

Ying et al. tested WTP for three different health insurance programmes: 1) MCDI would reimburse 80 per cent of health expenditure when the insured suffered from a catastrophic disease; 2) IEI would cover 100 per cent of the enrolees' health expenditures on in-patient health services; and 3) OEI would cover 60 per cent of health expenditure on outpatient health services. 43 per cent of respondents chose MCDI (WTP: 110.1 Chinese Yuan (US $17) = 2.2 per cent of annual income); 49 per cent chose IEI (WTP 100.2 RMB (US$15.50) = 2.0 per cent of annual income); and 25 per cent chose OEI (WTP 72.4 Chinese Yuan (US$11) =1.4 per cent of annual income). The price elasticity of the demand for MCDI was -0.27 (this indicates that demand for MCDI would decrease by 2.7 per cent if the premium increased by 10 per cent). The elasticity of demand for IEI and OEI was -0.34 and -0.42, respectively. In this experiment, the demand for MCDI was least elastic, and WTP highest, both nominally and relative to income. These results suggest that WTP for health insurance can reflect not only financial protection but also preferences for different kinds of services.

By contrast, Lofgren et al. elicited the WTP of their respondents in respect of different insurance products: 1) a health insurance that is based on compulsory affiliation with income-rated premium[11] and 2) health insurance that is based on

11 All households in the district are obliged to pay an annual premium to a local healthcare fund when crops are sold. There are no exemption cards. The fee is based on the households' income. The higher the income, the higher the fee. All members in the household are entitled to free healthcare at the Communal Health Station or District Health Centre and free medicine if it is prescribed by a doctor. If care at higher levels is needed, the insured patient will be supported by an amount based on the cost per bed-day at the District Health Centre level. The fund will be managed by the Commune People Committee (or elected representative)

voluntary affiliation with risk rated premium[12] Although when subjects were asked about their willingness to affiliate with either of these insurance products there was a slight preference for the compulsory affiliation, the mean WTP for both products was practically the same despite the fact that each household was presented with both options.

Dror et al. also examined the sensitivity of WTP to being packaged in a different way: each third of the sample was offered a different benefit package.[13] In that experiment, there was no difference in WTP for the three packages. This could be due to the different elicitation method, in which respondents were offered only one option and were not given a choice between options that they could compare or prefer. This suggests that WTP can, at least sometimes, be used as a tool for package design only when the same respondent can choose between options. This would work when the number of options is relatively small, but would be impracticable with the very many options that health insurance packages usually contain. Other methods were developed for benefit package design that enable respondents to choose from 10 or more options, but this is done within a finite budget, i.e. without soliciting the respondents' WTP. The methods that were applied in the context of CBHI in low income countries include simulation exercises (Dror et al.), Focus Group Discussions and structured interviews (De Allegri). We conclude that the available information on the impact of package composition on WTP is inconclusive.

12 Each household can choose to voluntarily pay an annual premium to a local healthcare fund when crops are sold. The fee is based on the number of people in the household and the fee is higher for children under five and elderly over 65 because they are expected to use more healthcare. All persons in the household paying the fee are entitled to free healthcare at the Communal Health Station or District Health Centre and free medicine if prescribed by the doctor. If care at higher levels is needed, the insured patient will be supported by an amount based on the cost per bed-day at the District Health Centre level. The fund will be managed by the Commune People Committee (or voted representative).

13 Version 1 included hospitalisation expenses up to INR 5000 (US$115) per year and person and reimbursement of costs for prescribed drugs up to INR 1000 (US$22.50) per year and person; version 2 included hospitalisation expenses up to INR 5000 (US$115) per year and person AND reimbursement of costs for general practitioners up to INR 1000 (US$22.50) per year and person; version 3 included reimbursement of costs for prescribed drugs up to INR 1000 (US$22.50) per year and person AND reimbursement of costs for general practitioners up to INR 1000 (US$22.50) per year and person.

7.7 Location of residence and WTP

The discussion presented above, based on the data reported in the cited studies, leads to the assertion that WTP for micro health insurance is highly influenced by various variables, notably the economic and socio-demographic status of respondents, their financial exposure to healthcare costs and availability of healthcare facilities. All these features vary markedly by location, within and between countries. A simple comparison of results of different studies, reviewed here, is impossible due to the dissimilarity in methods used to elicit WTP and to interpret the data. Specifically, the question arises as to whether the significant explanatory variables identified at the level of single households can account for the difference across locations. We submit that the way to address this question with confidence would be to include a "location variable" in multiple regressions performed to identify the explanatory variables at the level of single households when the dataset includes more than one location. Following this process could ensure that household features and WTP levels would be elicited using the same methodology. Only two of the studies reviewed have actually followed this procedure, Dror et al. (comparing seven locations in India) and Onwujekwe et al. (comparing six locations in Nigeria). Both studies reported that the location still remained a highly significant explanatory variable for the variation in WTP, even in a multivariate model including all the features of the individual households (economic and socio-demographic status and recent experience with healthcare cost). This finding suggests that the studies published so far on WTP for micro health insurance have not yet identified all of the reasons that explain differences in WTP for health insurance across communities; we cannot exclude that some features, e.g. those reflecting cultural or life-style choices, could explain some underlying reasons that have not been recognized hitherto. The impact of location as an explanatory variable will need to be explored more thoroughly in future research on WTP for HI.

7.8 Lessons learned and implications for practitioners

"We had to work backwards taking into consideration what the community could pay, while creating a long-term, self-sustaining scheme." This testimony of one of the practitioners of micro health insurance in India presents the essential role of WTP estimates, namely that members' WTP determines the income side, and by extension also what the insurer can offer by way of cover.

This review of field experiments has illustrated that all researchers agree that WTP must be explored locally, because there is no "one-size-fits-all" option to determine the income side of different micro health insurance units operating in different settings. The review has also shed light on the difficulties associated with obtaining WTP estimates that would be relevant locally. Such estimates require data that is usually obtained through household surveys and other costly and time-consuming investigations. These constraints make it impracticable to obtain local data in each place where a micro health insurance is launched.

However, if the income of the target population is known, it could serve as an anchor for initial estimation of WTP, based on the analysis of the studies reviewed here and shown in Table 7.2. It has been shown that WTP estimates (when expressed as a percentage of income) converge mostly to a relatively narrow range around two per cent of income.

It has also been shown in Tables 7.3, 7.4 and 7.5 that various other parameters influence WTP levels. Therefore, we might be able to extrapolate WTP levels known in one location to other comparable locations using knowledge of these parameters. For instance, if in one location we know the level of education of household heads as well as the WTP values, and in another location we only know that household heads have a higher level of education, we would expect WTP levels in that second location to be higher. Similarly, ample supply of quality healthcare, or higher cost of care, or higher morbidity would all be expected to lead to higher WTP.

We have also seen that WTP levels are sensitive to benefit package design. Therefore we would expect that involving the target population in the design phase would increase WTP levels.

However, for the time being, it is impossible to devise a simple standard model to predict WTP everywhere, because of the large diversity of methods used to elicit and estimate WTP in the different studies reviewed in this chapter. Such a model could hopefully be devised in line with the methods used to determine WTP and standardized for the purpose of analysing explanatory variables.

Chapter 5.2

Estimating Willingness-to-Pay for Health Insurance Among Rural Poor in India by Reference to Engel's Law*

Main Messages

- Even the rural poor, with very little money, education or experience with (health) insurance consider health insurance as a necessity good (akin to food).
- On an average, willingness to pay (WTP) for community-based health insurance (CBHI) was around 4.5% of food expenditures in the studied locations.
- The average expenditure on food can serve as a better data series for the estimation of WTP for health insurance (HI) than either overall income or discretionary income.

*This chapter is reproduced from *Social Science and Medicine* (2012), 76, 67–73, Open Access, available at https://www.researchgate.net/publication/233535279_Estimating_Willingness-to-Pay_for_health_insurance_among_rural_poor_in_India_by_reference_to_Engel's_law.

Focus Points

- The nature of relationship between WTP for HI and income is comparable to Engel's Law which expresses the same kind of relationship between food expenditures and income.
- WTP for HI could be estimated as a percentage of average food expenditure in the target communities.
- WTP for HI could be estimated without having to conduct household surveys, as only information on average food expenditures in the community is required.
- Average food expenditure data can be obtained through cheap and fast research methods, such as focus group discussions with target communities or, if sufficiently accurately available, existing data.

Structured Abstract

Introduction

Estimating WTP for HI among the rural poor involves significant cost and time if it requires a household survey to be conducted. The quest to identify a parameter that would generate the most consistent estimate of WTP without resorting to a household survey prompted the authors to identify a coherent anchor for local estimation of WTP.

Method

Data for the study were sourced from household surveys that were conducted in rural areas of six Indian locations (total 7874 households) in 2008–2010. Respondents were asked how much they were willing to pay for HI per person per month, under the condition that all members of the household would enroll by paying a premium. It was observed that in all locations, WTP increased with nominal income, and when expressed as a percentage of income it decreased with household income. As this was akin to Engel's law on food expenditures,[1] the study investigated possible anchors. WTP was calculated as a percentage of three anchors: income-proxy, food

[1]Engel's Law: As income increases, the proportion of income spent on food decreases, even if actual expenditure on food rises (Engel, 1957).

expenditure, and discretionary income. The authors thereafter compared these estimates of WTP by calculating the coefficient of variation (for inter-community variation) and concentration indices (for intra-community variation).

Box 1: Data and Methods

Survey locations

2008 Warangal, Karimnagar (Andhra Pradesh)
2009 Kalahandi, Khorda and Malkangiri (Odisha)
2010 Gaya (Bihar)

Sampling

Two-stage sampling procedure

- Selection of villages
- Households were sampled randomly in each selected village

Two-cohorts

- Member households (Households were defined as "Members" if at least one person participated in a Self-Help-Group linked to partner-NGOs)
- Non-member households (unaffiliated households)

Descending Bidding Game method (to obtain maximum WTP values)

Step 1: The interviewer explained what health insurance is, how it works and the coverage of the package: "To buy a health insurance you have to pay a premium per month for your whole household. This health insurance will then pay you back some of the money you spend on health care costs for your household members. Suppose we offer you a health insurance that will cover part of the cost of hospital, medicines, tests, consultations, and maternity? How much would you agree to pay for that? If you are willing to pay more, you will get more benefits and if you are willing to pay less, you will get fewer benefits. But the condition is that all household members must join."

Step 2: The interviewer started with the relatively high opening bid of INR 30 per person per month (around PPP$ 1.8), again emphasizing that all household members have to join and their premium must be paid every month. Every time the bid was not accepted, it was lowered by INR 1 until it was accepted or reached INR 0. The accepted bid was recorded as the WTP level.

Findings

The coefficient of variation values were 0.36, 0.43, and 0.50 for WTP as a percent of food expenditures, overall income, and discretionary income, respectively. This implied that WTP expressed as a percentage of food expenditures varied the least across locations.

The consistency of indicators within locations was observed by calculating the concentration indices of the WTP indicators. In all six locations, the concentration index for WTP as a percentage of food expenditures was the lowest. Thus, food expenditures had the most consistent relationship with WTP within each location and across the six locations.

WTP for HI could, therefore, be estimated as a percentage of average food expenditure in the target communities. Estimates based on data collected in the six rural locations in India placed WTP at 4.5% of average food expenditures.

The findings revealed that the amount a household spends on food is a much better predictor of WTP for HI than the amount available to the household for spending after paying for food.

Conclusion

The study concludes that the level of WTP for HI could be estimated based on each community's food expenditures, and these expenses are much better known to all and can be obtained easily through focus group discussions or from data published routinely and in the public domain. Estimating WTP through this method thus saves on time and cost involved in otherwise conducting household surveys.

The key finding of this study is that, like food, HI is considered a necessity good even by people with very low income and no prior experience with HI. While further research could verify whether WTP is 4.5% of food expenditure everywhere, the authors expect the relationship to food expenditure to offer best-fit elsewhere as well.

Estimating Willingness-to-Pay for health insurance among rural poor in India by reference to Engel's law

Erika Binnendijk[a], David M. Dror[a,b,*], Eric Gerelle[c], Ruth Koren[d]

[a] Erasmus University Rotterdam, Institute of Health Policy and Management, P.O. Box 1738, 3000 DR Rotterdam, The Netherlands
[b] Micro Insurance Academy, New Delhi
[c] Geneva, Switzerland
[d] Tel Aviv University, Felsenstein Medical Research Center, Sackler Faculty of Medicine, Ramat Aviv, Tel Aviv, Israel

ARTICLE INFO

Article history:
Available online 2 November 2012

Keywords:
India
Willingness to pay
Low-income populations
Community-based health insurance
Micro health insurance
Engel's law

ABSTRACT

Community-Based Health Insurance (CBHI) (a.k.a. micro health insurance) is a contributory health insurance among rural poor in developing countries. As CBHI schemes typically function with no subsidy income, the schemes' expenditures cannot exceed their premium income. A good estimate of Willingness-To-Pay (WTP) among the target population affiliating on a voluntary basis is therefore essential for package design. Previous estimates of WTP reported materially and significantly different WTP levels across locations (even within one state), making it necessity to base estimates on household surveys. This is time-consuming and expensive. This study seeks to identify a coherent anchor for local estimation of WTP without having to rely on household surveys in each CBHI implementation. Using data collected in 2008–2010 among rural poor households in six locations in India (total 7874 households), we found that in all locations WTP expressed as percentage of income decreases with household income. This reminds of Engel's law on food expenditures. We checked several possible anchors: overall income, discretionary income and food expenditures. We compared WTP expressed as percentage of these anchors, by calculating the Coefficient of Variation (for inter-community variation) and Concentration indices (for intra-community variation). The Coefficient of variation was 0.36, 0.43 and 0.50 for WTP as percent of food expenditures, overall income and discretionary income, respectively. In all locations the concentration index for WTP as percentage of food expenditures was the lowest. Thus, food expenditures had the most consistent relationship with WTP within each location and across the six locations. These findings indicate that like food, health insurance is considered a necessity good even by people with very low income and no prior experience with health insurance. We conclude that the level of WTP could be estimated based on each community's food expenditures, and that this information can be obtained everywhere without having to conduct household surveys.

Introduction

Policy makers across the world have recognized that adequate access to health services is important for the entire population and that this cannot be achieved without a well-functioning health financing system. Member States of the World Health Organization committed in 2005 to develop their health financing systems so that all people have access to services and do not suffer financial hardship paying for them (World Health Assembly resolution 58.33). Health financing policies across the world promote risk pooling mechanisms in order to move away from direct payments (out-of-pocket spending at the point of delivery) and achieve universal health coverage (James & Savedoff, 2010; World Health Organization, 2010).

Most developing countries cannot mandate affiliation to health insurance because the vast majority of the population is living and working in the "informal sector" (Bacchetta, Ernst, & Bustamante, 2009; Pratap & Quintin, 2006). This is also why these countries cannot fully subsidize health insurance forever for all people in the informal sector. Thus, voluntary affiliation to a contributory scheme like Community-Based Health Insurance (CBHI) or micro health insurance is the most likely route to achieve broad-based health insurance coverage in settings where governments can neither

* Corresponding author. Present/permanent address: Micro Insurance Academy, 52B Okhla Industrial Estate Phase III, New Delhi 110020, India. Tel.: +91 99 5820 6633; fax: +91 11 43799117.
E-mail addresses: binnendijk@bmg.eur.nl (E. Binnendijk), daviddror@socialre.org (D.M. Dror), ericgerelle@gmail.com (E. Gerelle), rkoren@post.tau.ac.il (R. Koren).

mandate nor subsidize the full cost. India is a case in point, as a large share of its population lives in rural areas, works in the informal sector and does not pay taxes. Notwithstanding a policy of delivering healthcare through the public sector, these facilities commonly suffer from shortages in qualified staff and supplies, especially in rural and peripheral areas (Berman, 1998; Peters et al., 2002; Reddy et al., 2011). Therefore, the rural poor mostly seek care with private practitioners (National Sample Survey Organization, 2006) and have to bear the costs of care out of pocket at the point of delivery. It has been shown that often, rural poor pay for this care by resorting to borrowing or selling assets (Binnendijk, Koren, & Dror, 2012). Additionally, rural poor cannot easily find health insurance in rural areas; the more likely option to become insured in rural areas is through CBHI providing affordable (but partial) health insurance coverage (Ahuja, 2005; Bhat & Jain, 2006; Devadasan, 2006; National Commission on Macroeconomics and Health, 2005). CBHI schemes are organized mostly by NGOs serving poorer segments of society on a not-for-profit voluntary basis. One of the strengths of CBHI is keeping transaction costs low and tailoring the benefits to suit local needs (Ahuja, 2005; Bhat & Jain, 2006). Typically, CBHI schemes do not benefit from premium subsidy. Therefore, the expenditure on benefits is limited to premium income of single schemes. It is self-explanatory that people will buy health insurance voluntarily only if the package suits their needs, the premium is affordable, and if they expect the contract to be executed as promised. Estimating what people are willing to pay for health insurance (WTP) before the insurance can be launched is thus essential because it defines the financial boundaries within which a to design the package.

Contingent valuation is the method used most often to get information regarding WTP; people are asked to declare their WTP for something that is not yet available in the market (Dror & Koren, 2012). It should be noted that the query about WTP is not an offer to sell a product; it is a hypothetical question about a product that does not yet exist, i.e. it precedes the offer of insurance. This query has often been part of a household survey. However the time and cost needed to conduct household surveys render this method of data acquisition impractical for generalized implementation of CBHI. Furthermore, it has been found, both in India and Nigeria, that WTP for health insurance differs significantly and materially across locations even within the same country or district (Dror, Radermacher, & Koren, 2007; Onwujekwe et al., 2010), suggesting that it is necessary to estimate WTP for every location separately. The purpose of this study is to identify a coherent anchor for such local estimation of WTP without having to carry out a household survey.

Several studies have looked at factors influencing the level of WTP for health insurance in developing countries, such as economic and socio-demographic status of respondents, availability of healthcare facilities, financial exposure to healthcare costs. However, variables that significantly explain WTP in one study were not significant in other studies (Dror & Koren, 2012). Household income (or income-proxy) turned out to be a positive predictor of WTP in many studies (Asenso-Okyere, Osei-Akoto, Anum, & Appiah, 1997; Asfaw & von Braun, 2004; Barnighausen, Liu, Zhang, & Sauerborn, 2007; Binam, Nkama, & Nkenda, 2004; Dong, Kouyate, Cairns, Mugisha, & Sauerborn, 2003; Dong, Kouyate, Cairns, & Sauerborn, 2005; Dong, Kouyate, Snow, Mugisha, & Sauerborn, 2003; Dror et al., 2007; Gustafsson-Wright, Asfaw, & van der Gaag, 2009; Lofgren, Thanh, Chuc, Emmelin, & Lindholm, 2008; Masud, Farooq, & Ghaffar, 2003; Mathiyazhagan, 1998; Onwujekwe et al., 2010; Ying et al., 2007). This finding is not surprising and tallies with the prevalent practice in developed countries to price social health insurance premiums as a fixed percentage of household income (Saltman, Busse, & Figueras, 2004). On the other hand, it has also been shown that while nominal WTP increases with income, when expressed as a percentage of income, WTP decreases as income increases. This relationship between WTP and income reminds of Engel's Law, the important observation in economics stating that the proportion of income spent on food decreases as income increases, even if actual expenditure on food rises (Engel, 1957; Perthel, 1975). This finding relating to WTP for health insurance suggests that similar to food, health insurance should be considered a 'necessity good' rather than a 'luxury good', i.e. goods that people cannot live without and the demand for which is not easily reduced even when times are tough. We therefore queried whether the cost of a necessary commodity like food could serve as a better anchor for estimation of WTP, rather than disposable income or total household income. We tested our hypotheses by comparing data from six rural locations in India to identify the anchor that, in every location separately (intra-community) as well as across the locations (inter-community), showed the most consistent relation with WTP.

Data and methods

Setting and sampling

We used data from household surveys we conducted in rural areas of six Indian locations. Two were undertaken in 2008 in Warangal and Karimnagar districts in Andhra Pradesh; three in 2009 in Kalahandi, Khorda and Malkangiri districts in Odisha; and the last in 2010 in Gaya district in Bihar. These surveys formed part of a baseline study prior to launching a development project among members of local Non-Government Organizations (NGOs), and the locations were selected in agreement with the implementing local NGOs: CDF in Andhra Pradesh; Madhyam Foundation in Odisha (comprising 11 grassroots NGOs: Parivartan, PUSPAC, SOMKS, SDS, ODC (Malkangiri); Mahashakti Foundation, DAPTA, Lok Yojana, Sanginee (Kalahandi); MVPS, DSS (Khorda)) and BASIX in Bihar.

We followed a two-stage sampling procedure in each location. In stage one, villages were selected; In Warangal and Karimnagar the survey was conducted in 8 and 12 villages respectively listed by the local NGOs; in Kalahandi, Khorda and Malkangiri respectively 27, 22 and 31 villages were randomly sampled from lists provided by the local NGOs; and in Gaya, 50 villages were selected randomly from the Census 2001 registry of villages. In stage two, in each selected village, households were sampled randomly by applying the "four winds" (or "line sampling") technique (Som, 1996). The overall response rate of the survey was 100% because most people were keen to participate and there was always a willing adult in the household who could respond.

The households (except in Gaya) were sampled in two cohorts of equal size: member and non-member households. Households were defined as "Members" if at least one person participated in a Self-Help-Group linked to partner-NGOs; unaffiliated households were "Non-members". In Gaya only non-member households were sampled. As we found no significant difference in WTP levels between the "member" and "non-member" sub-cohorts in the same locations, we aggregated the two sub-cohorts for the purpose of the analysis reported here. Sample size was 625 households in Warangal (2429 individuals), 1089 in Karimnagar (4328 individuals), 1805 in Kalahandi (8173 individuals), 1758 in Khorda (9049 individuals), 1597 in Malkangiri (7326 individuals), and 1000 in Gaya (6607 individuals). 100% of the sampled households were rural.

The survey questionnaire was translated from English into the local languages (Telugu, Oriya and Hindi respectively for AP, Odisha and Bihar), back translated for verification, and pre-tested among 80 households per language. Surveyors fluent in local dialects conducted the interviews. We obtained verbal informed consent of the respondents prior to interviews, and kept confidential participants' names in data recording and analysis. Our research tools were reviewed for ethical compliance by an ad-hoc advisory committee, as at the time of the rollout of the survey there was no local ethics committee in place in Odisha, India. We however held a two-day workshop in preparation of the study in which we discussed the ethical aspects of the study with scholars and senior scholars from India and other countries.

Data

With the use of the household survey questionnaire we queried about expenditures on many items of household consumption in order to obtain a proxy for household income (Grosh & Glewwe, 2000). We followed the method as adopted by the Indian National Sample Survey Organization (National Sample Survey Organization, 2008). These items of consumer expenditures included expenditures on food, tobacco, alcohol, fuel, gas, electricity, transportation, household disposables, toilet articles, entertainment, telephone, internet, (house) rent, consumer taxes, water fees and domestic servants for last 30 days and expenditures on bedding, clothing, footwear, education, household durables, agricultural equipment/inputs, life-stock, business inputs, repair/ maintenance, holidays, functions and insurance premiums for last 12 months. All these expenditure items, normalized per person per month, serve as our proxy for socio-economic status and are labelled 'income-proxy'. Our income-proxy does not include health expenditure, unlike the National Sample Survey Organization (Flores, Krishnakumar, O'Donnell, & van Doorslaer, 2008; Wagstaff, 2008).

We also estimated "discretionary income", i.e. the income available to households after paying for food (Imber & Toffler, 2008). Stated differently, discretionary income is income-proxy minus food expenditures per person per month. Discretionary income is sometimes defined as disposable income, i.e. total income minus necessities. For people living in the Western world expenditures on water, fuel and electricity are considered necessities besides food. For the rural poor populations we dealt with in this paper, paying for necessities meant something quite different. For example, the water consumed is sourced from wells or streams and does not command payment. Most of the necessary fuel (to cook or heat for instance) is gathered from sources that do not require payment, e.g. cow dung cakes, crop residue or wood collected in the field; most of the other fuel is not a necessity good as most people don't have motorized transportation. And finally, electricity does not exist everywhere and is not always paid for. Therefore food is the only generally applicable necessity good which is retained in this analysis.

In the survey questionnaire we also queried about caste, education and occupation of the household head, household size and other indicators of demographics and socio-economic status of the household. The government of India has "scheduled" certain backward Indian classes or groups in order to promote their welfare: Scheduled Tribes (Ministry of Law India, 1950b), Scheduled Castes (Ministry of Law India, 1950a), and "Other Backward Castes". Scheduled Tribes (tribals or adivasis) are mostly not Hindu and thus out of the caste system and are considered the most disadvantaged economically. Scheduled Castes (Dalits and those sometimes labelled "untouchable") are considered at the bottom of caste hierarchy. The list of Other Backward Castes is quite dynamic and changes from time to time in many states. All other castes are described here as General Caste.

Finally, we queried about WTP for health insurance using the Descending Bidding Game method in order to obtain the maximum values. First the interviewer explained what health insurance is, how it works and the coverage of the package: "To buy a health insurance you have to pay a premium per month for your whole household. This health insurance will then pay you back some of the money you spend on healthcare costs for your household members. Suppose we offer you a health insurance that will cover part of the cost of hospital, medicines, tests, consultations and maternity? How much would you agree to pay for that? If you are willing to pay more, you will get more benefits and if you are willing to pay less, you will get fewer benefits. But the condition is that all household members must join." Then the interviewer started with the relatively high opening bid of INR 30 per person per month (around PPP$ 1.8), again emphasizing that all household members have to join and their premium must be paid every month. Every time the bid was not accepted, it was lowered by INR 1 until it was accepted or reached INR 0. The accepted bid was recorded as the WTP level.

Analysis

We conducted all analyses at household level (reflecting the condition that in this experiment health insurance was available only when the whole household joined). For the analysis we used only households for which WTP and all expenditure items were available (in Warangal 1.4% of households had at least one expenditure item missing, in Karimnagar 1.0%, Kalahandi 3.5%, Khorda 6.4%, Malkangiri 2.6% and Gaya 0.2%). We also only included households whose WTP level was higher than zero; in context, households that were unwilling to join health insurance at any price could only express that through WTP equal to zero; as they are out of scope for voluntary affiliation of health insurance they were not included. The resulting sample is: Warangal 609 households (2.6% excluded), Karimnagar 1051 households (3.5% excluded), Kalahandi 1698 households (5.9% excluded), Khorda 1592 households (9.4% excluded), Malkangiri 1524 households (4.6% excluded), and Gaya 862 households (13.8% excluded).

We calculated WTP in several ways: as percentage of income-proxy; as percentage of food expenditure; and also as percentage of discretionary income. The effect of income on these different expressions of WTP was checked separately for each location by using a concentration index, which measures how equitably an indicator is distributed across households with different income. The closer the concentration index is to zero, the more equitable the indicator is (O'Donnell, van Doorslaer, Wagstaff, & Lindelow, 2008).

We used STATA version 11 for all analyses.

All amounts, reported in Indian Rupee (INR) during the surveys were converted into international dollars (purchasing power parity, PPP$) using the exchange rate of PPP$1 = INR 16.130 for the survey conducted in 2008, INR 16.692 for the 2009 survey and 18.073 for the 2010 survey (International Monetary Fund, 2012).

Findings

Socio-economic profile

The socio-economic profile of the studied populations is summarized in Table 1. With income-proxies between PPP$ 1.0 and PPP$ 2.7 per person per day, all locations can be considered poor but the differences in poverty are quite considerable across the different locations. Food expenditure was on average about half of the total income-proxy (ranging from 36% to 57%). This percentage was lower in the higher income cohorts, as one could expect by reference to Engel's law.

Table 1
Socio-economic profile of the studied locations.

	Warangal	Karimnagar	Kalahandi	Khorda	Malkangiri	Gaya
	Mean (±SEM)					
Income-proxy pppm	79.77 (±2.62)	79.17 (±2.13)	29.46 (±0.48)	35.65 (±0.52)	29.97 (±0.47)	50.24 (±1.15)
Food expenditures pppm	31.34 (±0.81)	28.59(±0.85)	14.68(±0.20)	20.49 (±0.30)	15.92 (±0.23)	23.09 (±0.47)
Household size	3.89 (±0.06)	4.01 (±0.05)	4.52 (±0.04)	5.15 (±0.05)	4.58 (±0.05)	6.62 (±0.10)
	% of total					
Caste						
Scheduled tribe	1.0%	2.8%	22.0%	6.7%	64.6%	2.2%
Scheduled caste	16.7%	20.5%	15.3%	28.5%	21.6%	35.3%
Other backward caste	73.1%	54.2%	52.7%	33.2%	7.7%	43.0%
General caste	9.2%	22.6%	10.0%	31.6%	6.2%	19.5%
Education of household head						
No education	42.3%	47.6%	53.9%	32.5%	69.1%	43.4%
Class 1–5	13.3%	12.3%	21.2%	29.5%	16.0%	12.2%
Class 6–10	29.0%	25.4%	22.4%	34.1%	13.7%	33.2%
Class 11 and higher	15.3%	14.8%	2.5%	3.8%	1.2%	11.3%
Occupation of household head						
Self-employed agriculture	17.9%	33.0%	43.5%	26.8%	48.3%	28.8%
Self-employed business/trade	18.4%	14.1%	9.0%	32.7%	5.8%	7.0%
Regular salaried employee	11.0%	5.5%	3.3%	4.8%	3.9%	4.5%
Daily wage labourer	46.8%	39.0%	38.1%	19.3%	35.8%	47.9%
Not working	5.9%	8.4%	6.2%	16.4%	6.1%	11.8%

In all locations, the majority of household heads have no or very little education (below class 5), but there is a marked difference across the locations in the percentage of household heads with higher education. The occupation of the majority of household heads differs across locations from self-employed in agriculture to daily wage labourers and self-employed in business/trade. The distribution of the castes is very different across locations with some locations having a very small minority Scheduled Tribe (1–3%) while in Malkangiri nearly 65% of households were Scheduled Tribe.

WTP for health insurance

Respondents of the household survey were asked how much they were willing to pay for health insurance per person per month, under the condition that the entire household had to be included in the insurance and the premium had to be paid for every person in the household. The average WTP values as reported in the different locations are displayed in Fig. 1.

From the data in Fig. 1 it can be seen that average WTP for health insurance varies greatly (nearly three-fold) across the locations; this finding tallies with previous reports (Dror et al., 2007; Onwujekwe et al., 2010).

Fig. 2 shows the average WTP values by quintiles of income-proxy in each location. It is clear that nominal WTP increases

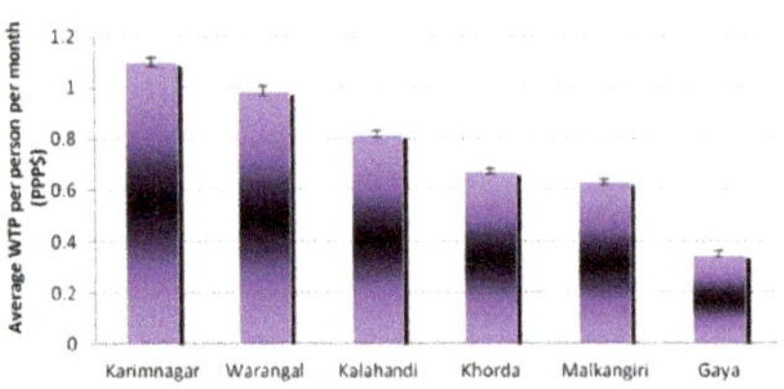

Fig. 1. Nominal WTP per person per month in the six study locations WTP values for the sampled households in the six study locations were obtained through the bidding game method and the data are presented as mean ± standard error.

when the income of the household increases and thus that there is also great variation of WTP for health insurance across income groups within the locations.

In all the locations studied, WTP values increased with income; this finding tallies with earlier reports. We wandered whether a fixed percentage of income could serve as an anchor to predict WTP of households for health insurance? We therefore expressed WTP as a percentage of income-proxy and checked whether this resulted in a constant percentage across locations and within locations (Fig. 3).

As can be seen, there is a strong intra- and inter-location variation in WTP as percentage of income-proxy. Even though relative WTP decreases in all locations as income increases, the decrease is not identical across locations (or relative to income quintiles).

Anchor for determination of WTP

Fig. 2 illustrated that richer households were willing to pay higher premiums for health insurance in nominal term, but the higher amounts represented a smaller percentage of income compared to poorer households in the same location (see Fig. 3). As mentioned before, the relation between WTP and income

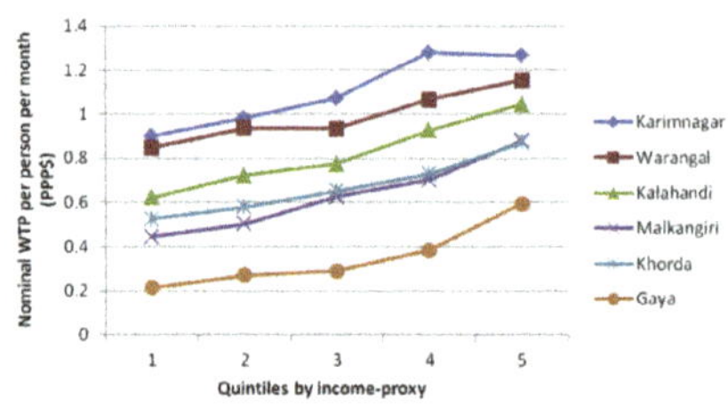

Fig. 2. Nominal WTP as a function of income-proxy WTP values for the sampled households in the six study locations were obtained through the bidding game method. Mean values for each income quintile in each of the six study locations are shown.

E. Binnendijk et al. / Social Science & Medicine 76 (2013) 67–73

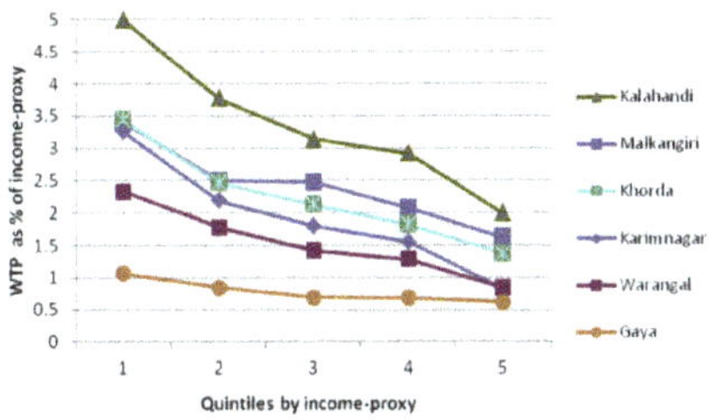

Fig. 3. WTP as percentage of income-proxy as a function of income-proxy WTP values for the sampled households in the six study locations were obtained through the bidding game method. For each household values were expressed as percentage of income-proxy for the same household. Mean values are shown for each income quintile in each of the six study locations.

reminded of Engel's Law, an observation in economics stating that as income increases the proportion of income spent on food decreases, even if actual expenditure on food rises (Engel, 1957; Perthel, 1975). Prais and Houthakker (1955) introduced the concept that the shape of Engel's curve can reflect a distinction between luxury and necessity goods like food. We therefore examined the notion that actual spending on one necessity (food) can serve as an anchor for the estimation of WTP for another necessity (health insurance). To this end we checked the consistency of WTP as percentage of reported food expenditures within and across locations. For a more robust comparison we also examined the opposite notion, that WTP is considered a 'luxury good' a household can only buy when it has enough money to spare. To this end we calculated discretionary income (income-proxy minus food expenditures) and checked the consistency of WTP as percentage of discretionary income within and across locations. Fig. 4 shows the averages of both indicators for all six locations.

The data in Fig. 4 indicates that the variation in WTP as percentage of discretionary income across locations (average values) is more pronounced than the variation in WTP expressed as percentage of food expenditures. This consistency across locations was quantified by calculating the coefficient of variation (the ratio of the standard deviation to the mean). The overall average WTP as percentage of food expenditure was 4.6% (with a standard deviation of 1.6%), and the overall average WTP as percentage of discretionary income was 5.0% (with standard deviation of 2.5%).

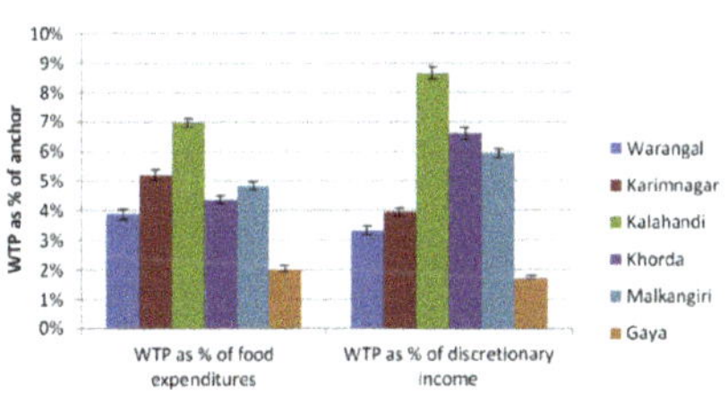

Fig. 4. WTP as percentage of food expenditures and discretionary income in the six study locations WTP values for the sampled households were obtained through the bidding game method. For each household values were expressed as percentage of food expenditure and as percentage of discretionary income for the same household. The results for each of the six study locations are presented as mean ± standard error.

The coefficient of variation of WTP expressed as percentage of food expenditure was 0.36 and of WTP expressed as percentage of discretionary income was 0.50. For reference, the coefficient of variation of WTP as percentage of income was 0.43. This means that WTP expressed as percentage of food expenditure varied the least across locations.

We also examined the consistency of the indicators within locations, by calculating the concentration indices of the WTP indicators. This measure can show whether an indicator is distributed equitably across households with different income within the same location (O'Donnell et al., 2008). The more equitable the determinant of WTP (concentration index closer to zero), the better it can serve as an anchor across income groups in a location (least income-dependent).

WTP expressed as percentage of food expenditure has a lower concentration index than WTP expressed as percentage of discretionary income in all locations (Fig. 5). This means that the amount a household spends on food is a much better predictor of WTP for health insurance than the amount available to the household for spending after paying for food.

Discussion

The purpose of this study is to find an anchor to obtain initial estimates of WTP for community-based health insurance (CBHI) under conditions of voluntary affiliation. The WTP represents the price that the household was willing to pay per person per month for health insurance that would cover part of the healthcare expenditures, within the WTP level. The prevailing practice has hitherto been to estimate WTP based on specific questions included in household surveys. We aim to identify the parameter that would yield the most consistent estimate of WTP and which could be established without resorting to household surveys, as these are costly and time-consuming.

We compared data from six locations in rural India; we found a positive relation between WTP and income, but this relation was neither consistent across income-groups within locations, nor across the locations. In a previous study it had been shown that there is a positive relation between nominal increase in income and in WTP, but a negative relation when WTP is expressed as share of income (Dror et al., 2007). This characteristic of the relationships is remindful of Engel's Law which expresses the same kind of relationship between food expenditures and income (Engel, 1957; Perthel, 1975). In our study, the described relationships between

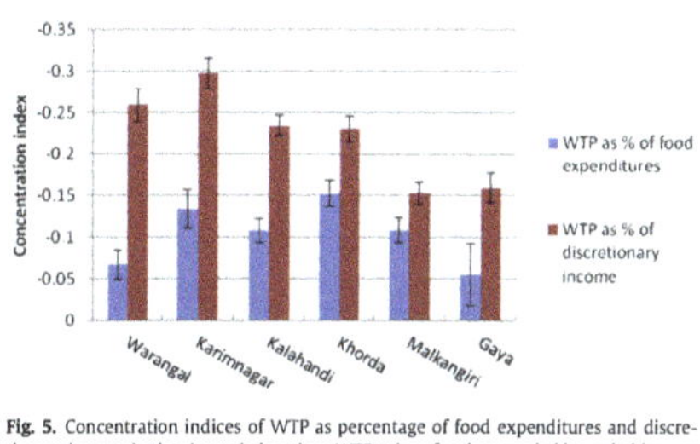

Fig. 5. Concentration indices of WTP as percentage of food expenditures and discretionary income in the six study locations WTP values for the sampled households were obtained through the bidding game method. For each household values were expressed as percentage of food expenditure and as percentage of discretionary income for the same household. Concentration indices were calculated for each of the six study locations and are presented as the value ± standard error.

income and WTP repeated itself in all the locations, leading us to consider that (WTP for) health insurance behaves like a typical necessity good, like food.

We therefore checked the relationship between WTP and food expenditures and between WTP and discretionary income (the amount available after paying for food). We measured inter-community differences by using the coefficient of variation, and intra-community variations with the concentration index. The most important insight gained from these calculations has been that average household spending on food provided a good indication of the WTP for health insurance of the studied populations in all locations as well as across the locations. WTP estimations based on food expenditure were most consistent, more so than overall income and better than discretionary income. That said, this higher consistency in the measure of WTP across and within locations does not mean that the actual values reported across locations are uniform; naturally they are not, as can be seen e.g. that Gaya is a clear outlier; the differences in values are likely to reflect other (cultural, demographic) parameters.

It has been shown that on average WTP for health insurance can be estimated at around 4.5% of food expenditures. This estimation means that a simple and cost-effective method to establish average food expenditures in a target community would also provide a reliable handle for WTP prior to the launch of contributory CBHI. This is a simplification of current practices, with no sacrifice to quality of estimates of WTP. This method would obviate the need to conduct costly and time-consuming WTP studies through household surveys, and would also remove confounding information (e.g. inconsistent WTP as percentage of overall income or discretionary income, revealed in this study). The only reference data that would be needed would be food expenditure, which – being everyday expenditures – are much better known to all, and can be obtained easily through focus group discussions or from data published routinely and in the public domain.

WTP estimated at 4.5% of average food expenditures was obtained based on data collected in six rural locations in India, which of course differ from each other in several socio-economic and demographic features. Before our findings can be generalized for other places, further research would be needed to validate that the estimated WTP is similar elsewhere. The actual anchor could differ from this 4.5% of food expenses in other countries, but we expect that the expression of WTP relative to food expenditure will remain the most consistent compared to other measurements. Further research to test that the relationship to food expenditures applies elsewhere would be able to confer a more general validity to our findings in rural India. Finally, further research could also refine the most effective method to extract information on average food expenditures in a community, for instance through focus group discussions.

The finding that WTP for health insurance behaves like a necessity good rather than a luxury good is quite surprising. Intuitively one could have expected health insurance to be a luxury good, in particular as the rural poor that were the focus of our study had such very low income, and hardly any experience with health insurance or insurance in general. However, these insights actually flow quite logically from a previous finding of the same authors that health-related hardship financing among rural poor populations (i.e. borrowing with high interest or selling assets) was considerable (Binnendijk et al., 2012). Therefore, it seems logical that people who are exposed to such financial risk would seek to reduce illness-related financial shocks, and would consider affordable and relevant solutions as essential. It follows that the scoping of WTP levels among rural poor prior to launching CBHI can proceed successfully even among cohorts that are inexperienced with the financial instrument, when given coherent explanations.

Conclusion

The first and most striking insight gained through this study in six locations in India is that WTP for health insurance could be estimated as a percentage of average food expenditure in the target communities. This is related to the second important finding that the relationship between income and food expenditures is similar to the relation between income and WTP for health insurance, indicating that even rural poor, with very little money, education or experiences with (health) insurance consider health insurance as a necessity good (akin to food). The average expenditure on food can serve as a better data series for the estimation of WTP for health insurance than either overall income or discretionary income. Thirdly, the detailed calculations show that the level of WTP for community-based health insurance (CBHI) was approximately 4.5% of food expenditure in the six locations we studied in India. Further research could verify whether the same percentage applies everywhere; but we expect the relationship to food expenditure to offer best-fit elsewhere as well. Finally, the analysis described in this article strongly suggests that it is possible to estimate WTP for health insurance without having to conduct household surveys to obtain essential data first; the only data source needed would be information on average food expenditures in the community. We submit that this can be obtained through cheaper and faster research methods, such as focus group discussions with target communities or, if sufficiently accurately available, existing data sources. This means that it would be much easier, faster and cheaper to implement CBHI among rural poor populations (in India) than hitherto, as one of the critical needs that required doing a baseline is obviated by the new method presented in this article.

Acknowledgements

The authors gratefully acknowledge funding support from the Netherlands Organization for Scientific Research (NWO), under WOTRO Integrated Programme grant No. W01.65.309.00. Additional funding for the household survey in Odisha was obtained from the German Federal Ministry for Economic Cooperation and Development (through a contract between AWO International, Madhyam Foundation Orissa, and the Micro Insurance Academy New Delhi). The sponsors had no influence or role in study design, in the collection, analysis and interpretation of data; in the writing of the article; and in the decision to submit the article for publication. We benefited from logistical and research support from the Micro Insurance Academy, New Delhi, India. The following organizations provided logistical support at the research sites: CDF in Andhra Pradesh; Madhyam Foundation (and its 11 affiliated NGOs (Parivartan, PUSPAC, SOMKS, SDS, ODC, Mahashakti Foundation, DAPTA, Lok Yojana, Sanginee, MVPS, DSS) in Odisha; and BASIX in Bihar. Last but not least, we acknowledge all the respondents for their participation in the study. Thanks also to two anonymous peer reviewers that offered useful suggestions how to improve this article.

References

Ahuja, R. (2005). *Health insurance for the poor in India: An analytical study*. Working Paper No. 161. New Delhi, India: Indian Council for Research on International Economic Relations (ICRIER).

Asenso-Okyere, W. K., Osei-Akoto, I., Anum, A., & Appiah, E. N. (1997). Willingness to pay for health insurance in a developing economy – a pilot study of the informal sector of Ghana using contingent valuation. *Health Policy, 42*(3), 223–237.

Asfaw, A., & von Braun, J. (2004). Can community health insurance schemes shield the poor against the downside health effects of economic reforms? The case of rural Ethiopia. *Health Policy, 70*(1), 97–108.

Bacchetta, M., Ernst, E., & Bustamante, J. P. (2009). *Globalization and informal jobs in developing countries*. Switzerland: Economic Research and Statistics Division, World Trade Organization & International Institute for Labour Studies, International Labour Office.

Barnighausen, T., Liu, Y., Zhang, X., & Sauerborn, R. (2007). Willingness to pay for social health insurance among informal sector workers in Wuhan, China: a contingent valuation study. *BMC Health Services Research, 7*, 114.

Berman, P. A. (1998). Rethinking health care systems: private health care provision in India. *World Development, 26*(8), 1463–1479.

Bhat, R., & Jain, N. (2006). *Factoring affecting the demand for health insurance in a micro insurance scheme*. IIMA Working Papers WP2006-07-02. Ahmedabad: Indian Institute of Management.

Binam, J., Nkama, A., & Nkenda, R. (2004). *Estimating the willingness to pay for community health prepayment schemes in rural area: A case study of the use of contingent valuation surveys in centre Cameroon*. Available at. Yaounde: Institute of Agricultural Research for Development (IRAD) http://www.csae.ox.ac.uk/conferences/2004-GPRAHDIA/papers/4h-Binam-CSAE2004.pdf.

Binnendijk, E., Koren, R., & Dror, D. M. (2012). Hardship financing of healthcare among rural poor in Orissa, India. *BMC Health Services Research, 12*(1), 23.

Devadasan, N. (2006). *Health insurance in India: Current status and some suggestions for the future*. India: Government of India.

Dong, H., Kouyate, B., Cairns, J., Mugisha, F., & Sauerborn, R. (2003). Willingness-to-pay for community-based insurance in Burkina Faso. *Health Economics, 12*(10), 849–862.

Dong, H., Kouyate, B., Cairns, J., & Sauerborn, R. (2005). Inequality in willingness-to-pay for community-based health insurance. *Health Policy, 72*(2), 149–156.

Dong, H., Kouyate, B., Snow, R., Mugisha, F., & Sauerborn, R. (2003). Gender's effect on willingness-to-pay for community-based insurance in Burkina Faso. *Health Policy, 64*(2), 153–162.

Dror, D. M., & Koren, R. (2012). The elusive quest for estimates of willingness to pay for micro health insurance among the poor in low-income countries. In C. Churchill, & M. Matul (Eds.), *Micro insurance compendium* (pp. 211–261).

Dror, D. M., Radermacher, R., & Koren, R. (2007). Willingness to pay for health insurance among rural and poor persons: field evidence from seven micro health insurance units in India. *Health Policy, 82*(1), 12–27.

Engel, E. (1957). Die Productions- und Consumtionsverhaltnisse des Konigreichs Sachsen. *Zeitschrift Des Statistischen Bureaus Des Koniglich Sachsischen Ministeriums Des Inner, 8 and 9*, 1–5454, It was reprinted as an appendix to Die Lebenskosten Belgischer Arbeiter Familien fruher und jetzt. Bulletin de l'Institut International de Statistique (1895), 9, premiere livraison.

Flores, G., Krishnakumar, J., O'Donnell, O., & van Doorslaer, E. (2008). Coping with health-care costs: implications for the measurement of catastrophic expenditures and poverty. *Health Economics, 17*(12), 1393–1412.

Grosh, M., & Glewwe, P. (Eds.), (2000). *Designing household survey questionnaires for developing countries: Lessons from 15 years of the living standards measurement study* (1st ed.). Washington, DC, USA: The World Bank.

Gustafsson-Wright, E., Asfaw, A., & van der Gaag, J. (2009). Willingness to pay for health insurance: an analysis of the potential market for new low-cost health insurance products in Namibia. *Social Science & Medicine (1982), 69*(9), 1351–1359.

Imber, J., & Toffler, B. A. (2008). *Dictionary of marketing terms* (4th ed.). New York, USA: Barron's Educational Series.

International Monetary Fund. (2012). *World economic outlook database*. Retrieved June 24, 2012 from. http://www.imf.org/external/pubs/ft/weo/2012/01/weodata/index.aspx.

James, C., & Savedoff, W. (2010). *Risk pooling and redistribution in health care: An empirical analysis of attitudes toward solidarity*. Geneva, Switzerland: World Health Organization, World Health Report 2010, Background Paper No. 5. Available at http://www.who.int/healthsystems/topics/financing/healthreport/SolidarityNo5FINAL.pdf.

Lofgren, C., Thanh, N. X., Chuc, N. T., Emmelin, A., & Lindholm, L. (2008). People's willingness to pay for health insurance in rural Vietnam. *Cost Effectiveness and Resource Allocation, 6*, 16.

Masud, T. I., Farooq, N., & Ghaffar, A. (2003). Equity shortfalls & failure of the welfare state: community willingness to pay for health care at government facilities in Jehlum (Pakistan). *Journal of Ayub Medical College, 15*(4), 43–49.

Mathiyazhagan, K. (1998). Willingness to pay for rural health insurance through community participation in India. *The International Journal of Health Planning and Management, 13*(1), 47–67.

Ministry of Law India. (1950a). *The constitution (scheduled castes) order, 1950 (C.O.19)*. Retrieved June 14, 2009 from. http://lawmin.nic.in/ld/subord/rule3a.htm.

Ministry of Law India. (1950b). *The constitution (scheduled tribes) order, 1950 (C.O.22)*. Retrieved June 14, 2009 from. http://lawmin.nic.in/ld/subord/rule9a.htm.

National Commission on Macroeconomics and Health. (2005). *Financing and delivery of health care services in India*. National Commission on Macroeconomics and Health Background papers. New Delhi: Ministry of Health and Family Welfare, Government of India.

National Sample Survey Organization. (2006). *Morbidity, health care and the condition of the aged*. Report No. 507 (60th round January–June 2004). New Delhi: National Sample Survey Organization, Ministry of Statistics and Programme Implementation, Government of India.

National Sample Survey Organization. (2008). *Household consumer expenditure in India, 2006–07*. Report No. 527. New Delhi: National Sample Survey Organization, Ministry of Statistics and Programme Implementation, Government of India.

O'Donnell, O., van Doorslaer, E., Wagstaff, A., & Lindelow, M. (2008). *Analyzing health equity using household survey data*. Washington DC: The World Bank.

Onwujekwe, O., Okereke, E., Onoka, C., Uzochukwu, B., Kirigia, J., & Petu, A. (2010). Willingness to pay for community-based health insurance in Nigeria: do economic status and place of residence matter? *Health Policy and Planning, 25*(2), 155–161.

Perthel, D. (1975). Engel's law revisited. *Revue Internationale De Statistique [International Statistical Review], 43*(2), 211–218.

Peters, D. H., Yazbeck, A. S., Sharma, R. P., Ramana, G. N. V., Pritchett, L. H., & Wagstaff, A. (2002). *Better health systems for India's poor: Findings, analysis and options*. Washington (DC): World Bank.

Prais, S. J., & Houthakker, H. S. (1955). *The analysis of family budgets* (2nd 1971 ed.). Cambridge: Cambridge University Press.

Pratap, S., & Quintin, E. (2006). *The informal sector in developing countries: Output, assets and employment*. WIDER Research Paper 2006/130. Helsinki: Finland: United Nations University – World Institute for Development Economics Research (UNU-WIDER).

Reddy, K. S., Patel, V., Jha, P., Paul, V. K., Kumar, A. K., Dandona, L., et al. (2011). Towards achievement of universal health care in India by 2020: a call to action. *Lancet, 377*(9767), 760–768.

Saltman, R. B., Busse, R., & Figueras, J. (Eds.), (2004). *Social health insurance systems in Western Europe* (1st ed.). Berkshire, England: Open University Press.

Som, R. K. (1996). *Practical sampling techniques* (2nd ed.). New York: Marcel Dekker.

Wagstaff, A. (2008). *Measuring financial protection in health*. Report No. 4554. Washington, DC: World Bank.

World Health Organization. (2010). *Health systems financing: The path to universal coverage*. The World Health Report 2010. Geneva, Switzerland: World Health Organization.

Ying, X. H., Hu, T. W., Ren, J., Chen, W., Xu, K., & Huang, J. H. (2007). Demand for private health insurance in Chinese urban areas. *Health Economics, 16*(10), 1041–1050.

Chapter 5.3

Systematic Review of Willingness to Pay for Health Insurance in Low and Middle Income Countries*

Main Messages

- The first systematic review of willingness to pay (WTP) of individuals or households for health insurance (HI) in low- and middle-income countries (LMICs).
- The first-ever study attempting to express WTP estimates as a percentage of GDP per capita of the respective country or as a percentage of national net income per capita.
- Review of literature based on 16 studies (21 articles) from 10 countries.

Focus Points

- A systematic review of the literature on WTP for social and community-based (non-commercial) health insurance (CBHI) in LMICs.
- The WTP for HI among rural households in LMICs was just below 2% of the GPD per capita per household per year.

---

*This chapter is reproduced from *PLoS ONE* (2016), Open Access, doi: 10.1371/journal.pone.0157470, available at https://www.researchgate.net/publication/304662855_Systematic_Review_of_Willingness_to_Pay_for_Health_Insurance_in_Low_and_Middle_Income_Countries.

- Factors which were consistently correlated with higher WTP for insurance included family size, education level, income, past hospitalization and perceived poor health status.
- Low WTP suggests that LMICs seeking universal health coverage should not rely on households' premiums as a major financing source, but invest in also increasing their fiscal capacity for an equitable health care system using other sources.

Structured Abstract

Introduction

The low penetration rates of HI in LMICs have prompted various studies on WTP among the target population. The authors draw upon the findings of these studies in an attempt to estimate WTP as a percentage of GDP per capita and net national income per capita. The other objective of the study is to identify the variables that consistently affected WTP for HI in different settings.

Method

The literature search included academic and grey literature. The authors systematically searched databases up to February 2016 and included studies of individual or household WTP for HI in one or more LMICs. A total of 16 studies (21 articles) from 10 countries met the inclusion criteria. Besides the data extracted from these studies, the study also uses data on country-specific GDP per capita, net national income, and population in the year of the study from the World Bank's list of indicators.

For the analysis, WTP was estimated as a percentage of GDP per capita, and adjusted net national income per capita of each country. The study used two analytical approaches:

— meta-analysis to calculate WTP means and confidence intervals,
— vote-counting to identify the variables that more often affected WTP.

Box 1: Data Analysis and Synthesis

A meta-analysis synthesis to assess WTP

- Estimating effect size: WTP annual values converted to US$; WTP estimated as a percentage of GDP/Net National Income per capita.
- Estimating standard error of the effect size: Standard error (SE) of the effect size was estimated from the SE of the WTP values.
- Weights: SEs of the effect size were used as weights.
- Estimating summary effect: The summary effect was obtained by averaging the effect sizes, after applying weights.

Vote counting

- Identified different objective variables that influenced willingness to pay as assessed in regression analyses reported in the included studies.
- Categorized the variables by those that had significant positive, significant negative or non-significant effects on WTP in their respective study sample.
- Each study casts a "vote" in support of the above relationships and the numbers of the votes were counted.
- If a variable obtained a minimum of three votes, it was considered that the variable was likely to affect the WTP for HI.

Findings

The meta-analysis yielded results suggesting that WTP amounted to just below two percent of GDP per capita per household per year, with a lower figure obtained for individuals' WTP. This may be considered as a minimal expression of WTP as several studies included in the meta-analysis reported data originating from rural areas of low-income countries, where an understanding of insurance is limited.

The study could not find sufficient evidence associating WTP to factors such as the price of insurance, degrees of risk aversion, the magnitude of expected loss from illness or the probability of illness. Instead, the analysis indicated that other factors which were consistently correlated with higher WTP for insurance included family size, education level, income, past hospitalization and perceived poor health status. The elderly were correlated with reduced WTP, which can be attributed to their lower capacity to pay rather than the lower perception of risk. It was also observed that low awareness of the value proposition of insurance is associated with a lower WTP.

Most of the reviewed studies used "bidding game" methods for the estimation of WTP. Although this method is simple to execute, it has some inherent disadvantages. The initial anchor (or 'price' offered) in a bidding game may influence the WTP estimate to be higher than that identified using the other contingent valuation methods.

Conclusion

The findings of the study suggest that following the classical theoretical precepts on demand for health insurance is not very helpful since only a limited set of empirical variables corresponding to the theory-driven factors consistently affected the WTP for insurance. Moreover, the low WTP estimated by the study indicates that LMICs seeking universal health coverage should not rely on households' premiums as a major financing source. Instead, they must also focus on increasing their fiscal capacity for an equitable health care system using other sources.

The findings can serve as a general guide for national policymakers as well as donors in deciding the amount they should provide over and above the resources that households might be required and willing to contribute toward the provision of non-commercial health insurance.

RESEARCH ARTICLE

Systematic Review of Willingness to Pay for Health Insurance in Low and Middle Income Countries

Shirin Nosratnejad[1,2]*, Arash Rashidian[3,4], David Mark Dror[5,6]

1 Iranian Center of Excellence in Health Services Management, School of Management and Medical Informatics, Tabriz University of Medical Sciences, Tabriz, Iran, 2 Tabriz Health Services Management Research Center, Department of Health Services Management, School of Management and Medical Informatics, Tabriz University of Medical Sciences, Tabriz, Iran, 3 Department of Health Management and Economics, School of Public Health, Tehran University of Medical Sciences, Tehran, Iran, 4 Knowledge Utilization Research Center, Tehran University of Medical Sciences, Tehran, Iran, 5 Micro Insurance Academy, New Delhi, India, 6 Former hon. Professor, Erasmus University Rotterdam, Rotterdam, Netherland

* Sh_nosratnejad@yahoo.com

Abstract

Objective

Access to healthcare is mostly contingent on out-of-pocket spending (OOPS) by health seekers, particularly in low- and middle-income countries (LMICs). This would require many LMICs to raise enough funds to achieve universal health insurance coverage. But, are individuals or households willing to pay for health insurance, and how much? What factors positively affect WTP for health insurance? We wanted to examine the evidence for this, through a review of the literature.

Methods

We systematically searched databases up to February 2016 and included studies of individual or household WTP for health insurance. Two authors appraised the identified studies. We estimated the WTP as a percentage of GDP per capita, and adjusted net national income per capita of each country. We used meta-analysis to calculate WTP means and confidence intervals, and vote-counting to identify the variables that more often affected WTP.

Result

16 studies (21 articles) from ten countries met the inclusion criteria. The mean WTP of individuals was 1.18% of GDP per capita and 1.39% of adjusted net national income per capita. The corresponding figures for households were 1.82% and 2.16%, respectively. Increases in family size, education level and income were consistently correlated with higher WTP for insurance, and increases in age were correlated with reduced WTP.

Conclusions

The WTP for healthcare insurance among rural households in LMICs was just below 2% of the GPD per capita. The findings demonstrate that in moving towards universal health

OPEN ACCESS

Citation: Nosratnejad S, Rashidian A, Dror DM (2016) Systematic Review of Willingness to Pay for Health Insurance in Low and Middle Income Countries. PLoS ONE 11(6): e0157470. doi:10.1371/journal.pone.0157470

Editor: Ulla Kou Griffiths, London School of Hygiene and Tropical Medicine, UNITED KINGDOM

Received: November 13, 2015

Accepted: May 30, 2016

Published: June 30, 2016

Data Availability Statement: All relevant data are within the paper.

Funding: The authors have no support or funding to report.

Competing Interests: The authors have declared that no competing interests exist.

coverage in LMICs, governments should not rely on households' premiums as a major financing source and should increase their fiscal capacity for an equitable health care system using other sources.

Introduction

The interest in Willingness To Pay (WTP) for health insurance arises in settings where on the one hand access to healthcare is mostly contingent on Out-Of-Pocket Spending (OOPS) by health seekers, and on the other hand health insurance schemes must know upfront how much they could charge as premium, to ensure their financial sustainability. This is particularly relevant in Low- and Middle-Income Countries (LMICs); by one estimate, only 5–10% of population in sub-Saharan Africa and South Asia are covered by social healthcare schemes that are funded by the state [1], and in many middle-income countries the effective cost coverage of mandatory health insurance schemes ranges from 20 to 60% [1], leaving even insured persons exposed to considerable OOP.

In 2012 the UN General Assembly, in the framework of the Resolution on 'universal health coverage', called upon Member States "*to ensure that health financing systems evolve so as to avoid significant direct payments at the point of delivery and include a method for prepayment of financial contributions for health care and services as well as a mechanism to pool risks among the population in order to avoid catastrophic health-care expenditure and impoverishment of individuals as a result of seeking the care needed*" [2]. This framing would require many LMICs to raise enough funds to achieve universal health insurance coverage. This poses a number of questions: are individuals or households willing to pay for health insurance, and how much? What factors positively affect WTP for health insurance? And is the role of governments obviated when private health insurance is offered? This study focuses on reviewing the evidence about WTP for social or other non-commercial health insurance (including community-based mutual health insurance) with the view to offer policymakers an estimate of the resources that can be generated from uninsured population segments were health insurance offered, based on the evidence from pilot experiments reported in the existing literature from low- and middle income countries.

There are two approaches to estimating WTP: "Revealed Preferences" (RP) [3], and "Stated Preferences" (SP)[4]. RP is a predictive, modeling approach to WTP, based on studying actual purchasing behavior of products from which we wish to estimate the WTP for the product for which no purchasing information exists and that we are interested in. Unfortunately, we could not find any published study using the RP method to estimate WTP for health insurance in LMIC.

The alternative option, SP, is to ask people what they would be willing to pay for insurance cover that they do not yet have, and that is perhaps not even on the market. Several SP methods evolved to value non-market goods. One of the most frequently used, called "Contingent Valuation" (CV)[3, 4] consists of using survey methods to present respondents with hypothetical scenarios about an intervention under evaluation (or insurance product in our case). Respondents are required to think about the contingency (or feasibility) of an actual market for the benefits, and state the maximum they would be willing to pay for them. This method assumes that prospective clients are given a detailed description of the product for which they are asked how much they would be willing to pay. However, if the price determines the product, and is not yet known, how then is it possible to guarantee that the described product would actually be the one delivered?

WTP is presumably mediated by ability to pay and by individual and cultural aspects that determine how the utility of insurance is perceived. We wanted to examine the evidence for this, through a review of the literature. Different authors have used different anchors to measure the WTP against (e.g. income, disposable income, food expenditure etc.). In the interest of comparison across countries and different socioeconomic contexts, we propose to assess WTP levels against per capita GDP.

This article is structured as follows: section 2 contains methodological notes. Results of the review are presented in Section 3, and a discussion and conclusions in the 4th and last section.

Methods

Information Sources

The literature search (conducted in February 2016) included academic and gray literature. The academic thematic databases included Pubmed, Science Direct and Scopus and search engine of Google scholar. The gray literature was searched manually, through citation tracking.

Search Strategy

Search strategies for electronic databases were developed by one of the authors (SN) and peer-reviewed by other authors. One of the authors conducted the search. We used "willingness to pay" and "insurance" as the key terms, with no limits for study designs and date of publication, while limiting the searches to English language for practical reasons. The search identified studies published until 2016. The complete Medline/PubMed search strategy is available as Supporting Information (S1 Text).

Eligibility Criteria (Inclusion/Exclusion)

Primary studies that assessed households or individuals' WTP for health insurance in LMIC were eligible for inclusion. Studies were considered eligible for inclusion if:

1. Collected data from individuals or households living in one or more LMIC.
2. Estimated individuals or households' WTP for health insurance using monetary value or as a percentage of income
3. Reported data on WTP for social, national or community health insurance.

These selection criteria meant that studies that focused solely on insurance of other risks, or health insurance that was based on individual risk rating and without any aspect of community rating for the purpose of defining the level of payment requested from the individual (e.g. private actuarial insurance) were not eligible for inclusion. Finally, studies that assessed WTP for certain health care services (e.g. insurance for dental care or complementary inpatient insurance) were not eligible for inclusion.

A priori, we considered any previously published systematic review studies of WTP for health insurance as eligible for inclusion in this review, if they answered the same questions. No other article adopted the exact same inclusion criteria; we found one study on the same topic which did not expressly exclude private health insurance but was also focused in LMIC, where private health insurance is rare[5].Those articles retained 13 articles within the date range from 1996 to 2010, of which 12 are also included in this systematic review; this review includes 11 additional studies (for a total of 23 articles). And its analysis followed a different method[5]. Hence, we do not have a previous study to which we can compare our results.

Data Extraction

One author extracted data from included studies and entered them into the data extraction sheet that was then checked by another author for accuracy and completeness. Data extracted included location and year of study, sample size, response rate, target population, household size, data collection method, variables that significantly affected WTP, and WTP values (per individual and per household) reported in the study. Additionally, we collected data on country specific Gross Domestic Product (GDP) per capita, net national income and population in the year of the study from the World Bank's list of indicators[6]

Critical appraisal of studies: quality assurance process

Quality assurance was maintained in four stages: (1) All duplicates were eliminated, using End-Note software version 7 (http://endnote.com/) (2). The titles and the abstracts of identified papers were screened, and those that were obviously unrelated to our review were excluded. (3) Two authors assessed the full texts of the retained articles and any discrepancies between them resolved through discussion. (4) The critical appraisal of included studies was done by the STROBE tool [7] and in this stage we also considered some methodological recommendations in appraisal of studies (S1 Table) [8, 9].

Data Analysis and Synthesis

We used two analytical approaches

1. A meta-analysis synthesis to assess WTP
2. A vote counting to identify the main attributes that affect WTP.

A meta-analytic synthesis of the studies, conducted with sub-topics as follows:

Estimating effect size. The included studies in this meta-analysis reported WTP values. We used the following way to convert these values into the effect size: the values were transformed to annual values and converted to US$ using the exchange rate for the study year, as reported in the study. If not reported, we used the International Monetary Fund (IMF) values [10]. In the next step, we estimated the WTP of individuals or households as a percentage of GDP per capita and as a percentage of adjusted net national income per capita of each country.

Estimating standard error of the effect size. Standard error (SE) of the effect size was estimated from the SE of the WTP values by applying similar transformation used for estimating the effect size. Some authors reported the 95 percent confidence intervals instead of the SE. For these studies we first computed the SE of the values and then computed the SE of the effect size by using the following way.

Some authors did not report the SE, CI (Class Interval). Therefore, we could not estimate the SE of the effect size for these studies [11–13]

Weights. The standard practice in meta-analysis is to apply weights proportional to the variances of the effect size for estimating the summary effect. In this meta-analysis we applied the SEs of the effect size as a weight.

Estimating summary effect. When a WTP values were computed in the same way by all studies, the summary effect was obtained by averaging the effect sizes, after applying weights. We used fixed and random effect meta-analysis techniques to calculate summary effect, based on the level of heterogeneity between the included studies.

A descriptive vote-counting approach conducted with sub-topics as follows [14, 15]:

- We identified Different objective variables that influenced willingness to pay as assessed in regression analyses reported in the included studies

- We categorized the variables by those that had significant positive, significant negative or non-significant effects on WTP in their respective study sample.
- Each study casts a "vote" in support of the above relationships and the numbers of the votes were counted
- If a variable obtained a minimum of three votes, we considered that variable likely to affect the WTP for health insurance.

We follow the PRISMA approach in performing this systematic review, and we attached the PRISMA form as appendix (S1 Appendix).

Results

Search result

Our academic database searches yielded 1411 hits and the gray literature searches another 8 articles. After screenings of the titles and abstracts, we kept58 studies for full-text review (Fig 1), and thereafter retained 23 articles for detailed review [11–13, 16–35]. Of these, two articles [26] and [20] were excluded after quality assessment.

The remaining 21 articles relate to 16 distinct studies in the following ten countries: In Asia: Bangladesh [34], China [27], India [18, 19, 28, 33], Iran [21, 32] and Vietnam [12]. In Sub- Saharan African: Burkina Faso [16], Cameroon [22, 30], Ethiopia [13], Ghana [11], and Nigeria [17, 29]. The studies altogether had surveyed about 1050 households plus about 9857 individuals.

Consequently, in Table 1 we included 17 studies (as the study of the scheme in Burkina Faso is considered by reference to two articles by Dong et al (one relating to households and the other to individual WTP in the same scheme). In Table 2, we only listed the 12 out of 16 distinct studies which had adequate data for Meta-analysis. And in Table 3 we list only 16 studies, since the variables under consideration allowed considering Burkina Faso as a single study.

Quality Assessment result

Details of the quality of studies are presented in appendix (S2 Appendix). The overall methodological quality of included empirical studies was good, with more than half of studies meeting all criteria. Two studies [20, 26] that did not rank suitably according to this appraisal were excluded from further analysis.

Studies characteristics

Table 1 contains information on study characteristics.

The sample sizes of the studies varied greatly, from 300 to 3,070 individuals. Seven studies were conducted in rural settings[12, 13, 19, 21, 22, 29, 30], four studies on rural and urban residents [11, 16, 17, 28], one study on urban residents [32], three studies on urban informal sector employees [27, 33, 34] and one study on the urban poor [18]. Most of the studies involved face-to-face interviews with the respondents. All of the identified studies used contingent valuation for WTP estimation: bidding game (eight), open ended (five), double-bounded (five), payment cards (two) and single bounded (one) methods, including four studies that used more than one method.

WTP for health insurance

We were able to calculate the WTP as percentages of GDP and net national income per capita for all except one included study; that one exception estimated the WTP only as a percentage of household income and did not report monetary values[18]. Four studies that measured

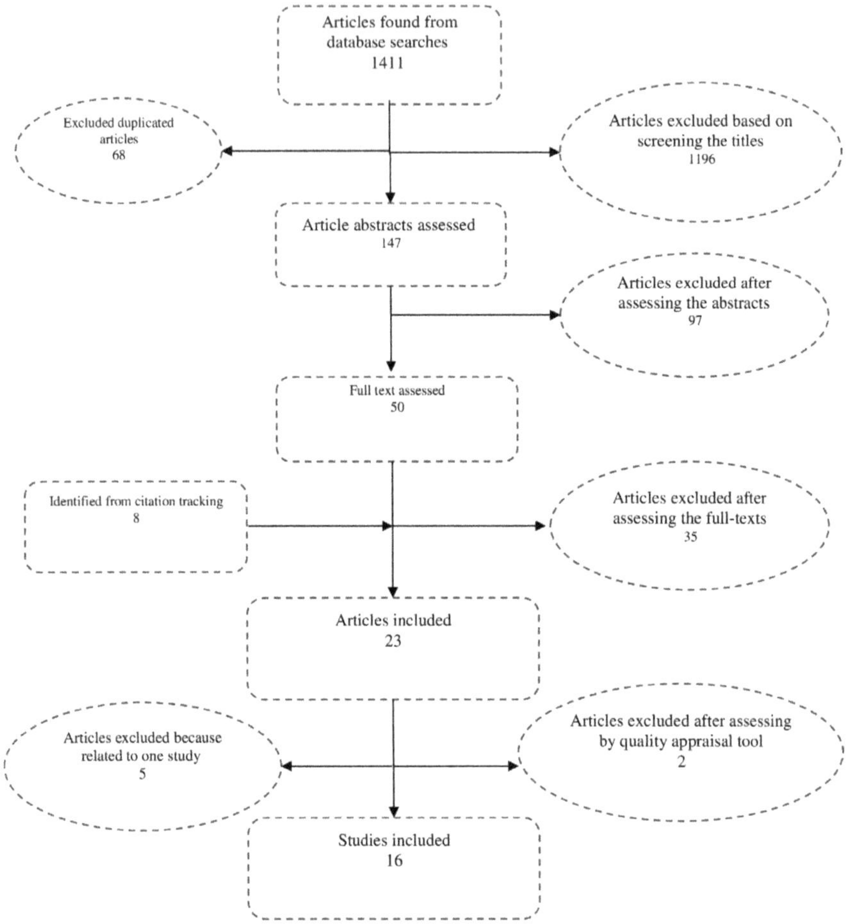

Fig 1. Article flowchart for studies of WTP for insurance demonstrating the studies identified assessed and included in the systematic review.

doi:10.1371/journal.pone.0157470.g001

household WTP provided enough data to enable us to calculate the corresponding individual WTP[11, 12, 19, 29].

Out of 15 studies, ten studies provided enough data to conduct a meta-analysis of WTP at individual level, using national GDP data: 1.18% of GDP per capita (95% CI: 1.13–1.24) and 1.39% of adjusted net national income per capita (95% CI: 1.34–1.44). Out of five studies, four

Table 1. Summary of articles conducted in different countries on willingness to pay for health insurance.

	Author (year)	Country	Year	Population	Household or individual	Sample size	Measurement method of WTP	WTP as a percentage of GDP per capita	WTP as a percentage of net national income per capita
1	**Asenso-Okyereet al., 1997** [11]	Ghana	1992	Rural and urban	Household	306	bidding game	8.07	9.13
					individual			1.61	1.83
2	**Mathiyazhagan et al., 1998** [19]	India	1995	Rural	Household	918	open-ended questions	0.84	1.01
3	**Barnighausen et al., 2007**	China	2000	Urban	Individual	651	payment card	6.07	7
4	**Dong et al., 2003** [16]	Burkina Faso	2001	Rural and urban	Household	705	bidding game	5.86	6.28
5	**Dong et al., 2004** [23]	Burkina Faso	2001	Rural and urban	Individual	2414	bidding game	2.15	2.3
							Take- it- or leave—it		
6	**Asgary et al., 2004** [21]	Iran	2001	Rural	Household	2139	bidding game	1.9	2.82
7	**Binam et al., 2004** [22]	Cameroon	2002	Rural	Individual	471	bidding game	2.23	2.61
8	**Lofgren et al., 2008** [12]	Vietnam	2004	Rural	Household	2063	Biding game	1.85	2.36
					individual		open- ended question	0.41	0.53
9	**Dror et al., 2007** [28]	India	2005	Rural and urban	Household	3024	bidding game	1.82	2.12
					individual			0.39	0.46
10	**Ataguba et al., 2008** [29]	Nigeria	2007	Rural	Household	309	payment card,	2.15	3.06
					Individual		double bounded dichotomous choice	0.35	0.51
							open- ended question		
11	**Onwujekwe et al., 2010** [17]	Nigeria	2007	Rural and urban	Individual	3070	bidding game	2.32	3.3
12	**Donfouet et al., 2010–2011** [30, 31]	Cameroon	2009	Rural	Individual	399	double bounded dichotomous choice	1.98	2.52
							open -ended question		
13	**Ghosh et al., 2011 [De 18]**	India	2010	Urban	Individual	1502	double bounded dichotomous choice	–	–
14	**AbayAsfaw et al., 2004** [13]	Ethiopia	2001	Rural	Household	550	double bounded dichotomous choice	12.2	-
15	**Kumar et al., 2015** [33]	India	2008	Urban	Individual	500	open -ended question	0.45	0.54
16	**Sayem Ahmed et al., 2016** [34]	Bangladesh	2011	Urban	Individual	557	bidding game	1.63	2.05
17	**Nosratnejad et al., 2014** [32]	Iran	2016	Urban	Individual	300	double bounded dichotomous choice	0.99	1.33

doi:10.1371/journal.pone.0157470.t001

Table 2. WTPs as a percentage of GDP and net national income: the results of meta-analysis of the included studies.

Variable	Method	Pooled estimate	95% confidence interval	P-value	N of studies [ref]
WTP household (% GDP per capita)	Fixed effect	1.82	1.5–2.15	0.000	4 [16, 19, 21, 29]
WTP Household (% net national income per capita)	Fixed effect	2.16	1.83–2.50	0.000	4 [16, 19, 21, 29]
WTP of individual (% GDP per capita)	fixed effect	1.18	1.13–1.24	.0.000	10 [16, 17, 22, 27–30, 32–34]
WTP of individual (% net national income per capita)	fixed effect	1.39	1.34–1.44	0.000	10 [16, 17, 22, 27–30, 32–34]

doi:10.1371/journal.pone.0157470.t002

studies provided enough data to conduct a meta-analysis of WTP at household level: 1.82% of GDP per capita (95% CI: 1.5–2.15) and 2.16% of adjusted net national income per capita (95% CI: 1.83–2.50)(Table 2) (Fig 2). All the meta-analysis resulted in small p-values suggesting that the findings were unlikely to have occurred due to chance, noting the studies were conducted in different times and different countries.

We repeated the analyses after excluding the studies conducted in urban areas that reported substantially higher WTPs, but this did not affect the meta-analysis results.

Variables that influenced WTP for healthcare insurance

We categorized all objective variables that were assessed for their influence on WTP for health insurance into five groups, as follows:

- Demographic determinants. 'Marital status' and 'having a child under five in the household' did not affect willingness to pay. 'Male gender' (5 to 2) and a larger 'family size' (8 to 1) were linked with higher willingness to pay, while 'older age' (6 to 1) was correlated with lower willingness to pay for health insurance.
- Socioeconomic determinants. The 'income level' (11 to 1) and 'education level' (9 to 1) higher than primary education or highest grade educations were linked with an increased willingness to pay. We found equivocal evidence of the potential effects of 'living in rural areas' and 'employment statuses on willingness to pay.
- Health services determinants. The results for effects of 'distance to the nearest or preferred hospital' on willingness to pay were equivocal.
- Perceived needs determinants. A 'past experience of hospitalization' (4 to 0) and a 'perceived poor health status' (3 to 0) were linked with a higher willingness to pay. The findings for 'past health care expenditure' were equivocal.
- Insurance related variables. Effects of 'experience of having insurance' (2 to 0) were linked with a higher willingness to pay (See "S2 Text" for more details). Fourteen variables were included in at least three studies each and were included in vote-counting analyses.

Discussion

Our study is the first systematic review of WTP of individuals or households for health insurance in LMICs. We identified 21 articles (16 distinct studies) assessing households or individuals' WTP. Our study had two main objectives that we discuss in turn: identifying the variables that consistently affected WTP for insurance in different settings, and a transferrable estimation of the level of WTP in LMICs (as a percentage of GDP or net income per capita).

Table 3. Variables that influenced WTP in the included studies[$].

	Demographic					Socio- economic				Health service	Perceived need			Insurance related
	Male gender	Age	Married	Family size	Having children under 5	Income	Education	Employment statues	Living in rural areas	Distance to preferred health facility	Past health expenditure	Incidence of hospitalization	Poor health status	Insurance experience
Asenso-Okyere et al., 1997	↓↓	↑	↑	↑↑	-	↓↓	↓↓	↓	↓	↑	↓↓	-	-	↓
Mathiyazhagan et al., 1998	-	↓	-	↑↑	-	↑↑	-	↑↑	-	↑↑	-	↑↑	↑↑	-
Barnighausen et al., 2007	↓↓	↓↓	-	-	-	↑↑	↑	↓↓	-	-	↑↑	-	-	-
Dong et al., 2003	↑↑	↓↓	↑	↑	↑	↑↑	↑↑	-	↑↑	↓↓	↑↑	-	↓	-
Asgary et al., 2004	↑	↑↑	-	↓	-	↑	↑↑	-	↓↓	↑↑	-	-	-	↓
Binam et al., 2004	↑↑	↑	↓	↑↑	-	↑↑	↑	-	-	-	-	↑↑	↑↑	-
Lofgren et al., 2008	↑	↓↓	-	↑↑	↑	↑↑	↑↑	↓	-	-	-	-	-	↑
Dror et al., 2007	↑↑	↓↓	-	↑↑	↑	↑↑	↑↑	-	$$	↓↓	-	↑↑	-	↑↑
Ataguba et al., 2008	↑↑	↓	-	-	-	-	↑	-	-	↑↑	-	-	↑	-
Onwujekwe et al., 2010	↑↑	-	-	↓↓	-	-	↑↑	-	↓↓	-	-	-	-	-
Donfouet et al., 2010–2011	↑	↓↓	-	↑	-	↑↑	↑	↓↓	-	-	-	-	↑	-
Ghosh et al., 2011	-	↓	-	-	-	↑↑	↑	-	-	-	-	↑↑	↑↑	-
AbayAsfaw et al., 2004	↑	↓	-	↑↑		↑↑	↑↑						↑	
Kumar et al.,2014		↓	↑	↑	-	-	↑↑	-	-	-	-	-	-	-
Sayem Ahmed et al., 2016	↑	↓↓	↑	↑↑	-	↑↑	↑↑	-	-	-	-	-	↑	-
Nosratnejad et al., 2014	↑	↑	-	↑↑	↑	↑↑	↑↑	↑↑	-	-	-	↑	↓	↑↑

[$] Variables that mentioned in more than 3 studies are indicated in the Table.

[$$] The study had conflicting results (i.e. different rural and urban regions provided varying WTP estimates).

[↑↑] the effect of variable is positive and significant.

[↓↓] the effect of variable is negative and significant.

[↓] the effect of variable is negative and non- significant.

[↑] the effect of variable is positive and non-significant.

doi:10.1371/journal.pone.0157470.t003

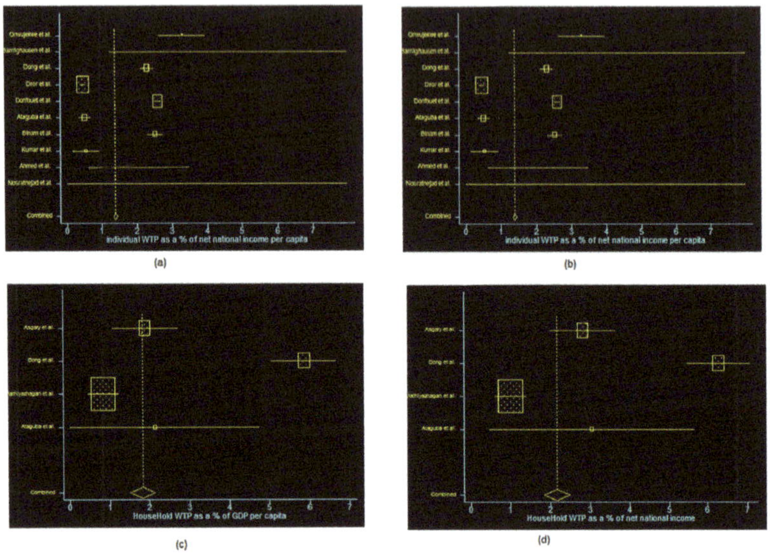

Fig 2. The reported Willingness to pay for health insurance in different studies, and the overall estimated WTP of individual as a % of GDP (a), and as a % of net national income (b), WTP for household as a % of GDP (c) and as a % of net national income (d).

doi:10.1371/journal.pone.0157470.g002

Different demand theories explain decisions to purchase health insurance [36, 37]. According to these theories, factors such as the price of insurance, degrees of risk aversion, household ability to pay and income, the magnitude of expected loss from illness (i.e. user fees), the probability of illness, and the expected performance of the insurer (the service coverage and the amount of pay-off) might affect the decision to insure and the WTP for insurance. While these theories are generally unequivocal in their expectation of the impact of different variables on WTP for insurance, our findings suggested that only a limited set of empirical variables corresponding to the theory driven factors consistently affected the WTP for insurance. This finding upholds the newest study on theory of demand for health insurance [38].

Our findings suggest that increase in family size, education level, income, past hospitalization and perceived poor health status were consistently correlated with higher WTP for insurance. Increased household income enables the households to purchase more health insurance and increase the demand for health insurance [39]. A previous study estimated that a 1% increase in national income might lead to a 0.9% increase in health spending after controlling for other factors [40]. We also noted that increases in age were correlated with reduced WTP. This seems surprising as it is widely assumed that older people incur higher health expenditure [41]; however, a recent review noted that the effects of older age on health care were lesser than argued in the past [40]. Another recent study suggested that older people might have less capacity to pay for needed health care [36], and to pay for health insurance. These different views suggest that our finding of lower WTP for health insurance among older people requires further study.

Other factors may also affect WTP. For example, when the concept / value proposition of "insurance" is unclear, or when households consider their ability to avail health care as slim (e.g. because the service provider is too far away, or because of previous negative experiences), they may report a lower WTP [42]. Similarly, when their past experience suggests improvements in health status because of the service (even if it is far away) they may be willing to pay more for the insurance. Hence it may be difficult to separate the impact of hypothetical scenario or access barriers on WTP. We did not observe a consistent picture in different studies.

The results of the meta-analysis suggest that WTP amounted to just below two per cent of GDP per capita per household per year. A lower figure was obtained for individuals' WTP. WTP, by definition, is the maximum amount people are willing to spend to acquire a service [17]. Despite this theoretical underpinning of the WTP concept, we should interpret the findings of this review with care. Many of the studies included in the meta-analysis originated from rural areas of low-income countries. Rural residents may have a limited understanding of insurance and risk management, and this may affect their WTP. Also as they generally have a lower socioeconomic status than the rest of the country, they may have a lower WTP. The six studies that included urban residents reported WTP values higher than other studies, although the three studies conducted after 2012 reported lower WTP values as a proportion of GDP per capita [32–34].

In many LMICs, households with a lower socioeconomic status spend substantial amounts out-of-pocket on essential needs for health care [43]. Hence they may be willing to pay for health insurance, if they have a positive expectation that health insurance would provide effective social protection against health-induced poverty and catastrophic expenditures [44]. Others [12, 29] have suggested that the surveys may underestimate WTP; one way this was explained has been that households facing high out-of-pocket medical expenses and risk catastrophic health care expenditure may state lower WTP for insurance [12]. Another argument has been that in some LMICs people may have a higher WTP if the payment is in kind and via commodities, but lower when WTP must be made as cash payment [29].

Most of the included studies used bidding game methods for the estimation of WTP. While the bidding game is simple to conduct, it has some inherent disadvantages. The initial anchor (or 'price' offered) in a bidding game may influence the WTP estimate to be higher than that identified using the other contingent valuation methods [24].

This is the first study proposing to express WTP estimates as a percentage of GDP per capita of the respective country, or as a percentage of national net income per capita. The idea is that such estimates might provide a powerful tool for policymakers in planning revenue generation through a national social or other broad format of non-commercial health insurance program. Estimating a rough figure that is linked to the general economic status of a country should only act as a starting point where local specific data is not available. While many countries lack national representative data to enable them to assess average WTP for health insurance, the review findings might be preferable than basing these estimates on small samples in a limited area of a country.

There might be other benefits for having such estimates. While LMICs may use past experiences of other countries and the advice of donors and international organizations for setting benefit packages, they often face the challenges of having few financial resources to cover the costs. Estimating the WTP as a percentage of GDP can help foresee what resources might be available from households, resources that are often untapped and if generated could sustainably provide an affordable benefit package. Our overall estimate of WTP for health insurance should be interpreted as a likely minimum value, which could increase over time when the social or community-based health insurance delivers compelling results. That said, households with a low socioeconomic status would perhaps find it very difficult to pay the same level of national community rated contribution.

Conclusions

This systematic review of the literature on willingness to pay for social and community-based (non-commercial) health insurance in low- and middle income countries has shown that following the classical theoretical precepts on demand for health insurance is not very helpful, since only some but not all "assumed predictors" are actually borne out by the empirical evidence. From our study we conclude that we cannot find sufficient evidence linking WTP to factors such as the price of insurance, degrees of risk aversion, the magnitude of expected loss from illness or the probability of illness. Our findings point that factors which were consistently correlated with higher WTP for insurance include family size, education level, income, past hospitalization and perceived poor health status. We also noted that people of elderly age were correlated with reduced WTP, which is probably due to lower capacity to pay rather than lower perception of risk. We also conclude that low awareness to the value proposition of insurance is associated with a lower WTP.

The results of our meta-analysis suggest that WTP amounted to just below two per cent of GDP per capita per household per year, with a lower figure obtained for individuals' WTP. Considering that many of the studies included in the meta-analysis reported data originating from rural areas of low-income countries, and considering the cumulative effect of a limited understanding of insurance and a lower socioeconomic status among rural populations, one might treat the results as a minimal expression of WTP.

The findings might provide a general guide for national policy makers as well as donors in deciding the amount they should provide over and above the resources that households might be required and willing to contribute toward the provision of social or community-based health insurance.

Supporting Information

S1 Appendix. The PRISMA checklist.
(DOC)

S2 Appendix. Quality appraisal of included studies.
(XLSX)

S1 Table. Methodological recommendations in appraisal of studies.
(DOCX)

S1 Text. The complete PubMed search strategy.
(DOCX)

S2 Text. The full list of variables that were assessed in primary studies for their influence on willingness to pay for health insurance.
(DOC)

Author Contributions

Conceived and designed the experiments: AR DD SN. Performed the experiments: AR DD SN. Analyzed the data: AR DD SN. Contributed reagents/materials/analysis tools: AR DD SN. Wrote the paper: AR DD SN.

References

1. World Health Organization. The World Health Report–Health Systems Financing: The Path to Universal Coverage. Geneva: World Health Organisation, 2010.
2. Soini EJ. Contingent valuation of Eight new treatments: What is the clinician's and politician's willingness to pay? The Open Complementary Medicine Journal. 2012 Apr 20; 4(1):1–11S.
3. Ciriacy-Wantrup SV. Capital returns from soil-conservation practices. Journal of farm economics, 1947. 29(4 Part II): p. 1181–1196.
4. Hanley N, Ryan M, Wright R. Estimating the monetary value of health care: lessons from environmental economics. Health economics, 2003. 12(1): p. 3–16. PMID: 12483757
5. Dror DM, Koren R. Micro Insurance Compendium II. Churchill C, Matul M, editors. Geneva: ILO; 2012. The Elusive Quest for Estimates of Willingness to Pay for Health Micro Insurance among the Poor in Low-Income Countries; p. 156–73.
6. Van der Star SM, Van den Berg B. Individual responsibility and health-risk behaviour: A contingent valuation study from the ex ante societal perspective. Health Policy. 2011 Aug; 101(3): p. 300–311. doi: 10.1016/j.healthpol.2010.10.001 PMID: 21168930
7. Von Elm E. The strengthening the reporting of observational studies in Epidemiology (STROBE) statement: Guidelines for reporting observational studies. Annals of Internal Medicine. 2007 Oct 16; 147 (8):573. PMID: 17938396
8. Smith RD. Construction of the contingent valuation market in health care: A critical assessment. Health Economics. 2003; 12(8):609–628. PMID: 12898660
9. Carson RT. Contingent Valuation: A User's Guide. Environmental Science & Technology, 2000. 34(8): p. 1413–1418.
10. Iskedjian M, Iyer S, Librach SL, Wang M, Farah B, Berbari J. Methylnaltrexone in the treatment of Opioid-Induced constipation in cancer patients receiving palliative care: Willingness-to-pay and cost-benefit analysis. Journal of Pain and Symptom Management. 2011 Jan; 41(1):104–15. doi: 10.1016/j.jpainsymman.2010.04.012 PMID: 20832981
11. Asenso-Okyere WK, Osei-Akoto I, Anum A, Appiah EN. Willingness to pay for health insurance in a developing economy. A pilot study of the informal sector of Ghana using contingent valuation. Health Policy. 1997 Dec; 42(3):223–37. PMID: 10176302
12. Lofgren C, Thanh NX, Chuc NT, Emmelin A, Lindholm L. People's willingness to pay for health insurance in rural Vietnam. Cost Effectiveness and Resource Allocation. 2008; 6(1):16.
13. Asfaw A, von Braun J. Can community health insurance schemes shield the poor against the downside health effects of economic reforms? The case of rural Ethiopia. Health policy, 2004.Oct; 70(1): p. 97–108. PMID: 15312712
14. Davenport CF, Elley KM, Fry-Smith A, Taylor-Weetman CL, Taylor RS. The effectiveness of routine dental checks: A systematic review of the evidence base. British Dental Journal. 2003 Jul 26; 195 (2):87–98. PMID: 12881749
15. Centre for Reviews and Dissemination. Systematic reviews: CRD's guidance for undertaking reviews in health care. 3rd ed. York: University of York NHS Centre for Reviews & Dissemination; 2009 Feb. ISBN: 9781900640473.
16. Dong H, Kouyate B, Cairns J, Mugisha F, Sauerborn R. Willingness-to-pay for community-based insurance in Burkina Faso. Health Economics. 2003; 12(10):849–62. PMID: 14508869
17. Onwujekwe O, Okereke E, Onoka C, Uzochukwu B, Kirigia J, Petu A. Willingness to pay for community-based health insurance in Nigeria: Do economic status and place of residence matter? Health Policy and Planning. 2009 Oct 26; 25(2):155–61. doi: 10.1093/heapol/czp046 PMID: 20156920
18. Ghosh S, Mondal S. Morbidity, health expenditure and willingness to pay for health insurance amongst the urban poor: A case study. Journal of Health Management. 2011 Nov 14; 13(4):419–37.
19. Mathiyazaghan K. Willingness to pay for rural health insurance through community participation in India. The International Journal of Health Planning and Management. 1998 Jan; 13(1):47–67. PMID: 10178583
20. Gumber A, Kulkarni V. Health insurance for informal sector: Case study of Gujarat. Economic and Political Weekly. 2000 Oct 6; 35(40):3607–13. Available: http://www.jstor.org/stable/4409810 doi: 10.2307/4409810
21. Asgary A, Willis K, Taghvaei AA, Rafeian M. Estimating rural households? Willingness to pay for health insurance. The European Journal of Health Economics, formerly: HEPAC. 2004 Sep; 5(3):209–15.
22. Binam JN, Nkama A, Nkendah R. Estimating the willingness to pay for community health prepayment schemes in rural area: A case study of the use of contingent valuation surveys in centre Cameroon. [place unknown: publisher unknown]; 2004.

23. Dong H, Mugisha F, Gbangou A, Kouyate B, Sauerborn R. The feasibility of community-based health insurance in Burkina Faso. Health Policy. 2004 Jul; 69(1):45–53. PMID: 15484606

24. Dong H. Differential willingness of household heads to pay community-based health insurance premia for themselves and other household members. Health Policy and Planning. 2004 Feb 1; 19(2):120–6. PMID: 14982890

25. Dong H, Kouyate B, Snow R, Mugisha F, Sauerborn R. Gender's effect on willingness-to-pay for community-based insurance in Burkina Faso. Health Policy. 2003 May; 64(2):153–62. PMID: 12694952

26. Edoh D, Brenya A. A community-based feasibility study of national health insurance scheme in Ghana. African Journal of Health Sciences. 2004 Aug 12; 9(1)p. 41–50.

27. Bärnighausen T, Liu Y, Zhang X, Sauerborn R. Willingness to pay for social health insurance among informal sector workers in Wuhan, china: A contingent valuation study. BMC Health Services Research. 2007; 7(1):114.

28. Dror DM, Radermacher R, Koren R. Willingness to pay for health insurance among rural and poor persons: Field evidence from seven micro health insurance units in India. Health Policy. 2007 Jun; 82 (1):12–27. PMID: 16971017

29. Ataguba J, Ichoku EH, Fonta W. Estimating the willingness to pay for community healthcare insurance in rural Nigeria. SSRN Electronic Journal.

30. Donfouet HPP, Makaudze E, Mahieu P-A, Malin E. The determinants of the willingness-to-pay for community-based prepayment scheme in rural Cameroon. International Journal of Health Care Finance and Economics. 2011 Aug 28; 11(3):209–20. doi: 10.1007/s10754-011-9097-3 PMID: 21874541

31. Donfouet HP, Edimo J-RE, Mahieu P-A, Malin E. Social capital and willingness-to-pay for community-based health insurance in rural Cameroon. Global Journal of Health Science. 2011 Apr 5; 3(1).

32. Nosratnejad S, Rashidian A, Mehrara M, Akbari Sari A, Mahdavi G, Moeini M. Willingness to pay for the social health insurance in Iran. Global Journal of Health Science. 2014 May 30; 6(5).

33. Kumar N, Tiwari VK, Kumar K, Nair KS, Raj S, Nandan D. Evolving social health scheme for workers in unorganized sector: Key evidences from study of cycle rickshaw pullers in Delhi, India. The International Journal of Health Planning and Management. 2014 Mar 27; 30(4):366–81. doi: 10.1002/hpm.2244 PMID: 24677059

34. Ahmed S, Hoque ME, Sarker AR, Sultana M, Islam Z, Gazi R, et al. Willingness-to-pay for community-based health insurance among informal workers in urban Bangladesh. PLOS ONE. 2016 Feb 1; 11(2): e0148211. doi: 10.1371/journal.pone.0148211 PMID: 26828935

35. Asfaw A, von Braun J. Innovations in health care financing: New evidence on the prospect of community health insurance schemes in the rural areas of Ethiopia. International Journal of Health Care Finance and Economics. 2005 Sep; 5(3):241–53. PMID: 16082517

36. Scheil-Adlung X, Bonan J. Gaps in Social Protection for Health Care and Long Term Care in Europe: Are the Elderly Faced with Financial Ruin? International Social Security Review, 2013. Jan; 66(1): p. 25–48.

37. Folland S, Goodman AC, Stano M. The Economics of health and health care. New Jersey: Pearson Prentice Hall; 2007.

38. Dror DM, Firth LA. The demand for (micro) health insurance in the informal sector. The Geneva Papers on Risk and Insurance Issues and Practice. 2014 Jul 16; 39(4):693–711.

39. Nosratnejad S, Rashidian A, Mehrara M, Jafari N, Babamohamadi H, Moeeni M. Factors Influencing Basic and Complementary Health Insurance Purchasing Decisions in Iran: Analysis of Data From a National Survey. World Medical & Health Policy, 2016. In press.

40. Savedoff WD, de Ferranti D, Smith AL, Fan V. Political and economic aspects of the transition to universal health coverage. The Lancet. 2012 Sep; 380(9845):924–3.

41. Getzen TE. Population aging and the growth of health expenditures. Journal of Gerontology. 1992 May 1; 47(3):S98–S104. PMID: 1573213

42. Spaan E, Mathijssen J, Tromp N, McBain F, Have A, Baltussen R. The impact of health insurance in Africa and Asia: A systematic review. Bulletin of the World Health Organization. 2012 Sep 1; 90 (9):685–92. doi: 10.2471/BLT.12.102301 PMID: 22984313

43. Kavosi Z, Rashidian A, Pourreza A, Majdzadeh R, Pourmalek F, Hosseinpour AR, et al. Inequality in household catastrophic health care expenditure in a low-income society of Iran. Health Policy and Planning. 2012 Jan 25; 27(7):613–23. doi: 10.1093/heapol/czs001 PMID: 22279081

44. Schneider P. Why should the poor insure? Theories of decision-making in the context of health insurance. Health Policy and Planning. 2004 Nov 1; 19(6):349–55. PMID: 15459160

Chapter 6

Hardship Financing of Health Care Among Rural Poor in Orissa, India*

Main Messages

- Survey of 5,383 rural households representing 25,606 individuals.
- Use of multivariate analysis to investigate factors influencing the risk of households to need hardship financing to finance their health care costs.
- The study refutes common economic theory that borrowing or selling assets would have immediate welfare gains in the sense that the ill person could be treated.
- Welfare gain from treatment of an ill person comes at a cost of welfare loss that extends over a much longer period of time if health care is financed by borrowing from moneylenders.

Focus Points

- Around 25% of the households (with any health care cost) had hardship financing.

---

*This chapter is reproduced from *BMC Health Services Research* (2012), **12,** 23, Open Access, available at https://www.researchgate.net/publication/221784516_Hardship_financing_of_healthcare_among_ruralpoor_in_Orissa_India.

- Hardship financing occurs not only in cases of expensive hospitalizations (40%) but also in many cases of expenditures for outpatient (23%) and maternity care (25%).
- Hardship financing is correlated to the asset-index, occupation of household head, SHG membership, household source of water, health expenditure and household illness incidents in the previous year.
- Policy interventions aiming to ensure health-related financial protection need to demonstrate that they have reduced both the frequency and the volume of hardship financing.

Structured Abstract

Introduction

The authors define "hardship financing" as having to borrow money with interest or to sell assets to pay out-of-pocket health care costs. The objective of this study is to identify the parameters affecting households' risk to resort to "hardship financing".

Method

The study uses survey data of 5,383 low-income, rural households in Orissa, one of the poorest states of India. The survey questionnaire included questions on socioeconomic status, health care utilization, and health care cost.

Those households that reported financing health care by selling assets or borrowing money with interest, were categorized as having had hardship financing. On the other hand, households that reported using only current income and/or savings and/or borrowing from relatives or friends/neighbors were defined as having had no hardship financing.

A multivariate analysis was used to investigate factors influencing the risk of households to need hardship financing to finance their health care costs. The authors applied a logistic regression (logit model) as the outcome variable was binary in nature (yes/no hardship financing).

Box 1: Proxies for Socioeconomic Status

Household income-proxy

- Followed the method adopted by the Indian Sample Survey Organization[1] to obtain a proxy (monthly per capita consumer expenditure) through questions on many items of household expenditure (on food, clothing, fuel, etc.).
- Did not include health expenditure because study was interested in identifying patterns of financing of health care.

Asset-index

- Performed a principal component analysis (PCA)[2] on various aspects of household assets.
- Variables included
  - binary variables — house type, the source of lighting, a way of cooking, land ownership, various consumer durables (radio, motorcycle, telephone, etc.),
  - continuous variables — possession of animals (cattle, sheep, chickens, etc.), size of land.
- Factor scores of each of the variables from the first principal component used as weights to compute a total for each household: *the household's socioeconomic score*.

Findings

The survey revealed that overall, about 25% of the households (with any health care cost) had hardship financing during the year preceding the survey. If we consider households that experienced a hospitalization, nearly 40% had hardship financing. Surprisingly, 23% of households

[1]National Sample Survey Organization: Household Consumer Expenditure in India, 2006–07. 2008, Report No. 527, National Sample Survey Organization, Ministry of Statistics and Programme Implementation, Government of India, New Delhi.

[2]Vyas, S. and Kumaranayake, L. (2006). 'Constructing socio-economic status indices: How to use principal components analysis', *Health Policy Plan*, **21**(6), 459–468.

that incurred outpatient costs also reported that they had to use hardship financing sources to pay for this outpatient care. Of the households that had a maternity case in the reference period, 25% had hardship financing.

The authors explored the factors which could influence the risk of households to need hardship financing to meet health care costs.

1. Asset-index: Highly significant and negative predictor
2. Occupation of household held: Higher likelihood of hardship financing if self-employed in agriculture, self-employed in business, a daily wage laborer, or does not work due to any reason; Lower likelihood if household head is a regular salaried employee.
3. The minority of households with a better source of water are less likely to have hardship financing.
4. The logarithm of the total health expenditures during the year preceding the survey is a significant and positive predictor of hardship financing.
5. Having a chronically ill person in the household, or having experienced one or more events of hospitalization in the year preceding the survey are both significant independent predictors.

An analysis of the impact of SHG membership on hardship financing revealed that households, where someone is a member of an SHG, have a higher propensity to have hardship financing. The authors suggested this may be a fallout of SHG members relying significantly more often on microfinance as a source of borrowing than non-members when paying for all health expenditures.

Furthermore, data revealed that the district in which a household resides remains a major predictor of the likelihood to have hardship financing.

Conclusion

The considerable financial hardship that the rural poor households are subject to due to out-of-pocket health care costs cannot be overlooked and calls for a policy solution that would limit that exposure both in quantum and in time. The authors, therefore, emphasize that policy intervention aiming to ensure health-related financial protection need to demonstrate that they have reduced both the frequency and the volume of hardship financing.

Binnendijk et al. BMC Health Services Research 2012, 12:23
http://www.biomedcentral.com/1472-6963/12/23

BMC Health Services Research

RESEARCH ARTICLE Open Access

Hardship financing of healthcare among rural poor in Orissa, India

Erika Binnendijk[1], Ruth Koren[2] and David M Dror[1,3*]

Abstract

Background: This study examines health-related "hardship financing" in order to get better insights on how poor households finance their out-of-pocket healthcare costs. We define hardship financing as having to borrow money with interest or to sell assets to pay out-of-pocket healthcare costs.

Methods: Using survey data of 5,383 low-income households in Orissa, one of the poorest states of India, we investigate factors influencing the risk of hardship financing with the use of a logistic regression.

Results: Overall, about 25% of the households (that had any healthcare cost) reported hardship financing during the year preceding the survey. Among households that experienced a hospitalization, this percentage was nearly 40%, but even among households with outpatient or maternity-related care around 25% experienced hardship financing. Hardship financing is explained not merely by the wealth of the household (measured by assets) or how much is spent out-of-pocket on healthcare costs, but also by when the payment occurs, its frequency and its duration (e.g. more severe in cases of chronic illnesses). The location where a household resides remains a major predictor of the likelihood to have hardship financing despite all other household features included in the model.

Conclusions: Rural poor households are subjected to considerable and protracted financial hardship due to the indirect and longer-term deleterious effects of how they cope with out-of-pocket healthcare costs. The social network that households can access influences exposure to hardship financing. Our findings point to the need to develop a policy solution that would limit that exposure both in quantum and in time. We therefore conclude that policy interventions aiming to ensure health-related financial protection would have to demonstrate that they have reduced the frequency and the volume of hardship financing.

1. Background

While we know that the biggest part of health expenditures in India is paid by health-seekers themselves when getting care, we know much less about how those costs are met. Evidence confirms that out-of-pocket spending on healthcare absorb more than one quarter of household resources net of food costs in at least one-tenth of all households in India [1]. All over India, the level of out-of-pocket spending is 69.5% of total health expenditures [2]. This considerable burden warrants a better understanding of how poor households finance these out-of-pocket healthcare costs. This article focuses on this very question, using data from Orissa, where out-of-pocket spending represents nearly 80% of health expenditure [2].

The literature dealing with financing of out-of-pocket healthcare cost includes definitions of "catastrophic" healthcare expenditures when spending exceeds an essentially arbitrary threshold. Xu et al. [3] fix the threshold at 40% of disposable income net of subsistence needs; Russell [4] and Van Doorslaer et al. [1] use a threshold of 10% of total annual household income. However, these methods fail to recognize that a uniform threshold might represent varying levels of hardship. For example, spending 10% by a poor household could mean withdrawing a child from school or skipping a meal, while the same spending level would not entail any immediate consequence for a richer household [5,6]. Also the timing of the payment could cause different cash-flow problems. As most rural poor households in India have irregular flows of income, they would find it easier to pay during

* Correspondence: daviddror@socialre.org
[1]Institute of Health Policy and Management, Erasmus University Rotterdam, P.O. Box 1738, 3000 DR Rotterdam, The Netherlands
Full list of author information is available at the end of the article

harvest season (when they have income from selling the crop or from work as agricultural labourers) than in other times of the year. Morduch and Rutherford [7] reported this cash-flow pattern to hold true in most low-income countries.

We therefore assess the hardship a household faces as a consequence of health expenses not merely by the amount spent, but by the additional costs to the direct cost of healthcare related to how the out-of-pocket spending is financed. This is in line with notions put forward by Flores et al. [8] and Kruk et al. [5].

Three sources of financing out-of-pocket healthcare costs can be distinguished: paying from current income or savings; borrowing with zero interest (e.g. from family and friends), and borrowing with interest or selling assets. The first two categories may be regarded as less burdensome than the third [5,9,10], because selling assets or borrowing money with interest usually entails a cost. This cost is self-explanatory in the case of interest on loans [11]. Selling assets also generates costs, such as losses when assets are sold at less than optimal price, or future income loss due to the sale of income-generating assets (like land or livestock). Thus, we say that households incur "hardship financing" when they are exposed to a less stable or worsened financial state brought about by additional costs/losses due to borrowing or selling assets. This definition follows Kruk et al. [5], with the notable modification that we only consider borrowing with interest instead of any borrowing. Our adjustment is in agreement with previous findings [12] and with our investigations that confirmed that borrowing from family/friends for healthcare purposes is indeed mostly interest-free.

Many of the previous publications regarding the financing sources for out-of-pocket payments for healthcare in developing countries, and in India, are related to financing of care for specific diseases [4,13-19] and mostly based on small-scale surveys. Some studies look at specific population segments [9,20], others used data available on a whole country level [5,8,10,21]. Kruk et al. [5], whom we follow in the definition of "hardship financing", looked at nationally representative household surveys of 40 low- and middle-income countries, whereas we look at rural (and largely tribal) poor in three districts of Orissa, one of the poorest states in India. By focusing on this target population, we examine hardship financing of out-of-pocket payments for healthcare expenditures among the most vulnerable segment of society in India. Our goal is to identify the parameters affecting households' risk to resort to hardship financing.

2. Methods

2.1. Setting and Sampling

We used data from a household survey undertaken early in 2009 in the rural areas of Kalahandi, Khorda, and Malkangiri districts of the state of Orissa. Orissa, the eleventh largest state of India by population (41,947,358) with 83% of population being rural [22,23], is located on the Bay of Bengal at the east coast of India. The average monthly per capita consumer expenditure (MPCE) of INR459 (PPP$30.6) for rural Orissa, is the lowest of all states [24]. The household survey questionnaire was translated into Oriya (the local language), back translated for verification, and pre-tested among 80 households in the area. Surveyors who spoke local dialects fluently conducted the survey.

We followed a three-stage sampling procedure. (i) The sites in Orissa were selected due to a relationship with 11 NGOs[1] that invited the research team to conduct a baseline study (prior to launching a development project among their members). (ii) Within each district, villages were selected randomly from among those selected by the NGOs for the development project (27 villages in Kalahandi, 22 in Khorda, 31 in Malkangiri). (iii) Stage three entailed random sampling of two equal sub-cohorts in each village: 'member households' and 'non-member households' (comparator group). Member households (i.e. households that included at least one person who was a member of a Self-Help Group (SHG[2]) linked to one of the respective NGOs) were selected randomly out of the membership list. Non-member households were sampled randomly with the use of line sampling (from the centre of the village 4 lines were drawn in the four winds directions, "the four winds technique") [25]. We interviewed a total of 5,383 households representing 25,606 individuals (with a similar number of member and non-member households in every village, totalling 2,688 member and 2,695 non-member households and with a similar number of households from each district, totalling 1820 households from Kalahandi, 1763 households from Khorda and 1800 households from Malkangiri). 100% of the sample interviewed was rural.

At the time of the rollout of the survey there was no local ethics committee in place in Orissa, India. We however held a two-day workshop in preparation of the study in which we discussed the ethical aspects of the study with scholars and senior scholars from India. Informed consent of the respondents was obtained at the beginning of the interviews and we kept participants' names confidential in data recording and analysis.

2.2. Data

The household survey questionnaire included questions on socioeconomic status: education of household head, occupation of household head, source of drinking water, toilet facility and caste. Under the Constitution of India, the government has "scheduled" certain backward Indian classes or groups [hence Scheduled Castes [26] or Scheduled Tribes [27], and "Other backward castes"], with the view to promoting their welfare. Scheduled Tribes (Tribals or Adivasis) are mostly not Hindu and thus out of the caste system and are considered the most disadvantaged economically. Scheduled Castes (Dalits and those sometimes labelled "Untouchable") are considered at the bottom of caste hierarchy. The list of Other Backward Castes is quite dynamic and changes from time to time in many states. All other castes are described here as General Caste.

For household income, we followed the method adopted by the Indian National Sample Survey Organization to obtain a proxy (monthly per capita consumer expenditure) through questions on many items of household expenditure (expenditures on food, clothing, fuel, etc.) [24]. In our study, unlike the National Sample Survey Organization, we did not include health expenditure, because we seek to identify patterns of financing of healthcare [6,8]. We label this proxy for socioeconomic status as "income-proxy".

We also developed an asset-index as proxy for socioeconomic status by performing a principal component analysis (PCA) on various aspects of household assets, following the guidelines of Vyas and Kumaranayake [28]. PCA is a statistical technique used for data reduction. We included the following variables: house type, source of lighting, way of cooking, land ownership, various consumer durables (radio, motor cycle, telephone, etc.), possession of animals (cattle, sheep, chickens, etc.). Size of land and possession of animals were included as continuous variables, the other variables as binary (yes/no) variables. We then used the factor scores of each of the variables from the first principal component as weights and computed a total for each household: the household's socioeconomic score. Characteristic of this score is that it has a mean equal to zero and a standard deviation equal to one; the higher the score, the higher the implied socioeconomic status or wealth of that household. As we deal in this paper with health-related issues, source of drinking water and toilet facility were not included in the PCA given their possible direct relation with health status [28,29].

Besides indicators of socioeconomic status, the household survey questionnaire included questions on healthcare utilization and cost. The households were asked whether they had incurred expenditures for outpatient care, hospital admittances and maternity-related care in the year preceding the survey. Hospital admittances reflected cases with inpatient stay exceeding 24 hours. Stays in hospital of less than 24 hours were counted under outpatient care, together with consultations with a healthcare practitioner, and payment for medicines or tests in an outpatient setting. Maternity-related utilization included delivery and pre- and post-natal care. Respondents were asked to estimate total direct medical expenditures of the household in the year preceding the survey, as well as the expenditures for hospital admittances in the household in the year preceding the survey. More detailed information on outpatient care utilization and cost was queried for one month preceding the survey. Chronic illness in the household was identified by a set of questions related to symptoms, length of illness and regular medicine use.

We asked households also what hospital they would go to in case of a hospitalization of more than 24 hours, what kind of hospital this is, and the distance (travel time in minutes) to this hospital. Similar questions were asked related to the practitioner for outpatient care.

Households that reported healthcare costs for hospitalizations, outpatient care, or maternity-related care during the year preceding the survey were asked how they financed each type of these cost. Sources of financing included using current income, money received as gift, savings, money obtained from selling assets, money obtained through borrowing (borrowing options included relatives, friends/neighbours, bank, moneylender, or microfinance e.g. local microfinance institution or SHG), health insurance, and other sources. Households could report as many sources of financing as relevant. With respect to borrowing we also queried how much was borrowed from each of these sources to pay for healthcare costs. In this paper we ignore three sources since they turned out to be negligible (e.g. 1.4% of households with any health expenditure reported gifts, 0.02% reported health insurance and 0.7% reported "other").

We categorized a combination of financing sources as hardship financing: selling assets or borrowing money with interest from bank, microfinance or moneylender. If a household had reported using at least one of these financing sources, this household was categorized as having had hardship financing. Households that reported using only current income and/or savings and/or borrowing from relatives or friends/neighbours were defined as having had no hardship financing.

2.3. Analysis

We investigated factors influencing the risk of households to need hardship financing when paying for healthcare costs with the use of a multivariate analysis. We applied a logistic regression (logit model) as the outcome variable is a binary variable (yes/no hardship financing). Only households that had healthcare costs in the year preceding the survey were included in the regression. The explanatory variables were included in the model in a stepwise inclusion procedure

Data is analyzed using STATA version 11. The unit of analysis is the household, reflecting the fact that in rural low-income countries, many decisions on paying for healthcare are taken at that level rather than by individuals [30].

Statistical significance of difference has been shown at levels of 10%, 5% and 0.1% throughout the paper. When ANOVA is used we show significance with *, ** and *** respectively; when Pearson Chi-square is used we show significance with†, †† and††† respectively. In case of the logistic regression statistical significance of the coefficient (Z-test) is shown at levels of 5%, 1% and 0.1% with *, ** and *** respectively.

All amounts, reported in Indian Rupee (INR) during the survey, were converted into international dollars (Purchasing Power Parity, PPP$) using the exchange rate of PPP$1 = INR 16.389 for 2009 [31].

3. Results

3.1. Socioeconomic profile

The socioeconomic profile of the sampled population is summarized in Table 1. The majority of the studied population is from Scheduled Caste or Tribe. The majority of the household heads have no or very little education and work as daily wage labourers or are self-employed in agriculture. The income of our sampled population in Orissa was on average below the extreme poverty anchor of PPP$1.08 per person and day (defined by the World Bank in 1993, equalling PPP$1.71 p.p.p.d. when adjusted to the survey year 2009 and to India) [32,33]. Most households have no toilet and get drinking water from a shared tap in the village or hand pump/well. The households consist on average of 4.8 persons of which 8% are infants (0-4 years old) and 8% are elderly (60 years and older).

The socioeconomic status indicators from the National Sample Survey Organization for rural Orissa show similar patterns as our aggregated total population (table 1): income-proxy PPP$ 28.9 p.p.p.m., household size 4.6 persons) [24].

Table 1 Demographics & socioeconomic status

	Mean (± SE)[a]
Income-proxy p.p.p.m (PPP$)[b]	32.41 (± 0.29)*****
Asset-index[c]	0.00 (± 0.03)*****
Household size	4.76 (± 0.02)*****
Ratio infants (0-4) in household	0.082 (± 0.002)****
Ratio elderly (60 and older) in household	0.075 (± 0.002)****
	% of total
Caste[d]	
Scheduled Tribe	30.0
Scheduled Caste	22.3
Other Backward Caste	31.3
General Caste	16.5
Education level household head	
No education	51.4
Class 1-5	22.2
Class 6-10	23.8
Class 11 and higher	2.7
Occupation household head	
Self-employed agriculture	38.7
Self-employed business/trade	16.1
Regular Salaried employee	4.6
Daily wage labourer	30.8
Not working	9.9
Source of drinking water	
Own tap	9.9
Shared tap	53.9
Hand-pump/well	36.2
Toilet facility	
Own flush toilet	4.4
Own pit toilet	4.9
Shared toilet	1.0
No toilet	89.7

[a] SE = Standard Error.
[b] Income is proxied as monthly per capita consumer expenditure through questions on many items of household expenditure and expressed in Purchasing Power Parity International Dollar.
[c] Asset-index is a proxy for socioeconomic status based on various aspects of household assets. The index is calculated using a principal component analysis (PCA).
[d] Caste is a proxy for socioeconomic status in India. Scheduled Castes (Dalits and those sometimes labelled "untouchable") are considered at the bottom of caste hierarchy. The list of Other Backward Castes is quite dynamic and changes from time to time in many states. All other castes are described here as General Caste.

3.2. Morbidity, healthcare availability, utilization and cost

Information on morbidity, availability of healthcare, utilization of healthcare and healthcare expenditures of the sampled population are summarized in Table 2.

Around 85% of the sampled households had health expenditures in the year preceding the survey, and almost 24% of households had to meet hospitalization costs in the same period. Around 10% of the sampled households have a chronically ill person in the household.

Average health expenditures represented about 9% of the average income-proxy for the sampled population (income-proxy p.p.p.m. and household size table 1 total health expenditure for the household last year table 2).

Households usually go to a public facility for hospitalizations of more than 24 hours. In about half of the cases they go to a public facility for outpatient care. To go to the facility where they would go to for a hospitalization takes a little bit more than 50 minutes travel time; the facility for outpatient care is on average 30 minutes away from their homes.

In Additional Files 1 and 2 the same information of Table 1 and 2 is shown separate for the member and non-member sub-cohorts (defined in the methods section). The difference between SHG members and non-members

Table 2 Morbidity, healthcare availability, utilization and cost in the sampled population

	Mean (± SE)[a]
Total health expenditure last year for household (PPP$)[b]	167.34 (± 5.14)
Distance to preferred hospital (in minutes)	52.48 (± 0.54)
Distance to preferred primary care practitioner (in minutes)	30.40 (± 0.40)
	% of total
Household with chronic ill person	10.5
Household with hospitalization costs last year	23.5
Household with outpatient care costs last year	83.8
Household with maternity costs last year	14.4
Household with any healthcare costs last year	85.1
Hospital household usually goes to	
Private	6.3
Public	93.7
Preferred primary care practitioner household usually goes to	
Traditional healer	36.6
Government facility	50.4
Unqualified private doctor (non-MBBS)[c]	7.6
AYUSH practitioner[d]	3.2
Qualified private doctor/specialist (MBBS)	2.2

[a] SE = Standard Error.
[b] Total health expenditure last year for household expressed in Purchasing Power Parity International Dollar.
[c] Unqualified private doctor (non-MBBS) is a doctor practicing allopathic medicine without having a medical degree (Medical Bachelor and Bachelor of Surgery).
[d] AYUSH is the aggregate of all qualified systems of traditional medicines in India: Ayurveda, Yoga and Naturopathy, Unani, Siddha and Homeopathy.

in morbidity, healthcare utilization and cost is not significant for most indicators. The difference in socioeconomic profile between the member and non-member cohorts seems to be significant, pointing to a higher socioeconomic status for SHG members. However, for the indicators that are significantly different, this difference is rather small and probably immaterial. Therefore we aggregated the two sub-cohorts for the descriptive statistics, but included the membership variable in the regression analysis.

3.3. Healthcare financing

We asked respondents how they financed their healthcare costs (Figure 1). The majority of the households reported to have used at least (some) of their current income and savings to pay for their health expenditures. However, the multiplicity of sources shows that households were often unable to fund all their health expenditures from their current income and savings alone.

Households selling assets or borrowing money with interest in order to finance their healthcare were defined as households with hardship financing. Households that were able to finance their healthcare costs solely from current income, savings and/or borrowing without interest (from relatives or friends/neighbours) are defined as households with no hardship financing. Figure 2 shows the shares of households paying healthcare costs with hardship financing versus households that did not have to use hardship financing.

Overall, about 25% of the households (with any healthcare cost) had hardship financing during the year preceding the survey. Among households that experienced a hospitalization this percentage is much higher, nearly 40% had hardship financing. Quite unexpectedly, 23% of household that incurred outpatient costs also reported that they had to use hardship financing sources to pay for this outpatient care, as well as 25% of the households that had a maternity case in the reference period.

3.4. Parameters influencing the risk of hardship financing

We explored with the use of a logistic regression the factors that could influence the risk of households to need hardship financing when paying for healthcare costs (Table 3).

Socioeconomic and demographic parameters

We found that, whereas the logarithm of the income-proxy was not a significant predictor of hardship financing, the asset-index was a highly significant and negative predictor (i.e. households with a lower asset-index have a higher propensity to have hardship financing). The education of the household head did not influence the probability to have hardship financing while his occupation did; households where the household head is self-employed in

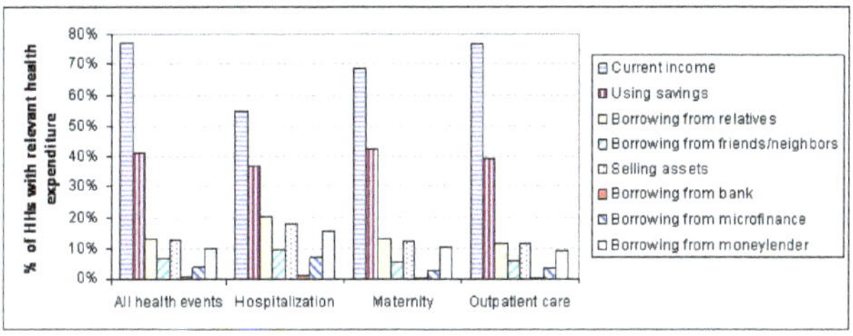

Figure 1 Healthcare financing.

agriculture, self-employed in business, a daily wage labourer, or does not work due to any reason all have a significant higher likelihood to have hardship financing than households where the household head is a regular salaried employee. Caste, household size, the ratio of infants or the ratio of elderly in the household did not have a significant impact on hardship financing.

The minority (10%) of households with a better source of water are less likely to have hardship financing. The type of toilet used was not a significant explanatory variable.

Morbidity parameters & health expenditures

The logarithm of the total health expenditures during the year preceding the survey is a significant and positive predictor of hardship financing. Interestingly, having a chronically ill person in the household, or having experienced one or more events of hospitalization in the year preceding the survey are both significant independent predictors even after the overall health expenditures has been taken into account in the regression analysis.

3.5. Impact of SHG membership on hardship financing

The logistic regression (table 3) revealed that households where someone is a member of an SHG have a higher propensity to have hardship financing. This we found somewhat unexpected as we did not observe a big difference between the member and non-member sub-cohorts in demographics, socioeconomic status, morbidity, healthcare utilization and costs. Also the direction of the influence is somewhat unexpected. When looking at the demographics, SHG member households have a slightly higher asset-index, have more household heads that are salaried employees and more often have their own tap than non-member households (i.e. less poor households). And, from the logistic regression (table 3) it can be seen that, as expected, less poor households are less likely to have hardship financing. But, when controlled for these variables in the regression itself, it seems that SHG members are more likely to have hardship financing.

When looking at the financing sources used by members and non-members, we found that SHG members rely significantly more often on microfinance as a source of borrowing than non-members when paying for all health expenditures, hospital expenditures, or outpatient expenditures (4.4% vs. 2.3%, $p < .001$; 8.5% vs. 4.7%, $p < 0.01$; 3.7% vs. 2.1%, $p < .01$ respectively, Chi2). Non-members

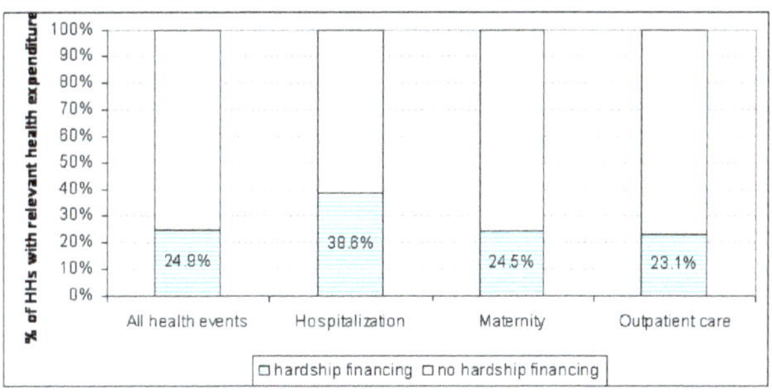

Figure 2 Hardship financing.

Table 3 Factors that influence the risk of hardship financing for households with healthcare costs (logistic regression)

	Coefficient	95% Confidence interval	
Socioeconomic and demographic parameters			
Log income-proxy[a]	0.1197	-0.0694	0.3089
Asset-index[b]	-0.1176***	-0.1698	-0.0655
Employment household head			
Salaried employee	*Reference*		
Self-employed in agriculture	0.8420**	0.3307	1.3533
Self-employed in business/trade	0.7521**	0.2176	1.2866
Daily wage labourer	0.9204**	0.4005	1.4404
Not working	0.7824**	0.2145	1.3503
Education household head			
No education	*Reference*		
Class 1-5	-0.0831	-0.2991	0.1329
Class 6-10	-0.1719	-0.3930	0.0492
Class 11 and higher	-0.0340	-0.6023	0.5343
Caste[c]			
Scheduled Caste	-0.1293	-0.4347	0.1761
Scheduled Tribe	0.2173	-0.0632	0.4978
Other Backward Caste	-0.1570	-0.4255	0.1116
General Caste	*Reference*		
Household size	0.0370***	-0.0135	0.0876
Ratio infants (0-4) in household	0.2015	-0.4490	0.8520
Ratio elderly (60+) in household	0.1851	-0.3583	0.7284
Source of water			
Own tap	*Reference*		
Shared tap	0.4873**	0.1733	0.8013
Hand pump/Well	0.3540*	0.0286	0.6794
Type of toilet			
Own flush toilet	*Reference*		
Own pit toilet	0.0556	-0.5192	0.6305
Shared toilet	0.7037	-0.2623	1.6697
No toilet	-0.0607	-0.4942	0.3728
Morbidity parameters and health expenditures			
Log health expenditures last year	0.7232***	0.6365	0.8099
Chronic illness in household			
No chronic ill	*Reference*		
Chronic ill	0.3779**	0.1301	0.6257
Hospitalization in household last year			
No hospitalization	*Reference*		
Hospitalization	0.7225***	0.5335	0.9116
SHG membership in household			
No SHG member	*Reference*		
SHG member[d]	0.2184**	0.0536	0.3833
Location of residence			
Khorda district	*Reference*		
Kalahandi district	1.3776***	1.1376	1.6176
Malkangiri district	0.1739	-0.0947	0.4424
Constant	-9.5496***	-11.1226	-7.9766
N	4121		
Likelihood ratio test:			
LR chi2(27)	1025.76		

Table 3 Factors that influence the risk of hardship financing for households with healthcare costs (logistic regression) *(Continued)*

Prob > chi2	0.00
Pearson goodness-of-fit test:	
Pearson chi2(4091)	3930.87
Prob > chi2	0.96

*** Significance of coefficient p < 0.05 (Z-test)

*** Significance of coefficient p < 0.01 (Z-test)

*** Significance of coefficient p < 0.001 (Z-test)

[a] Income is proxied as monthly per capita consumer expenditure through questions on many items of household expenditure and expressed in Purchasing Power Parity International Dollar.

[b] Asset-index is a proxy for socioeconomic status based on various aspects of household assets. The index is calculated using a principal component analysis (PCA).

[c] Caste is a proxy for socioeconomic status in India. Scheduled Castes (Dalits and those sometimes labelled "untouchable") are considered at the bottom of caste hierarchy. The list of Other Backward Castes is quite dynamic and changes from time to time in many states. All other castes are described here as General Caste.

[d] A household was defined as SHG member if at least one person in the household was a member of a Self-Help Group (SHG) linked to one of the related NGOs.

on the other hand make more frequently use of their savings in order to pay for hospital expenditures than members (23.8% vs. 17.0%, p < .01, Chi2).

3.6. Impact of location on hardship financing

When controlled for all features of individual households as variables included in the logistic regression, still the district in which a household resides remains a major predictor of the likelihood to have hardship financing (table 3). Therefore we explored this further. Figure 3 shows the difference in hardship financing between the districts.

By using a step-by-step inclusion procedure for the different variables in the regression, we found that the healthcare costs explained the difference in hardship financing between households in Malkangiri and Khorda districts. No other variable had this effect. The difference between Kalahandi on the one hand and Khorda and Malkangiri on the other hand remained unexplained with the current set of variables.

In the course of the examination we also checked other variables (e.g. preferred type of hospital, preferred practitioner for outpatient care, and distance (in minutes of travel time) to both preferred hospital and preferred outpatient practitioner) which were eliminated from the model as they did not proof to be statistically significant and weakened the overall model.

In order to find an explanation for the difference across the districts, we looked at alternative morbidity-related parameters. From our household survey we also have information on illness episodes and related costs for last month that cannot be annualized at the level of the single household. Therefore these parameters can serve to estimate morbidity of the district, but cannot be included in the regression analysis (Table 4).

In both Kalahandi and Khorda around 62% of the households reported an illness last month and around 60% had outpatient treatment (in the form of consultation, medicines and/or tests) for that illness. In Malkangiri this percentage is lower: 51% of the households reported an illness last month and 49% had some form of outpatient treatment for that illness. The average cost of the outpatient treatment is the highest in Khorda (PPP$71.74), a bit lower in Kalahandi (PPP$56.65) and much lower in Malkangiri (PPP$34.78).

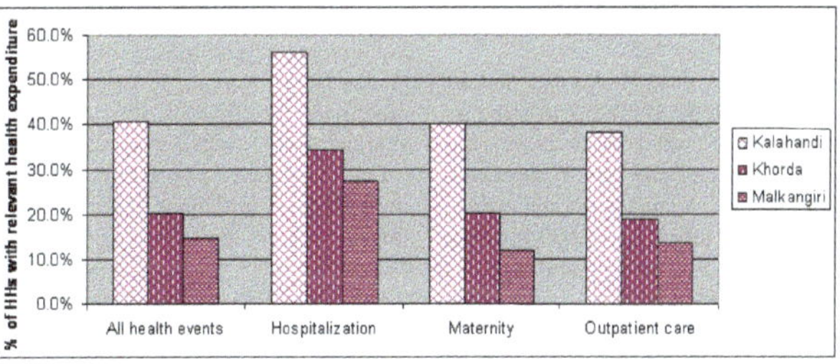

Figure 3 Hardship financing in the three districts.

Table 4 Additional explanatory variables across the three districts.

Parameter	Kalahandi	Khorda	Malkangiri
% of sampled household that reported illness last month	62.3%	61.6%	51.3%[†††] [d]
% of sampled household that had outpatient treatment last month	60.7%	59.8%	49.1%[†††] [d]
Outpatient cost of household that reported illness last month (± SE) (PPP$)[a]	56.65 (± 2.21)	71.74 (± 3.39)	34.78 (± 1.77) ***[e]
Income-proxy p.p.p.m. (± SE) (PPP$)[b]	29.94 (± 0.48)	36.16 (± 0.54)	31.35 (± 0.46) ***[b)]
Asset-index (± SE)[c]	-0.70 (± 0.04)	1.36 (± 0.06)	-0.62 (± 0.05) ***[f]
% of household with healthcare expenditures that reported borrowing from relatives and/or friends	15.6%	23.7%	14.2%[†††] [g]

*** Significance of overall difference across the three districts p< 0.001 (ANOVA)

††† Significance of overall difference across the three districts p< 0.001 (Pearson Chi-square)

[a] Average outpatient costs ± Standard Error, expressed in Purchasing Power Parity International Dollar.

[b] Income is proxied as monthly per capita consumer expenditure through questions on many items of household expenditure and expressed in Purchasing Power Parity International Dollar.

[c] Asset-index is a proxy for socioeconomic status based on various aspects of household assets. The index is calculated using a principal component analysis (PCA). SE = Standard Error

[d] The difference between Kalahandi and Khorda is not significant for both indicators, p = .687 and p = .593 respectively Chi2

[e] For each of the three districts the average cost is significantly different from any other district, p < .001 ANOVA

[f] The difference in average asset-index between Kalahandi and Malkangiri is not significant (p = .163 ANOVA)

[g] The difference in share between Kalahandi and Malkangiri is not significant, p = .282 Chi2

Although the parameters of the socioeconomic status of individual households were included in the regression, we wondered whether the average socioeconomic status of the district is associated with the risk of hardship financing. Therefore we also show the average socioeconomic status (income-proxy and asset-index) for each of the three districts in table 4. We found that the sampled population in Khorda is on average wealthier than the other two districts which are similar to each other.

Finally we examined whether the access of households to a social network of family and/or friends that can provide interest-free loans is different in the three districts. We checked this through the share of households with health expenditures that borrowed from family and/or friends (table 4). We found that households in Khorda had a better access to such a social network than households in Kalahandi and Malkangiri. It is interesting to note that a higher average asset-index is positively associated with higher interest-free borrowing from family/friends.

4. Discussion

In this study we found that many households experienced hardship financing. We defined hardship financing as being exposed to a less stable or worsened financial state brought about by additional costs/losses due to borrowing or selling assets. Based on the information in our household survey we cannot quantify losses due to selling assets. However, using the amounts borrowed from different sources as reported in our household survey and assuming a standard period of 12 months for all loans, an equal monthly repayment regime, and the following interest rates per annum (48% - moneylenders, 24% - microfinance, 12.5% - banks [12,34]), we can estimate the additional cost of the interest payment on the loans. Households that borrowed with interest from a bank, moneylender or microfinance paid, under the above assumptions, a mean interest amount of PPP$64. This adds almost 24% to their healthcare costs, and represents on average nearly 5% of overall annual household expenditure excluding health expenditure. Unlike common economic theory that borrowing or selling assets would have immediate welfare in the sense that the ill person could be treated, that welfare gain comes at a cost of welfare loss that extends over a much longer period of time. The added welfare comes at varying prices, which reflects not the value of the additional consumption (in this case the cost of care) but the varying cost of financing, which is more expensive for those that resort to moneylenders than those that can resort to cheaper sources of borrowing or do not have to borrow at all.

Hardship financing occurs not only when facing the high cost of inpatient care (nearly 40%) but also outpatient care (23%). This finding is in line with a previous study where it was found that the aggregated costs of outpatient care can exceed those of inpatient care among low-income households in India [35]. Interestingly our results reveal that maternity-related expenditures also cause hardship financing for a quarter of the households, although these events are known in advance and theoretically the household could save money and prepare for them. When considering the entire target population, the impact of hardship financing of outpatient care can be considered more severe than of inpatient care since 84% of the sampled households reported expenses due to outpatient care and only 24% had expenses due to inpatient care. Berman et al. [36] have reached a similar conclusion using a different methodology. These authors compared the number of households below poverty line before and after healthcare payment as a definition of impoverishment and found that outpatient care was more impoverishing than inpatient care for households in India.

Peters [37] reported that 40% of hospitalized patients (all-India average) had to sell assets or borrow money to pay for hospital costs. Duggal [38] found that among the poorest quintile in India, this percentage was 50%. One would expect our result for the rural poor communities of Orissa to be similar to the percentage found for the lowest quintile. The discrepancy however could be due to the difference in definition, as we considered as hardship financing only borrowing with interest. According to these and other results [5] it is reasonable to assume that poorer households have a higher risk to experience hardship financing. We wondered whether this difference still holds within our study-population, all of which is poor. We addressed this issue in our multivariate logistic regression by including two measures for wealth (income-proxy and asset-index). Interestingly we found that whereas a lower asset-index was associated with a higher risk of hardship financing, the association with income-proxy was not significant. This may well reflect the situation that in the informal economy many transactions are not monetized and the possession of assets is a more reliable indicator of socioeconomic status [39]. The negative association between asset-index and hardship financing could be due to asset-rich households for instance having a better chance of accessing social networks that would be more likely to give interest-free loans (non-hardship financing). It cannot be excluded though that the lower asset-index may be a result of, rather than the cause for, hardship financing, as we measure the asset-index after the health event.

Households where the household head is a salaried employee were least likely to need hardship financing compared to households where the head was self-employed in business or in agriculture, was a daily-wage labourer or did not work. As income was included in the regression as a separate parameter, the reason for the correlation with employment cannot be attributed solely to a difference in income. Perhaps the difference is due to having a steady rather than erratic flow of income. This finding would then be in agreement with our hypothesis that hardship financing can sometimes be caused by a time-gap between the inflow of income and outflow of health expenses.

From our logistic regression it turned out, as could be intuitively expected, that health expenditures in the last year were significantly associated with the risk for hardship financing. However, interestingly, having had a chronic illness or hospitalization in the household in the last year were also independent significant indicators for hardship financing. This means that the presence of chronic illness or hospitalization affected the risk of hardship financing in a way which was independent of the related expenses. Both chronic illness and hospitalization generate many indirect costs (loss of income of the chronic ill patient, loss of income of the hospitalized patient and/or caretaker and transportation costs) which could independently aggravate the situation leading to hardship financing. The recurring nature of outpatient expenditures related to a chronic illness could cause depletion of savings and attrition of goodwill of others to give interest-free loans and thus increase the need for hardship financing. In the case of hospitalizations one should note that poor households usually have to pay (some) costs upfront before admission to or treatment in hospital [38]. Therefore the unpredictable timing of hospital care and immediate need for large funds associated with such an event could increase the risk of hardship financing.

SHG membership surprisingly reported increased likelihood to have hardship financing, even though we have seen that SHG members are slightly better off than non-members (Additional File 1) and that better off households need less hardship financing. The explanation for this phenomenon might be that members have their savings tied up in the scheme and can therefore not liquefy those savings when needed. On the other hand, SHG members have an easier access to low-interest loans while non-members cannot easily access microfinance and low-interest loans. Therefore it is possible that SHG members would prefer this low-interest loan over borrowing from relatives/friends who may not be able to spare the money for a long time.

Finally it becomes very clear from the regression that the difference in hardship financing across the three districts could not be fully explained by the many household features included in the model. We found that the district where the household resides has a big significant independent effect on the risk of hardship financing. Using the step-wise regression method we found that when healthcare costs are introduced into the model, the difference in the risk of hardship financing between Malkangiri and Khorda became insignificant. The difference in hardship financing between Kalahandi on the one hand and Khorda and Malkangiri on the other hand remained unexplained with the current set of variables: living in Kalahandi could be associated with increased likelihood of hardship financing, because of higher utilization and costs of outpatient care compared to Malkangiri. In Khorda, both utilization and costs of outpatient care were similar to those observed in Kalahandi, yet the risk of hardship financing was significantly lower. This could be linked to the related finding that average income-proxy and asset-index in Khorda are higher than in Kalahandi (the asset index introduced in the regression takes into account the wealth of the individual household but the average asset index in the district reflects the wealth of the social network). This difference could suggest that households in Khorda have access to richer family/friends (better social network) that can provide more interest-free loans. This assumption gains credibility from the finding that a higher percentage of households in Khorda borrowed from relatives/friends, compared to Kalahandi (table 4).

While this study can play an important role in advancing the notion of hardship financing as a measure of the effectiveness of health financing policy alternative to the catastrophic spending method, there are some limitations to this study. Without adequate data one cannot conclude that the same findings would apply elsewhere. And, as the source of data is interviews with respondents, the regular limitations of self-reporting of incidence of illness and cost of care apply.

5. Conclusions

Our study sheds light on a hitherto understudied dimension of hardship of very poor rural groups occasioned by the need to raise funds to pay for healthcare out-of-pocket. We defined "hardship financing" as borrowing with interest or selling assets. The extra cost due to the interest payable on money borrowed with interest is far from negligible. We estimated the additional costs due to interest on loans to pay for illness-related costs at 24% of the health expenditure, a cost that represented nearly 5% of households' annual overall expenditure. The monetary value of the loss due to selling assets is also not zero, but hard to estimate. The hardship associated with these costs extends well beyond the duration of the health event.

This analysis has shown that hardship financing occurs not only in cases of expensive hospitalizations (40%) but also in many cases of expenditures for outpatient (23%) and maternity care (25%). Taking into account that the frequency of outpatient utilization is much higher, many more people actually face hardship financing due to outpatient care than due to inpatient care.

We have shown that possession of assets and having regular income-flow are predictors of lower expected hardship financing, and better predictors than the income-proxy of the household used in this study. The first parameter indicates the aggregate financial strength of the household in an environment where many economical transactions are not monetary. The second parameter is self-explanatory, as regular income makes it easier to plan future expenses based on stable future income. Interestingly, not only the assets of the households with out-of-pocket healthcare costs were negatively associated with hardship financing, but also the average wealth in the community in which the households resides. This indicates that hardship financing is also influenced by attributes of the social network the household can access; better access to a wealthier social network seems to increase the likelihood of obtaining interest-free loans.

Our study adds a qualitative dimension to understanding health-related financial exposure among rural poor households. Hardship financing is explained not only by how much is spent out-of-pocket on healthcare in nominal terms or relative to income or assets, but also by when the payment occurs, and, as is the case with chronic illness, its frequency and duration. This important finding that rural poor households are subjected to considerable and protracted financial hardship due to the indirect and longer-term deleterious effects of how they cope with out-of-pocket healthcare costs points to the need to develop a policy solution that would limit that exposure both in quantum and in time. We therefore conclude that policy interventions aiming to ensure health-related financial protection would have to demonstrate that they have reduced the frequency and the volume of hardship financing.

Endnotes

1) The 11 grassroots NGOs linked with Madhyam Foundation, Bhubaneswar, Orissa included: (i) in Malkangiri: Parivartan, PUSPAC, SOMKS, SDS, ODC; (ii) in Kalahandi: Mahashakti Foundation, DAPTA, Lok Yojana, Sanginee; and (iii) in Khorda MVPS, DSS.

2) SHGs represent a unique approach to financial intermediation in communities. The approach combines access to low-cost financial services with a process of self-management and development for the SHG members. SHGs are seen to confer many benefits, both economic and social.

Additional material

Additional file 1: Demographics & socioeconomic status disaggregated for members and non-members. This file contains the same information of Table 1 on demographics and socioeconomic status but separate for the member and non-member sub-cohorts (as defined in the methods section).

Additional file 2: Morbidity, healthcare availability, utilization and cost disaggregated for members and non-members. This file contains the same information of Table 2 on morbidity, healthcare availability, utilization and cost but separate for the member and non-member sub-cohorts (as defined in the methods section).

List of abbreviations

INR: Indian Rupee; MPCE: Monthly Per Capita Consumer Expenditures; NGO: Non-Government Organization; PCA: Principal Components Analysis; PPP$: Purchasing Power Parity International Dollar; p.p.p.m: per person per month; SE: Standard Error; SHG: Self-Help Group.

Acknowledgements and funding

The authors gratefully acknowledge funding support from the Netherlands Organization for Scientific Research (NWO), under WOTRO Integrated

Programme grant No. W01.65.309.00. Additional funding for the household survey was obtained from the German Federal Ministry for Economic Cooperation and Development (through a contract between AWO International, Madhyam Foundation Orissa, and the Micro Insurance Academy New Delhi). The authors wish to thank Prof. Frans Rutten (Erasmus University Rotterdam) for reading the manuscript and offering helpful comments, and to Prof. P.R. Sodani (Indian Institute for Health Management Research-IIHMR, Jaipur, India) for his advice and support throughout the project. We benefited from logistical and research support from the Micro Insurance Academy, and from Madhyam Foundation Bhubaneswar, Orissa and its 11 affiliated NGOs (Parivartan, PUSPAC, SOMKS, SDS, ODC, Mahashakti Foundation, DAPTA, Lok Yojana, Sanginee, MVPS, DSS). Last but not least, we acknowledge all the respondents for their participation in the study. The sponsors had no influence or role in study design, in the collection, analysis and interpretation of data; in the writing of the article; and in the decision to submit the article for publication.

Author details
[1]Institute of Health Policy and Management, Erasmus University Rotterdam, P.O. Box 1738, 3000 DR Rotterdam, The Netherlands. [2]Felsenstein Medical Research Center, Tel Aviv University Sackler Faculty of Medicine, Ramat Aviv, Tel Aviv, Israel. [3]Micro Insurance Academy, 246 Sant Nagar, East of Kailash, New Delhi 110065, India.

Authors' contributions
DMD is the lead researcher and responsible for overall project management. EB, DMD and RK are responsible for the study concept and design. EB supervised the fieldwork and was responsible for the data management of the household survey. EB, RK and DMD (in order of contribution) analysed and interpreted the data and drafted the manuscript. All authors read, revised and approved the final version of the manuscript.

Authors' information
This work represents part of the requirements for the PhD thesis of EB at Erasmus University Rotterdam.
DMD, in addition to acting as principal investigator on this grant within his position as hon. Professor at Erasmus University Rotterdam, is also the Chairman of the Micro Insurance Academy.

Competing interests
The authors declare that they have no competing interests.

Received: 12 September 2011 **Accepted:** 27 January 2012
Published: 27 January 2012

References
1. Van Doorslaer E, O'Donnell O, Rannan-Eliya RP, Somanathan A, Adhikari SR, Akkazieva B, Garg CC, Harbianto D, Herrin AN, Huq MN, Ibragimova S, Karan A, Lee T, Leung GM, Lu JR, Ng CW, Pande BR, Racelis R, Tao S, Tin K, Tisayaticom K, Trisnantoro L, Vasavid C, Zhao Y: **Paying out-of-pocket for health care in Asia: Catastrophic and poverty impact.** 2005, EQUITAP Project: Working Paper #2.
2. Ministry of Health and Family Welfare India: **National Health Accounts, India - 2004/2005.** National Health Accounts Cell, Ministry of Health and Family Welfare, Government of India, New Delhi; 2009.
3. Xu K, Evans DB, Kawabata K, Zeramdini R, Klavus J, Murray CJL: **Household catastrophic health expenditure: A multicountry analysis.** *The Lancet* 2003, **362(9378)**:111-117.
4. Russell S: **The economic burden of illness for households in developing countries: A review of studies focusing on malaria, tuberculosis, and human immunodeficiency virus/acquired immunodeficiency syndrome.** *Am J Trop Med Hyg* 2004, **71(Suppl 2)**:147-55.
5. Kruk ME, Goldmann E, Galea S: **Borrowing and selling to pay for health care in low- and middle-income countries.** *Health Aff (Millwood)* 2009, **28(4)**:1056-1066.
6. Wagstaff A: **Measuring financial protection in health 2008.**, Report No. 4554, World Bank, Washington (DC).
7. Morduch J, Rutherford S: **Microfinance: Analytical issues for India.** World Bank; 2003.
8. Flores G, Krishnakumar J, O'Donnell O, van Doorslaer E: **Coping with health-care costs: implications for the measurement of catastrophic expenditures and poverty.** *Health Econ* 2008, **17(12)**:1393-1412.
9. Asfaw A, Lamanna F, Klasen S: **Gender gap in parents' financing strategy for hospitalization of their children: Evidence from India.** *Health Econ* 2010, **19(3)**:265-79.
10. Steinhardt LC, Waters H, Rao KD, Naeem AJ, Hansen P, Peters DH: **The effect of wealth status on care seeking and health expenditures in Afghanistan.** *Health Policy Plan* 2009, **24(1)**:1-17.
11. Krishna A: **Escaping poverty and becoming poor: Who gains, who loses, and why?** *World Dev* 2004, **32(1)**:121-136.
12. Kochar A: **An empirical investigation of rationing constraints in rural credit markets in India.** *J Dev Econ* 1997, **53(2)**:339-371.
13. Adhikari SR, Maskay NM, Sharma BP: **Paying for hospital-based care of Kala-azar in Nepal: Assessing catastrophic, impoverishment and economic consequences.** *Health Policy Plan* 2009, **24(2)**:129-39.
14. Khun S, Manderson L: **Poverty, user fees and ability to pay for health care for children with suspected dengue in rural Cambodia.** *International Journal for Equity in Health* 2008, **7(1)**:10.
15. Van Damme W, Van Leemput L, Por I, Hardeman W, Meessen B: **Out-of-pocket health expenditure and debt in poor households: Evidence from Cambodia.** *Trop Med Int Health* 2004, **9(2)**:273-80.
16. Wyss K, Hutton G, N'Diekhor Y: **Costs attributable to AIDS at household level in Chad.** *AIDS Care* 2004, **16(7)**:808-16.
17. Mock CN, Gloyd S, Adjei S, Acheampong F, Gish O: **Economic consequences of injury and resulting family coping strategies in Ghana.** *Accident Analysis & Prevention* 2003, **35(1)**:81-90.
18. Nahar S, Costello A: **The hidden cost of 'free' maternity care in Dhaka, Bangladesh.** *Health Policy Plan* 1998, **13(4)**:417-22.
19. Sauerborn R, Adams A, Hien M: **Household strategies to cope with the economic costs of illness.** *Soc Sci Med* 1996, **43(3)**:291-301.
20. Bonu S, Rani M, Peters DH, Jha P, Nguyen SN: **Does use of tobacco or alcohol contribute to impoverishment from hospitalization costs in India?** *Health Policy Plan* 2005, **20(1)**:41-9.
21. Leive A, Xu K: **Coping with out-of-pocket health payments: Empirical evidence from 15 African countries.** *Bulletin of the World Health Organization* 2008, **86(11)**:849-56.
22. Census of India: **Provisional Population Totals Paper 1 of 2011 India.** Office of the Registrar General & Census Commissioner, India; 2011.
23. Census of India: **Provisional Population Totals Paper 2 of 2011 India.** Office of the Registrar General & Census Commissioner, India; 2011.
24. National Sample Survey Organization: **Household Consumer Expenditure in India, 2006-07.** 2008, Report No. 527, National Sample Survey Organization, Ministry of Statistics and Programme Implementation, Government of India, New Delhi.
25. Som RK: *Practical sampling techniques.* 2 edition. New York: Marcel Dekker; 1996.
26. **The constitution (scheduled castes) order, 1950 (C.O.19), Ministry of Law India.** [http://lawmin.nic.in/ld/subord/rule3a.htm].
27. **The constitution (scheduled tribes) order, 1950 (C.O.22), Ministry of Law India.** [http://lawmin.nic.in/ld/subord/rule9a.htm].
28. Vyas S, Kumaranayake L: **Constructing socio-economic status indices: How to use principal components analysis.** *Health Policy Plan* 2006, **21(6)**:459-468.
29. Dunteman GH, Lewis-Beck MS: **Principal Components Analysis.** Sage Publications, Newbury Park, California; 1989.
30. Sauerborn R, Ibrango I, Nougtara A, Borchert M, Hien M, Benzler J, Koob E, Diesfeld HJ: **The economic costs of illness for rural households in Burkina Faso.** *Trop Med Parasitol* 1995, **46(1)**:54-60.
31. **World Economic Outlook Database.** [http://www.imf.org/external/pubs/ft/weo/2009/01/weodata/index.aspx].
32. **OECD statistics consumer price indices India.** [http://stats.oecd.org/mei/default.asp?lang=e&subject=8&country=IND].
33. Sillers D: **National and international poverty lines: An overview.** 2005, USAID.
34. Basu P: *Improving access to finance for India's rural poor:* Washington, D.C.: The World Bank; 2006.
35. Dror DM, van Putten-Rademaker O, Koren R: **Cost of illness: Evidence from a study in five resource-poor locations in India.** *Indian J Med Res* 2008, **127(4)**:347-361.
36. Berman PA, Ahuja R, Bhandari L: **The impoverishing effect of healthcare payments in India: New methodology and findings.** *Economic and Political Weekly* 2010, **45(16)**:65-71.

37. Peters DH, Yazbeck AS, Sharma RP, Ramana GNV, Pritchett LH, Wagstaff A: *Better health systems for India's poor: Findings, analysis and options* Washington (DC): World Bank; 2002.
38. Duggal R: **Financing healthcare in India - Prospects for health insurance.** *Express Healthcare Management* 2004, (1st to 15th March).
39. Moser C, Felton A: **The construction of an asset index measuring asset accumulation in Ecuador.** 2007, CPRC Working Paper #87, Chronic Poverty Research Centre, Washington DC.

Pre-publication history

The pre-publication history for this paper can be accessed here: http://www.biomedcentral.com/1472-6963/12/23/prepub

doi:10.1186/1472-6963-12-23

Cite this article as: Binnendijk *et al.*: **Hardship financing of healthcare among rural poor in Orissa, India.** *BMC Health Services Research* 2012 12:23.

Part 2

Methods

Chapter 7

Illness Mapping: A Time and Cost Effective Method to Estimate Health Care Data Needed to Establish Community-based Health Insurance*

Main Messages

- This chapter describes a cheaper and faster method to derive quantitative estimates of health care events through qualitative approaches.
- Intervention involved small group discussions with 18 women's and 17 men's groups, and a household survey conducted in 50 villages with 1,000 randomly selected households (6,656 individuals).
- The IM method of sourcing local data represented a reduction of 59% in work-days, implying lesser time and costs when compared to a household survey.

Focus Points

- Household surveys can be replaced by an "Illness Mapping (IM)" technique which could source local data at acceptably accurate levels, and much faster and cheaper than the survey method.

---

*This chapter is reproduced from *BMC Medical Research Methodology* (2012), **12**, 153, Open Access, available at https://www.researchgate.net/publication/232221834_Illness_Mapping_A_time_and_cost_effective_method_to_estimate_healthcare_data_needed_to_establish_community-based_health_insurance.

- It is possible to accumulate estimates of morbidity and health care utilization for the entire village by a judicious use of the knowledge of villagers that is readily available at no cost.
- IM can be extracted from interactions with either gender of respondents, as there is no statistical difference between the estimates given by men's and women's groups; it is easier to assemble groups of women than men.
- There was a very good agreement between the two methods on the incidence of deliveries, and good agreement on the overall prevalence of illnesses (in the last one month) and on the prevalence of acute and chronic illnesses, as well as on the share of deliveries in hospitals.
- For incidence of hospitalizations, the IM provided a lower estimate (1.1%) than the HHS (2.6%).

Structured Abstract

Introduction

Community-based health insurance (CBHI) schemes run on small budgets, and it is expensive and time-consuming to obtain relevant information on local morbidity, health care utilization and other information for the design and pricing of a customized insurance package. This chapter seeks to find an alternative to household surveys to derive estimates of health care data needed to establish micro health insurance (MHI). The study was conducted in Gaya District of Bihar state, India.

Method

The intervention comprised of two exercises: the IM and a household survey (HHS). The IM included 18 women's and 17 men's groups. The HHS was conducted in 50 villages with 1,000 randomly selected households (6,656 individuals). The households were selected randomly by applying the "four winds technique", or "line sampling".

For the IM, small group discussions were held in the villages with men and women who were marginally literate and numerate, but nonetheless experts or valid representatives of their village communities. In the HHS, besides other questions, respondents were asked about illness episodes in the household during the month preceding the survey, and on the basis of their replies illnesses were classified into four categories: acute, chronic, accidents and undefined.

To assess the potential of the IM method, the results obtained by this method were compared to those obtained through the household survey on the basis of three parameters which are important for the implementation of MHI: the prevalence of illness for acute and chronic illnesses, the incidence of hospitalization, and the incidence of deliveries, especially hospital deliveries.

Findings

The results of the intervention showed very good agreement between the two methods on the incidence of deliveries, and good agreement on the overall prevalence of illnesses (in the last one month) and on the prevalence of acute and chronic illnesses, as well as on the share of deliveries in hospitals. However, for the incidence of hospitalizations, we obtained a lower estimate from the IM (1.1%) than from the HHS (2.6%). This discrepancy could be attributed to two types of memory effects that can lead to erroneous reporting by respondents: errors of omission (omitting to report an episode entirely) and of telescoping (remembering and reporting an event as having occurred more recently than it actually had).

Box 1: Findings

- Overall prevalence of illness (IM: 25.9% ±3.6; HHS: 31.4%); Good agreement
- Prevalence of acute illnesses (IM: 76.9%; HHS: 69.2%); Good agreement
- Prevalence of chronic illnesses (IM: 20.1%; HHS: 16.6%); Good agreement
- Incidence of deliveries (IM: 3.9% ±0.4; HHS: 3.9%); Very good agreement
- Hospital deliveries (IM: 61.0%.±5.4; HHS: 51.4%); Good agreement
- Hospitalizations (IM: 1.1%.±0.4; HHS: 2.6%); Significant difference

The key advantage of the IM method was that it represented a reduction of 59% in work-days, implying lesser time and costs when compared to a household survey, and could thus replace a household survey for estimating local data on morbidity and health care utilization.

Another finding is that there is no statistical difference between the estimates given by men's and women's groups. IM can, therefore, be extracted from interactions with either gender of respondents, and it is easier to assemble groups of women than men.

Conclusion

The study shows that IM could be used as an alternative to household surveys for faster and cheaper resourcing of essential local data, at acceptably accurate levels. This method can be useful in extracting local data for introducing health insurance among low-income persons as the premium and benefits package needs to be customized to local conditions.

Binnendijk *et al. BMC Medical Research Methodology* 2012, **12**:153
http://www.biomedcentral.com/1471-2288/12/153

BMC
Medical Research Methodology

RESEARCH ARTICLE **Open Access**

Illness Mapping: a time and cost effective method to estimate healthcare data needed to establish community-based health insurance

Erika Binnendijk[1], Meenakshi Gautham[1], Ruth Koren[2] and David M Dror[1,3*]

Abstract

Background: Most healthcare spending in developing countries is private out-of-pocket. One explanation for low penetration of health insurance is that poorer individuals doubt their ability to enforce insurance contracts. Community-based health insurance schemes (CBHI) are a solution, but launching CBHI requires obtaining accurate local data on morbidity, healthcare utilization and other details to inform package design and pricing. We developed the "Illness Mapping" method (IM) for data collection (faster and cheaper than household surveys).

Methods: IM is a modification of two non-interactive consensus group methods (Delphi and Nominal Group Technique) to operate as interactive methods. We elicited estimates from "Experts" in the target community on morbidity and healthcare utilization. Interaction between facilitator and experts became essential to bridge literacy constraints and to reach consensus.

The study was conducted in Gaya District, Bihar (India) during April-June 2010. The intervention included the IM and a household survey (HHS). IM included 18 women's and 17 men's groups. The HHS was conducted in 50 villages with1,000 randomly selected households (6,656 individuals).

Results: We found good agreement between the two methods on overall prevalence of illness (IM: 25.9% ±3.6; HHS: 31.4%) and on prevalence of acute (IM: 76.9%; HHS: 69.2%) and chronic illnesses (IM: 20.1%; HHS: 16.6%). We also found good agreement on incidence of deliveries (IM: 3.9% ±0.4; HHS: 3.9%), and on hospital deliveries (IM: 61.0%. ± 5.4; HHS: 51.4%). For hospitalizations, we obtained a lower estimate from the IM (1.1%) than from the HHS (2.6%). The IM required less time and less person-power than a household survey, which translate into reduced costs.

Conclusions: We have shown that our Illness Mapping method can be carried out at lower financial and human cost for sourcing essential local data, at acceptably accurate levels. In view of the good fit of results obtained, we assume that the method could work elsewhere as well.

Keywords: India, Community based health insurance (CBHI), Micro health insurance, Illness prevalence, Incidence of hospitalization, Illness Mapping

* Correspondence: daviddror@socialre.org
[1]Institute of Health Policy and Management, Erasmus University Rotterdam, P.O. Box 1738, Rotterdam 3000 DR, the Netherlands
[3]Micro Insurance Academy, 52B Okhla Industrial Estate Phase III, New Delhi 110020, India
Full list of author information is available at the end of the article

Background

A large part of health care spending in developing countries is private and out of pocket (OOP). India is typical: 70% of spending is private, of which 86% is OOP [1,2]. Moreover, private insurance rates remain below 5% [3]. The dearth of insurance is surprising, given the high frequency and cost of borrowing from moneylenders even for outpatient care and maternity [4] in addition to inpatient care [4,5], and the inability of rural poor to pay for non-communicable diseases [6] even as the prevalence of NCDs increases in low-income countries [7,8]. One possible explanation for low insurance penetration is that poorer individuals in the informal sector doubt their ability to enforce contracts with insurance companies. A solution to the problem is community-based health insurance schemes (CBHI) [9-12]. These schemes are owned and run locally, at village level [12,13]. One of the hurdles to launching CBHI schemes is obtaining relevant information on local morbidity, healthcare utilization and other information that would inform the design and pricing of a relevant and affordable insurance package. A number of experiments with micro health insurance have relied on household surveys to obtain reliable local actuarial estimates and other information required for package design and pricing [14-16]. Obtaining accurate local data is essential both because the income of CBHI is often limited and because of significant differences across locations in the number and type of illness episodes [17-19]. However, household surveys are both expensive and time consuming. Thus a faster and cheaper method would be instrumental in promoting the expansion of micro health insurance.

Our study is located in Gaya district, Bihar state, India. The main source of data on incidence/prevalence of illnesses and hospitalisations is the Indian National Sample Survey (NSS) [20]. The NSS however provides information only at state level and not at district or block level, which are the more relevant units for CBHI. In addition, the most recent edition of NSS with information on morbidity and healthcare utilization dates to 2004 [20] with an earlier survey in 1995/96 [21]. And, health information sourced from local medical record-keeping does not provide sufficiently accurate location-specific data.

This paper contains a description of a cheaper and faster method to derive quantitative estimates of healthcare events through qualitative approaches [22]. The experiment we conducted is inspired by previous methodologies aiming to achieve similar objectives. For instance, Auray and Fonteneau [23] suggested possible group methods using consensus-building techniques, notably the Delphi and the Nominal Group Technique (NGT), to derive estimates from expert opinions on prevalence of hospitalizations, incidence of illness etc.

In the Delphi method, individual experts that are not in contact with each other first provide their quantitative estimate to a query; then, each expert is informed about other experts' replies, and invited to adjust the value (but each expert does so alone, without interacting with the others); this process can be repeated several iterations until consensus is reached [22,24]. In the NGT, experts that are assembled in the same place at the same time individually write down their views on the topic in question and present one idea to the facilitator which is recorded. There is a group discussion to clarify and evaluate each idea and following this discussion each participant privately ranks each idea. This ranking is tabulated and presented. The group then discusses the overall ranking to reach consensus [22,25,26]. It is noted that while there is some interaction between NGT group members to discuss or clarify ideas, other major group processes, such as idea generation and final rankings, are conducted silently and individually [26]. So, while both the Delphi and NGT are methods to reach consensus, both unfold among *non-interacting groups* (participants do not interact and discuss with each other during the group process) [26,27]. In interacting groups on the other hand, participants are allowed to interact and discuss with each other at each step of the process (generation of information, ideas, views, evaluation and final consensus) [27]. Interacting groups are usually unstructured (participants have complete freedom to think, review and synthesize together); examples are Brainstorming discussions and Focus Group Discussions [28]. Non-interacting groups however, are usually structured (participants receive systematic procedural guidance) [24,26].

Research in the 1960s and 70s compared non-interacting groups with interacting groups [26,27,29,30]. Delphi and NGT have been found superior to interacting groups for finding solutions to problems [26], but when group interactions were structured to enhance exchanges among the participants during thinking, visualizing and estimating, results were better than with unstructured interactions [31,32]. Moreover, Van de Ven and Delbecq [27] found that the most optimal group processes occurred when a structured procedure entailed interactive discussions after the initial exposé of ideas/views. Bouchard [30] found that group-results were enhanced when the groups consisted of carefully selected individuals who had some prior knowledge of each other and some practice of working or being together (where differences that might inhibit group effectiveness were minimized).

Our study entailed a variation of an interactive group technique, inspired by the non-interactive group techniques. We elicited expert opinion in which our experts were members of the target community that knew each other, whose opinions were obtained in a structured, interactive group situation. The purpose of the inquiry has been to derive estimates of healthcare data needed to establish micro health insurance. We call this method "Illness Mapping". With the view to verifying robustness of results of the Illness Mapping method, we compared them to household survey data from the same locations and period. Our working assumption was that if the Illness Mapping delivered useful comparator data in this case, this method could be used elsewhere as an alternative to household surveys for faster and cheaper resourcing of the context-relevant essential data.

Methods

Setting and sampling

The study was conducted in Gaya District of Bihar state, India. Gaya district is subdivided into 24 blocks. We selected 7 contiguous blocks purposively because this is where a local partner Non-governmental Organization (NGO) intended to implement a micro health insurance scheme. The intervention included two exercises: the Illness Mapping and a household survey. Both activities were conducted during April-June 2010.

For the Illness Mapping, we divided the 7 blocks into 3 clusters (northern, middle and southern) and selected 6 villages in each cluster based on distance from the nearest government primary health centre (0–5 kms; 5.1-8 kms; and more than 8 kms). Our total sample included 18 villages, (7 villages in the 0–5 kms category; 6 villages in the 5.1-8 kms category; and 5 villages in the >8 kms category). In consultation with the field partner, we selected a male group and a female group in each village, each with about 10 participants. The groups were gender homogenous to enable participants to speak freely on the given subject. There were 18 women's groups (263 participants) and 17 men's groups (147 participants).

The household survey was conducted in 50 villages across Gaya district, selected randomly (using census list of villages) from all 24 blocks in the district, proportional to the number of villages in each block. Within each village, we interviewed 20 households, selected randomly by applying the "four winds technique", or "line sampling" (selecting households according to a predetermined staggering e.g. every second/third household starting from the centre of the village and progressing in the four cardinal directions) [33]. In total, 1,000 households were interviewed, representing 6,656 individuals.

Verbal informed consent was obtained from respondents of the household survey at the beginning of the interviews, and from participants of the Illness Mapping before the discussions began. 100% of the interviewed sample was rural.

Illness mapping

The Illness Mapping technique is an adaptation of two non-interactive consensus group methods (Delphi process and Nominal Group Technique – NGT) operated in an interactive manner. The adaptation was necessary because it was impossible to apply the Delphi and NGT as is (i.e. sending our experts a questionnaire and/or requesting each to write ideas individually) due to the limited literacy of the population. Rather, interaction between the facilitator and the group members became essential, especially as the option of reaching decisions by vote was discarded, in light of the finding in one of our previous studies in India that rural participants preferred to reach a consensus [34].

Like the Delphi and NGT techniques, Illness Mapping relies on the knowledge of experts. Prior to the selection of the experts, our research team met with key informants in the village [health/development workers such as the Accredited Social Health Activist (ASHA), Aanganwadi Worker (AWW) or Auxiliary Nurse Midwife (ANM), representatives of Self Help Groups, etc.] to get an overview of the village, its size, social segmentation, and a general impression of its socio-economic status. Using this knowledge, we selected our experts by applying the following criteria:

1. They should be living in different parts of the village.
2. They should be sociable, outgoing and interacting frequently with their neighbours, so that they would be knowledgeable about people and events in the village. Not surprisingly, participants with higher interpersonal skills have been found to perform better in group discussions [30].
3. Group members should reflect similar social or income groups.

In the Illness Mapping facilitators (of the same gender as the participants) guided group meetings to enhance recall of the parameters needed for the calculation of the prevalence of illnesses and utilization of health services. Such facilitated recall procedure does not occur either in the Delphi or the NGT, but publications suggested that compared to unstructured interventions, participants recall the relevant parameters better when procedures are structured during the thinking, visualizing and estimating stage of the interaction with the facilitator [31,32]. Considering that people with motivation or training have been reported to perform better in group interactions [30], we motivated our participants by explaining that they were selected for this discussion from the entire village, and that the information they provided would help develop the right kind of health insurance benefits for them and the entire village.

With each group, we first obtained a rough estimate of the number of households in different parts of the village, the rough household size (i.e. number of family members that ate from the same pot), and the total population of the village. Then we asked the number of persons who had been sick over the last one month, and the nature of their illness. We then asked every participant to name, one after the other, all the illnesses they could remember. To facilitate recall, the facilitator prompted periodically by asking about specific illnesses by name, both common and not so common ones. We also enquired about incidence of hospitalizations and deliveries (during the last 12 months) including information whether the delivery occurred at home or in an institute.

Consensus was reached through a structured group discussion of the final tallies, similar to the final round of the NGT. We presented to each group the final tallies of the main illness categories and frequencies of illnesses, hospitalizations and deliveries, and asked for feedback on the illness tallies (presented both as a number and as a percentage of the total village population). Usually participants chose to increase the final cumulative percentage. In the few instances where the group was not able to arrive at a single estimate, we noted the different estimates (usually 2–3 different estimates) and averaged them.

Similar to the Delphi method, our facilitator combined all responses and fed those back to the experts, who then ranked all opinions/solutions to obtain a new "agreed value", which was again combined and distributed. Like in the Delphi, the experts can re-evaluate their ranking and possibly change their original opinions/ solutions [22].

As in NGT, our Illness Mapping process occurs in a meeting. And, like NGT interaction is limited in the first part of the process when each expert gives their response to the facilitator (in NGT this is done in writing). A group discussion follows, to clarify and evaluate responses, and reach consensus (in NGT, unlike our Illness Mapping, before discussion to reach consensus each expert ranks responses separately, and the ranking is tabulated and presented) [22,25].

Data obtained in group discussions were recorded on pre-designed data sheets; a second person, other than the facilitator recorded the responses. Names and frequencies of illnesses[i] were recorded; we classified the illnesses reported as acute, chronic, accidents, and undefined. 18 groups from 14 villages provided 8 or more names of illnesses; only these groups were retained for the analysis of illness types. Hospitalizations and deliveries were counted and presented separately.

Household survey

The household survey questionnaire included questions on general demographics (age, gender, education, economic activity), socio-economic status (queried through questions on many items of household expenditures) and health status of household members. Following the method of the Indian National Sample Survey Organization [35], we consider the monthly per capita consumer expenditure excluding healthcare costs as a proxy for income. Respondents were asked about illness episodes in the household during the month preceding the survey. Using the replies regarding the illness (related to symptoms, length of illness, recurrence, medication etc.), we classified illnesses into four categories: acute, chronic, accidents and undefined. Respondents were asked about hospital admissions in the year preceding the survey and deliveries in the two years preceding the survey including where the delivery took place (home or hospital). The household survey questionnaire was translated into Hindi (the local language), back translated for validation, and pre-tested among 80 households in the area. Surveyors who spoke the local language fluently conducted the survey.

Data presentation and statistical analysis

We used Stata (version 11) for a descriptive analysis of the household survey. We used MS Excel (version 2003) for the Illness Mapping data tabulation and analysis.

The incidence of illness and health care utilization derived from the household survey are represented in percentages by dividing the number of cases by the overall number of members of the sampled households. The estimates derived from the Illness Mapping are presented as the mean and standard error of the mean (SEM) of all the group estimates arrived through consensus (male/ female groups separately and all groups). We compared information obtained from male vs. female groups to ascertain that familiarity with local illnesses was comparable, and significance of this difference was assessed by Student's t-test. When comparing the results from the Illness Mapping with the results from the household survey we considered as "good fit" results of the Illness Mapping that were less than two SEM of the household survey data and as "very good fit" the results that were less than one SEM.

Findings

Socioeconomic and demographic profile of the sampled population

The information on socioeconomic and demographic status of the sampled population in Gaya (one of the districts of Bihar state) is summarized in Table 1. As can be seen, the population is resource-poor (income is about PPP$ 1.53 per person per day), poorly educated (44% with no schooling whatsoever), and the main source of earning is daily wage labour (60%) and self-employed in agriculture (24%). As a comparison, monthly per capita consumer expenditure (not including medical expenditures) was INR 753 in rural Bihar according to NSS (=PPP$ 1.39 per person per day) [36].

Table 1 Socioeconomic and demographic information obtained

	Mean (± SE[a])
Income-proxy per person per month[b] (INR)	832.62 (± 7.05)
Household size	7.97 (± 0.04)
	Share of population
Education of population (15 years and older)	
No schooling	43.67%
Class 1-5	12.08%
Class 6-10	34.55%
Class 11 and higher	9.69%
Economic activity of income earners (15 years and older)	
Daily wage labourer	60.43%
Self-employed in agriculture	24.30%
Self-employed in business/trade	7.89%
Regular salaried employee	7.38%

[a] *SE* = Standard Error.
[b] monthly per capita consumer expenditure – our proxy for income – is obtained through questions on many items of household expenditure (excluding healthcare expenditures).

Prevalence of illnesses

Local prevalence of illnesses is one of the main parameters for designing and pricing health insurance. We compared the estimate of prevalence of illnesses (the percentage of persons ill in the last month) from the Illness Mapping methodology with the conventional household survey (Table 2). The comparison of the mean value of prevalence of illness obtained through the Illness Mapping and that obtained through the household survey were less than two SEM, and provided "good fit". Furthermore, the results obtained from groups composed of males and females were not significantly different from each other (*t* test).

Types of illnesses

The proportion of acute and chronic illnesses in the Illness Mapping and the household survey data is shown in Table 3. Acute illnesses represented most of the morbidity under both counts (76.9% of all illnesses based on the Illness Mapping compared to 69.2% derived from the household survey). Chronic illnesses were 20.1% and 16.6% respectively. The proportion of accidents in the Illness Mapping (2.0%) was lower than that reported in the household survey (5.0%). There were fewer undefined illnesses in the Illness Mapping than in the household survey (1% vs. 9.1%).

Hospitalizations

The Illness Mapping estimate of incidence of hospitalization was 1.1% (±0.4) and the household survey estimate was 2.6% (Table 4). Data from the household survey gave a much higher estimate than the Illness Mapping. The difference was significant and material even after taking the standard errors into account.

Deliveries

Data on incidence of deliveries and on percentage of hospital deliveries is presented in Tables 5 and 6. We found very good agreement between the Illness Mapping data and the household survey data on incidence of deliveries: 3.9% (±0.4) in the Illness Mapping data for all groups combined and 3.9% in the HH survey.

The Illness Mapping estimate of hospital or institutional deliveries was 61.0% (±5.4) for all groups combined, while the household survey estimate was 51.4% (Table 6). The two data series were within the good fit limit, but results

Table 2 Estimates of prevalence of illness from Illness Mapping and household survey

Proportion of ailing persons (last month) obtained from the Illness Mapping			Proportion of ailing persons (last month) obtained from the household survey
Male and female groups combined (±SE[a])	Male groups only (±SE[a])	Female groups only (±SE[a])	
25.9% (±3.6%)	24.5% (±4.8%)	28.5% (±5.4%)	31.4%
	p = 0.587[b]		

[a] *SE* = Standard Error.
[b] Test of significance between male and female groups (*t*-test).

Table 3 Estimates of types of illness from Illness Mapping and household survey

	Illness types as share of illnesses:			
	Acute	Chronic	Accidents	Undefined
Data obtained from the Illness Mapping	76.9%	20.1%	2.0%	1.0%
Data obtained from the household survey	69.2%	16.6%	5.0%	9.1%

Note: The above percentages for illness types were calculated for all groups together. Standard errors for these values are therefore not available.

reported by the female groups were in closer agreement (very good fit).

Cost and time comparison between household survey and Illness Mapping

Table 7 gives a record of the time and human resources required for the household survey of 1,000 households compared to the Illness Mapping for 35 groups. The comparison is limited to the core activities related to the two methods, since the exact related costs could presumably be context dependent (salaries, traveling conditions, accommodations, will be different in different locations). The table shows that Illness Mapping represented a reduction of 59% in work-days, i.e. requires less time and less costs than conducting a household survey.

Discussion

In this study we set out to develop a reliable method that may in future enable us to access the necessary data for the establishment of a micro health insurance in low income rural communities where data would not be available otherwise. The objective before us was to find a way to overcome the two constraints associated with data sourcing through household survey, namely, the cost and time required. The Illness Mapping method we describe here seems to meet this objective. The information given in Table 7 illustrates the advantage of the Illness Mapping method in terms of human resources and time required, which obviously translate into differences in costs (e.g. salaries, travel, accommodation etc.).

The design of an insurance product requires estimates of the prevalence/incidence of the events covered by the insurance. Our previous studies showed that: (i) the incidence of illness episodes, and prevalence of hospitalizations and delivery is strongly context-dependent and varies across locations even in the same country [19] making it necessary to obtain local data. (ii) Prospective clients of health insurance in rural India are exposed to hardship financing not only in cases of hospitalizations but also in cases of outpatient treatment and in deliveries [4]. In fact, this is even more pronounced in case of chronic illnesses [6]. (iii) When expressing their priorities regarding benefits that should be covered by insurance, prospective clients expressed a clear wish to include both inpatient and outpatient benefits [34,37]. It is thus clear that the information obtained through Illness Mapping regarding the prevalence/incidence of prioritized cost generating events is essential for the design and pricing of context-relevant health insurance.

We followed a strategy of soliciting local information from groups rather than from individuals. We were inspired by group techniques, assuming that the small cosmos of a village community could be captured through harvesting the knowledge that is readily available to its inhabitants free of charge. Having failed to find a ready-made suitable method in the published literature, we opted to utilize a combination of established methods and adapt them to our settings. Group approaches such as the Delphi and NGT have been used successfully and with high accuracy for business forecasting as well as for public policy [38,39]. We adopted the criteria for resourcing quantitative information from qualitative non-interacting groups such as Delphi and NGT [22,26], and modified those to take account of the advantages of interactive group situations in which the discussions are moderated and facilitated rather than left to chance (as often happens in exploratory brainstorming groups or focus groups [28]). Such structured group methods are based on the principle of collective intelligence [40], or group intelligence that emerges through managed consensus decision making [31].

Our method was based on small group discussions with people who were marginally literate and numerate, but nonetheless experts or valid representatives of their village communities. They were chosen (with the help of

Table 4 Estimates of incidence of hospitalization from Illness Mapping and household survey

Percentage of hospitalized persons (last year) obtained from the Illness Mapping			Percentage of hospitalized persons (last year) obtained from the household survey
Male and female groups combined (±SE[a])	Male groups only (±SE[a])	Female groups only (±SE[a])	
1.1% (±0.4%)	1.6% (±0.8%)	0.5% (±0.1%)	2.6%
	$p = 0.213$[b]		

[a] *SE* = Standard Error.
[b] Test of significance between male and female groups (*t*-test).

Table 5 Estimates of incidence of deliveries from Illness Mapping and household survey

Number of deliveries per 100 persons (last year) obtained from the Illness Mapping			Number of deliveries per 100 persons (last year) obtained from the household survey[b]
Male and female groups combined (±SE[a])	Male groups only (±SE[a])	Female groups only (±SE[a])	
3.9% (±0.4%)	4.4% (±0.7%)	3.4% (±0.6%)	3.9%
	p = 0.293[c]		

[a] SE = Standard Error.
[b] Based on the reported number of children less than or equal to 1 year in the household.
[c] test of significance between male and female groups (t-test).

our partner NGO staff who had prior access to the village) for their social attributes and their knowledge of households in their own neighbourhood in the village. In each village we carefully identified such participants and facilitated their interaction to obtain estimates for the prevalence of illness for the entire village. Other key contacts in the village such as teachers, village head, and health workers could also be recruited to provide similar information if there were no prior links with the village.

We organized gender homogenous groups in each village to ensure that both men and women would be able to express themselves freely. We thought that women, who are usually caregivers, might be more familiar with illnesses than men. However we found no statistical difference between the estimates given by men's and women's groups. We found it more difficult to assemble men's groups as men were usually away during the day. From this experience we infer that Illness Mapping could be extracted from interactions with either gender of respondents, and that women's groups are likely to be easier to assemble than men.

Our method had to be adjusted to the field reality of low literacy which meant that written consensus and voting was not the best option and so we employed a strategy which involved everyone in a sequential and structured interaction. Our structure emerged from the motivation, explanations, and facilitation techniques that we used to encourage accurate recall and steer discussions towards final consensus.

We examined the potential of our new Illness Mapping method by comparing the results obtained with those derived through a household survey. We compared three parameters which are important for implementation of micro health insurance: (i) prevalence of illness for acute and chronic illnesses, both of which entail cost implications which can be much higher in the case of chronic illnesses [18], (ii) incidence of hospitalization, as this cost is included in most health insurance programmes, and (iii) incidence of deliveries, especially hospital deliveries. We found very good agreement between the two methods on incidence of deliveries, and good agreement on prevalence of illnesses (in the last one month) and on prevalence of acute and chronic illnesses, as well as on the share of deliveries in hospital.

We obtained a lower estimate of incidence of hospitalization from the Illness Mapping than from the household survey (1.1% (±0.4) from the first source versus 2.6% from the second source). This discrepancy could be the result of two types of memory effects that can lead to erroneous reporting by respondents: errors of omission and of telescoping [41]. While omission means forgetting or omitting to report an episode entirely, telescoping works in the opposite direction, i.e. the respondent remembers and reports an event as having occurred more recently than it actually had. The telescoping effect increases the total number of events reported in a given period. It has also been found that telescoping may be greater in face to face interviews as the presence of an interviewer and the face to face interaction may prod the respondent to give "too much rather than too little information" [41]. It is possible that the telescoping effect may have resulted in an *overestimation* of hospitalizations in our household survey. In contrast, hospitalizations may have been *underestimated* in the Illness Mapping method as the group members may have only been aware of the longer duration hospitalizations in their communities and those due to major procedures such as surgeries. They may have omitted the shorter and less severe hospitalizations. This

Table 6 Estimates of percentage of hospital deliveries from Illness Mapping and household survey

Percentage of hospital deliveries obtained from the Illness Mapping			Percentage of hospital deliveries obtained from the household survey
Male and female groups combined (±SE[a])	Male groups only (±SE[a])	Female groups only (±SE[a])	
61.0% (±5.4%)	67.3% (±7.8%)	55.4% (±7.3%)	51.4%
	P=0.275[b]		

[a] SE = Standard Error.
[b] Test of significance between male and female groups (t-test).

Table 7 Number of working days required for Illness Mapping and household survey

	Illness Mapping	Household survey
Preparation (including translation of tools, training of interviewers and pre-test)	3 days	8 days
Field work (with 1 supervisor and 4 or 5 interviewers)	18 days	30 days
Data entry (1 person)	1 day	20 days
Data cleaning and analysis (1 person)	8 days	14 days

view is supported by prior evidence that longer duration stays and surgeries are more positively associated with recall than other hospitalizations [42]. We do not have a definitive basis to determine which of these estimates is more pronounced, and only actual utilization data could indicate which estimate is the more accurate prediction.

Data obtained either from Illness Mapping or from a household survey would usually be treated by insurers with some reserve, as both methods are less reliable than actual claims data over a long period of time. The Illness Mapping did not, a-priori, show any difference on this count relative to the data obtained from the household survey. In insurance business, it is therefore common practice to include a safety loading in premium calculations, to account for errors in assumptions or inaccuracy of estimates.

The main advantage of the Illness Mapping method is that it is cheaper and faster to operate, and could replace a household survey for estimating morbidity and healthcare utilization, especially where local data is needed but not readily available. While we have tested this method in rural settings in India, we have no reason to think that it could not be equally effective in urban settings (e.g. slums), or in other countries. The estimates about morbidity and healthcare utilization are of course essential not only for insurance purposes, but also for health policy choices more generally. Limitations of this method include the need to establish good contacts with the study communities in order to identify the most suitable community experts. Secondly, high quality group facilitation is essential, by facilitators that must speak the local language and understand the local social settings (and probably be local). Finally, as the estimates obtained by both methods are predictive, one powerful way to evaluate the robustness of the estimates obtained would be to examine both Illness Mapping data and household survey data against actual claims data. Such a follow-up examination is needed to validate the accuracy of the Illness Mapping as a generally applicable alternative to household surveys for the data in question.

Conclusions

The effort to introduce health insurance among low income persons in areas in the informal economy requires that the benefit packages as well as the premiums payable will be customized to local conditions. Evidence has shown that those local conditions are context-specific and that one-size-fits-all simply will not do. This customization therefore is contingent on obtaining at least some local data on such pieces of information as prevalence of illness, hospitalizations, chronic and acute illnesses, and deliveries. We have explored the Illness Mapping method on the assumption that it can deliver a cheaper and faster resourcing of the essential local data, at acceptably accurate levels. We have shown in this study that the results obtained through the Illness Mapping method were comparable to those obtained through household survey. We have also shown that obtaining these results costs less time and money than conducting a household survey. We therefore conclude that for as long as health insurance solutions must be adapted to context relevant conditions and that these differ from one location to the next significantly, the Illness Mapping method tested in this study and explained in this article may serve the purpose.

Endnotes

[i]The following conditions were usually included: (i) acute: fevers, diarrheas, body pains, respiratory conditions (not including asthma/COPD), TB and skin problems; (ii) chronic: asthma/COPD, diabetes, hypertension, kidney diseases, and cardiovascular problems.

Abbreviations

ASHA: Accredited social health activist; HHS: Household survey; IM: Illness mapping; NGO: Non-governmental organization; NGT: Nominal group technique; NSS: National sample survey; SE: Standard error.

Competing interests

The authors declare that they have no competing interests.

Authors' contributions

DMD and RK were responsible for the study concept and design. MG was responsible for the Illness Mapping fieldwork and data management; EB was responsible for the household survey fieldwork and data management. MG, EB, RK and DMD analysed and interpreted the data. EB, MG and RK prepared the draft of the manuscript. All authors read, revised and approved the final version of the manuscript.

Authors' information

MG was a Post-Doctoral Fellow, and EB a Ph.D. student with the Institute of Health Policy and Management, Erasmus University, Rotterdam, while

developing this article. This work represents part of the requirements for the PhD thesis of EB at Erasmus University.
DMD, in addition to acting as principal investigator on this grant within his position as hon. Professor at Erasmus University Rotterdam, also acted as supervisor of MG in the Post-Doctoral fellowship and EB in the PhD studies. He is also the Chairman of the Micro Insurance Academy.

Acknowledgements
The authors gratefully acknowledge funding support from the Netherlands Organization for Scientific Research (NWO), under WOTRO Integrated Programme grant No. W01.65.309.00. The sponsors had no influence or role in study design, in the collection, analysis and interpretation of data; in the writing of the article; and in the decision to submit the article for publication.
The authors gratefully acknowledge logistical and research support from the Micro Insurance Academy New Delhi, and logistical support from the BASIX Units at Gaya and Patna. Last but not least, we acknowledge all the respondents for their participation in the study.

Author details
[1]Institute of Health Policy and Management, Erasmus University Rotterdam, P.O. Box 1738, Rotterdam 3000 DR, the Netherlands. [2]Felsenstein Medical Research Centre, Tel Aviv University Sackler Faculty of Medicine, Ramat Aviv, Tel Aviv, Israel. [3]Micro Insurance Academy, 52B Okhla Industrial Estate Phase III, New Delhi 110020, India.

Received: 3 April 2012 Accepted: 19 September 2012
Published: 9 October 2012

References

1. World Development Indicators:: ; Retrieved 09/13, 2012 from [http://data.worldbank.org/data-catalog/world-development-indicators].
2. Karan AK, Selvaraj S: **Why publicly-financed health insurance schemes are ineffective in providing financial risk protection.** *Econ Polit Wkly* 2012, **47**(11):61.
3. Ma S, Sood N: *A comparison of the health systems in China and India.* Santa Monica, USA: Rand Corporation, Center for Asia Pacific Policy; 2008.
4. Binnendijk E, Koren R, Dror DM: **Hardship financing of healthcare among rural poor in Orissa.** *India. BMC health services research* 2012, **12**(1):23.
5. Peters DH, Yazbeck AS, Sharma RP, Ramana GNV, Pritchett LH, Wagstaff A: *Better health systems for India's poor: Findings, analysis and options.* Washington (DC): World Bank; 2002.
6. Binnendijk E, Koren R, Dror DM: **Can the rural poor in India afford to treat non-communicable diseases.** *Tropical Medicine & International Health* 2012, doi: 10.1111/j.1365-3156.2012.03070.x. [Epub ahead of print]
7. Lopez AD, Mathers CD, Ezzati M, Jamison DT, Murray CJ: **Global and regional burden of disease and risk factors, 2001: Systematic analysis of population health data.** *Lancet* 2006, **367**(9524):1747–1757.
8. World Health Organization: *Global status report on noncommunicable diseases 2011.* Geneva, Switzerland: World Health Organization; 2010.
9. Ahuja R: *Health insurance for the poor in India.* New Delhi, India: Working paper No. 123, Indian Council for research on International Economic Relation (ICRIER); 2004.
10. Ahuja R: *Health insurance for the poor in India: An analytical study.* New Delhi, India: Working Paper No. 161, Indian Council for Research on International Economic Relations (ICRIER); 2005.
11. Bhat R, Jain N: *Factoring affecting the demand for health insurance in a micro insurance scheme.* Ahmedabad: IIMA Working Papers WP2006-07-02, Indian Institute of Management; 2006.
12. National Commission on Macroeconomics and Health: *Financing and delivery of health care services in India.* New Delhi: National Commission on Macroeconomics and Health Background Papers, Ministry of Health and Family Welfare, Government of India; 2005.
13. Dror DM, Radermacher R, Khadilkar SB, Schout P, Hay FX, Singh A, Koren R: **Microinsurance: Innovations in low-cost health insurance.** *Health Aff (Millwood)* 2009, **28**(6):1788–1798.
14. Doyle C, Panda P, Van de Poel E, Radermacher R, Dror DM: **Reconciling research and implementation in micro health insurance experiments in India: Study protocol for a randomized controlled trial.** *Trials* 2011, **12**(1):224.
15. Dong H, Mugisha F, Gbangou A, Kouyate B, Sauerborn R: **The feasibility of community-based health insurance in Burkina Faso.** *Health Policy* 2004, **69**(1):45–53.
16. AC Nielsen ORG-MARG Pvt Ltd: *Needs and demands for healthcare and health insurance amng landless agriculture laborers in Burdwan district, West Bengal.* Kolkota, India: Final Report submitted to GTZ Technical Assistance Team, Health Sector Support, Kolkata, AC Nielsen ORG-MARG Pvt Ltd; 2001.
17. Dror DM: **Why "one-size-fits-all" health insurance products are unsuitable for low-income persons in the informal economy in India.** *Asian Economic Review* 2007, **49**(1):47–56.
18. Dror DM, van Putten-Rademaker O, Koren R: **Cost of illness: Evidence from a study in five resource-poor locations in India.** *Indian J Med Res* 2008, **127**(4):347–361.
19. Dror DM, van Putten-Rademaker O, Koren R: **Incidence of illness among resource-poor households: Evidence from five locations in India.** *Indian J Med Res* 2009, **130**(2):146–154.
20. National Sample Survey Organization: Morbidity, health care and the condition of the aged. 2006, Report No. 507 (60th round January-June: *National Sample Survey Organization, Ministry of Statistics and Programme Implementation.* New Delhi: Government of India; 2004.
21. National Sample Survey Organization: Morbidity and treatment of ailments. 1998, Report No. 441 (52th round July 1995-June: *National Sample Survey Organization, Ministry of Statistics and Programme Implementation.* New Delhi: Government of India; 1996.
22. Jones J, Hunter D: **Consensus methods for medical and health services research.** *BMJ* 1995, **311**(7001):376–380.
23. Aurey JP, Fonteneau R: **Local consensus and estimates of medical risk.** In *Social Reinsurance, A new approach to sustainable community health financing.* Edited by Dror DM, Preker AS. Geneva: The World Bank and the International Labour Organisation; 2002:187–222.
24. Woudenberg F: **An evaluation of Delphi.** *Technol Forecast Soc Chang* 1991, **40**(2):131–150.
25. Sample JA, Nominal Group Technique: **An alternative to brainstorming.** *J Ext* 1984, **22**(2): accessed at: http://www.joe.org/joe/1984March/iw2.php.
26. Van de Ven AH, Delbecq AL: **The effectiveness of nominal, Delphi, and interacting group decision making processes.** *Acad Manag J* 1974, **17**(4):605–621.
27. Van de Ven AH, Delbecq AL: **Nominal versus interacting group processes for committee decision-making effectiveness.** *Acad Manag J* 1971, **14**(2):203–212.
28. Kitzinger J: **Qualitative research: Introducing focus groups.** *BMJ* 1995, **311**(7000):299–302.
29. Bouchard TJ: **Personality, problem-solving procedure, and performance in small groups.** *J Appl Psychol* 1969, **53**(1 (supplement 1):1–29.
30. Bouchard TJ: **Training, motivation, and personality as determinants of the effectiveness of brainstorming groups and individuals.** *J Appl Psychol* 1972, **56**(4):324–331.
31. Hart S, Boroush M, Enk G, Hornick W: **Managing complexity through consensus mapping: Technology for the structuring of group decisions.** *Acad Manag Rev* 1985, **10**(3):587–600.
32. Lowry PB: *Research on process structure for distributed, asynchronous collaborative writing groups.* Dallas: Proceedings of the 8th Annual Americas Conference on Information Systems; 2002:2172–2179.
33. Som RK: *Practical sampling techniques.* 2nd edition. New York: Marcel Dekker; 1996.
34. Danis M, Binnendijk E, Vellakkal S, Ost A, Koren R, Dror DM: **Eliciting health insurance benefit choices of low income groups.** *Econ Polit Wkly* 2007, **42**(32):3331–3339.
35. National Sample Survey Organization: *Household Consumer Expenditure in India, 2006–07.* New Delhi: Report No. 527, National Sample Survey Organization, Ministry of Statistics and Programme Implementation, Government of India; 2008.
36. National Sample Survey Organization: *Level and pattern of consumer expenditure, 2009–2010.* New Delhi: Report No. 538, National Sample Survey Organization, Ministry of Statistics and Programme Implementation, Government of India; 2011.
37. Dror DM, Koren R, Ost A, Binnendijk E, Vellakkal S, Danis M: **Health insurance benefit packages prioritized by low-income clients in India: three criteria to estimate effectiveness of choice.** *Soc Sci Med* 2007, **64**(4):884–896.

38. Basu S, Schroeder RG: **Incorporating judgments in sales forecasts: Application of the Delphi method at American Hoist & Derrick.** *Interfaces* 1977, **7**(3):18–27.
39. Hilbert M, Miles I, Othmer J: **Foresight tools for participative policy-making in inter-governmental processes in developing countries: Lessons learned from the eLAC Policy Priorities Delphi.** *Technol Forecast Soc Chang* 2009, **76**(7):880–896.
40. Surowiecki J: *The wisdom of crowds*. USA: Double Day (Random House Inc); 2004.
41. Sudman S, Bradburn NM: **Effects of time and memory factors on response in surveys.** *J Am Stat Assoc* 1973, **68**(344):805–815.
42. Harlow SD, Linet MS: **Agreement between questionnaire data and medical records: The evidence for accuracy of recall.** *Am J Epidemiol* 1989, **129**(2):233–248.

Chapter 8

A Model to Estimate the Impact of Thresholds and Caps on Coverage Levels in Community-based Health Insurance Schemes in Low-Income Countries*

Main Messages

- Knowledge of the distribution of health care costs is essential in order to match costs with local levels of willingness-to-pay (WTP) for health insurance (HI), in order to predict (simulate) the expected performance of the community-based health insurance (CBHI).
- This knowledge of the distribution makes it possible to determine at the stage of package design the optimal levels of thresholds and/or caps for each benefit-type included.
- A theoretical model was built, fitted with data obtained from 11 household surveys conducted between 2008 and 2010 in rural locations (9 in India and 2 in Nepal).

---

*This chapter is reproduced from *Health* (2014), **6**, 822–835, Open Access, available at https://www.researchgate.net/publication/261179132_A_Model_to_Estimate_the_Impact_of_Thresholds_and_Caps_on_Coverage_Levels_in_Community-Based_Health_Insurance_Schemes_in_Low-Income_Countries.

- The mean cost and probability of health care utilization in the 11 locations were very different, yet the standardized distributions of expenditures on hospitalization and tests in the 11 locations were very similar.
- The model could be applied more generally.

Focus Points

- A theoretical model of health care costs based on a lognormal distribution can be used to calculate the impact of thresholds and caps on the share of costs and bills that would be reimbursable.
- It is possible to simulate the expected performance of the CBHI in the local context at the stage of package design, and determine not only which components should be included but also the optimal level of threshold and cap that would meet the expressed levels of WTP best.
- The distribution of locally relevant health care costs can be estimated without cumbersome and expensive data collection in the field.

Structured Abstract

Introduction

CBHI schemes manage to offer affordable HI to the rural poor by limiting the coverage they offer both by the types of care considered, and by applying thresholds and/or caps to costs reimbursed. This chapter seeks to develop a model to estimate insurance coverage under CBHI. While this requires that the distribution of the expected costs is known, the authors demonstrate that the distribution can be predicted even without cumbersome and expensive data collection in the field. Such a predictive method has particularly important ramifications in the context of introducing HI to the rural poor in low-income countries, where data is usually missing and collection of the required data entails a high cost, which often cannot be borne as part of implementation costs in these settings.

Method

The study focuses on health care expenditure (hospitalization and tests) in low-income settings and compares the simulated distributions to empirical data obtained through 11 household surveys conducted between 2008 and 2010 prior to launching CBHI schemes in several rural locations (9 in India and 2 in Nepal).

The authors observed the consequences of different levels of caps and thresholds on

(a) the percentage of overall costs that the insurance would reimburse, and
(b) the percentage of bills covered by the insurance.

Findings

Only costs of hospitalization and tests were considered in this study. A large variation was observed in the incidence/prevalence of illness, utilization of health care, its cost and WTP for HI across the 11 locations studied. Since the mean cost of the two benefits differed significantly across the locations, the authors made an attempt to study the shape of the distributions independently of the mean costs. On considering the shape of the distributions, it was found to be very similar in all 11 locations for both benefits, and this could be represented by a model based on a lognormal distribution.

The findings suggested a marked similarity between the theoretical model and the empirical data in the prediction of the percentage of total costs that the insurance needs to cover (mostly within 10% difference). A comparison of predicted versus empirical data on the percentage of bills covered by insurance also yielded a marked similarity when the caps were set at 100% or 200% of the mean. The agreement was, however, lower with only 5 out of 11 locations in good agreement when the cap was assumed to be 50% of the mean.

This satisfactory comparison between empirical data and the theoretical model strengthened the conviction of the authors that the lognormal model can provide a good approximation for the data.

Box 1: Theoretical Model Predictions Compared with Empirical Data

- Marked similarity between the theoretical model and the empirical data in the prediction of the percentage of total costs that the insurance needs to cover.
- When the cap is assumed to equal 100% of the mean, the predicted outcome was less than 10% different from the empirical outcome ("good agreement") in 8 out of the 11 locations.
- In two more examples (when the cap was assumed to be 0.5 times the mean, and when the cap was assumed to be 2 times the mean), the study observed good agreement in 9 out of the 11 locations.
- The theoretical and empirical values were in good agreement in all locations when comparing the effect of introducing a threshold without a cap (two examples shown: thresholds of 10% or 20% of the mean).
- A comparison of predicted versus empirical data on the percentage of bills also yielded a marked similarity when the caps were set at 100% or 200% of the mean (good agreement in 9 and 11 cases out of 11, respectively).
- The agreement was lower, with only 5 out of 11 locations in good agreement, when the cap was assumed to be 50% of the mean.
- With a threshold of 10% of the mean, 10 out of 11 cases were in good agreement, and with a threshold of 20% of the mean, 7 out of 11 were in good agreement.

Conclusion

The study demonstrates how a theoretical model of health care costs based on a lognormal distribution can be used to assess the impact of thresholds and caps on the share of reimbursable costs and bills. The valuable information obtained from such an analysis can provide useful inputs to enhance premium calculations of community-based health insurance (CBHI) schemes in low-income countries, without cumbersome and expensive data collection in the field.

Using this model, it is possible to simulate the expected performance of the CBHI in the local context at the stage of package design, and identify not only which components should be included but also the optimal level of threshold and cap that would meet the expressed levels of WTP best.

A Model to Estimate the Impact of Thresholds and Caps on Coverage Levels in Community-Based Health Insurance Schemes in Low-Income Countries

Erika Binnendijk[1], **Ruth Koren**[2], **David M. Dror**[1,3*]

[1]Institute of Health Policy and Management, Erasmus University Rotterdam, Rotterdam, The Netherlands
[2]Felsenstein Medical Research Center, Sackler Faculty of Medicine, Tel Aviv University, Tel Aviv, Israel
[3]Micro Insurance Academy, New Delhi, India
Email: *daviddror@socialre.org

Received 7 January 2014; revised 10 February 2014; accepted 19 February 2014

Abstract

Background: Community-based health insurance (CBHI) schemes are increasingly implemented in low-income settings. These schemes limit the coverage they offer both by the types of care considered, and by applying thresholds and/or caps to costs reimbursed. The consequences of these thresholds and/or caps on insurance coverage have hitherto been usually ignored, for lack of data on the distributions of healthcare costs or understanding of their impact on effective coverage levels. This article describes a theoretical model to obtain the distributions even without data collection in the field, and demonstrates the quantitative impact of thresholds and/or caps on claim reimbursements. Methods: This model applies to applications on healthcare expenditures in low-income settings, following research methods examined in the Western world. We looked at hospitalizations and tests; we compared the simulated distributions to empirical data obtained through 11 household surveys conducted between 2008 and 2010 in rural locations (9 in India and 2 in Nepal). Results: We found that the shape of the distributions was very similar in all locations for both benefits, and could be represented by a model based on a lognormal distribution. The agreement between theoretical and empirical results was satisfactory (mostly within 10% difference). Conclusions: The model makes it possible to simulate the expected performance of the CBHI (represented by the percentage of costs or bills covered). The aim is to match costs with local levels of willingness-to-pay for health insurance. This model makes it possible to determine at the stage of package-design the optimal levels of thresholds and/or caps for each benefit-type included.

*Corresponding author.

Keywords

Distributions; Healthcare Costs; Community-Based Health Insurance; Micro Health Insurance; Thresholds; Caps

1. Introduction

Most healthcare spending in developing countries is borne by healthcare-seekers out-of-pocket (OOP). India is a good example: 70% of health spending is private, 86% of which is OOP [1] [2]. Households in India frequently finance such OOP spending, not only for inpatient care but also for outpatient care and even for maternity-related costs, by borrowing money with interest or selling assets [3]. This inequitable and inefficient health financing situation persists in other low-income countries as well [4]. The solution proposed by WHO and other international bodies has been to strive toward universal health coverage, notably through prepayment and risk pooling mechanisms in lieu of payments at the point and time of service delivery [5] [6]. Yet, penetration of health insurance in most low-income countries remains very low [7]; in India, insurance uptake is below 5% [8]. One possible explanation for low insurance uptake is that poorer individuals in the informal sector doubt their own ability to enforce contracts with insurance companies. A solution to the problem is for people to own and run community-based health insurance (CBHI) schemes at village level [9]-[13].

Typically, CBHI schemes do not benefit from premium subsidy. Therefore, these stand-alone schemes must ensure that benefit expenditures would be limited to premium income (reflecting willingness-to-pay levels).This can be done through the application of a threshold (the predetermined amount above which the insurance reimburses the rest of the bill) and/or a cap (the predetermined amount up to which the insurance reimburses the bill). For premium calculations, information is needed on the probability of healthcare utilization by insured persons and the cost of that utilization. The consequences of applying thresholds and/or caps on the expected average pay-out of insurance, and thus on the premium, can be calculated only when the distribution of the costs of healthcare utilization is known. It is self-explanatory that when low caps are applied, the effective protection of insured persons for costs above the cap is diminished. The lower the cap, the more likely the situation of reduced insurance cover, which could lead to a perception that the insurance will not provide the protection the clients seek. Such perception could greatly dampen willingness to affiliate. It is recalled that the actual assessment of the effects of caps on the protection provided by the insurance can be known in advance only if the distribution of costs is known.

Our study builds on previous research, which confirmed the imperative need to obtain information locally [14] because locations differ significantly in the number and type of illness episodes [15], cost of healthcare [16] and the willingness-to-pay (WTP) for health insurance [17]-[19]. Location-specific data cannot be extracted accurately from national data; one source would be actual claims data (fixing premiums based on such information is called "experience rating"), but this can apply only to schemes already in operation. Projections for new schemes must rely on household surveys. Indeed, a number of experiments with CBHI have relied on baseline data collection (mainly household surveys) to obtain reliable local estimates required for package design and pricing [20]-[25]. However, the time and money required to obtain information through household surveys prior to launching CBHI impede the replication of new CBHIs. To reduce these impediments preceding the launch of CBHI, we have developed faster and cheaper methods to estimate morbidity and healthcare utilization through a quick intervention method we called "Illness Mapping" [26], as well as estimates of WTP [18]. This article deals with estimating the distributions of healthcare costs, which is the third piece of information needed.

The purpose of this paper is to develop a method for premium calculation of locally relevant health insurance packages that apply a threshold and/or a cap to benefits, and to show that this can be done even without cumbersome and expensive data collection efforts in each location where CBHI is implemented.

2. Data and Methods

2.1. Setting and Sampling

The study is based on data obtained from 11 household surveys conducted in the following periods and locations:

2008, in Warangal and Karimnagar districts, Andhra Pradesh, India; 2009, in Kalahandi, Khorda and Malkangiri districts, Odisha, India; and in Dhading and Banke districts, Nepal; and 2010, in Kanpur Dehat and Pratapgarh districts, Uttar Pradesh, India; and Vaishali and Gaya districts, Bihar, India.

All locations were selected purposively, in agreement with local Non-Government Organizations (NGOs, listed in the acknowledgement) implementing a development project among their members, for which these surveys formed part of the baseline study.

We followed a two-stage sampling procedure: in stage one, villages were selected; 8 were selected in Warangal, 12 in Karimnagar and 42, 15 and 34 villages respectively in Kanpur Dehat, Pratapgarh and Vaishali (from a list given by the local NGO); 27, 22, 31, 9 and 17 villages were randomly sampled in Kalahandi, Khorda, Malkangiri, Dhading and Banke respectively (from lists provided by the local NGOs); and 50 villages were selected randomly in Gaya (from lists provided by the local NGO) plus 50 villages that were selected randomly from the Census 2001 registry of villages. In stage two, households were sampled randomly in each selected village by applying the "four winds" (or "line sampling") technique [27] (except in Kanpur Dehat, Pratapgarh and Vaishali). The households were sampled in two cohorts of equal size: member and non-member households. Households were defined as "Members" if at least one person participated in a Self-Help-Group linked to partner-NGOs; other households were "Non-members". We aggregated the two sub-cohorts for the purpose of the analysis reported here. In Kanpur Dehat, Pratapgarh and Vaishali stage two entailed inclusion of all member households, rather than sampling.

Sample sizes were 625 households (2464 individuals) in Warangal, 1089 (4384) in Karimnagar, 1805 (8258) in Kalahandi, 1758 (9110) in Khorda, 1597 (7448) in Malkangiri, 1000 (5275) in Dhading, 1008 (5741) in Banke, 1751 (10,220) in Kanpur Dehat, 1541 (9374) in Pratapgarh, 1922 (10,286) in Vaishali and 2006 households (13,320 individuals) in Gaya. It is noted that sampling was intended to represent the target population for the CBHI programme rather than the entire population in either state or district. 100% of the sampled households were rural. The overall response rate was 100% because there was always a willing adult respondent in the household.

The survey questionnaire was translated from English into the local languages (Telugu, Oriya, Hindi and Nepali, respectively for AP, Odisha, UP and Bihar, and Nepal), back translated for verification, and pre-tested among 80 households per language. Surveyors fluent in local dialects conducted the interviews. These surveyors were hired through local survey companies. The interviews were conducted orally at the houses of the sampled respondents as the respondents mostly were illiterate. The answers provided were recorded by the interviewers. Informed consent of the respondents was obtained and recorded prior to interviews. Participants' names were kept confidential in data recording and analysis. The research tools were reviewed for ethical compliance by an ad-hoc advisory committee composed of scholars and senior scholars from India and other countries that held a two-day workshop in New Delhi in 2006 in preparation of the study, and discussed ethical compliance of the study. It is recalled that at the time of the rollout of the survey there was no local ethics committee in place in India or Nepal.

2.2. Data

We queried about general demographics and socio-economic status of households. Respondents to the household survey were asked, among others, to report the age, gender, education and economic activity of every household member. For our "income-proxy" we followed the method as adopted by the Indian National Sample Survey Organization [28] to note expenditures on many items of household consumption. Our income-proxy does not include health expenditure as recommended in previous studies related to determinants of health expenditure [29] [30].

Besides demographics and socio-economic status, we also queried about hospital admissions (exceeding 24 hours) in the year preceding the survey, as well as the direct medical costs related to each admission. These expenditures included the hospital bill, and other consumables from outside sources used during the hospitalization and directly related to it e.g. expenditures for medicines or tests. We also queried about costs of diagnostic tests performed in an outpatient setting in the month preceding the survey.

2.3. Method

We define the following variables:

X = the costs per event of an insurance benefit, such as hospitalization or tests;
$f(x)$ = the density function of X;
t = threshold value, c = cap value, we assume $t < c$;
$E(X)$ = the expected costs of an insurance benefit;
$E_{0,c}(X)$ = the expected pay-out by an insurer for a policy covering the costs of an insurance benefit up to cap c;
$E_{t,\infty}(X)$ = the expected pay-out by an insurer for a policy covering the costs of an insurance benefit above threshold t;
$E_{t,c}(X)$ = the expected pay-out by an insurer for a policy covering the costs of an insurance benefit above threshold t and below cap c.

We assume the density function of healthcare expenditures to be a continuous distribution describing the healthcare expenditures per cost generating event. Previous research has shown that the distribution of positive healthcare expenditures per person per year can be approximated by a lognormal model [31]-[34]. We therefore investigate in this article to what extent a lognormal model can be used to approximate the distribution of the healthcare costs per event. The density function of a lognormal distribution $f(x)$ is:

1) $$f(x) = \frac{1}{x\sigma\sqrt{2\pi}} e^{-\frac{1}{2}\left(\frac{\ln(x)-\mu}{\sigma}\right)^2}$$

If X follows a lognormal distribution with parameters μ and σ, the natural logarithm of X ($\ln(X)$) follows a normal distribution with parameters μ and σ and consequently, the variable $Y = (\ln(X) - \mu)/\sigma$ follows the standard normal distribution.

Given a certain sample we first estimate the values for parameters μ and σ of the lognormal distribution. For this, we only need the mean costs of the benefit and its standard deviation. We denote the mean costs by $\bar{X}$ and the standard deviation by S. Then the parameters μ and σ of the lognormal distribution are estimated as:

2) $$\sigma = \sqrt{\ln\left(\frac{S}{\bar{X}}\right)^2 + 1}$$

3) $$\mu = \ln(\bar{X}) - \frac{1}{2}\sigma^2$$

Insurance companies commonly introduce thresholds and/or caps for reimbursement to assure their long-term survival. We can also calculate the expected pay-out by the insurer with a certain cap or threshold (or both), after we have estimated the parameters μ and σ. Subsequently, $E_{0,c}(X)$, $E_{t,\infty}(X)$ and $E_{c,t}(X)$ would be calculated as follows:

4) $$E_{0,c}(X) = E(X)\cdot\Phi(d-\sigma) + c\cdot(1-\Phi(d)),$$

5) $$E_{t,\infty}(X) = E(X)\cdot(1-\Phi(e-\sigma)) - t\cdot(1-\Phi(e)),$$

where $d = \frac{\ln(c)-\mu}{\sigma}$, $e = \frac{\ln(t)-\mu}{\sigma}$ and $\Phi(z)$ is the cumulative density function of the standard normal distribution [33] [34].

In Formula (4), the first part equals the expected pay-out by the insurer when the costs of the insurance benefit was lower than the cap value; the second part equals the expected pay-out when the costs of the benefit was equal to the cap, or above it. The first part of Formula (5) equals the expected pay-out by the insurer when the benefit costs exceed the threshold. The second part of the formula equals the costs that are excluded from the insurance policy.

Subsequently we can calculate $E_{t,c}(X)$ as:

6) $$E_{t,c}(X) = (E_{0,c}(X) + E_{t,\infty}(X)) - E(X)$$

The design of an insurance product with a cap and/or threshold requires understanding of the quantitative consequences of these measures. We use two outcome measures to assess the quantitative consequences of caps and/or thresholds. The first is the percentage of the total costs that is reimbursed by the insurance (Formula (7)). This indicates the income required by the insurance company, assuming an actuarially fair premium, in order to break even.

7) Percentage of costs covered:

a) Situation with only a cap: $\frac{E_{0,c}(X)}{E(X)}$;

b) Situation with only a threshold: $\frac{E_{t,\infty}(X)}{E(X)}$;

c) Situation with both a threshold and a cap: $\frac{E_{t,c}(X)}{E(X)}$.

The second outcome measure is the percentage of bills covered by the insurance (*i.e.* percentage of bills below cap, above threshold and between threshold and cap in the situation with only a cap, only a threshold and both a threshold and a cap respectively, Formula (8)). This second outcome measure can serve as an indicator of the satisfaction of prospective clients.

8) Percentage of bills covered:

a) Situation with only a cap: $\Phi(d)$;

b) Situation with only a threshold: $1-\Phi(e)$;

c) Situation with both a threshold and a cap: $\Phi(d)-\Phi(e)$.

2.4. Analysis

The unit of analysis is individual cases of hospitalizations and tests.

The analysis is based on hospitalizations with non-zero costs (95% of all hospitalizations reported) as those are the ones relevant for insurance payouts. For the analysis of tests, all outpatient tests had costs and were included.

We used STATA version 11 and MS Excel (version 2010).

All amounts, reported in Indian Rupee (INR) during the surveys were converted into international dollars (purchasing power parity, PPP\$) using the exchange rate of PPP\$1 = INR 16.130 for the survey conducted in 2008, INR 16.692 for the 2009 survey and 18.073 for the 2010 survey [35]. The amounts reported in Nepalese Rupee (NPR) were converted into PPP\$ using the exchange rate of PPP\$1 = NPR 29.222 [35].

3. Results

3.1. Socio-Economic Status of Studied Populations

The studied populations are characterized by low income and low educational levels (Table 1). The income-proxy of the population varies from PPP\$ 1.0 to PPP\$ 2.6 per person per day; and more than 40% of persons aged 15 years or more had no or very little education (below Class 5). At the same time, the percentage of people with higher education differed markedly across locations. Most people were engaged in self-employment in agriculture, daily wage labour and self-employment in business/trade.

3.2. Reported Costs for Hospitalizations and Tests

Information about expenditures for hospitalizations and tests is self-reported (Table 2). The incidence of hospitalizations ranges from 0.02 to 0.15, and for tests the range was between 0.02 and 0.10. The mean costs of hospitalizations and tests also differ markedly across the locations studied: a 6-fold difference in the mean costs of hospitalizations (from PPP\$109 in Malkangiri to PPP\$685 in Karimnagar) and a 5-fold difference in mean costs of tests (ranging from PPP\$6 in Malkangiri to PPP\$29 in Karimnagar). This large variation in healthcare costs across locations is in line with our previous findings in five other rural locations in India [16].

In this study, we want to examine whether the distributions of costs, not just cost levels, differ across locations. This could be done when the mean of the distributions could be standardized while maintaining the shape of each distribution. We "standardized" the costs by dividing reported costs in each location by that location's av-

Table 1. Socio-economic profile of the studied populations.

	Warangal	Karimnagar	Kalahandi	Khorda	Malkangiri	Kanpur Dehat	Pratapgarh	Vaishali	Gaya	Dhading	Banke
Income-proxy per person per month (PPP$)[a]											
Mean	77.99	74.49	27.79	33.41	27.98	59.76	47.28	56.58	43.84	70.58	56.87
Standard error	1.21	0.97	0.22	0.22	0.22	0.67	0.53	0.40	0.28	0.70	0.48
Education of adult population (15 years and older)											
No education	40.1	42.5	51.7	27.4	68.6	31.5	35.2	45.5	46.3	37.5	34.3
Class 1 - 5	9.1	8.4	16.8	20.3	13.5	11.8	12.5	14.5	12.3	18.8	13.8
Class 6 - 10	28.3	26.8	25.5	42.3	15.9	41.1	37.7	31.2	33.0	28.9	35.6
Class 11 and higher	22.5	22.2	6.1	10.1	2.0	15.6	14.6	8.9	8.4	14.8	16.2
Economic activity of adult population (15 years and older)											
Self-employed in agriculture	9.8	19.9	20.6	10.6	27.9	31.0	10.9	12.9	12.3	31.8	24.06
Self-employed in business/trade	10.0	7.5	5.4	17.1	3.7	4.0	7.7	9.8	3.6	14.17	8.35
Regular salaried employee	7.0	4.5	2.2	4.2	2.6	2.7	3.8	1.6	2.9	8.39	11.2
Casual wage labourer	39.7	31.5	26.3	12.5	27.5	8.1	15.2	19.5	33.0	4.21	8.91
Domestic duties	10.9	10.6	29.5	38.3	28.4	31.5	32.7	35.5	28.4	13.6	21.66
Not working	22.5	25.9	15.9	17.4	9.9	22.7	29.7	20.8	19.9	27.83	25.82

[a]Income is proxied as monthly per capita consumer expenditure through questions on many items of household expenditure and expressed in Purchasing Power Parity International Dollar.

Table 2. Socio-economic profile of the studied populations.

	Hospitalizations				Diagnostic tests			
	Incidence of cases with cost > 0 (n)	Mean costs (PPP$[a])	Standard deviation (PPP$[a])	Coefficient of variation (CV)	Incidence of cases with cost > 0 (n)	Mean costs (PPP$[a])	Standard deviation (PPP$[a])	Coefficient of variation (CV)
Warangal	0.15 (377)	625.49	1267.03	2.03	0.05 (124)	23.12	43.98	1.90
Karimnagar	0.15 (654)	685.52	1414.20	2.06	0.06 (271)	28.86	41.57	1.44
Kalahandi	0.06 (469)	183.34	268.93	1.47	0.10 (799)	5.76	12.41	2.15
Khorda	0.06 (523)	345.71	563.96	1.63	0.05 (490)	9.67	13.77	1.42
Malkangiri	0.06 (468)	108.94	185.62	1.70	0.04 (304)	5.53	5.28	0.95
Kanpur Dehat	0.02 (245)	681.91	1129.76	1.66	0.03 (328)	20.52	31.88	1.55
Pratapgarh	0.02 (143)	356.44	588.56	1.65	0.02 (196)	14.50	24.95	1.72
Vaishali	0.03 (331)	272.92	369.14	1.35	0.06 (605)	18.84	30.01	1.59
Gaya	0.03 (353)	372.10	610.53	1.64	0.02 (272)	13.75	18.00	1.31
Dhading	0.04 (204)	502.31	657.07	1.31	0.03 (139)	23.28	30.40	1.31
Banke	0.04 (218)	437.58	717.58	1.64	0.04 (255)	14.04	21.37	1.52

[a]PPP$ = Purchasing Power Parity International Dollar.

erage cost, obtaining the same mean cost of one in all locations, while the Coefficient of Variation (CV) of each distribution remained unchanged. These standardized distributions are shown in Figure 1 (for hospital expenditures) and in Figure 2 (for expenditures on tests).

To our surprise, the standardized distributions of hospital expenditures in the 11 locations were really similar; the same clear similarity across locations was also observed with the distributions of expenditures on tests.

We then proceeded to elaborate a model describing the best-fit for all distributions. It is recalled that previous research has successfully used the lognormal distribution as a good approximation for empirical distributions of

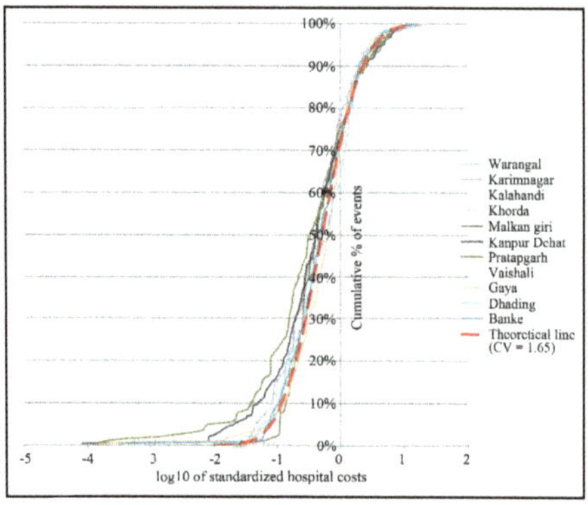

Figure 1. Distributions of hospital costs.

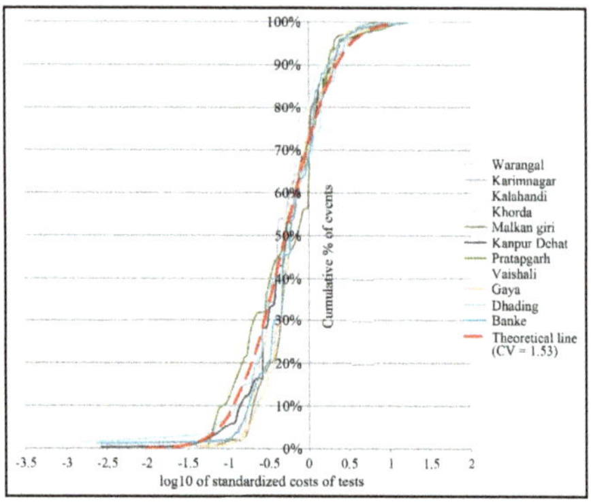

Figure 2. Distributions of costs on diagnostic tests.

healthcare costs [31]-[34]. We therefore created a theoretical lognormal curve (Equation (1)) with mean of one and a CV which is the arithmetic average for the 11 locations (1.65 for hospital costs and 1.53 for tests, Table 2). The resulting theoretical curve is plotted in Figure 1 for hospitalization expenditures and in Figure 2 for expenditures on tests.

3.3. Outcome Measures as Predicted by the Theoretical Model and Compared with Empirical Data

The model needs to predict the financial performance of CBHI schemes functioning with different levels of caps and thresholds. We observed the consequences of different levels of caps and thresholds on 1) the percentage of over all costs that the insurance would reimburse; and 2) the percentage of bills covered by the insurance.

As a reminder, all bills and all costs are reimbursable fully only when neither threshold nor cap apply. Moreover, most insured persons do not claim at all (and these would not be shown in the distributions); and many bills entail low costs, with only very few very high cost bills. Both a threshold and a cap will be effective in reducing the average reimbursement per insured. In many cases, the insurance product is limited both by a threshold and by a cap.

Tables 3 and 4 contain both the results obtained by applying our theoretical model and those obtained by applying the same caps/thresholds to the empirical data derived from the household surveys in all 11 locations. It should be noted that these caps/thresholds are per event (*i.e.* hospitalization or test).

We observe marked similarity between the theoretical model and the empirical data in the prediction of the percentage of total costs that the insurance needs to cover. For instance, when the cap is assumed to equal 100% of the mean, the predicted outcome was less than 10% different from the empirical outcome ("good agreement") in 8 out of the 11 locations (Table 3). In two more examples (when the cap was assumed to be 0.5 times the mean, and when the cap was assumed to be 2 times the mean), we observed good agreement in 9 out of the 11 locations. And, the theoretical and empirical values were in good agreement in all locations when comparing the effect of introducing a threshold without a cap (two examples shown: thresholds of 10% or 20% of the mean).

A comparison of predicted versus empirical data on the % of bills also yielded a marked similarity when the caps were set at 100% or 200% of the mean (good agreement in 9 and 11 cases out of 11, respectively). On the other hand, the agreement was lower, with only 5 out of 11 locations in good agreement, when the cap was assumed to be 50% of the mean. With a threshold of 10% of the mean, 10 out of 11 cases were in good agreement and a threshold of 20% of the mean 7 out of 11 were in good agreement.

A similar pattern was observed when comparing the theoretical model with the empirical data relating to tests (Table 4).

4. Discussion

This article deals with developing a model to estimate insurance coverage under CBHI. If a threshold and/or a cap limits the payout of any benefit then the evaluation of coverage can be done only when the distribution of the expected costs is known. Because thresholds and caps are not rare but a standard feature of benefit packages, we are keen to develop a method to predict the distribution in each case. A predictive method has particularly important ramifications in the context of introducing health insurance to rural poor persons in low income countries, where data is usually missing and collection of the required data entails high cost, which often cannot be borne as part of implementation costs in these settings.

In this study, we examine the distributions of the costs of two benefits (hospitalizations and diagnostic tests) derived from eleven household surveys conducted prior to launching CBHI schemes (nine in India and two in Nepal). As the mean cost of the benefits differed significantly across the locations, we wished to study the shape of the distributions independently of the mean costs. The shape of the distribution is determined by the relative frequency of small bills versus high/outlier bills: for two data series with the same mean costs but with very different ratios of small bills to large bills, the consequences of applying the same threshold and/or cap could be completely different in terms of insurance coverage.

We were not surprised to find in this study large differences across locations in incidence/prevalence of illness, utilization of healthcare, its cost and different levels of WTP for health insurance (Table 2), as this corroborated previous relevant research [15]-[17]. On the other hand, when—in our search for a theoretical model of the distributions—we "standardized" the eleven data series by dividing costs reported in each location by that loca-

Table 3. Theoretical model vs. empirical data for hospitalizations.

		Cap			Threshold	
Theoretical model	Fraction of mean	0.5	1.0	2.0	0.2	0.1
(Assumed CV[a] = 1.65)	% of cost covered	38%	57%	75%	82%	90%
	% of bills covered[b]	49%	72%	88%	80%	92%
Warangal	Cap/threshold (PPP$[c])	313	625	1250	125	63
	% of cost covered	35%	53%	67%	82%	90%
	% of bills covered[b]	57%	81%	93%	69%	85%
Karimnagar	Cap/threshold (PPP$[c])	343	685	1371	137	69
	% of cost covered	34%	50%	66%	83%	90%
	% of bills covered[b]	58%	78%	89%	69%	85%
Kalahandi	Cap/threshold (PPP$[c])	92	183	366	36	18
	% of cost covered	39%	59%	77%	82%	90%
	% of bills covered[b]	46%	74%	89%	82%	92%
Khorda	Cap/threshold (PPP$[c])	173	346	691	69	35
	% of cost covered	37%	56%	75%	82%	90%
	% of bills covered[b]	46%	71%	88%	78%	90%
Malkangiri	Cap/threshold (PPP$[c])	54	109	218	22	11
	% of cost covered	36%	53%	71%	81%	90%
	% of bills covered[b]	56%	75%	87%	78%	98%
Kanpur Dehat	Cap/threshold (PPP$[c])	341	682	1364	136	68
	% of cost covered	33%	50%	69%	83%	91%
	% of bills covered[b]	57%	72%	89%	69%	84%
Pratapgarh	Cap/threshold (PPP$[c])	178	356	713	71	36
	% of cost covered	31%	50%	69%	84%	91%
	% of bills covered[b]	57%	70%	87%	62%	77%
Vaishali	Cap/threshold (PPP$[c])	136	273	546	55	27
	% of cost covered	38%	58%	77%	82%	91%
	% of bills covered[b]	46%	70%	87%	80%	89%
Gaya	Cap/threshold (PPP$[c])	186	372	744	74	37
	% of cost covered	39%	61%	79%	82%	90%
	% of bills covered[b]	42%	70%	90%	82%	92%
Dhading	Cap/threshold (PPP$[c])	251	502	1005	100	50
	% of cost covered	36%	59%	80%	82%	90%
	% of bills covered[b]	48%	63%	87%	75%	91%
Banke	Cap/threshold (PPP$[c])	219	438	875	88	44
	% of cost covered	37%	56%	74%	82%	90%
	% of bills covered[b]	51%	72%	90%	77%	91%

[a]CV = Coefficient of Variation; [b]Percentage of bills covered by the insurance: percentage of bills below cap or above threshold in the situation with only a cap or only a threshold respectively; [c]PPP$ = Purchasing Power Parity International Dollar.

Table 4. Theoretical model vs. empirical data for outpatient diagnostic tests.

		Cap			Threshold	
Theoretical model	Fraction of mean	0.5	1.0	2.0	0.2	0.1
(Assumed CV[a] = 1.53)	% of cost covered	39%	58%	77%	80%	90%
	% of bills covered[b]	47%	71%	88%	80%	94%
Warangal	Cap/threshold (PPP$[c])	11.6	23.1	46.2	4.6	2.3
	% of cost covered	42%	58%	72%	80%	90%
	% of bills covered[b]	41%	79%	90%	94%	99%
Karimnagar	Cap/threshold (PPP$[c])	14.4	28.9	57.7	5.8	2.9
	% of cost covered	40%	58%	76%	80%	90%
	% of bills covered[b]	54%	70%	86%	92%	99%
Kalahandi	Cap/threshold (PPP$[c])	2.9	5.8	11.5	1.2	0.6
	% of cost covered	44%	62%	75%	79%	90%
	% of bills covered[b]	30%	71%	91%	88%	98%
Khorda	Cap/threshold (PPP$[c])	4.9	9.7	19.3	1.9	1
	% of cost covered	41%	60%	77%	81%	90%
	% of bills covered[b]	43%	74%	90%	87%	98%
Malkangiri	Cap/threshold (PPP$[c])	2.8	5.5	11	1.1	0.6
	% of cost covered	45%	70%	89%	80%	89%
	% of bills covered[b]	26%	57%	88%	97%	98%
Kanpur Dehat	Cap/threshold (PPP$[c])	10.3	20.5	41	4.1	2.1
	% of cost covered	40%	60%	77%	81%	90%
	% of bills covered[b]	43%	70%	89%	86%	95%
Pratapgarh	Cap/threshold (PPP$[c])	7.3	14.5	29	2.9	1.4
	% of cost covered	37%	57%	75%	82%	91%
	% of bills covered[b]	48%	72%	93%	72%	89%
Vaishali	Cap/threshold (PPP$[c])	9.4	18.8	37.7	3.8	1.9
	% of cost covered	42%	64%	81%	80%	90%
	% of bills covered[b]	40%	69%	91%	97%	100%
Gaya	Cap/threshold (PPP$[c])	6.9	13.7	27.5	2.7	1.4
	% of cost covered	44%	65%	84%	81%	90%
	% of bills covered[b]	39%	68%	85%	96%	99%
Dhading	Cap/threshold (PPP$[c])	11.6	23.3	46.6	4.7	2.3
	% of cost covered	38%	60%	81%	81%	90%
	% of bills covered[b]	45%	66%	86%	84%	94%
Banke	Cap/threshold (PPP$[c])	7	14	28	2.8	1.4
	% of cost covered	43%	64%	80%	81%	90%
	% of bills covered[b]	45%	67%	91%	95%	98%

[a]CV = Coefficient of Variation; [b]Percentage of bills covered by the insurance: percentage of bills below cap or above threshold in the situation with only a cap or only a threshold respectively; [c]PPP$ = Purchasing Power Parity International Dollar.

tion's average cost (a practice common in natural sciences) we were surprised to see that the shape of the distributions was remarkably similar. This led us to develop a theoretical model based on the assumption that the distributions are lognormal [31]-[34] and its shape is determined by the Coefficient of Variation (CV = standard deviation/mean). The CV of the theoretical model was assumed to be the arithmetic average of the CVs of the eleven locations.

Previous research has shown that the distribution of positive healthcare expenditures per person per year can be fitted by a lognormal model [31]-[34]. Several researchers have investigated the influence of different covariates on healthcare costs in order to find ways to make an even better fit of the lognormal model [36] [37]. The purpose of this article is to estimate the distribution of locally relevant healthcare costs without cumbersome and expensive data collection. In the context of this article we therefore don't make use of that knowledge as this would require more data inputs which are not (easily) at hand in rural India and would therefore diminish the advantage we seek in the modelling.

When we compared the theoretical model against the predications based on empirical data we obtained satisfactory predictions of the consequences of applying thresholds and/or caps on the expected financial performance of CBHI, both in the case of hospitalizations and tests (Tables 3 and 4). The outcome measures were the percentage of bills covered and the percentage of costs reimbursed by the insurance under different assumptions for caps and/or thresholds. Given this satisfactory comparison between empirical data and the theoretical model we were strengthened in our belief that the lognormal model can provide a good approximation for this data.

The arithmetic averages of the CVs of the two benefits under study were remarkably similar even though one benefit was related to inpatient care and the other to a component of outpatient care. We do not know if this similarity might apply also to other benefits, or is a coincidence. This would have to be examined against the distributions of additional cost components of outpatient care.

Applying the theoretical model requires an estimate of the mean cost of the benefit(s) in question. We believe that it should be easy enough to obtain mean costs in each new location as part of the investigation to estimate the probability of healthcare utilization based on facilitated interactive group discussions which we developed, called "Illness Mapping" [26].

In designing health insurance there is always the tension between the desire to include more benefits and the wish to keep the premium amount affordable. The reasons for introducing a threshold and/or a cap seem rather straight forward: thresholds can reduce the administrative burden of many small claims, caps can protect the insurance from very high outlier bills. However, both measures could reduce the willingness to join, especially when insured persons must still borrow money or sell assets to pay for healthcare bills [3]. Setting caps and/or thresholds is therefore a delicate issue. The percentage of bills covered can be used as an outcome measure that could serve as an indicator of the expected satisfaction of prospective clients.

The theoretical model developed in this paper is based on nine Indian and two Nepalese locations. These eleven locations are very different in mean cost and probability of healthcare utilization of the studied benefits (Table 2). The satisfactory fit of the empirical distributions with the distributions derived on the basis of the theoretical model supports the notion that the model could be applicable for all Indian and Nepalese rural poor cohorts. More generally, the theoretical model presented here makes it possible to simulate the expected performance of the CBHI in the local context at the stage of package design, and determine not only which components should be included but also the optimal level of threshold and cap that would meet the expressed levels of WTP best. To the best of our knowledge, this has never before been done in development projects aiming to develop CBHI with suitable health insurance coverage under severe rationing rules.

A look at the distributions in the eleven locations studied (both of hospitalizations and tests) makes clear that the distributions are less similar at the left tail. This scattering in the range of the small bills may reflect a variation in health seeking behaviour in less severe illnesses (due to healthcare availability/proximity and/or education). It may also be caused by recall bias which can be expected to be more pronounced in the case of small bills [38]. This problem could be reduced by applying a threshold.

It would be interesting to replicate this research in other developing countries where CBHI schemes are implemented or considered, in order to establish whether the distributions of costs follow a similar pattern.

5. Conclusion

The analysis in this paper has shown that a theoretical model of healthcare costs based on a lognormal distribution can be used to calculate the impact of thresholds and caps on the share of costs and bills that would be reimbursable. This information, hitherto ignored, can be used to refine premium calculations of community-based health insurance schemes in low income countries and foretell expected client satisfaction with locally relevant health insurance packages that define a threshold and/or a cap. Application of the model makes it possible to obtain the local data required faster and cheaper than by conducting household surveys.

Acknowledgements

The authors gratefully acknowledge funding support from the Netherlands Organization for Scientific Research (NWO), under WOTRO Integrated Programme grant No. W01.65.309.00 to Prof. Dror. This grant funded the household surveys in Warangal, Karimnagar, and Gaya in full, plus partial funding of the household survey in Malkangiri, Kalahandi and Khorda, for which additional funding was obtained from the German Federal Ministry for Economic Cooperation and Development (through a contract between AWO International, Madhyam Foundation Odisha, and the Micro Insurance Academy New Delhi). The household survey in Nepal (Dhading and Banke districts) was funded through a grant by the Rockefeller Foundation (2008 PSH 229) to Prof. Dror plus another grant by an anonymous donor to Save the Children USA/Nepal. The household surveys in Kanpur Dehat, Pratapgarh and Vaishali were funded by the European Commission 7th Framework Program, grant ID HEALTH-F2-2009-223518. The sponsors had no influence or role in study design, in the collection, analysis and interpretation of data; in the writing of the article; and in the decision where to submit the article for publication. We benefited from logistical and research support from the Micro Insurance Academy, New Delhi, India. The following organizations provided logistical support at the research sites: CDF in Warangal and Karimnagar; Madhyam Foundation (comprising 11 grassroots NGOs: Parivartan, PUSPAC, SOMKS, SDS, ODC (Malkangiri); Mahashakti Foundation, DAPTA, Lok Yojana, Sanginee (Kalahandi); MVPS, DSS (Khorda)); Shramik Bharti in Kanpur Dehat; BAIF in Pratapgarh; Nidan in Vaishali; BASIX in Gaya; DEPROSC in Dhading; and NIRDHAN in Banke. Last but not least, we acknowledge all the surveyors and the respondents for their participation in the study.

References

[1] World Development Indicators (2012)
http://data.worldbank.org/data-catalog/world-development-indicators

[2] Karan, A.K. and Selvaraj, S. (2012) Why Publicly-Financed Health Insurance Schemes Are Ineffective in Providing Financial Risk Protection. *Economic and Political Weekly*, **47**.

[3] Binnendijk, E., Koren, R. and Dror, D.M. (2012) Hardship Financing of Healthcare among Rural Poor in Orissa, India. *BMC Health Services Research*, **12**, 23.

[4] Kruk, M.E., Goldmann, E. and Galea, S. (2009) Borrowing and Selling to Pay for Health Care in Low- and Middle-Income Countries. *Health Affairs (Millwood)*, **28**, 1056-1066. http://dx.doi.org/10.1377/hlthaff.28.4.1056

[5] James, C. and Savedoff, W. (2010) Risk Pooling and Redistribution in Health Care: An Empirical Analysis of Attitudes toward Solidarity. World Health Report 2010, World Health Organization, Geneva.

[6] World Health Organization (2010) Health Systems Financing: The Path to Universal Coverage. The World Health Report 2010, World Health Organization, Geneva.

[7] Staib, D. and Bevere, L. (2011) World Insurance in 2010: Premiums Back to Growth, Capital Increases. *Swiss Re Sigma*, **2011**, 1-44.

[8] Ma, S. and Sood, N. (2008) A Comparison of the Health Systems in China and India. Rand Corporation, Center for Asia Pacific Policy, Santa Monica.

[9] Ahuja, R. (2005) Health Insurance for the Poor in India: An Analytical Study. Indian Council for Research on International Economic Relations (ICRIER), New Delhi.

[10] Bhat, R. and Jain, N. (2006) Factoring Affecting the Demand for Health Insurance in a Micro Insurance Scheme. Indian Institute of Management, Ahmedabad.

[11] Dror, D.M., Radermacher, R., Khadilkar, S.B., Schout, P., Hay, F.X., Singh, A. and Koren, R. (2009) Microinsurance: Innovations in Low-Cost Health Insurance. *Health Affairs (Millwood)*, **28**, 1788-1798.
http://dx.doi.org/10.1377/hlthaff.28.6.1788

[12] National Commission on Macroeconomics and Health (2005) Financing and Delivery of Healthcare Services in India. National Commission on Macroeconomics and Health Background Papers, Ministry of Health and Family Welfare,

Government of India, New Delhi.

[13] Dror, D.M. and Jacquier, C. (1999) Micro-Insurance: Extending Health Insurance to the Excluded. *International Social Security Review*, **52**, 71-97. http://dx.doi.org/10.1111/1468-246X.00034

[14] Dror, D.M. (2007) Why "One-Size-Fits-All" Health Insurance Products Are Unsuitable for Low-Income Persons in the Informal Economy in India. *Asian Economic Review*, **49**, 47-56.

[15] Dror, D.M., van Putten-Rademaker, O. and Koren, R. (2009) Incidence of Illness Among Resource-Poor Households: Evidence from Five Locations in India. *Indian Journal of Medical Research*, **130**, 146-154.

[16] Dror, D.M., van Putten-Rademaker, O. and Koren, R. (2008) Cost of Illness: Evidence from a Study in Five Resource-Poor Locations in India. *Indian Journal of Medical Research*, **127**, 347-361.

[17] Dror, D.M., Radermacher, R. and Koren, R. (2007) Willingness to Pay for Health Insurance among Rural and Poor Persons: Field Evidence from Seven Micro Health Insurance Units in India. *Health Policy*, **82**, 12-27. http://dx.doi.org/10.1016/j.healthpol.2006.07.011

[18] Binnendijk, E., Dror, D.M., Gerelle, E. and Koren, R. (2013) Estimating Willingness-to-Pay for Health Insurance among Rural Poor in India by Reference to Engel's Law. *Social Science & Medicine*, **76**, 67-73. http://dx.doi.org/10.1016/j.socscimed.2012.10.006

[19] Dror, D.M. and Koren, R. (2012) The Elusive Quest for Estimates of Willingness to Pay for Micro Health Insurance among the Poor in Low-Income Countries. In: Churchill, C. and Matul, M., Eds., *Protecting the Poor—A Micro Insurance Compendium Volume* 2. *Volume Chapter* 7. International Labour Organization, Geneva, 156-173.

[20] Doyle, C., Panda, P., Van de Poel, E., Radermacher, R. and Dror, D.M. (2011) Reconciling Research and Implementation in Micro Health Insurance Experiments in India: Study Protocol for a Randomized Controlled Trial. *Trials*, **12**, 224. http://dx.doi.org/10.1186/1745-6215-12-224

[21] Dong, H., Mugisha, F., Gbangou, A., Kouyate, B. and Sauerborn, R. (2004) The Feasibility of Community-Based Health Insurance in Burkina Faso. *Health Policy*, **69**, 45-53. http://dx.doi.org/10.1016/j.healthpol.2003.12.001

[22] AC Nielsen ORG-MARG Pvt Ltd. (2001) Needs and Demands for Healthcare and Health Insurance among Landless Agriculture Laborers in Burdwan District, West Bengal. Final Report Submitted to GTZ Technical Assistance Team, Health Sector Support, AC Nielsen ORG-MARG Pvt Ltd., Kolkata.

[23] De Allegri, M., Pokhrel, S., Becher, H., Dong, H., Mansmann, U., Kouyate, B., Kynast-Wolf, G., Gbangou, A., Sanon, M., Bridges, J. and Sauerborn, R. (2008) Step-Wedge Cluster-Randomised Community-Based Trials: An Application to the Study of the Impact of Community Health Insurance. *Health Research Policy and Systems*, **6**. http://dx.doi.org/10.1186/1478-4505-6-10

[24] Mwaura, J.W. and Pongpanich, S. (2012) Access to Health Care: The Role of a Community Based Health Insurance in Kenya. *The Pan African Medical Journal*, **12**. http://www.panafrican-med-journal.com/content/article/12/35/full

[25] Onwujekwe, O., Onoka, C.A., Uguru, N., Nnenna, T., Uzochukwu, B.S., Eze, S., Kirigia, J. and Petu, A. (2010) Preferences for Benefit Packages for Community-Based Health Insurance: An Exploratory Study in Nigeria. *BMC Health Services Research*, **10**, 162. http://dx.doi.org/10.1186/1472-6963-10-162

[26] Binnendijk, E., Gautham, M., Koren, R. and Dror, D.M. (2012) Illness Mapping: A Time and Cost Effective Method to Estimate Healthcare Data Needed to Establish Community Based Health Insurance. *BMC Medical Research Methodology*, **12**, 153.

[27] Som, R.K. (1996) Practical Sampling Techniques. 2nd Edition, Marcel Dekker, New York.

[28] National Sample Survey Organization (2008) Household Consumer Expenditure in India, 2006-07. Ministry of Statistics and Programme Implementation, Government of India, New Delhi.

[29] Flores, G., Krishnakumar, J., O'Donnell, O. and van Doorslaer, E. (2008) Coping with Health-Care Costs: Implications for the Measurement of Catastrophic Expenditures and Poverty. *Health Economics*, **17**, 1393-1412. http://dx.doi.org/10.1002/hec.1338

[30] Wagstaff, A. (2008) Measuring Financial Protection in Health. World Bank, Washington DC.

[31] Newhouse, J.P. and The Insurance Experiment Group (1993) Free for All? Lessons from the RAND Health Insurance Experiment. Harvard University Press, Cambridge.

[32] Van der Laan, B.S. (1988) Modelling Total Costs of Claims of Non-Life Insurances: With Applications to Health Insurance and to Motor Insurance. Erasmus University, Rotterdam.

[33] Van Vliet, R.C. (2000) A Statistical Analysis of Mandatory Pooling across Health Insurers. *Journal of Risk and Insurance*, **67**, 197-217. http://dx.doi.org/10.2307/253771

[34] Van Vliet, R.C. (2004) Deductibles and Health Care Expenditures: Empirical Estimates of Price Sensitivity Based on Administrative Data. *International Journal of Health Care Finance and Economics*, **4**, 283-305.

http://dx.doi.org/10.1023/B:IHFE.0000043759.93644.c0

[35] World Economic Outlook Database (2012) http://www.imf.org/external/pubs/ft/weo/2012/01/weodata/index.aspx

[36] Manning, G.W., Basu, A. and Mullahy, J. (2005) Generalized Modeling Approaches to Risk Adjustment of Skewed Outcomes Data. *Journal of Health Economics*, **24**, 465-488. http://dx.doi.org/10.1016/j.jhealeco.2004.09.011

[37] Gilleskie, D.B. and Mroz, T.A. (2004) A Flexible Approach for Estimating the Effects of Covariates on Health Expenditures. *Journal of Health Economics*, **23**, 391-418. http://dx.doi.org/10.1016/j.jhealeco.2003.09.008

[38] Harel, Y., Overpeck, M.D., Jones, D.H., Scheidt, P.C., Bijur, P.E., Trumble, A.C. and Anderson, J. (1994) The Effects of Recall on Estimating Annual Nonfatal Injury Rates for Children and Adolescents. *American Journal of Public Health*, **84**, 599-605. http://dx.doi.org/10.2105/AJPH.84.4.599

Chapter 9

Do Micro Health Insurance Units Need Capital or Reinsurance? A Simulated Exercise to Examine Different Alternatives*

Main Messages

- Study based on a data set of a large health insurer in Ireland, containing more than 1.3 million insureds.
- Novel approach adopted of splitting the large data source into 535 small "virtual micro insurance units (MIUs)" to analyze each as a stand-alone entity.
- By having run 1,005 iterations of the original data set to obtain 535 virtual MIUs in each run, the total data yield in this experiment has been 537,675 virtual MIUs.

---

*This chapter is reproduced from *Geneva Papers on Risk and Insurance* (2006), **31**, 739–761, Open Access, available at https://www.researchgate.net/publication/5221840_Do_Micro_Health_Insurance_Units_Need_Capital_or_Reinsurance_A_Simulated_Exercise_to_Examine_Different_Alternatives.

Focus Points

- A steep increase in capital loading can be expected when the group size decreases or when the confidence levels are increased.
- The impact of changes in confidence levels is weaker than the impact of changes in the number of insureds on capital loading levels.
- The cost of reinsurance is much lower than the minimum capital needed to assure the solvency of MIUs for all group sizes.

Structured Abstract

Introduction

In low-income countries, the amount of premium charged is one of the limiting factors for extension of health insurance (HI) since affordability is a key deciding factor in enrolling for insurance. Besides covering the cost of the pure risk, insurance premiums normally include capital loading and loading for administration. Through this study, the authors seek to estimate the capital needs of MIUs, analyze the impact of group size on capital requirements, and compare the cost of retaining capital with the cost of a reinsurance premium.

Method

By carrying out a simulation exercise, the authors are able to compare the capital requirements of one large pool with the capital requirements of many small sub-pools of varying sizes. The dataset used in the study belongs to a large health insurer in Ireland, comprising of more than 1.3 million insureds.

The data source was split into 535 small "virtual MIUs", each with a membership of 200–5,500 insureds. The level of capital required was calculated by comparing the difference in costs per insured in a single large pool of 1.3 million insureds with the same cost when the same persons are distributed randomly over 535 virtual MIUs of different sizes and at different confidence levels.

Box 1: Assumptions of the Study

Income

- We assume that all virtual MIUs derive their income from premiums only.
- We also assume that the premiums are calculated in relation to the long-term average cost of claims.
- The proxy for the long-term average cost is the average community-rated premium for the original dataset. We call this benchmark the "market average per-capita cost".

Cost experience of virtual MIUs

- The actual cost each virtual MIU must bear (in each of the 1,005 iterations) is the sum of the total cost of health care used by all members of each virtual MIU in each iteration, copied from the original dataset.
- The cost experience of each MIU was then compared to the benchmark market average per-capita cost

Method of calculating capital requirements

- We assume that the original dataset must have had the capital to cover the aggregate loss experience in the given year.
- Similarly, each virtual MIU needs surplus capital to cover its accumulated losses.
- As the market average per-capita cost is assumed to be the sole source of income, we consider the shortfall in the capital of a virtual MIU compared to that benchmark as the indicative measure for capital needs.

Independence

- It is assumed that the virtual MIUs are independent of each other, i.e., no interactions or correlations between them exist.

Confidence levels

- Confidence levels considered: 99.9, 99.5, 99.0, and 95.0 percent.

Findings

Like in the case of commercial insurers, MIUs also strive to pay all underwritten claims at all times. While the premium income is sufficient to cover normal claims, insurers need surplus capital as a buffer against the risk of insolvency when they experience outlier costs. The study reveals that although adding a capital loading to premiums also represents a risk that clients might consider the premiums unaffordable, it is still less than the risk of insolvency. MIUs, therefore, need capital for their sustenance.

The authors also analyzed the association between group size and capital requirements. On the basis of the observed benefit cost of 537,675 virtual MIUs, it was evident that capital loading is very sensitive to group size, and causes a considerable increase in the premium, especially for small group-sizes such as MIUs.

The recorded values of capital loading were in the range of 23.7% (at a confidence level of 95% and average group size 2,426 insureds) to 75.3% (at a confidence level of 99.9% and average group size of 620 insureds). Data also suggested that the impact of changes in confidence levels is weaker than the impact of changes in the number of insureds on capital loading levels.

A comparison was made between two options available to MIUs which can help them operate on a sustainable basis: reinsurance and partial subsidization. Reinsurers consider MIUs as unprofitable partners and therefore show less interest in this low-income market. On the other hand, MIUs are reluctant to pay a premium to reinsurers as they are not convinced that ceding risks to a reinsurer is beneficial to them. In such a situation, the government can subsidize the premium by funding the capital loading, thus bringing the premium closer to the more affordable cost of pure risk.

The study reveals that the cost of reinsurance is much lower than the minimum capital needed to assure the solvency of MIUs for all group sizes.

Conclusion

The simulation exercise leads us to the conclusion that an increase in portfolio size increases diversification of risk, and that without capital loading, the MIUs are vulnerable to the risk of insolvency. In this context, reinsurance provides a cheaper substitute to holding solvency capital directly.

The Geneva Papers, **2006**, **31**, (739–761)

www.palgrave-journals.com/gpp

Do Micro Health Insurance Units Need Capital or Reinsurance? A Simulated Exercise to Examine Different Alternatives*

David M. Dror and John Armstrong
rte de Frontenex 39b, CH-1207 Geneva, Switzerland.
E-mail: daviddror@socialre.org, johnarmstrong@eircom.net

The purpose of this article is to provide a technical discussion of capital loading that "micro health insurance units" (MIUs) must add to the premium to maintain financial sustainability. MIUs offer benefit packages and require prepayment, that is, they create a rudimentary community-based health insurance for poor people in low-income countries. We broke up the 2001 data set of a health insurer containing upward of 1.3 million insureds into 535 "*virtual MIUs*"; and running 1,005 iterations, we got a data yield of 537,675 virtual MIUs. Capital loading levels increased steeply with decreasing group size and higher confidence levels. The impact of group size remains strong even with groups of 25,000 plus, and is stronger than the impact of changes in confidence levels. We discuss options to correct size-related premium bias through government subsidies, and conclude that reinsurance is cheaper than capital loading and a preferable solution for governments compared to other alternatives.
The Geneva Papers (2006) **31,** 739–761. doi:10.1057/palgrave.gpp.2510107

Keywords: reinsurance; capital requirement; health insurance; micro health insurance units; social reinsurance; low-income countries

Introduction

The purpose of this article is to provide a technical basis for the discussion, both among market innovators in the insurance industry and among policy-makers, of financial sustainability of nascent insurance mechanisms that emerge at grassroots level in low-income countries, known as "micro health insurance units" (MIUs).

One of the limiting factors for extension of health insurance in low-income countries is the price of the premium. It is clear that the premium must reflect the aggregate risk borne by the insurer, regardless of the rating method applied. However, insurance premiums normally cover much more than the cost of the pure risk, as they must include capital loading (reflecting the cost associated with regulatory surplus requirements and with uncertainty of the risk calculations) and loading for administration (reflecting transaction costs associated with product design, premium

* This article incorporates elements from an earlier partial version (Dror *et al.*, 2005a). The calculations presented here differ from previous findings as they are based on a new and much larger set of iterations of the empirical data, and a complete revision of the text, tables, figures and references. Useful comments of four anonymous peer reviewers are gratefully acknowledged.

collection, cost of reinsurance and profits). The loadings for operational and business risks such as mispricing of underwriting and claims adjudication can be both large and difficult to measure (they are not dealt with here). Additionally, the technical assumptions used to determine profit are not always stated. Therefore, many risk-based capital models include large loads over the measurable statistical fluctuations (in the order of two to three times or more). In most low- and middle-income countries, this practice nourishes a perception that insurance premiums prioritize profits of rich insurers over protecting poor clients from financial havoc, and could thus be excessive and unfair. Hence, a reasoned discussion of loading to insurance premiums can contribute to transparency, credibility, understanding and acceptance of insurance practices, and by extension to insurance penetration in low-income countries as well as to "making insurance work for the poor".

Additionally, in many low-income countries health insurance is increasingly sold by or through community-based groups, also known as MIUs. In terms of insurance modeling, MIUs represent a multitude of fragmented, relatively small sub-pools, which are not combined into one large set. We seek to investigate the capital needs of MIUs to cover outlier costs, comparing alternative solutions, in particular own capital and reinsurance, bearing in mind the impact of the fragmentation on capital loading. This is done through a simulation exercise, which enables us to compare the capital requirements of one large pool with the capital requirements of many small sub-pools of varying sizes. The many small sub-pools are treated here as "*virtual* micro health insurance units" (virtual MIUs).

The article is structured as follows: the first section offers a short overview of why MIUs are of interest, their role, impact and estimated outreach today. The following section presents the methods employed in this study, and the next section provides the findings of the simulation. The following section contains the discussion of the findings, followed by a discussion of whether reinsurance can be an alternative to capital loading, and potential advantages of this alternative. The article then presents the limitations of the model, and in the last section it offers the authors' policy conclusions.

Background information on micro health insurance in low-income countries

The phenomenon of insuring by or through MIUs is relatively new but by no means negligible. The attraction to deal with MIUs finds its origin in the thought that, just as micro finance enabled poor people to gain access to capital, micro insurance might provide the platform to make health insurance work for the poor. The term "micro insurance" can be found in the literature for the first time in 1999,[1] but other terms have also been used before and since, including community-based health financing schemes, mutual health insurance schemes, etc.[2] In the last few years there has been new published research on the strength of MIUs in gaining clients' trust, based on the social capital of the group.[3] Several inventories of MIUs suggest that they have

[1] Dror and Jacquier (1999)
[2] Atim *et al.* (2005); Derriennic *et al.* (2005)
[3] Preker *et al.* (2002); Burdine *et al.* (1999)

developed mainly in West Africa,[4] in India,[5] Philippines,[6] and Bangladesh,[7] although quite a few MIUs operate also in other South Asian countries (e.g., Nepal[8]) and elsewhere.[9] Overall outreach is now counted in the millions of insureds.[10] Much of the literature looks at MIUs as health systems: for example, what impact do MIUs have on access to healthcare,[11] or how well do these bodies perform in terms of equality of access among members,[12] their contribution to capturing additional resources for healthcare,[13] on expressed willingness to join[14] and willingness to pay for such health insurance.[15] Also, it has been reported that MIUs usually cover a partial benefit package and that clients are sometimes involved in defining benefit packages.[16] Systematizing this practice necessitated the development and testing of a method to elicit clients' preferred priorities,[17] and to assess the judiciousness of clients' choices.[18] A fuller summary of the accumulated knowledge on MIUs would take too much space and would be beyond the scope of this paper; therefore, the purpose of this brief review is simply to point interested readers in the direction where they can find more information on this nascent form of health insurance.

Other recent developments regarding micro insurance include public–private partnership in commissioning a series of field case studies on good and bad microinsurance practices, holding an international conference in October 2005 on this topic, and the publication of a comprehensive book that summarizes the knowledge gained through the previous two activities.[19] This book includes a chapter on the definition of micro insurance, written by Craig Churchill; according to him, MIUs are financial arrangements to protect low-income people against specific perils, covering a variety of different risks (e.g., illness, death, property loss, etc) in exchange for regular premium payments that are usually small and proportionate to the likelihood and cost of the risk involved.[20] Another chapter provides an analysis of the distinct organizational models of MIUs.[21] Considering that many MIUs deal with a wide range of heads-of-damage, and operate either as agents or as friendly societies or as mutuals, we wish to limit our reference in this paper to MIUs that cover *health* risks and that *underwrite* the risk at least in part, that is, MIUs that can be compared to

[4] ILO (2002a, b)
[5] ILO/STEP (2005a)
[6] ILO/STEP (2005b)
[7] ILO/STEP (2003a)
[8] ILO/STEP (2003b)
[9] ILO/STEP (2003c)
[10] Devadasan *et al.* (2006)
[11] Dror *et al.* (2005a)
[12] Dror *et al.* (2005b)
[13] Preker *et al.* (2002)
[14] Zhang *et al.* (2006)
[15] Habbani *et al.* (2006); Dong *et al.* (2005); Dror *et al.* (2006c)
[16] Miller Franco *et al.* (2004); Preker *et al.* (2002); Danis *et al.* (2004); Loewenson (1999)
[17] Danis *et al.* (June 2006)
[18] Dror *et al.* (2006a)
[19] Churchill (2006a)
[20] Churchill (2006b)
[21] Radermacher and Dror (2006)

mutual insurers (regardless of whether they are formally licensed as cooperative insurers). Finally, it is noted that the International Association of Insurance Supervisors (IAIS) and the World Bank's Consultative Group to Assist the Poorest (CGAP) have recently embarked on drafting an *Issue Paper on the Regulation and Supervision of Microinsurance*, which could offer a framework for possible regulatory provisions for the operation of micro insurance. The aggregate impact of growing outreach, better research, and new thinking on regulation of this form of insurance clearly suggests that micro insurance is on the radar screen of those wishing to see the development of insurance penetration into the informal economy and among low-net-worth persons.

Yet there is painfully little literature on how MIUs perform in terms of insurance economics. Bonnevay *et al.*[22] examined the theoretical basis for the long-term viability of MIUs and concluded that MIUs need reinsurance and that reinsurance of MIUs can work. Feeley *et al.*[23] wrote an evaluation of the regulatory framework for providing reinsurance to MIUs, and Fairbank[24] wrote an organizational evaluation of Bonnevay's mathematical elaboration, suggesting that the very small client-base of MIUs explained why no reinsurer accepts the risks of MIUs today. We could not find any other economic analysis of the insurance function of MIUs (except an earlier version of this paper). This article takes the economic analysis beyond the theoretical study of Bonnevay *et al.* while retaining the essential economic assumption that MIUs operate as stand-alone entities. The focus of this article is on the following economic evaluation of MIUs: (i) an estimate of their capital needs; (ii) quantitative estimates of the impact of group size on capital requirements, relative to overall cost of the claim load; and (iii) a comparison of the cost of retaining capital with the cost of a reinsurance premium.

Data and methods employed in this study

Database

The objective of the exercise here is to compare the capital requirements that apply to insurers with different sizes of insureds, all other things being equal. Ideally, one would wish to use actual data of sufficient size and quality emanating from MIUs. Unfortunately, we were unable to analyse actual claims data of MIUs operating in the field, as the number of MIUs and their sizes in reality are much smaller than the scope of this simulation. Additionally, we have no valid basis to assume uniform rates of mortality, morbidity and duration of illnesses or unit- and claims costs for all MIUs. Therefore, using actual data of MIUs could raise questions whether we are comparing equal with equal, a condition that is required for an analysis of the impact of group size under the condition of *ceteris paribus*. Bonnevay *et al.* (see footnote 22) used as source for their simulations a dataset obtained through a random-number generator assuming that the incidence is distributed according to Poisson distribution and the unit cost in χ^2 distribution function. The difficulty with this option is

[22] Bonnevay *et al.* (2002)
[23] Feeley *et al.* (2002)
[24] Fairbank (2003)

that it would require postulating many complex assumptions about distributions and incidence of events and costs, as well as dependence or independence between events, if we would wish the artificial data to resemble real-life situations; and no matter how complex the assumptions, it would be impossible to verify the quality of fit-to-reality.

Fortunately, we have been able to access the 2001 data set of a large health insurer in Ireland, containing upward of 1.3 million insureds, which is sufficiently large, and for which practically all claims were settled ("the original data set"). We consider this data set to be robust because of its size and the stable nature of the claims profile experienced by this insurer. We thus performed the analysis by using an empirical distribution of health care expenditure of that health insurer in Ireland and broke up the large data source into many small "virtual MIUs", and looked at each as a stand-alone entity. Using this alternative obviated the need to make assumptions on the relationships between events or on the costs incurred, as these are inherent in the data set.

We wish to emphasize that we do not ignore the huge differences in health care settings, disease profiles and levels of claim control in low-income rural areas compared to conditions that prevail in Ireland. For one, we do not assert that the Irish data is indicative of insurance experience in low-income countries where MIUs operate. We state more on this in the section describing the limitations of the model. However, we think that the Irish dataset is superior to laboratory-generated data for the purpose of disaggregating a large pool of insureds into smaller units through repeated re-sampling without replacement (bootstrap) and counting the frequencies of excess loss for each smaller unit, because the sub-groups are perfectly comparable to each other in terms of morbidity, claim experience, unit costs and levels of claim control.

Data yield

We split the original data set into smaller groups; the number of the smaller groups was determined randomly. We obtained 535 "*virtual MIUs*". With the view to emulating the likely range of sizes of MIUs,[25,26] we applied a decision rule that each group had to count no less than 200 and no more than 5,500 insureds; within this rule, the size of membership of each group was determined randomly, and was kept unchanged throughout the experiment.

The modelling exercise (iterations)

We ran over 1,000 iterations (1,005 to be precise) of the database; in each round, we assigned individuals randomly from the original data set to one of the virtual MIUs. For each individual that was assigned, we copied the total claims cost from the original

[25] With the notable exception of Yeshasvini Trust (see reference in footnote 26), a "micro" health insurance in Karnataka (India) that has upward of a million members, all other documented cases mention the size of MIUs to be a few hundred to a few thousand members. We are guided here by this range.

[26] Radermacher *et al.* (2005)

Table 1 Data Yield (A breakdown of the number of virtual MIUs)

Size of MIU (persons)	*No. of MIUs*	*Iterations*	*Number of MIUs (all iterations)*
200–1000	95	1,005	95,475
1000–2000	123	1,005	123,615
2000–3000	121	1,005	121,605
3000–4000	120	1,005	120,600
4000–5500	76	1,005	76,380
All	**535**	**1,005**	**537,675**

data set to the relevant virtual MIU for the entire year. As stated earlier, the number of virtual MIUs remained unchanged throughout the 1,005 iterations; and the number of individuals in each virtual MIU remained constant as well. In this way, we obtained a random and different composition of persons in each virtual MIU at each iteration, reflecting a distinctive membership structure by age, gender, health status and all other risk factors affecting the level of health care utilization. Consequently, by having run 1,005 iterations of the original data set to obtain 535 virtual MIUs in each run, the total data yield in this experiment has been 537,675 virtual MIUs. The breakdown of this number of virtual MIUs by membership size is shown in Table 1.

Assumptions

Income
We assume that all virtual MIUs derive their income from premiums only. We further assume that the premiums are calculated in relation to the long-term average cost of claims, rather than relative to individual risk (risk rating) or to annual experience rating for each year separately (community rating). The proxy for the long-term average cost is the average community-rated premium for the original dataset (rather than an MIU-specific community or another rate).[27] We call this benchmark the "*market average per-capita cost*". This benchmark premium may be lower than the MIU-specific community rate.

Cost experience of virtual MIUs
The actual cost each virtual MIU must bear (in each of the 1,005 iterations) is the sum of the total cost of health care used by all members of each virtual MIU in each iteration, copied from the original data set. The cost experience of each MIU was then compared to the benchmark market average per-capita cost.

Method of calculating capital requirements
We assume that the original data set must have the capital to cover the aggregate loss experience in the given year. Similarly, each virtual MIU needs surplus capital to cover

[27] The pool-wide community rate acts as equalizer of some of the risk across the MIUs, and in reality a mechanism must be established for this equalization, which will reallocate amounts between MIUs and cover the possible difference between the sum of MIU-specific community rates and the pool-wide community rate.

its accumulated losses. As the *market average per-capita cost* is assumed to be the sole source of income, we consider the shortfall in capital of a virtual MIU compared to that benchmark as the indicative measure for capital needs.

Incidences where the costs of virtual MIUs exceeded the benchmark were noted for all virtual MIUs in all iterations. With the exception of three of the 1,005 iterations, over 90 per cent of average claims for each MIU occur within ± 25 per cent of the mean cost;[28] however, as expected, the distribution of these differences changed somewhat across iterations, and tails were skewed (meaning that the extreme situations occur more often than predicted by a perfectly normal distribution). We are interested here in the right side of the tail; the longer the tail, the greater the eventuality that claims exceeding the market average per-capita cost (outlier claims) could occur, and the greater the amount of capital the virtual MIUs need. Using the overall distribution of the deviations of costs from the benchmark,[29] and applying an adjusted form of the statistical boot-strap method,[30] we calculated the amount that needs to be added to the premiums to secure the solvency of each virtual MIU at a given level of confidence (this amount is equated here to loading for capital accumulation).

Independence

As each virtual MIU is defined by the number and characteristics of its "members" (which change from one iteration to another), we assume that the virtual MIUs are independent from each other, that is, no interactions or correlations between them exist. As we are using data of a real health insurer, we need not postulate any assumptions about the independence of cost-generating events or about possible correlations between different causes of morbidity. Possible correlations, if any, are already embedded in the claims data used. For the same reason we can also forego any assumption on the statistical distribution functions of the costs.

Confidence levels[31]

We look at confidence levels of 99.9, 99.5, 99.0 and 95.0 per cent.

---

[28] In the three cases 89 per cent of claims for each MIU were within this range.

[29] The difference between the mean claims cost of the single MIU and the market average per-capita cost, divided by the market average per capita cost.

[30] The method pioneered by Efron (1979) uses repeated samples as a basis for calculating the underlying statistical distribution of the random variable. Combined with this, the Law of Large Numbers postulates that when observations are independently and identically distributed, the sample statistics converge to the underlying population value as the number of iterations n becomes "large" (Athreya (1983)). This method is described in more detail by Chernick (1999) and Green (1997).

[31] The Confidence level is the probability value $(1-\alpha)$ associated with a confidence interval. It is often expressed as a percentage. Confidence intervals are usually calculated at 95 per cent, but one can produce 90, 99, 99.9 per cent (or whatever) confidence levels for the unknown parameter. For example, if $\alpha=0.05=5$ per cent, then the confidence level is 95 per cent$=(1-0.05)=0.95=95$ per cent. The interval gives an estimated range of values for an unknown parameter, calculated from a given set of sample data. If independent samples are taken repeatedly from the same population, and a confidence interval calculated for each sample, then a certain percentage of the intervals (confidence level) will include the unknown population parameter.

Findings

The level of capital was calculated by comparing the difference in costs per insured in a single large pool of 1.3 million insureds with the same cost when the same persons are distributed randomly over 535 virtual MIUs of different sizes and at different confidence levels. In this exercise, both the overall size of the population of the original dataset and the number of virtual MIUs remained steady (with an average size of 2,426 individuals). In addition, we created 53 medium-sized virtual MIUs (each counting no less than 2,000 and no more than 55,000 insureds, that is, 10 times larger than the 535 virtual MIUs, with average size of 24,492 individuals), and 10 large virtual MIUs (each counting no less than 10,600 and no more than 291,500 insureds, with average size of 129,808 persons), also simulated 1005 times. The purpose of these very large virtual MIUs has been to enlarge the observations of the impact of different group sizes on capital requirements, in addition to the question of capital required by these virtual MIUs. Capital requirements are expressed as a percentage of the overall average cost. The results are presented in Table 2.

As can be seen in Table 2, a higher confidence level is associated with a higher capital requirement. For example, a virtual MIU must load 44.5 per cent to its total annual cost in order to have sufficient funds to pay all its costs at 99.9 per cent of the cases, but only 37.1 per cent of annual costs at confidence level of 99.5 per cent, and only 23.7 per cent at confidence level of 95.0 per cent.

It is not surprising that a higher confidence level requires more capital (as it means less tolerance that virtual MIUs would go bankrupt). In this example, when confidence levels are lowered from 99.9 to 95.0 per cent, capital requirements drop very sharply, by almost 50 per cent. One might expect that the reduction in the probability of insolvency by a factor of 50 times would have a very significant effect, which would preclude a linear risk-return shape; and considering that in a normal distribution we would expect about 68.2 per cent of the observations to occur within one standard deviation, 95.4 per cent within two SD and 99.6 per cent of the occurrences within three SD of mean, the steep drop in capital requirement as the confidence level is lowered demonstrates a similar phenomenon. One could explain the sharp decline also in another way: the very rare cases are at the right tail of the distribution and thus the more costly ones. Therefore it costs so much more to ensure full financial cover for the most expensive 5 per cent of outliers. This finding could have important policy implications.

Table 2 also illustrates that at an identical confidence level, small groups must secure a much higher level of capital than large groups. For example, at confidence level of 99

Table 2 Capital requirements for different group sizes and at different confidence levels

Number of virtual MIUs to which the sample was divided	535	53	10
Average number of insureds per virtual MIU	2,426	24,492	129,808
Mean variation from overall average cost	0.03%	0.00%	0.00%
Standard deviation from average cost	14.40%	1.09%	0.20%
Capital requirements at 99.9 per cent confidence level	44.52%	3.38%	0.61%
Capital requirements at 99.5 per cent confidence level	37.12%	2.82%	0.51%
Capital requirements at 99.0 per cent confidence level	33.53%	2.54%	0.46%
Capital requirements at 95.0 per cent confidence level	23.72%	1.80%	0.33%

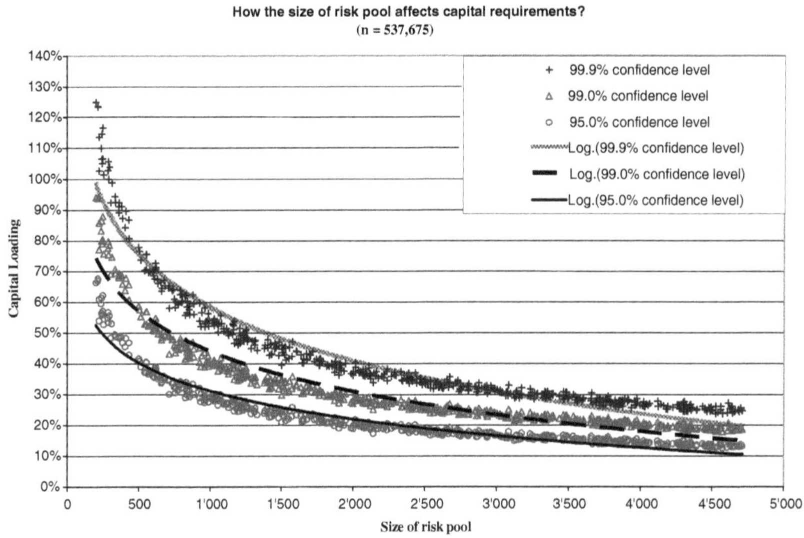

Figure 1. Capital loading and group size.

per cent, virtual MIUs with an average size of 2,426 members must load 33.5 per cent of annual cost to ensure adequate capital reserves, compared to <0.5 per cent for virtual MIUs with 129,808 insureds. This result shows the huge impact of increasing group size on reducing the standard deviation of the variation of the average cost of the virtual MIUs compared to the overall average cost of the pool of 1.3 million insureds. As we consider this variation to be a proxy measure for capital requirements, we conclude that group size has a determining influence on capital loading. We have also plotted the results for the entire dataset of 537,675 small virtual MIUs as an additional illustration of the relationship between group size and capital loading levels (Figure 1). This insight could also have policy repercussions.

Capital requirements for smaller virtual MIUs (typical for the initial period of activity)

We anticipate that when MIUs start operating, they are likely to induct few insureds (and, incidentally, fewer MIUs are likely to exist so the pool will also be smaller). We therefore estimate the capital required under the scenario that both the size of membership and the number of MIUs will increase gradually.

For this illustration, we filtered from the original dataset the virtual MIUs that were randomly assigned small group sizes: in the first year, we looked at the data of the 95 virtual MIUs with up to 1,000 insureds; in year 2, we looked at the data of the 218 virtual MIUs with up to 2,000 insureds; in year 3, we looked at the data of the 339 virtual MIUs with up to 3,000 insureds; in year 4, we looked at the data of the 459 virtual MIUs with up to 4,000 insureds; and in year 5, we looked at all the 535 MIUs, each with up to 5,500 insureds. The calculated estimates, at the same confidence levels that were used before, are given in Table 3. The bold numbers in Table 3 are identical to data already shown in Table 2, reproduced here for ease of comparison of the smaller virtual MIUs to the 535 virtual MIUs.

Table 3 provides data that amplifies the insight that capital requirements are considerably higher for virtual MIUs with fewer insureds, and that capital requirements drop also when the confidence level is lowered. For example, at confidence level of 99.9 per cent, capital loading above average costs is 75.3 per cent when average group size is under 1,000 members and drops to 44.5 per cent when average group size increases to 5,500. And when the confidence level is relaxed to 95 per cent, the corresponding loading factors drop to 40.0 and 23.7 per cent, respectively.

Consequences of retaining insufficient capital

MIUs that retain low or no capital reserves run the risk of insolvency. An estimate of this risk is presented in Tables 4 and 5. Table 4 contains the expected solvency of the 535 virtual MIUs in the original dataset; Table 5 presents the expected insolvency rates for smaller virtual MIUs.

The bold-highlighted figures in Table 4 are identical to those shown in Table 2, and are repeated here for ease of reference. This table shows that if the average capital retained by the simulated 535 virtual MIUs is lower than the required 23.7 per cent, the expected probability of insolvencies grows quite dramatically. And, as could be expected, it would be even higher when smaller virtual MIUs fail to keep adequate capital levels. These calculations are presented in Table 5.

Table 5 provides the demonstration that average group size also influences the risk of insolvency due to insufficient capital. For example, when capital retention is 20 per cent, the larger groups (average group size 2,426) have 8.3 per cent risk of insolvency, whereas smaller virtual MIUs (with average membership of 620) incur 21.6 per cent risk of insolvency. Interestingly, the gap between larger and smaller groups diminishes as capital inadequacy becomes more pronounced, and disappears altogether in the extreme case that the virtual MIUs keep no capital at all. In such situation, all virtual MIUs run an identical risk of insolvency of 50 per cent, regardless of their size. It should be noted that the risk of insolvency increases over time as well: even if an MIU

Table 3 Capital requirements for smaller MIUs with fewer insureds

Year	1	2	3	4	5
Number of virtual MIUs in the pool	95	218	339	459	535
Number of insureds per virtual MIU	⩽1,000	⩽2,000	⩽3,000	⩽4,000	⩽5,500
Avg number of insureds per virtual MIU	620	1,092	1,594	2,103	2,426
Mean variation from overall average cost	0.16%	0.11%	0.06%	0.05%	0.00%
Standard deviation from average cost	24.20%	19.30%	16.80%	15.20%	14.40%
Capital requirements at 99.9 per cent confidence level	75.30%	59.90%	52.00%	47.00%	44.52%
Capital requirements at 99.5 per cent confidence level	62.60%	49.90%	43.40%	39.20%	37.12%
Capital requirements at 99.0 per cent confidence level	56.60%	45.10%	39.20%	35.30%	33.53%
Capital requirements at 95.0 per cent confidence level	40.00%	31.90%	27.70%	25.00%	23.72%

Table 4 Expected insolvency rates at various levels of capital shortage

Margin of retained capital (above average market cost)	*Expected proportion of all schemes becoming insolvent*
23.72%	5.0%
20%	8.3%
10%	24.5%
5%	36.5%
1%	47.3%
0%	50.0%

Table 5 Expected insolvency rates of small MIUs

MIUs in simulation	*Average MIU Size*	*Insureds*	*Retained Capital*				
			0%	*1%*	*5%*	*10%*	*20%*
			Expected proportion of all schemes becoming insolvent				
95	620	⩽1,000	50.00%	48.60%	42.10%	34.20%	21.60%
218	1,092	⩽2,000	50.00%	48.10%	40.00%	30.40%	15.20%
339	1,594	⩽3,000	50.00%	47.80%	38.20%	27.40%	11.80%
459	2,103	⩽4,000	50.00%	47.50%	37.30%	25.60%	9.50%
535	2,426	⩽5,500	50.00%	47.30%	36.50%	24.50%	8.30%

with insufficient capital survives the first year, its aggregated probability to survive two years is lower, three years even lower, etc.

Before concluding this section we wish to remind that this analysis is expressly limited to estimating capital loading in respect of *underwriting risks*, that is, the capital required to cover outlier cost of benefits above the expected average per insured. We are aware that the prevailing practice in the insurance industry is to base the calculations on additional components of operational risk. More on this point is explained in the section that deals with the limitations of the model.

Discussion of the findings

Micro health insurance units need capital

It was stated earlier that this paper focuses on MIUs that underwrite health risks. MIUs that underwrite risk fill the institutional role of providing insurance in surroundings where affordable and pertinent insurance products are usually hard to get. Although the business process and the value chain of MIUs differ from those of commercial insurers, some fundamentals are nevertheless similar. One of these fundamental essentials is the ability of MIUs to pay all underwritten claims at all times. Capital loading is one way to secure that such an engagement is kept. Insurers collect premiums that should normally pay for their customers' losses in full. This implies that when insured losses exceed premium income, insurers must pay for losses out of their own capital. Therefore, insurers need surplus capital as a buffer against insolvency when they experience outlier costs. The higher the uncertainty about the characteristics of the covered risk, the more difficult it is to calculate premiums accurately. In these circumstances, insurers usually increase the capital loading to reduce their risks. The theoretical explanation for capital needs is that outlier costs can occur due to statistical fluctuations in the number or in the cost of claims or both ("underwriting risk"), but also due to other reasons. Incidentally, the same logic applies to operational risks, which are however outside the focus of this article.[32]

It has been shown that MIUs operating with insufficient or no capital are exposed to a considerable risk of insolvency. We must recognize that adding a capital loading to premiums also represents a risk that clients might consider the premiums unaffordable or unfairly high. However, we feel that insolvency is the bigger of the two risks, because default on benefit payment is a bigger dampener of trust, and without trust there is no insurance. We therefore conclude that MIUs need capital (or foolproof capital relief, e.g., external deficit guarantees).

Impact of group size on capital requirement

What we have seen in this study, based on the observed benefit cost of 537,675 virtual MIUs, leads us to say that capital loading is very sensitive to group size, and causes considerable increase in the premium, observed in particular for small group-sizes that are typical of MIUs. The observed values of capital loading range from a low of 23.7 per cent (at confidence level of 95 per cent and average group size 2,426 insureds) to a high of 75.3 per cent (at confidence level of 99.9 per cent and average group size of 620 insureds) (see Tables 3 and 5).

An earlier analysis of the impact of group size[33] linked the phenomenon to two statistical characteristics: first, at an identical risk, small groups have a wider distribution, and thus a higher likelihood of outlier claims. Secondly, when the probability drops, small groups benefit less from that drop, because of the larger variance. That study (based on theoretical assumptions of risk distributions of two virtual MIUs, one of 100 and the other of 1,000 members) concluded that a major source of uncertainty of MIUs was their small group size. This study suggests that the impact of group size does not disappear even when groups number about 25,000 insureds, or 25 times larger than in the theoretical analysis. The relevant data is shown in Table 2: a tenfold increase from 2,426 to 24,492 insureds resulted in the lowering of the standard deviation from 14.1 to 1.1 per cent but this was still much higher than 0.2 per cent, which was registered for the virtual MIU with 129,808 members. This insight is new, and is probably linked to a lower decline in the variance due to unit cost than to the variance due to the incidence.

---

[32] We refer here to "operational risks" but shall not deal with these here, other than to point out that there is no uniform and generally accepted definition of operational risk. Incidentally, there is much debate on how this risk can be quantified and whether it should be counted in the risk-based capital requirements of the insurer.

[33] Dror (2001); Dror and Preker (2002).

Impact of confidence interval

The second important insight gained from this study is that the impact of changes in confidence levels is weaker than the impact of changes in the number of insureds on capital loading levels. For example, an increase in the number of insureds from 2,426 to 24,492 reduced capital requirement from 44.5 to 3.4 per cent (about 13-fold), whereas a decrease of the confidence interval from 99.9 to 95 per cent brought about a reduction in capital requirements from 44.5 to 23.7 per cent (less than two-fold) (Table 2).

Impact of insufficient reserving

When capital reserves are lower than required the risk of insolvency increases rapidly. Considering that small MIUs must load higher levels, they have a more difficult job to get clients to pay a loading factor of, for example, 25 per cent than 30 or 40 per cent. Consequently, small MIUs are more likely to be insufficiently capitalized, and therefore also more exposed to the risk of insolvency and bankruptcy. It is of course self-explanatory that when the virtual MIUs do not retain any capital at all, their group size no longer influences their risk of insolvency, which is a uniform 50 per cent.

Alternatives to maintaining capital

We refrain from discussing the desirable but hypothetical option of government funding of social health insurance, which would obviate the phenomenon of MIUs in low-income countries. We focus on the reality of health financing in low-income countries, which includes MIUs; and we are interested to explore what can be done to enable them to operate on a sustainable basis, which is also in line with tried-and-tested mechanisms in use by the insurance industry. Two options seem the most likely: reinsurance and partial subsidization. Needless to say, these two options are not mutually exclusive. However, for the sake of clarity of the discussion, we treat each separately.

Reinsurance

The original purpose of reinsurance is to enable primary insurers to limit their exposure to the (more affordable) average cost of the underwritten risk, while transferring to another risk-carrier the costs linked to unexpected changes in the portfolio or business environment. This relationship is based on two fundamental processes: (i) Reinsurance enlarges the pool of insureds captured by its clients, the primary insurers, for better diversification. This upward move along the insurance "production chain" (which looks like an inverted pyramid) translates to a higher absolute claim-load and a smaller difference between actual and expected results. (ii) Reinsurance simplifies primary insurers' access to reinsurers' larger supply of capital and information. Reinsurers may actually be exposed to more outlier risks than primary insurers, but can nevertheless improve the value chain because they can enjoy lower cost of capital through better leveraging; one very tangible aspect is that reinsurers are required to meet lower/different levels of solvency compared to primary insurers. Therefore, they can underwrite more risk for every dollar of capital/surplus.[34]

Secondly, reinsurers have a unique inside view of the insurance industry, particularly in markets where they interact with a large number of primary insurers. Therefore, they can share with clients an understanding of how best to address underwriting challenges and management concerns about expanding (or reducing) their existing product lines. This expertise is valuable for primary insurers who are particularly exposed to the risk of error in estimating the underwritten average risk or the cost of claims of a new product ("innovation error").

How prevalent is reinsurance? Considering that the global insurance market is largely concentrated in very few rich countries,[35] and bearing in mind that only one lower-middle income country has high insurance penetration[36] but not a single low-income country, we can well assume that reinsurers are not all that familiar with the context of MIUs. There are of course reinsurers in several low-income countries, such as General Insurance Company (GIC) in India, which serve their commercial insurance companies, and which sometimes even enjoy monopoly or quasi-monopoly status. However, these country-specific reinsurers have very little exposure to reinsurance of health insurance. Hence, the expertise in health reinsurance is relatively modest, their acquaintance with risk profiles of MIUs is rather cursory, and the offer of reinsurance is very rare indeed.

MIUs have limited experience in underwriting risk professionally, and virtually no experience with ceding risks to reinsurance. In fact, two obstacles stand in the way of exploiting this option: the legal/regulatory barrier, and the doubts about clear win-win relations. The regulatory obstacle consists of requiring reinsurers to do business only with registered/licensed insurers; many MIUs are not registered as insurers, would probably be unable to qualify for such license due to various financial and formal barriers to entry. For instance, in India, where quite a number of MIUs operate, the regulatory requirement for insurance license includes depositing Rs 1 billion (~US$ 22 million), an amount that is prohibitive, disproportional to the risk that the MIU would underwrite, and which excludes any MIU from qualifying for formal recognition. Consequently, neither side can negotiate or sign treaties. Secondly, in most low-income countries, just as most poor people cannot buy insurance, MIUs cannot buy reinsurance. This has been explained by the Chairman of the Supervisory Board of Munich Re, Dr. Hans-Jürgen Schinzler, in his address to the Microinsurance Conference in October 2005: "Premium income is low, administrative costs are relatively high, and infrastructure for insurance is lacking; that's why commercial insurers have not taken more interest in this market".[37] But even if the reinsurers would decide to show more interest in the low-income market, MIUs would also need

---

[34] Capital/Surplus=Admissible Assets – Liabilities

[35] In 2005, 85 per cent of global premium volume was concluded in only 10 countries (U.S.A., Japan, U.K., Germany, France, Italy, South Korea, Canada, Spain and The Netherlands) of which five countries captured almost 75 per cent of global insurance premiums (U.S.A., Japan, U.K., Germany, France). Source: Swiss Re (2006).

[36] The notable exception is South Africa, a middle-income country, which has the highest rate of premiums as percentage of GDP in the world.

[37] Churchill *et al.* (2006)

to be convinced that they can gain from ceding the major part of their risks to reinsurance. It is not quite clear who should provide the technical support for such a development. The insurance industry seems in unison that cooperation with MIUs will occur only when reinsurers can earn a profit from it; and most MIUs find it difficult to understand why their poor clients should add to the profits of reinsurers that are much wealthier than the clientele of MIUs. For the time-being, neither governments nor development agencies have agreed to facilitate the development of win–win relations. The purpose of this paper is to show that there is substantive basis for doing so. The following section has more on this.

Government subsidies

It is taken as a given here that subsidies are an effective tool in directing public financing. There is more experience with subsidizing access to health care, but some proposals have been formulated to subsidize access to health insurance. For instance, the Commission on Macroeconomics and Health (in 2001) suggested "to offer local communities an incentive scheme, in which each $1 that the community raises for pre-paid health coverage would be augmented, at some rate of co-financing, by the national government (backed by donor assistance)".[38]

This proposal to subsidize premiums would probably be complicated to implement due to the known difficulties in efficient targeting and controls against fraud. The analysis of capital loading opens up an alternative route for subsidization of health insurance: reducing the capital loading payable by insureds. This subsidy can be implemented for MIUs, which in any case operate in low-income and rural sub-groups, and which are unlikely to induct persons who live far away from their centre of activity or earn much higher income. The internal logic of why governments should subsidize the equivalent of capital loading resides in taking a risk-equalizing measure that puts MIUs at par with larger groups in terms of financial solvency. Stated differently, if the government had a single (national) pool, its sheer size would have reduced the rate of capital loading; MIUs offering health insurance in lieu of a national social health insurance should not be exposed to higher vulnerability due to small group size, and their members, who are mostly low-net-worth, should not have to subsidize the cost of government inaction in this domain. In fact, government funding of the capital loading would bring the premium closer to the more affordable cost of pure risk, and this subsidy would be available only to those who agree to pay the (lower) premium. As the insureds would be unable to manipulate this capital loading or convert it into an income-related subsidy in the form of a voucher, this subsidy would be much easier and much cheaper to administer. The cost of capital loading would also compare very favourably for governments with the cost of delivering even a modest form of health insurance, because the cost of the loading is in all cases lower than the total amount of the premium. A practical way of implementing this form of subsidization would be through a reinsurer, namely through the affiliation of MIUs to a designated reinsurer that would offer reinsurance (e.g., stop loss or excess loss) at concessionary rates that reflect no or minimal capital loading.

[38] Sachs (2001, p. 60).

The authors are aware that such a proposal has not yet been implemented anywhere. However, the idea of tying resource generation (by collecting a premium) to partial subsidization (by reducing component costs of the premium) offers a strong internal logic, coupled with lower public expenses, which nevertheless offer an improvement over the prevalent situation as it is known today.

This logic suggests that governments should be keen to support links between MIUs and a reinsurance facility, either by creating such facility directly or by enabling a nongovernmental social reinsurance to function. And one way to encourage such development is through subsidies. At least four reasons justify using government subsidies to reduce MIUs' reinsurance premiums: (i) as discussed earlier in this paper, the cost of the risk diminishes when the group is larger. The more MIUs join the reinsurance pool, the larger the overall group size, and the lower the community-rated reinsurance premium payable. All MIUs that participate in the reinsurance pool will capture sizeable savings compared to scheme-specific community-rated premium. However, no MIU would accept to absorb the cost of covering the risk of other MIUs. Therefore, the pooling arrangement can work if the difference between the pool-wide community rate and the MIU-specific risk rate is subsidized. The subsidy amount will in fact ensure that more risky and smaller MIUs will de facto enjoy a higher subsidy, and this targeting is very efficient because it does not require any additional administrative adjustment to base the subsidy on the inherent characteristics of reinsured health risk. (ii) One way of reducing the reinsurance premium and the contribution of the MIU is to reduce to zero the loading for capital requirements plus interest. This can be done if the necessary capital is supplied from another source, either as an upfront cash payment or by way of concessionary drawing rights in case of need. This subsidy can be limited in time to the first few years of operation of the MIU and the social reinsurer. (iii) MIUs have no experience with reinsurance, and the higher the reinsurance premium, the more likely their reluctance to pay it. Yet MIUs are most vulnerable financially precisely in the first few years, when they need reinsurance most, both for surplus relief and for technical assistance. A subsidy can reduce their status-quo bias. (iv) One of the arguments against supporting small MIUs is their inadequate administrative capacity. MIUs need capacity building and technical assistance, which they cannot pay for but which can be cheaper and more effective when provided by the reinsurance. This support is customary in the reinsurance industry, because it is not only cost-effective but enhances adherence to the industry rules on reporting and audit. The classical sharing of responsibilities entrusts front-office activities with the MIU (to capture their relative advantage in low-cost collection of contributions and social pressure to reduce free-riding), and back-office functions with the reinsurer in a pool-wide service centre (to process claims, analyse costs for actuarial, costing and product development purposes, negotiate with providers of health care, etc).

In closing, one should recall that there are a few examples of governments' role in support of the development of insurance through subsidies. For example, in Ghana the subsidy covers part of the health insurance premium;[39] in Mexico, the government

[39] Atim *et al.* (2001)

subsidizes part of the reinsurance premium of crop reinsurance (Agroasemex);[40] in Turkey the government has created a reinsurance facility for earthquake risks.[41] This list of examples is by no means exhaustive. And there are other measures that could be suitable, for example, guaranteeing drawing rights in case of catastrophic exposure.

Tradeoff between reinsurance and accumulating capital

Reinsurance is an alternative to holding contingency reserves (capital), and its cost is easily measured by the premium payable. All other things being equal, if the two alternatives are equal, they should be interchangeable. However, considering that capital markets are imperfect and that there is less than perfect information about the underlying risk of each insurer, the monetary cost of both options is unlikely to be equal.[42] In addition, the reinsurance premium is calculated differently according to whether the reinsurance contract is proportional or non-proportional. For proportional reinsurance contacts, the larger the "ceding commission" the insurer receives from the reinsurer, the cheaper the net reinsurance premium. For non-proportional reinsurance contracts, pricing is based on the reinsurer's estimate of expected underlying losses, plus loading for administration costs and profit. One of the key questions is how the cost of reinsurance compares with that of retaining reserves.

As we cannot model the exact levels of reinsurance premiums in the way we have done for capital loading, we resort to the only model that we have found in the literature, the *Social Re* model, which claims that the minimum reinsurance premium is equal to half the standard deviation of the average cost of stand-alone MIUs (see footnote 30). Taking the values of the standard deviation given in Table 2, one can see that the premium would be lower than the loading for capital in all cases reviewed. However, it should be recalled also that at that premium level, the reinsurer can survive only if 20 MIUs or more are reinsured after five years. The numbers are shown in Table 6. Of course these numbers are merely indicative, and in reality it would be necessary to base the premium on the value of the standard deviation applying to each MIU specifically. But, as illustrated in Table 6, the gap between capital loading and reinsurance premium is so large that a small margin of error (due to the possible difference between average value of the SD and the specific value) does not fundamentally alter the conclusion.

The main insight is that the cost of reinsurance is much lower than the minimum capital needed to assure the solvency of MIUs for all group sizes. As a reminder, Table 2 shows that capital loading will be only 0.33 per cent when the size of the insured population reaches 129,808 clients at 95 per cent confidence level. Needless to say, this extremely large size is irrelevant as a comparison for most MIUs, and the only lesson one can draw from this information is that subsidizing the reinsurance premium can be done by comparison to a notional large group that would be akin to the pool of

[40] World Bank Institute (2004); AGROAsemex (2006)
[41] Gurenko (2000); Selamet (nd)
[42] In fact given the operational risk associated with MIUs the cost of acquisition of external capital may be prohibitive.

Table 6 Comparison between reinsurance premiums and capital loading

Size of MIUs	*Standard deviation from average cost (%)*	*Estimated reinsurance premium under the* Social Re *model (%)*	*Capital loading (at 95% confidence) (%)*
⩽5,500	14.40	7.20	23.70
⩽4,000	19.30	9.65	25.00
⩽3,000	16.80	8.40	27.70
⩽2,000	19.30	9.65	31.90
⩽1,000	24.20	12.10	40.00

a universal health insurance. Hence the extra large group of insureds shown in Table 2 could be a relevant benchmark.

Similarly, there could be an option to subsidize the difference in capital loading due to the application of a higher versus a lower confidence level. The same logic applies: all parties have an interest that MIUs should remain solvent. The cost of applying the difference is relatively low, and this subsidy cannot be subject to the habitual concerns of abuse, free riding or misappropriation, in so far as the reduction in the loading translates into a reduced premium, and this reduction can be captured only by those who agree to pay the premium but by nobody else.

Limitations of the model

This paper focuses on the risk of random clustering of cost-generating events, which is greatly affected by the claim-load, which in turn is directly associated with membership size. The exposure to these issues is one of the defining characteristics of MIUs.

The novelty of this study resides in using an actual database that reflects real health events, real costs, real statistical distributions and the real correlations between events. However, all these "real" components relate to the reality of Ireland, which is quite different from the reality of MIUs. We nevertheless used this database because the prospect of using real empirical data of MIUs, desirable as it is, is unrealistic for the time being due to lack of sufficient data and lack of standardization of definitions of relevant parameters. We felt that the Irish data set is superior to an artificial database obtained through a random number generator, plus a series of assumptions about distributions and interdependencies. We recognize that the model we present should not be construed to suggest that we present an accurate approximation of the costs of real MIUs. The real costs could be calculated with exact information on the relevant epidemiological situations, morbidity, definitions of benefits covered by insurance and the costs of care. In particular, the incidence of infectious diseases is higher in most low-income countries, and can be much more prone to fluctuations than in Ireland, but by no means uniform for all low-income countries. Secondly, statistical fluctuations are strongly dependent on the actual claim load, which is smaller in MIUs because of the compound effect of small group size and of the limited benefit package. That said, it is also clear that the trends affecting capital loading will be the same in Ireland and in areas where MIUs operate, even if absolute values differ.

Specifically, a steep increase in capital loading can be expected when the group size decreases or when the confidence levels are increased.

Hence, this exercise is useful in terms of weighing economic alternatives of loading a capital factor to premiums or obtaining capital through reinsurance. The exact details will vary from only one MIU to another, relative to the specific risk exposure and the specific size and benefit package it offers.

In addition, we have dealt here only with capital loading within the definition given in this article. We specifically excluded additional loading related to operational risk, because its definition is not uniform even in the countries with high insurance activity.

While we recognize that group size is somehow related to topics such as propensity to join MIUs and willingness to pay, we formulate no assumptions on these issues because they are beyond the topic at hand. Nor do we deal with the difference in adverse selection or moral hazard on claim loads, because we used a dataset that already reflected the possible impact of these elements and did not require these assumptions for a relevant simulation exercise.

Finally, this simulation looked at a single year of operation. Were it not for logistical limitations, we would have liked to run multi-year results, notably in order to measure the effect of a longer time-series on capital requirements. That said, the size of the data being so large, it is unlikely that the results would change considerably from year to year.

Conclusions

This article set out to examine capital needs of "micro health insurance units" to ensure financial sustainability, and examine alternatives to satisfy these needs.

The detailed analysis of the impact of group size on capital needs of MIUs suggests that for an identical risk-exposure and an identical premium, MIUs may go bankrupt when larger groups will not. This quantitative illustration is extremely important for two reasons:

- First, it demonstrates that the poor are acting logically in refusing insurance that offers them lower financial protection for the same price that ensures higher financial protection to other insureds. Some would argue that the poor should be allowed to pay a lower premium, reflecting their lower ability to pay. But even those who reject this approach and plead for equal cost for the same level of risk-mitigation must surely agree that it is unreasonable to expect the poor to pay a higher premium for an identical insurance product, emanating from a higher capital loading due to smaller group size. This illustration of the premium bias suggests that the market alone does not offer an automatic corrective measure; thus, insurance regulators would have a role to play in ensuring fair pricing that would not disadvantage clients of MIUs.
- Secondly, this is the first illustration of inherent reasons why MIUs must break away from stand-alone operations if they are to keep the cost of transfer of risk at affordable levels. The cost of transferring risk is linked to the size of the pool, and conceptually different from the cost of diversification.

The analysis has shown that governments have many options to correct the premium bias caused by the higher capital requirement that MIUs must meet. Some of the options would be to subsidize the difference in capital loading that is directly related to small group size, by applying the capital loading rate that would apply to a large (national) group rather than the higher rate applicable to smaller MIUs. Governments could also create a facility that would allow MIUs to draw loans to meet their capitalization requirements in bad years. Additionally, governments could subsidize the difference in the cost of applying a lower confidence level by offering insolvency protection at a higher confidence level. This is of course very similar to reinsurance.

It should be stressed that interventions aiming to correct the size-related premium bias of MIUs address the cost of risk transfer (from individuals to small groups and from small groups to larger ones) without influencing the cost of risk bearing (which relates to the pure risk component of the premium).

It has been shown that the solution of reinsurance is cheaper capital loading (by reference to a model that provided a generalized formula for the cost of reinsurance relative to standard deviation). And it has been shown that MIUs need capital from inception. This leads us to suggest that MIUs cannot forego reinsurance from inception.

Reinsurance is a safer solution for governments compared to other alternatives, such as rolling out a modest version of social health insurance. The cost of universal cover under social health insurance is forbidding for most low-income countries, and can put governments under heavy pressure to constantly increase budget allocations as the needs grow. On the other hand, government facilitation of access to reinsurance, notably by subsidization of part of the reinsurance premium, mitigates governments' risk that they might have to pay without cap in cases where MIUs fail financially. By opening the tried-and-tested route that links MIUs to reinsurance, governments would have no more risk related to MIUs than they have in respect of any commercial insurer. The option of subsidizing the reinsurance premium would also be a more interesting alternative for governments than setting up social health insurance, because the subsidy of the reinsurance premium would be payable only in conjunction with premium payment by – and thus revenue generation from – the end beneficiaries of these subsidies. Such balance between revenues and payments would be very difficult to ensure through the alternative route of social insurance for the poor. Also, the accounting and accountability of flows of funds between insurer and reinsurer is much more stringent than can be expected in a publicly funded social health insurance.

In conclusion, the simulation exercise reported here shows that an increase in portfolio size increases diversification of risk (and vice versa); that without capital loading, the MIUs are exposed to an unacceptable risk of insolvency and bankruptcy; and that reinsurance is a cheaper substitute to holding solvency capital directly. These findings confirm that the basic principles underlying the success of insurance apply equally well to MIUs, which are in an embryonic form of underwriting risk and are usually composed of small groups. This confirmation is very important in determining the role of MIUs, and shows that if the barriers-to-ceding-risks to reinsurance that

MIUs face today were removed, MIUs could offer a relevant and sustainable vehicle for extension of insurance penetration among low-income persons in low-income countries.

References

AGROAsemex (2006) 'Retrocession in AGROAsemex', http://www.agroasemex.gob.mx/english/acerca/A4_01.html (accessed July 2006).

Athreya, K.B. (1983) 'Strong law for the bootstrap', *Statistics and Probability Letters* **1**: 147–150.

Atim, C., Diop, F. and Bennett, S. (2005) *Determinants of the Financial Stability of Mutual Health Organizations: A Study in the Thies Region of Senega*, Bethesda, MD: The Partners for Health Reform*plus* Project, Abt Associates Inc.

Atim, C., Grey, S., Apoya, P., Anie, S. and Aikins, M. (2001) 'A survey of health financing schemes in Ghana', available online: http://www.phrplus.org/Pubs/Tech013_fin.pdf,accessed 15 July 2006.

Bonnevay, S., Dror, D.M., Duru, G. and Lamure, M. (2002) 'A model of microinsurance and reinsurance' (chapter 7), in D.M. Dror and A.S. Preker (eds) *Social Reinsurance: A New Approach to Sustainable Community Health Financing*, Washington: World Bank & ILO, pp. 153–186.

Burdine, J.N., Felix, M.R.J., Wallerstein, N., Abel, A.L., Wiltraut, C.J., Musselman, Y.J. and Stidley, C. (1999) 'Measurement of social capital', *Annals of the New York Academy of Sciences* **896**(1): 393.

Chernick, M. (1999) *Bootstrap Method: A Practitioner's Guide*, Hoboken, NJ: Wiley & Sons (Wiley Series in Prob. & Statistics).

Churchill, C. (ed) (2006a) *Protecting the Poor: A Microinsurance Compendium*, Geneva: ILO.

Churchill, C. (2006b) 'What is insurance for the poor?' (Chapter 1.1), in C. Chuchill (ed) *Protecting the Poor: A Microinsurance Compendium*, Geneva: ILO, pp. 12–24.

Churchill, C., Reinhard, D. and Qureshi, Z. (2006) 'Into action: microinsurance – report summary microinsurance conference', Munich, Washington and Geneva: Munich Re Foundation, CGAP Working Group on Microinsurance and ILO, January (online at: http://www.munichre-foundation.org/NR/rdonlyres/A7C0E563-3F94-41A5-B7A7-1CAC19C85F96/0/IntoAction01_2006_Microinsurance_E.pdf).

Danis, M., Biddle, A. and Goold, S. (2004) 'Enrollees choose priorities for medicare', *The Gerontologist* **44**(1): 58–67, available online: http://gerontologist.gerontologyjournals.org/cgi/content/abstract/44/1/58,accessed 4 October 2005.

Danis, M., Binnendijk, E., Ost, A., Vellakkal, S., Koren, R. and Dror, D.M. (2006) 'Eliciting the health insurance Benefit choices of low-income populations in India with the CHAT exercise', submitted for publication in *Health Services Management Research*.

Derriennic, Y., Wolf, K. and Kiwanuka-Mukiibi, P. (2005) *An Assessment of Community-Based Health Financing Activities in Uganda*, Bethesda, MD: The Partners for Health Reformplus Project, Abt Associates Inc.

Devadasan, N., Ranson, K., Van Damme, W., Acharya, A. and Criel, B. (2006) 'The landscape of community health insurance in India: an overview based on 10 case studies', *Health Policy* **78**(2–3): 224–234.

Dong, H., Kouyate, B., Cairns, J. and Sauerborn, R. (2005) 'Inequality in willingness-to-pay for community-based health insurance', *Health Policy* **72**(2): 149–156.

Dror, D.M. (2001) 'Reinsurance of health insurance for the informal sector', *Bulletin of the World Health Organisation* **79**(7): 672–678.

Dror, D.M., Armstrong, J. and Kalavakonda, V. (2005a) 'Why micro health insurance schemes cannot forego reinsurance', *Journal of Insurance and Risk Management* (special issue on micro health insurance) (Greater Noida, India) **4**(7): 1–29.

Dror, D.M. and Jacquier, Ch. (1999) 'Micro-insurance: extending health insurance to the excluded', *International Social Security Review* **52**(1): 71–97.

Dror, D.M., Koren, R., Ost, A., Binnendijk, E., Vellakkal, S. and Danis, M. (2006a) 'Health insurance benefit packages prioritized by low-income clients in India: Three criteria to estimate effectiveness of choice, submitted for publication in *Social Science and Medicine*, May 2006.

Dror, D.M., Koren, R. and Steinberg, D.M. (2006b) 'The impact of filipino micro health insurance units on income-related equality of access to healthcare', *Health Policy* **77**(3): 304–317, doi:10.1016/j.healthpol.2005.08.001.
Dror, D.M. and Preker, A.S. (eds) (2002) *Social Reinsurance: A New Approach to Sustainable Community Health Financing*, Washington: World Bank & ILO, pp xvii + 518.
Dror, D.M., Radermacher, R. and Koren, R. (2006c) 'Willingness to pay for health insurance among rural and poor persons: field evidence from seven micro health insurance units in India', in *Health Policy* (in press), doi: 10.1016/j.healthpol.2006.07.11.
Dror, D.M., Soriano, E.S., Lorenzo, M.E., Sarol Jr., J.N., Azcuna, R.S. and Koren, R. (2005b) 'Field based evidence of enhanced healthcare utilization among persons insured by micro health insurance units in Philippines', *Health Policy* **73**(3): 263–271.
Efron, B. (1979) 'Bootstrap method: another look at the jackknife', *Annals of Statistics* **7**: 1–26.
Fairbank, A. (2003) *Sources of Financial Instability of Community-Based Health Insurance Schemes: How Could Social Reinsurance Help?*, Technical Report No. 024. Bethesda, MD: The Partners for Health Reform*plus* Project, Abt Associates Inc.
Feeley, F.G., Gasparro, D.J. and Snowden, K. (2002) 'Assessment of piloting social reinsurance in the Philippines', in D.M. Dror and A.S. Preker (eds) *Social Reinsurance: A New Approach to Sustainable Community Health Financing*, Washington: World Bank & ILO, pp. 423–441.
Green, W.H. (1997) *Econometric Analysis* 3rd Edn, Upper Saddle River, NJ: Prentice Hall.
Gurenko, E.N. (2000) *The Role of World Bank in Supporting Turkish Catastrophe Insurance Pool* World Bank Conference on Innovations in Managing Catastrophic Risks, Washington DC http://www1.worldbank.org/finance/assets/images/DCconference.pdf,accessed December 2004.
Habbani, K., Groot, W. and Jelovac, I. (2006) 'Household health-seeking behaviour in Khartoum, Sudan: the willingness to pay for public health services if these services are of good quality', *Health Policy* **75**(2): 140–158.
ILO (2002a) *Extending Social Protection in Health Through Community-Based Health Organizations*, Community-Based Schemes Working papers.
ILO (2002b) *Micro-assurance santé: Guide d'introduction aux mutuelles de santé en Afrique*, Guides and Manuals.
ILO/CGAP, (forthcoming) *Book On Micro Finance*, Geneva: ILO.
ILO/STEP (2003a) *Micro Insurers: Inventory of Micro-Insurance Schemes in Bangladesh*, Community-Based Schemes Working paper, Geneva.
ILO/STEP (2003b) *An Inventory of Micro-Insurance Schemes in Nepal*, Community-Based Schemes Working papers.
ILO/STEP (2003c) *Extending maternity protection to women in the informal economy. An overview of community-based health-financing schemes*, Community-Based Schemes Working papers, Geneva.
ILO/STEP (2005a) *India: An inventory of micro insurance schemes* Community-Based Schemes Working Paper no. 2, Geneva.
ILO/STEP (2005b) *Inventory of Micro-Insurance Schemes in the Philippines*, Community-Based Schemes Working paper no. 1, Geneva.
Loewenson, R. (1999) *Public Participation in health: Making people matter*, IDS Working Paper 84, available online: http://www.ids.ac.uk/ids/bookshop/wp/wp84.pdf,20 June 2005.
Miller Franco, L., Mbengue, C. and Atim, C. (2004) *Social Participation in the Development of Mutual Health Organizations in Senegal*, Bethesda, MD: The Partners for Health Reformplus Project, Abt Associates Inc, Available online: http://www.phrplus.org/Pubs/Tech056_fin.pdf [09.06.05].
Preker, A., Carrin, G., Dror, D.M., Jakab, M., Hsiao, W. and Arhin, D. (2002) 'Effectiveness of community health financing in meeting the cost of illness', *Bulletin of the World Health Organization* **80**(2): 143–150, available online: http://www.scielosp.org/pdf/bwho/v80n2/a10v80n2.pdf, accessed 27 May 2005.
Radermacher, R. and Dror, I.H. (2006) 'Institutional options for delivering health insurance', chapter (4.4) in C. Churchill (ed) *Protecting the Poor: A Microinsurance Compendium*, Geneva: ILO, pp. 401–423.
Radermacher, R., Wig, N., van Putten-Rademaker, O., Müller, V. and Dror, D.M. (2005) *Good and Bad Practices in Microinsurance: Yeshasvini Co-Operative Farmers Health Scheme*, Karnataka, India, Report commissioned by ILO Social Finance Unit and CGAP, Sept 2005.

Sachs, J. (Chairperson) (2001) *Macroeconomics and Health: Investing in Health for Economic Development*, Report of the Commission on Macroeconomics and Health, World Health Organization, Geneva, p. 60.

Selamet, Y. (nd) *The Turkish Catastrophe Insurance Pool (TCIP) and the Compulsory Earthquake Insurance Scheme*, available online: http://info.worldbank.org/etools/docs/library/114715/istanbul03/docs/istanbul03/11yazici3-n per cent5B1 per cent5D.pdf.

Swiss Re (2006) 'World Insurance 2005', *Sigma Insurance Research* 5/2006, http://www.swissre.com/ (accessed Jul 2006).

World Bank Institute (2004) 'Presentation of Agroasemex', http://www.worldbank.org/wbi/banking/insurance/natdisaster/pdf/, accessed December 2004.

Zhang, L., Wang, H., Wang, L. and Hsiao, W. (2006) 'Social capital and farmer's willingness-to-join a newly established community-based health insurance in rural China', *Health Policy* **76**(2): 233–242.

Part 3

Evidence

Chapter 10

Health Insurance Benefit Packages Prioritized by Low-Income Clients in India: Three Criteria to Estimate Effectiveness of Choice*

Main Messages

- A total of 302 individuals from a number of villages and towns, organized in 24 groups, participated in a consensus-building exercise.
- Health care utilization data originated from 2,049 households that reported at least one illness episode during 3 months prior to the survey.
- The choices made by the respondents were reviewed using three criteria — the "reimbursement criterion", the "fairness criterion", and the "catastrophic protection criterion".
- Such an exercise of simulating the impact of different rationing choices on household expenditure for health care, and the three criteria formulated to evaluate different choices, has not been attempted prior to the publication of this chapter.

---

*This chapter is reproduced form *Social Science & Medicine* (2016), **64**(4), 884–896, available at https://www.researchgate.net/publication/6656925_Health_insurance_benefit_packages_prioritized_by_low-income_clients_in_India_Three_criteria_to_estimate_effectiveness_of_choice.

Focus Points

- The poor can actively participate in designing their own insurance package without compromising on the judiciousness of rationing choices.
- By using the CHAT tool, it has been possible for predominantly illiterate and innumerate groups in India (with almost no experience with health insurance), to compose benefit packages for health insurance with a limited budget of INR 500 (USD 11) per household per year.
- About 88% of respondents chose at least three out of four 'major' benefits that are directly related to vital care in case of illness and which also cost the most.
- Respondents preferred a wide range of benefits at basic levels of coverage, rather than a narrow choice of benefit types with higher coverage levels.
- The results implied a desire to improve one's quality of life and avoiding situations causing severe morbidity.
- The choices made by respondents revealed a preference for their long-term needs and those of their communities, over and above the needs of those with acute illnesses only.

Structured Abstract

Introduction

The target population for microinsurance comprises largely of illiterate and innumerate persons with no prior experience with insurance. This chapter puts forward the findings of an experiment directed at understanding the rationing choices of this population segment in India when given the opportunity to compose an affordable health insurance package for themselves. The authors aim to draw policy insights from the analysis of these insurance choices made by the poor.

Method

The chapter adopts an innovative consensus-building exercise called 'Choosing Healthplans All Together (CHAT)'. CHAT was conducted in Nov–Dec 2005 in Karnataka and Maharashtra with around 302 participants organized in 24 groups. Participants had the option to choose from

10 benefit types, and for most benefit types, they could choose three coverage levels: basic, medium and high.

Since CHAT packages were not part of an insurance contract, the authors had to use the data of utilization and cost sourced from a household survey as proxy. The utilization data originated from 2,049 households that reported at least one illness episode during 3 months prior to the survey (out of 3,531 households where we could obtain valid answers for the set of questions on spending on illness). The incidence and distribution of unit costs of hospitalizations, consultations, diagnostic tests, and purchase of prescribed drugs were estimated based on the household survey, with adjustments made by an actuary with field experience in India.

The choices made by the participants were juxtaposed with actual costs related to illness episodes incurred by a comparable cohort. The results were reviewed using three criteria — the "reimbursement criterion", the "fairness criterion", and the "catastrophic protection criterion".

Box 1: Three Criteria to Determine the Perceived Effectiveness of Benefit Packages

Reimbursement criterion

- Assumes that the poor wish to be reimbursed some part of every bill, irrespective of whether the absolute level of expenditure is low or high
- Measure: Mean reimbursement rate

Fairness criterion

- States that the insured would like insurance to pay a small part when the bill is small and a big part when the bill is big[1]
- Measure: Extent and direction of the correlations between expenditures and the rate of reimbursements

(Continued)

[1] Toth, W. (2005). Satisfaction is job one. Insurance & Technology (July 2005).

Box 1: (*Continued*)

Catastrophic protection criterion

- States that the insured wish to be covered against catastrophic exposure[2]
- Measure: the extent of compensation for the outlier cases

Findings

Analysis of data from the CHAT exercise revealed that 88.4% of the participants chose a package that included at least three of the "major benefits", and their choices were at the basic level of coverage. The remaining 11.6% of the participants opted for only two of the major benefits, with coverage levels higher than basic in some cases.

It was observed that the most frequently chosen packages scored highly on all three criteria, and thus rationing choices were confirmed as judicious. A key finding was that respondents preferred a wide range of benefits at basic levels of coverage, rather than a narrow choice of benefit types with higher coverage levels. The preference was for packages which provide coverage for expensive care, irrespective of whether the expense was the result of a few rare and expensive events or a result of frequent events each costing modest amounts.

The pattern of choices made by respondents showed that they were willing to trade off optimal coverage of major benefits in return for coverage of minor benefits. This can be interpreted as a desire to improve one's quality of life, and avoiding situations causing severe morbidity. It also highlights that respondents' value their long-term needs and those of their communities, over and above the needs of those with acute illnesses only.

Conclusion

The CHAT exercise provides a means to actively involve community members in the design of their health insurance packages, albeit their

[2]Radermacher, R. (2006). Health insurance for the poor — Examples from India. Unpublished monograph.

low levels of literacy and numeracy. This tool can be used by policy-makers in resource-poor countries to encourage participation in voluntary health insurance, by supporting benefits that the respondents prioritize through a subsidy of medium cover at the cost of basic coverage.

Health insurance benefit packages prioritized by low-income clients in India: Three criteria to estimate effectiveness of choice ☆

David Mark Dror[a,*], Ruth Koren[b], Alexander Ost[c], Erika Binnendijk[d], Sukumar Vellakkal[e], Marion Danis[f]

[a]*Erasmus University Rotterdam, Institute for Health Policy & Management, rte de Frontenex 39B, 1207 Geneva, Switzerland*
[b]*Tel Aviv University Medical School, Tel Aviv, Israel*
[c]*University of Cologne, Cologne, Germany*
[d]*Erasmus University Rotterdam, Institute for Health Policy & Management, The Netherlands*
[e]*Institute for Social and Economic Change, Bangalore, India*
[f]*National Institutes of Health, Bethesda, MD, USA*

Available online 4 December 2006

Abstract

We applied a decision tool for rationing choices, with a predetermined budget of about US$11 per household per year, to identify priorities of poor people regarding health insurance benefits in India in late 2005. A total of 302 individuals organized in 24 groups, participated from a number of villages and neighborhoods of towns in Karnataka and Maharashtra. Many individuals were illiterate, innumerate and without insurance experience. Involving clients in insurance package design is based on an implied assumption that people can make judicious rationing decisions. Judiciousness was assessed by examining the association between the frequency of choosing a package and its perceived effectiveness. Perceived effectiveness was evaluated by comparing respondents' choices to the costs registered in 2049 illness episodes among a comparable cohort, using three criteria: '*reimbursement*' (reimbursement regardless of the absolute level of expenditure), '*fairness*' (higher reimbursement rate for higher expenses) and '*catastrophic coverage*' (insurance for catastrophic exposure). The most frequently chosen packages scored highly on all three criteria; thus, rationing choices were confirmed as judicious. Fully 88.4% of the respondents selected at least three of the following benefits: outpatient, inpatient, drugs and tests, with a clear preference to cover high aggregate costs regardless of their probability. The results

☆This CHAT experiment was jointly implemented by the project 'Strengthening Micro Health Insurance Units for the Poor in India' and the National Institutes of Health of the US Public Health Service (NIH). The European Commission within the EU–India Economic Cross-Cultural Programme funded the project. The household survey was partly funded by the Deutsche Gesellschaft für Technische Zusammenarbeit (GTZ India). NIH funded the development of CHAT materials, and personnel training and facilitation of the exercise. Logistical support was provided by the Birla Institute for Management Technology, Greater Noida (India). Persons who contributed include: D. Garand, S. Khare, A. Joshi, N. Badwe, A. Rao, F. Hay and K. Shailabh, Dr. Sudarshan, and the leaders and residents of the villages that participated. O. Koren provided research assistance in data mining. R. Radermacher, and O. van Putten Rademaker provided essential logistical support. The opinions expressed are those of the authors, and do not reflect positions of the institutions they are associated with.

*Corresponding author. Tel.: +41 78 790 6789; fax: +41 22 788 2288.

E-mail addresses: daviddror@socialre.org (D.M. Dror), rkoren@post.tau.ac.il (R. Koren), alexander.ost@gmx.de (A. Ost), erikabinnendijk@gmail.com (E. Binnendijk), sukumar109@rediffmail.com (S. Vellakkal), mdanis@nih.gov (M. Danis).

D.M. Dror et al. / Social Science & Medicine 64 (2007) 884–896 885

show that involving prospective clients in benefit package design can be done without compromising the judiciousness of rationing choices, even with people who have low education, low-income and no previous experience in similar exercises.

Keywords: India; Benefit package design; Low-income population; Rationing choices; Access to healthcare; Health insurance

Introduction

The purpose of this article is to draw policy insights from the analysis of choices made by prospective clients among the poor in India on benefit-package composition for health insurance.

Many authors agree that if the poor are to accept insurance, it must respond to their needs (Ahuja & Jütting, 2004; Gumber, 2002; Leftley, 2005; Radwan, 2005). However, these authors advocate that the industry design different insurance products for the poor, but do not refer to perceived priorities of the clients themselves. The literature on consumer-driven healthcare has so far dealt mainly with the situation in rich countries. Coast (2001) investigated whether citizens want to make rationing decisions in healthcare in the context of universal coverage in the UK. Her findings suggest inter alia that the potential distress that denying care may cause increases citizens' desire to be directly involved in such decisions. Following this logic, poor population segments in low-income countries, who can at best buy only severely rationed health insurance packages, would presumably be exposed to high potential distress due to limited access to healthcare, and would therefore wish to be involved in rationing decisions. In developing countries, there is a general shortage of information and data about the preferences of households (Asfaw, 2003). Specifically, there is very little literature on the preferences of prospective clients of health insurance who personify simultaneously low-income, low-education, low-numeracy and low- or no experience with insurance. The few studies we were able to identify concluded that 'groups of low-income uninsured individuals [in the USA] are able to identify acceptable benefit packages that are comparable in cost but differ in benefit design from managed care contracts offered to many US employees' (Danis, Biddle, & Goold, 2002); that clients' satisfaction with benefit-package design in a community-based health insurance scheme in West Africa contributed to a higher willingness to enroll (De Allegri, Sanon, Bridges, & Sauerborn, 2006); and that in the same area, there were strong preferences for inclusion of high-cost health services such as operation, essential drugs and consultation fees in the benefit package (Dong, Mugisha, Gbangou, Kouyate, & Sauerborn, 2004). Finally, one study, carried out in India on a somewhat related topic, suggested that most households would prefer a comprehensive benefit package over partial coverage (Mathiyazhagan, 1998). However, this falls short of evidence-based reporting of the preferences of such population segments in India. Thus, our article offers new information on the expressed priorities of households that were asked to compose the health insurance package of their choice.

In India today, out-of-pocket spending by households for healthcare represents about 73% of total health expenditure (WHO, 2006); another estimate puts that rate at more than 80% (Devadasan, Ranson, Van Damme, Acharya, & Criel, 2005). This high rate exposes many households to unexpected and unaffordable healthcare costs for which insurance can be an attractive and cheaper alternative (Ray, Pandav, Anand, Kapoor, & Dwivedi, 2002). However, at present only about 3% of India's population, mostly in the formal sector, benefit from some form of health insurance and the role of grassroots community-based schemes is prominent in the informal economy relative to the alternatives offered by the public sector or by commercial insurers (Devadasan et al., 2005; Tabor, 2005).

Furthermore, community-based health insurance schemes in India cover a partial benefit package that reflects the assumption that premiums are the main source of financing. If the poor are to pay for insurance, the package must be attractive in two regards: it must meet clients' perceived needs and be affordable to them (Radwan, 2005; Wiesmann & Jütting, 2000). Since affiliation to grassroots schemes is voluntary, and considering that willingness to join such schemes may increase when prospective clients are satisfied with the benefit package and identify with it (De Allegri et al., 2006; Fleck, 1994; Schone & Cooper, 2001), it is important to develop a tool to assess prospective clients' priorities.

The novelty of the experiment described in this article is that it divulges information on the rationing choices of low-income, low-education population segments in India who were given the opportunity to compose an affordable benefit package.

Methods

Study design

The 'Choosing Healthplans All Together' (CHAT) experiment described here is based on a modified version of an original CHAT tool developed and tested in the USA (Danis et al., 2002; Danis, Biddle, & Goold, 2004; Goold, Biddle, Klipp, Hall, & Danis, 2005; Keefe & Goold, 2004). Around 302 individuals organized in 24 groups participated in the exercise. The exercise was carried out in November–December 2005, in Karnataka and Maharashtra. Selection of the villages or neighborhoods of towns where the interviews were conducted was purposive, based on contacts the research group established through a household survey conducted earlier in 2005. Participation in the groups was voluntary, and depended on availability of persons at the day and time of assembly rather than on sampling techniques. In reality, most people in the locations wanted to participate. The material was translated into several local languages; local facilitators were trained to read out instructions and provide explanations so that illiterate persons could nevertheless participate. We saw no evidence that illiterate persons were less intelligent or less capable of making choices once they were given help to overcome the objective limitation of illiteracy.

The CHAT exercise enabled participants to choose from 10 benefit types; for most benefit types, participants could choose three coverage levels: basic, medium and high. The choice was limited to basic or high coverage level for three benefit types (see Table 1 for benefit types; and see algorithms of coverage levels below).

If the most expensive options were selected for all benefits, the estimated actuarial cost of the package would have been INR 1470 per household. This amount is far too high for most low-income households in India. We set the predetermined budget of the package at INR 500 (~US$11) per household per year, which approximates the level of willingness-to-pay (WTP) obtained from a survey

Table 1
Sticker cost of benefits

Benefit types	Coverage level		
	Basic	Medium	High
Drugs (D)	18	18+12	18+12+12
Outpatient medicine (OP)	11	11+6	11+6+10
Hospitalization (IP)	10	10+6	10+6+8
Tests (T)	8	8+5	8+5+5
Dental care (DEN)	7	7+4	7+4+5
Medical equipment (ME)	5	5+3	5+3+3
Preventive care (P)	1	1+1	1+1+1
Maternity (M)	1		1+1
Indirect costs (IC)	1		1+1
Mental health care (MH)	1		1+1

conducted by the same research group simultaneously and reported elsewhere (Dror, Radermacher, & Koren, 2006). This WTP study suggested that about half the sampled population was willing to pay around 1.35% of annual HH income. We also checked the median HH income of the populations in the areas where the CHAT experiment unfolded; in Maharashtra, median income for the comparable cohort was INR 48,000; and in Karnataka, median income was INR 39,800. By determining a premium of INR 500 for this CHAT experiment, we ensured that it did not exceed 1.3% of income for 50% of the target population, i.e. within the range of the expressed WTP values. This estimate is also supported by the findings of Gumber (2002) that annual WTP in rural areas in India ranged from INR 80 to 95 per person per year for hospitalization, chronic care, specialist consultations; and that WTP was some 10% higher if medicines, diagnostic tests and transportation were added.

We would have liked to examine the judiciousness of rationing decisions of CHAT participants by applying actual reimbursement decisions. As the CHAT packages were not part of an insurance contract, we used as proxy the data of utilization and cost obtained from a household survey conducted by the same research group in 2005 in India (and which was also the source of data for the WTP study mentioned above). The utilization data originate from 2049 households that reported at least one illness episode during 3 months prior to the survey (out of 3531 households where we could obtain valid answers for the set of questions on spending on illness). This dataset is relevant for the CHAT experiment because the socio-economic–

demographic characteristics of the cohorts were comparable. We applied the CHAT business rules to this proxy.

Algorithms for the calculation of coverage levels

Basic level of coverage: covers 50% of all costs; 50% is paid out-of-pocket

Medium level of coverage: benefit increases as the bill increases, according to the following formula:

a. bill under median cost: insurance pays 50% of bill,
b. bill between median and 70th percentile: insurance pays

$$(\text{Median}/2) + (\text{bill} - \text{median} * 0.9).$$

c. bill higher than 70th percentile: insurance pays:

$$(\text{Median}/2) + (\text{p70} - \text{median}) * 0.9 + (\text{bill} - \text{p70}) * 0.95.$$

High level of coverage: 100% of all costs; zero out-of-pocket payment.

We did not expect the participants to understand these complex algorithms, and explained the reimbursement rules using easy-to-understand examples. For instance, the explanation for hospitalization was as follows: '*Basic level*: Insurance pays half your bill. *Medium level*: You pay half the cost of low amounts, but as your bill increases your insurance payments increase even more. For example, when your bill is INR 1000 you pay INR 500, but when the bill is INR 10,000 you pay only INR 1275. *High level*: Insurance pays your entire bill'.

Definitions of what is included under the various benefit types

The cost of drugs (**D**) includes only prescribed allopathic drugs but excludes the cost of traditional (homeopathic or ayurvedic) drugs and unprescribed drugs.

The cost of outpatient care (**OP**) includes payments for consultations with a general practitioner, pediatrician and with specialists, but excludes consultations with traditional practitioners.

Inpatient care (**IP**) costs reflect all out-of-pocket costs that are required during periods of IP, including surgery in hospital (note: antenatal & postnatal care & confinement for delivery are categorized as maternity benefits, not IP).

The cost of diagnostic tests (**T**) includes lab tests and medical imaging.

The cost of dental care (**Den**) includes all care given by a dentist.

The cost of medical equipment (**ME**) includes eye glasses, hearing aids, wheelchairs, crutches and ambulance.

The cost of preventive care (**P**) includes preventive services for household members older than 1 year.

The cost of maternity (**M**) includes mother's care before, during and after delivery in hospital, and child's care until 1 year; also includes family planning.

The cost of indirect costs (**IC**) covers INR 50 or INR 100 (for basic or high levels of coverage, respectively) per day of hospitalization (compensating wage loss and transportation of patient and care giver). IC also covers the cost of continuing the health insurance coverage if the HH head died or is permanently disabled (3 months coverage at basic level and 6 months' extension at high level).

The cost of mental health (**MH**) covers treatment for mental illnesses, alcohol or drug abuse.

Actuarial estimates of costs

The incidence and distribution of unit costs of hospitalizations, consultations, diagnostic tests and purchase of prescribed drugs was estimated based on the HH survey, and adjusted as necessary by an actuary with field experience in India. The incidence and distribution of unit costs of P, Den, mental care, ME and M was estimated by the same actuary. The estimated incidence of IC was established by the actuary. The adjustments made to the data were based on actuarial experience with various insurance schemes in India and other countries considering the overall national household expenditures for health in India.

The actuarial calculations that determine the cost of the benefits were expressed in monetary terms, which were converted to stickers. Respondents received a budget of 50 stickers (each sticker reflected the value of INR 10). The 'sticker values' of each benefit type and each level of coverage that was available in this experiment are shown in Table 1.

The choices that clients could make

The version of the CHAT exercise consisted of two rounds. In the *first round*, each participant composed a benefit package that met his/her and her/his families' priorities separately, by selecting benefit types and the level of coverage (basic, medium or high). Players indicated their choices by gluing stickers on circles drawn on a board. In the *second round* of the game, the whole group (group sizes ranged from 10 to 17 respondents) composed a benefit package that reflected the choice of the entire group; at this stage, group discussions continued until a consensus had been reached. During the discussions, the facilitator mediated the process to ensure that preferences of all participants were considered. In cases when facilitators noted attempts of certain respondents to dominate the discussion, they intervened and requested those individuals to respect the feeling of others. The opinions of all participants on the fairness of the process were solicited through an exit questionnaire; 72% strongly agreed and 27% agreed with the statement: 'the way the group reached its decision was equally fair to each member of the group'. More details on the group dynamics and participants' satisfaction with the process are provided elsewhere (Danis et al., 2006).

The process of choice offered in the CHAT exercise obliged respondents to make a yes–no choice first; if respondents did not choose a particular benefit, the outcome was termed 'nothing'. For every benefit chosen, participants had to select the basic level of benefits first, and add stickers for the choice of a higher level of coverage thereafter.

At the end of round one, players picked *health event cards* that contain a scenario/story of an illness episode and what it costs. Participants could then estimate what they would have received from the insurance according to the coverage level they selected (basic, medium or high) if they had experienced the same scenario. The validation of choices against a concrete scenario was read out aloud and thus enabled participants to assess their choices, or change them in the next round.

Data

The choices noted by players on the CHAT boards were uploaded to an electronic file. The dataset retained the identification of each group of players, as well as a separate record of replies in round one and in round two. The structure of the record ensured confidentiality, as replies were not traceable back to any specific respondent.

Analysis

Statistical analysis of the data was performed by using SPSS statistical software.

Findings

Choices made by participants

The choices of respondents (the number of replies and percent of total population that selected the benefit types, as well as levels of service) are recorded in Table 2.

The number of positive replies (including basic, medium or high levels) is significantly higher (χ^2 test) than the negative ones (who preferred excluding that benefit), for all benefits except Den and ME. We observe more choices at the basic level (1626), followed by high level (521) and fewest choices of medium level of coverage (49). If benefit types are ranked according to the frequency of positive replies, the ranking is as follows: M (100% positive replies); drugs (92.7%); IC (90.4%); tests (83.8%); IP (82.1%); P (77.8%); OP (56.6%); MH (56.0%); ME (45.7%); and Den (42.1% positive replies).

Major benefits

The facilitators who observed the entire experiment reported that most respondents started the selection process by choosing two, three or four of the following: D, OP, IP and T. Non-access to these four benefits can spell disaster in case of illness, and paying for this access out-of-pocket could significantly deplete household finances because they represent the highest aggregate expenses. The high cost of these services was also reflected in the high sticker cost (shown in Table 1). They were thus denoted here as 'major benefits'.

In Table 3 we show the combinations of major benefits that respondents selected in this CHAT experiment. The cost of the combination including all four major benefits at basic level of coverage was 47 stickers of the available 50. This leaves very few stickers for other benefit. Participants were thus confronted with the question whether to select all four major benefits at basic level or to forego one or more of the 'major four' in order to buy higher coverage levels for the remaining major benefits and/or include minor benefits in their package. Participants chose only eight combinations that

Table 2
Choices of the participants

Type of benefits	Nothing		Basic		Medium		High	
	Replies	% of total	Replies	% of total	Replies	% of total	Replies	% of total
Drugs (D)	22	7.28	280	92.72	0	0.00	0	0.00
Out patient medicine (OP)	131	43.38	171	56.62	0	0.00	0	0.00
Hospitalization (IP)	54	17.88	225	74.50	13	4.30	10	3.31
Tests (T)	49	16.23	231	76.49	12	3.97	10	3.31
Dental care (DEN)	175	57.95	115	38.08	12	3.97	0	0.00
Medical equipment (ME)	164	54.30	138	45.70	0	0.00	0	0.00
Preventive care (P)	67	22.19	105	34.77	12	3.97	118	39.07
Maternity (M)	0	0.00	144	47.68	0	0.00	158	52.32
Indirect costs (IC)	29	9.60	130	43.05	0	0.00	143	47.35
Mental health care (MH)	133	44.04	87	28.81	0	0.00	82	27.15
Totals	824		1626		49		521	

Table 3
Packages chosen

	Choice[a]	No. of groups	No. of individuals	% of all individuals	Sticker cost (%)	Stickers left for minor benefits
1	OP(b) + IP(b) + T(b) + D(b)	6	81	26.8	47	3
2	IP(b) + T(b) + D(b)	8	96	31.8	36	14
3	OP(b) + T(b) + D(b)	3	42	13.9	37	13
4	OP(b) + IP(b) + D(b)	3	36	11.9	39	11
5	OP(b) + IP(b) + T(b)	1	12	4.0	29	21
6	IP(m) + D(b)	1	13	4.3	34	16
7	T(m) + D(b)	1	12	4.0	31	19
8	IP(h) + T(h)	1	10	3.3	42	8

[a]OP = outpatient; IP = inpatient; T = tests; D = drugs; (b) = basic; (m) = medium; (h) = high.

include one or more of the four major benefits, described in Table 3. Many other permutations were theoretically possible.

The data in Table 3 show that 88.4% of the participants chose a package that includes at least three of the 'major benefits' and all choices are at the basic level of coverage. The remaining 11.6% of the participants chose only two of the major benefits, but at coverage levels that were sometimes higher than basic.

Criteria to determine the perceived effectiveness of benefit packages

The entire proposition of involving clients in benefit-package design is based on an implied assumption that a group of people acting as a cohesive social unit can relate, better than any outsider, needs and priorities to the location-specific conditions, prevalent activities and level of resources (Dror & Jacquier, 1999). It also implies that people are capable of judicious rationing decisions. We propose that a positive association between the frequency of a choice of a package and its perceived effectiveness would signify a 'judicious rationing decision'.

We define the following criteria as the quantitative expressions of the 'perceived effectiveness of a benefit package':

(1) *The reimbursement criterion*: suggests that insured wish to be reimbursed some part of every bill, regardless of whether the absolute level of expenditure is low or high. This attribute is important for people who perceive insurance as useless when there is no reimbursement in case

of an illness episode (Gumber, 2002; Insure.-com). This criterion can be gauged by the mean reimbursement rate.

(2) *The fairness criterion*: postulates that the insured would like insurance to pay a small part when the bill is small and a big part when the bill is big (Toth, 2005). This criterion can be gauged by the extent and direction of the correlations between expenditures and the rate of reimbursement.

(3) *The catastrophic protection criterion*: states that the insured wish to be covered against catastrophic exposure (Radermacher, 2006); this criterion can be measured by the extent of compensation of the outlier cases.

It has been explained under the 'Methods/Study design' section that utilization and cost data obtained in the HH survey were used to evaluate the effectiveness of the CHAT choices. For each illness episode we summed the costs related to the 'major benefits' and these sums were considered as the total expenditure. We then applied the CHAT business rules to each expenditure item, and obtained the estimated reimbursable amount for each package. This was repeated for all eight packages and for each of the 2049 episodes. The details of expenses and reimbursements are shown in Table 4.

Examining the reimbursement criterion

Table 4 provides the reimbursement levels of healthcare expenses both in INR and in percentages (the rates were shown relative to the total expenditure of each episode). The mean and maximum rates of reimbursement for the first five packages cannot exceed 50%, as the applicable business rule is that reimbursement at the basic level of coverage is 50% of expenses.

In looking at the mean percent of reimbursements, it is clear that selecting all four 'major benefits' at the basic level (package 1) yielded the best returns. Interestingly, the mean reimbursement rate per illness episode was very similar to package 4, in which T was dropped. Surprisingly, when IP is dropped (package 3) the mean level of reimbursement is lower by less than 5%; a likely explanation for this small reduction is the low probability of being hospitalized. On the other hand, dropping OP (package 2) caused a dramatic drop in mean reimbursement rate. And giving up D (package 5) caused a drop of about half the mean reimbursement rate. Similar results were noted when OP and T are dropped, even though IP coverage was increased to medium level (package 6). Finally, when both OP and D were dropped (package 8), mean reimbursement was only 11.1% of expenses during an illness episode, even though IP and T were covered at high level.

The strong impact of dropping either OP (package 2) or D (package 5) on reimbursement rates, and the minor impact of dropping IP (package 3) or T (package 4) is even more apparent when looking at median levels of reimbursement: whereas 50% of those who chose packages 3 or 4 received the same reimbursement level that they would have received had they chosen package 1,

Table 4
Hypothetical reimbursements for the different packages

No.	Combination	Reimbursed (in INR)			Reimbursement % of expense[a]		Percentile of reimbursements (%)			
		Mean	SE±	Median	Mean[b]	SE±	10th	25th	Median	90th
1	OP+IP+T+D	489	±30	125	46.80	±0.27	50.0	50.0	50.0	50.0
2	IP+T+D	393	±26	90	30.72	±0.38	0.0	20.0	35.7	50.0
3	OP+T+D	322	±15	115	41.97	±0.34	12.5	41.7	50.0	50.0
4	OP+IP+D	447	±28	120	44.26	±0.30	28.5	47.8	50.0	50.0
5	OP+IP+T	305	±26	40	23.46	±0.37	0.0	10.0	21.7	50.0
6	IP(m)+D(b)	432	±38	75	22.72	± 0.37	0.0	7.6	22.6	45.3
7	T(m)+D(b)	225	±12	60	19.41	±0.34	0.0	4.7	18.8	41.7
8	IP(h)+T(h)	418	±45	0	11.10	± 0.46	0.0	0.0	0.0	42.9

OP = outpatient; IP = inpatient; T = tests; D = drugs; levels of benefit: (b) = basic; (m) = medium; (h) = high.

[a]Expenses per illness episode were calculated on the basis of responses to the HH survey. Of the 2049 illness episodes, 131 cases did not report any expenses for any of the 'major benefits' types. The nominal values of all illness episodes were: mean INR 1045 (SE ±63) and median INR 290.

[b]HH that reported zero expenditure for the 'major benefits' types were considered as obtaining zero reimbursement (and zero %); this explains why the mean reimbursement figures (calculated for the entire population) are lower than 50% of expenses, even for package 1.

half the people who chose packages 2 or 5 obtained considerably lower reimbursements. Choosing packages 6 or 7, which included only two of the major benefits, resulted in median reimbursement of less than half the percentage payable for package 1. The most dramatic effect is observable with package 8, where the reimbursement rate was zero in half the illness episodes. It is noteworthy that 10% of the episodes would not generate any reimbursement at all under packages 2 or 5 or 6 or 7; and 10% of those who selected packages 3 or 4 would have been entitled to much lower reimbursement than under package 1.

Examining the fairness criterion

The situation whereby 10% of the population is getting low or no reimbursement may be acceptable when it applies to inexpensive episodes. However, such an outcome would be unsatisfactory if it caused low reimbursement rates to those who incur high healthcare costs. From the data presented so far it is not clear which illness episodes received low reimbursement when respondents forego one or more of the 'major benefits'. The answer to this question can be found by looking at the correlations between the level of reimbursement and the absolute level of expenses. A positive correlation means that people who incur higher expenses are entitled to higher compensation (in %); and a negative correlation means that those with higher expenses are entitled to lower compensation, which is an undesirable outcome.

In package 1 there is no correlation between expenses and reimbursement (expressed as % of total costs) because the rule is to always reimburse 50%, regardless of cost. As can be seen in Table 5, the coverage of IP is associated with significant and positive correlations (packages 8, 6, 2, 5). Dropping IP from the benefit package resulted in a negative correlation (which is strong for package 3, but much weaker for package 7). An interesting case is package 4, which contains IP at the basic level of coverage but does not include T; it is associated with a significant negative correlation which is however much weaker than package 3.

Examining the catastrophic protection criterion

So far, the calculations were based on the entire sample. We now wish to examine which package would yield the highest reimbursement when the most expensive episodes occur. This question was analyzed by reference to the most costly decile, i.e. 195 illness episodes that cost more than INR 2400. The results are shown in Table 6:

The package including all 'major benefits' secured the highest mean reimbursement rate in the case of outliers as before, followed by package 4, with packages 2 and 8 tagging closely behind. The difference between the packages is more pronounced when one looks at the lowest 10th percentile of reimbursement: whereas package 4 guarantees up to 37.1% reimbursement, package 2 provides only up to 26.9% and package 8 (composed only of IP and T at high coverage level) a mere 3.4% reimbursement. The explanation for this low reimbursement rate under Package 8 is found in its composition: high coverage level for IP and T offers no protection for high expenses due to D or OP. And, contrary to what one might have expected, outlier cases (top 10% of expenses) cannot automatically be assumed to involve hospitalizations, even if it is true that the highest outlier cases do involve IP.

Table 5
Correlations between expenses and reimbursement levels (in %)

No.	Combination	Correlation coefficient (Pearson)	Significance
1	OP+IP+T+D	0.0	
2	IP+T+D	0.1766	$P<0.0001$
3	OP+T+D	−0.3947	$P<0.0001$
4	OP+IP+D	−0.0801	$P<0.0005$
5	OP+IP+T	0.1431	$P<0.0001$
6	IP(m)+D(b)	0.2848	$P<0.0001$
7	T(m)+D(b)	−0.0598	$P<0.001$
8	IP(h)+T(h)	0.4081	$P<0.0001$

Comparing the effectiveness of the benefit packages according to the three criteria

We wish to compare the effectiveness of the different benefit packages in the light of the three criteria elaborated earlier. For this purpose, we developed a ranking system whereby the package that scores highest under each criterion was assigned the score of 1 and the package that scored lowest was assigned the value of zero. All other packages were assigned a value between zero and one, reflecting their relative position on a linear scale. For the *reimbursement criterion*, packages were scored according to the mean reimbursement rate (in %)—values noted in Table 4 column 6—and package 1 was assigned the score of 1, while

Table 6
Expenses and reimbursement levels—outlier cases

No.	Combination	Reimbursed			Reimbursement % of expense[a]		Percentile of reimbursements			
		Mean (INR)	SE± (INR)	Median (INR)	Mean (%)	SE± (%)	10th	25th	Median	90th
1	OP+IP+T+D	3298	±226	2125	50.0	±0.0	50.0	50.0	50.0	50.0
2	IP+T+D	2765	±209	1725	41.7	±0.7	26.9	37.7	45.8	50.0
3	OP+T+D	1761	±100	1425	31.7	±1.1	10.3	17.0	34.4	50.0
4	OP+IP+D	2990	±213	1950	44.3	±0.6	37.1	42.9	46.8	50.0
5	OP+IP+T	2377	±219	1500	32.4	±1.0	10.0	22.2	35.9	50.0
6	IP(m)+D(b)	3312	±337	1700	34.9	±1.3	14.3	20.9	32.3	61.3
7	T(m)+D(b)	1261	±86	1000	18.4	±1.1	2.1	5.8	14.2	41.4
8	IP(h)+T(h)	3688	±406	2300	38.9	±2.0	3.4	13.8	36.4	78.1

OP = outpatient; IP = inpatient; T = tests; D = drugs; levels of benefit: (b) = basic; (m) = medium; (h) = high.
[a]Expenses per illness episode were calculated on the basis of responses to the HH survey, based on 195 illness episodes that represented the top 10%. The values of all illness episodes were: mean (INR 6595), SE (±452) and median (INR 4250).

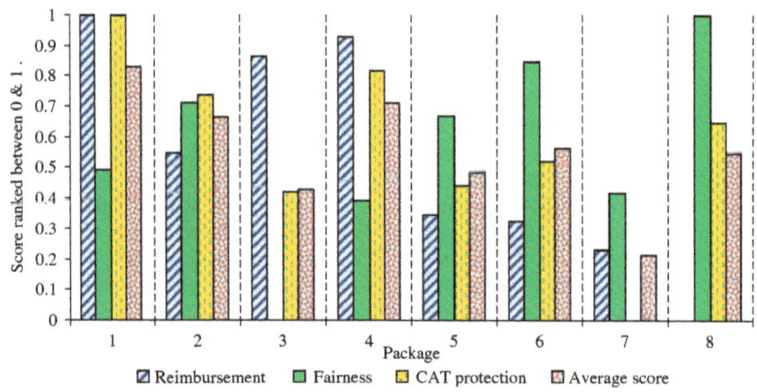

Fig. 1. Weighted ranking of benefit packages according to the three criteria.

package 8 scored zero. For the *fairness criterion*, packages were scored according to the correlation coefficients—noted in Table 5 column 3—and package 8 was assigned the score of 1, while package 3 was assigned the score of zero. For the *catastrophic protection criterion*, packages were scored according to the mean reimbursement of outlier cases (in %)—values noted in Table 6 column 6—and package 1 was assigned the score of 1, while package 7 was assigned the score of zero. As we have no information on the relative value that clients attach to the three criteria, we consider them to be of equal importance. Fig. 1 shows the scores for all three criteria, as well as the average score for each package.

Fig. 1 shows that the three packages with the highest average score were 1, 2 and 4. These packages include IP and D, plus at least one other major benefit. Package 1 had the highest average score, yet package 2 was the most popular, maybe because the latter left a balance of 14 stickers with which to buy 'minor' benefits compared to only 3 stickers for package 1 (Table 3). Packages 2 and 4 have similar average scores, but the former scored above average on all three criteria, whereas the latter scored above average on two criteria but below average on the fairness criterion. Another explanation for the difference in the popularity between packages 2 and 4 might be that the former included T (but not OP), while the latter included OP but not T. Indeed, the facilitators who accompanied the experiment reported that the respondents explained their preference for T by saying they were much less sure of the cost of tests, some of which could be very expensive, but knew the expected costs of OP.

Packages 3 and5 also include three of the four major benefits, but unlike packages 2 and 4, did not include one of the critical components: IP or D. They scored below average. Packages 6, 7 and 8 are composed of only two major benefits, which prevented them from scoring high (except on the fairness criterion); these packages were selected by only one group each.

In summary, the analysis shown in Fig. 1 helps distill an important insight on the effective composition of the benefit packages: IP and D have a higher significance than the other major benefits. And a composition of three major benefits that includes these two and that scores well on all three criteria is the most interesting for the clients.

Minor benefits

The balance of the sticker-budget after the major benefits are chosen determines the choices of minor benefits. The balance of sticker-budget and the number of possible combinations to select minor benefits are shown in Table 7 for each of the packages. The large gap between the number of possible combinations and the number of the combinations actually chosen indicates a coherent set of priorities rather than random distribution of choices.

It should be noted that two of the minor benefits (ME and Den) are more costly than the other four which offer basic coverage with one sticker and high coverage with 2 or 3 stickers only (Table 1). This price difference has an impact on the possible choices. For instance, respondents with a balance of less than five stickers must buy the cheap minor benefits. And respondents who have more than nine stickers must buy at least one of the costly minor benefits, because the cost of buying all the cheap minor benefits at the high level is exactly nine stickers.

Table 8 presents the choices of minor benefits that were recorded during the experiment. The choices are represented here as scores, where '0' means that the benefit was not chosen, and '1', '2' and '3' that the benefit was chosen at the basic, medium and high level of coverage, respectively.

The average scores shown at the bottom of Table 8 are weighted according to the number of respondents in each of the 24 groups. As can be seen, in the choice between the two costly minor benefits (Den and ME) the score was the same for both. And in the choice of the less costly minor benefits, groups consistently favored M, followed by IC, followed by P, and mental care came last.

Discussion and conclusions

The main finding of this study is that rural, poor, predominantly illiterate and innumerate groups in India, many of whom have little experience with health insurance, have been able to compose benefit packages for health insurance with a limited budget of INR 500 (~US$11) per household per year.

The study shows that about 88% of respondents chose at least three out of four benefits that are directly related to vital care in case of illness and which also cost the most: D, IP, OP and T (denoted here as 'major benefits'). 92.7% of the respondents chose to cover D, and 82.1% chose IP. 70.5% of the respondents chose benefit packages that included both IP and D (Table 3). Interestingly, these choices echo findings from Africa that people clearly preferred a benefit package that included high-cost

Table 7
The number of possible combinations and the number actually chosen

	Package	Stickers left for minors	Possible combinations	Combinations chosen	No. of groups
1	OP(b) + IP(b) + T(b) + D(b)	3	17	3	6
2	IP(b) + T(b) + D(b)	14	52	4	8
3	OP(b) + T(b) + D(b)	13	48	2	3
4	OP(b) + IP(b) + D(b)	11	55	3	3
5	OP(b) + IP(b) + T(b)	21	53	1	1
6	IP(m) + D(b)	16	48	1	1
7	T(m) + D(b)	19	53	1	1
8	IP(h) + T(h)	8	21	1	1

Table 8
The choices recorded for the various minor benefits

	Package	Group	n	Medical equipment	Dental care	Preventive care	Indirect cost	Mental care	Maternity
1	OP(b) + IP(b) + T(b) + D(b)	1	12	0	0	1	1	0	1
		2	17	0	0	1	1	0	1
		3	12	0	0	1	1	0	1
		4	13	0	0	0	1	1	1
		5	13	0	0	1	1	0	1
		6	14	0	0	1	1	0	1
2	IP(b) + T(b) + D(b)	7[a]	12	0	0	3	3	3	3
		8	12	0	1	3	1	1	3
		9	12	1	0	3	3	3	3
		10	12	1	1	0	1	0	1
		11	12	0	1	2	3	1	3
		12	12	1	0	3	3	3	3
		13	13	1	0	3	3	3	3
		14	11	1	0	3	3	3	3
3	OP(b) + T(b) + D(b)	15	16	1	1	0	0	0	1
		16	13	1	1	0	0	0	1
		17	13	0	1	1	3	1	3
4	OP(b) + IP(b) + D(b)	18	12	1	0	1	3	1	3
		19	12	0	1	1	3	0	1
		20	12	1	0	3	1	0	3
5	OP(b) + IP(b) + T(b)	21	12	1	1	3	3	3	3
6	IP(m) + D(b)	22	13	1	1	0	1	1	3
7	T(m) + D(b)	23	12	0	2	3	3	1	3
8	IP(h) + T(h)	24	10	0	0	3	3	3	1
	Weighted average score			0.46	0.46	1.60	1.85	1.10	2.05
	SE ±			0.104	0.12	0.24	0.22	0.24	0.19

[a]This group decided not to use all their stickers and to stop the game when they had five stickers left.

health services, e.g. operations, drugs and consultation fees (Dong et al., 2004).

This pattern of choices reflects the reality whereby the aggregate cost of drugs is higher than the aggregate cost of IP, even though the average cost of drugs per illness is much lower than the average cost of an IP episode. We note that the respondents, that were poor, prioritized protection against the aggregate costs of illness as much as protection against rare and costly medical events. This observation is consistent with experience in other areas of insurance where WTP for rare catastrophic events (e.g. life insurance) is often significantly reduced in comparison with readiness to pay for coverage of events that are more likely to happen with greater frequency (e.g. crop insurance) (Preker et al., 2002). It also fits with the finding that it is harder to sell only catastrophic coverage to clients who do not fully understand the value of insurance, and covering only common health events raises the question of whether the poor would be better off with a flexible savings account rather than insurance. The solution is to provide coverage for a mix of hospitalization and primary healthcare services—this helps make the insurance service more desirable to target beneficiaries since all are likely to make some use of the scheme during the course of a year (Tabor, 2005).

In exercising choices, the respondents had to trade off a diversity of benefit types against levels of coverage. The respondents have shown clearly that they prefer a wide range of benefits at basic levels of coverage over a narrow choice of benefit types with higher coverage levels (Table 2). The paradigm emerging from these findings is that respondents seek coverage for expensive care, regardless of whether the expense is generated by a few rare and costly events or by frequent events bearing each a moderate cost. This pattern of choice suggests that health insurance covering only low-probability-&-high-cost care would probably not be attractive to this target population. On the other hand, benefit packages that also include high-probability-&-low-cost care would find takers.

As this benefit-package composition challenges the prevailing thought that health insurance can be operated for low-probability-&-high-cost care but less so for high-probability-&-low-cost care (Churchill, Liber, McCord, & Roth, 2003; Morduch, 2006), we examined the judiciousness of the choices people make.

The literature on public involvement in healthcare priority setting cites a range of methods to elicit people's preferences regarding rationing priorities within a fixed budget (Coast, 2001; Mullen, 1999; Ryan et al., 2001). However, we have been unable to find reports using quantitative methods to examine the judiciousness of choices made, let alone in a relevant context. Hence, the exercise of simulating the impact of different rationing choices on HH expenditure for healthcare, and the criteria we formulated to evaluate different choices, are novel to the best of our knowledge.

We juxtaposed the choices respondents made with costs related to actual illness episodes that were registered within a comparable cohort among poor people in India. Three criteria were employed for the assessment of the results: the '*reimbursement criterion*' (which is based on the assumption that respondents will reject insurance when costs that they associate with the insurance are not reimbursed, regardless of the absolute level); the '*fairness criterion*' (the underlying assumption of which is that people prefer a higher share of reimbursement when higher costs are incurred, even when costs are not catastrophically high); and the '*catastrophic protection criterion*' (which is based on the concept that insurance should provide adequate protection against catastrophes).

The results confirm that the packages chosen most frequently satisfied all three criteria. Including IP contributed most to protection against catastrophic costs and to fairness, and including drugs was critical for the reimbursement criterion.

The analysis also showed that respondents were willing to trade off optimal coverage of major benefits (package 1) in return for coverage of minor benefits. The choice of minor benefits in lieu of major benefits reflects a wish to improve quality of life (by including ME) and prevent situations of severe morbidity (by including P). This trade off also reflects the ability of the respondents to address their long-term needs as well as the needs of entire communities, rather than the needs of people with acute illnesses only.

However, one should recall that contributory health insurance schemes depend on a broad-based willingness to affiliate, which is presumably associated with clients' satisfaction with the composition of the benefit package. Hence, there would be a strong case for considering the choices of prospective clients as a basis for benefit-package design. And this experiment provides encouraging proof that the CHAT method offers a workable way to elicit respondents' choices effectively.

The CHAT decision tool imposes the rule that respondents must choose benefits until they exhaust a predetermined sticker budget; respondents can neither buy additional stickers nor forego stickers in exchange for a premium reduction. Nor can respondents negotiate the prices of the benefits in the setting of the game. This double inflexibility could bias the choices of benefits when respondents are left with a small number of stickers that they must 'get rid of'. The bias occurs when respondents select benefits they do not really prioritize because this is their only option to dispose of the residual stickers ('the residual sticker bias'). For instance, 77.8% of the respondents chose P, but would as many have made the same choice if P had cost more than 1 to 3 stickers, or if they could have obtained a premium reduction in lieu of the residual stickers?

In conclusion, the results of this analysis demonstrate that respondents can participate actively in the design of their health insurance packages; that they make judicious choices even at their present level of literacy and numeracy; and that the CHAT exercise provides a means to identify clients' perceived priorities. Therefore, it seems an attractive tool for engaging potential clients in the launch of voluntary health insurance. This tool opens up options for policy makers in resource-poor countries wishing to encourage the successful implementation of contributory health insurance among low-income populations by supporting benefits that the clients prioritize through a subsidy of medium cover at the cost of basic cover. Such policy choice would have the added advantage that it does not dampen the willingness to affiliate and to pay, and limits the subsidy to those who commit their own resources in improving their access to healthcare through health insurance.

References

Ahuja, R., & Jütting, J. (2004). *Are the poor too poor to demand health insurance?*. New Delhi: Indian Council for Research on International Economic Relations.

Asfaw, A. (2003). Cost of illness, demand for medical care, and the prospect of community health insurance schemes in the rural areas of Ethiopia. *Development Economics and Policy*, p. 131.

Churchill, C., Liber, D., McCord, M., & Roth, J. (2003). *Making insurance work for microfinance institutions: A technical guide to developing and delivering microinsurance*. Geneva: International Labour Organization.

Coast, J. (2001). Citizens, their agents and health care rationing: An exploratory study using qualitative methods. *Health Economics*, *10*(2), 159–174.

Danis, M., Biddle, A. K., & Goold, S. D. (2002). Insurance benefit preferences of the low-income uninsured. *Journal of General Internal Medicine*, *17*(2), 125–133.

Danis, M., Biddle, A. K., & Goold, S. D. (2004). Enrollees choose priorities for Medicare. *Gerontologist*, *44*(1), 58–67.

Danis, M., Binnendijk, E., Ost, A., Vellakkal, S., Koren, R., & Dror, D. M. (2006). Eliciting the health insurance benefit choices of low-income populations in India with the CHAT exercise. *Health Services Management Research*, submitted for publication.

De Allegri, M., Sanon, M., Bridges, J., & Sauerborn, R. (2006). Understanding consumers' preferences and decision to enroll in community-based health insurance in rural West Africa. *Health Policy*, *76*(1), 58–71.

Devadasan, N., Ranson, K., Van Damme, W., Acharya, A., & Criel, B. (2005). The landscape of community health insurance in India: An overview based on 10 case studies. *Health Policy*.

Dong, H., Mugisha, F., Gbangou, A., Kouyate, B., & Sauerborn, R. (2004). The feasibility of community-based health insurance in Burkina Faso. *Health Policy*, *69*(1), 45–53.

Dror, DM., & Jacquier, C. (1999). Micro-insurance: Extending health insurance to the excluded. *International Social Security Review*, *52*(1), 71–97.

Dror, D. M., Radermacher, R., & Koren, R. (2006). Willingness to pay for health insurance among rural and poor persons: Field evidence from seven micro health insurance units in India. *Health Policy*, in press, doi:10.1016/j.healthpol.2006.07.011.

Fleck, L. M. (1994). Just caring: Health reform and health care rationing. *Journal of Medicine and Philosophy*, *19*(5), 435–443.

Goold, S. D., Biddle, A. K., Klipp, G., Hall, C. N., & Danis, M. (2005). Choosing healthplans all together: A deliberative exercise for allocating limited health care resources. *Journal of Health Politics Policy and Law*, *30*(4), 563–601.

Gumber, A. (2002). *Health insurance for the informal sector: Problems and prospects*. New Delhi: Indian Council for Research on International Economic Relations.

Insure.com. *The 2004 national homeowners insurance study*. Browsed 21 May 2006 〈http://info.insure.com/home/jdpower1101.html〉.

Keefe, C. W., & Goold, S. D. (2004). Designing health plan benefits: A simulation exercise. *Medical Education*, *38*(11), 1196.

Leftley, R. (2005). Technical assistance for the promotion of micro insurance—The experience of opportunity international. *Good and bad practices in microinsurance*. CGAP Working Group on Microinsurance.

Mathiyazhagan, K. (1998). Willingness to pay for rural health insurance through community participation in India. *International Journal of Health Planning and Management*, *13*(1), 47–67.

Morduch, J. (2006). Micro-insurance: The next revolution? In Banerjee, A., Benabou, R., & Mookherjee, D. (Eds.), *Understanding Poverty* (chapter 22). Oxford: University Press, April 2006, ISBN: 9780195305203.

Mullen, P. M. (1999). Public involvement in health care priority setting: An overview of methods for eliciting values. *Health Expect*, *2*(4), 222–234.

Preker, A. S., Carrin, G., Dror, D., Jakab, M., Hsiao, W., & Arhin-Tenkorang, D. (2002). Effectiveness of community health financing in meeting the cost of illness. *Bulletin of the World Health Organization*, *80*(2), 143–150.

Radermacher, R. (2006). *Health insurance for the poor – Examples from India*. Unpublished monograph.

Radwan, I. (2005). *India: Private health services for the poor, a policy note*. Washington, DC: World Bank.

Ray, T. K., Pandav, C. S., Anand, K., Kapoor, S. K., & Dwivedi, S. N. (2002). Out-of-pocket expenditure on healthcare in a north Indian village. *National Medical Journal of India*, *15*(5), 257–260.

Ryan, M., Scott, D. A., Reeves, C., Bate, A., van Teijlingen, E. R., Russell, E. M., et al. (2001). Eliciting public preferences for healthcare: A systematic review of techniques. *Health Technology Assessment*, *5*(5), 1–186.

Schone, B. S., & Cooper, P. F. (2001). Assessing the impact of health plan choice. *Health Affairs (Millwood)*, *20*(1), 267–275.

Tabor, S. R. (2005). *Community-based health insurance and social protection policy, Social Protection Discussion Paper Series*. Washington, DC: WorldBank.

Toth, W. (2005). *Satisfaction is job one*. Insurance & Technology (July 2005), Browsed 21 May 2006 〈http://www.insurancetech.com/news/showArticle.jhtml?articleID=166402239〉.

WHO. (2006). *The World Health Report 2006: Working together for health*. Geneva World Health Organization.

Wiesmann, D., & Jütting, J. (2000). The emerging movement of Community Based Health Insurance in Sub-Saharan Africa: Experiences and lessons learned. *Afrika Spectrum*, *35*(2), 193–210.

Chapter 11

What Factors Affect Voluntary Uptake of Community-based Health Insurance Schemes in Low- and Middle-Income Countries? A Systematic Review and Meta-Analysis*

Main Messages

- Around 54 rigorously screened articles were retained for the systematic review, and they present evidence from 20 countries.
- The evidence is discussed based on meta-analysis and thematic synthesis.
- The largest number of studies dealt with community-based health insurance (CBHI) schemes in Sub-Saharan Africa.

Focus Points

- The demand-side factors which positively affect enrolment in CBHI schemes in low- and middle-income countries (LMICs) include

---

*This chapter is reproduced from *PLoS ONE* (2016), Open Access, available at https://www.researchgate.net/publication/307544280_What_Factors_Affect_Voluntary_Uptake_of_Community-Based_Health_Insurance_Schemes_in_Low-and_Middle-Income_Countries_A_Systematic_Review_and_Meta-Analysis.

education, age, female household heads, and the socioeconomic status of households.

- Supply-side factors acting as enablers of enrolment include trust in the scheme management and trust in the insurance scheme and quality of health care.
- Decisions regarding CBHI membership renewal are most influenced by trust in the insurer.
- The poor are more likely to enroll in CBHI on a voluntary basis when governments formulate an enabling environment for the development and expansion of CBHI.

Testimonials

Box 1: Benefits Package

- "People with chronic diseases receive care from the doctor at the ambulatory; they get their drugs from the pharmacy where they often have to pay for the drugs. They can be a burden on their families; it is difficult to afford the drugs for many people. CBHI should cover these costs if possible."
- "The neediest people in our community especially the orphans, the disabled and the elderly still pay in the schemes. They have more health needs and should be excused."

Cultural Beliefs

- "Paying before you fall sick is like buying a disease."
- "In our culture, it is only when someone becomes sick that we ask the community to contribute financially to help a person."

Structured Abstract

Introduction

The contribution of CBHIs in providing a financial risk management mechanism to the rural poor is indisputable. However, if we wish to view CBHI as part of social protection policies, such schemes will have to shift from niche to scale by enlisting and retaining more members. This chapter delves on the demand and supply-side factors influencing initial voluntary uptake of CBHIs in low- and middle-income countries (LMIC), and renewal decisions. It is based on a literature search conducted from May to November 2013 that included academic and gray literature.

Method

The authors conducted a comprehensive search of academic and gray literature following the PRISMA[1] protocol. The academic thematic databases included social science, economics and medical sciences, and other electronic resources. The quantitative studies included randomized controlled trials, quasi-experimental studies, experimental designs with control groups, and observational studies that analyzed factors affecting enrolment and renewal/dropout.

The qualitative studies considered were case studies, interviews/key informant interviews (KIIs), and focus groups with participants (who enrolled, did not enroll, renewed or dropped out) and scheme managers/policymakers. Out of the initial search yields of 15,770 hits, the authors zeroed in on 54 relevant studies for the analysis.

The quantitative synthesis (informed by meta-analysis) and the qualitative analysis (informed by thematic synthesis) were compared to draw a coherent synthesis of the findings.

Findings

Results of the meta-analysis suggest that enrolments in CBHI were positively associated with household income, education and age of the household head (HHH), female-headed household and chronic illness episodes in the household. The impact of household size and HHH marital status is only localized.

The thematic synthesis identifies certain factors as enablers for enrollment. These include knowledge and understanding of insurance

---

[1]PRISMA (Preferred Reporting Items for Systematic Reviews and Meta-Analyses) is an evidence-based minimum set of items for reporting in systematic reviews and meta-analyses.

Box 1: Stages of Analysis

Stage 1: Coding of quantitative studies and qualitative studies by key features:

- Study objectives
- Design
- Sample size
- Analytical methods
- Context
- Findings

Stage 2: Meta-analysis of the quantitative studies

- Estimating effect size
- Estimating standard error of the effect size
- Estimating summary effect

Stage 3: Thematic synthesis of qualitative studies

- Review and analysis of quotations and other relevant texts, and development of codes
- Redefining codes with additional data
- Theme charts were populated by all the studies, an analytical framework was developed and findings were analyzed to explain factors associated with enrolment or renewal decisions.

Stage 4: Comparison of analysis

- The qualitative synthesis (Stage 3) and quantitative synthesis (Stage 2) were compared, to gain insight for an overall synthesis of findings/statements.

and CBHI, quality of health care, and trust in the insurance scheme, and trust in the scheme management. The factors which can pose as barriers to enrolment include an inappropriate benefits package, cultural beliefs, affordability, distance to a health care facility, lack of adequate legal and policy frameworks to support CBHI, and stringent rules of some CBHI schemes.

Decisions pertaining to member renewals were positively associated with HHH education, household size and trust in the scheme management. Renewals were also prompted by factors such as knowledge and understanding of insurance and CBHI, health care quality, and receipt of an insurance payout the previous year.

The barriers to renewal decisions included stringent rules of some CBHI schemes, inadequate legal and policy frameworks to support CBHI, and inappropriate benefits package.

Conclusion

One of the findings of this systematic review is that the poor are more likely to enroll in CBHI on a voluntary basis when governments formulate an enabling environment for the development and expansion of CBHI. This suggests that although low-income governments may be unable to act as funders and providers of services, they can contribute in a significant capacity by acting as regulators. By leveraging people's willingness to exercise voluntary and contributory enrolment in a CBHI, the government can seek to effectively broaden their outreach to grassroots groups that are otherwise excluded from social protection.

RESEARCH ARTICLE

What Factors Affect Voluntary Uptake of Community-Based Health Insurance Schemes in Low- and Middle-Income Countries? A Systematic Review and Meta-Analysis

David Mark Dror[1,2☯¤]*, S. A. Shahed Hossain[3‡], Atanu Majumdar[1☯], Tracey Lynn Pérez Koehlmoos[4‡], Denny John[5‡], Pradeep Kumar Panda[6☯]

1 Micro Insurance Academy, New Delhi, India, 2 Erasmus University Rotterdam, Rotterdam, Netherlands, 3 International Centre for Diarrheal Disease Research, Dhaka, Bangladesh, 4 The Uniformed Services University of the Health Sciences, Bethesda, MD, United States of America, 5 Peoples Open Access Education Initiative (Peoples-Uni), Delhi, India, 6 International Institute of Health Management Research, Dwarka, Delhi, India

☯ These authors contributed equally to this work.
¤ Current address: 86 Okhla Industrial Estate Phase 3, New Delhi 110020, India
‡ These authors contributed equally to this work.
* daviddror@socialre.org

OPEN ACCESS

Citation: Dror DM, Hossain SAS, Majumdar A, Pérez Koehlmoos TL, John D, Panda PK (2016) What Factors Affect Voluntary Uptake of Community-Based Health Insurance Schemes in Low- and Middle-Income Countries? A Systematic Review and Meta-Analysis. PLoS ONE 11(8): e0160479. doi:10.1371/journal.pone.0160479

Editor: Dan Weary, University of British Columbia, CANADA

Received: January 1, 2016

Accepted: July 20, 2016

Published: August 31, 2016

Data Availability Statement: All relevant data are within the paper and its Supporting Information files.

Funding: Grant from 3ie and Grant No. SR4/1009. The funders had no role in study design, data collection and analysis, decision to publish, or preparation of the manuscript.

Competing Interests: The authors have declared that no competing interests exist.

Abstract

Introduction

This research article reports on factors influencing initial voluntary uptake of community-based health insurance (CBHI) schemes in low- and middle-income countries (LMIC), and renewal decisions.

Methods

Following PRISMA protocol, we conducted a comprehensive search of academic and gray literature, including academic databases in social science, economics and medical sciences (e.g., Econlit, Global health, Medline, Proquest) and other electronic resources (e.g., Eldis and Google scholar). Search strategies were developed using the thesaurus or index terms (e.g., MeSH) specific to the databases, combined with free text terms related to CBHI or health insurance. Searches were conducted from May 2013 to November 2013 in English, French, German, and Spanish. From the initial search yield of 15,770 hits, 54 relevant studies were retained for analysis of factors influencing enrolment and renewal decisions. The quantitative synthesis (informed by meta-analysis) and the qualitative analysis (informed by thematic synthesis) were compared to gain insight for an overall synthesis of findings/statements.

Results

Meta-analysis suggests that enrolments in CBHI were positively associated with household income, education and age of the household head (HHH), household size, female-headed household, married HHH and chronic illness episodes in the household. The thematic synthesis suggests the following factors as enablers for enrolment: (a) knowledge and understanding of insurance and CBHI, (b) quality of healthcare, (c) trust in scheme management. Factors found to be barriers to enrolment include: (a) inappropriate benefits package, (b) cultural beliefs, (c) affordability, (d) distance to healthcare facility, (e) lack of adequate legal and policy frameworks to support CBHI, and (f) stringent rules of some CBHI schemes. HHH education, household size and trust in the scheme management were positively associated with member renewal decisions. Other motivators were: (a) knowledge and understanding of insurance and CBHI, (b) healthcare quality, (c) trust in scheme management, and (d) receipt of an insurance payout the previous year. The barriers to renewal decisions were: (a) stringent rules of some CBHI schemes, (b) inadequate legal and policy frameworks to support CBHI and (c) inappropriate benefits package.

Conclusion and Policy Implications

The demand-side factors positively affecting enrolment in CBHI include education, age, female household heads, and the socioeconomic status of households. Moreover, when individuals understand how their CBHI functions they are more likely to enroll and when people have a positive claims experience, they are more likely to renew. A higher prevalence of chronic conditions or the perception that healthcare is of good quality and nearby act as factors enhancing enrolment. The perception that services are distant or deficient leads to lower enrolments. The second insight is that trust in the scheme enables enrolment. Thirdly, clarity about the legal or policy framework acts as a factor influencing enrolments. This is significant, as it points to hitherto unpublished evidence that governments can effectively broaden their outreach to grassroots groups that are excluded from social protection by formulating supportive regulatory and policy provisions even if they cannot fund such schemes in full, by leveraging people's willingness to exercise voluntary and contributory enrolment in a community-based health insurance.

Introduction

Healthcare-seekers, through out-of-pocket (OOP) spending at the time and place of treatment, defray most healthcare costs in developing countries. In India, private funds pay for 70 percent of all healthcare, and OOP spending represents 86 percent of it [1,2]. This inequitable and inefficient health financing situation pervades other LMICs as well. The solution proposed by the World Health Organization (WHO) and other international bodies has been to strive toward universal health coverage (UHC), notably through health insurance. However, few low-income countries have been able to mount mandated funding solutions for UHC that truly cover their entire populations [3]. Attempts to subsidize large population segments have been rare and stopped short of UHC [4,5].

One way to enhance coverage could be through Community Based Health Insurance (CBHI) schemes [6], which are local mutual aid schemes that put in place arrangements for mobilizing, pooling, allocating and managing or supervising members' resources for healthcare [7, 8]. CBHI schemes have been effective in reducing OOP and improving access to healthcare services [9]. However, such schemes are usually small. If CBHI should be viewed as part of social protection policies, such schemes will have to move from niche to scale by enlisting and retaining more members.

To see how this might happen, the *International Initiative on Impact Evaluation* (3ie) commissioned a Systematic Review of the literature, and the *Evidence for Policy and Practice Information and Co-ordinating Centre* (EPPI-Centre) assisted the authors in elaborating the Protocol [10]. This article, summarizing the full report [11] answers the following questions relating to voluntary uptake (and renewal) of CBHI enrolment in LMICs

1. Demand-side factors
   a. Which household and individual characteristics affect CBHI uptake?
   b. Which social-capital–related factors in the community affect uptake?
2. Supply-side factors
   a. Which scheme-related factors affect access to CBHI?
   b. Which institutional factors (e.g., governance, marketing, self-help group (SHG) membership) play a role in increasing uptake?
   c. Which other health-related supply-side factors enhance CBHI uptake?
3. What factors affect CBHI renewal and retention of clients?

Previous systematic reviews of the literature on CBHI bear testimony to the persistent interest in this health financing mechanism over many years. Ekman [12] examined 15 peer-reviewed articles plus 21 unpublished papers and reports (grey literature) dating from 1980 to 2003, in English, French, Portuguese and Spanish. Ekman concluded that there was then strong evidence that CBHI provided some financial protection by reducing OOP spending, moderate evidence that such schemes improved cost-recovery and that there was still insufficient agreement on outcome indicators that should be followed. Robyn PJ, Sauerborn R, Bärnighausen T. [13] conducted a systematic review of 34 publications (dealing with 17 schemes in South Asia, 10 in sub-Saharan Africa, 4 in East Asia and 1 in Latin America) on provider payment methods used by CBHI, published up to January 2010. These authors concluded that the evidence on the influence of one of five provider payment systems (fee-for-service, salaries, coverage ceiling, capitation and co-insurance) on customer demand and population enrollment, risk pooling or financial sustainability of CBHI was limited and not particularly strong, as most studies were observational rather than based on trials or on quasi-experimental research. The most recent systematic review, by Adebayo et al [14] included 25 studies published in English between 2003 and 2013 (18 quantitative, six qualitative and one mixed method) on factors affecting uptake of CBHI in LMIC, many of which were about measuring willingness to pay. Considering that studies dealing with WTP must be treated as unreliable sources of evidence of actual enrolment, we applied a different selection criterion whereby WTP studies were included in our review only when they also dealt with willingness-to-enrol, as our investigation is about factors affecting uptake (enrolment) and renewal of membership in CBHI. Thus, Readers asking *why do we need another review for CBHI?* will be interested to know that 44 out of the 54 included in our review were considered only in our review, and only 10 articles were considered for the review also by Adebayo et al. Moreover, our study is the first and only following the rigorous research protocol that has been approved by EPPI centre and 3ie that included both thematic synthesis of qualitative articles and meta-analysis of quantitative studies covering many more publications (reflecting notably a longer time-frame and four languages rather than only one), thus obtaining stronger external validity of the findings and conclusions on this topic. We also show, in the conclusion section of this article, how our conclusions differ from those of earlier systematic reviews of the CBHI literature.

Methods

Information Sources

The literature search (conducted from May to November 2013) included academic and gray literature. The academic thematic databases included social science, economics and medical sciences (Business Source Premier [EBSCO], Econlit [EBSCO], Global health [OVID], ISI web of knowledge, Medline [OVID], ProQuest, Scopus, Sociological Abstracts) and other electronic resources (e.g., Eldis and Google Scholar). The gray literature was searched manually, through citation tracking and personal communications.

Search Strategy

Following the PRISMA protocol (S1 Table), search strategies for electronic databases were developed by one of the authors (SH) and peer-reviewed by search specialists at 3ie and EPPIA. The complete Medline/PubMed search strategy is appended (S1 Text). The search identified studies published from 1990 to 2013, in English, Spanish, French and German. The search strategy was translated by an information specialist for use in other databases using the appropriate controlled vocabulary. Electronic search results or publications available digitally in '.ris' format were uploaded to review software (*EPPI-Reviewer 4*), for screening, reviewing, coding and further processing by the review team.

Eligibility Criteria (Inclusion/Exclusion)

The *inclusion criteria* were determined by "*PICOS*". **P**articipants invited to join CBHIs voluntarily in LMICs (World Bank definitions 2012) were included, whether they decided to enroll or not. Also included were voluntary, contributory and community-based **I**nterventions (when in LMICs); **C**omparisons between individuals who do and who do not join CBHI schemes and those who renew or dropout); **O**utcomes when related to determinants of demand (e.g., socio-economic characteristics or social capital in the community) or supply (e.g., scheme-related factors, institutional factors or other health-related factors that enhance CBHI uptake). The review also included factors affecting renewal (or dropout) in CBHI schemes. **S**tudy design influenced the inclusion. Among quantitative studies included were randomized controlled trials, quasi-experimental studies, experimental designs with control groups, and observational studies (quantitative surveys, cohort studies, case-controlled studies and case studies) that dealt with factors affecting enrolment and renewal/dropout. The qualitative studies included case studies, interviews/key informant interviews (KIIs), and focus groups with participants (who enrolled, did not enroll, renewed or dropped out) and scheme managers/policymakers.

Studies were *excluded* if (a) published before 1990; (b) a policy analysis or opinion piece; (c) dealing with a non-LMIC country; (d) dealing with other health insurance mechanisms (private, social or mandatory); and (e) examining only the impact of already functioning CBHI schemes.

Data Extraction

Using a coding tool characterizing studies by context, mechanism and outcomes (S2 Text: Data Extraction Sheet), two researchers independently extracted information about study characteristics (e.g., research country, focal research area, population characteristics, study design, sample size, analytical framework and findings).

Critical appraisal of studies: quality assurance process

Quality assurance was maintained in six stages: (1) potential citations were imported to *EPPI-Reviewer 4* and duplicates removed; (2) studies were scanned on the basis of title and abstract, (3) and (4) two of the authors independently appraised the studies; any discrepancies in the critical appraisal were resolved through discussion, and any issue that could not be resolved was discussed with a third author (5) studies retained were consolidated with studies published after the search strategy had been applied, and these studies were added manually; (6) the assessment of the "Remaining Included Studies" was done following checklists for critical appraisal of quality (S2 Table) and separated into:

1. *Randomized control trial studies*: Risk of Bias Assessment Tool, Table 8.5d –Cochrane Handbook for SRs of Interventions [15]; *Cohort studies*: Critical Appraisal Skills Programme (CASP) checklist for cohort studies [16]; *Quantitative studies* (case-control and cross-sectional): Critical Appraisal Checklist [17].
2. *Qualitative studies*: Critical Appraisal Skills Programme (CASP) checklist for qualitative studies [18,19]
3. *Mixed method studies*: Quantitative and qualitative components of the study were judged on quality using their respective checklist adopted for each component separately.

Analysis: Overall Approach to Synthesis

The studies retained for detailed analysis were processed through four stages: (1) *coding of quantitative studies* (including quantitative data from mixed-method studies) and qualitative studies (including qualitative data from mixed-method studies) by key features (study objectives, design, sample size, analytical methods, context, and findings) (S3 Table). (2) *a meta-analytic synthesis* of the quantitative studies (hereafter meta-analysis), with subtopics as follows:

(2A) Estimating effect size: Most studies included in this meta-analysis reported odds ratios or the coefficients of regression of the logit or probit model [20]. We used the following formulas to convert these measures into the effect size.

$$\textit{Effect Size} = \frac{\ln(OR)}{1.81}, \textit{ where OR is the odds ratio estimated by a logit model}$$

$$\textit{Effect Size} = \frac{\textit{Coefficient of Regression}}{1.81}, \textit{ where the coefficient of regression is estimated by a logit model}$$

$$\textit{Effect Size} = \textit{Coefficient of Regression}, \textit{ where the coefficient of regression is estimated by a probit model}$$

(2B) Estimating standard error of the effect size: Standard error (SE) of the effect size was estimated from the SE of the odds ratio or the coefficients of regression of Logit or Probit model, by applying similar transformation used for estimating the effect size. Some authors reported the 95 percent confidence intervals instead of the SE. For these studies we first computed the 95 percent confidence interval of the effect size by applying similar transformations and then computed the SE of the effect size by using the following formula.

$$\textit{Standard Error of the Effect Size} = \frac{95\,\textit{percent CI of ES (Upper Limit)} - 95\textit{percent CI of ES (Lower Limit)}}{2 * 1.96}$$

Some studies did not report the confidence intervals but reported the t-statistic for the coefficient of regression. For these studies we first estimated the SE of the coefficient of regression by using the following formula

$$\textit{Standard Error of the Coefficient of Regression} = \frac{\textit{Coefficient of Regression}}{\textit{t statistic}}$$

and then estimated the SE of the effect size by using the same transformation used to estimate effect size.

Some authors did not report the SE, CI (Class Interval) or the t-statistic. Therefore, we could not estimate the SE of the effect size for these studies [21,22].

Sample size: Sample size was reported by all the studies.

Weights: The standard practice in meta-analysis is to apply weights *proportional to the variances* of the effect size for estimating the summary effect. But this could not be applied in this meta-analysis exercise as the SEs of the effect size for a few studies could not be estimated. It was also not wise to exclude because they were based on large samples. Therefore, we applied weights *proportional to the sample size* to estimate the summary effect by combining the effect size estimated from individual studies.

(2C) Estimating summary effect: When a characteristic or a trait influencing a household's enrolment behavior was reported in the same way by all studies, the summary effect was obtained by averaging the effect sizes, after applying weights. However, the studies included in this meta-analysis reported the same characteristic in different ways (e.g., as continuous and categorical variables), and authors used heterogeneous categories for analyzing data when it was a categorical variable (Box 1).

Handling this heterogeneity was the major challenge of the meta-analysis. Averaging the effects across very heterogeneous studies with weights was not an option. Instead, we applied an innovative technique to obtain the summary effect. Effect size for a continuous variable is basically the transformation of the regression slope line, and it implies the amount of increase in the effect size for unit increment in the independent variable. Thus, the effect size for a particular category of a categorical variable should be uniform for that category. Multiple categories can be considered as a step function of the independent variable. To combine the effect sizes estimated from individual studies, we first simulated the effect sizes from each study over a domain of interest (= range of values of the independent variable), then merged them in a single dataset and fitted a linear regression over the merged dataset. We consider the coefficient of regression (of the merged dataset) as the summary effect, the average increase in the effect size for unit increment in the independent variable, now a combination of continuous and categorical variable. We applied this technique to estimate the summary effect of four variables: household head's age and educational status, household size and income/expenditure/assets quintile. This method has been referred to as the regression method for obtaining summary effect.

Standard Error (SE) of the summary effect estimated using the regression method has been computed by Stata with the following command:

$$\text{Regress } \{\text{Dependent Variable}\}\ \{\text{Independent Variable}\}\ [\text{Pweight} = \text{SampleSize}]$$

(3) In the third stage, we performed a thematic synthesis of qualitative studies (hereafter thematic synthesis) following [3]. First, two researchers' independently reviewed and analyzed quotations and other relevant texts and developed codes by labeling the data. Second, codes

Box 1. Heterogeneity across Studies: The Major Challenge to Meta-Analysis

Oriakhi (Edo State, Nigeria), Kuwawenaruwa (Tanzania) and Panda (India, 3 sites) used the household head's age as a continuous variable in logit model. Other authors used that age as a categorical variable. But different authors had different base categories and estimated odds ratios for multiple but non-uniform categories. Ranson (Gujrat, India) assumed three categories of age (18–29 years (base); 30–39 years; and 40 years and above). Gumber (Gujrat, India) assumed five categories for age: (16–25 years (base); 26–35 years; 36–45 years; 46–55 years; and 56 years and above). De Allegri (Burkina Faso, 2006) created three categories (20–40 years (base); 41–60 years; and 61 years and above). Gnawali (Burkina Faso, 2009) also used three categories (the same base category as Allegri; 41–64 years; and 65 years and above). Schneider (Rwanda) had two (Below 40 years (base) and 40 years and above). Chankova (Ghana, Mali and Senegal) created four categories (less than 40 years (base); 40–49 years; 50–59 years; and 60 years and above). Mathiyazaghan (Karnataka, India) mentioned three categories: youthful (base), middle-aged and old-aged, without any mention of age-brackets. Based on a thorough literature search we concluded that in the Indian context youthful was 15 to 29 years; middle aged = 30 to 59 years; and old aged were 60 years and above.

were redefined with additional data. These codes led to the thematic framework for examination of common elements across studies. Finally, theme charts were populated by all the studies, an analytical framework was developed and findings were analyzed to explain factors associated with enrolment or renewal (dropout) decisions.

(4) In the final stage, the qualitative synthesis (informed by thematic synthesis) and quantitative synthesis (informed by meta-analytic synthesis) were compared, to gain insight for an overall synthesis of findings/statements.

Results

Study Selection

The flow of study selection is shown in Fig 1.

Study Characteristics

The 54 papers [21–74] describing 56 countries retained for the SR (listed in S3a, S3b and S3c Table) present evidence from 20 countries (Afghanistan, Armenia, Benin, Burkina-Faso [x7], Cambodia, Cameroon [x2], China [x3], Democratic Republic of Congo, Ecuador, Ghana [x5], Guinea-Conakry, India [x9], Malaysia, Mali, Nigeria [x7], Rwanda [x2], Senegal [x4], Sri Lanka, Tanzania [x3], and Uganda [x4]). The largest number of CBHI uptake studies was conducted in Sub-Saharan Africa (SSA), followed by Asia, with only few studies in other countries. Thirty-two studies were conducted in rural settings, 7 in an exclusively urban environment, and 15 involved both rural and urban settings. Most studies were conducted in low-income countries, a few studies in lower-middle income countries, and 3 studies in upper-middle income countries (China, Malaysia and Ecuador). Of the 54 studies, 4 examined CBHI schemes operating at national level, 39 at regional level and 11 at local level. All 7 studies in Burkina-

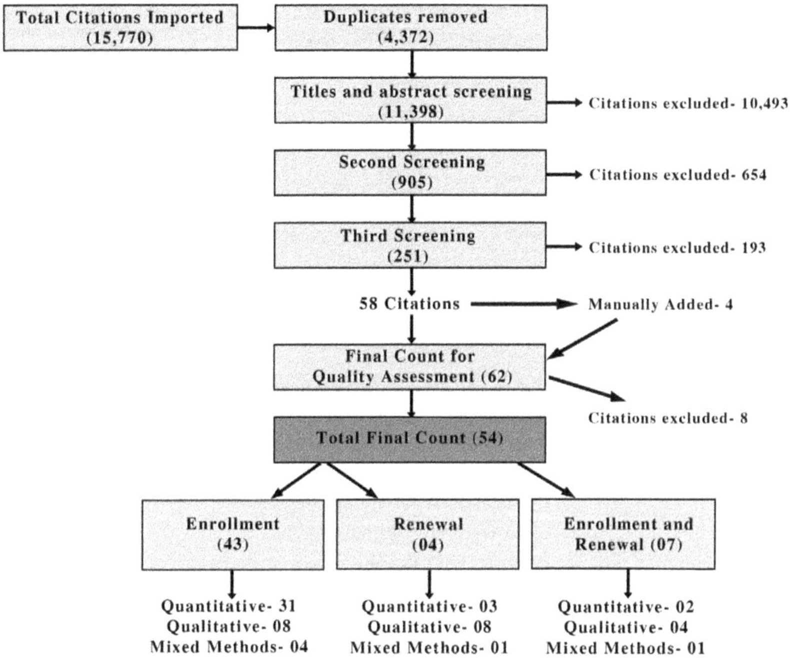

Fig 1. PRISMA Flowchart Diagram of Study Selection.

doi:10.1371/journal.pone.0160479.g001

Faso dealt with the Nouna Health District CBHI scheme (regional level). Studies in Nigeria studied mostly the schemes in Anambra and Enugu districts.

In terms of timing, CBHI research has taken off only in the last decade: few studies were undertaken in the 1990s, and most publications date to 2005–06 and 2009–11.

Out of the 42 quantitative studies (36 quantitative [21,23,27–29,36–37,39–47,49–52,54–59,61,63,65–66,68–69,73–74] and 6 mixed methods with quantitative (and qualitative) data [25,38,60,62,70,72]) one dealt with a randomized control trial (RCT), 5 with case-control methods and cohort studies, and the remaining 31 were cross-sectional surveys based on random samples. Twenty-nine studies examined correlates of uptake and renewal using multivariate analyses (logit/probit/tobit). One study was based on panel data, and used fixed effect and random effect models. Eleven studies used descriptive statistics with statistical tests, and one descriptive study used no statistical test.

Out of the 18 qualitative studies (12 qualitative [30–35,48,64,67,71,75–76] and 6 mixed-methods with qualitative (and qualitative) data [25,38,60,62,70,72]), 10 used both focus groups

Table 1. Summary Effects for the Variables Influencing Enrolment (Combined Regional and Overall).

Variables	Summary effect			Method of estimating summary effect
	Asia	Sub-Saharan Africa	All	
Socioeconomic percentile	0.2379	0.5209	0.4626	Regression
Presence of acute illnesses	0.1169	-	-	Averaging
Presence of chronic illnesses	0.0909	0.0495	0.0597	Averaging
Household head's educational level	0.0153	0.0555	0.0443	Regression
Household size	-0.0036	0.0414	0.0323	Regression
Household head's marital status	0.1543	-0.0027	0.1403	Averaging
Household head's age	0.0082	0.0042	0.0048	Regression
Presence of elderly person	-0.1847	-0.1614	-0.1731	Averaging
Gender	-0.0635	-0.4083	-0.3556	Averaging

doi:10.1371/journal.pone.0160479.t001

and interviews, and four each used either focus groups or interviews with different participants (insured, uninsured, renewed or dropped out) and with scheme managers and healthcare providers to elicit in-depth understanding of the reasons for uptake and renewal in CBHI schemes.

Results of Quantitative Synthesis (Meta-Analysis)

Meta-analysis was conducted for 18 [21–23,28,35,40,44–45,49–50,52,61,63,65,68–69,73–74] quantitative studies. We studied in depth the following variables:

- Socioeconomic status of household
- Presence of acute illness in household
- Presence of chronic illness in the household
- Household head's educational level
- Household size
- Household head's marital status
- Household head's age
- Presence of elderly people (above 65 years) in household
- Household head's gender
- Trust in insurer

The results of the meta-analysis (pooled effect size and 95 percent confidence intervals) are summarized in Table 1 for enrolment and Table 2 for renewal/dropout. We report the

Table 2. Summary Effects for the Variables Influencing Renewal/Drop-Out.

Variable	Type of variable	Summary effect		
		Asia	Sub-Saharan Africa	All location combined
Household head's gender	Cat: Female = 0, Male = 1	0.4500	0.0072	0.1581
Trust in insurer	Cat: No trust = 0, trust = 1	0.1800	0.7700	0.5076
Household size	Con	0.0200	-0.0400	0.0135
Household head's education	Con: years of education	0.0542	0.013	0.0460
Socioeconomic status	Con: socioeconomic percentile	-	-0.0341	-

doi:10.1371/journal.pone.0160479.t002

summary effects for each region separately and also after clubbing them together, for enrolment and renewal/dropout decisions.

The results show that the determinant influencing enrolment most in CBHI, in both regions, is socioeconomic status (SES) of households. Next is heavy incidence of chronic illnesses in households, which are more likely to join the CBHI (the effect is stronger in SSA than in Asia). Similarly, educated, mature and female household heads attach more value to CBHI membership; gender matters most, followed by education and age. Presence of elderly people negatively influences enrolment. The two variables that behave differently across the two regions are household size and Household head's marital status. Household size has a negative effect in Asia but a positive effect in SSA. The effect of Household head's marital status is close to zero (negative) in SSA and positive and somewhat higher in Asia. These results suggest that SES, education, gender and age have similar effects universally, whereas marital status and household size have only localized impact.

The direction of the impact on enrolment is the same for most variables (except household size and marital status).

As regards renewal/dropout decisions, trust in the insurer had the largest effect, followed by male heading of household and household head's education. While trust in the insurer had a stronger effect in SSA, household head's gender and education had a greater influence on renewal decisions in Asia.

The small R-square values for the fitted regressions (estimating the summary effects) for some of the variables indicate localized behaviors may rule out any meaningful combining of the results of several studies.

In the next section more details are presented on each variable considered in the meta-analysis.

Socioeconomic Status of Household. Ten studies [21–22,35,44–45,50,63,65,68,73] reported that the key variable influencing enrolment in CBHI was the SES, but different authors use different variables as reference: Some refer to income as the indicator of SES; others consider expenditure level; and yet others construct socioeconomic categories based on household assets. We presume that notwithstanding the differences between income, expenditure and assets, all three can throw light on the SES of a household, and we consider the categories based on either of them (in absence of any uniform measure) as an indicator of SES of a household. See Fig 2.

The forest-plot diagram for the variable indicates a positive association between household SES and the likelihood of its joining the CBHI. It can also be seen that the effect size increases as SES increases in SSA, but the shift in the effect size is not unidirectional in Asian locations. Effect is positive when the household ranks above the poorest category, but that effect size diminishes as the household SES is higher.

Authors classified the SES categories of households based on income, expenditure or asset, but the categories were not identical across all studies. For instance, some classified the households on the basis of tertiles, others on the basis of quartiles, and some created quintiles. The heterogeneity of these categories made it impossible to use a standard methodology to estimate the summary effect. Hence we assumed (i) uniform effect size within a given category (tertile, quartile or quintile) and (ii) the distribution of households over the domain of socioeconomic *percentile* (instead of tertile, quartile or quintile). We then applied the regression method of obtaining summary effect by fitting a linear regression of effect size on the percentile values.

The SE of the summary effect for all locations combined is 0.001 which implies that the effect is significantly different from zero (p-value = 0.000). We estimate the summary effect of socioeconomic percentile for Asian and SSA locations as 0.258 and 0.5209, respectively (Table 1).

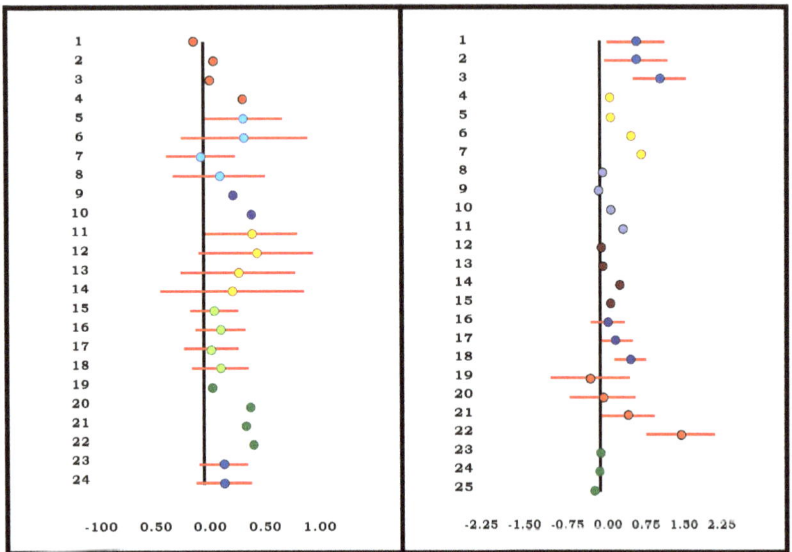

Note: The horizontal line denotes the 95 percent confidence interval. The markers of same shape and shade imply the effect of multiple categories estimated from the same study

Fig 2. Forest-Plot for Socioeconomic Status.

doi:10.1371/journal.pone.0160479.g002

In line with the meta-analysis, similar results appear in findings of all the quantitative studies. In 84 percent of quantitative studies, HH socioeconomic status is positively associated with enrolment.

Presence of Acute Illnesses in Household. Only 2 studies [63,65] involving 4 Asian locations (and none from SSA) reported on acute illnesses (during the month preceding the survey) as a determining factor for enrolment in CBHI. One of those showed a positive association between the presence of acute illnesses and enrolment, and this effect was significantly higher than zero. Acute illnesses in the household were treated as a continuous variable, estimated at 0.138. However, the results are only indicative and not conclusive as the SE for the summary effect size could not be calculated (Fig 3). In four-fifths of the full range of quantitative studies, enrolment is positively associated with the presence of acute illness in the household, suggesting similar results from meta-analysis and vote count.

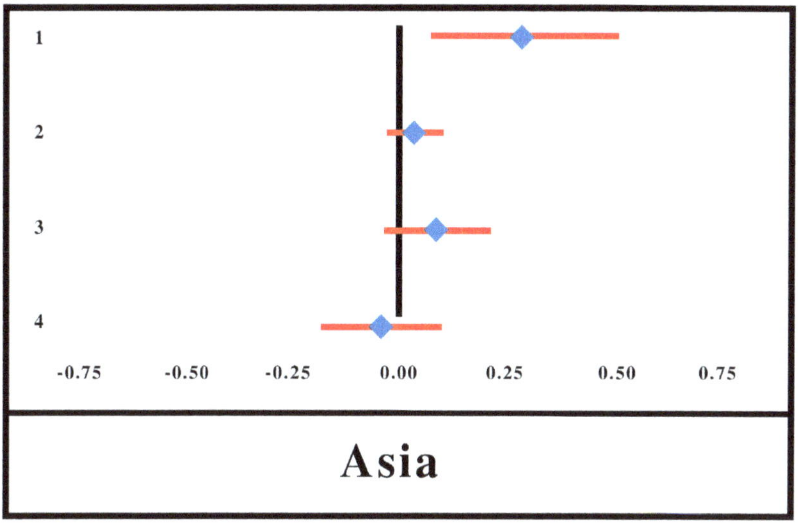

Fig 3. Forest-Plot for Presence of Acute Illnesses in Household.

doi:10.1371/journal.pone.0160479.g003

Presence of Chronic Illnesses in Household. Three studies [23,45,63] involving 5 Asian locations and 3 studies [21,35,44] involving 4 locations in SSA reported the effect of chronic illnesses in the household on enrolment. The forest-plot is displayed in Fig 4. The Asian studies report a positive association between chronic illnesses in the household and enrolment in CBHI, but only one was significantly different from zero. In SSA the effects are close to zero and one is significantly negative. We estimate the summary effects 0.097, 0.0495 and 0.0601, respectively, for Asia, SSA and all locations combined together (Table 1).

Household Head's Education. Many studies reported a positive association between household head's educational level and enrolment in CBHI, and the effect size is apparent in the forest-plot diagram (Fig 5).

Some authors did not report the SE of their results, and others reported seemingly counter-intuitive results, whereby with increased educational level, the effect size is reported to be both positive and negative. However, as a whole the association appears positive, with effect size not always significantly different from zero.

Three authors [23,61,68] measured education in terms of number of years in school, and considered it a continuous variable. The rest [10,21, 22,35,44,45,49,50,65,73] treated it as a categorical variable. All of them assumed the same base category (no experience of schooling), but dealt with multiple heterogeneous categories for the educational level (e.g., primary, secondary, middle, upper-middle). To estimate the summary effect of Household head's educational level, we applied the regression method for obtaining summary effect (as described in the methods

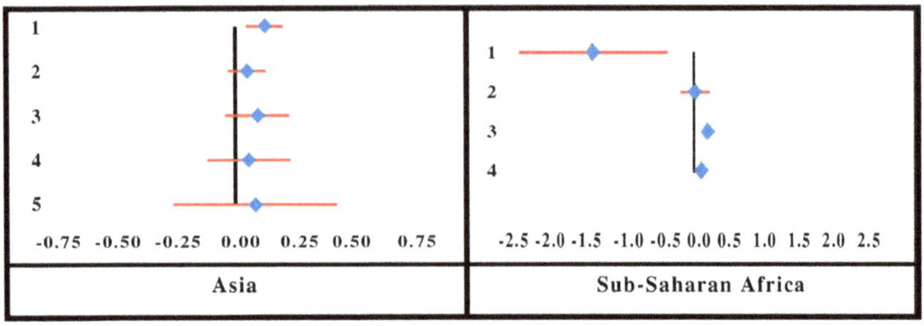

Fig 4. Forest-Plot for Presence of Chronic Illnesses in Household.

doi:10.1371/journal.pone.0160479.g004

section) over a domain of 0 to 15 years of schooling. The summary effect size of education, after applying weights (proportional to the sample sizes), is estimated as 0.0167 for Asia, 0.0555 for SSA and 0.0451 when two regions are clubbed together (Table 1). R-square for the weighted OLS is estimated at 0.069 (for two regions combined). SE of the summary effect for all locations combined is estimated at 0.0002, which implies that it is significantly different from zero (p-value = 0.000).

In line with meta-analysis, the vote count results of the full range of quantitative studies support the positive association between education of the head of household and enrolment in 81 percent of cases.

Household Size. As is evident from the forest-plot diagram (Fig 6), that household size has a negative association with enrolment in Asia and a positive association in SSA. The variable has been treated differently by different authors—continuous as well as categorical with many non-uniform categories. Hence we apply regression method to estimate the summary effect—for regions as well as all locations combined and report the coefficient of regression as the summary effect.

We estimate the summary effects -0.0040 for the Asian locations [22,23,45,63,65] and 0.0414 for the SSA locations [21, 49,50,61,68]. The summary effect for all locations combined is estimated at 0.0328 with R-square value = 0.059 (Table 1) and SE = 0.0002. The small SE implies that the effect significantly differs from zero (p-value = 0.000).

The vote count findings of all quantitative studies suggest a positive relationship between household size and enrolment in three-fifths of the studies. However, the estimate of the summary effect in meta-analysis might have been influenced by large sample size used in some studies.

Household Head's Marital Status. Three studies [45,65,73] involving five locations from Asia and two studies [49,61] from SSA probed household head's marital status as a determinant of enrolling in CBHI (Fig 7). Four studies from Asia and one study from SSA reported a positive association (a household with a married head is more likely to join the CBHI than one with an unmarried head). Overall summary effect for the variable is estimated positive for Asia (0.1543) and negative for SSA (-0.0027). Estimated summary effect for the variable for all locations combined was 0.1403 (Table 1). However, the results are only indicative and not conclusive as the SE for the summary effect size could not be calculated.

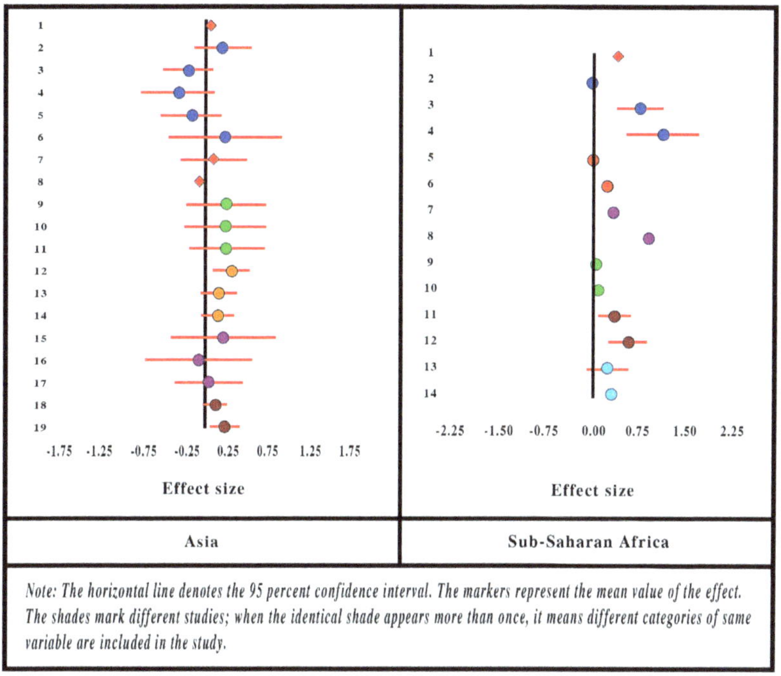

Fig 5. Forest-Plot for Household Head's Education.

doi:10.1371/journal.pone.0160479.g005

Similar to the results of the meta-analysis, vote count results suggest that 86 percent of all the quantitative studies found a positive association between households with a married household head and enrolment.

Household Head's Age. Eight authors [21,22,35,44,45,63,65,68] have studied household head's age associated with the enrolment in CBHI. Again, the variable was treated differently by different authors—continuous and categorical with heterogeneous categories.

The forest-plot diagram for the household head's age (Fig 8) indicates a positive association between the age of the head of household and enrolment in CBHI in SSA. In Asian locations, it is a mixture of positive and negative associations. For those studies where the age has been treated as a continuous variable, the slope of the regression is almost zero.

We apply the regression method to obtain summary effect and fit a regression of the effect size on household head's age ranging from 16 to 65 years, with weights proportional to the sample size. We estimate the summary effect of the variable as 0.0048 with R-square value of

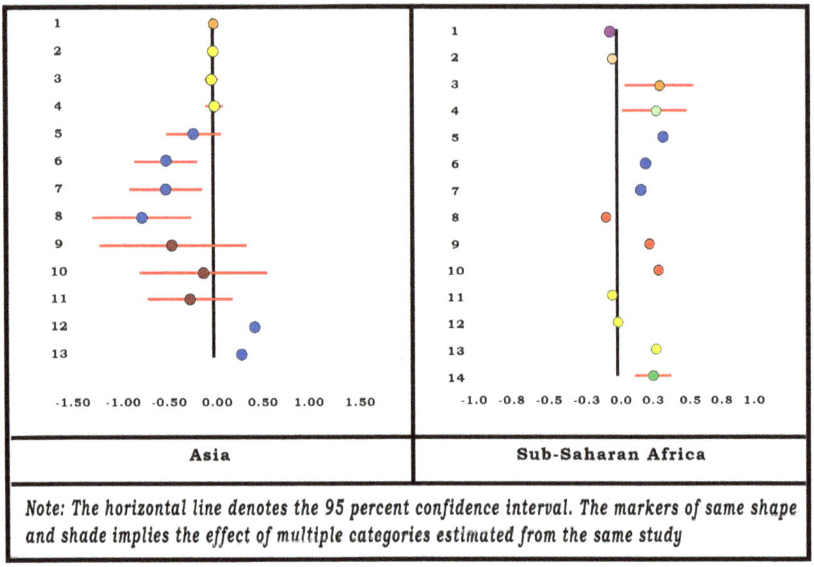

Fig 6. Forest-Plot for Household Size.

doi:10.1371/journal.pone.0160479.g006

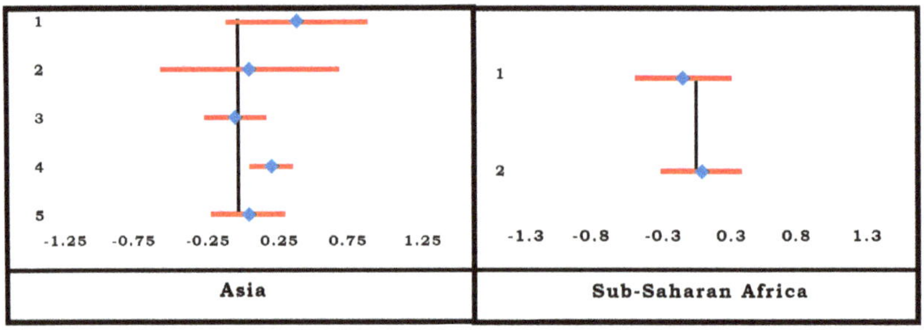

Fig 7. Forest-Plot for Household Head's Marital Status.

doi:10.1371/journal.pone.0160479.g007

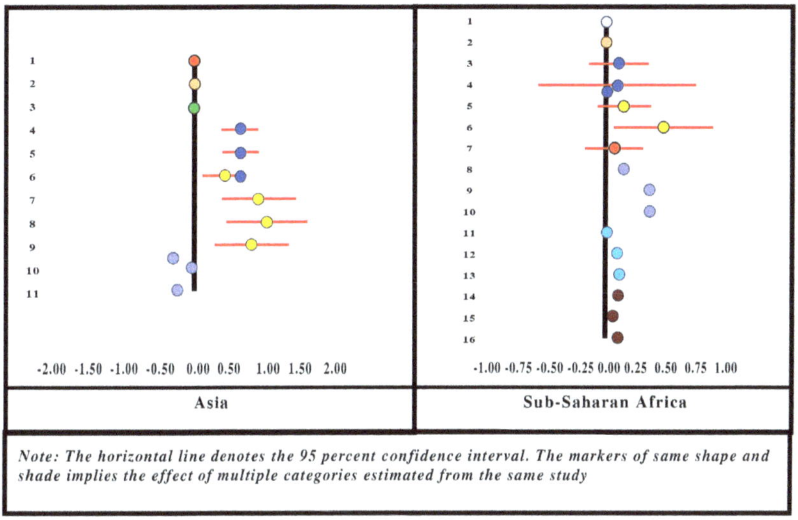

Fig 8. Forest-Plot for Household Head's Age.

doi:10.1371/journal.pone.0160479.g008

0.15 for all locations combined (Table 1). The SE of the summary effect is estimated to be very small (8.43E-06) implying that the effect significantly differs from zero (p-value = 0.000). Separate estimates of the summary effect for Asian and SSA locations are estimated at 0.0092 and 0.0042, respectively.

When the association between household head's age and enrolment is considered in all quantitative studies, we find a positive relationship in half of the studies.

Presence of Elderly People in Household. Only one study [63] involving three locations for Asia and two studies [44,49] from SSA probed the effect of elderly household members on enrolment in CBHI (Fig 9). All studies in the Asian locations indicate a negative association between the two. One of the two studies in SSA reported a negative association and the other reported a slightly positive association. Overall the summary effects are estimated to be negative for both regions (-0.212 for Asia and -0.1614 for SSA) and also for all locations combined (-0.181) (Table 1). However, the results are only indicative and not conclusive because the SE for the summary effect size could not be calculated.

The vote count results from the full range of quantitative studies contradict the findings of the meta-analysis. In three-fifths of all the quantitative studies, we find a positive association between enrolment and the presence of elderly people in the household while the relationship was negative in meta-analysis. This discrepancy could be explained by the small number of studies involved or that the vote count does not take into consideration sample size.

Household Head's Gender. Household head's gender was reported by many authors as a factor influencing enrolment in CBHI (Fig 10). Two studies [63,73] involving 4 locations for

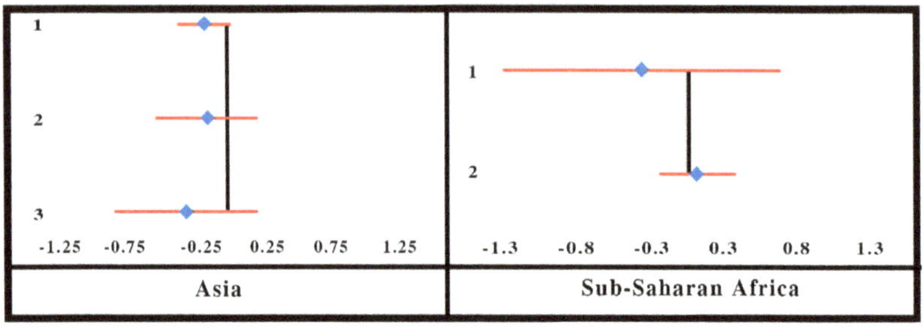

Fig 9. Forest-Plot for Presence of Elderly People in Household.

doi:10.1371/journal.pone.0160479.g009

the Asia region and 7 studies [21, 36, 44,49,50,61,68] involving 9 locations for the SSA region examined the variable in detail. A household with a female head in Asia was more likely to enroll in CBHI than one headed by a male. The result was uniform across the region although the absolute values of the effect size and its confidence intervals (CIs) varied. In the SSA region

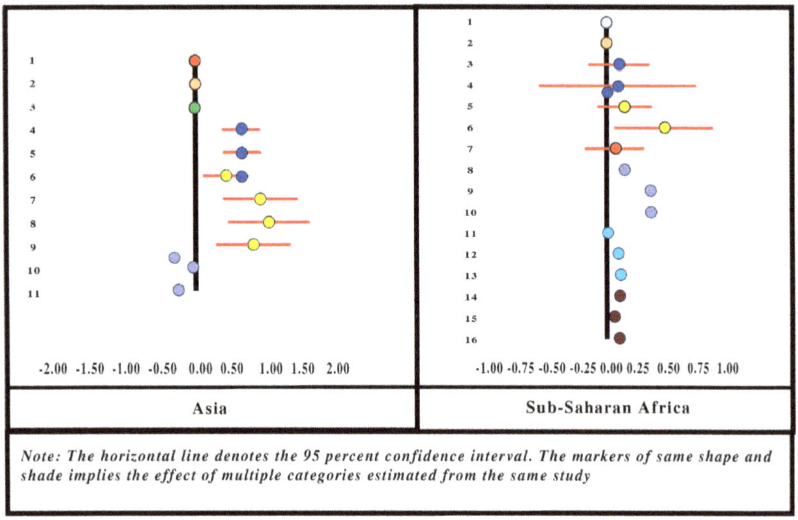

Fig 10. Forest-Plot for Household Head's Gender.

doi:10.1371/journal.pone.0160479.g010

on the other hand the result was not uniform. Three [49, 61,68] of nine studies in the SSA region reported a positive association between the enrolment in CBHI and male-headed household, but the remaining studies reported almost zero, or highly negative association between the two. The summary effect is estimated as negative for both regions (-0.0505 for Asia, -0.3556 for SSA) and for the two regions combined (-0.359) (Table 1). However, the results are only indicative and not conclusive because the SE for the summary effect size could not be calculated.

In line with the results in meta-analysis, the vote count results show a similar pattern of relationship between female-headed households and enrolment—four-fifths of all quantitative studies show a positive association between the two.

Results of Qualitative Synthesis (Thematic Synthesis)

18 qualitative studies [25, 30–32, 33–35,38,48,60,62,64,67,70,71,72,75,76] have been used for the thematic synthesis; we identified nine major themes: knowledge and understanding of insurance principles and CBHI, quality of healthcare, trust, benefit package, rules of CBHI schemes, cultural beliefs, affordability, distance to health facility, and legal and policy framework (Fig 11 and S3b Table).

Theme 1—Knowledge and understanding of insurance principles and CBHI. This theme encompasses knowledge and understanding of prepayment, risk-pooling, redistribution of financial resources, CBHI managerial structure, responsibilities of different management levels, and CBHI benefits (including scheme features). Eleven studies reported knowledge and understanding of insurance principles and CBHI [30–32, 33,34,35,62,67,70,71,76].

Inadequate knowledge and understanding of insurance principles and CBHI were reported to be an obstacle to enrolment in 4 studies [31,33,48,62]. Limited understanding of the principles of CBHI by both beneficiaries and health providers and managers of CBHI was reported

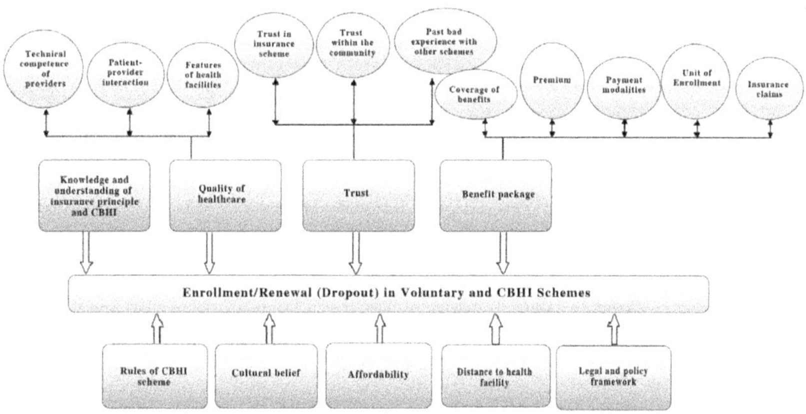

Fig 11. Themes and Subthemes Identified in CBHI Uptake and Dropout.

doi:10.1371/journal.pone.0160479.g011

to be a barrier to enrolment in one study [30]. However, failure to understand the principles of CBHI did not explain low enrolment rates in one study [33]. A good understanding of the benefits of insurance was a facilitator of enrolment decision in 1 study [75]. Health insurance was poorly understood by some people as a form of "lotto" in 1 study [75]. Even in specific contexts where people had a broad understanding of insurance and CBHI, some legal terms (e.g., collaboration between CBHI and providers are regulated by a contract; CBHIs are managed following their by-laws) were not understood in 1 study [67] and some technical aspects of insurance (e.g., the risk of adverse selection; the advantages of large risk pool) were not fully understood in another study [33]. Although respondents comprehended the principle of insurance, they could not recall specific elements of scheme features including the CBHI managerial structure in 1 study [35]. In addition, one study reported poor knowledge and understanding of CBHI activities by key policy makers and health service managers [75,31]. Lack of clear understanding of insurance and prepayment mechanisms was reported to hamper scale-up of CBHI activities in 1 study [71]. Poor knowledge and understanding of CBHI was also reported to be a barrier to renewal in 2 studies [33,70].

Theme 2—Healthcare quality. The issues related to healthcare quality include three aspects: providers' technical competence, patient-provider interactions and providers' attitude and health facility features. Twelve studies reported these dimensions of quality of healthcare [25, 31,76,33,34,35, 48,64,67,71,72, 75]. Low healthcare quality was recognized by participants in one study [70] as one of the most important constraints to enrolment and membership renewal.

Healthcare providers' lack of technical competence was reported to be a barrier to enrolment in two studies [33,67]. In one study it was argued that dropping out of the CBHI scheme could be explained by providers' lack of technical expertise. [67]. The negative attitude of healthcare providers was reported to be a barrier to enrolment in five studies [31,33,48,71,75]. Participants expressed dissatisfaction with the negative attitude of providers toward patients in five studies [25, 34,67,72, 76]. The dissatisfaction was occasioned by long waiting queues, provider rudeness, preference given to cash-paying uninsured patients, and differential treatment depending on patient's SES.

One study reported that 30 percent of members left a scheme because of providers' negative behaviors [71]. Another study also reported that members dropped-out of the schemes due to providers' rude behavior [40]. Four studies linked low enrolment to adverse features of a healthcare facility (dirty premises, unavailability of diagnostics, unavailability or shortage of prescribed medicines) [31,33,64,71]. In addition, two studies highlighted participants' concerns about these poor features of healthcare facilities although they did not relate these features directly to either enrolment or renewal decisions [67,72].

Theme 3—Trust. This theme includes trust in insurance scheme management, trust within community and distrust associated with past bad experience of other schemes or collective arrangements. Fifteen studies commented on aspects relating to trust [25, 30,31, 33,34,35,48,62,64,67,70,71,72,75,76]

People's trust in CBHI management was reported to be a facilitator of insurance enrolment decisions in four studies [25,34,62,67] and distrust a barrier to enrolment in five studies [30,35,71,72,75]. In addition, four studies highlighted the role of trust, although this was not in reference to specific enrolment/renewal decisions: poor involvement of the community in a hospital-based scheme [31]; lack of community participation in premium setting and managing funds [76]; criticism by respondents that the scheme failed to reach its objectives, defend its members, and keep its promises [33]; and low community participation an obstacle to sustaining the scheme [48]. In one study [70], members who renewed their membership had much stronger linkages with the scheme's grassroots workers than did dropouts. Greater contact led to greater trust by scheme members.

Trust within the community was reported to be a facilitator of enrolment decision in one study [34], and also a facilitator of renewal decision in another study [70]. In both studies, participants highlighted that they joined because other villagers had joined or renewed, so they trusted the insurance scheme. Lack of trust within the community led to skepticism about who would manage the CBHI funds [35]. One study reported strong social capital or trust within the community, but limited trust outside the community and toward the government [64]. Lack of solidarity among community members was reported to be among the main reasons for non-enrolment in one study [67]. Previous bad experience and lack of trust in local financial organizations or other collective arrangements led communities to distrust the CBHI management and thus, not to enroll in the schemes in five studies [30,31,34,62,67]. The communities in such contexts were suspicious of the CBHI scheme and preferred 'to wait and see whether CBHI would keep its promises before enrolling [67]. In fact, one study reported that past bad experience did not explain low enrolment because over time people gained confidence about scheme transparency and management's trustworthiness [31].

Theme 4—Benefits package. This theme involves benefits package composition, premium, payment modalities, enrolment units and insurance claims. Twelve studies reported on aspects of benefits package [25, 31, 34,35, 38,60,64,67,70,71,75,76].

People's dissatisfaction with the insurance benefits package was reported to be a major cause of low enrolment and membership renewal in three studies [31,48,71]. Exclusion of chronic diseases from the benefits package was reported to be a major weakness in four studies [31,48,64,72]. In one study, scheme dropouts suggested that the benefits package should cover out-patient care [70]. Participants voiced concerns about the provision of only second-level care (hospitalization) and lack of access to primary care at the healthcare centers in two studies [75,76]. Participants in four studies reported that the premium was fair and not too high [25,33–35]. One study reported that a high premium deterred people from joining the scheme [64]. The uninsured in another study reported that they did not join the scheme because they considered the premium too high [75]. However, in the same study, an equally high percentage of uninsured reported that they did not join due to an inappropriate registration period. Therefore, premium per se was not a decisive issue. As reported in two studies [48,76] participants criticized the flat-rate premium, in one case the same for children and adults [76] and in another case the same for both rich and poor, with no exemptions for the most vulnerable [48]. In fact, the participants in one study appreciated that CBHI has set different premiums for adults and children [35].

Paying the premium for the whole family at once was reported to be a major deterrent to enrolment in five studies [25, 34,35,71, 75] and a deterrent to renewal in one study [70]. Conversely, as reported in one study, payment by installment was an enabler for enrolment [30]. The timing of premium collections was noted as an enabler in one study: it was important for villagers to receive the CBHI card before being asked to pay for premiums [62]. In one study, participants criticized the inappropriate registration period and the fact that payment could not spread out over time [76].

Family/household enrolment was the norm in most of the schemes. Six studies reported that family enrolment for large families discouraged enrolment [25, 31,34,35,71,75]. In one study, enrolment was limited to four household members, which excluded larger families from the scheme and the coverage level was low [48]. One study found that a good claim experience could motivate renewal [70].

Theme 5—Rules of CBHI schemes. Arbitrary restrictions were found to inhibit CBHI enrolment and renewal [25,30,31,34,35,48]. Stringent rules imposed by management inhibited participation, both enrolment and renewal, four studies reported [25,30,31,48]. Many large families were reported to be excluded from some CBHI schemes due to restrictions on the number of persons that can be covered under a family membership (e.g., only up to four members can enroll) [48]. One study reported that unemployed or homeless persons are excluded from healthcare—most of the poorest segments of society [25]. Three studies reported difficulties in interesting the minimum number of people in CBHI membership so that enrolment could begin: 60 percent of a group or 100 families per village [30,31,48].

Theme 6—Cultural belief. Various sociocultural factors can either facilitate or act as barriers to enrolment in CBHI. One study reported that all the participants acknowledged that setting money aside for healthcare may be perceived as attracting diseases [34]. Some participants in that study further stated that when they save they do not talk about diseases. Prepayment before illness was associated with "inviting disease" in a study [31]. In another cultural context, participants reported that it is only when someone becomes sick that they ask the community to contribute financially to help a person [71]. In some cultures, women seek permission from their husbands to enroll [70]. See Box 2.

Box 2. Non-Subscribers Views on Benefits Packages, CBHI Rules, Cultural Belief

Benefits Package

"People with chronic diseases receive care from the doctor at the ambulatory; they get their drugs from the pharmacy where they often have to pay for the drugs. They can be a burden on their families; it is difficult to afford the drugs for many people. CBHI should cover these costs if possible." [64]

"Some services are included and some are excluded. They have excluded some services because the money would not be enough to pay for them. I would like if one day, they could cover all services, but today it is good as it is, so that the insurance can have money till the end of the year." [35]

Rules of CBHI Schemes

"If the CBHI people had said that I could divide the whole amounts in parts, I could have managed to enroll.' [34]

"We did all we could to pay the entire premium. We looked for the money and we managed to find it. But for large families, this is very hard. It would be better if they could pay little by little. So, when they have some money, they turn that in. Then, when they find the rest, they pay again." [35]

"The neediest people in our community especially the orphans, the disabled and the elderly still pay in the schemes. They have more health needs and should be excused." [48]

"Rules should be change[d] so that those who don't fall sick get something from the scheme." [31]

"Why [can't] the body of a subscriber who has died in hospital be transported to the villages?" [76]

Cultural Beliefs

"Paying before you fall sick is like buying a disease." [31]

"It is the old people who say that if you keep an idea in your head, this thing will happen, but nowadays we do not think like this anymore." [34]

"In our culture, it is only when someone becomes sick that we ask the community to contribute financially to help a person." [71]

Theme 7—Affordability. Affordability involves people's ability to pay the premium. All the studies noted that the poorest had been excluded from the CBHI scheme due to their inability to raise sufficient funds to pay the premium. Eleven studies commented on aspects of affordability [25,30,31, 33,34,35,62,64,70,75,76]. Lack of financial means was the most common reason for people not enrolling in CBHI schemes, mentioned in 11 studies [25, 30,31, 33–35, 62,64,70,75,76]. Lack of affordability was also a reason for people dropping out of the scheme [65]. However, one study reported that lack of money was not a major issue for renewal decision [70]. While lack of money was a common response for not being able to join the scheme, especially for poor households, many studies noted that the real issue was the unavailability of funds at the time when payment was collected [25, 34,70,75].

Theme 8—Distance from health facility. Travel and transport, too, can act as facilitators or barriers in accessing healthcare at the facilities contracted by the CBHI scheme [25,27,31,34,64,71]. One study reported that 25 percent of the unenrolled could not join the scheme because there was no facility nearby [25]. Long distance from the communities to a healthcare facility was reported to be an obstacle to enrolment in one study [27]. Two studies reported that high transport cost was a reason for low enrolment [64,71].

Theme 9—Legal and policy framework. Various legal and policy frameworks with enrolment/renewal decisions were evident. Nine studies discussed this theme affecting uptake in CBHI [30,32,48,62,64,67,70,71,72]. Four studies highlighted the absence of a coherent legal, regulatory and policy framework as a direct obstacle to maximizing CBHI membership [62,67,70,71]. One study reported that many insured members had dropped out of the CBHI schemes as they were skeptical about CBHI operations without appropriate legislative backup from the government [48]. The importance of legal and policy framework was discussed in the context of the sustainability of CBHI schemes in three studies [32,67,72].

Box 3 contains testimonials on the above themes.

Discussion

The systematic review of the literature set out to provide evidence on demand- and supply-side factors affecting uptake of CBHI memberships in LMIC. The evidence, originating from 54 rigorously screened articles, is discussed here based on the meta-analysis and a thematic synthesis.

Demand-Side Factors

On the demand side, the strongest factor affecting uptake of CBHI is the socioeconomic status (SES) of the household. The results of meta-analysis confirm a positive association of SES with enrolment (summary effect is significantly higher than zero), regardless of whether the SES is expressed in terms of income, expenditure or asset ownership. The importance of this factor is strengthened by the obverse evidence from the thematic synthesis that low affordability was one of the barriers to enrolment or renewing membership. Interestingly, lack of affordability was not synonymous with low income in all cases, but could also mean inability to pay the annual premium upfront (i.e., compliance with administrative modalities) or the inability to pay at the time premiums were collected (e.g., before the harvest season).

In Asia, the second most prominent demand-side factor affecting enrolment is the marital status of the household head (but significance could not be confirmed as some authors did not report the SE of their estimates). It emerged clearly from the meta-analysis that Asian married household heads were more disposed to enroll, and that this factor was not equally weighty in Africa. Female-headed households (in Asia) were more likely to enroll than male-headed

Box 3. Barriers to Health Insurance: Affordability, Distance, Inadequate Legal and Policy Framework

Affordability-

"We are not refusing to pay, but we cannot afford to" [76]

"I wanted to enroll, but I did not find the means, maybe next year. . .." [34]

"The only reason for not joining is money. If we had money we would join, but our village is the poorest of the poor." [64]

"If people cannot afford to pay now, how will they afford to pay if you increase the premiums?" [64]

Why should it be the same premium for everyone, when there are different charges for adults and children at the health centre and the hospital? [76]

"Out here in the countryside, the availability of money poses a problem. . .. . .. we, the farmers, have money after the harvest, but by the time the rainy season arrives, we have nothing left in our hand and out here you cannot find where to borrow money. [35]

Distance to Health Facility-

"It was expensive for me to travel 27 Km to and from Ishaka hospital." [31]

"Transport is a problem. Our village is isolated, and the road is not good. In winter it is very difficult to even get to Vayk." [64]

"If there was a doctor in our village, more people would enroll. . .. To have a doctor right at your side would encourage many to enter." [34]

Quality of Care

"The care given to us at the hospital is good but we cannot afford joining the scheme." [30]

Legal and Policy Framework-

"For me, the solution is that [health insurance] becomes obligatory and that there's a real constraint to enroll. Without this, MHOs [mutual health organizations] will not survive." [71]

"It should be feasible to roll-out CBHI schemes nationally, but technical and managerial oversight would be needed. There is no role for the government in this; it should be provided by NGOs." [64]

"No policy yet but CHI [community health insurance] is a component of the ministerial policy statement." [30]

"Health is something that everyone needs to maintain, and therefore CHI has a place in Uganda. Let us start with national policies facilitating CHI. . .. Regulations are very important and gradual implementation is needed." [32]

households (source: meta-analysis), but also more likely to drop out. This may reflect possible dynamics toward female household heads within schemes. Neither marital status nor gender of the household head emerged as factors in the thematic synthesis.

Education of the household head, another individual attribute, was positively correlated with both enrolment and renewal decisions in CBHI schemes (meta-analysis), and this summary effect was significantly higher than zero. The thematic synthesis brought to light that knowledge and understanding of insurance principles and the functioning of the CBHI facilitated both enrolment and renewal decisions. In communities where literacy is low and information scarce, low enrolment and renewal decisions may be related to people's low understanding of CBHI. While education can be counted as a demand-side factor, efforts made by insurance companies to explain their value proposition reflect supply-side factors to acquire potential clients that are free to enroll or not. Low enrolment linked to low familiarity with CBHI operations may be counted as a supply-side factor.

Another demand-side factor that enables enrolment to CBHI (confirmed through meta-analysis) is prevalence of chronic illness in the household (caveat: statistical significance of the summary effect could not be established as some studies did not provide information on SE). The importance of this factor must be considered in the context that such diseases are on the rise in all LMIC, and augmented by the increase of life expectancy. The household head's age was confirmed to be a facilitator of enrolment (in meta-analysis but not in the thematic synthesis) but the presence of elderly persons in the household was a barrier to enrolment. These results might at first seem contradictory, but are really quite complementary. It is self-explanatory why household head age is positively associated with enrolments; and it seems also self-explanatory that when elderly people cannot expect to obtain services they want from their CBHI scheme they obviously would not see reason to enroll. A similar effect could be expected of chronically ill: higher propensity to enroll when the scheme covers at least part of their higher costs, and lower enrolments when schemes do not cover their needs. These factors have a supply-side angle in that responsibility for benefits package design is vested with schemes. The benefits limitations that CBHI schemes observe arise from the need to remain sustainable even as they keep premiums low (a clear plus point for enrolments) and cannot normally rely on subsidy income.

Finally, household size was positively associated with enrolment in the meta-analysis (and the summary effect was significantly higher than zero) but in the thematic synthesis was flagged as a barrier to enrolment, when large households could not pay premiums for all their members at one go. The seemingly conflicting information may be due to the inclusion of different pricing practices of some CBHI in the quantitative analysis, for example, premium discount to large households. The meta-analysis suggests that household size was a facilitator of renewal as well. None of the qualitative studies looked at this aspect.

Supply-Side Factors

We now come to supply-side factors. The thematic synthesis found that *trust in the scheme management* was a significant enabler of enrolment. This aspect was not considered in the meta-analysis, but the closely related *trust in insurance scheme* was, and found to facilitate renewal decisions. Two closely related themes had similar effects: when the rules of CBHI schemes were perceived as rigid, and when people felt there was lack of clarity about the legal or policy framework, they were less inclined to enroll and renew. All these factors show that, when a scheme is trusted, considered accommodating, and enjoys support from policymakers, it attracts higher enrolments.

Other supply-side factors that emerged in the thematic synthesis (and not at all considered in the meta-analysis) include the self-explanatory situation that when healthcare services were considered of good quality they were an important enabler of enrolment and renewal decisions. And distance from residence to healthcare facility was found to be an obstacle to enrolment in the thematic synthesis.

This systematic review deals with voluntary and contributory enrolment and renewal; SES was shown to be an enabling factor, but as people's SES improves, they may consume more of everything and also of healthcare services, beyond what the CBHI covers. Thus, just as there might be a positive association between enrolment and SES, there could be a negative association between increased SES and renewal, if the gap grows between what a household can afford and what the CBHI offers. This was established through the meta-analysis. However, the net effect would be influenced by other operational practices of the CBHI, such as its track record in paying claims promptly and correctly. The thematic synthesis confirmed that positive experience with how the CBHI settled claims was an important enabler of renewal decision.

Conclusions and Policy Implications

This systematic review examined the evidence of factors affecting voluntary uptake of community-based health insurance schemes in low- and middle-income countries, with a view to including CBHI as part of a strategy to extend the outreach of social protection. The evidence shows that certain factors affecting voluntary uptake in CBHI are basically demand-driven, while others are driven by conditions controlled by the supply-side or by policy.

The first major insight relates to demand-side factors positively affecting enrolment in CBHI, as well as renewals: Education, age, female household heads, and the socioeconomic status of households are all factors that positively affect enrolments. Moreover, when individuals understand insurance principles in general, and how their CBHI functions, they are more likely to enroll; when people have a positive claims experience, they are more likely to renew. A higher prevalence of chronic conditions enhances the likelihood of enrolling; the perception that healthcare is of good quality and nearby acts as a factor enhancing enrolment, and the perception that services are distant or deficient leads to lower enrolments. All this reflects common-sense. Moreover, the finding that having to pay annual premiums upfront creates financial stress which was not limited to poor households suggests that this problem affecting uptake and renewal in CBHI is inherently solvable, as it originates mainly from administrative convenience, and could be resolved or at least significantly reduced, when arrangements are put in place to spread premium payment over the entire coverage period. Such arrangements are commonly in place in social health insurance, and could be applied at CBHI level as well, either through regulation and/or through suitable arrangements with local MFIs.

The second insight is that many supply side issues that are within the control of CBHI schemes and related organizations can be adjusted to enhance enrolment and renewals as well. Trust in the *scheme management* and trust in the *insurance scheme* emerged as significant enablers of enrolment. Schemes viewed by the target population as applying rules rigidly (i.e., unfairly) attract fewer enrolments. Stated simply, the evidence indicates that even community-based schemes must maintain a positive image, or risk alienation from their catchment communities.

The third insight is that clarity about the legal or policy framework also acts as a factor influencing enrolments, and lack of clarity dampens uptake. The evidence discovered through this systematic review offers for the first time a clear indication that the prospective members of CBHIs harbor two balancing expectations: on the one hand, an expectation (from governments and the development community) to recognize that CBHI schemes function within a legitimate framework, and by implication that CBHIs are fulfilling a desirable social role; and on the other hand, an expectation from the CBHI to operate a client-centric scheme at local level, with measures to ensure clients that the insurance contract can and will be enforced fairly, rather than being complementary to, or dependent on other schemes or vertical programs or external governance. This conclusion differs fundamentally from that of Ekman [12] who claimed that CBHI were at best *complementary to other more effective systems of health financing*. There is no contradiction between the wish of the population to take advantage of benefits from a local scheme, while simultaneously expecting the authorities to provide a coherent framing to recognize such local scheme as legitimate. This very pragmatic nexus suggests that people recognize that they must pay for health insurance, and prefer localized operations through which they stand a better chance to gain welfare by being involved not merely in paying but also in priority-setting and in scheme governance. This is also fundamentally different from conclusions reached by Adebayo et al [14] that the challenges of CBHI are captured by *lack of funds, poor quality of care, and lack of trust*, i.e. three deficiencies reflecting unmet expectations from others: funders, providers and administrators. Our analysis has shown that the target population has expectations to influence priority-setting or governance when they participate voluntarily in CBHI schemes. This expectation of the target population suggests that governments—especially in low income countries—could leverage people's willingness to exercise voluntary and contributory enrolment in a community-based health insurance, by acting as regulators even when they cannot act as funders and providers. The limitations of low-income governments to act as funders and providers of services are well known and there are no easy solutions at hand today; our conclusions that people at the base of the pyramid are more likely to enroll in CBHI on a voluntary basis when governments formulate an enabling environment for the development and expansion of CBHI offer an important unexplored opportunity to facilitate the growth of this form of health financing from niche to mass.

Limitations

This research report was limited by the number, quality and themes of the published literature. Thus, the filtering process could deal only with the quality of articles, but not with the meager number or with the themes that were chosen by the various authors. As the largest number of studies dealt with CBHI schemes in Sub-Saharan Africa, the conclusions might be more relevant for the African context. This is particularly limiting in the case of a nascent activity like CBHI, where the history of publications spans barely a decade and relies mainly on the African experience but where much of the growth in activities now occurs in Asia. On the quality of publications, other than the 8 articles that were considered unsuitable and excluded, all the studies retained for full text analysis were then considered as equal in terms of quality [26] suggested that this could possibly bias the pooled results. A number of authors did not report the SEs or their estimates. Hence, we applied weights proportional to the sample size (instead of inverse of the variance, which is the standard practice of meta-analysis) while estimating the summary effect. We also recognize the somewhat weak internal validity of certain studies due to flaws in study methodology. Although we attempted to account for this utilizing the PRISMA protocol for the search strategy, this corrective approach has its limitations. Sample sizes for some of the studies were large [21] and sensitivity analysis shows that it does have some influence on the estimated summary effect. For some variables, the results are only indicative and not conclusive as the SE was not reported in all studies, and consequently the summary effect size could not be calculated.

Supporting Information

S1 Table. PRISMA Checklist.
(DOCX)

S2 Table. Quality Assessment of Included Studies.
(DOCX)

S3 Table. Characteristics of Included Studies (Quantitative; Qualitative; Mixed-method papers).
(DOCX)

S1 Text. Search Strategy.
(DOCX)

S2 Text. Data Extraction Sheet.
(DOCX)

Acknowledgments

The authors express their sincere appreciation to Kanika Garg, Anuj Pratap Singh, Tanuka Endow, Sunetra Ghatak, Isha Chaudhry, Sachin Hans and Shraddha Srivastava, researchers at the Micro Insurance Academy, New Delhi, for their immense contributions to various drafts of the report which formed the basis of this article. We would like to thank Hugh Waddington, Birte Snilstveit, John Eyers and Ami Bhavsar of International Initiative for Impact Evaluation (3ie) and Mukdarut Bangpan and Carol Vigurs of EPPI Centre, for guidance and technical assistance at every step during the completion of the full report which is summarized in this article. Last but not least, we thank the external peer reviewers for their valuable comments that have enriched the report.

Author Contributions

Conceptualization: DMD TPK PP.

Data curation: AM PP SASH DJ.

Formal analysis: AM PP SASH.

Funding acquisition: PP DMD TPK.

Investigation: DJ SASH AM PP DMD.

Methodology: PP SASH AM TPK.

Project administration: PP DMD.

Resources: SASH TPK.

Software: AM DJ.

Supervision: DMD.

Validation: TPK DMD.

Visualization: AM.

Writing - original draft: DMD AM DJ PP.

Writing - review & editing: DMD TPK.

References

1. Selvaraj S, Karan A. Why publicly-financed health insurance schemes are ineffective in providing financial risk protection. Economic & Political Weekly. 2012; 47(11):61.
2. Bank World. How we classify countries. 2009 [cited 2015 Dec 21]. Available from: http://data.worldbank.org/about/country-classifications.
3. Stuckler D, Feigl A, Basu S, McKee M. The political economy of universal health coverage. Geneva: Background Paper -HSR/BCKGRT for the Global Symposium on Health Systems Research, Technical Report. WHO, Health Systems Research; 2010.
4. Dror DM, Vellakkal S. Is RSBY India's platform to implement universal hospital insurance? Indian Journal of Medical Research. 2012; 135(56–63):56–63.
5. Gottret P E, Schieber G. Health financing revisited: A Practitioner's guide. Washington, DC: World Bank Publications; 2006.

6. Dror DM, Jacquier C. Micro-insurance: Extending health insurance to the excluded. International Social Security Review. 1999; 52(1):71–97.
7. Dror DM, Jambhekar S (Editors): *Microinsurance Business Processes Handbook.* New Delhi, Micro Insurance Academy, Jan 2016. ISBN 978-81-909841-7-1, xxii+144 pp
8. Dror DM. (2014) *Health Microinsurance Programs in Developing Countries* in Culyer A. J. (ed.) *Encyclopaedia of Health Economics.* United States: Elsevier Science, Vol 1. pp. 412–421
9. Tabor S. Community-Based Health Insurance and Social Protection Policy. Washington D.C.: Social Protection Discussion Paper Series No 0503, The World Bank; 2005.
10. Panda P, Dror I, Koehlmoos T, Hossain S, John D, Khan J, et al. What factors affect take up of voluntary and community-based health insurance programmes in low- and middle- income countries? A systematic review (Protocol). London: EPPI-Centre, Social Science Research Unit, Institute of Education, University of London.; 2013.
11. Panda P, Dror I, Koehlmoos T, Hossain S, John D, Khan J, et al. What factors affect uptake of voluntary and community-based health insurance schemes in low- and middle-income countries? A Systematic Review and Meta-Analysis. Delhi: 3ie Systematic Reviews—SR4/1009 Review, the International Initiative for Impact Evaluation (3ie); 2015.
12. Ekman B. Community-based health insurance in low-income countries: a systematic review of the evidence. Health Policy Plan. 2004 Sep; 19(5):249–70. Review. PMID: 15310661.
13. Robyn PJ, Sauerborn R, Bärnighausen T. Provider payment in community-based health insurance schemes in developing countries: a systematic review. Health Policy Plan. 2013 Mar; 28(2):111–22. doi: 10.1093/heapol/czs034. Epub 2012 Apr 19. Review. PMID: 22522770; PubMed Central PMCID: PMC3584992.
14. Adebayo EF, Uthman OA, Wiysonge CS, Stern EA, Lamont KT, Ataguba JE. A systematic review of factors that affect uptake of community-based health insurance in low-income and middle-income countries. BMC Health Serv Res. 2015 Dec 8; 15:543. doi: 10.1186/s12913-015-1179-3 PMID: 26645355; PubMed Central PMCID: PMC4673712
15. Higgins J, Green S, editors. Cochrane Handbook for Systematic Reviews of Interventions Version 5.1.0 [updated March 2011]. The Cochrane Collaboration: [publisher unknown]; 2011 [cited 2015 Dec 21]. Available from: www.cochrane-handbook.org.
16. Critical Appraisal Skills Programme. 12 questions to help you make sense of cohort study. England: Public Health Resource Unit; 2013.
17. Waddington H, Snilstveit B, Hombrados G.J, Vojtkova M, Anderson J, White H. Protocol: Farmer Field Schools for Improving Farming Practices and Farmer Outcomes in Low- and Middle-income Countries: A Systematic Review. 2012 [cited 2015 Dec 21]. Available from: http://campbellcollaboration.org/lib/project/203/.
18. Thomas J, Harden A. Methods for the thematic synthesis of qualitative research in systematic reviews. BMC Medical Research Methodology. 2008; 8(45).
19. Critical Appraisal Skills Programme. 10 questions to help you make sense of qualitative research. England: Public Health Resource Unit; 2006.
20. Chinn S. A simple method for converting an odds ratio to effect size for use in meta-analysis. *Statistics in Medicine*. 2000; 19(22):3127–3131. doi: 10.1002/1097-0258(20001130)19:22<3127::aid-sim784>3.0.co;2-m PMID: 11113947
21. Chankova S, Sulzbach S, Diop F. Impact of mutual health organizations: Evidence from West Africa. Health Policy and Planning. 2008; 23(4):264–276. doi: 10.1093/heapol/czn011 PMID: 18480126
22. Mathiyazaghan K. Willingness to pay for rural health insurance through community participation in India. The International Journal of Health Planning and Management. 1998 Jan; 13(1):47–67. PMID: 10178583
23. Aggarwal A. Achieving equity in health through community-based health insurance: India's experience with a large CBHI Programme. Kobe: Discussion Paper Series- DP2010-31, RIEB, Kobe University; 2010 Nov 10.
24. Akotey OJ, Osei K A, Gemegah A. The demand for micro insurance in Ghana'. Journal of Risk Finance (Emerald Group Publishing Limited). 2011; 12(3):182–194.
25. Alatinga K, Fielmua N. The impact of mutual health insurance scheme on access and quality of health care in northern Ghana: The case of Kassena-Nankana east scheme'. Journal of Sustainable Development. 2011; 4(5):125–138.
26. Bai A, Shukla V, Bak G, Wells G. Quality assessment tools project report. Ottawa: Canadian agency for drugs and technologies in health; 2012.
27. Bendig M, Arun T. Enrollment in micro life and health insurance: evidences from Sri Lanka. Bonn: IZA Discussion Paper No. 5427, Institute for the Study of Labor; 2011.

28. Bhat R, Jain N. Factors affecting the demand for health insurance in a micro insurance scheme. Ahmedabad: IIMA Working Paper No. 2006-07-02; 2007.

29. Bonan J, Dagnelie O, LeMay-Boucher P, Tenikue M. Is it all about money? A Randomized evaluation of the impact of insurance literacy and marketing treatments on the demand for health Microinsurance in Senegal. Geneva: Research paper No. 14, International labour Office and Microinsurance Innovation Facility; 2012.

30. Basaza R, Criel B, Van der Stuyft P. Low enrolment in Ugandan community health insurance schemes: Underlying causes and policy implications. BMC Health Services Research. 2007; 7(1):105.

31. Basaza R, Criel B, Van der Stuyft P. Community health insurance in Uganda: Why does enrolment remain low? A view from beneath. Health Policy. 2008; 87(2):172–184. doi: 10.1016/j.healthpol.2007.12.008 PMID: 18280608

32. Basaza R, Criel B, Van der Stuyft P. Community health insurance amidst abolition of user fees in Uganda: The view from policy makers and health service managers. BMC Health Services Research. 2010; 10(1):33.

33. Criel B, Waelkens MP. Declining subscriptions to the Maliando mutual health Organisation in Guinea-Conakry (West Africa): What is going wrong? Social Science & Medicine. 2003; 57(7):1205–1219.

34. De Allegri M, Sanon M, Sauerborn R. To enrol or not to enrol? A qualitative investigation of demand for health insurance in rural west Africa. Social Science & Medicine. 2006a; 62(6):1520–1527.

35. De Allegri M, Sanon M, Bridges J, Sauerborn R. Understanding consumers' preferences and decision to enrol in community-based health insurance in rural west Africa. Health Policy. 2006b; 76(1):58–71.

36. De Allegri M, Kouyate B, Becher H, Gbangou A, Subhash P, Sanon M, et al. Understanding enrollment in community health insurance in sub-Saharan Africa: a population-based case-control study in rural Burkina Faso', Special issue: Contracting and Health Services. Bulletin of the World Health Organization. 2006c; 84(11):852–858.

37. Donfouet HPP, Jeanty P W, Malin É. Accounting for spatial interactions in the demand for community-based health insurance: A Bayesian spatial Tobit analysis. Paper presented at the 11th International Workshop Spatial Econometrics and Statistics, France. 2012.

38. Dong H, Mugisha F, Gbangou A, Kouyate B, Sauerborn R. The feasibility of community-based health insurance in Burkina Faso. Health Policy. 2004; 69(1):45–53. PMID: 15484606

39. Dong H J, Kouyate B, Cairns J, Sauerborn R. Inequality in willingness-to-pay for community-based health insurance. Health Policy. 2005; 72(2):149–156. PMID: 15802150

40. Dong HJ, De Allegri M, Gnawali D, Souares A, Sauerborn R. Dropout analysis of community-based health insurance membership at Nouna, Burkina Faso. Health Policy. 2009; 92(2–3):174–179. doi: 10.1016/j.healthpol.2009.03.013 PMID: 19394105

41. Dror DM. Voluntary affiliation to micro health insurance and social capital among resource-poor persons: initial evidence from India. Global Risk Forum GRF Davos. 2010.

42. Eckhardt M, Forsberg B, Wolf D, Crespo B A. Feasibility of community-based health insurance in rural tropical Ecuador. Rev Panam Salud Publica. 2011; 29(3):177–184. PMID: 21484017

43. Fonta W M, Eme I H, Ataguba J E. Paying for community-based health insurance schemes in rural Nigeria: the use of in-kind payments. African Review of Money Finance and Banking. 2010; 36(1):109–128.

44. Gnawali D, Pokhrel S, Sié A, Sanon M, De Allegri M, Souares A, et al. The effect of community-based health insurance on the utilization of modern health care services: Evidence from Burkina Faso. Health Policy. 2009; 90(2–3):214–222. doi: 10.1016/j.healthpol.2008.09.015 PMID: 19036467

45. Gumber A. Hedging the health of the poor: the case for community financing in India. Washington DC: HNP Discussion Paper, World Bank.; 2001.

46. Ito S, kono H. Why is the take-up of microinsurance so low? Evidence from a health insurance scheme in India. Chiba: Project, Institute of Developing Economies (IDE-JETRO); 2009.

47. Jutting J. Health insurance for the poor? Determinants of participation in community-based health insurance schemes in rural Senega. France: Working Paper No. 204, OECD Development Centre; 2003.

48. Kyomugisha E, Buregyeya E, Ekirapa E, Mugisha J, Bazeyo W. Strategies for sustainability and equity of prepayment health schemes in Uganda. African Health Sciences. 2009; 9(2):59–65.

49. Kuwawenaruwa A, Macha J, Borghi J. Willingness to pay for voluntary health insurance in Tanzania. East African Medical Journal. 2011; 88(2):54–64. PMID: 24968592

50. Lammers J, Warmerdam S. Adverse selection in voluntary micro health insurance in Nigeria, Rotterdam: AIID Research Series, 10–06, University of Amsterdam, Amsterdam Institute for International Development, Ecorys; 2010.

51. Liu H, Sun Q, Zhao Z. Social learning and health insurance enrollment: evidence from China's new cooperative medical scheme. Bonn: IZA Discussion Paper No. 7251, Institute for the Study of Labor; 2013.

52. Mladovsky P. Why do people drop out of community-based health insurance? Findings from an exploratory household survey in Senegal. Social Science & Medicine. 2014 Apr; 107:78–88.

53. Moher D, Liberati A, Tetzlaff J, Altman D, The PRISMA Group. Preferred Reporting Items for Systematic Reviews and Meta-Analyses. The PRISMA Statement. PLoS Med. 2009 Jul 21; 6(7):e1000097. doi: 10.1371/journal.pmed.1000097 PMID: 19621072

54. Msuya J, Jutting J, Asfaw A. Impacts of community health insurance schemes on healthcare provision in rural Tanzania: membership in Tanzanian community health funds drastically improving access to healthcare. Bonn: ZEF-Discussion Papers on Development Policy: 82; 2004.

55. Msuya J M, Jütting J P, Asfaw A. Impact of community health funds on the access to health care: Empirical evidence from rural Tanzania. International Journal of Public Administration. 2007; 30(8–9):813–833.

56. Noubiap JJN, Joko WYA, Obama JMN, Bigna JJR. Community-based health insurance knowledge, concern, preferences, and financial planning for health care among informal sector workers in a health district of Douala, Cameroon. Pan African Medical Journal. 2013; 16.

57. Nsiah-Boateng E, Aikins M. Performance assessment of Ga district mutual health insurance scheme, greater Accra region, Ghana. Value in Health Regional Issues. 2013; 2(2):300–305.

58. Onwujekwe O, Onoka C, Uzochukwu B, Okoli C, Obikeze E, Eze S. Is community-based health insurance an equitable strategy for paying for healthcare? Experiences from southeast Nigeria. Health Policy. 2009 Sep; 92(1):96–102. doi: 10.1016/j.healthpol.2009.02.007 PMID: 19349091

59. Onwujekwe O, Uzochukwu B, Kirigia J. Basis for effective community-based health insurance schemes: investigating inequities in catastrophic out-of-pocket health expenditures, affordability and altruism. African Journal of Health Economics. 2011; 1:1–11.

60. Onwujekwe O, Onoka C, Uguru N, Nnenna T, Uzochukwu B, Eze S, et al. Preferences for benefit packages for community-based health insurance: An exploratory study in Nigeria. BMC Health Services Research. 2010 Jun 12; 10(1):162.

61. Oriakhi H, Onemolease E. Determinants of rural household's willingness to participate in community based health insurance scheme in Edo State, Nigeria. Studies on ethno-medicine. 2012; 6(2):95–102.

62. Ozawa S, Walker Damian G.. Innovations in Health System Finance in Developing and Transitional Economies (Advances in Health Economics and Health Services Research, Volume 21). Chernichovsky D, Hanson K, editors. United Kingdom: Emerald Group Publishing Limited; 2009. Trust in the context of community-based health insurance schemes in Cambodia: Villagers' trust in health insurers; p. 107–132.

63. Panda P, Chakraborty A, Dror DM, Bedi A. Enrolment in community-based health insurance schemes in rural Bihar and Uttar Pradesh, India. Health Policy and Planning. 2013; 29(8):960–974. doi: 10.1093/heapol/czt077 PMID: 24162838

64. Poletti T, Balabanova D, Ghazaryan O, Kamal Y, Kocharyan H, Karen A, et al. Options for scaling up community-based health insurance for rural communities of Armenia. Health System Development Program. London: Health System Development Program, London School of Hygiene and Tropical Medicine; 2007.

65. Ranson K. The impact of Sewa's medical insurance fund on hospital utilization and expenditure: a household survey. Washington D.C.: HNP Discussion Paper, The World Bank; 2001.

66. Rao K D, Waters H, Steinhardt L, Alam S, Hansen P, Naeem A J. An experiment with community health funds in Afghanistan. Health Policy and Planning. 2009; 24(4):301–311. doi: 10.1093/heapol/czp018 PMID: 19474086

67. Schneider P. Trust in micro-health insurance: An exploratory study in Rwanda. Social Science & Medicine. 2005; 61(7):1430–1438.

68. Schneider P, Diop F. Synopsis of results on the impact of community-based health insurance on financial accessibility to healthcare in Rwanda. Washington D.C.: HNP Discussion Paper, The World Bank; 2001.

69. Shafie A A, Hassali M A. Willingness to pay for voluntary community-based health insurance: Findings from an exploratory study in the state of Penang, Malaysia. Social Science & Medicine. 2013; 96:272–276.

70. Sinha T, Patel F, Gandhi F. Understanding Member Dropout in VIMO SEWA. Ahmedabad.: Indian Institute of Management; 2006.

71. Turcotte-Tremblay A-M, Haddad S, Yacoubou I, Fournier P. Mapping of initiatives to increase membership in mutual health organizations in Benin. International Journal for Equity in Health. 2012 Dec 5; 11 (1):74.

72. Uzochukwu B, Onwujekwe O, Eze S, Ezuma N, Obikeze E, Onoka C. Community Based Health Insurance Scheme in Anambra State, Nigeria: an analysis of policy development, implementation and equity effects. Nigeria: Consortium for Research on Equitable Health Systems Article, Health Policy research Group, University of Nigeria; 2009.

73. Wang H, Winnie Y, Licheng Z, Lusheng W, William H. Community-based health insurance in poor rural china: The distribution of net benefits'. Health Policy and Planning. 2005; 20(6):366–374. PMID: 16143589

74. Zhang L, Wang H, Wang L, Hsiao W. Social capital and farmer's willingness-to-join a newly established community-based health insurance in rural china'. Health Policy. 2006; 76(2):233–242. PMID: 16046027

75. Atim C, Madjiguene S. An external evaluation of the Nkoranza community financing health insurance scheme, Ghana. Technical Report No. 50, Bethesda, MD: Partnerships for Health Reform Project, Abt Associates Inc.; 2000.

76. Criel B, Dormael V, Lerberghe V. Voluntary health insurance in Bwamanda, democratic republic of Congo. An exploration of its meanings to the community. Tropical Medicine and International Health. 1998; 3(8):640–653. PMID: 9735934

Chapter 12

Building Awareness to Health Insurance Among the Target Population of Community-based Health Insurance Schemes in Rural India*

Main Messages

- First known published analysis of awareness campaigns associated with community-based health insurance (CBHI) or microinsurance.
- Assessment of the awareness campaign/insurance education programmes conducted prior to the launch of three CBHI schemes in rural northern India.
- Data sourced from a baseline survey (2010) and a follow-up survey (2011) of more than 800 households in the pre- and post-campaign periods.

Focus Points

- The study provides empirical evidence that the awareness campaigns were successful in enhancing understanding of health insurance (HI) among treatment groups.

---

*This chapter is reproduced from *Tropical Medicine & International Health* (2015), Open Access, doi:10.1111/tmi.12524, available at https://www.researchgate.net/publication/275054564_Building_awareness_to_health_insurance_among_the_target_population_of_community-based_health_insurance_schemes_in_rural_India.

- Higher awareness of CBHI is associated with higher propensity to enroll in the program.
- Increase of one unit in the average score of CBHI understanding increased the proportion of members enrolled in a household by 3–7%.
- Enhanced general understanding of insurance, although positively correlated with understanding of CBHI, did not contribute significantly to enrolment in CBHI, implying that in promoting enrolment, it is more effective to impart knowledge about context-specific schemes and their operational rules than about *general* principles of insurance.
- Higher awareness of CBHI was associated with higher propensity to take up health insurance cover program: Increase of one unit in the average score of CBHI understanding increased the proportion of members enrolled in a household by 3–7%.
- Enhanced general understanding of insurance did not contribute significantly to enrolment in CBHI The lesson: in promoting enrollment, it is more effective to impart knowledge about *context-specific schemes* and their operational rules than about *general* principles of insurance.
- Interactive activities were liked most and considered best. Advertising and printed material were least liked and least effective.
- Communicating the concepts may require repeated interactions. The treatment cohort had low scores (3.3 of 7 or 47%) on CBHI understanding even after participation in the awareness campaign.
- Improvements in awareness after the campaigns were independent of the level of education. This differs from most other studies which treated education level as a proxy for insurance literacy.

Structured Abstract

Introduction

In an attempt to understand the impact of an awareness campaign carried out before the launch of three CBHI schemes in rural India, the study seeks to answer three questions:

1. Has the awareness campaign been successful in enhancing participants' understanding of health insurance?

2. What awareness tools were most useful from the participants' point of view?
3. Has enhanced awareness resulted in higher enrollment?

Method

The analysis was based on data from a baseline survey (2010) and a follow-up survey (2011) of more than 800 households in the pre- and post-campaign periods. The authors adopted the difference-in-differences (DID) method to evaluate the impact of awareness activities on insurance understanding. This method evaluated the change in the percentage of insurance understanding in the pre- and post-awareness campaign. An ordinary least square (OLS) regression analysis was conducted to understand whether insurance knowledge and CBHI understanding had an impact on enrolment in CBHI.

Box 1: Awareness Campaign

Group interventions

- Treasure pot: A game-like tool that demonstrates the benefits of pooling
- Customized picture books
- Posters and wall paintings
- Films

Household-level intervention

- Choosing Health-plan All Together (CHAT): Exercise to choose benefits package

Assessment of awareness tools

- Respondents stated that they enjoyed the Treasure-Pot game and household-level discussions the most.
- CHAT I process was the most instructive in communicating that insurance coverage is always limited by a cap and that the premium amount determines both the type of benefits that can be included and the depth of coverage.

Findings

On the basis of responses to a set of six questions, aimed at assessing the understanding of insurance concepts, it was revealed that the level of insurance understanding was poor among the target population. After awareness campaigns were introduced for the treatment groups, the intervention cohort demonstrated substantially higher understanding of insurance concepts than the control group, and understanding of CBHI was a positive determinant for enrolment. The evaluation of the awareness tools was reviewed based on the treatment groups' self-reported responses, including qualitative answers. Among the insurance awareness tools, the respondents considered the "Treasure-Pot" tool (an interactive game) as most useful in enhancing insurance awareness.

The study estimated that an increase of one unit in the average score of CBHI understanding increased the proportion of members enrolled in a household by 3–7% in Pratapgarh, Vaishali and the pooled data.

An interesting finding was that enhanced *general* understanding of insurance, although positively correlated with an understanding of CBHI, did not contribute significantly to enrolment in CBHI. This suggests that in promoting enrolment, it is more effective to impart knowledge about context-specific schemes (like CBHI) and their operational rules rather than about general principles of insurance.

Data from Kanpur-Dehat suggested that while CBHI knowledge had no significant effect on the proportion of household members enrolled, the education level of the SHG member was a positive and significant determinant. Data revealed that an increase in 1 year of education was associated with 3.6% higher proportion of members enrolled.

It is a concern that the treatment cohort had low scores (3.3 of 7 or 47%) on CBHI understanding even after participation in the awareness campaign. This indicates that communicating the concepts may require repeated interactions.

Conclusion

The study concludes that understanding awareness campaigns are important prerequisites to the successful launch of CBHI among the poor in rural

India. The authors postulate that as opposed to most other studies which treated education level as a proxy for insurance literacy, their evidence indicates that improvements in awareness after the campaigns were independent of the level of education. There is also a need to differentiate between understanding insurance principles and understanding CBHI.

Building awareness to health insurance among the target population of community-based health insurance schemes in rural India

Pradeep Panda[1], **Arpita Chakraborty**[1] **and David M. Dror**[1,2]

1 *Micro Insurance Academy, New Delhi, India*
2 *Erasmus University Rotterdam, Rotterdam, The Netherlands*

Abstract

OBJECTIVE To evaluate an insurance awareness campaign carried out before the launch of three community-based health insurance (CBHI) schemes in rural India, answering the questions: Has the awareness campaign been successful in enhancing participants' understanding of health insurance? What awareness tools were most useful from the participants' point of view? Has enhanced awareness resulted in higher enrolment?

METHODS Data for this analysis originates from a baseline survey (2010) and a follow-up survey (2011) of more than 800 households in the pre- and post-campaign periods. We used the difference-in-differences method to evaluate the impact of awareness activities on insurance understanding. Assessment of usefulness of various tools was carried out based on respondents' replies regarding the tool(s) they enjoyed and found most useful. An ordinary least square regression analysis was conducted to understand whether insurance knowledge and CBHI understanding are related with enrolment in CBHI.

RESULTS The intervention cohort demonstrated substantially higher understanding of insurance concepts than the control group, and CBHI understanding was a positive determinant for enrolment. Respondents considered the 'Treasure-Pot' tool (an interactive game) as most useful in enhancing awareness to the effects of insurance.

CONCLUSIONS We conclude that awareness-raising is an important prerequisite for voluntary uptake of CBHI schemes and that interactive, contextualised awareness tools are useful in enhancing insurance understanding.

keywords community-based health insurance, insurance education, health microinsurance, awareness campaign, rural India

Introduction

There is international consensus that all people should have access to affordable, quality healthcare services [1], which can be achieved by applying prepayment and pooling of funds to replace/reduce direct out-of-pocket payments [2]. However, in India in 2009–2010, only ~26% of the population had access to health insurance (HI), including Rashtriya Swasthya Bima Yojna (RSBY) [3]. This raises the question why such a small proportion of the population is insured. One explanation is perhaps implied in results of a study conducted by the National Council of Applied Economic Research [4], which reported that when households were asked 'what is insurance?' ~20% of the rural uninsured households and 16% of urban counterparts had nothing to say. This implies that awareness of the benefits of insurance is low. In urban India and among the salaried class, [life] insurance is largely used as a tax saving tool, rather than for protection against risk; and as most rural people in India cannot draw tax benefits as they do not pay taxes, they may think that insurance is not useful for them. Moreover, another study from India claimed that lack of awareness was the second most important barrier to the uptake of health insurance, after lack of funds [5]. Lack of consumer awareness could relate to many issues (e.g. what options exist, whether other people decide to enrol, where to get HI, its cost).

We set out to examine whether activities to impart awareness, knowledge or understanding about HI at village level can provide the information leading to enrolment. Only few published studies deal with awareness in the context of CBHI. De Allegri *et al.* [6] found that a non-performing communication and sensitisation programme in Burkina Faso resulted in people's disinterest in enrolling. Basaza *et al.* [7] reported from Uganda that lack of good information about the scheme was mentioned as a reason for not enrolling. Similarly, Thornton *et al.* [8] reported that lack of awareness reduced demand in Nicaragua. Others suggested that success in transmitting how insurance protects was compromised when the awareness programme was unattractive or ill-adapted to less educated people [9]. Chankova *et al.* [10], who studied the impact of micro-HI (MHI) in four West African countries concluded that promotion of the schemes played a crucial role in their success among the less educated. In case of government-based social insurance in Mexico, King *et al.* [11] found that awareness campaigns increased enrolment rates. Bonan *et al.* [12] found that a customised insurance literacy module had no significant effect on households' purchasing decisions, but financial incentives in the form of vouchers generated positive results. Khan and Ahmed [13] reported from Bangladesh that educational intervention among urban informal workers had a positive impact on demand for HI. Similarly, Matul *et al.* [14] claimed that consumer education might positively affect the demand for index insurance, and information spread by peers had more potential to increase enrolment in health microinsurance. Gine *et al.* [15] concluded that lack of understanding of the product was the most frequently cited reason for non-participation in rainfall insurance in India, and demand for rainfall insurance was positively and significantly associated with financial education [16] and with understanding of the insurance product [17]. These studies did not describe details of what the awareness programmes consisted of or whether they measured differences in awareness before and after campaigns.

We address three research questions: firstly, has the awareness campaign been successful in enhancing people's understanding of health insurance? Secondly, what awareness tools were testified as most useful from the participants' point of view? And thirdly, has enhanced awareness among the treatment groups resulted in higher enrolment in the CBHI schemes?

Our investigation was located in rural northern India, where the Micro Insurance Academy launched three community-based health insurance (CBHI) schemes in collaboration with three grassroots NGOs (BAIF in Pratapgarh, Uttar Pradesh; Shramik Bharti in Kanpur-Dehat, Uttar Pradesh; and Nidan in Vaishali district, Bihar) as part of a 5-year project (2009–2014) that included also an assessment of the impact of being insured on financial literacy, inclusion, protection and healthcare utilisation. The enrolment discussed here was designed as a step-wedge experiment compliant with cluster randomised controlled trial (CRCT) sampling [18].

Our article offers detailed information on several elements of the awareness campaigns that we conducted in 2011, before the CBHI schemes were launched. The insurance awareness campaigns lasted for 4 months and were followed by an in-depth analysis of the responses on a range of questions. Considering that India is a large arena of CBHI activity [19, 20], our findings may be relevant for many other schemes as well.

Methods

Background on the CBHI schemes, treatment and control groups

The study relates to members of households with at least one woman affiliated in March 2010 to a self-help group (SHG). The awareness study was conducted during first wave of the 3-year study, when one-third of the sample served as treatment group and two-thirds as controls (Appendix 1). The treatment group was offered to join a CBHI. CBHI is based on the premise that a community (similar in geographical, occupational, ethnic, gender) owns and operates a non-profit or profit-sharing (health) insurance scheme [21]. The community of insured bears its risk, and premiums are independent of individual health status [22, 23]. The CBHI schemes described here follow the mutual model: enrolment is voluntary and contributory; members are involved in package design, pricing and claims administration; coverage is renewable year after year; and a detailed description can be found elsewhere [24]. The benefit packages (detailed in Appendix 2) complement government-run schemes, notably the RSBY, and include outpatient-care consultations [25].

All sites are rural, located 50–100 kms outside urban agglomerations. The households reported low income and low level of education (Table 1). The treatment and control cohorts are comparable, considering key socio-economic indicators.

Awareness campaign

The awareness campaign was the eighth of a 17-step implementation process [24]; it unfolded from November 2010 to February 2011. Treatment groups were exposed to general messages on HI and detailed ones on CBHI (including its operational aspects). The campaign tools were developed in cooperation with the local target population during a preparatory workshop (6th step of the 17-step process). The stories and folklore evoked in flipbooks,

Table 1 Socio-economic characteristics of the survey households (mean and standard error of mean)

Indicators	Pratapgarh Treatment	Pratapgarh Control	Pratapgarh Difference (-C)	Kanpur-Dehat Treatment	Kanpur-Dehat Control	Kanpur-Dehat Difference (T-C)	Vaishali Treatment	Vaishali Control	Vaishali Difference (T-C)	Total Treatment	Total Control	Total Difference (T-C)
Social												
Schedule caste/ Schedule tribe households	0.29 ± 0.03	0.31 ± 0.05	−0.02	0.31 ± 0.03	0.27 ± 0.06	0.04	0.34 ± 0.03	0.41 ± 0.06	−0.07	0.31 ± 0.02	0.33 ± 0.03	−0.02
Economic condition of household												
Monthly per capita expenditure (Rs.)	1176 ± 64	1362 ± 84	−186.00	1798 ± 203	2037 ± 139	−235.00	1606 ± 191	1602 ± 93	4.00	1470 ± 87	1657 ± 62	−187.00
Owns a savings account	0.57 ± 0.03	0.55 ± 0.53	0.02	0.46 ± 0.03	0.38 ± 0.07	0.08	0.28 ± 0.03	0.24 ± 0.05	0.04	0.44 ± 0.02	0.40 ± 0.03	0.04
Has life insurance	0.28 ± 0.05	0.19 ± 0.03	0.09	0.16 ± 0.05	0.24 ± 0.03	−0.08	0.14 ± 0.04	0.13 ± 0.02	0.0	0.20 ± 0.03	0.19 ± 0.01	0.01
Enrolled in RSBY	0.16 ± 0.02	0.15 ± 0.04	0.01	0.23 ± 0.03	0.12 ± 0.05	0.11	0.35 ± 0.03	0.41 ± 0.06	−0.06	0.25 ± 0.02	0.23 ± 0.03	0.02
Characteristics of household head												
Age	47.4 ± 0.91	48.1 ± 1.50	−0.70	46.9 ± 0.99	45.2 ± 2.03	1.73	42.4 ± 0.85	44.7 ± 1.75	−2.25	45.5 ± 0.54	46.3 ± 1.00	−0.75
Male–headed household	0.77 ± 0.03	0.76 ± 0.05	0.01	0.88 ± 0.02	0.82 ± 0.06	0.06	0.65 ± 0.03	0.68 ± 0.06	−0.03	0.76 ± 0.02	0.75 ± 0.03	0.01
Years of education	5.48 ± 0.34	5.11 ± 0.49	0.37	5.97 ± 0.34	6.77 ± 0.69	−0.80	3.64 ± 0.30	5.11 ± 0.64	−1.47**	5.00 ± 0.19	5.49 ± 0.34	−0.49
Characteristics of SHG member												
Age	43.1 ± 0.85	42.7 ± 1.48	0.41	40.4 ± 0.97	39.3 ± 1.60	1.10	37.1 ± 0.81	38.6 ± 1.56	−1.51	40.2 ± 0.51	40.5 ± 0.91	−0.36
Years of education	2.50 ± 0.29	2.10 ± 0.41	0.40	4.83 ± 0.33	3.31 ± 0.57	1.52*	1.95 ± 0.23	2.75 ± 0.47	−0.80	3.04 ± 0.17	2.60 ± 0.27	0.44
Access to health facility												
Travel time for inpatient services(mins)	42.9 ± 2.4	40.7 ± 3.4	2.29	117.8 ± 6.0	125.4 ± 13.4	−7.69	34.0 ± 1.7	28.0 ± 3.4	5.99*	63.2 ± 2.6	55.8 ± 4.5	7.39
Travel time for outpatient services(mins)	20.3 ± 1.0	17.2 ± 1.2	3.08*	28.6 ± 2.1	39.5 ± 5.8	−10.9*	17.8 ± 1.2	15.6 ± 2.0	2.17	22.0 ± 0.9	21.8 ± 1.7	0.27
Household health events												
No. of chronic illness	1.14 ± 0.07	1.56 ± 0.10	−0.42**	0.82 ± 0.06	0.80 ± 0.12	0.02	0.81 ± 0.05	0.85 ± 0.13	−0.04	0.93 ± 0.04	1.15 ± 0.07	−0.22***
No. of acute illness	1.04 ± 0.07	1.24 ± 0.12	−0.20	1.26 ± 0.08	1.56 ± 0.16	−0.30	0.90 ± 0.06	1,24 ± 0.14	−0.34*	1,06 ± 0.04	1.31 ± 0.08	−0.25***
No. of hospitalisation	0.12 ± 0.02	0.16 ± 0.05	−0.04	0.17 ± 0.03	0.18 ± 0.06	−0.01	0.21 ± 0.03	0.24 ± 0.06	−0.03	0.17 ± 0.02	0.20 ± 0.03	−0.03
Sample Size	117	195		72	188		120	205		309	588	

***$P < 0.01$, ** $P < 0.05$, * $P < 0.1$ of *t*-test.

posters and wall paintings differed across locations, based on local understanding of insurance and risk-pooling. All the awareness campaign tools were translated from English to Hindi (local language), and all messages and meetings were conducted in Hindi. The campaign was composed of group-level and household-level activities.

Group interventions

The group interventions occurred at SHG meetings, in the form of group discussion on insurance, followed by playing 'Treasure-Pot', and subsequent discussions of key messages on exposure to risks, insurability of health risks, benefits of insurance, the non-profit nature of CBHI, community governance of CBHI, trust relations between the insured and the CBHI, etc. Picture books, posters, wall painting, movie and songs were used to illustrate the messages.

The *Treasure-Pot* is a game-like tool that demonstrates the benefits of pooling. The game simulates exposure to risks (players draw cards representing real-life events) and costs (candy symbolising money). The game is run in two rounds: first without pooling of resources, followed by pooling. A facilitator and SHG members manage the game (illustrating group governance).

Customised picture books communicate consequences of health situations on insured and uninsured persons. *Posters and wall paintings* serve a similar purpose and were shown to SHG members during group meetings and displayed for public viewing on walls of village houses and in offices of local implementing partners. MIA produced a *full-length film with authentic contemporary village-life images and cast*, narrating how a village succeeded to introduce a new CBHI. The plot follows folkloric style and 'hero–villain/intrigue–calamity' scenarios that entertain and show how support for the common goal of the village is reached. The film was projected to larger village audiences (not just treatment cohorts), and facilitators also played songs in local languages/dialects on CBHI schemes before and after the projections.

Household-level intervention

After group discussions and Treasure-Pot games at SHG level, facilitators visited SHG members at home, to facilitate discussions among household members and reply to questions raised on benefits and operational rules of the CBHI.

Choosing Health-plan All Together (CHAT) is another simulator of benefit packages (and premium) that members can choose from [26]. The CHAT exercise is conducted in three stages: CHAT I: entails inviting each SHG member to shortlist their 1st and 2nd choice of benefit package, from 4 to 6 options presented on CHAT boards; CHAT II: entails confirmation of the choices by groups, after the SHG members had the opportunity to discuss the options with their family; and CHAT III: entails narrowing the choice to one benefit package that would apply to all CBHI members, which is the package chosen by most groups (see Appendix 1 for the chosen benefit packages).

Data

A baseline survey was conducted in March–May 2010 with a sample of 3685 SHG households, of which 1335 households were 'treatment', and 2350 households were 'control' during wave I of the project (Appendix 1). For the purpose of the awareness campaign study, we drew around 25% of these cohorts as respondents. We conducted the survey both before and after the awareness campaign: *Before*: During the baseline, 897 households (randomly drawn from the sample of 3685) were administered a questionnaire on insurance understanding. About 309 of these 897 households were included as treatment, and 588 were control (Appendix 1). *After:* One year later, in March 2011, we asked the same households to reply to the same questions. A total of 811 of the 897 HHs replied (attrition of 9%), 291 HHs from treatment and 520 HHs from control cohorts.

An in-depth analysis comparing the socio-economic characteristics of the respondents' group to those who dropped out revealed no statistically significant differences. The *after* questionnaire included additional questions on CBHI understanding, which awareness tools the respondents used and which they considered most useful.

Methods

The impact of awareness activities on peoples' understanding of insurance was assessed using the difference-in-differences (DID) method, based on the change in percentage of correct answers given by the respondents (henceforth 'percentage of insurance understanding') from the treatment and control cohorts, in the *before* and *after* surveys (i.e. pre- and post-awareness campaign).

In addition, a DID regression was performed for insurance understanding, using the following specification:

$$\mathrm{IU}_{ht} = \alpha'\mathrm{TRT}_h + \beta'\mathrm{POST}_t + \gamma'\mathrm{INTR}_{ht} + \delta'\mathrm{CONFOUNDER}_{ht_0} + \varepsilon'_{ht}, \tag{1}$$

where IU is the percentage of insurance understanding by household h in time t; TRT is a dummy variable for treatment households (one for households who were part of awareness campaign and then offered to join CBHI, else 0); POST signifies the dummy for time period (0 and 1 for pre-and post-campaign period, respectively); INTR is the interaction term between TRT and POST (*INTR=TRT*POST*); and CONFOUNDER includes the socio-economic indicators of the household (caste, log of monthly per capita expenditure (LMPCE), dummies for ownership of savings account and subscription to life insurance and RSBY), characteristics of the head of the household (age, gender and years of education) and SHG member (age and years of education), access to health services (travel time for inpatient and outpatient services), and locational dummies. Descriptive statistics were used to evaluate how the treatment group rated various awareness tools as enjoyable and useful.

Finally, the relationships between the proportion of household members enrolled in the CBHI and various parameters (notably understanding of insurance and CBHI) were examined through ordinary least square (OLS) regression. The information on enrolment was drawn from the management information system of the CBHI schemes.

The study design and all questionnaires were submitted to the independent ethics committee of Cologne University, and ethical clearance for this experiment was obtained.

Results

Impact of awareness campaign on understanding of insurance and CBHI

We assess respondents' understanding of insurance concepts based on responses to a set of six questions. Answers were scored as 1 (correct) or as 0, and respondents' scores could range from 0 to 6. Average scores are shown in Appendix 3 (for the treatment and control groups, before and after awareness campaign). Correct responses on insurance understanding prior to the awareness campaign were rare (Table 2) and increased after the campaign, both among the treatment and the control groups. We applied the DID method on percentage of insurance understanding, to neutralise possible indirect effects of awareness activities, that unfolded in the public domain or through family discussions (e.g. the increase in insurance understanding in Pratapgarh among the treatment cohort was 18.6 percentage points higher compared to their control counterparts). Results of the treatment groups were significantly and materially higher than those of the control groups (paired *t*-test), in all three locations and for the pooled data. The only exception was among the control cohort in Pratapgarh, where differences were not significant. The DID between the treatment and control groups was highly significant: 20.7 in Kanpur-Dehat, 18.6 in Pratapgarh and 8.8 in Vaishali.

However, respondents' insurance knowledge can be influenced by externalities, such as experience with life insurance or RSBY. To neutralise that, we performed a DID regression with the percentage of insurance understanding as dependent variable [see equation (1)]. The regression results (Table 3) indicate that the time dummy and the interaction variable between time and treatment dummies were positively and significantly associated with the percentage of insurance understanding for all three locations and at the pooled data. LMPCE and subscription to RSBY had positive effect on insurance understanding for the pooled data. Ownership of savings account (proxy for financial literacy) positively influenced insurance understanding in Pratapgarh, Vaishali and overall, whereas subscription of life insurance had a positive impact on insurance understanding in Kanpur-Dehat. Also, households in Pratapgarh and Vaishali had lower propensity to gain awareness from the campaign, compared to Kanpur-Dehat. On the whole, the interac-

Table 2 Difference-in-difference (DID) in the percentage of correct insurance understanding among treatment and control groups †,‡

Year	Group	Pratapgarh	Kanpur-Dehat	Vaishali	All
Pre (2010)	Control	47.3 ± 2.2	47.7 ± 2.0	40.6 ± 2.1	44.9 ± 1.2
Post (2011)		64.5 ± 2.1	64.4 ± 2.1	59.8 ± 2.3	62.9 ± 1.3
Pre (2010)	Treatment	40.1 ± 3.4	44.9 ± 4.3	41.3 ± 4.4	41.7 ± 2.4
Post (2011)		75.9 ± 3.3	82.3 ± 2.1	69.3 ± 3.4	75.2 ± 1.9
Difference in control		17.2	16.7*	19.2**	18.0***
Difference in treatment		35.8***	37.4***	28.0***	33.5***
Difference-in-Difference (DID)		18.6***	20.7***	8.8***	15.5***
No. of respondents	Control	163	188	169	520
	Treatment	115	72	104	291

†Percentage of correct response to the total of six questions.
‡Mean and standard error of mean is presented.
*** $P < 0.01$, ** $P < 0.05$, * $P < 0.1$ of *t*-test.

Table 3 DID regression results of insurance understanding based on initial conditions

Indicators	Pratapgarh	Kanpur–Dehat	Vaishali	Total
Treatment Group				
Treatment (base = control)	−7.106 (4.344)	−1.543 (4.799)	1.033 (4.828)	−2.623 (2.660)
Time				
Post–intervention (base = pre-campaign)	9.808*** (3.147)	16.91*** (2.801)	8.097*** (3.070)	11.35*** (1.756)
Interaction				
Treatment*time	18.87*** (5.994)	19.90*** (6.455)	21.01*** (6.646)	19.41*** (3.676)
Social				
Schedule caste/Schedule tribe households (base = general caste)	2.354 (3.160)	−5.115* (3.046)	−4.056 (3.270)	−1.715 (1.809)
Economic Condition of Household				
Log of monthly per capita expenditure	3.111 (2.330)	0.683 (2.206)	3.346 (2.485)	2.562* (1.337)
Enrolled in RSBY	6.165 (3.979)	4.768 (3.397)	3.919 (2.984)	4.728** (1.907)
Owns a savings account	5.597* (3.011)	3.220 (2.759)	7.526** (3.398)	5.507*** (1.729)
Has life insurance	3.180 (3.466)	5.819* (3.268)	1.354 (4.397)	3.431 (2.097)
Characteristics of Head of Household				
Age	−0.145 (0.153)	−0.0717 (0.136)	−0.248 (0.186)	−0.041 (0.0900)
Male	5.236 (3.862)	−5.348 (4.295)	4.099 (3.376)	3.145 (2.140)
Years of education	0.508 (0.390)	0.289 (0.360)	−0.510 (0.445)	0.144 (0.223)
Characteristics of SHG Member				
Age	0.0929 (0.156)	0.0539 (0.145)	−0.103 (0.197)	0.0265 (0.0944)
Years of education	−0.0269 (0.398)	0.346 (0.367)	0.959* (0.559)	0.292 (0.244)
Access to health facility				
Travel time for inpatient services (mins)	−0.0242 (0.0405)	−0.0157 (0.0163)	0.0124 (0.0576)	−0.0155 (0.0155)
Travel time for outpatient services (mins)	−0.138 (0.100)	0.0495 (0.0439)	−0.150* (0.0870)	−0.0126 (0.0376)
Locational characteristics†				
Pratapgarh				−5.130** (2.419)
Vaishali				−9.830*** (2.522)
Constant	29.23 (17.95)	44.97** (17.49)	26.04 (17.54)	35.24*** (10.48)
Observations	278	260	273	811

Standard errors in parentheses.
†Base is Kanpur-Dehat.
*** $P < 0.01$, ** $P < 0.05$, * $P < 0.1$.

tion term (treatment*time) yielded the strongest impact in enhancing insurance understanding.

These findings (Tables 2 and 3) signify that the level of insurance understanding is poor (see average scores in Appendix 3), but also that the awareness campaign was successful in imparting conceptual understanding of HI among the study population generally and among the treatment group in particular. We conclude that awareness could be improved through more activities.

Understanding of CBHI

In addition to the awareness campaign (aimed at the treatment groups but with knowledge spillovers to others), we sought to assess understanding of the CBHI among the control and treatment groups. Seven questions were presented, and answers were scored as 1 (when correct) or 0, with the total per respondent score ranging from 0 to 7. Questions and scores are shown in Table 4. The average scores of the treatment groups on understanding of CBHI were markedly higher than those of the control groups, and the differences were statistically significant (*t*-test). The treatment cohort in Kanpur-Dehat recorded the highest average score (3.47; compare to 1.66 of control group), followed closely by Vaishali (3.39 for treatment and 1.24 for control) and Pratapgarh (3.11 for treatment *vs.* 1.16 for control). The difference in average score between the treatment and control groups was highest in Vaishali (2.15).

Overall, around 76% of respondents in the treatment groups understood the meaning of *en-bloc affiliation* (compared to only 28% among the control group), but

Table 4 Understanding of CBHI for the control and treatment group (mean and standard error of mean)†

Understanding of CBHI	Cohort	Pratapgarh	Kanpur-Dehat	Vaishali	Total
If a SHG wants to join, everyone in this group, and everyone in their household, has to join (right)	Control	0.24 ± 0.03	0.39 ± 0.03	0.20 ± 0.03	0.28 ± 0.02
	Treatment	0.80 ± 0.04	0.78 ± 0.05	0.69 ± 0.05	0.76 ± 0.03
	Difference	0.56***	0.39***	0.49***	0.48***
CBHI will not allow people above 65 and children below 5 years to enrol (wrong)	Control	0.14 ± 0.02	0.17 ± 0.03	0.17 ± 0.03	0.16 ± 0.01
	Treatment	0.32 ± 0.04	0.39 ± 0.06	0.33 ± 0.05	0.34 ± 0.03
	Difference	0.18***	0.22***	0.16***	0.18***
Premium will be collected by someone from outside your community (wrong)	Control	0.24 ± 0.03	0.28 ± 0.03	0.26 ± 0.03	0.26 ± 0.02
	Treatment	0.68 ± 0.04	0.58 ± 0.06	0.59 ± 0.05	0.62 ± 0.03
	Difference	0.44***	0.3***	0.33***	0.36***
Premium will be collected annually (right)	Control	0.06 ± 0.02	0.27 ± 0.03	0.16 ± 0.03	0.17 ± 0.01
	Treatment	0.23 ± 0.04	0.68 ± 0.06	0.76 ± 0.04	0.53 ± 0.03
	Difference	0.17**	0.41***	0.60***	0.36***
The CBHI scheme will be run by staff from Baif/Shramik Bharti/Nidan (wrong)	Control	0.05 ± 0.02	0.07 ± 0.02	0.09 ± 0.02	0.07 ± 0.01
	Treatment	0.20 ± 0.04	0.10 ± 0.04	0.25 ± 0.04	0.19 ± 0.02
	Difference	0.15**	0.03	0.16*	0.12***
A group of community members will decide whether or not to repay the claims that members of the scheme make (right)	Control	0.33 ± 0.03	0.37 ± 0.03	0.31 ± 0.03	0.34 ± 0.02
	Treatment	0.77 ± 0.04	0.74 ± 0.05	0.72 ± 0.04	0.75 ± 0.03
	Difference	0.44***	0.37***	0.41***	0.41***
Those who are sick will have all of their medical bills paid for by the CBHI scheme, no matter how big their bills are (wrong)	Control	0.07 ± 0.02	0.10 ± 0.02	0.06 ± 0.02	0.08 ± 0.01
	Treatment	0.37 ± 0.05	0.26 ± 0.05	0.27 ± 0.04	0.31 ± 0.03
	Difference	0.30***	0.16***	0.21***	0.23***
Average of total CBHI knowledge score	Control	1.16 ± 0.10	1.66 ± 0.11	1.24 ± 0.11	1.36 ± 0.06
	Treatment	3.11 ± 0.18	3.47 ± 0.21	3.39 ± 0.23	3.30 ± 0.12
	Difference	1.95***	1.81***	2.15***	1.94***
No. of respondents	Control	163	188	169	520
	Treatment	115	72	104	291

†Respondents were asked to say whether the statements were right or wrong; the correct answer (right/wrong) is given in parentheses against each statement.
*** $P < 0.01$, ** $P < 0.05$, * $P < 0.1$ of *t*-test.

only ~34% of the treatment group knew that affiliation to the local CBHI would be open to all ages.

Most of the treatment respondents understood the governance structure of the CBHI schemes, notably that premiums would be collected by community members, that the claims committee was both appointed by and composed of SHG members and that it had the authority to adjudicate claims. Furthermore, upward of 76% of the treatment cohort in Vaishali and around 68% in Kanpur-Dehat were aware that the annual premium was payable upfront. In Pratapgarh, a lower share of respondents (23%) gave the correct reply on this question, perhaps because the implementing partner agreed that members could join by paying 30% of the annual premium and engaging to pay the rest in eight interest-free instalments during the year.

However, only a minority of respondents (31%) understood that each benefit type was capped by an upper limit. And only 19% understood that day-to-day operations would be run by the members of the scheme, not by implementing partners.

We conclude from these results that while the understanding of CBHI following the awareness campaign was higher for the treatment than the control group, some gaps in knowledge remained, for example on the community's role in governance of day-to-day CBHI operations, on caps of benefits and on eligibility of all ages to enrol. The Kanpur-Dehat and Vaishali respondents were relatively better-informed about the CBHI compared to Pratapgarh. We note that the average score (3.3 of 7 or 47%) is low.

Assessment of the awareness tools

We review the evaluation of the awareness tools, based on the treatment groups' self-reported responses, including qualitative answers.

Participation, enjoyability and usefulness of various awareness activities

Overall, around 70–75% of the respondents stated that they participated in group discussions and Treasure-Pot game

Table 5 Participation in various awareness campaign tools

Participation/ Usefulness	Pratapgarh	Kanpur-Dehat	Vaishali	Total
Group discussion				
Participated	73.9	69.4	73.1	72.5
Among them				
Enjoyed	77.6	76.0	72.4	75.4
Found it useful	75.3	78.0	64.5	72.0
Treasure-Pot				
Participated	76.5	73.6	76.9	76.0
Among them				
Enjoyed	86.4	86.8	87.5	86.9
Found it useful	79.5	75.5	85.0	80.5
Picture Books				
Have seen	68.7	63.9	75.0	69.8
Among them				
Enjoyed	70.9	71.7	62.8	68.0
Found it useful	57.0	80.4	56.4	62.1
Household-level Intervention				
Local NGO visited the HH	70.4	59.7	68.3	67.0
Among them				
Enjoyed	77.8	88.4	80.3	81.0
Found it useful	76.5	86.0	76.1	78.5
Poster/wall painting				
Have seen	74.8	48.6	74.0	68.0
Among them				
Enjoyed	46.5	37.1	32.5	39.4
Found it useful	37.2	42.9	24.7	33.3
Movie/songs				
Attended the movie/song show	53.9	62.5	68.3	61.2
Among them				
Enjoyed	75.8	71.1	80.3	76.4
Found it useful	72.6	71.1	74.6	73.0
No. of Respondents	115	72	104	291

and saw picture books and poster/wall paintings (Table 5). Around two-thirds reported that facilitators visited their homes to create awareness. And about 60% said they watched the movie/song show. Fewer participated in awareness activities in Kanpur-Dehat than in Pratapgarh or Vaishali. Most respondents participated in most activities, but, surprisingly, the movie attracted the lowest number of participants from the treatment group.

Interestingly, the responses to the questions about 'enjoyment' and 'usefulness' were highly correlated ($r = 0.82$, significant at 5% level), indicating that awareness activities are perceived as useful when they are fun.

Respondents stated that they enjoyed most the Treasure-Pot game and household-level discussions, which they also found most useful. In their view, the game successfully conveyed the advantages of risk-pooling, and household discussions created the opportunity to involve household members in the decision process, which provided the necessary assurances to women (the SHG members) that male decision-makers participate in the financial decision and endorse the decision to join the CBHI.

Participation in CHAT

CHAT is relevant only for persons who have decided to enrol with CBHI. Most of the groups in all three locations (~75% of the SHG members) stated they attended the CHAT process following the awareness campaign (Table 6). The CHAT I process was the most instructive in communicating that insurance coverage is always limited by a cap and that the premium amount determines both the type of benefits that can be included and the depth of coverage. The direct involvement of the treatment cohort in choosing the benefits ensured that the awareness campaign served to get clear understanding of the essential information. Interestingly, fewer people participated in CHAT II (67% in CHAT II, *vs.* 76% in CHAT I). The reasons for this are not fully clear.

Relation between insurance understanding and enrolment

We performed an OLS regression analysis to assess whether better knowledge about insurance, gained during the awareness campaign, resulted in higher enrolment in the CBHI. The proportion of household members enrolled was the dependent variable for the treatment group. The regressions were performed separately for the three locations and for the pooled data.

The percentage increase in *insurance understanding* from pre- to post-campaign (Appendix 3) and the average scores of *CBHI understanding* (Table 4) were the two variables tested to explain the enrolment in CBHI. Other possible explanatory variables were socio-demographic and economic characteristics of the household [caste, household size, LMPCE; age, years of education of household head and SHG member (Table 1)]; households with a savings account; subscription to RSBY; access to health care (both inpatient and outpatient services); and recent health events (number of chronic and acute illness and hospitalisation events in the household). Locational dummies were used to examine whether there was any variation among the three trial areas, when the analysis was performed using the pooled data.

The results shown in Table 7 confirm that the respondents' understanding of CBHI was positively and significantly associated with enrolments. Increase of one unit in the average score of CBHI understanding increased the proportion of members enrolled in a household by 3–7%

Table 6 Evaluation of CHAT process – Treatment group

Participation/ usefulness	Pratapgarh	Kanpur-Dehat	Vaishali	Total
CHAT I				
Participated in CHAT	80.9	72.2	72.1	75.6
NGO staff explain different packages on CHAT board*	100.0	100.0	100.0	100.0
Explanation was useful†	66.7	67.3	68.0	67.3
CHAT board was given to take home	96.8	86.5	92.0	92.7
Discussed insurance with family members	93.5	88.5	89.3	90.9
CHAT II				
Participated in CHAT	73.9	62.5	62.5	67.0
No. of Respondents	115	72	104	291

*Of those, who participated in CHAT.
†Of those, who reported that the NGO staff explained different packages on CHAT boards.

in Pratapgarh, Vaishali and the pooled data. It follows that more efforts to improve awareness on CBHI could be very useful in enhancing enrolments, all the more so as scores were generally relatively low (3.3 of seven overall). On the other hand, general insurance understanding was not significantly correlated with enrolment. The correlation between the percentage change in insurance understanding and CBHI understanding was not very high ($r = 0.27$, significant at 5% level). When the regressions were performed separately for the percentage increase in insurance understanding and average scores of CBHI understanding, neither was significant. This could suggest that the understanding of the detailed operational aspects of CBHI was essential in facilitating that decision, but understanding insurance principles *per se* would not have led to enrol in the CBHI.

In Kanpur-Dehat, CBHI knowledge has no significant effect on proportion of household member enrolled. However, education level of the SHG member was a positive and significant determinant. An increase in 1 year of education was associated with 3.6% higher proportion of members enrolled. In Kanpur-Dehat, the proportion of members enrolled in CBHI was positively associated with the household size.

In Vaishali, a higher proportion of scheduled caste/ scheduled tribe households were more likely to enrol in the CBHI than general caste households. Male-headed households in Vaishali were less likely to enrol in CBHI than female-headed ones.

Travel time to outpatient care and past experience of hospitalisation were positive predictors of the proportion of household members joining the CBHI in Kanpur-Dehat. It is recalled that in this location, outpatient and inpatient services were included in the benefit package. This strengthens the link between understanding the coverage provided by CBHI and enrolment.

Similarly, the negative correlation in Vaishali between past hospitalisation and enrolment may be due to the exclusion of inpatient care from the benefit package and high RSBY penetration rate (35% – Table 1). No other household features were significant explanatory variables for enrolment in CBHI.

As awareness campaigns preceded the enrolment, we submit that understanding of the CBHI is exogenous. However, we wanted to verify that general understanding of insurance before the awareness campaigns did not affect the enrolment decision. We tested this using the pre-campaign insurance understanding scores as a predictor of enrolment, after controlling for other confounding factors. This regression analysis did not return any significant association between pre-campaign insurance understanding and enrolment in CBHI.

Limitations

We recognise three limitations of this study. First, the impact of the awareness campaign could not be restricted to the treatment group, as some insurance awareness activities unfolded in public and some knowledge spillover could have reached the control group. However, the awareness activities that unfolded in the public domain included placing posters and wall paintings (depicting insurance related messages), whereas the Treasure-Pot and follow-up door-to-door discussions were only available to the treatment groups. Secondly, the information on participation in the awareness campaign was self-reported rather than objectively verified. That said, considering that several awareness activities were deployed in each location, a significant majority would have participated in one or another awareness session. Finally, as this study targeted women members of self-help groups, our findings are not generalisable. However, as SHG households are usually low income and have a pan-Indian spread, the findings have important policy implications for poor rural populations.

Discussion

This study set out to assess the awareness campaign/ insurance education programmes, conducted prior to the launch of three CBHI schemes in rural northern India.

Table 7 OLS regression estimates of proportion of household members enrolled in CBHI

Explanatory variables	Pratapgarh	Kanpur-Dehat	Vaishali	All
Insurance understanding				
Percentage increase in insurance understanding	0.000765 (0.000908)	0.000595 (0.00529)	0.00140 (0.00612)	3.68e-05 (0.000597)
Average score of CBHI understanding	0.0687** (0.0265)	0.0502 (0.0288)	0.0333* (0.0232)	0.0444*** (0.0145)
Socio-demographic characteristic of the household				
Schedule caste/schedule tribe (base = general caste)	−0.0727 (0.0956)	0.190 (0.127)	0.113 (0.0993)	0.0715 (0.0593)
Household size	−0.0307 (0.0205)	0.0631** (0.0268)	0.0332 (0.0235)	0.0129 (0.0127)
Economic condition of household				
Log of MPCE	−0.123 (0.0773)	0.138 (0.0906)	−0.0633 (0.0804)	−0.0172 (0.0458)
Owns a savings account	−0.000900 (0.00387)	−0.0271 (0.0964)	0.0349 (0.0884)	−0.00129 (0.00376)
Enrolled in RSBY	−0.0404 (0.125)	−0.0753 (0.182)	0.0496 (0.100)	0.0282 (0.0678)
Characteristics of head of household				
Age	0.00449 (0.00465)	0.00353 (0.00442)	−0.00859 (0.00597)	0.000401 (0.00268)
Male-headed household	0.0338 (0.105)	−0.0771 (0.188)	−0.220** (0.107)	−0.0712 (0.0628)
Years of education	0.0161 (0.0108)	−0.0107 (0.0113)	0.0150 (0.0121)	0.00416 (0.00609)
Characteristics of SHG member				
Age	−0.00140 (0.00456)	0.00553 (0.00634)	0.00806 (0.00677)	0.00276 (0.00305)
Years of education	−0.0144 (0.0110)	0.0355*** (0.0113)	−0.0153 (0.0162)	0.00590 (0.00710)
Access to health facility				
Travel time for inpatient services (mins)	0.00244 (0.00163)	−0.000826 (0.000713)	0.00362 (0.00222)	−9.52e-05 (0.000607)
Travel time for outpatient services (mins)	−0.00538 (0.00436)	0.00372** (0.00141)	−0.00187 (0.00325)	0.00147 (0.00130)
Household health events				
No. of chronic illness	−0.00776 (0.0392)	−0.0351 (0.0462)	−0.00534 (0.0383)	−0.00801 (0.0232)
No. of acute illness	−0.0218 (0.0327)	−0.00871 (0.0413)	−0.00674 (0.0370)	−0.000612 (0.0207)
No. of hospitalisation	0.0165 (0.0786)	0.156* (0.0906)	−0.182* (0.0949)	−0.00756 (0.0483)
Locational characteristics†				
Pratapgarh				0.0795 (0.0772)
Vaishali				0.0905 (0.0812)
Constant	0.924 (0.609)	−1.647** (0.740)	0.683 (0.627)	−0.00133 (0.375)
Observations	115	72	104	291
R−squared	0.1646	0.4099	0.2266	0.0715

Standard errors in parentheses.
†Base is Kanpur-Dehat.
*** $P < 0.01$, ** $P < 0.05$, * $P < 0.10$.

The awareness campaigns were administered only to the treatment groups. Results of knowledge scores were compared with relevant control groups. This study provides empirical evidence that the awareness campaigns were successful in enhancing understanding of health insurance among treatment groups; the regression results show the treatment groups demonstrated higher scores of insurance understanding and understanding of CBHI than the control cohorts after the awareness campaign.

Moreover, both the treatment and the control subcohorts had higher scores after the awareness campaigns on questions reflecting understanding of insurance principles. The increased knowledge among the control group may reflect spillover effects of messages posted publicly (posters/wall paintings on health insurance). However, understanding of the CBHI did not have the same spillover effect as exposure to this topic was limited to the treatment groups. We conclude that raising awareness prior to enrolment serves an essential purpose in imparting knowledge of health insurance to people with no such prior exposure, as higher awareness of CBHI was associated with higher propensity to enrol in the programme. These findings are important for policymakers and development practitioners wishing to promote voluntary enrolment in CBHI. In addition, our study also informs policymakers in India that awareness campaign and insurance education can enhance enrolment in RSBY. We note that we could not find published previous analysis of awareness campaigns associated with CBHI or micro-insurance, and thus, we submit that our study fills a gap in in-depth empirical analysis of the effect of insurance education campaign on enrolment, mentioned by Defourny and Failon [9].

On the question whether enhanced awareness resulted in higher enrolment in the CBHI schemes among the treatment groups, we found positive and significant correlation between knowledge and understanding of this type of insurance and the proportion of household members enrolled in CBHI. Increase of one unit in the CBHI knowledge score increased the proportion of household members enrolled by 3% to 7% in Pratapgarh, Vaishali and the pooled data. However, enhanced general understanding of insurance, although positively correlated with understanding of CBHI, did not contribute significantly to enrolment in CBHI. This finding suggests that in promoting enrolment, it is more effective to impart knowledge about context-specific schemes and their operational rules than about general principles of insurance.

Qualitative analyses of similar schemes in other developing countries in Africa and Central America found that lack of understanding of insurance and CBHI is one of the reasons for non-enrolment [6–8]; Thornton *et al.* 2010).

Even after participation in the awareness campaign, the scores on CBHI understanding among the treatment cohort left much to be desired (3.3 of seven), suggesting that communicating the concepts may require repeated interactions.

Thirdly, we found that the interactive sessions were perceived as enjoyable and were rated as most useful by the participants. This included the group interactions when playing the Treasure-Pot game (to understand the benefits of pooling) and CHAT (to understand rationing of benefits), as well as the facilitated discussions with household members. On the other hand, mass media, general messages and printed material were reported as less enjoyable or useful. This leads to the conclusion that advertising, even via TV, may not be useful in enhancing awareness or enrolment among rural poor populations.

The results confirm that the awareness tools were found useful by respondents, independent of education status of the target group, and the material was equally well understood by all rural poor, when explanations were customised to suit less educated populations.

Conclusion

Awareness campaigns are important prerequisites to the successful launch of CBHI among the poor in rural India. We also submit that, as opposed to most other studies which treated education level as a proxy for insurance literacy, our evidence points that improvements in awareness after the campaigns were independent of the level of education. There is a real difference between understanding insurance principles and understanding CBHI. Studies seeking to add more evidence on these aspects, notably for a better understanding of the demand for CBHI, should examine the attributes of CBHI separately from general knowledge about insurance and specifically focus on the role of awareness campaigns in deciding to enrol in CBHI.

Acknowledgements

David M. Dror and Pradeep Panda gratefully acknowledge funding provided by European Commission 7th Framework Programme [HEALTH-F2-2009-223518]. The authors gratefully acknowledge the extensive and substantive contribution of the Micro Insurance Academy and its staff in data collection and cleaning as well as in analytical inputs; and the implementing partners (BAIF, Shramik Bharti and Nidan) as well as the respondents, for their ongoing willingness to share information on the implementation.

References

1. United Nations General Assembly. *Adopting Consensus Text, General Assembly Encourages Member States to Plan, Pursue: Transition of National Health Care Systems Towards Universal Coverage.* United Nations General Assembly: New York, USA, 2012.
2. World Health Organisation. *Health Systems Financing: The Path to Universal Coverage.* The World Health Report 2010, World Health Organisation: Geneva, Switzerland, 2011.
3. Planning Commission. *Steering Committee Report for Health for 12th Five Year Plan.* Government of India: New Delhi, India, 2012.
4. National Council of Applied Economic Research. *Pre-launch Survey Report of Insurance Awareness Campaign.* National Council of Applied Economic Research: New Delhi, India, 2011.
5. Bawa SK, Verma S. Awareness and willingness to pay for health insurance: an empirical study with reference to Punjab, India. *Int J Hum Soc Sci* 2011: **1**: 100–108.
6. De Allegri M, Sanon M, Sauerborn R. To enrol or not to enrol? A qualitative investigation of demand for health insurance in rural West Africa. *Soc Sci Med* 2006: **62**: 1520–1527.
7. Basaza R, Criel B, Van der Stuyft P. Community health insurance in Uganda: why does enrolment remain low? A view from beneath. *Health Policy* 2008: **87**: 172–184.

8. Thornton R, Hatt L, Field E *et al.* Social security health insurance for the informal sector in Nicaragua: a randomized evaluation. *Health Econ* 2010: **19**: 181–206.
9. Defourny J, Failon J. Community-based health insurance schemes in Africa: Which factors really induce membership? Paper presented at the 8th International Conference for Third Sector Research. University of Barcelona, Barcelona (July 9), 2008http://hdl.handle.net/2268/11566.
10. Chankova S, Sulzbach S, Diop F. Impact of mutual health organisations: evidence from West Africa. *Health Policy Plan* 2008: **23**: 264–276.
11. King G, Gakidou E, Imai K *et al.* Public policy for the poor? A randomised assessment of the Mexican universal health insurance program. *The Lancet* 2009: **373**: 1447–1454.
12. Bonan J, Dagnelie O, Boucher PL, Tenikue M . Is it all about money? A randomized evaluation of the impact of insurance literacy and marketing treatments on the demand for health micro insurance in Senegal. DEMS Working Papers No. 216, Department of Economics, University of Milano-Bicocca" Milan, 2012http://www.ilo.org/public/english/employment/mifacility/download/repaper14.pdf.
13. Khan JAM, Ahmed S. Impact of educational intervention on willingness-to-pay for health insurance: a study of informal sector workers in urban Bangladesh. *Health Econ Rev* 2013: **3**: 1–10.
14. Matul M, Dalal A, Bock OD, Gelade W. Why people do not buy microinsurance and what can we do about it. Microinsurance Paper No. 20. International Labour Organisation: Geneva, 2013. http://www.ilo.org/public/english/employment/mifacility/download/mpaper20_buy.pdf
15. Gine X, Townsend R, Vickery J. Patterns of rainfall insurance participation in rural India. *World Bank Econ Rev* 2008: **22**: 539–566.
16. Gaurav S, Cole S, Tobacman J. Marketing complex financial products in emerging markets: evidence from rainfall insurance in India. *J Mark Res* 2011: **48**: S150–S162.
17. Cole S, Gine X, Tobacman J *et al.* Barriers to household risk management: evidence from India. *Am Econ J Appl Econ* 2013: **5**: 104–135.
18. Doyle C, Panda P, Poel EVD, Radermacher R, Dror DM. Reconciling research and implementation in micro health insurance experiments in India: Study protocol for a randomized controlled trial. *Trials* 2011: **12**: 1–15.
19. Acharya A, Vellakkal S, Taylor F *et al.* The impact of health insurance schemes for the informal sector in low- and middle-income countries: a systematic review. *World Bank Res Obs* 2013: **27**: 236–266.
20. Michielsen J, Criel B, Devadasan N *et al.* Can health insurance improve access to quality care for the Indian poor? *Int J Qual Health Care* 2011: **23**: 471–486.
21. Dror DM. Health microinsurance programs in developing countries. In: Culyer AJ (ed.). *Encyclopaedia of Health Economics*. Elsevier: San Diego, 2014, 412–421.
22. Criel B, Waelkens MP, Soors W, Devadasan N, Atim C. Community health insurance in developing countries. In: Heggenhougen K Quah S (eds). *International Encyclopaedia of Public Health*. Academic Press: San Diego, 2008, 782–791.
23. Radermacher R, Dror I. Institutional options for delivering health microinsurance. In: Churchill C (ed). *Protecting the Poor: A Microinsurance Compendium*. International Labour Organisation: Geneva, 2006, 401–423.
24. Dror DM, Majumdar A, Panda P, John D, Koren R. Implementing a participatory model of micro health insurance among rural poor, with evidence from Nepal. *Geneva Papers* 2014a: **39**: 280–303.
25. Panda P, Chakraborty A, Dror DM, Bedi AS. Enrolment in community-based health insurance schemes in rural Bihar and Uttar Pradesh, India. *Health Policy Plan* 2014: **29**: 960–974.
26. Dror DM, Panda P, May C, Majumdar A, Koren R. "One for all and all for one": consensus-building within communities in rural India on their health microinsurance package. *Risk Manag Healthc Policy* 2014b: **7**: 139–153.

Appendix 1

Table A1 Timeline for the awareness campaign and first year of CBHI implementation

2010	March–May	• Baseline survey of 3685 SHG households (enumeration of all the SHG member HHs, affiliated to the partner NGOs under the experimental geographical location as on March 2010) • Pre-campaign insurance understanding survey of 897 households (around 25%), randomly chosen from 3685 households
2010	June	• Clustering of the 3685 HHs using baseline survey data so that each cluster contains roughly equal number of HHs (total 48 clusters); each cluster was then randomly assigned in three waves of implementation (1/3rd in each wave). ○ Year 1 of implementation – Wave 1 clusters in treatment; waves 2 and 3 clusters in control ○ Year 2 of implementation – Wave 2 clusters in treatment; Wave 3 clusters in control ○ Year 3 of implementation – Wave 3 clusters in treatment; ○ For Year 1 of implementation (discussed here), 1335 HHs (Wave 1) were treatment and 2350 HHs (wave 2 & 3) were control ○ For awareness campaign analysis (described here), 309 HHs (of Wave 1) were treatment and 588 HHs (of waves 2 & 3) were control
2010–2011	November–February	• Awareness campaign rolled out to the treatment population (1335 HHs of Wave 1)
2011	March	• Post-campaign insurance understanding survey (of 811 HHs of 897 HHs of pre-campaign survey) • Enrolment process in CBHI for the treatment group (Wave 1 HHs)
2011	Apr	• CBHI scheme launched

Appendix 2

Table A2 Description of benefit packages

Indicators	Pratapgarh	Kanpur-Dehat	Vaishali
Annual CBHI premium per person/per year (Rs.)*	176	192	197
Coverage for hospitalisation			
Fees (cap per person per event, Rs.)	6000	3000	–
Wage loss (per day, Rs.)	100	75	100
Wage loss days	3rd–6th	4–13th	4–9th
Transport (maximum coverage per episode, Rs.)†	100	100	–
Coverage for outpatient care			
Fees (Rs.)	–	Unlimited	Unlimited
Lab tests (per year, Rs.)‡	–	–	200
Imaging tests (per year, Rs.) ‡	–	–	300
Coverage for maternity care			
Caesarean (per episode, Rs.)	5000	–	-

'–' indicates 'not Included in package'.
*In Pratapgarh, the households could pay 30% of total premium upfront to join CBHI and pay remaining 70% in eight equal interest-free instalments; in Vaishali, the per-person premium amount was Rs. 197 for up to five members from a household, Rs. 188 for 6–8 members from a household and Rs. 169 for 9 members and above
†For hospitalisation of more than 24 h.
‡Maximum amount, per person per year.

Appendix 3

Table A3 Changes in insurance understanding from pre- and post-awareness campaign (mean ± standard error of mean)†

Questions	Year	Pratapgarh		Kanpur-Dehat		Vaishali		Total	
		Control	Treatment	Control	Treatment	Control	Treatment	Control	Treatment
Insurance provides protection against the health risks in your life (right)	Pre	0.59 ± 0.03	0.51 ± 0.05	0.52 ± 0.03	0.44 ± 0.06	0.51 ± 0.03	0.54 ± 0.06	0.54 ± 0.02	0.50 ± 0.03
	Post	0.81 ± 0.03	0.91 ± 0.03	0.79 ± 0.03	0.99 ± 0.01	0.76 ± 0.03	0.82 ± 0.04	0.79 ± 0.02	0.90 ± 0.02
	Change	0.22***	0.40***	0.27***	0.55***	0.25***	0.28**	0.25***	0.40***
With insurance you pay money upfront, but you do not know whether you will get something out of it (right)	Pre	0.51 ± 0.03	0.48 ± 0.05	0.42 ± 0.03	0.36 ± 0.06	0.50 ± 0.03	0.51 ± 0.06	0.47 ± 0.02	0.45 ± 0.03
	Post	0.67 ± 0.03	0.72 ± 0.04	0.70 ± 0.03	0.82 ± 0.05	0.57 ± 0.03	0.72 ± 0.04	0.64 ± 0.02	0.75 ± 0.03
	Change	0.16***	0.24*	0.28***	0.46***	0.07	0.21**	0.17***	0.30***
If I do not claim, I will get my premium back (wrong)	Pre	0.33 ± 0.03	0.20 ± 0.04	0.39 ± 0.03	0.39 ± 0.06	0.25 ± 0.03	0.23 ± 0.05	0.33 ± 0.02	0.27 ± 0.03
	Post	0.35 ± 0.03	0.63 ± 0.05	0.38 ± 0.03	0.50 ± 0.06	0.41 ± 0.03	0.43 ± 0.05	0.38 ± 0.02	0.53 ± 0.03
	Change	0.02	0.43***	−0.01	0.11	0.16***	0.20*	0.05*	0.26***
If you do not claim, your money can be used to help pay the claim of someone else in your community (right)	Pre	0.25 ± 0.03	0.26 ± 0.05	0.31 ± 0.03	0.32 ± 0.05	0.32 ± 0.03	0.30 ± 0.06	0.29 ± 0.02	0.29 ± 0.03
	Post	0.46 ± 0.04	0.73 ± 0.04	0.47 ± 0.03	0.83 ± 0.04	0.37 ± 0.03	0.68 ± 0.05	0.43 ± 0.02	0.74 ± 0.03
	Change	0.21***	0.47***	0.16**	0.51***	0.05	0.38***	0.14***	0.45***
Insurance can help you and your family afford health care when health problem arises (right)	Pre	0.65 ± 0.03	0.59 ± 0.05	0.66 ± 0.03	0.64 ± 0.06	0.52 ± 0.03	0.55 ± 0.06	0.61 ± 0.02	0.59 ± 0.03
	Post	0.81 ± 0.03	0.90 ± 0.03	0.82 ± 0.03	0.99 ± 0.01	0.78 ± 0.03	0.80 ± 0.04	0.80 ± 0.02	0.89 ± 0.02
	Change	0.16***	0.31***	0.16***	0.35***	0.26***	0.25**	0.19***	0.30***
Only the rich can afford insurance (wrong)	Pre	0.50 ± 0.03	0.39 ± 0.05	0.59 ± 0.03	0.58 ± 0.06	0.35 ± 0.03	0.35 ± 0.06	0.48 ± 0.02	0.44 ± 0.03
	Post	0.78 ± 0.03	0.86 ± 0.03	0.71 ± 0.03	0.85 ± 0.04	0.71 ± 0.03	0.74 ± 0.04	0.73 ± 0.02	0.81 ± 0.02
	Change	0.28***	0.47***	0.12**	0.27***	0.36***	0.39***	0.25***	0.37***
No. of respondents	Pre	195	117	188	72	205	120	588	309
	Post	163	115	188	72	169	104	520	291

†Respondents were asked to say whether the statements were right or wrong, the correct answer (right/wrong) is given in parentheses against each statement.
*** $P < 0.01$, ** $P < 0.05$, * $P < 0.1$ of t-test.

Corresponding Author: Pradeep Panda, Micro Insurance Academy, 52-B, Okhla Industrial Estate, Phase III, New Delhi – 110020, India. Tel.: +91 11 4379 9100; Fax: +91 11 4379 9117; E-mail: pradeep@mia.org.in

Chapter 13

Mobilizing Community-based Health Insurance to Enhance Awareness and Prevention of Airborne, Vectorborne, and Waterborne Diseases in Rural India*

Main Messages

- Data were collected from two surveys, each of 300 randomly selected households drawn from a community-based health insurance (CBHI) project sample of 3,685 households.
- The awareness campaign resulted in a significant increase both in awareness (34%) and in preventive practices (48%).
- The awareness campaigns were part of a larger project carried out by Micro Insurance Academy, New Delhi, India, that included the launch of three CBHI schemes.

---

*This chapter is reproduced from *The Indian Journal of Medical Research* (2015), **142**, 151–164, Open Access, available at https://www.researchgate.net/publication/281446317_Mobilizing_Community-based_Health_Insurance_to_Enhance_Awareness_Pvention_of_Airborne_Vector-borne_Waterborne_Diseases_in_Rural_India.

Focus Points

- Well-structured health educational campaigns can be effective in raising awareness and promoting health-enhancing practices in resource-poor settings.
- The education of women SHG members was a positive and significant determinant of awareness and reported practices.
- Affiliation to CBHI had a significant positive influence on awareness and on practice scores in the post-campaign period.
- CBHI schemes can serve as a platform to enhance awareness about diseases and encourage preventive practices.

Structured Abstract

Introduction

Health awareness campaigns were conducted in order to enhance the knowledge of the target groups about diseases, so that they adopt preventive practices and also seek timely health care if required. This study aims to evaluate the effectiveness of such awareness campaigns in enhancing knowledge about airborne, vector-borne and waterborne diseases, as well as enhancing preventive practices among rural communities. The objective is to identify and confirm possible associations between key demographic and socio-economic factors and awareness and/or preventive practices. The study was conducted in Pratapgarh and Kanpur-Dehat districts in Uttar Pradesh and Vaishali district in Bihar, India.

Method

Data for this analysis were collected twice, once before the awareness campaign and the second time following it. Each survey had 300 randomly selected households drawn from a sample of 3,685 households (SHG members) who were invited to join CBHI schemes. The degree of awareness was measured by scoring replies to a series of questions about the diseases and habits regarding practices to reduce exposure or prevent these illnesses. Descriptive statistics were used for the analysis of changes in respondents' awareness and practice responses. Differences between pre- and post-campaign were assessed by using student t-test. By using ordinary least squares (OLS) regression, the authors examined the factors explaining the overall awareness and practice scores, both before and after the awareness campaigns.

Findings

The study revealed a significant increase in people's knowledge about the risks of airborne, vector-borne and waterborne diseases after the campaign. There was an increase of 14–58% in the average awareness score after the campaign. There was also an increase of 30–65% in the average practice score following the awareness campaign, suggesting that the campaign improved reported preventive practices. The average practice scores were, however, lower than the average awareness scores, even after the campaign. Another observation was that the campaign was more effective in raising awareness about airborne and waterborne diseases (an improvement of almost 50% in the post-campaign score), as compared to vector-borne diseases (an improvement of about 33% in the post-campaign score). Preventive practice scores were generally lower (between 28 and 35%).

The education level of the respondents (women SHG members) was positively associated with both awareness and practice scores. Affiliation to CBHI was another factor which had a significant positive influence on awareness and on practice scores in the post-campaign period. Since enrollment was open to women SHG members, and the CBHI entails participatory practices, it is possible that this nurtured regular interaction and dissemination of information on the diseases and their prevention practices.

Box 1: Changes in Practices to Prevent Airborne, Vector-borne and Waterborne Diseases

Airborne diseases

- An increased number of respondents adopted preventive practices, e.g. washing hands with soap after defecation and after coughing and sneezing.

(Continued)

Box 1: (*Continued*)

- 60% of the respondents reported that they were covering their face while coughing and sneezing, and 69% consulted a doctor when their coughing persisted for more than two weeks.

Vectorborne diseases

- Notable increase in applying three methods to control mosquito breeding: removing water collections once a week, spray kerosene on stagnant water, and keeping surroundings clean.
- Sleeping under ITBN (insecticide-treated bed nets) was extremely rare in all three locations, even after the campaign.

Waterborne diseases

- More than half of the respondents reported after the campaign that they purified their water by boiling and filtering it, but only a few used chlorination and alum.
- Most people reported using homemade solutions for diarrhea prevention and care.
- Although 44% reported using ORS (oral rehydration salts) for diarrhea post-campaign, only a few reported following the suitable practice to prepare ORS, even after the campaign.

Conclusion

Health educational campaigns can be effective in creating awareness and instilling health-enhancing practices in resource-poor settings. Repeating the campaigns may reinforce preventive practices among the target population. Since affiliation to CBHI has a positive impact on awareness and preventive practices, CBHI schemes can serve as a platform to enhance awareness about diseases, and promote preventive practices. It was also observed that as the implementation of CBHI schemes was based on targeting women members of SHGs, awareness campaigns can be organized more frequently through such groups.

Mobilizing community-based health insurance to enhance awareness & prevention of airborne, vector-borne & waterborne diseases in rural India

Pradeep Panda*, Arpita Chakraborty* & David M. Dror*,**

*Micro Insurance Academy, New Delhi, India & **Institute of Health Policy & Management, Erasmus University, Rotterdam, The Netherlands

Received April 17, 2014

***Background & objectives*: Despite remarkable progress in airborne, vector-borne and waterborne diseases in India, the morbidity associated with these diseases is still high. Many of these diseases are controllable through awareness and preventive practice. This study was an attempt to evaluate the effectiveness of a preventive care awareness campaign in enhancing knowledge related with airborne, vector-borne and waterborne diseases, carried out in 2011 in three rural communities in India (Pratapgarh and Kanpur-Dehat in Uttar Pradesh and Vaishali in Bihar).**

***Methods*: Data for this analysis were collected from two surveys, one done before the campaign and the other after it, each of 300 randomly selected households drawn from a larger sample of Self-Help Groups (SHGs) members invited to join community-based health insurance (CBHI) schemes.**

***Results*: The results showed a significant increase both in awareness (34%, $P<0.001$) and in preventive practices (48%, $P=0.001$), suggesting that the awareness campaign was effective. However, average practice scores (0.31) were substantially lower than average awareness scores (0.47), even in post-campaign. Awareness and preventive practices were less prevalent in vector-borne diseases than in airborne and waterborne diseases. Education was positively associated with both awareness and practice scores. The awareness scores were positive and significant determinants of the practice scores, both in the pre- and in the post-campaign results. Affiliation to CBHI had significant positive influence on awareness and on practice scores in the post-campaign period.**

***Interpretation & conclusions*: The results suggest that well-crafted health educational campaigns can be effective in raising awareness and promoting health-enhancing practices in resource-poor settings. It also confirms that CBHI can serve as a platform to enhance awareness to risks of exposure to airborne, vector-borne and waterborne diseases, and encourage preventive practices.**

Key words Airborne disease - awareness campaign - community-based health insurance - preventive healthcare - rural India - vector-borne disease - waterborne disease

Despite remarkable reduction in airborne, vector-borne and waterborne diseases, the morbidity and mortality associated with these conditions continue to be high in India. India accounted for 21 per cent of the world's burden of disease in 2010[1]. Diseases such as tuberculosis, malaria, filariasis, dengue, diarrhoea, typhoid, *etc.* are endemic in India[2]. According to Cohen[3], 1.6 million deaths were caused in India by indoor and outdoor air pollution in 2010. Similarly, India had close to one million confirmed cases of malaria, and many malaria deaths (estimates varied from 15,000[4] to 200,000 individuals every year[5]). On waterborne diseases (*e.g.* cholera, acute diarrhoea, typhoid and viral hepatitis) the estimates vary widely because of a lack of reporting and poor surveillance, yet one report estimated that around 14 million people suffered from some of these conditions in 2012[6].

Many such diseases are preventable through low-cost preventive practices. Public health experts and researchers have recognised that health education is an important tool to encourage individual health-promoting choices[7-9]. However, the evidence is inconsistent. One study reported that an awareness campaign in Vietnam was successful in enhancing people's early access to health care after they acquired more knowledge about avian influenza[9]. Another study reported that in China, short-term health education was not associated with adoption of health protecting behaviour[10]. In the Indian scenario, one study found that information, education and communication (IEC) campaigns were effective in enhancing awareness on tuberculosis[11]. Another, in Karnataka, informed that local folk theatre generated a significant impact on awareness, which led to a reduction in malaria incidence[7]. A study in tribal areas of Odisha concluded that after the awareness campaign about mosquito bites, most participants adopted the recommended preventive measure of using insecticide treated bed nets (ITBN)[12]. In rural Tamil Nadu, awareness generation to waterborne diseases left gaps in understanding the connection between using contaminated drinking water and disease[13]. Finally, in high chikungunya prevalent areas in urban India, there was no significant association between respondents' education level and emptying/drying of water containers[14].

In this study, we evaluated the effectiveness of awareness campaigns in increasing knowledge about airborne, vector-borne and waterborne diseases, as well as enhancing preventive practices among rural communities. The study was conducted in Pratapgarh and Kanpur-Dehat districts in Uttar Pradesh and Vaishali district in Bihar, India; all located in humid semi-arid climate in the Ganges River plain[15]. All the three sites are predominantly rural and more than the one-third of the population is illiterate (Table I). Crude death rates and under five mortality rates are higher than the all India rural average.

Material & Methods

Project background: The awareness campaigns were part of a larger project carried out by Micro Insurance Academy, New Delhi, India, that included the launch of three community-based health insurance (CBHI) schemes in 2011 in these locations. The CBHI schemes under this project were designed as a cluster randomized control trial[20], located 50-100 km outside major urban centres in poor rural areas. There were three waves of enrollment, in 2011, 2012 and 2013. In total, 3,685 households (1,283, 1,039 and 1,363 from Pratapgarh, Kanpur-Dehat and Vaishali, respectively) were selected as treatment cohorts, and all filled the condition that in each household, at least one woman was registered in March 2010 as a member of a Self-Help Group (SHG) facilitated by the three field partners. The treatment groups were exposed to insurance education programmes prior to being invited to join the schemes. Households were characterised by low levels of education, and limited access to healthcare (Table II).

The CBHI schemes targeted communities sharing a common background (geographical, economic, occupational, ethnic, gender, *etc.*). The communities were involved in the design and selection of the benefit packages. The schemes were characterized by low premium and mutual-aid structure, *i.e.* the CBHI schemes were owned and managed by the enrolled community members and operated on a not-for-profit basis[21]. The prevalence was estimated by using the baseline data (collected prior to the launch of CBHIs); more than half of the households had experienced at least one chronic illness episode, and more than two-third reported an acute illness in the family during one month before the survey. More specifically to our study, more than 25 per cent of the sampled households reported an airborne or a vector-borne or a waterborne ailment. Hence, the awareness campaigns were launched, which were open to insured and uninsured households alike.

Table I. Key indicators on living conditions and demographics of the study locations and India

	Pratapgarh	Kanpur-Dehat	Vaishali	India
Socio-demographic profile*,**				
Rural population (%)	94.5	90.3	93.3	68.9
Population density (population per sq. km)	826.9	551.9	1632.2	268.8
Sex ratio	1001.8	862.0	895.1	949.0
Literacy rate (%)	59.6	64.7	54.6	57.9
Male	69.5	71.7	62.1	65.8
Female	49.8	56.5	46.2	49.6
Crude death rate (/1000 population)	24.2	20.0	7.5	7.0
Infant mortality rate (/1000 live births)	85.0	68.0	39.0	42.0
Under five mortality rate (/1000 live births)	107.0	98.0	59.0	52.0
Living conditions†				
Access to drinking water (%)				
Tapwater from treated sources	14.1	10.6	1.4	17.9
Covered well	1.1	0.9	0.8	1.5
Handpump	64.1	77.4	89.4	43.6
Tubewell/borehole	0.6	0.3	1.4	8.3
Separate kitchen (%)	44.6	25.7	14.6	52.8
Type of latrine facility (%)				
Access to toilet	12.5	24.4	26.1	32.7
Open defecation	87.5	75.6	73.9	67.3

*For population and literacy rate (*Source*: Ref. 16)
**For crude death rate, infant mortality rate and under five mortality rate (*Sources*: Refs 17-19)
†Figures are for percentage of households (*Source*: Ref. 16)

The awareness campaigns: The campaigns on awareness to preventive care were an application of the theory of "reasoned action and planned behaviour" (a theory about the link between beliefs and behaviour, which suggests that a person's behaviour is determined by his/her intention to perform the behaviour, which in turn reflects his/her attitudes and his/her subjective norms)[22]. The awareness campaigns entailed training of all the SHG groups that were under the CBHI project. The campaign was organized as a Training of Trainers (ToT) activity; trainers from the lead institution trained representatives of the three field partners about the use of various tools and the key messages; this unfolded during September-October 2011 in all three locations. The field partners' trainers, in turn, trained representatives selected by the SHG members at clusters of villages. These trained SHG members conducted group discussions at SHG meetings on awareness to airborne, vector-borne and waterborne diseases; messages included key identifiable symptoms and associated preventive measures that everyone could practice on a daily basis without reliance on professional assistance or supervision. Pursuant to group discussions, practical exercises followed, like preparation of ORS (oral rehydration solution). Following group discussions, the trainers facilitated follow up discussions at household level of families of SHG members, to cascade the effect of the campaign beyond only the SHG participants.

The campaign tools included group discussion and flipbooks. The flipbooks contained written and pictorial messages, developed by trained physicians of the lead institution, with inputs from the community representatives of the three sites on local beliefs and practices. The flipbooks were written in English, translated into Hindi (the local language).

Table II. Socio-economic characteristics of the households/respondents for all locations together - percentage/mean and standard error of mean*

Characteristics	Pre-campaign	Post-campaign
Household socio-economic characteristics		
% of schedule caste/schedule tribe households	28 (3)	33 (3)
Monthly per capita expenditure (₹)**	1426 (67)	1399 (114)
% households enrolled in CBHI	39 (3)	40 (3)
Household experiencing diseases†		
Airborne diseases	12 (2)	11 (2)
Vector-borne diseases	4 (1)	4 (1)
Waterborne diseases	13 (2)	4 (1)***
Head of household characteristics		
Age (yr)	44.6 (0.7)	44.3 (0.7)
% male	78 (2)	73 (3)
Years of education	5.4 (0.3)	5.1 (0.3)
Employment (%)		
Self-employed	50 (3)	48 (3)
Others	27 (3)	33 (3)
Not working	19 (4)	19 (2)
SHG member characteristics		
Age (yr)	39.4 (0.7)	39.1 (0.6)
Years of education	2.7 (0.2)	2.8 (0.2)
Employment (%)		
Paid labour	13 (2)	17 (2)
Domestic worker	79 (2)	79 (2)
Not-working	5 (1)	3 (1)
Access to health care facilities		
Travel time for IPD services (min)	65.2 (4.1)	72.3 (4.7)
Travel time for OPD services (min)	21.8 (1.3)	19.8 (1.4)
Sample size	300	300

*Figures denote mean (SEM); ***$P<0.01$
**Price adjusted for inflation with 2010 as base; †Household with at least one person experiencing airborne, vector-borne and waterborne diseases in the last 30 days respectively prior to pre- and post-campaign survey; CBHI, community-based health insurance; IPD, in-patient department; OPD, out-patient department

Data and methodology: Two sources of data were used for this study:

Pre-campaign survey data - In August 2011, 300 households (100 each in Pratapgarh, Kanpur-Dehat and Vaishali), randomly selected from the CBHI project sample of 3,685, were asked to respond to questions as to how airborne, vector-borne and waterborne diseases could be identified, how these spread and how these could be prevented. Information of the socio-economic characteristics of respondents, health events in the household during one month prior to the survey and about their access to healthcare facilities was also collected. All data collection tools were pretested and finalized. Trained researchers collected information from the selected households, and the female SHG members were the respondents, using the non-prompted questionnaire.

Post-campaign survey data - In August 2012, the same questionnaire was re-used to probe 300 randomly selected households (not necessarily the same, but selected randomly from the CBHI project sample of 3,685 households; 100 households each in Pratapgarh, Kanpur-Dehat and Vaishali).

Comparison of pre- and post-campaign respondents: Although only seven of the 300 households were sampled in both the pre- and the post-campaigns, the two groups of households were comparable considering the key household indicators, incidence rates, characteristics of household heads and SHG members and access to health care facilities (Table II). Participation in the survey was based on informed consent, voluntary and confidential.

Calculation of awareness and practice scores: We measure the degree of awareness about preventive care and habits regarding preventive practices by scoring replies to a series of questions. Each correct answer was assigned a value of one and each incorrect reply a value of zero. For questions where multiple correct responses were possible, a score of one was assigned for each correct response. All individual scores were added for a single total score per respondent, reflecting all replies relating to airborne, vector-borne and waterborne diseases. Thus, the total scores for awareness could range from zero to 38 (0-12, 0-11 and 0-15 for airborne, vector-borne and waterborne, respectively); and for practice, the total scores could range between 0 and 25 (0-8, 0-8 and 0-9 for airborne, vector-borne and waterborne, respectively). For ease of comparison and comprehension, all total individual scores were divided by the number of questions, to obtain the average scores per question, which now range from zero to one.

Statistical analysis: Descriptive statistics were used for the analysis of changes in respondents' awareness and practice responses. Differences between pre- and post-campaigns were assessed by using student t-test. Ordinary least square (OLS) regression was used to examine the factors explaining the overall awareness and practice scores, both in pre-campaign and post-campaign.

Results

Changes in awareness and practice scores: After the campaign, the results (Table III) showed that the average awareness scores on airborne diseases increased moderately, 20 per cent but significantly

Table III. Changes in awareness and practice scores from pre- to post-campaign - All locations

			Pratapgarh	Kanpur-Dehat	Vaishali	Total
Airborne	Awareness	Pre-campaign	0.44 (0.03)	0.52 (0.02)	0.42 (0.02)	0.46 (0.01)
		Post-campaign	0.46 (0.01)	0.64 (0.02)***	0.57 (0.02)***	0.55 (0.01)***
	Practice	Pre-campaign	0.10 (0.01)	0.30 (0.02)	0.20 (0.01)	0.20 (0.01)
		Post-campaign	0.20 (0.01)***	0.34 (0.02)	0.29 (0.01)***	0.28 (0.01)***
Vector-borne	Awareness	Pre-campaign	0.19 (0.01)	0.32 (0.01)	0.22 (0.01)	0.24 (0.01)
		Post-campaign	0.29 (0.01)***	0.41 (0.02)***	0.35 (0.01)***	0.35 (0.01)***
	Practice	Pre-campaign	0.17 (0.01)	0.26 (0.01)	0.12 (0.01)	0.18 (0.01)
		Post-campaign	0.23 (0.02)*	0.36 (0.01)***	0.22 (0.01)***	0.27 (0.01)***
Waterborne	Awareness	Pre-campaign	0.38 (0.01)	0.40 (0.01)	0.27 (0.01)	0.35 (0.01)
		Post-campaign	0.46 (0.02)***	0.45 (0.02)*	0.52 (0.02)***	0.48 (0.01)***
	Practice	Pre-campaign	0.30 (0.01)	0.26 (0.02)	0.18 (0.01)	0.25 (0.01)
		Post-campaign	0.39 (0.02)***	0.35 (0.02)***	0.32 (0.02)***	0.35 (0.01)***
Over all	Awareness	Pre-campaign	0.36 (0.01)	0.41 (0.01)	0.31 (0.01)	0.35 (0.01)
		Post-campaign	0.41 (0.02)***	0.50 (0.01)***	0.49 (0.01)***	0.47 (0.01)***
	Practice	Pre-campaign	0.19 (0.01)	0.27 (0.01)	0.17 (0.01)	0.21 (0.01)
		Post-campaign	0.28 (0.02)***	0.35 (0.01)***	0.28 (0.01)***	0.31 (0.01)***
	Sample size	Pre-campaign	100	100	100	300
		Post-campaign	100	100	100	300

Figures in parentheses are standard error of mean

$P^{*}<0.05$, $^{***}<0.001$ compared with pre-campaign

($P<0.001$) for the entire sample and for Kanpur-Dehat and Vaishali. As for practice scores on airborne diseases, average scores increased significantly in all three locations after the campaign (+40% on reported practice score for the entire sample).

The average post-campaign awareness scores about vector-borne diseases were significantly higher in all three locations (Kanpur-Dehat 0.41; Vaishali 0.35; and Pratapgarh 0.29). The average practice scores increased by about 50 per cent in all locations after the campaign ($P<0.001$), but only 27 per cent of the sample reported practicing prevention post-campaign.

For waterborne diseases, the average awareness scores increased by +37 per cent ($P<0.001$); this reflected a very pronounced increase in Vaishali (+92%; $P<0.001$), and a modest improvement in Kanpur-Dehat (+12.5%; $P<0.05$). Combining all three diseases, the average awareness post-campaign scores were higher than the pre-campaign scores (increase by 34%, $P<0.001$). This was the case for all three locations, but the extent of the increase was different (in Vaishali it was +58%, in Kanpur-Dehat it was +22%, and in Pratapgarh the change was merely +14%). As for the practice scores, the average scores increased by 48 per cent in the post-campaign for the entire sample ($P<0.001$); and in all three locations compared to the pre-campaign scores, but they were quite lower than the awareness scores, both before and after the campaign (Table III). It is noted that the campaign led to a higher improvement in practice scores than in awareness scores, with percentage changes of +65 per cent in Vaishali, +30 per cent in Kanpur-Dehat, and +47 per cent in Pratapgarh.

Changes in awareness and practices for airborne, vector-borne and waterborne diseases: The overall low scores even after the campaign (less than one-third correct replies), especially for practice, necessitated further analysis, which is shown in Tables IV, V and VI for airborne, vector-borne and waterborne diseases, respectively, for the entire sample.

Airborne diseases: Overall, an increased number of respondents in the post-campaign period were aware that airborne diseases spread through sneezing and coughing (Table IV). Most of the respondents understood that washing hands before and after eating, and after defecation, prevented diseases. More than 60 per cent of the respondents recognized that fever and extended coughing (more than two weeks) were symptoms of TB, but most did not know, even after the campaign, that weight and appetite-loss were also possible indications of TB (less than 30%).

An increased number of respondents reported having adopted preventive practices, *e.g.* washing hands with soap after defecation (increase from 38 of 58%; $P<0.01$) and after coughing and sneezing (28% in post-campaign vs. 8% in pre-campaign; $P<0.05$). In addition, 60 per cent of the respondents reported that they were covering faces while coughing and sneezing, and 69 per cent consulted a doctor when their coughing persisted for more than two weeks (Table IV).

The increase in awareness about airborne diseases from pre-campaign to post-campaign was much higher in Vaishali and Kanpur-Dehat than Pratapgarh (data not shown). But when it came to practicing preventive methods for airborne diseases, in Kanpur-Dehat respondents were well behind those from Pratapgarh and Vaishali.

Vector-borne diseases: The respondents' awareness rose significantly post-campaign about the effectiveness of spraying insecticide inside houses and cattle sheds to prevent malaria/filariasis (+18% of correct replies; $P<0.01$) (Table V), and about the places that are prone to mosquito breeding. Awareness to various curative methods of filariasis also increased significantly. As regards practices, an increased number of respondents reported post-campaign that they were controlling mosquito breeding by removing water collections once a week (32%; $P<0.01$), using kerosene in stagnant water (30%; $P<0.05$) and keeping surroundings clean (49%; $P<0.01$). Close to two-thirds of the respondents reported that they kept drinking water containers covered.

The increase in awareness about vector-borne diseases was significantly higher in Vaishali, followed by Pratapgarh and Kanpur-Dehat (data not shown). Awareness to curative methods of filariasis also increased significantly in Pratapgarh and Vaishali (but remained very low even after the campaign).

The most notable increase in practices was in applying three methods to control mosquito breeding: removing water collections once a week, use of kerosene in stagnant water, and keeping surroundings clean. However, sleeping under ITBN was extremely rare in all three locations, even after the campaign (Table V).

Waterborne diseases: After the campaign, awareness increased on three of the four sources of water

Table IV. Changes in awareness and practice about airborne diseases in pre- and post-campaign phase (percentage of correct response and standard error of mean) - All locations

Indicators	Pre-campaign	Post-campaign
Awareness		
Modes of spread of air-borne diseases		
Sneezing	37 (3)	44 (3)
Coughing	38 (3)	50 (3)**
Talking	24 (2)	25 (2)
Spiting	7 (2)	11 (2)
When hand washing should be done		
Before and after eating	80 (2)	89 (2)**
After defecation	90 (2)	94 (1)
After coughing and sneezing	8 (2)	18 (2)**
After playing	8 (2)	9 (2)
Symptoms of tuberculosis		
Fever	45 (3)	60 (3)**
Coughing more than two weeks	53 (3)	68 (3)**
Weight loss	23 (2)	29 (3)
Loss of appetite	13 (2)	22 (2)**
Practice		
Precautions to prevent spread of airborne diseases		
Wash hands with soap after defecation	38 (3)	58 (3)**
Wash hands after coughing and sneezing	8 (2)	28 (3)*
Avoid spiting in open place	8 (2)	12 (2)
Maintain distance with infected person	34 (3)	44 (3)
Covers face while		
Coughing	12 (2)	20 (2)
Sneezing	17 (2)	13 (2)
Coughing and sneezing	45 (3)	60 (3)
Consults doctor in case of cough more than 2 wk	57 (3)	69 (3)
Sample size	300	300

Figures in parentheses are standard error of mean
$P^{*}<0.05$, $^{**}<0.01$ compared with pre-campaign values

contamination, and on the three ways to prevent worm infection and two of the three symptoms of scabies (Table VI). Respondents exhibited better knowledge on how long ORS can be kept in store, how to clean clothes of scabies patients, and minimum time for boiling of drinking water and cooking non-vegetarian dishes. Moreover, in post-campaign replies, about 70 per cent of the respondents knew that babies with diarrhoea should be breastfed (Table VI).

More than half of the respondents reported after the campaign that they purified their water by boiling and filtering it, but only a few used chlorination and alum. Most people reported using homemade solutions for diarrhoea prevention and care (like salt and sugar solutions, *daal-paani*, *etc*.). Although 44 per cent reported using ORS for diarrhoea post-campaign, only a few reported following the suitable practice to prepare ORS, even after the campaign. The effect of the campaign on enhancing awareness and practices relating to waterborne diseases was most pronounced in Vaishali, compared to Pratapgarh and Kanpur-Dehat (data not shown).

Table V. Changes in awareness and practice about vector-borne diseases in pre- and post-campaign phase (percentage of correct response and standard error of mean) - All locations

Indicators	Pre-campaign	Post-campaign
Awareness		
Methods of prevention of malaria/filariasis		
Application of mosquito repellent	38 (3)	34 (3)
Creating smoke by burning Neem leaves	43 (3)	50 (3)
Insecticide spray	15 (2)	33 (3)**
Places of insecticide spray		
Inside house	35 (3)	66 (3)**
In cattle sheds	12 (2)	25 (2)**
In the streets of village	12 (2)	16 (2)
Various places of mosquito breeding		
Stagnant water	73 (3)	82 (2)
Garbage	6 (1)	30 (3)**
Methods of care in case of filariasis		
Wash swollen area with soap and water everyday	12 (2)	14 (2)
Use antibacterial cream on wound	21 (2)	30 (3)
Elevate and exercise swollen arm of leg	2 (1)	8 (2)**
Practice		
Methods to control mosquito breeding		
Removing all water collection once a week	13 (2)	32 (3)**
Beating collection of water with stick regularly	33 (3)	36 (3)
Use of kerosene oil in stagnant water collections	19 (2)	30 (3)*
By keeping surroundings clean	26 (3)	49 (3)**
Always uses ITBN	0 (0)	1 (1)
Covers the stored water kept for		
Drinking	52 (3)	65 (3)**
Washing	1 (0)	2 (1)
Bathing	0 (0)	3 (1)*
Sample size	300	300

Figures in parentheses are standard error of mean
ITBN, insecticide treated bed nets
$P^*<0.05$, $^{**}<0.01$ compared with pre-campaign values

Determinants of awareness and practices in the pre- and post-campaign periods: While the average scores of awareness and reported practice were higher after the campaign (Table III), those scores were still quite low. We, therefore, analysed other factors that could influence people's scores. The overall average awareness and practices scores (combined average scores of airborne, vector-borne and waterborne diseases - Table III) for the OLS regressions were used as dependent variable, and regression was performed both for the pooled data (Table VII) and for the three locations separately (data not shown). Several explanatory variables were considered, *e.g.* household characteristics, households experiencing diseases, head-of-household characteristics, access to health services, SHG member characteristics and locational characteristics. It was also tested whether awareness led to reported practice, by considering the average awareness score as an explanatory variable for the determinants of reported practice.

Table VI. Changes in awareness and practice about waterborne diseases in pre- and post-campaign phase (percentage of correct response and standard error of mean) - All locations

Indicators	Pre-campaign	Post-campaign
Awareness		
Different ways of water contamination		
Mixing of human & animal excreta with water	34 (3)	36 (3)
Collecting drinking water in unclean container	26 (3)	47 (3)**
Keeping drinking water uncovered	53 (3)	61 (3)
Dipping unclean & dirty hands into vessel	50 (3)	62 (3)**
Methods to prevent worm infestation		
Hand washing	31 (3)	47 (3)**
Wearing slippers	4 (1)	18 (2)**
Eating fruit & vegetable after washing	17 (2)	25 (2)*
ORS can be used/kept up to 24 h	18 (2)	24 (2)
Mother should breast feed in case of diarrhoea of child	58 (3)	70 (3)**
Symptoms of scabies		
Rash	60 (3)	58 (3)
Itching	67 (3)	82 (2)**
Ulcer due to scratching	36 (3)	46 (3)**
Clothes of scabies patient to be cleaned in hot water	50 (3)	67 (3)**
Water should be boiled for 15-20 min for purification	16 (2)	30 (3)**
Eats non-veg after at least 30 min of cooking	7 (1)	49 (3)**
Practice		
Methods of water purification		
Boiling	32 (3)	53 (3)**
Chlorination	5 (1)	11 (2)**
Filtering	38 (3)	51 (3)**
Using alum	1 (1)	6 (1)**
Things to be given in case of diarrhoea		
ORS	30 (3)	44 (3)**
Salt & sugar solution prepared at home	58 (3)	74 (3)**
Plain water	3 (1)	3 (1)
Daal-pani, rice water, coconut water, *etc*.	40 (3)	60 (3)**
ORS preparation method - 1 packet ORS in one litre water	15 (2)	17 (2)
Sample Size	300	300

Figures in parentheses are standard error of mean
ORS, oral rehydration solution
$P^{*}<0.05$, $^{**}<0.01$ compared with pre-campaign values

Determinants of preventive care awareness: Before the campaign, awareness was positively associated with prior exposure of the households to vector-borne and waterborne diseases (Table VII). The education of the SHG member was significantly and positively linked with awareness (but the education of the household head and the monthly per-capita expenditure (log of MPCE) were not significant explanatory variables). Residents of Pratapgarh and Vaishali had lower awareness than residents of Kanpur-Dehat.

After the campaign, affiliation to CBHI increased the probability of higher awareness ($P<0.01$). Similar to the pre-campaign results, education levels of SHG membership were positively associated with awareness. Households in Pratapgarh demonstrated lower effect of the campaign as scores did not change very much

Table VII. Regression results with total preventive care awareness and practice score in pre- and post-campaign period - All locations

Independent variables	Awareness		Practice	
	Pre-campaign	Post-campaign	Pre-campaign	Post-campaign
Knowledge of preventive health care				
Awareness score			0.0122**	0.0128**
			(0.00112)	(0.00114)
Household (HH) characteristics				
HH belongs to SC/ST	0.0234	0.0195	0.0212	0.0101
	(0.0164)	(0.0169)	(0.0115)	(0.0123)
HH enrolled in CBHI	-0.0148	0.0485**	0.0116	0.0556**
	(0.0139)	(0.0174)	(0.00973)	(0.0128)
Log of monthly per capita expenditure	0.0165	0.0101	-0.0136	0.00319
	(0.0130)	(0.0148)	(0.00908)	(0.0107)
HH experiencing diseases				
Experienced airborne diseases	0.0181	0.0156	-0.00287	-0.0103
	(0.0201)	(0.0253)	(0.0140)	(0.0184)
Experienced vector-borne diseases	0.0885*	0.0467	-0.00232	0.0357
	(0.0359)	(0.0388)	(0.0253)	(0.0282)
Experienced waterborne diseases	0.0380	0.0181	0.00340	0.0184
	(0.0194)	(0.0406)	(0.0137)	(0.0294)
Head of household characteristics				
Age	0.000502	0.000860	0.000652	0.0000427
	(0.000791)	(0.000993)	(0.000553)	(0.000720)
Years of education	-0.000292	-0.00279	0.00361**	-0.00229
	(0.00173)	(0.00222)	(0.00121)	(0.00161)
Gender - male	0.0228	0.0000079	-0.0198	0.0359*
	(0.0204)	(0.0241)	(0.0143)	(0.0175)
Employment - self-employed	0.0226	-0.00146	0.0106	-0.0181
	(0.0201)	(0.0269)	(0.0141)	(0.0195)
Employment - others	0.0254	0.0132	-0.00651	-0.0180
	(0.0214)	(0.0262)	(0.0150)	(0.0190)
Access to health services				
Travel time for IPD services	-0.000123	0.0000964	0.0000420	0.000182*
	(0.000122)	(0.000119)	(0.0000853)	(0.0000860)
Travel time for OPD services	-0.000210	-0.000409	-0.000319	0.0000750
	(0.000327)	(0.000339)	(0.000229)	(0.000246)
SHG member characteristics				
Age	-0.000241	-0.000871	-0.000703	-0.0000847
	(0.000852)	(0.00113)	(0.000595)	(0.000822)
Years of education	0.00798**	0.0114**	0.00257	0.00712**
	(0.00193)	(0.00238)	(0.00139)	(0.00179)
Employment - paid labour	-0.0277	0.0492	-0.00416	0.0325
	(0.0361)	(0.0506)	(0.0252)	(0.0368)

Contd...

Independent variables	Awareness		Practice	
	Pre-campaign	Post-campaign	Pre-campaign	Post-campaign
Employment - domestic worker	-0.0426	0.0483	0.0279	0.0588*
	(0.0327)	(0.0465)	(0.0229)	(0.0338)
Locational characteristics				
Pratapgarh	-0.0629**	-0.0762**	-0.0370*	0.00300
	(0.0204)	(0.0230)	(0.0145)	(0.0170)
Vaishali	-0.105**	-0.0258	-0.0455**	-0.0612**
	(0.0215)	(0.0244)	(0.0157)	(0.0177)
Constant	0.275**	0.325**	0.127*	-0.0385
	(0.105)	(0.120)	(0.0744)	(0.0881)
Observations	100	100	100	100
R-squared	0.229	0.216	0.518	0.533

Figures in parentheses are standard errors
P *<0.05, **<0.01
SC, scheduled caste; ST, scheduled tribe; CBHI, community-based health insurance; IPD, in-patient department; OPD, out-patient department

compared to Kanpur-Dehat, and for Vaishali the dummy turned out to be insignificant.

The comparison across locations showed that before the campaign, households in Kanpur-Dehat were aware to airborne, vector-borne or waterborne diseases in cases they reported prior exposure to these conditions (data not shown). In Vaishali, the average awareness score was negatively associated with travel time for inpatient care (IPD). And, in all three locations, the education of SHG members was a positive and significant determinant of awareness.

In post-campaign results, enrollment in CBHI and income (proxy used was per capita monthly expenditure (log of monthly per capita expenditure) were positively associated with awareness in Kanpur Dehat. In addition, in Kanpur-Dehat and in Pratapgarh, awareness was also positively associated with prior exposure to airborne diseases. Travel time to outpatient care (OPD) was negatively associated with awareness in Kanpur-Dehat.

Determinants of reported preventive care practices: In the pre-campaign phase, reported preventive care practices were positively and significantly determined by awareness ($P<0.01$) (Table VII). Scheduled caste/scheduled tribe households were more likely to practice preventive health as compared with household from higher castes. Education of both head of households ($P<0.01$) and the SHG member ($P<0.1$) were positive and significant determinants of reported practices. Households in Kanpur-Dehat were more likely to report preventive practices, compared to households in Pratapgarh and Vaishali.

After the campaign, practice scores continued to be positively and significantly associated with awareness scores ($P<0.01$). Affiliation to CBHI had a positive effect on practice scores ($P<0.01$). Male-headed households were more likely to report preventive health practices than female-headed households ($P<0.05$). An increase in average travel time to IPD services was associated with an increase in the reported practice scores ($P<0.05$). As in the pre-campaign phase, educational level of the SHG members was positively associated with practice scores ($P<0.01$). SHG members that were domestic workers had higher practice scores than non-working members ($P<0.1$). Households in Vaishali were less likely to practice preventive health compared to households in Kanpur-Dehat.

The average awareness scores were the most consistent explanatory variable for the practice scores in all locations, both before and after the campaign. CBHI-enrolled households were more likely to obtain higher practice scores in Pratapgarh before and after the campaign, while in Vaishali such positive relationship was observed only after the campaign (data not shown). The education of SHG member had a significant and positive effect on practice scores in Pratapgarh and Vaishali after the campaign.

Discussion

This study was carried out to establish the evidence on three research questions: First, was the campaign to enhance people's awareness to the risks of airborne, vector-borne and waterborne diseases effective? Secondly, were the campaigns also effective in inculcating preventive practices? Thirdly, is it possible to identify and confirm the associations between key demographic and socio-economic factors and awareness and/or preventive practices?

The findings offered a clear response to the first research question: the average awareness score was 14-58 per cent higher after the campaign, an improvement in people's awareness to the risks of airborne, vector-borne and waterborne diseases. The findings on the second question were equally compelling: the post-campaign average practice score was higher by 30-65 per cent compared to pre-campaign score showing that the campaign improved reported preventive practices. But the campaign was not equally effective everywhere: it was more effective in Vaishali than in Pratapgarh and Kanpur-Dehat.

The score improvements differed for the three types of diseases studied. For airborne diseases, the increase in average practice score was 40 per cent, but these results were better in Kanpur-Dehat and Vaishali, lesser in Pratapgarh. Awareness about tuberculosis increased significantly, but remained low; our findings corroborated those reported in other studies[23,24]. For vector-borne diseases, the increase in awareness (46%) and practice (50%) was similar, but the absolute scores remained low, and the average practice score was lower than the one for awareness, even after the campaign. Other studies from developing countries suggested that the adoption of practices followed exposure to health incidence, even among people who were aware to the risks[24,25]. As for waterborne diseases, average awareness and practice scores increased by 37 and 40 per cent respectively after the campaign. The average scores increased in Vaishali more than in Pratapgarh and Kanpur-Dehat. The responses on the practice of using ORS were very low, confirming similar findings in India reported by others[26], even though awareness scores increased, especially in Vaishali. The post-campaign score on awareness about worm infection increased significantly, corroborating similar findings from China[27].

The disease specific analysis suggested that the campaign was effective in raising awareness about airborne and waterborne diseases (an improvement of almost 50% in post-campaign score) and less so about vector-borne diseases (an improvement of about 33% in post-campaign score). Preventive practice scores were generally lower (between 28 and 35%); Kanpur-Dehat respondents stood out as more aware and more engaged in preventive measures; and Vaishali respondents stood out for their impressive improvement post-campaign, both in better awareness and in higher practices.

It was shown that education of women SHG members was a significant determinant of better awareness (confirming similar findings by others[24,28]), which was assumed to facilitate adoption of preventive practices[29]. Affiliation to CBHI was one of the consistent determinants for higher awareness and practice scores after the campaign. As enrollment was open to female SHG members, and the CBHI entails participatory practices, these might have provided a platform for regular interaction and dissemination of information on the diseases and prevention.

It was concluded that campaigns organized as part of implementation of CBHI schemes targeting women members of SHGs in three locations in rural India enhanced awareness to the risks of airborne, vector-borne and waterborne diseases. The campaigns were effective in encouraging application of preventive practices (based on self-reported preventive practices), indicating that better awareness to the risks was a necessary first step to adoption of preventive practices. This also suggests that repeating the campaigns may lead to better adoption of preventive practices. The second important conclusion is that the CBHI schemes can serve as a platform to impart better awareness. This conclusion was based on the finding that better awareness and better practice were associated with membership in CBHI. Moreover, the CBHI activities provided the opportunity for regular gatherings and knowledge exchanges between the members. Thirdly, considering that the implementation of CBHI schemes was based on targeting women members of SHGs, the potential of success in achieving greater awareness to preventive care and subsequent adoption of suitable practices might be enhanced by organizing similar awareness campaigns through such groups on a wide scale.

Our study had certain limitations. Though almost similar results were observed in all three study locations, such a small study would not justify making generalizations that awareness campaigns led to improved preventive practices everywhere. Secondly, although our results were based on random samples of respondents drawn over two points in time, we did not assert a general pattern of cause-and-effect everywhere. Thirdly, due to the absence of a control group, it was not possible to conclude that the enhanced awareness and reported practice scores were solely due to the campaign. However, the fact that key socio-economic and demographic indicators, health incidence rates and access to health care facilities were similar in the pre- and post-campaign periods, the observed changes in awareness and reported practices might largely be attributed to the awareness campaigns. Fourthly, the information on preventive practices was sourced from self-reporting, so the habitual limitations of self-reporting must be considered. More research would be needed to confirm affirmatively the impact of better awareness on the adoption of preventive health practices, and in turn on the reduction of disease burden and the related healthcare costs.

Acknowledgment

The first (PP) and the last author (DMD) acknowledge funding provided by European Commission 7th Framework Programme; grant ID HEALTH-F2-2009-223518 – Community-based Health Insurance in India. The authors acknowledge substantive contribution of the Micro Insurance Academy and its staff in data collection and cleaning as well as in analytical inputs; and the implementing partners (BAIF, *Shramik Bharti* and *Nidan*) and the respondents, for their ongoing willingness to share information on the implementation. The authors thank Drs Nidhi Bhatt and Dinesh Baliga for their assistance in the development of awareness campaign materials and also for training.

Conflicts of interest: None.

References

1. World Health Organization: Country cooperation strategy at a glance: India 2012. Available from: *http://www.who.int/countryfocus/cooperation_strategy/ccsbrief_ind_en.pdf?ua=1*, accessed on April 9, 2014.
2. Government of India. *Report of the Working Group on Disease Burden for the 12th Five Year Plan.* New Delhi: Planning Commission; 2011.
3. Cohen AJ. Global Burden of Disease 2010. In: Global burden of disease 2010. New Delhi India: 2013. Available from: *http://www.cseindia.org/userfiles/global_burden_aaron.pdf*, accessed on March 18, 2014.
4. World Health Organization (WHO). *World malaria report 2008*; Geneva: WHO; 2008.
5. Dhingra N, Jha P, Sharma VP, Cohen AA, Jotkar RM, Rodriguez PS, *et al*; Million Death Study Collaborators. Adult and child malaria mortality in India: a nationally representative mortality survery. *Lancet* 2010; *376* : 1768-74.
6. Central Bureau of Health Intelligence (CBHI). *National health profile of India 2012.* New Delhi: CBHI, Directorate of Health Services, Government of India. 2013.
7. Ghosh SK, Patil RR, Tiwari S, Dash AP. A community-based health education programme for bio-environmental control of malaria through folk theatre (*Kalajatha*) in rural India. *Malar J* 2006; *5* : 123.
8. Aiello AE, Coulborn RM, Perez V, Larson EL. Effect of hand hygiene on infectious disease risk in the community setting: a meta-analysis. *Am J Public Health* 2008; *98* : 1372-81.
9. Manabe T, Pham TP, Vu VC, Takasaki J, Dinh TT, Nguyen TM, *et al.* Impact of educational intervention concerning awareness and behaviors relating to avian influenza (H5N1) in a high-risk population in Vietnam. *PLoS One* 2011; *6* : e23711.
10. Wang S, Carlton EJ, Chen L, Liu Y, Spear RC. Evaluation of an educational intervention on villagers' knowledge, attitude and behaviour regarding transmission of *Schistosoma japonicum* in Sichuan province, China. *Acta Trop* 2013; *127* : 226-35.
11. Sharma N, Taneja DK, Pagare D, Saha R, Vashist RP, Ingle GK. The impact of an IEC campaign on tuberculosis awareness and health seeking behaviour in Delhi, India. *Int J Tuberc Lung Dis* 2005; *9* : 1259-65.
12. Vijayakumar KN, Gunasekaran K, Sahu SS, Jambulingam P. Knowledge, attitude and practice on malaria: a study in a tribal belt of Orissa state, India with reference to use of long lasting treated mosquito nets. *Acta Trop* 2009; *112* : 137-42.
13. Gupta N, Mutukkanu T, Nadimuthu A, Thiyagaran I, Sullivan-Marx E. Preventing waterborne diseases: analysis of a community health worker program in rural Tamil Nadu, India. *J Community Health* 2012; *37* : 513-9.
14. Nagpal NB, Saxena R, Srivastava A, Singh N, Ghosh SK, Sharma SK, *et al.* Retrospective study of chikungunya outbreak in urban areas of India. *Indian J Med Res* 2012; *135* : 351-8.
15. Ranga V, Panda P. Spatial access to inpatient health care in northern rural India. *Geospatial Health* 2014; *8* : 545-56.
16. Census of India. Primary Census Abstract. 2011. Available from: *http://www.censusindia.gov.in/pca/default.aspx*, accessed on August 1, 2014.
17. Office of the Registrar General & Census Commissioner. *Annual health survey 2010-11*: Fact sheet, Bihar. New Delhi: 2012. Available from: *http://www.censusindia.gov.in/vital_statistics/AHSBulletins/AHS_Baseline_Factsheets/Bihar.pdf*, accessed on August 1, 2014.
18. Office of the Registrar General & Census Commissioner. *Annual health survey* 2010-11: Fact Sheet, Uttar Pradesh. New Delhi: 2012. Available from: *http://www.censusindia.gov.in/vital_statistics/AHSBulletins/AHS_Baseline_Factsheets/U_P.pdf*, accessed on August 1, 2014.
19. Sample Registration System. Vital rates: Figures at a glance, India 2012. New Delhi: Census of India; 2012. Available from: *http://www.censusindia.gov.in/2011-Common/Vital%20Rates.pdf*, accessed on August 1, 2014.
20. Doyle C, Panda P, Van de Poel E, Radermacher R, Dror DM. Reconciling research and implementation in micro health insurance experiments in India: study protocol for a randomized controlled trial. *Trials* 2011; *12* : 224.

21. Dror DM, Jacquier C. Micro-insurance: extending health insurance to the excluded. *Int Soc Secur Rev* 1999; *52* : 71-97.

22. Ajzen I, Fishbein M. *Understanding attitudes and predicting social behaviour*. New Jersey, USA: Prentice-Hall; 1980.

23. Sreeramareddy CT, Harsha Kumar HN, Arokiasamy JT. Prevalence of self-reported tuberculosis, knowledge about tuberculosis transmission and its determinants among adults in India: results from a nation-wide cross-sectional household survey. *BMC Infect Dis* 2013; *13* : 16.

24. Khandoker A, Khan MM, Krämer A, Mori M. Knowledge about tuberculosis transmission among ever-married women in Bangladesh. *Int J Tuberc Lung Dis* 2011; *15* : 379-84.

25. Oguonu T, Okafor HU, Obu HA. Caregivers's knowledge, attitude and practice on childhood malaria and treatment in urban and rural communities in Enugu, south-east Nigeria. *Public Health* 2005; *119* : 409-14.

26. Pahwa S, Kumar GT, Toteja GS. Performance of a community-based health and nutrition-education intervention in the management of diarrhoea in a slum of Delhi, India. *J Health Popul Nutr* 2010; *28* : 553-9.

27. Bieri FA, Gray DJ, Williams GM, Raso G, Li YS, Yuan L, *et al*. Health-education package to prevent worm infections in Chinese schoolchildren. *N Engl J Med* 2013; *368* : 1603-12.

28. Naing C, Ren WY, Man CY, Fern KP, Qiqi C, Ning CN, *et al*. Awareness of dengue and practice of dengue control among the semi-urban community: a cross sectional survey. *J Community Health* 2011; *36* : 1044-9.

29. Quick RE, Kimura A, Thevos A, Tembo M, Shamputa I, Hutwagner L, *et al*. Diarrhea prevention through household-level water disinfection and safe storage in Zambia. *Am J Trop Med Hyg* 2002; *66* : 584-9.

Reprint requests: Dr Pradeep Panda, Micro Insurance Academy, 86, Okhla Industrial Estate, Phase III,
New Delhi 110 020, India
e-mail: pradeep@mia.org.in

Chapter 14

Enrollment in Community-based Health Insurance Schemes in Rural Bihar and Uttar Pradesh, India*

Main Messages

- The target group for the entire project consisted of 3,686 SHG households.
- This study is based on data relating to the SHG households that joined in Wave one in the three locations (1,335 households representing 7,722 individuals).
- The analysis was based on 1,294 households (7,659 individuals) for which valid data could be collected in the baseline survey.
- Each community-based health insurance (CBHI) was governed by its members, who were also involved in the design of benefit packages, pricing and claims settlement.

Focus Points

- CBHI offered through SHGs is independent of a household's socio-economic status.

---

*This chapter is reproduced from *Health Policy and Planning* (2013), **29**, 960–974, Open Access, available at https://www.researchgate.net/publication/258102884_Enrolment_in_community-based_health_insurance_schemes_in_rural_Bihar_and_Uttar_Pradesh_India.

- Enrollment in the national hospitalization scheme (Rashtriya Swasthya Bima Yojana) does not affect enrollment in CBHI.
- Recent episodes of illness or self-assessed health status do not influence uptake of insurance.
- Offering insurance through women's SHGs pacifies concerns about the inclusiveness and sustainability of CBHI schemes.

Structured Abstract

Introduction

"Health Insurance" is a novel concept for most people in rural poor communities, and thus it is interesting to study the factors that influence uptake of insurance among these communities. This study aims to identify factors that drive enrolment in CBHI schemes launched in three rural locations in India in 2010–2011. It also examines the degree of inclusive practices of the schemes and the influence of health status on enrollment.

Method

Each of the CBHI schemes follows a three-wave implementation process, and this study is based on data relating to the SHG households that joined in Wave one in the three locations. In order to analyze the determinants of enrollment, two data sources were used: a baseline survey, and information maintained by MIA's management information system pertaining to actual enrolments, premium payments, and claims. The baseline survey included questions on socio-economic indicators, on self-reported illness events, on the treatment sought and expenditure incurred, and information on hospitalization or pregnancy in the 12 months preceding the survey.

To estimate the probability of enrolment, various factors were considered such as socio-economic status variables, formal health insurance and risk-pooling variables, travel time to the nearest inpatient and outpatient facility, variables indicating the total number of past health events, and variables to capture the age profile of the household. To assess intra-household resource allocation, additional variables were considered besides the above variables. These include SHG member, age, gender, marital status, education, employment status, relation to head of household, individual illness events and self-assessed health status.

Box 1: Variables Used in Estimating Probability of Enrollment in CBHI

Socio-economic status (SES)

- Caste, age, gender, education and employment status of the head of the household
- Expenditure quintile to which a household belongs

Formal HI and risk-pooling (FIRP)

- Access to formal HI — notably RSBY enrolment status
- Type of family (joint or nuclear)
- Size of household
- Whether incomes pooled within a household
- Current household "monthly per capita financial liabilities" (debt)

Supply-side factors (SS)

- Travel time to the nearest inpatient and outpatient facility

Total number of past health events (HE) and age profile

- Short-term illnesses, long-term illnesses, hospitalization experienced by members of the household
- The age profile of the household (presence of children younger than 12 years and adults older than 65 years)

Findings

A key finding of the study is that a household's socio-economic status did not appear to substantially inhibit uptake of insurance. Instead, in Pratapgarh, those belonging to an economically and socially disadvantaged community (SC/ST) had increased affiliation to the CBHI by 13%. It was also observed that households with greater financial liabilities considered insurance more attractive, whereas households with access to risk pooling mechanisms within their family network were less likely to enroll.

An interesting observation was that access to the national hospital insurance scheme (Rashtriya Swasthya Bima Yojana[1]) did not dampen CBHI uptake, suggesting that the potential for greater development of insurance markets and innovative products would respond to a need. On studying the data on individual illness, we saw that recent episodes of illness and self-assessed health status did not influence uptake of insurance. The study revealed that insurance coverage is prioritized within households, with the household head, the spouse of the household head and both male and female children of the household head, more likely to be insured as compared with other relatives.

Conclusion

The analysis suggests that there is an advantage in offering insurance through women's SHGs as it pacifies concerns about the inclusiveness and sustainability of CBHI schemes. The authors are of the view that since SHGs have a pan-Indian spread, providing insurance through such groups offers the potential to scale-up CBHI.

[1] In 2008, the Government of India introduced a hospitalization insurance scheme called Rashtriya Swasthya Bima Yojana (RSBY) which, for the time being, is heavily subsidized and open for affiliation mainly to persons confirmed as "below poverty-line" (BPL).

Enrolment in community-based health insurance schemes in rural Bihar and Uttar Pradesh, India

Pradeep Panda,[1,2]* Arpita Chakraborty,[1] David M Dror[1,3] and Arjun S Bedi[4,5]

[1]Micro Insurance Academy, New Delhi 110020, India, [2]Institute for Human Development, New Delhi 110002, India, [3]Erasmus University, Rotterdam, 3062 PA, The Netherlands, [4]International Institute of Social Studies, Erasmus University, Rotterdam, 2502 LT The Hague, The Netherlands and [5]Georgetown University, PO Box 23689, Doha, Qatar

*Corresponding author. Micro Insurance Academy, 52-B, Okhla Industrial Estate, Phase III, New Delhi 110020, India. Email: pradeep@mia.org.in

Accepted 20 September 2013

This article assesses insurance uptake in three community-based health insurance (CBHI) schemes located in rural parts of two of India's poorest states and offered through women's self-help groups (SHGs). We examine what drives uptake, the degree of inclusive practices of the schemes and the influence of health status on enrolment. The most important finding is that a household's socio-economic status does not appear to substantially inhibit uptake. In some cases scheduled caste/scheduled tribe households are more likely to enrol. Second, households with greater financial liabilities find insurance more attractive. Third, access to the national hospital insurance scheme Rashtriya Swasthya Bima Yojana does not dampen CBHI uptake, suggesting that the potential for greater development of insurance markets and products beyond existing ones would respond to a need. Fourth, recent episodes of illness and self-assessed health status do not influence uptake. Fifth, insurance coverage is prioritized within households, with the household head, the spouse of the household head and both male and female children of the household head, more likely to be insured as compared with other relatives. Sixth, offering insurance through women's SHGs appears to mitigate concerns about the inclusiveness and sustainability of CBHI schemes. Given the pan-Indian spread of SHGs, offering insurance through such groups offers the potential to scale-up CBHI.

Keywords Community-based health insurance, health microinsurance, enrolment, rural India, self-help groups, Bihar, Uttar Pradesh

KEY MESSAGES

- CBHI offered through SHGs is independent of a household's socio-economic status.
- Enrolment in the national hospitalization scheme (Rashtriya Swasthya Bima Yojana) does not affect enrolment in CBHI.
- Recent episodes of illness or self-assessed health status do not influence uptake.
- Offering insurance through women's SHGs appears to mitigate concerns about the inclusiveness and sustainability of CBHI schemes.

Introduction

Outpatient care represents the lion's share of health-care spending among resource-poor rural persons in India (Dror *et al.* 2008), and most of that cost is borne by health-care seekers out-of-pocket (OOP) (Selvaraj and Karan 2012; World Bank 2010a; Meghan 2010; WHO 2012). High OOP expenditure has been identified as a factor driving vulnerable households further into poverty (WHO 2000). The impoverishing effects of such expenditures in the Indian context have been highlighted by Berman *et al.* (2010); Shahrawat and Rao 2011 and Garg and Karan (2009). Binnendijk *et al.* (2012) have shown that households in question frequently finance such OOP spending by borrowing money with interest or selling assets, even for outpatient care, and this practice increases total OOP spending significantly. To reduce the inequity of such health financing (Kruk *et al.* 2009), it is now commonly agreed that risk pooling and prepayment should replace OOP spending when seeking care (James and Savedoff 2010; World Bank 2010b). In India, in 2008, the government has introduced a hospitalization insurance scheme called Rashtriya Swasthya Bima Yojana (RSBY) which, for the time being, is heavily subsidized and open for affiliation mainly to persons confirmed as 'below-poverty-line' (BPL). This scheme notwithstanding, health insurance mostly does not cover the cost of outpatient care and penetration is still low (Ma and Sood 2008).[1] The combined effect of excluding most outpatient care from health insurance, and general concerns of clients that they might not get suitable returns from insurance due to their inability to enforce the contract may explain the low penetration of health insurance (Dror and Vellakkal 2012).[2]

Since the late 1990s, community-based health insurance (CBHI) schemes at village level have been proposed as an alternative approach to increase access to insurance, replacing informal risk-pooling approaches. Special attention was drawn to CBHI that involved clients in establishing rationing rules and governing schemes (Dror and Jacquier 1999; WHO 2000; Wiesmann and Jutting 2001; Ahuja 2005; NCMH 2005; ILO/STEP 2006; Bhat and Jain 2006; UNDP 2007; Dror *et al.* 2009). This has led to the implementation of a number of CBHI schemes in several developing countries, including India (Dror *et al.* 2007; Gautham *et al.* 2011).[3]

Matching the roll-out of these schemes, there has been a proliferation of studies on various aspects, e.g. uptake, utilization of health care, financial protection and impact of such schemes (Gumber 2001; Jakab *et al.* 2001; Ranson 2001; Jutting 2004; Msuya *et al.* 2004; Chankova *et al.* 2008; Zhang and Wang 2008; Axelson *et al.* 2009; Gnawali *et al.* 2009; Wagstaff *et al.* 2009; Ito and Kono 2010; Thornton *et al.* 2010; Bendig and Arun 2011; Robyn *et al.* 2012). An early review was provided by Jakab and Krishnan (2001) and Preker *et al.* (2002) who concluded, based on 45 papers they reviewed, that there was convincing evidence that CBHI schemes were able to mobilize resources to finance health-care needs, albeit with substantial variation across schemes, and to reach low-income groups, although often not the very lowest-income groups. Ekman (2004) who carried out a systematic review of 36 studies published from 1980 to 2002, concluded that while such schemes provide financial protection for low-income groups, the magnitude of the effect is small and the lowest-income groups are excluded from enrolment. More recently, Mebratie *et al.* (2012) reviewed 36 papers (published between 1995 and 2011) that dealt with the determinants of CBHI uptake and, more specifically, social exclusion and adverse selection. They reported that most papers provide evidence that the lowest-income groups are excluded from CBHI schemes. They also reported that about 86% of the studies find that individuals suffering from pre-existing health conditions/poor health were more likely to join CBHI schemes as compared with those in good health, suggesting this is a proxy of adverse selection.

The purpose of this study is to examine and identify factors that drive enrolment in CBHI schemes launched in three rural locations (one in Pratapgarh, Uttar Pradesh, one in Kanpur Dehat, Uttar Pradesh and the third in Vaishali, Bihar) in India in 2010–11. This project is innovative in several aspects. First, households can enrol only through their female members who participate in a women's self-help group (SHG).[4] While focusing on SHG-affiliated households limits the generalizability of our estimates, in so far as women participating in SHG are usually from lower-income households,[5] we examine whether this enrolment strategy improves inclusiveness by offering resource-poor households non-competitive access to the CBHI schemes. Second, considering that the selection rule for membership (female participation in SHG) is unrelated to pre-existing medical conditions, does the evidence support the assumption that this affiliation strategy reduces the likelihood of adverse selection? Third, considering that the SHG women may enrol either alone or with other members of their household (but the others can only enrol if the SHG woman is enrolled), we examine intra-household resource allocation decisions relating to payment of insurance premiums. Fourth, notwithstanding the fact that the same enrolment rule applied to all three CBHI implementations, we observe variations in uptake, and assess the effect of some differences in design on enrolment.

The article unfolds by providing, in the section 'Methods', a description of the three CBHI schemes and a discussion of the data. This is followed by a discussion section of our analytical framework. The next section contains the empirical results. The final section of the article contains conclusions.

Methods

Household Scheme description, scheme uptake and data

The target group is defined as households with at least one woman registered as a member of an SHG in March 2010 (when the baseline study was conducted). The target group for the entire project consisted of 3686 SHG households (1284 in Pratapgarh, 1039 in Kanpur Dehat and 1363 in Vaishali) representing a total of 23 876 individuals (8933 in Pratapgarh, 7105 in Kanpur Dehat and 7838 in Vaishali).

Each of the CBHI schemes has been designed as a cluster randomized controlled trial (Doyle *et al.* 2011) and follows a three-wave implementation process. Each cluster is designed to contain an equal number of SHG-affiliated households and subsequently, each cluster is randomly assigned to one of the three waves of treatment. In each wave, one-third of clusters receive treatment (i.e. are offered to join the CBHI). This study is based on data relating to the SHG households that joined in

Wave 1 (affiliations from March 2011) in the three locations (1335 households or 7722 individuals)

The two states where the CBHI schemes are located, Uttar Pradesh (UP) and Bihar, are among India's most populated, poorest and least urbanized and display large gender differences.[6] All three CBHI sites are located in rural areas, about 75 km from the nearest urban centres (Figure 1).

At all locations, the project was implemented by the Delhi-based Micro Insurance Academy (MIA) in co-operation with a local non-governmental organization (NGO) or an implementing partner which has well-established relations with the SHGs.[7] In each location, the CBHI implementation followed MIA's four-phase process (initiating, involving, launch and post-launch) (Dror *et al.* 2013) that includes awareness building, insurance education, initial package design and premium pricing based on information obtained from a baseline survey, modification of package design and premium-setting on the basis of interactions with the SHGs during benefit option consultation workshops, and finally training of SHG members to manage the scheme ('creation of a local ground structure'). Following insurance education, the SHG members participated in benefit-package design through discussions within their family and at the SHG, in the form of a simulation game called CHAT (Choosing Health-plans All Together).[8] The activities were focused on female SHG members who were expected to spread information within their households and subsequently lead to enrolment of all household members in the scheme. In practice, while insurance was offered to an entire household, only some household members enrolled.

Baseline data from all eligible households were gathered during March to May 2010. Insurance education and preparatory activities took place between June 2010 and January 2011. Affiliation in wave I was open in Pratapgarh and Vaishali during February 2011. The schemes began operating in Pratapgarh and Vaishali in March 2011. No new enrolment was allowed between March 2011 and February 2012 in Pratapgarh and Vaishali. In Kanpur Dehat, affiliations were accepted in May 2011, and the scheme started operations in June 2011. No new affiliations were accepted from June 2011 to May 2012 in Kanpur Dehat.

Details on the benefit package selected at each CBHI scheme site are provided in Table 1. The packages in Pratapgarh and Kanpur Dehat are similar except that SHGs in Pratapgarh do not opt for coverage of outpatient care. Based on field experience it seems that SHGs in Pratapgarh appear to be more confident in being able to meet outpatient care expenses through OOP. SHGs in Vaishali district, which is relatively poorer as compared with the two districts in UP, opted not to include coverage of inpatient care. This may well be due to the relatively high enrolment in RSBY which covers BPL households (48%, as compared with 18% and 15%, respectively in Pratapgarh and Kanpur Dehat; see Table 2).

During the first wave of implementation, 525 households or 39% of the targeted households had at least one household member who was enrolled in the scheme (the corresponding number of individuals was 1806, or an enrolment rate of 23%). These figures translate into an insurance coverage of about 3.44 (1806/525) members per insured household. Given the average household size of 5.78 this implies that conditional on enrolment, 60% of a household is covered.

Figure 1 Location of the three CBHI projects

A closer look reveals considerable variation in enrolment across the three locations, ranging from 29% of households (15% of the individuals) in Kanpur Dehat to 46% (and 30%) in Vaishali, with Pratapgarh lying in the middle. Several factors may explain these differences. First, and perhaps most importantly, in Pratapgarh and Vaishali, the implementing partners have introduced innovations to enhance uptake; e.g. in

Table 1 CBHI schemes—enrolment and features of the scheme

Indicators	Pratapgarh	Kanpur Dehat	Vaishali
Scheme Name			
	Sanjivani	Jeevan Sanjivani	Swastha Kamal
Enrolment indicators			
Households offered insurance	433	378	524
At least one member of household is enrolled	174	109	242
Enrolment rate for households (%)	40	29	46
Individuals offered insurance	2594	2264	2864
Individuals enrolled	604	334	868
Enrolment rate for individuals (%)	23	15	30
Annual CBHI premium per person/per year (Rs)	176	192	197
Coverage for hospitalization			
Fees (cap per person per event, Rs)	6000	3000	–
Wage loss (per day, Rs)[a]	100	75	100
Transport (maximum coverage per episode, Rs)[b]	100	100	–
Coverage for outpatient care			
Fees (Rs)	–	Unlimited	Unlimited
Lab tests (per year, Rs)[c]	–	–	200
Imaging tests (per year, Rs)[c]	–	–	300
Coverage for maternity care			
Caesarean (per episode, Rs)	5000	–	–

Dashes indicate 'not included in package'.
[a]For Pratapgarh wages losses covered for the 3rd to 6th day, for Kanpur Dehat 4th to 13th day, for Vaishali 4th to 9th day.
[b]For hospitalization of more than 24 hours.
[c]Maximum amount, per person per year.

Pratapgarh, households were required to pay 30% of the annual premium on enrolment and the balance in eight equal interest-free instalments. In Vaishali, a discount was offered when several members of the same household enrol together. Finally, geographically, both Pratapgarh and Vaishali are located closer to urban areas compared with Kanpur Dehat, which means that health-care facilities are more proximate to these two locations (see Table 2). In Kanpur Dehat, the relatively lower supply of health-care services may explain lower interest in insurance.

Analysis of the determinants of enrolment is based on combining two data sources: (1) a baseline survey, and (2) information on actual enrolments, premium payments and claims, maintained by MIA's management information system (called 'Suchna'). The baseline survey which covered all eligible households included questions on socio-economic indicators, including demographic details of each household member, household consumption expenditures and household assets. In addition, data were collected on self-reported illness events, on the treatment sought and expenditure incurred. Information was also gathered on hospitalization or pregnancy in the 12 months preceding the survey.[9]

The analysis is based on 1294 households (417, 369 and 508 in Pratapgarh, Kanpur Dehat and Vaishali, respectively) and 7659 individuals (2562, 2239 and 2858 in Pratapgarh, Kanpur Dehat and Vaishali, respectively) for which valid data could be collected in the baseline survey and which were still alive/present when the scheme was launched.

A description of the variables used, and summary statistics, is provided in Table 2. Summary statistics conditional on insurance status are shown in the supplementary data (Tables A1–D1 and A2–D2). A comparison of key socio-economic variables across the three sites suggests that households in Kanpur Dehat are somewhat better off as compared with their counterparts in Pratapgarh and Vaishali. For instance, average monthly per capita expenditure is higher by more than 50% compared with the other sites. The majority are self-employed in agriculture (66%) when in the other locations casual wage work dominates (about 40%). However, Kanpur Dehat appears to be less well served in terms of access to health services when travel time to the nearest inpatient facility is considered: almost two hours from Kanpur Dehat compared with 44 min from Pratapgarh and 29 min from Vaishali. Access to outpatient care is more readily accessible in all three locations (12–20 min) and differences across the three districts are not material.[10]

Estimating enrolment

Affiliation to CBHI is voluntary and contributory. Therefore, we assume that some households that are offered the opportunity to affiliate would decline. We estimate the probability of enrolment considering various factors that are likely to influence both the demand for health insurance and for health care in the context of the three CBHI schemes in question. Since insurance was offered at the household level, we first estimate a household-level enrolment specification. However, in practice,

Table 2 Descriptive statistics (mean and standard deviation)

Variable	Pratapgarh		Kanpur Dehat		Vaishali	
	Mean	SD	Mean	SD	Mean	SD
SC/ST = 1 if household is schedule caste/tribe	0.36	0.48	0.26	0.44	0.41	0.49
Household size	5.99	2.73	5.99	2.23	5.47	2.1
Household enrolled in RSBY = 1	0.18	0.38	0.15	0.36	0.48	0.5
Quintile 2, 20–40 percentile based on monthly per capita expenditure – excluding health expenditure (Poor) = 1	0.24	0.43	0.13	0.34	0.21	0.41
Quintile 3, 40–60 percentile based on monthly per capita expenditure – excluding health expenditure (Middle) = 1	0.18	0.39	0.19	0.39	0.22	0.41
Quintile 4, 60–80 percentile based on monthly per capita expenditure – excluding health expenditure (Rich) = 1	0.19	0.39	0.25	0.43	0.17	0.38
Quintile 5, 80–100 percentile based on monthly per capita expenditure – excluding health expenditure (Richest) = 1	0.14	0.35	0.33	0.47	0.16	0.37
Per capita financial liability (monthly) in Rupees	333	479	459	838	467	1150
Per capita expenditure (monthly) in Rupees	1128	665	1793	1653	1205	947
If household pools income = 1	0.88	0.33	0.85	0.36	0.68	0.47
Joint family = 1	0.53	0.5	0.45	0.5	0.37	0.48
Household head age	46.18	12.98	44.87	12.37	41.94	12.48
Household head is male = 1	0.76	0.43	0.89	0.31	0.77	0.42
Household head has primary education = 1	0.18	0.38	0.12	0.32	0.16	0.37
Household head has middle level of education = 1	0.19	0.39	0.14	0.35	0.14	0.35
Household head has secondary education = 1	0.32	0.47	0.45	0.5	0.26	0.44
Household head is self-employed in agriculture = 1	0.21	0.41	0.66	0.47	0.18	0.39
Household head is self-employed in non-agriculture = 1	0.14	0.35	0.06	0.23	0.18	0.39
Household head is employed in other occupations (mainly casual wage work) = 1	0.4	0.49	0.14	0.35	0.4	0.49
Average time taken to reach the health facility in case of inpatient care	44.06	34.34	129.69	86.17	29.34	21.83
Average time taken to reach the health facility in case of outpatient care	19.31	11.56	12.02	17.23	15.73	27.72
Number of long-term illness events in the household, ill for more than 30 days	1.44	1	0.72	0.86	0.73	0.85
Number of short-term illness events in the household, ill for less than 30 days	1.18	1.12	1.33	1.06	1.08	0.99
Number of cases of hospitalization in the household in the last 12 months	0.14	0.4	0.19	0.49	0.18	0.43
Presence of child below 12 years in household = 1	0.78	342.81	0.75	0.43	0.85	0.36
Presence of adult above 65 in household = 1	0.26	0.41	0.19	0.39	0.19	0.4
Number of observations	433		378		524	

since households selected which members would be insured, we also estimate an individual-level specification.

Based on these considerations the insurance enrolment status of household *h* in location *j*, may be written as,

$$CBHI_{hj} = \alpha' SES_{hj} + \beta' FIRP_{hj} + \gamma' SS_{hj} + \delta' HE_{hj} + \varepsilon_{hj}, \quad (1)$$

where, $CBHI_{hj}$ is a binary variable with a value of 1 if at least one member of a household is enrolled in the CBHI scheme, and 0 otherwise. Socio-economic status (*SES*) is a set of variables that includes caste, age, gender, education and employment status of the head of the household and the expenditure quintile in which a household falls. Specifically, to assess the effect of economic conditions on enrolment, households were grouped into quintiles based on their monthly per capita consumption expenditure (MPCE) (excluding illness-related expenditures). *FIRP* (formal health insurance and risk-pooling) includes access to formal health insurance notably RSBY enrolment status, type of family (joint or nuclear), size of household and whether incomes are pooled within a household. This set of variables also includes current household monthly per capita financial liabilities (debt) which may provide an idea of a household's ability to borrow and cope with ill-health but it may also reflect the vulnerability of a household. To assess the effects of supply side (*SS*) factors we include two variables—travel time to the nearest inpatient and outpatient facility. Finally, to account for the incidence of past and potential illnesses on enrolment status we include a set of variables indicating the total number of past health events (*HE*) (short-term illnesses, long-term illnesses, hospitalization) experienced by members of the household and variables to capture the age profile of the household (presence of children younger than 12 years and adults older than 65 years).

To explore intra-household resource allocation we turn to an individual specification where the enrolment status of individual *i* in household *h* in location *j*, may be written as,

$$CBHI_{ihj} = \alpha' SES_{hj} + \beta' FIRP_{hj} + \gamma' SS_{hj} + \varphi' I_{ihj} + \varepsilon_{ihj}, \quad (2)$$

where, in addition to most of the variables included in (1) we add a set of individual traits (*I*) such as SHG member, age, gender, marital status, education, employment status, relation to head of household, individual illness events and self-assessed health status (SAHS).[11] Since SAHS is only available for individuals aged 13 years and above, we estimate variants of (2) with and without imposing this age restriction. Both (1) and (2) are estimated using a logit specification. In the case of (2), standard errors allow for intra-household correlations.

Results

Household-level marginal effect estimates based on a logit specification are provided in Table 3 while individual-level estimates are provided in Tables 4 and 5. Estimates are provided for all three locations separately and also for the pooled data.

Household-level estimates

Belonging to an economically and socially disadvantaged community (SC/ST) increased affiliation to the CBHI by 13 percentage points in Pratapgarh, but was statistically insignificant in the other two sites.[12] It is perhaps more important to state that in none of the three locations was there any evidence that low-caste communities were less likely to join a CBHI scheme. The effect of economic conditions of households on affiliations was analysed by grouping households into quintiles based on their monthly per capita consumption expenditure (excluding illness-related expenditures). In Pratapgarh, the households within the second and third quintile were substantially more likely to enrol (about 18–22 percentage points) as compared with the lowest quintile. In the other two sites there is no evidence that the poorest are less likely to enrol as compared with other quintiles. Other characteristics which indicate a household's socio-economic status are the education and occupation of its household head. While there is some evidence that household heads with some primary education, as compared with those who are illiterate, are more likely to join a CBHI scheme, the effect is restricted to Vaishali. Occupational status seems to have no bearing on insurance status. The main point emerging from this set of variables ('SES') is that the evidence does not suggest that the CBHI scheme is inaccessible even to the poorest households living in some of the poorest parts of rural India.

Turning to the set of variables clustered under FIRP, we find that belonging to a joint family or a larger household has no bearing on CBHI uptake. However, intra-household pooling of income, which is an indicator of risk-pooling and can help smooth consumption in the event of a shock, exerts a negative and large effect on enrolment. Households engaged in such pooling are about 11 percentage points less likely to join insurance with the effects emanating mainly from Pratapgarh (30 percentage point effect) and Kanpur Dehat (19 percentage point). In Vaishali the effect is also negative but small and statistically insignificant. Household financial liabilities may indicate household ability to access credit, which may have a negative effect on CBHI enrolment. On the other hand it may also be interpreted as a signal of inability to deal with past shocks through informal risk-pooling and hence the need for borrowing and in turn may have a positive effect on enrolment. Indeed, in two of the three sites, high household debt is positively linked to CBHI uptake. In Pratapgarh, a one standard deviation increase in financial liability (about Rs 500) is associated with a 7.2 percentage point increase (500×0.0154). In the case of Vaishali the figure is about 8.2 percentage points (1150×0.00711). Given the lack of development of credit markets in rural India and the usurious interest rates often charged by money lenders, outstanding household debt seems to increase risk aversion and to increase the demand for insurance. The effect of this variable highlights the need for financial protection and the need for further development of insurance markets in rural India. Finally, we see that household access to RSBY has no effect on CBHI uptake. Even in Vaishali where almost half the population is enrolled in RSBY, there is no effect on uptake. This finding supports the view that at least in the case of the schemes under analysis, national-level insurance schemes and community-based schemes are viewed as complementary in ensuring financial protection and access to health care.

While there are substantial differences in access to health services across sites, the two variables included in the specification to capture access to inpatient and outpatient care suggest that such considerations do not play a role in influencing insurance uptake. This may seem surprising but may be a feature of the participatory approach to choosing health-care plans. Since the plans cover transportation cost, at least in two sites, it is possible that this feature works towards reducing the potentially negative effect of accessibility on insurance uptake.

Turning to the effect of the incidence of past illnesses on insurance uptake we find that except for hospitalization, which increases the probability of enrolling in health insurance by 10 percentage points in Kanpur Dehat, there is no evidence that household decision-making is motivated by previous illness. However, households with children seem to be more risk averse and/or expect a higher need for health care and subsequently more likely to want to join insurance. The marginal effects are large (17 to 20 percentage point increase) in Pratapgarh and Vaishali. Finally, the marginal effect of older individuals in the family is negative (7 percentage points) and for the sample as a whole, statistically significant.

Individual-level estimates

Though we intended to apply 'en bloc' affiliation (i.e. all SHG household members would enrol together), in practice this was not followed, as households claimed that paying premiums for all members was too onerous. As we have seen, there is no evidence that even the poorest households are dissuaded from enrolling due to economic considerations, but there may well be systematic disparities within a household which lead to the exclusion of the aged, as well as the systematic inclusion of some members (children, those with poor health conditions). To explore these patterns, two variants of (2) are estimated. One of these is for the full sample and a second is restricted to the household members aged 13 years and above, since we only have information on self-assessed health status for such individuals.

The inclusion of the additional individual traits does not alter any of the earlier findings made based on the household-level estimates. There are several points which may be gleaned from

Table 3 Logit regression marginal effect estimates (standard errors) at the household level

Variable description	Pratapgarh	Kanpur Dehat	Vaishali	All
Household socio-economic status				
Caste				
Schedule caste/schedule tribe	0.127**	−0.0357	0.0653	0.0715**
	(0.0611)	*(0.0554)*	*(0.0520)*	*(0.0319)*
Economic status				
Poor by MPCE (quintile 2)	0.179**	0.0205	−0.0397	0.0381
	(0.0779)	*(0.127)*	*(0.0693)*	*(0.0452)*
Middle by MPCE (quintile 3)	0.219**	0.197	0.00237	0.0761
	(0.0885)	*(0.128)*	*(0.0703)*	*(0.0471)*
Rich by MPCE (quintile 4)	0.134	0.166	−0.0664	0.0287
	(0.0906)	*(0.124)*	*(0.0769)*	*(0.0484)*
Richest by MPCE (quintile 5)	0.0932	0.169	0.0516	0.0575
	(0.104)	*(0.119)*	*(0.0894)*	*(0.0522)*
Household head characteristics				
Household head				
Age	0.00186	0.000409	−0.000428	0.000747
	(0.00255)	*(0.00236)*	*(0.00237)*	*(0.00135)*
Male	−0.0465	−0.0554	−0.0464	−0.0677
	(0.0876)	*(0.106)*	*(0.0750)*	*(0.0476)*
Education				
Primary	0.105	0.0753	0.129*	0.133***
	(0.0868)	*(0.0916)*	*(0.0692)*	*(0.0450)*
Middle	0.0987	−0.0284	0.0274	0.0651
	(0.0884)	*(0.0792)*	*(0.0728)*	*(0.0454)*
Secondary and above	0.100	0.0133	0.0128	0.0609
	(0.0830)	*(0.0642)*	*(0.0671)*	*(0.0404)*
Employment				
Self-employed in agriculture	0.0831	0.00598	−0.0164	0.0119
	(0.0896)	*(0.0902)*	*(0.0829)*	*(0.0478)*
Self-employed in non-agriculture	0.0282	−0.00847	−0.142	−0.0534
	(0.102)	*(0.134)*	*(0.0823)*	*(0.0542)*
Other work (mainly casual wage work)	0.0869	0.0329	−0.0690	−0.00107
	(0.0848)	*(0.115)*	*(0.0772)*	*(0.0474)*
Formal insurance and risk pooling				
Joint family	−0.00281	−0.0237	0.0618	0.0147
	(0.0633)	*(0.0596)*	*(0.0629)*	*(0.0353)*
Shares income of all members	−0.300***	−0.194**	−0.0508	−0.111***
	(0.0820)	*(0.0793)*	*(0.0520)*	*(0.0365)*
Household size	−0.00566	0.00608	0.00351	0.00137
	(0.0135)	*(0.0157)*	*(0.0158)*	*(0.00799)*
Monthly per capita liability	0.000154**	0.00000043	0.0000711*	0.0000178
	(0.0000732)	*(0.0000298)*	*(0.0000391)*	*(0.0000177)*
Household enrolled in RSBY	0.0105	0.0190	0.00515	0.00782
	(0.0670)	*(0.0711)*	*(0.0493)*	*(0.0332)*
Supply-side indicators				
Average travel time for inpatient service	0.000972	0.0000763	0.00195	0.000344
	(0.000778)	*(0.000297)*	*(0.00111)*	*(0.000288)*
Average travel time for outpatient service	0.000515	0.000617	−0.00197	0.000322
	(0.00233)	*(0.000755)*	*(0.00148)*	*(0.000695)*

(continued)

Table 3 Continued

Variable description	Pratapgarh	Kanpur Dehat	Vaishali	All
Locational characteristics				
Pratapgarh				0.155***
				(0.0509)
Vaishali				0.201***
				(0.0509)
Age profile of household				
Presence of children <12 years	0.173***	−0.0695	0.197***	0.0899**
	(0.0619)	*(0.0699)*	*(0.0704)*	*(0.0388)*
Presence of adult >65 years	−0.0609	−0.102	−0.0223	−0.0690*
	(0.0688)	*(0.0624)*	*(0.0695)*	*(0.0383)*
Household's health events				
Number of long-term illness events	0.0387	0.0173	−0.00679	0.0183
	(0.0284)	*(0.0303)*	*(0.0299)*	*(0.0164)*
Number of short-term illness events	0.0396	−0.0141	0.0143	0.0161
	(0.0265)	*(0.0239)*	*(0.0246)*	*(0.0140)*
Number of hospitalization cases	0.00565	0.0987**	−0.0685	0.00801
	(0.0673)	*(0.0499)*	*(0.0565)*	*(0.0326)*
Observations	417	369	508	1294
Pseudo R^2	0.0814	0.0587	0.0518	0.0408

Note: ***$P < 0.01$, **$P < 0.05$, *$P < 0.1$.

these estimates. As may be expected and as the programme design requires, for the overall sample, SHG members are about 20 percentage points more likely to enrol in the scheme as compared with non-SHG members. With regard to intra-household priorities, across all three sites we see that household heads are substantially more likely (25 to 28 percentage points higher) to be covered as compared with 'other' household members (parents of head, siblings of the household head, spouses of siblings, in-laws of head, other relatives, non-relatives). Spouses of household heads, who are predominantly female and SHG members,[13] are 19 to 27 percentage points more likely to be covered as compared with 'others'. Notably, female children of the household head are as likely to be enrolled, if not more, as compared with their male counterparts (20 to 25 percentage points higher for female children and 18 to 22 percentage points higher for male children as compared with 'others'). Spouses of children of household head receive less priority as compared with the household head and his spouse, although more than other relatives, while grandchildren seem to be at the same level as 'other' members. The pattern supports the idea that vertical relationships tend to receive greater priority in terms of coverage as compared with horizontal and that the household head and his spouse receive the greatest priority within a household.

With regard to previous episodes of illness, while there are some instances, especially in Pratapgarh where individuals who have experienced short- or long-term illnesses during the baseline survey are more likely to be insured (5 to 6 percentage points higher), overall, it does not seem that such events play a large role in determining who is insured within a household. Estimates in Table 5 which control for illness events and self-assessed health status also do not support the idea that individuals with lower health status are more likely to be insured.

Conclusions

In India, illness-related expenditures have been identified as a key factor responsible for impoverishing vulnerable households. In the absence of a national insurance system covering all persons in the informal sector, CBHI has been proposed as a viable mechanism to achieve some degree of financial protection. This article analysed the factors that determine insurance uptake in three CBHI schemes that have been rolled out in two Indian states since 2011.

Affiliation to the CBHI schemes is offered to households and all their members through women's self-help groups. While focusing on such a target group limits the generalizability of our findings it also permits a focus on low-income groups. Indeed, since women participating in SHGs are typically from lower-income groups, this roll-out model is by design less susceptible to social exclusion on the basis of low income or low caste. Also, since CBHI is offered to groups who have come together for a different purpose, extending the social links that have already been established for other purposes (e.g. membership in SHG) reduces both the potential and the practical occurrence of adverse selection.

This article yielded several clear insights. There are sharp differences in uptake across the three sites, and we saw that local innovations in the business process, such as deferred payment plans and discounts for bulk purchases, created more attractive conditions for affiliation to the specific CBHI schemes. These innovations were possible because each CBHI was governed by its members, who were also involved in the design of benefit packages, pricing and claims settlement.

Table 4 Logit regression marginal effect estimates (standard errors) at the individual level

Variable description	Pratapgarh	Kanpur Dehat	Vaishali	All
Household socio-economic status				
Caste				
Schedule caste/schedule tribe	0.0913**	−0.0254	0.0784**	0.0565***
	(0.0387)	*(0.0267)*	*(0.0364)*	*(0.0203)*
Economic status				
Poor by MPCE	0.126**	0.0258	−0.00141	0.0422
	(0.0565)	*(0.0742)*	*(0.0490)*	*(0.0307)*
Middle by MPCE	0.176**	0.0962	0.0433	0.0748**
	(0.0704)	*(0.0717)*	*(0.0515)*	*(0.0326)*
Rich by MPCE	0.106	0.0835	−0.0460	0.0217
	(0.0707)	*(0.0631)*	*(0.0497)*	*(0.0316)*
Richest by MPCE	0.131*	0.113*	0.0531	0.0812**
	(0.0742)	*(0.0630)*	*(0.0647)*	*(0.0353)*
Formal and informal insurance (or risk) arrangement				
Joint family	0.0128	−0.0124	0.0684	0.0185
	(0.0398)	*(0.0313)*	*(0.0454)*	*(0.0225)*
Shares income of all members	−0.112**	−0.0885**	−0.0278	−0.0547**
	(0.0545)	*(0.0424)*	*(0.0369)*	*(0.0238)*
Household size	−0.00129	−0.00697	−0.0130	−0.00493
	(0.00543)	*(0.00627)*	*(0.0102)*	*(0.00409)*
Monthly per capita financial liability	−5.42e−05	6.30e−06	0.0000177**	8.42e−06
	(3.47e−05)	*(1.73e−05)*	*(7.05e−06)*	*(6.37e−06)*
Household enrolled in RSBY	−0.0266	−0.0118	−0.0155	−0.0169
	(0.0343)	*(0.0326)*	*(0.0343)*	*(0.0198)*
Supply-side indicators				
Average travel time for inpatient service	0.000791*	−5.38e−06	−2.20e−05	0.000170
	(0.000412)	*(0.000148)*	*(0.000732)*	*(0.000189)*
Average travel time for outpatient service	−0.000272	4.96e−05	−0.00130	−0.000226
	(0.00131)	*(0.000333)*	*(0.00101)*	*(0.000413)*
Locational characteristics				
Pratapgarh				0.128***
				(0.0344)
Vaishali				0.164***
				(0.0361)
Age profile of household				
Presence of children <12 years	0.102***	−0.0216	0.115**	0.0587**
	(0.0330)	*(0.0318)*	*(0.0479)*	*(0.0230)*
Presence of adult >65 years	−0.0145	0.00297	−0.0188	−0.00960
	(0.0420)	*(0.0375)*	*(0.0473)*	*(0.0248)*
Individual characteristics				
SHG membership	0.197***	0.133***	0.327***	0.222***
	(0.0358)	*(0.0358)*	*(0.0580)*	*(0.0247)*
Age	0.000351	−0.000544	0.00146	0.000532
	(0.00124)	*(0.000950)*	*(0.00136)*	*(0.000701)*
Gender				
Male	0.0339	0.0414	0.0339	0.0313
	(0.0340)	*(0.0381)*	*(0.0451)*	*(0.0225)*

(continued)

Table 4 Continued

Variable description	Pratapgarh	Kanpur Dehat	Vaishali	All
Marital status				
Married	0.0242	0.0661**	0.0287	0.0405*
	(0.0394)	*(0.0275)*	*(0.0520)*	*(0.0231)*
Relation to head				
Head	0.255***	0.245***	0.280***	0.264***
	(0.0915)	*(0.0817)*	*(0.103)*	*(0.0518)*
Male spouse of head	0.328	0.252	0.334**	0.307***
	(0.219)	*(0.169)*	*(0.141)*	*(0.0921)*
Female spouse of head	0.271**	0.189**	0.213*	0.232***
	(0.106)	*(0.0823)*	*(0.118)*	*(0.0578)*
Male child of head	0.196**	0.0966	0.220*	0.179***
	(0.0918)	*(0.0623)*	*(0.114)*	*(0.0525)*
Female child of head	0.248**	0.200**	0.248**	0.233***
	(0.107)	*(0.0906)*	*(0.106)*	*(0.0576)*
Spouse of child of head	0.273**	0.100	0.0714	0.163**
	(0.120)	*(0.106)*	*(0.114)*	*(0.0641)*
Grandchild of head	0.0877	0.0524	–0.0284	0.0383
	(0.117)	*(0.106)*	*(0.121)*	*(0.0633)*
Education				
Primary	0.0356	0.00422	0.0293	0.0345*
	(0.0350)	*(0.0220)*	*(0.0322)*	*(0.0179)*
Middle	0.0170	–0.0174	0.0201	0.0141
	(0.0337)	*(0.0190)*	*(0.0338)*	*(0.0176)*
Secondary and above	–0.00363	–0.0242	0.0517	0.0102
	(0.0355)	*(0.0198)*	*(0.0415)*	*(0.0196)*
Employment				
Self-employed	0.0185	–0.0134	–0.0236	–0.00341
	(0.0365)	*(0.0194)*	*(0.0367)*	*(0.0183)*
Other employment	0.00811	–0.0233	–0.0550	–0.0329
	(0.0318)	*(0.0305)*	*(0.0350)*	*(0.0181)*
Student	0.114**	0.0757**	0.224***	0.139***
	(0.0479)	*(0.0378)*	*(0.0606)*	*(0.0298)*
Pre-school children	0.108	0.0515	0.271***	0.171***
	(0.0691)	*(0.0487)*	*(0.0743)*	*(0.0413)*
Individual health indicators				
Number of long-term illness events	0.0468**	0.00820	–0.00873	0.0198
	(0.0224)	*(0.0231)*	*(0.0281)*	*(0.0147)*
Number of short-term illness events	0.0607***	0.000473	–0.00961	0.00453
	(0.0195)	*(0.00694)*	*(0.0109)*	*(0.00654)*
Number of hospitalization cases	0.0239	0.0210	0.0361	0.0260
	(0.0411)	*(0.0322)*	*(0.0454)*	*(0.0246)*
Number of pregnancy cases	0.0338	0.0273	0.0595	0.0349
	(0.0512)	*(0.0376)*	*(0.0511)*	*(0.0277)*
Observations	2562	2239	2858	7659
Pseudo R^2	0.0831	0.098	0.074	0.0806

Note: ***$P < 0.01$, **$P < 0.05$, *$P < 0.1$

Table 5 Logit regression marginal effect estimates (standard errors) at the individual level

Variable Description	Pratapgarh	Kanpur Dehat	Vaishali	All
Household socio-economic status				
Caste				
Schedule caste/schedule tribe	0.0886**	−0.0313	0.0409	0.0384*
	(0.0414)	*(0.0257)*	*(0.0371)*	*(0.0206)*
Economic status				
Poor by MPCE	0.139**	−0.0120	−0.0317	0.0325
	(0.0619)	*(0.0605)*	*(0.0468)*	*(0.0313)*
Middle by MPCE	0.196***	0.0913	−0.000954	0.0627*
	(0.0755)	*(0.0767)*	*(0.0508)*	*(0.0339)*
Rich by MPCE	0.118	0.0777	−0.0481	0.0295
	(0.0743)	*(0.0644)*	*(0.0507)*	*(0.0331)*
Richest by MPCE	0.137*	0.0873	0.0454	0.0704**
	(0.0769)	*(0.0611)*	*(0.0638)*	*(0.0353)*
Formal and informal insurance (or risk) arrangement				
Joint family	0.00955	0.00673	0.0130	0.00641
	(0.0402)	*(0.0308)*	*(0.0463)*	*(0.0223)*
Shares income of all members	−0.0984*	−0.119**	−0.0142	−0.0588**
	(0.0559)	*(0.0480)*	*(0.0372)*	*(0.0244)*
Household size	−0.000934	−0.00498	−0.00674	−0.00250
	(0.00563)	*(0.00664)*	*(0.0109)*	*(0.00407)*
Monthly per capita financial liability	−3.04e−05	1.20e−05	0.0000228***	0.0000136**
	(3.17e−05)	*(1.78e−05)*	*(6.32e−06)*	*(6.73e−06)*
Household enrolled in RSBY	−0.0162	−0.000848	−0.00535	−0.00660
	(0.0385)	*(0.0330)*	*(0.0350)*	*(0.0209)*
Supply-side Indicators				
Average travel time for inpatient service	0.000521	−5.06e−05	0.000834	0.000116
	(0.000418)	*(0.000154)*	*(0.000706)*	*(0.000189)*
Average travel time for outpatient service	0.000596	0.000174	−0.00171	−8.88e−05
	(0.00143)	*(0.000341)*	*(0.00115)*	*(0.000435)*
Locational characteristics				
Pratapgarh				0.108***
				(0.0351)
Vaishali				0.138***
				(0.0382)
Age profile of household				
Presence of children <12 years	0.0896**	−0.0379	0.109**	0.0471**
	(0.0368)	*(0.0340)*	*(0.0489)*	*(0.0238)*
Presence of adult >65 years	0.00815	−0.0144	−0.0146	−0.0109
	(0.0450)	*(0.0360)*	*(0.0460)*	*(0.0248)*
Individual characteristics				
SHG membership	0.191***	0.116***	0.337***	0.205***
	(0.0350)	*(0.0297)*	*(0.0645)*	*(0.0235)*
Age	−0.000261	−0.000230	0.00156	0.000484
	(0.00114)	*(0.00103)*	*(0.00137)*	*(0.000691)*
Gender				
Male	0.0321	−0.00507	0.0613	0.0175
	(0.0464)	*(0.0431)*	*(0.0643)*	*(0.0287)*

(continued)

Table 5 Continued

Variable Description	Pratapgarh	Kanpur Dehat	Vaishali	All
Marital status				
Married	0.0236	0.0709***	0.0353	0.0429**
	(0.0390)	*(0.0241)*	*(0.0472)*	*(0.0214)*
Relation to head				
Head	0.116**	0.258***	0.194**	0.182***
	(0.0588)	*(0.0756)*	*(0.0905)*	*(0.0395)*
Male spouse of head	0.182	0.362*	0.212	0.217**
	(0.195)	*(0.189)*	*(0.149)*	*(0.0887)*
Female spouse of head	0.134*	0.180**	0.132	0.149***
	(0.0739)	*(0.0715)*	*(0.103)*	*(0.0447)*
Male child of head	0.0106	0.111	0.126	0.0781*
	(0.0552)	*(0.0749)*	*(0.106)*	*(0.0429)*
Female child of head	0.0611	0.158*	0.246**	0.137***
	(0.0679)	*(0.0954)*	*(0.118)*	*(0.0502)*
Spouse of child of head	0.105	0.0729	0.0536	0.0908*
	(0.0725)	*(0.0858)*	*(0.102)*	*(0.0465)*
Education				
Primary	0.0257	−0.000144	0.0250	0.0268
	(0.0378)	*(0.0252)*	*(0.0408)*	*(0.0210)*
Middle	0.0364	0.00259	6.72e−05	0.0217
	(0.0378)	*(0.0244)*	*(0.0379)*	*(0.0199)*
Secondary and above	0.0222	−0.00332	0.0228	0.0186
	(0.0397)	*(0.0246)*	*(0.0437)*	*(0.0214)*
Employment				
Self-employed	0.0213	−0.000407	−0.0167	0.00277
	(0.0369)	*(0.0220)*	*(0.0359)*	*(0.0185)*
Other employment	0.0120	−0.00770	−0.0461	−0.0190
	(0.0327)	*(0.0339)*	*(0.0354)*	*(0.0189)*
Student	0.0985*	0.101**	0.258***	0.153***
	(0.0524)	*(0.0477)*	*(0.0681)*	*(0.0341)*
Individual health indicators				
Number long-term illness events	0.0413*	0.00191	0.00359	0.0195
	(0.0234)	*(0.0258)*	*(0.0331)*	*(0.0159)*
Number of short-term illness events	0.0638***	0.00272	−0.00173	0.0104
	(0.0242)	*(0.00751)*	*(0.0148)*	*(0.00791)*
Number of hospitalization cases	0.0344	−0.00416	0.0473	0.0297
	(0.0448)	*(0.0379)*	*(0.0511)*	*(0.0270)*
Number of pregnancy cases	0.0256	0.0262	0.0455	0.0313
	(0.0510)	*(0.0382)*	*(0.0507)*	*(0.0270)*
Self-assessed health rank				
Very good	0.0215	−0.0214	0.0404	0.00995
	(0.0593)	*(0.0397)*	*(0.0643)*	*(0.0330)*
Good	0.0336	−0.0320	0.0612	0.0187
	(0.0565)	*(0.0345)*	*(0.0639)*	*(0.0315)*
Moderate	−0.00288	−0.0136	−0.0351	−0.0158
	(0.0579)	*(0.0380)*	*(0.0575)*	*(0.0314)*
Observations	1748	1562	1678	4988
Pseudo R^2	0.0875	0.1233	0.0986	0.0878

Note: $^{***}P < 0.01$, $^{**}P < 0.05$, $^{*}P < 0.1$.

Another noteworthy insight is that, only at one of the sites did we find evidence that a household's economic position (as indicated by monthly per capita expenditure) limited the propensity to join the CBHI. Nor do any of the other socio-economic related variables, e.g. education and occupational status, limit access to the local CBHI scheme. Indeed, in the case of one of the schemes, SC/ST households are more likely to enrol. Additionally, based on the finding that past illnesses and self-assessed health status did not influence insurance uptake, we conclude that adverse selection is not a major issue. These two findings are in marked contrast to the bulk of the literature, as reviewed in Mebratie *et al.* (2012), which shows that often the lowest-income groups are excluded from CBHI schemes (in 9 out of 14 cases) and that individuals suffering from pre-existing health conditions/poor health are more likely to join CBHI schemes (in six out of seven cases).

Access to existing formal insurance and risk pooling mechanisms has a bearing on uptake; households that were better protected against financial risks through income pooling within their family network were less likely to enrol. On the other hand, households with greater financial liabilities found CBHI more attractive, and interestingly, enrolment in RSBY did not reduce enrolment to CBHI. Together these two aspects highlight (1) the need for greater development of self-governed and context-relevant insurance solutions that respond to perceived priorities of the population living and working in rural India; and (2) the importance of designing benefit packages which can complement existing insurance schemes.[14]

In terms of allocating household resources to pay the CBHI premium, there is a clear pecking order, with household head and spouse of the household head occupying the top slots, followed by their children—both male and female. There is no evidence that female children are less likely to be covered as compared with male children. Siblings of household heads and their wives are far less likely to be covered. These patterns suggest that access to CBHI reflects subtle intra-household prioritization decisions, which cannot simply be explained by generalities such as income, age and gender-related exclusion.

Based on the analysis reported here, we conclude that offering CBHI through women's SHGs mitigates common concerns that CBHI might be unsustainable or not sufficiently inclusive. Given the pan-Indian spread of SHGs, providing demand-driven and context-adapted CBHI schemes through SHGs and similar groups may be potentially an effective channel to scale up affordable access to health care through health insurance among India's rural poor.

Supplementary data

Supplementary data are available at *Health, Policy and Planning* online.

Acknowledgements

Research reported in this article has been funded by the European Union's FP7 programme, project–Community-Based Health Insurance in India, HEALTH-F2-2009-223518. The first author thanks ICSSR and NWO-WOTRO, for a visiting research fellowship which supported travel to the Netherlands (project no W07.04.030.231).

Conflict of interest

None declared.

Endnotes

[1] In the Indian context, it is estimated that in 2009–10, about 26% of the population had access to some form of health insurance either through the government, including the recently launched 'RSBY' (National Health Insurance Programme), or private insurance providers (Planning Commission 2012a).

[2] Recent studies which discuss various aspects of the RSBY scheme are Desai (2009), Prinja *et al.* (2012), Lagomarsino *et al.* (2012) and Rathi *et al.* (2012).

[3] Typically, such schemes are non-profit initiatives, and are intended for low-income households living in rural areas and/or for households living in urban areas and working in the informal sector. The schemes are designed to finance access to health care through a greater involvement of the target population (the community) in the design, management and governance of the scheme as compared to commercial or social health insurance schemes (Dror and Preker 2002).

[4] A self-help group (SHG) usually consists of between 10 and 20 poor women living in the same village who come together and agree to save a specific amount each period (see NABARD 2003). The savings of all SHG members are combined and deposited in a bank or a co-operative organization. Members may borrow from the pooled savings when the SHG agrees to give the loans. SHGs are usually supported and trained by NGOs. According to Garikipati (2012), there are about 40 million SHG members in India.

[5] The baseline data collected for the project confirms that the monthly per capita expenditure (proxy for income) of SHG members was about 6% lower than that of a comparator group composed of randomly surveyed non-SHG members in the same locations; and that educational attainment of the SHG members was about 7% lower than the comparator group.

[6] According to Census of India 2011, UP is India's most populated state (with close to 200 million) and Bihar is the third most populated state in the country (104 million). Literacy rates in UP and Bihar are 70 and 64%, respectively (compared with a national average of 74%). Bihar records the lowest literacy rate amongst the country's 35 states/union territories while UP is ranked 29 out of 35. Both states rank in the bottom five in terms of female literacy rates (59 and 53% in UP and Bihar, respectively). Male literacy rates are 65.5 and 73.4% in UP and Bihar, respectively. Both states are predominantly rural with 78 (UP) and 89 (Bihar)% of the population living in rural areas. Based on data from the Planning Commission (2012b) the incidence of poverty in UP is 37.7% and in Bihar it is 53.5% (compared with a national average of 29.8%).

[7] The three NGOs are Bharatiya Agro Industrial Foundation (BAIF) in Pratapgarh, *Shramik Bharti* in Kanpur Dehat and *Nidan* in Vaishali. Each implementing partner managed a pre-existing network of SHGs in the project area. For further details on project implementation see http://www.microinsuranceacademy.org/content/developing-efficient-responsive-community-based-health-insurance-cbhi-india.

[8] CHAT is a game-like tool, developed by MIA, which is designed to help communities manage the trade-offs, when considering health-care benefits. This tool allows community members to jointly choose the benefit package that is most relevant to their needs. The community members are provided with different options for benefit packages, which are based on actuarial calculations derived from the baseline data. The premium and benefits take into account local health-care costs, availability of facilities and risk of different health problems in the community, along with their socio-economic conditions. In the first stage of the CHAT exercise,

the community members choose a benefit package based on their family needs and based on discussions with their family members. Thereafter, the community members come together and mutually decide (sometimes on the basis of voting) on a single benefit package. This multiple-round exercise also enhances their knowledge of the CBHI scheme.

[9] Data collection was subcontracted to a professional data collection company, Sigma Research and Consulting; MIA supervised the collection process together with the implementing partner NGO. Approximately 20% of the questionnaires, randomly chosen, were verified in the field, and questionnaires re-administered, if needed. Data was electronically captured and verified in the field. Hard copies of the completed questionnaires are retained by MIA.

[10] The average distance to the nearest inpatient facilities is 9 km in the case of Pratapgarh, 44 km in the case of Kanpur Dehat and 4 km in Vaishali. For outpatient care, the corresponding figures are 1.7, 5.2 and 1.5 km for Pratapgarh, Kanpur Dehat and Vaishali, respectively.

[11] Health status is rated as good, moderate or bad. In cases where individuals were not present, a household member provided a response.

[12] SC/STs comprise 70% and 60% of the poorest 20% of the monthly per capita expenditure distribution in Pratapgarh and overall.

[13] Ninety-four per cent of the spouses of the household head are female and of them 91% are members of an SHG.

[14] At the moment the government is examining the possibility of extending access to outpatient care through the RSBY programme (see MoLE/GIZ 2012).

References

Ahuja R. 2005. *Health Insurance for the Poor In India: An Analytical Study*. ICRIER working paper. New Delhi: Indian Council for Research and International Economic Relations (ICRIER).

Axelson H, Bales S, Minh PD, Ekman B, Gerdtham U. 2009. Health financing for the poor produces promising short-term effects on utilization and out-of-pocket expenditure: evidence from Vietnam. *International Journal for Equity in Health* **8**: 1–17.

Bendig M, Arun T. 2011. *Enrolment in micro life and health insurance: evidences from Sri Lanka*. IZA Discussion Paper Series No 5427. Bonn: Institute for the Study of Labor.

Berman P, Ahuja R, Bhandari L. 2010. The impoverishing effect of healthcare payments in India: new methodology and findings. *Economic and Political Weekly* **45**: 65–71.

Bhat R, Jain N. 2006. *Factoring Affecting the Demand for Health Insurance in a Micro Insurance Scheme*. IIMA Working Paper No 2006-07-02. Ahmedabad: Indian Institute of Management Ahmedabad.

Binnendijk E, Koren R, Dror DM. 2012. Hardship financing of healthcare among rural poor in Orissa, India. *BMC Health Services Research* **12**: 1–41.

Chankova S, Sulzbach S, Diop F. 2008. Impact of mutual health organizations: evidence from West Africa. *Health Policy and Planning* **23**: 264–76.

Desai S. 2009. Keeping the 'health' in health insurance. *Economic and Political Weekly* **44**: 18–21.

Doyle C, Panda P, van de Poel E, Radermacher R, Dror DM. 2011. Reconciling research and implementation in micro health insurance experiments in India: study protocol for a randomized controlled trial. *Trials Journal* **12**: 1–15.

Dror DM, Jacquier C. 1999. Micro-insurance: extending health insurance to the excluded. *International Social Security Review* **52**: 71–97.

Dror DM, Koren R, Ost A *et al*. 2007. Health insurance benefit packages prioritized by low-income clients in India: three criteria to estimate effectiveness of choice. *Social Science and Medicine* **64**: 884–96.

Dror DM, Majumdar A, Panda P, John D, Koren R. 2013. *An Implementation Model of Community-Based Health Insurance with Evidence from Two Rural Schemes in Nepal*. New Delhi: Micro Insurance Academy, Mimeo.

Dror DM, Preker A (eds). 2002. *Social Reinsurance: A New Approach to Sustainable Community Health Financing*, World Bank and ILO. http://ssrn.com/abstract=1021682, accessed 28 February 2013.

Dror DM, Radermacher R, Khadilkar SB *et al*. 2009. Microinsurance: innovations in low-cost health insurance. *Health Affairs* **28**: 1788–98.

Dror DM, Radermacher R, Koren R. 2007. Willingness to pay for health insurance among rural and poor persons: field evidence from seven micro health insurance units in India. *Health Policy* **82**: 12–27.

Dror DM, van Putten O, Koren R. 2008. Cost of illness: evidence from a study in five resource-poor locations in India. *Indian Journal of Medical Research* **127**: 347–61.

Dror DM, Vellakkal S. 2012. Is RSBY India's platform to implementing universal hospital insurance? *Indian Journal of Medical Research* **135**: 56–63.

Ekman B. 2004. Community-based health insurance in low-income countries: a systematic review of the evidence. *Health Policy and Planning* **19**: 249–70.

Garg CC, Karan A. 2009. Reducing out-of-pocket expenditures to reduce poverty: a disaggregated analysis at rural-urban and state level in India. *Economic and Political Weekly* **24**: 116–28.

Garikipati S. 2012. Microcredit and women's empowerment: through the lens of time-use data from rural India. *Development and Change* **43**: 719–50.

Gautham M, Koren R, Binnendijk E, Dror DM. 2011. First we go to the small doctor: 1st contact healthcare providers of rural communities in Andhra Pradesh and Orissa, India. *Indian Journal of Medical Research* **134**: 627–38.

Gnawali DP, Pokhrel S, Sié A *et al*. 2009. The effect of community based health insurance on the utilization of modern health care services: evidence from Burkina Faso. *Health Policy* **90**: 214–33.

Gumber A. 2001. *Hedging the Health of the Poor: the Case for Community Financing in India*. HNP Discussion Paper. Washington, DC: World Bank.

ILO/STEP, GTZ. 2006. *The Role of Microinsurance as a Tool to Face Risks in the Context of Social Protection*. http://www.ilo.org/gimi/gess/RessShowRessource.do?ressourceId=93, accessed 16 January 2013.

Ito S, Kono H. 2010. Why is the take-up of microinsurance so low? evidence from a health insurance scheme in India. *The Developing Economics* **48**: 74–101.

Jakab M, Krishnan C. 2001. *Community Involvement in Health Care Financing: A Survey of the Literature on the Impact, Strengths and Weaknesses*. HNP Discussion Paper. Washington, DC: World Bank.

Jakab M, Preker A, Krishnan C *et al*. 2001. *Social Inclusion and Financial Protection through Community Financing: Initial Results from Five Household Surveys*. HNP Discussion Paper. Washington, DC: World Bank.

James C, Savedoff W. 2010. *Risk Pooling and Redistribution in Health Care: an Empirical Analysis of Attitudes towards solidarity*. Background Paper No 5. World Health Report 2010. Geneva: World Health Organization.

Jutting J. 2004. Do community-based health insurance schemes improve poor people's access to healthcare? Evidence from rural Senegal. *World Development* **32**: 273–88.

Kruk ME, Goldmann E, Galea S. 2009. Borrowing and selling to pay for health care in low- and middle-income countries. *Health Affairs* **28**: 1056–66.

Lagomarsino G, Garabrant A, Adyas A, Muga R, Otoo N. 2012. Moving towards universal health coverage: health insurance reforms in nine developing countries in Africa and Asia. *Lancet* **380**: 933–43.

Ma S, Sood N. 2008. *A Comparison of the Health Systems in China and India.* http://www.rand.org/pubs/occasional_papers/OP212, accessed 16 January 2013.

Mebratie AD, Sparrow R, Alemu G, Bedi AS. 2012. *Community-Based Health Insurance Schemes: A Systematic Review.* Rotterdam: International Institute of Social Studies, Erasmus University. Mimeo.

Meghan S. 2010. *Micro-Finance Health Insurance in Developing Countries.* Wharton Research Scholars Working Paper. Philadelphia: University of Pennsylvania.

MoLE/GIZ. 2012. *RSBY Connect.* New Delhi, India: Ministry of Labour and Employment, Government of India and German Development Cooperation. http://uhcforward.org/sites/uhcforward.org/files/RSBY_Connect_March2012_Issue_no.2.pdf, accessed 9 July 2013.

Msuya JM, Jutting JP, Asfaw A. 2004. *Impacts of Community Health Insurance Schemes on Health Care Provision in Rural Tanzania.* ZEF – Discussion Papers on Development Policy No 82. Bonn: Center for Development Research.

NABARD. 2003. *Banking with Self-Help Groups: How and Why? A Handbook for Branch Level Bankers.* Mumbai: National Bank for Agriculture and Rural Development (NABARD).

NCMH. 2005. *Report of the National Commission of Macro Economics and Health.* New Delhi: Ministry of Health and Family Welfare, Government of India.

Planning Commission. 2012a. *Steering Committee Report for Health for 12th Five Year Plan.* New Delhi: Planning Commission, Government of India.

Planning Commission. 2012b. *Press Note on Poverty Estimates, 2009–10.* New Delhi: Planning Commission, Government of India.

Preker AS, Carrin G, Dror DM *et al.* 2002. Effectiveness of community health financing in meeting the cost of illness. *Bulletin of the World Health Organization* **80**: 143–50.

Prinja S, Kaur M, Kumar R. 2012. Universal health insurance in India: ensuring equity, efficiency, and quality. *Indian Journal of Community Medicine* **37**: 142–49.

Ranson MK. 2001. *The Impact of SEWA's Medical Insurance Fund on Hospital Utilization and Expenditure – A Household Survey.* HNP Discussion Paper. Washington, DC: World Bank.

Rathi P, Mukherjee A, Sen G. 2012. Rashtriya Swasthya Bima Yojana: evaluating utilisation, roll-out and perceptions in Amaravati district, Maharashtra. *Economic and Political Weekly* **47**: 57–64.

Robyn PJ, Fink G, Sauerborn R. 2012. Health insurance and health-seeking behavior: evidence from a randomized community-based insurance rollout in rural Burkina Faso. *Social Science and Medicine* **75**: 595–603.

Selvaraj S, Karan A. 2012. Why publicly-financed health insurance schemes are ineffective in providing financial risk protection. *Economic and Political Weekly* **47**: 60–68.

Shahrawat R, Rao KD. 2011. Insured yet vulnerable: out-of-pocket payments and India's poor. *Health Policy and Planning* **27**: 213–21.

Thornton RL, Hatt LE, Field EM *et al.* 2010. Social security health insurance for the informal sector in Nicaragua: a randomized evaluation. *Health Economics* **19**: 181–206.

UNDP. 2007. *Building Security for the Poor: Potential and Prospects for Microinsurance in India.* Colombo: United Nations Development Programme.

Wagstaff A, Lindelow M, Jun G, Ling X, Juncheng Q. 2009. Extending health insurance to the rural population: an impact evaluation of China's new cooperative medical scheme. *Journal of Health Economics* **28**: 1–19.

WHO. 2000. *Health Systems: Improving Performance. The World Health Report 2000.* Geneva: World Health Organization.

WHO. 2012. *World Health Statistics 2012.* Geneva: World Health Organization.

Wiesmann D, Jutting JP. 2001. Determinants of viable health insurance schemes in rural Sub-Saharan Africa. *Quarterly Journal of International Agriculture* **40**: 361–78.

World Bank. 2010a. *Out of Pocket Health Expenditure.* (% of private expenditure on health) http://data.worldbank.org/indicator/SH.XPD.OOPC.ZS, accessed 16 January 2013.

World Bank. 2010b. *Immunization Financing Toolkit: A Resource for Policy-makers and Program Managers.* http://www.who.int/immunization_financing/tools/final_toolkit_2011.pdf, accessed 16 January 2013.

Zhang L, Wang H. 2008. Dynamic process of adverse selection: evidence from a subsidized community-based health insurance in rural China. *Social Science and Medicine* **67**: 1173–182.

Chapter 15

Implementing a Participatory Model of Micro Health Insurance Among Rural Poor with Evidence from Nepal*

Main Messages

- Data for the study were collected from three sources: a baseline study of 2,008 households, results of simulations, and actual results of the schemes.
- The prospective insurance beneficiaries designed the benefits package themselves through a game-like simulation method called CHAT.
- A novel alternative method to proxy WTP for health insurance estimated WTP as 4.5% of mean food expenditure.

Focus Points

- The two CBHI schemes studied were successful, considering four key performance indicator p: effective planning; affiliation (grew from 0 to ~10,000) and renewals (>65%); claims ratio (~50%); and promptness of claim settlement (~23 days).

---

*This chapter is reproduced from *Geneva Papers on Risk and Insurance* (2014), **00**, 1–24, Open Access, available at https://www.researchgate.net/publication/259575009_Implementing_a_Participatory_Model_of_Micro_Health_Insurance_among_Rural_Poor_With_Evidence_from_Nepal.

- The agreement between expected and observed number of claims for the three main benefit types was satisfactory, implying that the scheme was not exposed to adverse selection, moral hazard, or fraud.
- The study provides substantial evidence that contributory health insurance (HI) can be attractive to rural poor in a low-income country even without premium subsidies.

Structured Abstract

Introduction

The Government of Nepal proposes Universal Health Care for its rural citizens through implementation of health insurance. This paper presents a voluntary and contributory CBHI model that has been piloted in two districts of Nepal- Banke, and Dhading. It provides evidence to answers questions whether/how it is possible to operate sustainable health insurance in the informal sector in rural Nepal without premium subsidies, and what useful role communities can play in the self-governance of their insurance.

Method

Data for the study were collected from three sources: a baseline study of 2,008 households (Dhading: 1,000; Banke: 1,008), results of simulations at the design phase, and actual results of the schemes.

Baseline study

This included a household survey, focus group discussions (FGDs) and key informant interviews to gather information on socio-economic and demographic features, health-seeking patterns and how the local population financed access to health care.

Results of simulations at the design phase

During the preparatory stage, a series of simulation exercises were conducted with groups to obtain data on the benefits and compositions most suited to the population. These results served as a data source at various stages of the implementation process.

Actual results of the schemes

Data were obtained from the books of accounts (e.g. the number of paid-up members, premiums collected, and claims paid) and operational records of the CBHI schemes (notably information on the number of claims, the time needed to process those claims and number of meetings of the claims committees).

Box 1: Business Process of Implementation of this CBHI Model

Initiating (Baseline Survey)

- Success implies the garnering of adequate information needed for provision of sound actuarial and other technical advice.

Involving (awareness generation and engaging community in benefit-package-design)

- Success implies
  - the target groups are able to form a consensus on the design and pricing of the benefit package for their community
  - pursuant to participation in awareness and capacity-building activities

Launch (enrollment and training of selected community members)

- Success implies
  - CBHI members choose some members to be the office-bearers to manage and govern the scheme
  - enrolments reflect the community's consensus that insurance is better than no insurance

Post-launch (claims settlement, sustainability)

- Success implies
  - viable claims ratio
  - claims settled within a satisfactory time
  - adequate income to fund sustained operations
  - community consensus on the benefit package extends into subsequent years
  - CBHI has the capacity to meet ongoing technical support needs.

Findings

The two schemes scored well on four performance indicators: effective planning, affiliation, and renewals claims ratio, and promptness of claim settlement. The authors assess the results of these schemes against nine pieces of essential information.

Willingness to pay (WTP)

WTP was estimated using two methods. Using the descending bidding game method, the median WTP was NPR 10.0 in Dhading and NPR 10.5 in Banke. The second method estimated WTP based on mean food expenditure. By applying this method, the first approximation of WTP was NPR 41±1 in Dhading and NPR 38±1 in Banke.

Benefit package design and pricing

The community was involved in designing the benefits package through a preference elicitation method called CHAT (Choosing Healthplans All Together). The premium levels that were chosen by the groups were within the estimated range of WTP and closer to the higher limits. In designing the package, there was a clear desire to include both outpatient and inpatient coverage. To accommodate the cost of covering medicines in the package, a lower cap had to be chosen for hospital reimbursements.

Membership in the CBHI

Overall, membership numbers doubled from 2011 to 2012, with satisfactory renewal rates in Dhading, and relatively lower rates in Banke.

Household size of the insured population

There is a large difference in the mean household size when counting replies during the household survey (i.e. before households actually joined) and the average household size when counting the members enrolled in the CBHI schemes. On further investigation, it was seen that adult women were over-represented in the insured cohort, compared with men and with their proportion in the overall surveyed population. Also, young girls were under-represented among the insured, relative to their share of the population and compared to enrolled young boys.

Incidence of claims

The agreement between expected and observed number of claims for the three main benefit types was satisfactory, suggesting that the schemes were not exposed to adverse selection, moral hazard, or fraud. This is attributed to effective flow of information (including gossip) which enhances community governance.

Cost of reimbursable claims

The actual costs paid by the schemes were remarkably similar to the expected average costs estimated on the basis of the baseline data, except for significant differences in three cases.

Loss ratio (a.k.a. claims ratio)

The loss ratio for the two schemes was satisfactory and confirms that suitable premiums were collected.

Value for money

A low cap resulted in low coverage of claims with only 48% of hospitalization claims in Dhading being fully reimbursed in 2011. The rate was lower for Banke district with only 41% fully reimbursed claims. "Value for money" for the insured could improve by increasing the level of the cap.

Members' experience of the claims process

The promptness in processing and settling claims was remarkable. On an average, bills were paid within one month from claims submission, and only four claims were rejected.

Conclusion

The CBHI schemes have been successful in retaining most enrollees after the first year, and in attracting new enrollees. This is a remarkable achievement given that premiums we not subsidized and enrolment has been purely voluntary. Since the Government of Nepal is keen to achieve Universal Health Care through the implementation of health insurance, the CBHI model can help in achieving this social policy goal.

The Geneva Papers, **2014**, **00**, (1–24)
 1018-5895/2014
www.genevaassociation.org

Open

Implementing a Participatory Model of Micro Health Insurance among Rural Poor with Evidence from Nepal

David M. Dror[a,b], Atanu Majumdar[a], Pradeep Panda[a], Denny John[a] and Ruth Koren[c]

[a]Micro Insurance Academy, 52B Okhla Industrial Estate, Phase-3, New Delhi 110020, India.
[b]Erasmus University Rotterdam, Institute of Health Policy and Management, P.O. Box 1738, 3000 DR Rotterdam, The Netherlands.
E-mail: daviddror@socialre.org
[c]Tel Aviv University, Felsenstein Medical Research Center, Sackler Faculty of Medicine, Ramat Aviv, Tel Aviv, Israel.

This paper reports on two voluntary, contributory, contextualised, community-based health insurance (CBHI) schemes, launched in Dhading and Banke (Nepal) in 2011. The implementation followed a four-stage process: *initiating* (baseline survey), *involving* (awareness generation and engaging community in benefit-package-design), *launch* (enrolment and training of selected community members) and *post-launch* (viable claims ratio, settled within satisfactory time, sustainable affiliation). Both schemes were successful on four key parameters: effective planning; affiliation (grew from 0 to ~10,000) and renewals (>65 per cent); claims ratio (~50 per cent); and promptness of claim settlement (~23 days). This model succeeded in implementing CBHI with zero premium subsidies or subsidised health-care costs. The successful operation relied in large part on the fact that members trust that they can enforce this contract. Considerable insurance education and capacity development is necessary before the launch of the CBHI, and for sustainable operations as well as for scaling.
The Geneva Papers (2014) **0,** 1–24. doi:10.1057/gpp.2013.31

Keywords: Nepal; micro health insurance; community-based health scheme; benefit package design; health insurance performance indicators; microinsurance implementation process

Article submitted 8 May 2013; accepted 15 October 2013; advance online publication, 15 January 2014

The online version of this article is available Open Access

Introduction

In countries where governments can neither mandate contributory universal health coverage (UHC) nor subsidise its full cost, one of the great challenges is reducing private out-of-pocket expenditure (OPE) for health care payable at the point and time of service. This inequitable and inefficient health financing mechanism[1] persists in many low-income countries.[2] In Nepal, the third poorest country in Asia, OPE represents around 72 per cent

[1] Garg and Karan (2009).
[2] Xu *et al.* (2010).

of total health-care costs.[3] The World Health Organization proposes the introduction of prepayment and risk pooling as a way to solve this problem.[4] Several experiments with community-based health insurance (CBHI) have been reported[5,6,7]; in Nepal, experiments with CBHI have been carried out since 2004, both in rural and in urban settings.[8,9] Most projects depended on external subsidies and offered provider-based health insurance with a restricted choice of health-care services. Recently, the Government of Nepal has shown interest in universal health care (UHC) through implementation of health insurance[10]; however, it has neither launched a national scheme nor entered into arrangements with commercial insurers to secure an ample supply of health insurance, notably in difficult-to-reach locations. Rather, it has designated several "pilot" districts for experimentation with several models, notably CBHI. This paper addresses the question whether and how it is possible to operate sustainable health insurance in the informal sector in rural Nepal without premium subsidies, and what useful role communities can play in the self-governance of their insurance.

We present here the voluntary and contributory CBHI model that has been piloted in Nepal. The empirical scope covers CBHI operations from 2011 until 2013. The novelty of this implementation model is its combination of high-resolution data collection and analysis, reliance on revenue generation on a voluntary basis rather than on premium subsidies, and capacity development. The conceptual framework of this model includes tailoring benefits to local risks at premiums perceived locally as affordable; involving prospective beneficiaries in benefit package design to ensure that their perceived priorities are given voice; assigning responsibility for governance of the schemes to members, to reduce conflicts of interests and enhance the likelihood that benefits are paid as promised; and localising operations of the scheme at community level with suitable capacity development.

The paper is structured as follows: we provide details on the location, data and methods used in this study, followed by a description of the implementation model. The findings, reflecting the experience during two full years of operation using established performance indicators, follow. We interpret the findings in the discussion section, and end by formulating conclusions, notably on sustainability and scalability of this CBHI implementation model, and its potential contribution to achieving the social policy goals of the Government of Nepal.

Data and methods

The CBHI schemes studied

This paper describes the implementation of two schemes: *Saubhagya*, launched in January 2011 in Dhading district by a consortium composed of Development Project Service Centre

[3] World Bank (2007).
[4] World Health Organization (2011).
[5] Biener and Eling (2012).
[6] Mahal *et al.* (2013).
[7] Borghi *et al.* (2013).
[8] GIZ Health Sector Support Program, Department of Health Services (2012).
[9] Stoermer (2012).
[10] "National Health Insurance Policy 2012" of the Government of Nepal.

(DEPROSC),[11] Micro Insurance Academy (MIA)[12] and Save the Children Nepal (STC).[13] *Sanjeevni* was launched in June 2011 in Banke district by a consortium composed of Nirdhan Utthan Bank (Nirdhan),[14] MIA and STC.

Data sources

This paper is based on three data sources.

A baseline study

Conducted from January to April 2009, it included a household survey, focus group discussions (FGDs) and key informant interviews[15] to gather information on socio-economic and demographic features, health-seeking patterns and how the local population financed access to health care. A two-stage sampling method was applied. The first entailed purposive selection of "village development committees" (VDC) and wards (administrative divisions smaller than districts) to include the places the field partners designated for implementation of the CBHI schemes. The second stage included selection of intervention and control groups; the intervention groups included those to whom the CBHI was going to be offered (often organised as "self-reliant groups" (SRG) numbering about 15–20 people who were affiliated with DEPROSC in Dhading and with Nirdhan in Banke)[16]; the control groups, of equal size, were not invited to join. We call these sub-cohorts "members" and "non-members", respectively.

The sample consisted of 1,000 households from Dhading and 1,008 households from Banke. The sample size was calculated based on an error margin of 0.005 (for estimation of the hospitalisation rate with a prior estimated value of 0.04), a confidence interval of 80 per cent and a design effect of 2.[17] We interviewed a members sample comprised of 504 households randomly sampled from 17 VDCs in Banke (from Nirdhan's list), respecting a proportional number of members in the local ward population (member strength in Ward to member strength in VDC)[18]; and a random sample of 500 households in Dhading from the list of DEPROSC members (covering nine VDCs).[19] The non-members were selected randomly in each village, following the "four winds" method.[20]

For the purpose of analysis of the results of the implementation, only members' household baseline data are used.

---

[11] *http://www.deprosc.org.np/Home.aspx*

[12] *http://www.microinsuranceacademy.org/*

[13] *http://www.savethechildren.org/site/c.8rKLIXMGIpI4E/b.6150545/k.B8DE/Nepal.htm*

[14] *http://www.nirdhan.com/*

[15] Dror and Radermacher (2010).

[16] An SRG is a group of 10–15 women who agree to deposit a fixed amount every month in a common kitty. When a member is in need of money, she can borrow the amount from the common kitty. She pays a service charge (equivalent to interest) to the group fund. Each SRG has a bank account in the name of the group.

[17] Cochran (1977).

[18] With the following breakdown by VDC: 99 households in Bageswari, 33 in Banratuwa, 4 in Belbhar, 28 in Chisapani, 12 in Indrapur, 3 in Jaispur, 6 in Khajurapur, 124 in Kohalpur, 24 in Manikapur, 26 in Navabasta, 18 in Paraspur, 12 in Rajapur, 63 in Rajhaina, 10 in Sahigaon, 5 in Samserganj, 20 in Sitapur and 17 in Titanaria.

[19] Breakdown by VDCs was follows: 98 households in Baireni, 12 in Benighat, 21 in Bhumesthan, 21 in Dhusha, 43 in Gajuri, 86 in Jogimara, 42 in Kalleri, 70 in Kumpur, and 107 in Pida.

[20] Som (1996).

Table 1 Socio-demographic profile of respondents

	Dhading	*Banke*
MPCC (NPR)	2402 ± 77.6	1979 ± 58.2
MPCC (PPP$)	82 ± 2.65	68 ± 1.99
Total literacy	81%	82%
Female literacy	75%	75%
Average family size	5.24 ± 0.06	5.63 ± 0.08
House type (permanent structure)	13%	29%
Predominant religion	Hindu	Hindu
Predominant language	Nepali	Nepali

The average monthly per capita consumption (MPCC) of the members sub-cohorts as per the baseline was Napalese rupees (NPR) 2,402 ±77.6 (= purchasing power parity (PPP) $ 82±2.65) at Dhading and NPR 1,979 ±58.2 (= PPP$ 68±1.99) at Banke.[21] Estimated literacy rates of members sub-cohorts at Dhading and Banke were 81 and 82 per cent, respectively. The female literacy rate was 75 per cent in both places. The average family size was 5.63 (±0.08) in Banke and 5.24 (±0.06) in Dhading. In all, 29 per cent of houses in Banke were permanent housing structures ("pacca houses"), compared with only 13 per cent in Dhading (Table 1).

Results of simulations at the design phase
During the preparatory stage, a series of simulation exercises were conducted with groups (each of about 15 SRG members) to obtain data on the benefits and compositions that might suit best. The results of these simulation exercises were recorded and served as one data source at various stages of the implementation process.

Actual results of the schemes
Data was obtained from the books of accounts (e.g. number of paid-up members, premiums collected and payments made to members) and operational records of the CBHI schemes (notably information on number of claims, time needed to process those claims and number of meetings of the claims committees).

Essentials of the implementation model

The business process of implementation of this CBHI model follows four consecutive stages (see Appendix A).

Initiating: Initiating refers to the preparatory stage in which success implies the garnering of adequate information—on local willingness to pay, incidence of illness and costs—needed for provision of sound actuarial and other technical advice. In Nepal this information was gathered through the baseline study conducted in 2009.

[21] Conversion rate PPP$ 1 = NPR 29.25, in year 2009. The per capita per month GNI of Nepal was estimated at 100 PPP$ for the year 2009.

Involving: Involving refers to the stage in which success implies that the target groups are able to form consensus on the design and pricing of the benefit package for their community, pursuant to participation in awareness and capacity-building activities. This was done in 2010.

Launch: Launch refers to the stage in which success implies two things: that CBHI members choose some members to be the office-bearers to manage and govern the scheme, and that enrolments reflect the community's consensus that insurance (through the customised benefit package) is better than no insurance.

Post-launch: Post-launch refers to the stage in which success implies that the loss ratio is viable, that claims are settled in a contextually satisfactory time frame, that the income from membership (new and renewals) is adequate to fund sustained operations, that community consensus on the benefit package extends into subsequent years, and that the CBHI has the capacity to satisfy the community's ongoing technical support needs.

At the *Initiating* stage, the target community agrees to cooperate with an external body in surveying local conditions of risk exposure and perceptions of priorities about risk. Unremunerated interviewees share information; they expect a return, which (in this implementation model) is a promise to propose the insurance that could improve their lives. This engagement with the external organisers establishes agreed roles: the expert collects data and offers knowledge-based recommendations and the community decides on the action. Stated differently, the external expert (in this case the Micro Insurance Academy—MIA) acts as "change maker" and the local community acts as "decision-maker". The decisions are taken during the *Involving* stage, when the target group is engaged in benefit package design. The package that communities can compose may differ radically from anything offered by an insurer (if any offer exists at all). The assumption underlying this stage of the process is that, when prospective enrollees can participate in composing the package that reflects their perceived priorities, they will be more willing to affiliate and to pay. For as long as there is no willingness to pay (WTP), there can be no demand; asserting needs without solvent demand leads nowhere, and the necessary condition towards expanding health insurance coverage is that solvent demand exists where none existed before. The essential success of *Involving* is when the target group reaches consensus that being health-insured is "what we all do", at a price that we all are willing to pay. This also means that *Involving* is essentially a group decision rather than an individual choice.

Had there been ample competition in the supply of health insurance, the community could have shopped around for the package and price they wanted. But, the supply of insurance to the informal sector in Nepal is insufficient, both in terms of coverage and in terms of premium competition. Therefore, the *Launch* stage includes a decision by the community to act as "market maker" for the benefit package chosen by its members at the price they are willing to pay. As the community now needs the skills required to operate the scheme, the assistance must include a "competence chain" through which local persons are trained in skills they need to operate the insurance. The key roles are briefly described next.

The "*insurance activists*" (IAs) are the first line of managing the CBHI scheme; they move from village to village and door to door to enrol members, maintain direct contact with members, provide information, collect premiums, assist members to avail services (e.g. guide to certain health-care providers) and in submitting claims, etc. In Dhading each of the six IAs covers 150 members, while in Banke, each of the five IAs covers 455 members.

This large gap in member per IA reflects the time/effort required to reach the members in their villages in very different terrains. The IAs are employed by the CBHI and draw a monthly payment.

Another role is that of "*insurance coordinator*" (IC) who keeps membership records and books of accounts using a management information system provided by MIA, manages the bank account, and may also maintain relationships with health-care providers. From 2011 onwards, one IC was employed in Dhading and two in Banke.

Claims for reimbursement are adjudicated by the "*Claims Committee*" (CC). The CC is composed of one representative from each VDC where the members live, designated/elected by the "self-reliant groups" to sit on the CC. Candidates must be literate, understand the claims process and be able to make decisions promptly. In Dhading, seven CCs with 42 members were active in 2011, and eight CCs comprising 49 members in 2012, and the increase in 2012 was occasioned by the addition of two VDC populations; in Banke there were five CCs with seven members each operating in 2011 and in 2012. CC members meet once a month and receive a "sitting fee".

Finally, the "*Coordination Committee*" (CoCo) supervises the overall financial performance of the scheme. The CoCo meets monthly; reviews the financial performance; signs checks, policy documents and claim overview documents[22]; conducts client dispute resolution, etc. In Dhading there was one CoCo, with seven members in 2011 and eight members in 2012. In Banke (where the CoCo is called "Main Committee"), one committee operated with seven members in 2011 and 2012. CoCo members are paid a sitting fee by the scheme.

Results

The results of the Nepali CBHI schemes are examined here against nine pieces of essential information, some of which follow accepted performance indicators.[23]

Willingness to pay

Before launching a new CBHI, it is essential to have an estimate of WTP for health insurance among the target group (especially when the expected income from premium subsidies is zero) because WTP is used as a proxy for premiums that define the limits of the benefit package. The baseline survey includes elicitation of WTP. There are several methods to obtain this estimate[24]; we used the *descending bidding game* method,[25] which consisted of asking each interviewee how much she/he would *agree to pay for health insurance that would cover part of the cost of their health care on the basis that, if you are willing to pay more, you will get more benefits and, if you are willing to pay less, you will get fewer*

[22] The claim overview document is a document generated by the MIS application following submission of a claim. The system validates the claim amount under different benefit heads and calculates the amount payable based on the amount already received by the claimant. This calculation helps the CoCo to verify that decisions on the claim taken by the CC are fine.

[23] Wipf and Garand (2010).

[24] Dror and Koren (2012).

[25] Dror *et al.* (2007).

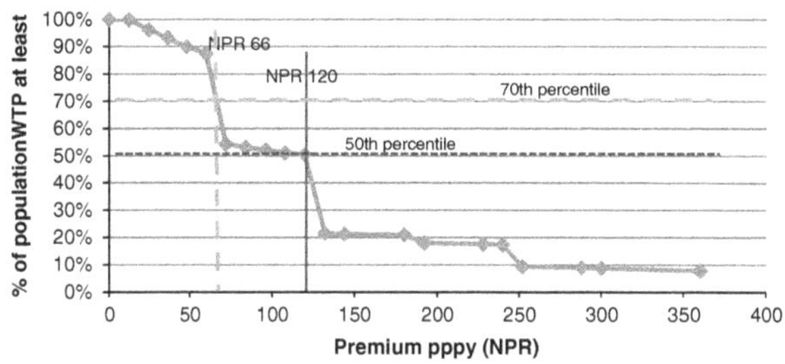

Figure 1. Results of the bidding game for WTP, *Saubhagya* Dhading.

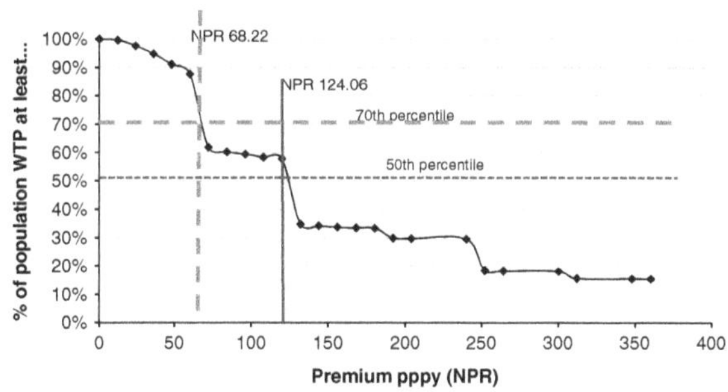

Figure 2. Results of the bidding game for WTP, *Sanjeevni* Banke.

benefits. The opening bid (of NPR 30 per person per month)[26] was intended to be refused as too high; when a bid was refused, a lower bid (1 NPR less) was offered, repeatedly, until a bid was accepted or the bid reached NPR 0. The accepted bid was recorded as the respondent's WTP. The median WTP was NPR 10.0 in Dhading and NPR 10.5 in Banke. All results of the bidding game are shown in Figures 1 and 2.

We also considered another method to estimate WTP, based on mean food expenditure.[27] The advantage of this method is that it bases the estimate of WTP on actual costs of known goods, rather than on unknown costs of uncertain services. By applying this method in Nepal, the first approximation of WTP was NPR 41$\pm$1 in Dhading and NPR 38$\pm$1 in Banke (about 4.5 per cent of mean food expenditure of the target population).

These two estimates of WTP, though markedly different, are taken as the lower and upper boundaries of scheme revenues within which the benefit package can be designed.

Benefit package design and pricing

It is known that benefit package design is an exercise in rationing limited resources.[28] Two key issues underlie this rationing exercise: firstly, the benefits must reflect local health needs

---

[26] An indicative exchange rate is 100 NPR=1 USD.
[27] Binnendijk *et al.* (2013).
[28] Ryan *et al.* (2001).

and local availability of health services; secondly, the people in the target population must agree to the rationing decisions, as they *can refuse* enrolment, which is voluntary.

We apply a modified version of a preference elicitation method called *CHAT* (Choosing Healthplans All Together) that has been successfully applied in many locations in rural India.[25,29] In the first stage of the process (known as the *design workshop* stage), the community (through its representatives) is shown many benefit package options, each with a particular premium. Through an iterative process of deliberations, the participants select four to five options that match the needs and WTP of the community. It is noted that the price reflects pure actuarial premiums plus about 30 per cent to cover risk loading and administrative expenses (incurred by the community in running the scheme), but without profit or any other cost (and no payment to MIA). The four or five benefit package options selected in the design workshop are then disseminated in the community (through pictorial paper boards called *CHAT Boards*; the CHAT board used in 2011 is attached as Appendix B for illustration), for discussion and decision. The package selected by the largest number of groups is retained for the entire scheme. A total of 47 such group discussions took place in Dhading and 81 in Banke. The CHAT and benefit/premium selection process is repeated each year, to allow the communities to adjust their priorities based on experience, and to increase coverage when WTP increases. Prior to preparation of new CHAT boards for 2012, a series of 24 FGDs were conducted in Dhading in June 2012 to elicit opinions on changes in the benefits and premiums for the next year. These FGDs led to proposals[30] which were considered during the "redesign workshop" by community representatives (CC and CoCo members). The CHAT exercises were administered among enrolled members and among non-members, with the view to enrolling more members.

The package options (those considered and those retained) for 2011 and 2012 are shown in Table 2.

Involving people in the CHAT exercises is a hands-on demonstration of the interplay between premiums on the one hand, and the width of benefits and depth of coverage, on the other. This experience helps manage expectations to realistic dimensions and minimises disappointments with reimbursements.

The premium levels that were chosen by the groups were within the estimated range of WTP (i.e. between NPR 10 and NPR 41±1 in Dhading, and between NPR 10.5 and NPR 38±1 in Banke) and closer to the higher limits.

As for the package design, the choices clearly favoured broad packages that included both outpatient and inpatient coverage. However, the cost of covering medicines was too high to be retained. The apparent trade-off was to choose a lower cap for hospital reimbursements.

It is also interesting to note that the benefit choices in Dhading and Banke were different from each other in Year 1 and converged towards more similarity in Year 2.

Based on the CHAT choices, the schemes implemented the packages described in Table 3.

It is noteworthy that the Dhading scheme changed the method of calculating caps, from a cap per person per year (pppy) to a dual cap per event (p.e.) and per family per year

[29] Danis *et al.* (2007).

[30] For example, in Dhading in 2012, the community mentioned injury to be a part of the benefit package, and later a survey among 455 members was conducted to calculate the probability and cost of injury.

Table 2 Benefit package options and premiums—including final selection per year per community (in Nepalese rupees)

Benefit options	*Dhading*										*Banke*								
	2011					*2012*					*2011*					*2012*			
	1	*2*	*3*	*4*	*5*	*1*	*2*	*3*	*4*	*5*	*1*	*2*	*3*	*4*	*5*	*1*	*2*	*3*	*4*
Hospitalisation	5,000	4,000	5,000	6,000	4,000	2,500	3,000	4,000	5,000	2,500	2,000	4,000	5,000	4,000	5,000	2,500	4,000	3,000	2,000
Imaging		500		400	500	400	600	700	600	400	250	500	1,000	1,000	1,000	300	250	400	600
Lab tests	600	250	400		250	250	400	500	400	250	200	250	250	500	1,000	200	200	250	400
Transport			200		400		300		200		100				100	200	200	200	200
Wage loss			@100/d											@100/d					
Medicines										500									
Premium PPPM[a]	23.1	24.5	24.7	25.4	26.2	21.1	28	31.7	34.3	76.4	20	30.3	35.1	36.1	38.8	28.3	33.3	33.8	35
Groups chose this	3/47	0	7/47	0	37/47	7/91	78/91	1/91	2/91	3/91	40/81	5/ 81	0	4/81	32/81	9/180	7/180	1/180	163/180
% of group choices	6%	0%	15%	0%	79%	8%	86%	1%	2%	3%	49%	6%	0%	5%	40%	5%	4%	1%	90%
Final selection					✓		✓				✓								✓

[a]Per person per month: During the CHAT, the premiums paid per month are shown to the community for the purpose of simplicity.

Table 3 The implemented benefits packages

Benefit type	*Conditions*	*Year 1*		*Year 2*	
		Banke Sanjeevni	*Dhading Saubhagya*	*Banke Sanjeevni*	*Dhading Saubhagya*
Hospitalisation benefit	All hospitalisations >24 h covered; only from selected hospitals: government and private; all direct hospital costs covered; hospital bill + medicines needed and bought during hospitalisation in pharmacy outside hospital + tests and imaging prescribed and done during hospitalisation in testing centre outside hospital	pppy[a]: NPR 2,000	pppy: NPR 4,000	pppy: NPR 2,000	p.e.[b]: 3,000; pfpy: 20,000
Transportation benefit	A one-time flat amount compensation for transportation costs for all hospitalisations of at least 24 h	NPR 100	NPR 400	NPR 200	NPR 300
Imaging tests benefit	Imaging test prescribed by the doctors of selected hospitals and done in an outpatient setting (not during hospitalisation of more than 24 h)	pppy: NPR 250	pppy: NPR 500	pppy: NPR 600	p.e.: NPR 600; pfpy[c]: 3,000
Lab tests benefit	Lab tests prescribed by the doctors of selected hospitals and done in an outpatient setting (not during hospitalisation of more than 24 h)	pppy: NPR 200	pppy: NPR 250	pppy: NPR 400	p.e.: NPR 400; pfpy: 3,000

[a]pppy = maximum amount insurance will pay out per person per year.
[b]p.e. = maximum amount insurance will pay per event.
[c]pfpy = maximum amount insurance will pay out per family per year.

(pfpy). This method of calculating the benefit, called "*family floater*",[31] increases the coverage amount available to sick individuals within a family unit; yet, there is no evidence thus far of adverse selection, with the notable exception that family size of the insured is smaller than expected, when larger family size could have been expected. One lesson might be to link the application of the family floater with an obligation to affiliate entire families, which could reduce the financial risk for the scheme and enhance the inclusive nature of the scheme.

Membership in the CBHI

Enrolment into the schemes was open during "affiliation periods" lasting two months; enrolment was not possible outside these affiliation periods. The evolution of membership numbers until 31 January 2013 is shown in Table 4.

Overall, membership numbers doubled from Year 1 (2011) to Year 2 (2012), with satisfactory renewal rates in Dhading, and relatively lower rates in Banke.

[31] In a family floater policy, the cap limits total payout to the family, instead of an event or an individual. In case someone becomes sick multiple times, she/he can take advantage of the higher per family cover.

Table 4 Membership in the CBHIs

Enrolment period	*Enrolment status*			*Total members per scheme*		*Renewal %*		*Total project*
	New	*Renew*	*Total*	*Saubhagya Dhading*	*Sanjeevni Banke*	*Saubhagya Dhading*	*Sanjeevni Banke*	
2011 January	514		514	514				514
2011 June	4,176				4,176			4,690
2011 July	394		394	908				5,084
2012 January	1,066	349	1,415	1,809		67.9%		5,985
2012 June	5,818	2,063			7,881		49.4%	9,690
2012 July	391	254	645	2,060		64.5%		9,941
2013 January	1,753	965	2,718	3,363		68.2%		11,244
31 Dec. 2011								5,084
31 Dec. 2012								9,941
31 Jan. 2013								11,244

Household size of the insured population

The mean household size of the members sub-cohort in the baseline survey was 5.24 ± 0.063 in Dhading and 5.63±0.075 in Banke (data sourced from baseline survey). Surprisingly, the average household size of enrolled members was significantly lower, at 2.85±0.035 in Dhading and 2.44±0.019 in Banke (obtained from membership records). This big difference raises the question which demographic segment has been excluded by families.

Table 5, providing the age and gender distributions of the two groups (the sampled "member" sub-cohort in the household survey vs the actual CBHI membership), shows clearly that adult women are over-represented in the insured cohort, compared with men and with their proportion in the overall population (household survey data). And, young girls are under-represented among the insured, compared both with young boys and with their share in the population.

Incidence of claims

We compare the expected and actual incidence of claims for the three main benefit types that formed the basis of members' benefits premium package choice, based on two years' experience. The results are summarised in Table 6.

The agreement between expected and actual incidence of hospital claims is very good in Banke and in the second batch of affiliation in Dhading; the first batch of enrollees in Dhading had lower incidence than expected, which may reflect that the number of enrolled was too small to represent the target group correctly.

As for imaging and lab claims, actual incidence was lower than expected in Banke, and this could explain the decision of both schemes to increase the cap for this benefit in Year 2, to offset the lower incidence by higher reimbursement at a similar premium. This suggests that the insured understood the pricing mechanism very well. The agreement between expected and observed number of claims suggests that adverse selection, moral hazard and

Table 5 Age and gender distribution ("members" cohort in the household survey vs insured population)

Age	*Dhading baseline members sample*		*Dhading insured*		*Significance of difference gender ratio in HHS vs insured*	*Banke baseline members sample*		*Banke insured*		*Significance of difference gender ratio in HHS vs insured*
	Male	*Female*	*Male*	*Female*	*p-value*	*Male*	*Female*	*Male*	*Female*	*p-value*
<6	11.7%	11.5%	13.3%	5.9%	0.000	9.6%	11.0%	16.6%	7.2%	0.000
6–15	25.3%	25.1%	25.6%	15.2%	0.000	22.9%	23.3%	32.5%	14.1%	0.000
15–59	56.5%	58.6%	55.4%	74.4%	0.000	61.3%	59.8%	46.7%	75.1%	0.000
60 +	6.4%	4.8%	5.7%	4.4%	0.000	5.7%	5.9%	4.2%	3.5%	0.000
Total	100%	100%	100%	100%	0.000	100%	100%	100%	100%	0.000
n	1,699	1,269	1,377	1,381	NA	7,927	4,154	1,452	1,478	NA

Table 6 Comparison between expected and actual incidence of claims

Incidence district	Hospitalisations			Imaging			Lab tests		
	Actual (%)	Expected (%)	p-value[a]	Actual (%)	Expected (%)	p-value[a]	Actual (%)	Expected (%)	p-value[a]
Dhading (January 2011)	2.1	3.7	0.225	13.4	15.9	0.484	10.5	18.5	0.001
Dhading (July 2011)	3.3	3.7	0.934	18.3	15.9	0.587	10.9	18.5	0.006
Banke (June 2011)	3.3	3.1	0.878	14.8	22.2	0.000	11.8	34.1	0.000

[a]Chi-square test.

Table 7 Comparison between expected and actual cost of claims

Mean cost per claim (NPR) district	Hospitalisations		Imaging		Lab	
	Actual (paid) ± SEM[a]	Expected ± SEM	Actual ± SEM	Expected ± SEM	Actual ± SEM	Expected ± SEM
Dhading (January 2011)	3094 ± 356	3303 ± 106	332 ± 18	395 ± 25	198 ± 10	197 ± 10
Dhading (July 2011)	3250 ± 302	3303 ± 106	313 ± 17	395 ± 25	217 ± 9	197 ± 10
Banke (June 2011)	1665 ± 45	1853 ± 34	225 ± 2	228 ± 6	162 ± 5	161 ± 6

[a]SEM= standard error of the mean.

fraud seem to be in good control. This is an interesting observation, which may reflect community governance of the scheme.

Cost of reimbursable claims

The actual costs paid by the CBHI schemes were compared with the expected costs that were simulated by using the members cohort in the household data, applying identical insurance rules (results shown in Table 7).

As can be seen, the actual and expected average costs per claim are remarkably similar, even though, in three cases, the difference is significant (unpaired Student's t-test). These results confirm that it is possible to base the actuarial calculations underlying package design on the baseline data.

Loss ratio (a.k.a. claims ratio)

Loss ratio (i.e. the amount paid as benefits divided by the total premium income) is a measure of the financial stability of the scheme, providing an indication of the adequacy of premiums charged relative to underwritten risk. The data shown (Table 8) refers to the first full year for which all claims were settled. The loss ratio is satisfactory and confirms that the two schemes collected suitable premiums. Note that in Dhading, the loss ratio of the second batch of enrollees was 56.7 per cent, higher by about 40 per cent from the first batch (with 40 per cent), but still within a very suitable range.

Table 8 Loss ratio (a.k.a. claims ratio) for the first year

Location	*No. of insured*	*Premium income (in NPR)*	*No. of claims*	*Claim amount (in NPR)*	*Loss ratio (%)*
Dhading (January 2011)	514	172,704	104	69,063	40.0
Dhading (July 2011)	394	132,384	104	74,998	56.7
Banke (June 2011)	4,177	1,052,352	810	461,830	43.9

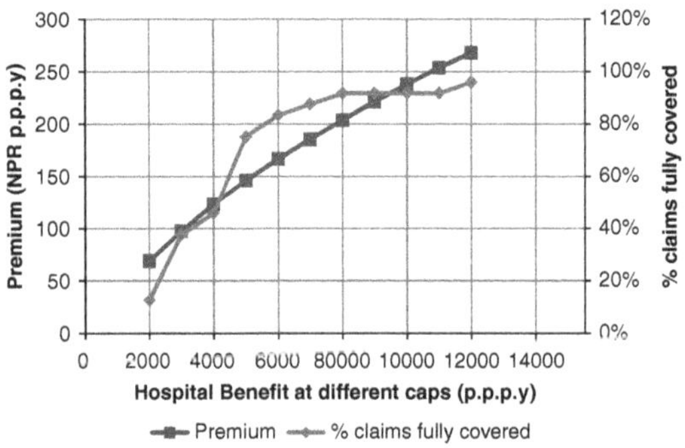

Figure 3. Coverage levels at different caps/hospitalisations (Dhading).

Value for money

One way to express "value for money" for the insured is to look at the probability that the claims submitted will be fully reimbursed. It is self-explanatory that the cap is designed to curtail some costs, and the probability of full reimbursement increases as the cap increases, but so do the premiums. The outcomes were as follows: in Dhading, in 2011 (the first year for which all claims were settled), 48 per cent of hospitalisations were fully reimbursed; in Banke, the rate was 41 per cent. This coverage seems too low. The share of claims that would have been fully paid at different levels of the cap, and the corresponding premiums are shown in Figures 3 and 4.

As can be seen, a small increase in a low cap occasions relatively better coverage for a modest premium increase, since the two lines in the graph are not parallel or linear (e.g. the range from 4,000 to 6,000 $\approx$ PPP$136.80 to PPP$205.10). For example, had the cap been increased from NPR 4,000 to NPR 5,000 in Dhading, 78 per cent of hospital claims would have been fully covered, while the premium would have increased by only NPR 23 pppy (from NPR 123 to 146).

In Dhading, some 89 per cent of imaging claims were fully covered with a cap of 500, and in Banke, only 24 per cent were fully covered when the cap was 250. It is interesting to note that both CBHI schemes chose a cap of 600 in 2012; this corrective choice seems suitable for Banke, but less necessary for Dhading. Finally, 45 per cent of lab claims in Dhading were fully covered (with a cap of 250), and 34 per cent in Banke (cap of 200). Both schemes chose to raise the cap to 400 in the following year. The involvement of communities in package

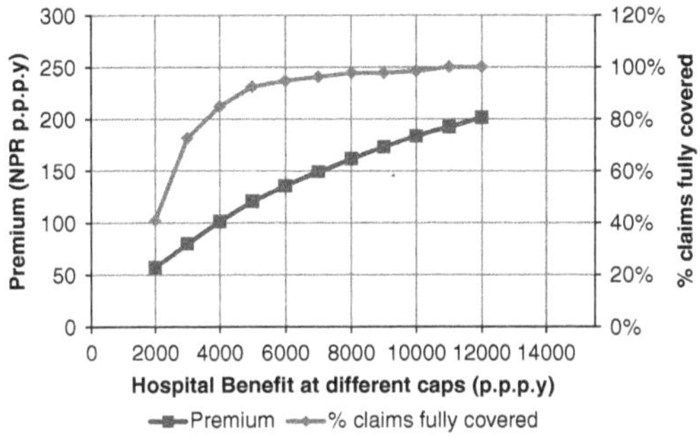

Figure 4. Coverage levels at different caps/hospitalisations (Banke).

Table 9 Promptness of claims reimbursement

Scheme district	*Enrolment period*	*Batch covered (months)*	*# Days from submission to CC decision*	*# Days from CC decision to payment*	*# Days from submission to payment*
			Mean ± SEM	*Mean ± SEM*	*Mean ± SEM*
Saubhagya Dhading	January 2011	12	14 ± 0.98	15 ± 0.72	28 ± 1.08
	July 2011	12	10 ± 0.80	12 ± 0.44	23 ± 0.85
	January 2012	10	10 ± 0.42	11 ± 0.22	21 ± 0.48
	July 2012	4	11 ± 0.95	12 ± 0.48	24 ± 1.21
Sanjeevni Banke	June 2011	12	13 ± 0.35	11 ± 0.27	24 ± 0.42
	June 2012	5	13 ± 0.38	10 ± 0.18	24 ± 0.46

revision offered the opportunity to adjust perceived value for money and the resulting interest to remain insured.

Members' experience of the claims process

Of 810 claims submitted in Dhading, only four claims were rejected (less than half of 1 per cent, due to client fraud or incomplete bills submitted by members). No claim rejections were registered in Banke.

Another way of measuring the experience of insured persons is the time interval between claim submission and reimbursement. We measured promptness in three distinct ways: firstly, how long it took from submission to the IA until the claims were decided by the CC; secondly, the delay from decision by the CC to actual payment to members; and thirdly, the promptness of the entire process from a member's claim submission until reimbursement. The results are shown in Table 9.

Bills were paid within one month on average. Considering that the CC meets once a month and that the IA needs to visit villages to collect claims and prepare them for decisions, and that cash payments are made to members at doorstep, the promptness of the process seems remarkable. Promptness could hardly improve if payments should continue to be made through personal interaction at doorstep, recalling the objective difficulties of travelling to remote villages and the scarce number of CBHI staff.

Discussion

This paper describes the implementation of two contributory, voluntary, context-adapted and demand-driven health insurance schemes in rural Nepal. The two locations differ from each other in many ways: Dhading is hilly whereas Banke is in the plain; Banke is relatively poorer in terms of MPCC, but has more availability of health-care providers. The differences were also reflected in the choice of benefit package. Owing to these reasons, instead of combining the results of two districts, we preferred to show them separately. These differences notwithstanding, the implementation of CBHI in both locations has been successful. The implementation model is founded on a partnership model (where all parties get a share of the productivity gains from pooling) through the application of the following components: (i) *trusted governance at local level*; mobilising local rules-in-use and local staff to manage the mutual model with no or few conflicts of interests typical to insurance; (ii) *combining "awareness chain"* (affiliation-enhancing insurance literacy[32] *with a "value chain"* (comprehensible value proposition of insurance) *and with a "competence chain"* (capacity development of local persons); (iii) *context-relevance in pricing and priority-setting of the risks covered*, enabling both a contextualised rationing of partial benefits and gaining credibility by involving prospective enrollees in design and pricing.

The unique feature of this implementation model is its design to achieve three objectives: (i) enabling target communities to take decisions that affect their members' lives (in context, this means deciding on the composition of their benefit package and its price); (ii) enabling communities to be in control of the money paid by members to the CBHI (to reduce concerns about leakages, fraud or corruption); and (iii) enabling communities to control that the pre-defined rules of the game are followed (in context, this means local governance of daily operations of the insurance). The following five critical conditions serve as benchmarks to review the success of the schemes in achieving these objectives.

The coverage should deal with risks of the insured

This condition means covering risks that the target group prioritises. The dialog with the target population on rationing, WTP and priority-setting must be based on local risk-exposure, that is, morbidity, provision and health-care costs. The data (Tables 6 and 7) demonstrate significant differences across the two locations, a situation already reported in other contexts.[33] The external *change maker* was responsible for structuring data acquisition and calculating premiums for different benefit options (a role requiring statistical and actuarial expertise), and the target community provided the information and then took the lead in making choices. The benefits (e.g. hospitalisation, imaging, lab tests, wage loss,

[32] Panda *et al.* (2013).
[33] Dror *et al.* (2008).

transportation, etc.) were chosen in two stages, first (rough cut) by community leaders, followed by a selection by small groups; the package selected by most groups was then retained as the one package applying to all. This interactive process of involving prospective insureds in package design, while time-consuming and labour-intensive, increased the population's understanding about the insurance. The "design workshop" (renamed "redesign workshop" when repeated the following year) enabled insured members to modify their choices based on their actual experience. For example, in Dhading in Year 2, members decided to increase the imaging cap from NPR 500 to 600 and in Banke, from NPR 250 to 600 (Table 2). It is noteworthy that in both schemes and in both years, the outpatient benefits included represented about half the premium cost (e.g. lab tests and imaging; premium data not shown). This package composition differs considerably from what most commercial schemes cover (only inpatient care). Recalling that low enrolment among commercial "microinsurance" schemes was due to the limited coverage of outpatient care,[34] the involvement of CBHI members in package design in these schemes led to a different priority-setting.

The price should be affordable

Affordability is what each target group considers as the acceptable price for its unique variant of health insurance. We assessed this by obtaining two estimates of WTP, one by applying a "descending bidding game" (one method of contingent valuation) as part of data collection, and the second by applying a novel alternative method to proxy WTP for health insurance as an estimated 4.5 per cent of mean food expenditure.[27] The premiums presented to the target groups in the design workshops were between these two estimates of WTP (see Figures 1 and 2). The members chose benefit packages that commanded premiums closer to the higher WTP estimate (premiums were NPR 26.2 and 28 in Dhading, and NPR 20 and 35 in Banke, respectively for the first and second enrolment periods; upper and lower WTP estimates were NPR 41 and NPR 10 pppm in Dhading; and NPR 38 and 10.46 pppm in Banke). We think that the lively group discussions (occasioned by involving so many community members in the process of choice) enhanced the understanding of the trade-off between premiums payable and the depth and width of coverage, and encouraged agreement to pay higher premiums in both schemes in the second year. This could suggest that WTP increases when the insured population gains useful experience with insurance over time (but the effect is not uniform). It is also noted that the premiums chosen in both locations even in Year 2 are lower than the highest estimate of WTP.

Another aspect of *affordability* is that administrative costs did not include profits to intermediaries or underwriters.

The value proposition of insurance should be positive and clear

We consider membership numbers (new and renewals, Table 4) as a strong indicator of a positive perception of the value proposition by the target population. In Dhading, membership rose from 514 to 2,060 (+300 per cent) in July 2012 and to 3,363 (+ 554 per cent) by end January 2013, and in Banke the membership rose from 4,176 in Year 1 to 7,881 in Year 2 (+90 per cent). Renewals were voluntary, and rates were around 66 per cent in Dhading and

[34] Pott and Holtz (2013).

49.4 per cent in Banke; there is scope for improvement. The household size of the target population was much larger than the average size of insured households (5.2 vs 2.9 lives in Dhading, and 5.6 vs 2.4 in Banke). The insured members (SRG women) did not avail of the opportunity to insure all their household members; the under-6 young girls were under-represented (Table 5). The traditional hierarchy in allocating resources within the family (lower allocation to girl children) is reflected in this context of considering the value proposition of insurance. Changing this perception will require more group discussions.

Another aspect of the value proposition of insurance is the share of premiums paid back to members (loss ratio); these ratios are of course very sensitive to caps, and the increases of caps for outpatient services that were adopted in Year 2 suggest that the target population fully understood this relationship. Finally, prompt reimbursement added to the sense of value, as members were less exposed to secure interim financing through loans.

The process is transparent and trusted by the insured

The transparency of the business process was enhanced by placing the operations of the scheme in the hands of members chosen by other members for their posts. Putting the operation and governance in the hands of members (formally a mutual-aid model) removes some conflicts of interest that exist in the partner-agent model, provided that the managers of the scheme run it well. The symbiosis between communities (the decision-makers) and the external facilitator (the change maker) made it possible to deliver tailored training to trusted officials that the community chose so that they would perform effectively, efficiently and locally. The training costs are not paid by the community, and the capacity-development activities are an essential part of this implementation model. The operative assumption underlying the inclusion of a "competencies chain" in the implementation model is that, with time, increased autonomy and self-reliance of communities in running their insurance schemes will allow the phasing out of technical assistance. And the development assumption is that the front-loaded costs in developing local capacity is a justified and essential phase towards achieving the development goals of better access to health care by rural people.

Viable supply and solvent demand could be established

The reports of other (micro) health insurance projects in Nepal (referenced earlier) suggest several unsuccessful attempts, even with external subsidies. The remarkable achievement reported here is that in similar terrain and difficult conditions, two rural communities, composed mostly of poor persons with low education and no prior exposure to health insurance, succeeded in organising and paying for a viable supply of health insurance where no (commercial) insurer was willing to underwrite risk. Moreover, they did this by respecting a perfect match between local solvent demand, and local prioritisation of benefits. Thirdly, the communities demonstrated their ability to govern a scheme transparently and responsibly. The net result was that the communities used new competencies to consolidate all the conditions to establish and operate a market for health insurance benefitting all concerned where none existed before. The implementation model does not entail any subsidy to premiums, yet operations have been sustainable and have grown from year to year. The technical and actuarial advice provided to the communities during the inception years was essential in ensuring viable insurance operations. These costs are in fact development costs, to create a nascent market for health insurance; they cannot and should not be borne by the rural poor, protagonists of this development. In passing, we add that the costs are lower than benchmarks for operating health insurance in other settings.

This study is subject to certain limitations as well. For one, this study described the successful operation of two stand-alone CBHIs. Previous studies flagged that small stand-alone schemes could have solvency issues.[35] The Nepali CBHIs are, of course, exposed to this risk as well. The solution could be creating a mutual reinsurance fund to pool outlier risks. That option might be politically more pertinent when more people become insured by CBHIs. Secondly, the analysis of the outcome is using claims data of the first full year, but the first year may differ from subsequent years.

Conclusions

The argument has been made that poor people demand a development process driven by their communities.[36] This article provides empirical evidence of the development of health insurance driven by the beneficiary communities in rural Nepal.

After more than two years of operation, the CBHI schemes have been successful in retaining many/most enrollees beyond the original one-year contract and in attracting many new enrollees. This was achieved without premium subsidies and on a voluntary basis, as members agreed to pay health insurance premiums. From a development perspective, this is a remarkable and rare demonstration that contributory health insurance without premium subsidies can be attractive to rural poor in a low-income country. It is also a demonstration that when the target population is involved in priority-setting and pricing, partial coverage is financially and administratively possible. This voluntary, contributory, needs-based and demand-driven implementation model met with a very good response at the grassroots level, and responds to the wishes of the communities to retain decisions, funds, priorities and operations locally. The experience offers evidence of success in overcoming the single most challenging obstacle to UHC in the informal sector in low-income countries, namely, generating contributions from rural poor populations.

This positive evaluation notwithstanding, the verdict is still out whether these CBHI schemes can keep a similar score in the long term. This is similar to the question, on many minds, whether the unknown sportsman that hit a new record is the new champion, or maybe just the one-off lucky beginner. The undisputed facts are the positive results posted and the small-scale size of these implementations. Can this model be replicated to provide health insurance coverage to the majority of the Nepalese population living on less than $2 per day? The answer is unclear at this stage, mainly because scaling will require financial resources to provide technical assistance to enable communities become the decision-makers and market makers. The social change of bringing rural persons to manage mutual insurance is not intuitive, and birthing it must be funded as development aid, not as administrative loading. Considering that the Government of Nepal intends to reach UHC and must generate resources through contributions from the beneficiaries, we submit and conclude that the

[35] Dror and Armstrong (2006).
[36] Narayan *et al.* (2000).

CBHI model described here could make a definite contribution to achieving social policy goals of Nepal.

Acknowledgements

The authors gratefully acknowledge the financial, technical and administrative support without which this study could not have been carried out, including: funding by Rockefeller Foundation New York[37] (grant No. 2008 PHS 229 to Prof. David Dror via Erasmus University Rotterdam) and a grant from an anonymous donor to Save the Children USA (sub-grant #31531-01) to complete the baseline study (development of questionnaires, data collection and cleaning, analysis and report writing) in 2009/2010; funding from the German Ministry of International Cooperation (BMZ) through MISEREOR (the German Catholic Bishops' Organisation for Development Cooperation[38]) (grant No. 323-900-1098 ZG, 2011) to support the costs of initiating, involving, launching and operating the schemes during 2010–2012, as well as the cost of Open Access publication. The Micro Insurance Academy has been providing steering, ongoing technical, statistical and other assistance to the CBHI project and to field partners at all the stages. Mr. Ralf Radermacher of MIA led the initial development stages; Ms. Dhriti Bhatta and later Mr. Vikram Patil (MIA staff) provided backstopping and project management of the implementation process. Save the Children (Nepal Country Office) provided logistical support; Dr. Harihar Dev Pant, Chairman of Nirdhan Utthan Bank Ltd and his team in Nepalganj branch, Banke, as well as Mr. Kailash Rijal, Deputy Director of DEPROSC and his team in Dhading, the field partners, were instrumental in securing the cooperation of the members and their field staff. Dr. Lucy Firth (lead economist, MIA) offered insightful in-house editorial peer-review before submission for publication. Two anonymous peer reviewers also offered useful comments. Thanks to all.

References

Biener, C. and Eling, M. (2012) 'Insurability in microinsurance markets: An analysis of problems and potential solutions', *The Geneva Papers on Risk and Insurance—Issues and Practice* 37(1): 77–107.

Binnendijk, E., Dror, D.M., Gerelle, E. and Koren, R. (2013) 'Estimating willingness to pay for health insurance among rural poor in India by reference to Engel's law', *Social Science and Medicine* 76(1): 67–73.

Borghi, J., Maluka, S., Kuwawenaruwa, A., Makawia, S., Tantau, J., Mtei, G, Ally, M. and Macha, J. (2013) 'Promoting universal financial protection: A case study of new management of community health insurance in Tanzania', *Health Research Policy and Systems* 11: 21.

Cochran, W.G. (1977) *Sampling Techniques*, 3rd edn, New York: John Wiley & Sons, p. 21.

Danis, M., Binnendijk, E., Vellakkal, S., Ost, A., Koren, R. and Dror, D.M. (2007) 'Eliciting the health insurance benefit choices of low income populations in India with the CHAT exercise', *Economic and Political Weekly* 42(32): 3331–3339.

Dror, D.M. and Armstrong, J. (2006) 'Do micro health insurance units need capital or reinsurance? A simulated exercise to examine different alternatives', *The Geneva Papers on Risk and Insurance—Issues and Practice* 31(4): 739–761.

Dror, D.M. and Koren, R. (2012) 'The elusive quest for estimates of willingness to pay for health microinsurance among the poor in low income countries', in C. Churchill and M. Matul (eds) *Protecting the Poor: A Microinsurance Compendium*, Vol. II, Geneva: International Labour Organization, pp. 156–173.

Dror, D.M., Koren, R., Ost, A., Binnendijk, E., Vellakkal, S. and Danis, M. (2007) 'Health insurance benefit packages prioritized by low-income clients in India: Three criteria to estimate effectiveness of choice', *Social Science and Medicine* 64(4): 884–896.

[37] http://www.rockefellerfoundation.org/.
[38] http://www.misereor.org/ http://www.misereor.org/.

Dror, D.M. and Radermacher, R. (2010) 'Financial inclusion opportunities for micro health insurance in Nepal', from *http://ssrn.com/abstract=1548870*, accessed 1 March 2013.

Dror, D.M., Radermacher, R. and Koren, R. (2007) 'Willingness to pay for health insurance among rural and poor persons: Field evidence from seven micro health insurance units in India', *Health Policy* 82(1): 12–27.

Dror, D.M., van Putten-Rademaker, O. and Koren, R. (2008) 'Cost of illness: Evidence from a study in five resource-poor locations in India', *Indian Journal of Medical Research* 127(4): 347–361.

Garg, C.C. and Karan, A.K. (2009) 'Reducing out of pocket expenditures to reduce poverty: A disaggregated analysis at rural–urban and state level in India', *Health Policy and Planning* 24(2): 116–128.

GIZ Health Sector Support Program, Department of Health Services (2012) *Review of Community-Based Health Insurance Initiatives in Nepal.* December 2012, Teku, Kathmandu: Commissioned by BMZ and P4H.

Mahal, A., Krishnaswamy, K., Ruchismita, R. and Babu, B.G. (2013) 'What is a health card worth? A randomized controlled trial of an outpatient health insurance product in rural India', *The Lancet* 381(sup.2): S87.

Narayan, D., Patel, R., Schafft, K., Rademacher, A. and Koch-Schulte, S. (2000) *Voices of the Poor: Can Anyone Hear Us?* New York: Oxford University Press (for the World Bank).

Panda, P., Chakraborty, A. and Dror, D.M. (2013) *Building Awareness to Health Insurance among the Target population of Community-Based Health Insurance Schemes in Rural India* (mimeo).

Pott, J. and Holtz, J. (2013) 'Value-added services in health microinsurance', Microinsurance Paper No 19, International Labour Organization, from *http://www.ilo.org/public/english/employment/mifacility/download/mpaper19_services.pdf*, accessed 1 March 2013.

Ryan, M., Scott, D.A., Reeves, C., Bate, A., van Teijlingen, E.R., Russell, E.M., Napper, M. and Robb, C.M. (2001) 'Eliciting public preferences for healthcare: A systematic review of techniques', *Health Technology Assessment* 5(5): 1–186.

Som, R.K. (1996) *Practical Sampling Techniques*, New York: M Dekker.

Stoermer, M. (2012) *Community based health insurance (CBHI) schemes in Nepal: An evaluation of their performance and potential contribution to healthcare financing*, paper presented at the 2012 European Conference on Health Economics, Zurich.

Wipf, J. and Garand, D. (2010) *Performance Indicators for Microinsurance: A Handbook for Microinsurance Practitioners*, Luxembourg: ADA asbl.

World Bank (2007) 'Out of pocket health expenditure (% of private expenditure on health)', from *http://data.worldbank.org/indicator/SH.XPD.OOPC.ZS*, accessed 1 March 2013.

WHO (2011) 'Health financing for universal coverage and social health protection: Bridging the health-care divide: A background paper for the development of national health financing strategy, Kathmandu', from *http://www.who.int/providingforhealth/countries/HFBackgroundPaper.pdf*, accessed 1 March 2013.

Xu, K., Saksena, P., Jowett, M., Indikadahena, C., Kutzin, J. and Evans, D.B. (2010) 'Exploring the thresholds of health expenditure for protection against financial risk', *World Health Report* 2010, Background paper No. 19.

Appendix A

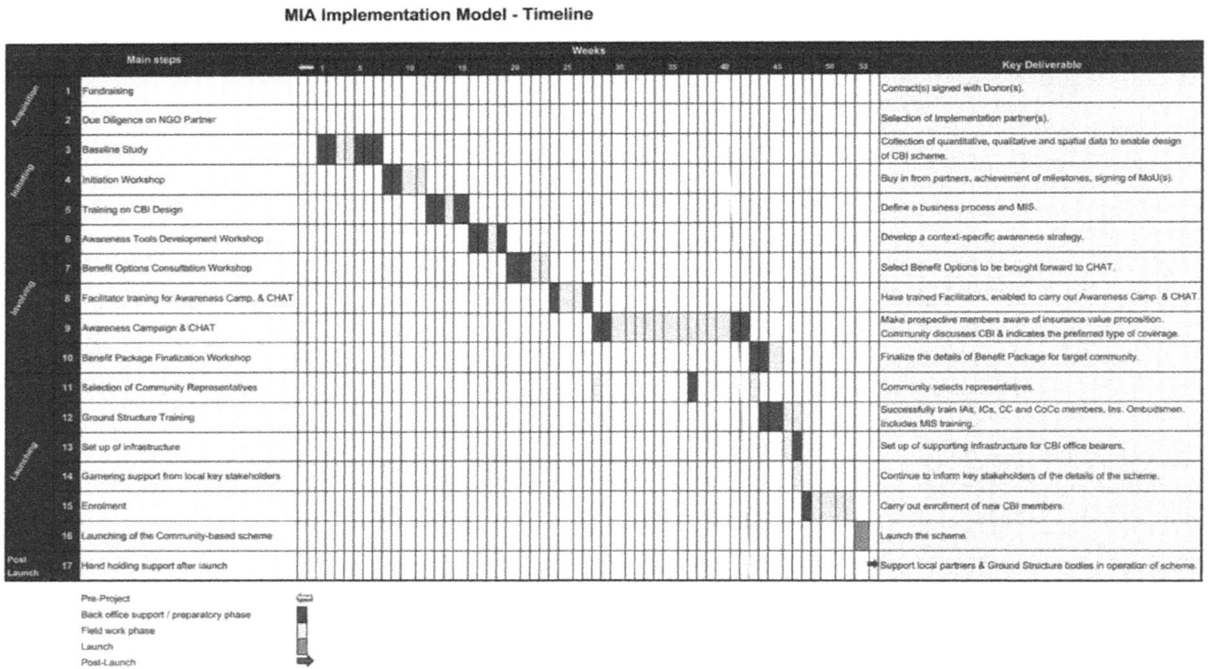

Figure A1. Details of the MIA implementation process.

Appendix B

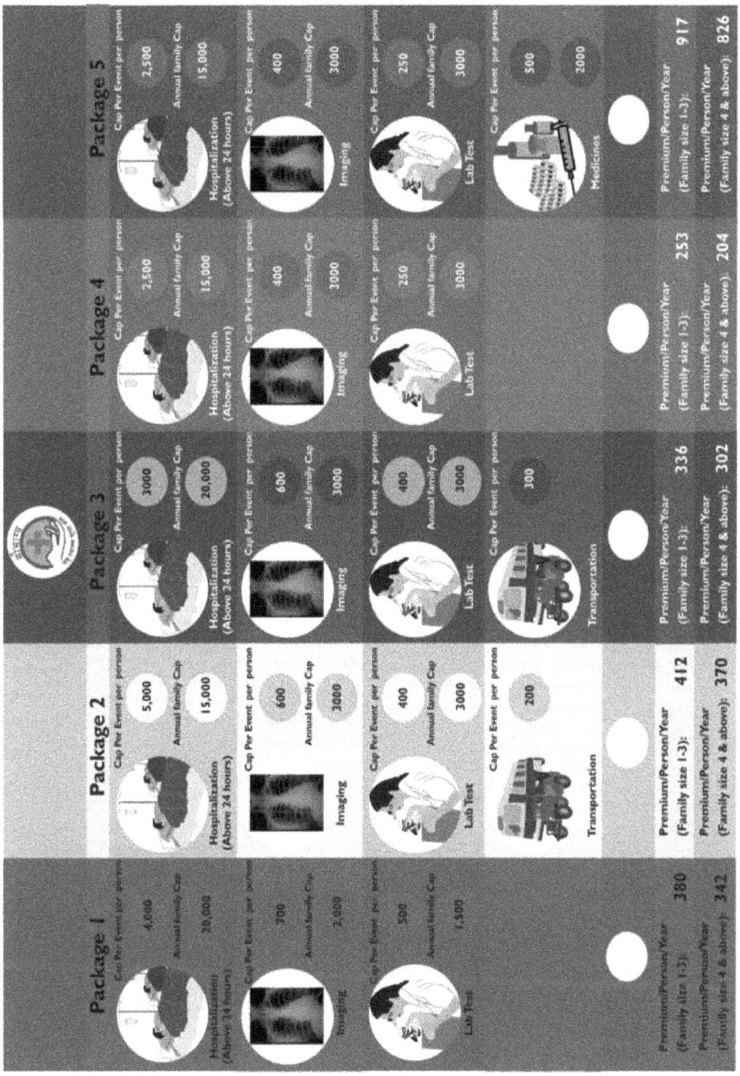

Figure B1. CHAT board describing various benefit packages, prepared by MIA.

Chapter 16

Microinsurance: Innovations in Low-Cost Health Insurance*

Main Messages

- Three microinsurance schemes in India are reviewed: two are member-operated and one is a commercial scheme.
- To review the microinsurance schemes, around 350 insured and 350 uninsured households were surveyed in each location, and scheme mangers were also interviewed.
- Analysis used parametric tests (t-test and one-way analysis of variance, or ANOVA) and non-parametric tests (median test and chi-square).

Focus Points

- Insurance with too low a cap was associated with inequity, whereas it should normally reduce inequity.
- Low caps and loss ratios are counterproductive in extending insurance coverage, financial protection, and high renewal rates among the poor.

---

*This chapter is reproduced from *Health Affairs* (2009), **28**(6), 1788–1798, Open Access, doi: 10.1377/hlthaff.28.6.1788, available at https://www.researchgate.net/publication/38065371_Microinsurance_Innovations_In_Low-Cost_Health_Insurance.

- Financial exposure was greatest, and protection was least, in the commercial scheme, which imposed the lowest caps on benefits and where income was the lowest.
- Inspite of less funding and professional resources than commercial insurers, MIUs have provided no less, and maybe more, protection to their insured populations, through mobilization of context-relevant social processes.

Structured Abstract

Introduction

Microinsurance schemes are designed to provide financial protection to the poor at affordable premium rates. In an attempt to keep premiums at low levels, these schemes have low benefit caps, and a low share of premiums is paid as benefits. In this paper, three microinsurance schemes are studied, two of which are member-operated and one a commercial scheme, to analyze the impact of low caps and loss ratios on extending insurance coverage, offering financial protection, and retaining members. The commercial scheme is Bharatiya Agro Industries Foundation (BAIF), and the member-operated schemes are UpLift Health and Nidan.

Method

Household surveys were conducted among 350 insured and 350 uninsured households in each of the locations covered by the three microinsurance schemes. The scheme managers were also interviewed regarding details about the microinsurance units.

In an attempt to distinguish pro-poor from pro-rich distribution of results, the study uses the World Bank method of concentration indexes. Comparisons were made between insured and uninsured cohorts, and among respondents across locations. The analysis used parametric tests (t-test and one-way analysis of variance, or ANOVA) and non-parametric tests (median test and chi-square). While p values less than 0.05 were considered significant, values of 0.05–0.10 were considered marginally significant.

The "incidence of illness" served as a proxy for perceived health status. It was calculated as the number and type of self-reported illness episodes during the three months preceding the survey, divided by the number of members. Respondents' descriptions of an episode were sorted into three types: acute illnesses, chronic illnesses, and accidents.

Findings

It was observed that in all three schemes, the low caps protected the insurance scheme rather than the resource-poor insured. Microinsurance with too low a cap was therefore associated with inequity whereas it should have normally reduced inequity.

Each of the three schemes adopted different methods to endure continuity of operations. BAIF followed a "relative benefit" plan which ensured that its microinsurance unit will never pay out more than its premium income. UpLift maintained a reserve fund, and vested the authority to control expenses with members acting as a committee and using local information, notably through case-by-case benefit curtailment. Nidan ran the highest risk of discontinuity of insurance as it depended on the commercial underwriter's decisions to (dis)continue business with this group, on which Nidan had no say.

All three schemes enrolled poor households and raised their use of hospital services. The schemes differed in target membership, benefits, and claims management practices. The findings suggest that financial exposure was greatest, and protection was least, in the commercial scheme, which imposed the lowest caps on benefits and where income was the lowest.

Box 1: Adequacy of Coverage

- Coverage has been limited to hospital bills upto a maximum of approximately US$112 in BAIF and UpLift, and approximately US$45 in Nidan Plan A.
- The degree of inadequacy of financial protection depends on the risk of incurring above-cap hospitalization costs, multiplied by the average out-of-pocket sum payable, relating this sum to income.

(Continued)

Box 1: (*Continued*)

- Financial exposure is calculated as the fraction of cases among the insured with costs above the cap, multiplied by the mean actual costs above the cap for the insured, divided by the mean income per household member in the insured cohort.
  - A value of zero denotes no financial exposure.
  - A low value means better financial protection.
- The higher the financial exposure index ratio, the higher the exposure to financial risk.

Conclusion

The authors conclude that low caps and loss ratios are counterproductive in extending insurance coverage, financial protection, and high renewal rates among the poor in India. Another inference drawn from this study is that microinsurance units, despite less funding and professional resources than commercial insurers enjoy, have provided no less, and maybe more, protection to their insured populations, through mobilization of context-relevant social processes.

MarketWatch

Microinsurance: Innovations In Low-Cost Health Insurance

Community-based arrangements offering low-cost health insurance can provide financial protection for poor households.

by David M. Dror, Ralf Radermacher, Shrikant B. Khadilkar, Petra Schout, François-Xavier Hay, Arbind Singh, and Ruth Koren

ABSTRACT: Microinsurance—low-cost health insurance based on a community, cooperative, or mutual and self-help arrangements—can provide financial protection for poor households and improve access to health care. However, low benefit caps and a low share of premiums paid as benefits—both designed to keep these arrangements in business—perversely limited these schemes' ability to extend coverage, offer financial protection, and retain members. We studied three schemes in India, two of which are member-operated and one a commercial scheme, using household surveys of insured and uninsured households and interviews with managers. All three enrolled poor households and raised their use of hospital services, as intended. Financial exposure was greatest, and protection was least, in the commercial scheme, which imposed the lowest caps on benefits and where income was the lowest. [Health Aff (Millwood). 2009;28(6):1788–98]

Increasing awareness in India about the value of health insurance has led to a diversity of plans, including "microinsurance." Microinsurance is low-cost health insurance based on a community or cooperative model, as distinct from conventional insurance. Microinsurance units can increase access to health care,[1] improve equality among members,[2] capture additional resources,[3] and promote social protection[4–9] and the development of financial systems.[10] Most of them require reinsurance.[11] Micro health insurance covered an estimated thirty-six million people worldwide in 2006.[12]

We report on a study of three microinsurance arrangements operating in two Indian states. The three differ in target membership, benefits, and claims management practices. We identify the strengths and shortcomings of the different approaches as judged by their im-

David Dror (daviddror@socialre.org) is professor of health insurance at the Institute of Health Policy and Management, Erasmus University Rotterdam in the Netherlands, and chairman of Micro Insurance Academy in New Delhi, India. Ralf Radermacher is director of research and training at Micro Insurance Academy. Shrikant Khadilkar is senior project coordinator for community health programs at BAIF Development Research Foundation in Maharashtra, India. Petra Schout is a project manager at the Dutch Federation of Patients and Consumer Organisations (NPCF) in Breda, the Netherlands. François-Xavier Hay was cofounder and director of UpLift Health in Pune, India, at the time of this study. Arbind Singh is founding director of Nidan in Patna, Bihar, India. Ruth Koren is professor of medical sciences, Sackler Faculty of Medicine, at the Felsenstein Medical Research Centre in Tel Aviv, Israel.

pact on financial protection and equitable access to expensive health care.

Unlike commercial insurers, affiliation with a microinsurance scheme is voluntary but is often open only to people who are linked with the group in other ways (which limits their scope for increasing membership). Some operate as mutual schemes, with members being both insured and carriers of risk. This model can attenuate potential conflicts of interest between insurer and insured. Solidarity-enhancing rules keep individual interests (which could increase adverse selection) restrained by group interests. We analyzed the microinsurance schemes' operational results by how well each benefited its members.

Description Of The Three Microinsurance Units

■ **Bharatiya Agro Industries Foundation (BAIF).** In 2002 the Development Research Foundation launched a commercial health insurance plan at its rural outpost in Pune, India, for women ages 18–70 participating in so-called self-help groups. The annual premium was INR 131.75 (US$3)[13] (plus an administrative fee of INR 25, or US$0.50); the benefit covered hospitalization up to INR 5,000 (US$113.65), plus concessionary prices for primary care at a BAIF center. Facing a 75 percent premium increase in 2003, the members launched a mutual scheme. The premium remained unchanged, with benefits capped at INR 5,000 (or less if all claims in any month exceeded one-twelfth of the annual premium). Claims not fully settled are eligible for reimbursement in future months when balances are positive. This "relative benefit" plan ensures that the scheme never runs a deficit; the claims loss ratio (the share of premiums used to pay claims) was 92 percent in 2005. A committee of members settles claims, monitors financial performance, and determines strategic direction. Membership grew when family members were added in 2004. By 2005, some 600 households had joined.

■ **UpLift Health.** UpLift Health began health insurance operations in 2003 in Pune City among slum-dwelling adults who borrowed from UpLift India's microfinance mechanism. Membership in 2005 was 16,356; premiums were age-related, then (in 2004) standardized at INR 100 (US$2.27) per person per year, discounted to 50 percent if entire households joined. UpLift's social workers collect premiums.

UpLift's microinsurance reimburses up to 80 percent of hospitalization costs, capped at INR 5,000 per person and year. Different maximum limits apply for specific illnesses.[14] Preexisting conditions and bills from out-of-network hospitals are excluded. UpLift pays income-loss compensation of INR 50 (US$1) per day (for days 3–18 of hospitalization). It negotiates discounts for outpatient care, organizes checkup camps and monthly prevention talks, and operates a 24/7 telephone "health hotline" giving medical guidance.

A members' claim committee decides reimbursement; it can authorize humanitarian reimbursements (from a "solidarity fund") for otherwise unqualified claims. The claims loss ratio was 42 percent in 2005.

■ **Nidan.** Nidan targets market vendors in Patna, Bihar; it had 10,189 members in 2005. Nidan's microinsurance unit was launched in 2001, through an association with the Self-Employed Women's Association (SEWA)[5,15] (a Gujarat-based nongovernmental organization that acts as an agent of a commercial insurer). Nidan's Plan A (chosen by 66 percent of members) costs INR 170 (US$3.86) per insured person plus spouse, and reimburses 80 percent of hospitalization costs (from accredited hospitals only, except for emergencies) up to INR 2,000 (US$45); Plan B costs INR 350 (US$7.95) for coverage up to INR 6,000 (US$136). Preexisting conditions and maternity-related costs are excluded. People ages 18–55 can join; renewal is possible until age sixty. Nidan self-help groups do not process claims or make strategic decisions. SEWA scrutinizes claims, paying after about two months. The claims loss ratio was 43.5 percent in 2005.

Study Data And Methods

■ **Data.** The study was based on 2005 household survey data, obtained in areas covered by the three microinsurance schemes. Sampling followed three stages: (1) purposively selected schemes; (2) several villages or urban areas at each location; and (3) random selection of about ten insured and ten uninsured households in each village. Some 350 insured and 350 uninsured households were surveyed in each location. The sample size was fixed to obtain statistical significance of differences of at least 50 percent between insured and uninsured cohorts, based on rates of morbidity and hospitalization from the Indian National Sample Survey.[16] Some details about the microinsurance units (for example, claims ratios) were obtained from their managers.

The questionnaire included household demographics, education, income (all sources of cash and in-kind), and expenditure (food, housing, apparel, transportation, and so forth), as well as health care use and costs (hospitalizations, number and cost of outpatient consultations, and drug costs). Respondents were also asked about their number of illness episodes in a specified time period. "Income per household member" and "non-health-related expenditure per member" were significantly correlated ($p < 0.01$).

■ Analysis methods. We calculated concentration indexes, following the World Bank method,[17, 18] to distinguish pro-poor from pro-rich distributions of results.[19] We compared insured and uninsured cohorts and compared respondents across locations (the latter including both insured and uninsured, unless otherwise stated). For brevity, we refer to these as, for example, "BAIF insured and uninsured," even though, by definition, there are no uninsured people in the BAIF microinsurance scheme. We used parametric tests (t-test and one-way analysis of variance, or ANOVA) and nonparametric tests (median test and chi-square). p values less than 0.05 were considered significant, and values of 0.05–0.10 were considered marginally significant. Data were analyzed using SPSS (version 12).

■ Health status. The number and type of self-reported illness episodes during the three months preceding the survey, divided by the number of members to enable comparisons across households of different sizes, served as a proxy for perceived health status. This parameter is called "incidence of illness." Respondents' descriptions of an episode were sorted into three types: acute illnesses, chronic illnesses, and accidents.[20]

Study Findings

■ Low socioeconomic status among clients. Respondents from all three schemes earned less than US$1 per day (Exhibit 1); incomes in urban areas were even below the official Monthly per Capita Consumer Expenditure,[16] reflecting UpLift's targeting slum dwellers and Nidan's targeting the very poor. The BAIF population (rural) seemed better off than average for residents of that state.[21] Differences between insured and uninsured people were significant only in Nidan (the uninsured were wealthier), and income levels differed significantly across the three microinsurance units. Thus, the evidence does not uphold the claim that "insurance is for the richer" or that the insured systematically enjoy higher socioeconomic status than the uninsured. The Nidan population (both insured and uninsured) was less educated than the two other groups, and the insured were less educated than the uninsured. In UpLift, the insured cohort had attained higher education levels than the uninsured.

In summary, the direction and extent of differences between the insured and the uninsured were inconsistent and depended (at least partly) on the targeting of the microinsurance units.

■ Dissimilar illness patterns across schemes. We observed significantly higher illness incidence among the insured cohort in BAIF and Nidan (supporting the notion that people who enrolled in health insurance perceived their health status as low),[22] but not in UpLift (Exhibit 2). There was no significant difference in incidence of illness between BAIF and UpLift populations, but a marked difference with Nidan, which reported more than double the incidence of the other two.

We examined the distribution of illnesses by type. Among both insured and uninsured in

EXHIBIT 1
Socioeconomic And Demographic Details Of The Insured And Uninsured Cohorts In Three Microinsurance Units, India, 2005

	BAIF		UpLift		Nidan	
Cohort	Insured	Uninsured	Insured	Uninsured	Insured	Uninsured
No. of households surveyed	349	459	347	353	349	351
Total population surveyed	1,958	1,942	1,606	1,763	2,250	2,110
Annual household income per member (median)						
Income per household member (mean INR; SE)	15,621 (±1,193)	13,410 (±873)	11,054 (±339)	10,854 (±503)	7,817 (±281)	9,225* (±376)
Income per household member (median INR)	11,120	10,172	10,500	9,600	6,615	7,500*
House type (percent of households; chi-square)						
Kaccha[a]	15.9%	20.6%***	2.6%	9.5%	63.3%	57.5%***
Semi-Pacca[b]	33.7	37.7***	38.8	35.1	26.8	23.1***
Pacca[c]	50.4	41.7***	58.6	55.4	9.9%	19.4***
Education of household head (years; chi-square)						
0	14.0%	12.7%	8.7%	8.1%***	57.1%	46.7%****
1–4	15.2	19.2	10.2	16.0***	13.9	12.5****
5–10	58.6	55.9	60.1	61.9***	26.7	30.2****
11+	12.2	12.2	21.0	14.0***	2.3	10.5****

SOURCE: Authors' 2005 household survey data.

NOTES: Significance denotes difference between insured and uninsured. INR is Indian rupees (in 2006, one U.S. dollar equaled 44 Indian rupees). SE is standard error.

[a] Self-built structures from bricks, plastered with a mud mixture, requiring much maintenance.

[b] Strong structures with a solid base, but impermanent roof or floor material, built partly professionally and partly by the dweller.

[c] Strong structures, firm roof and floor to which a second level can be added; more expensive, and found in middle- and upper-income segments, as well as in government housing sites.

$*p < 0.10$ $***p < 0.01$ $****p < 0.001$

all locations, 64–81 percent of episodes were acute illnesses. Chronic diseases were next (15–22 percent). There was no difference in the distribution of illness types between the insured and uninsured in BAIF and Nidan, but in UpLift the uninsured reported more chronic diseases than the insured. Although households were aware of prevalence and costs of chronic conditions, households with chronic illnesses were not more likely than others to enroll in the insurance program, perhaps because chronic conditions were excluded from coverage as "preexisting conditions."

■ **Higher use of hospitals among the insured.** The data confirm that hospitalization was more common among insured households than among the uninsured during the two years preceding the survey (Exhibit 3). When all of the cohorts are aggregated (not shown), the incidence of hospitalization was 4.2 percent among the insured and 2.8 percent among the uninsured (significantly higher in all three locations). Our result for the uninsured is comfortingly similar to the corresponding National Sample Survey rates of 2.3 percent in rural populations and 3.1 percent in urban populations.[23]

The greater use of hospitals is, however, associated with higher out-of-pocket spending. The average hospitalization cost before reimbursement for all insured people in BAIF was INR 4,868 (standard error: ±648); in UpLift, INR 4,515 (SE: ±699); and in Nidan, INR 3,764 (SE: ±454). However, some 25.5 percent of

EXHIBIT 2
Patterns Of Illness Among The Insured And Uninsured Cohorts In Three Microinsurance Units, India, 2005

	BAIF		UpLift		Nidan	
Incidence of illness (3 months)[a]	**Insured**	**Uninsured**	**Insured**	**Uninsured**	**Insured**	**Uninsured**
Illness episodes per household member (mean)	0.15	0.1***	0.14	0.13	0.34	0.24****
Type of illness[b]						
Acute	67.0%	64.4%	81.2%	66.0%****	68.5%	69.4%
Chronic	21.4	22.1	15.4	22.3****	18.2	18.3
Accidents	1.4	4.3	0.4	1.3	4.9	4.6
Undefined	9.9	9.1	3.0	10.5****	8.4	7.7

SOURCE: Authors' 2005 household survey data.
NOTE: A version of this exhibit showing standard errors is available in an appendix, online at http://content.healthaffairs.org/cgi/content/full/28/6/1788/DC1.
[a] Significance denotes difference between insured and uninsured (t-test).
[b] Significance denotes difference between insured and uninsured (chi-square).
***$p < 0.01$ ****$p < 0.001$

EXHIBIT 3
Use Of Health Care Services Among The Insured And Uninsured Cohorts In Three Microinsurance Units, India, 2005

	BAIF		UpLift		Nidan	
Hospitalizations (episodes per household member in the past 2 years)	**Insured**	**Uninsured**	**Insured**	**Uninsured**	**Insured**	**Uninsured**
Number of households	349	359	347	353	349	351
Mean incidence per household member	0.0776 (±0.007)	0.0479**** (±0.006)	0.0837 (±0.012)	0.0506* (±0.006)	0.0923 (±0.008)	0.0714*** (±0.007)
Number and costs of MD consultations and drugs per illness episode (3 months)						
Number of illness episodes	173	141	154	164	288	236
Consultations per episode						
Mean	2.99 (±0.389)	2.647 (±0.247)	2.54 (±0.265)	1.97 (±0.150)	1.53 (±0.078)	1.54 (±0.117)
Median	2	2	1	1	1	1
Consultation costs per illness episode (INR)						
Mean	311 (±56)	319 (±62)	178 (±26)	176 (±41)	95 (±7)	114 (±23)
Median	100	100	60	50	62	56
Drug costs per illness episode						
Mean	314.6 (±32)	525.7 (±91)	304.8 (±60)	287 (±46)	519.8 (±37)	520.5 (±47)
Median	200	150	80	60	333	300

SOURCE: Authors' 2005 household survey data.
NOTES: Significance denotes difference between insured and uninsured. INR is Indian rupees (in 2006, US$1 = INR 44).
*$p < 0.10$ ***$p < 0.01$ ****$p < 0.001$

hospitalized people in BAIF had to pay, on average, INR 8,204 as costs above the cap, approximately 17 percent and INR 8,734 in UpLift, and approximately 43 percent and INR 5,475 in Nidan.[24]

■ Use of other services and insurance status. We asked respondents about health care use during the three months preceding the survey (Exhibit 3), to explore whether insurance status was associated with different health care–seeking patterns (based on a proxy for needs-adjusted access to care). We asked about the number and cost of consultations and the cost of drugs per illness episode. None of the three proxy parameters of needs-adjusted use of primary care was associated with insurance status; the differences across the three locations were striking.

■ Preference for private providers. Our survey uncovered an overwhelming preference for private hospitals, physicians (consultations), and pharmacies, in all locations by insured and uninsured alike (Exhibit 4), even though the government's official policy is to provide free services. The difference between the insured and uninsured was noteworthy only with respect to hospitalizations among members of UpLift, where 18.2 percent of the uninsured but only 6.6 percent of the insured preferred public hospitals (UpLift reimbursed bills from many private hospitals).

■ Lower levels of inequality among the insured. Because insured people must pay expenses that exceed the cap of their coverage, does this imply that richer insured people would obtain more benefits than poorer insured people would? We examined income disparity by calculating Gini coefficients using income per household member.[25] The data on income are in Exhibit 1, and the Gini coefficients are in Exhibit 5.

In general, we found some income inequality in all cohorts; inequality was higher among the uninsured cohorts. BAIF had the highest inequality (Gini coefficient 0.46), and Nidan, the lowest (0.33). Income inequality among the insured was lower than among the uninsured in UpLift and Nidan; in BAIF, it was indistinguishable from that of the uninsured.

We also examined the association between income and illness patterns or access to services, using concentration indices for illness episodes, incidence of hospitalizations, consultations (incidence and costs), and drug

EXHIBIT 4
Type Of Provider (Public Versus Private) Preferred By Clients Among The Insured And Uninsured Cohorts In Three Microinsurance Units, India, 2005

	BAIF		UpLift		Nidan	
Provider type	**Insured**	**Uninsured**	**Insured**	**Uninsured**	**Insured**	**Uninsured**
Hospitalization						
Number (households)	343	352	318	336	347	345
Public	12.2%	14.8%	6.6%	18.2%****	17.9%	17.1%
Private	87.8	85.2	93.4	81.8****	82.1	82.9
MD consultations						
Number (households)	349	355	346	352	346	346
Public	8.0%	8.6%	1.2%	3.7%***	4.0%	3.8%
Private	92.0	90.3	98.8	96.3***	96.0	96.2
Drugs						
Number (households)	348	358	347	353	348	350
Public	2.9%	5.0%	0.3%	0.3%	1.1%	4.0%***
Private	97.1	95.0	99.7	99.7	98.9	96.0***

SOURCE: Authors' 2005 household survey data.
NOTES: Significance denotes difference between insured and uninsured. INR is Indian rupees (in 2006, US$1 = INR 44).
*$p < 0.10$ ***$p < 0.01$ ****$p < 0.001$

EXHIBIT 5
Income-Related Equality Between The Insured And Uninsured Cohorts In Three Microinsurance Units, India, 2005

	BAIF		UpLift		Nidan	
	Insured	Uninsured	Insured	Uninsured	Insured	Uninsured
Number in sample for illness episodes/hospitalizations	349	359	347	353	349	351
Gini coefficient[a]	0.480****	0.463****	0.303****	0.359****	0.290****	0.333****
Illness episodes (CI)	−0.059****	−0.094***	−0.079*	−0.133****	−0.008	−0.021
Hospitalizations (CI)	0.006	0.018	0.071	0.068	0.122*	0.075
Number in sample for MD consultations and drug costs	173	141	154	164	288	236
Consultations (CI)	−0.119	0.015	−0.042	−0.025	0.017	0.050
Cost of consultations (CI)	0.073	0.098	0.001	0.315***	0.009	0.199*
Cost of drugs (CI)	0.115***	0.028	0.066	0.134	0.147****	0.111***

SOURCE: Authors' 2005 household survey data.
NOTES: Significance denotes difference from zero for the sub-cohort mentioned above (t-test). CI is concentration index values. A version of this exhibit showing standard errors is available in an appendix, online at http://content.healthaffairs.org/cgi/content/full/28/6/1788/DC1.
[a] Gini coefficients are based on cash income per household member.
$*p < 0.10$ $***p < 0.01$ $****p < 0.001$

costs (Exhibit 5). In four cohorts (BAIF and UpLift insured and uninsured) the concentration indices for the incidence of illness episodes were negative, indicating that poorer households experienced more illness. The Nidan concentration indices did not differ from zero.

We then examined the income-related distribution of hospitalizations. Insured households reported more hospitalizations per member than uninsured households. If cost is limiting access to hospitalization, we would expect a pro-rich bias among the uninsured and a correction of that bias among the insured; a study among microinsurance units in the Philippines found this to be the case.[2] Concentration indices were not significantly different from zero in BAIF and UpLift, for both the insured and uninsured. In Nidan, the indices were positive and significantly different from zero for the insured but, curiously, not for the uninsured. This implies that in Nidan the more affluent insured households reported a higher increase in use of hospitals than the poorer households did, and far above their share in the population.

■ **Income and access to primary care.** We also examined the effect of income on needs-adjusted access to primary care. We measured first the concentration index for consultations per illness episode and found no deviation from income-related equality in either cohort in all locations. However, after examining the cost of consultations per illness episode, we found a positive and significant concentration index (pro-rich distribution) for the uninsured cohort in UpLift, absent in the insured cohort.

■ **Cost of drugs per illness.** Finally, we found a marginally significant positive concentration index, indicating pro-rich distribution, in the cost of drugs per illness episode (which the scheme does not cover) among the insured in BAIF. In Nidan, income was a significant determinant of purchases of medicines (a positive and significant pro-rich distribution in both cohorts). This could reflect the fact that compared to other areas, drugs were more expensive in Nidan (Exhibit 3), where the population was poorer (Exhibit 1).

Discussion

Limitations. A household was defined as *insured* when the respondent replied positively to the question, "Are you or any member of your household insured for health with the local [microinsurance unit]?" It is possible that some people counted as insured were in fact uninsured (even though there was supporting information that in most households more than one person was insured). Thus, we may have underestimated the impact of insurance.

We inquired about illness episodes during the three months preceding the survey and about hospitalizations during the previous two years. These intervals may have been subject to some recall bias.

Achievements of the units. All three microinsurance units aim to reduce their members' financial exposure to the cost of hospitalization. Their health insurance activity is an extension of other activities for which these organizations were originally created. None of these schemes is exclusively or primarily a health insurer; none has developed overriding commercial interests for the health insurance, such as increasing the membership beyond the original catchment area of its (core) activities; none "cherry picks" good risks to maximize profits; none has developed revenue streams from providers in return for guaranteed volumes; and none received any subsidy (other than some undocumented in-kind contribution of the supporting nongovernmental organizations' staff time). Therefore, we assessed their effectiveness first by their achievement in protecting their members' finances.

Adequacy of coverage. Coverage has been limited to hospital bills up to a maximum of approximately US$112 in BAIF and UpLift and approximately US$45 in Nidan Plan A (which was chosen by most members). These levels are adequate for costs up to the cap but inadequate for higher costs. The degree of inadequacy of financial protection depends on the risk of incurring above-cap hospitalization costs, multiplied by the average out-of-pocket sum payable, relating this sum to income. We have developed a financial exposure index, which we use to measure the performance of the schemes on this count.

Financial exposure is calculated as the fraction of cases among the insured with costs above the cap, multiplied by the mean actual costs above the cap for the insured, divided by the mean income per household member in the insured cohort. A value of zero denotes no financial exposure, and a low value means better financial protection. The higher the financial exposure index ratio, the higher the exposure to financial risk.[26, 27] These values[28] show that Nidan's insured members were more exposed to financial risk, reflecting the combined effect of a lower cap and lower mean income.[29]

The financial exposure index can be calculated without reference to premiums or to the parameters used for premium calculations, because it measures the unprotected share of costs rather than premium-to-coverage efficiency. The index is also independent of claims loss ratios reported by each microinsurance unit. For 2005, the loss ratios of BAIF, UpLift, and Nidan were 92 percent, 42 percent, and 43.5 percent, respectively; BAIF stands out as having performed best from the members' viewpoint. This was no accident or "statistical blip"; rather, it was inherent in the BAIF "relative benefit" plan. Although this plan could entail uncertainty as to the actual reimbursement rate if claims exceed premiums, the trade-off is a higher payout in other cases and a guarantee of financial sustainability.

Access to hospitalization. The insured cohorts of all three microinsurance schemes reported greater use of the hospital than the uninsured did. However, when we compared the difference in the incidence of illness (Exhibit 2) to the difference in hospitalization between the insured and uninsured (Exhibit 3), we saw that needs-adjusted rates of hospitalization were higher only among the UpLift insured cohort.

Because incidence was not higher in UpLift, there is no evidence of adverse selection (unlike in BAIF or Nidan); this suggests that UpLift's incentive to enroll entire families contributed to reducing adverse selection. The higher utilization may indicate a transition from underuse to normal use. This is an important positive effect, considering documented underuse among the poor without health insurance, suggested by 1995–96 National Sample Survey data showing that in India, hospitalization rates among households in the highest quartile of consumption spending were almost double those of the lowest quartile, and by the 2004 data stating that 28 percent of people in rural India said that they did not seek treatment when ill because of financial problems.[23]

■ **Equitability of increased use.** The prevalence of chronic illnesses (the only costs that can be predicted with certainty) was not higher in any of the insured cohorts in this study, offering another indication that the microinsurance units contributed to normalizing underuse rather than being exposed to adverse selection. The practice of reimbursing costs for using private providers, which were overwhelmingly preferred by the surveyed population in all locations, also favored higher utilization. However, private providers cost more than public providers, which raises the question of how equitable the utilization has been. We found no evidence of pro-rich bias in hospitalization among the three uninsured cohorts. However, we found a strong pro-rich bias in the access to hospitalization among the insured in Nidan. This suggests that only the more affluent members could afford the high out-of-pocket cost required. Because illness was pro-poor but spending on hospitalization (and medicines) was pro-rich in Nidan, much of this gap could probably have been narrowed had more members chosen Plan B (with higher caps and a higher premium). Insufficient clarity about the value of insurance could explain why members opted for the lower premium as an intuitive way to reduce their loss if they did not file any claims. More effort on the part of Nidan to explain the value proposition of alternative plans could probably persuade members to choose more suitable coverage.

■ **Adding and retaining enrollees.** The membership in all three microinsurance units has grown over time. Because they are active in only limited geographic areas, one way of increasing their size is high membership retention. However, renewal rates in UpLift and Nidan have been about 50 percent. In the UpLift cohort, 72.6 percent of insured households did not have a hospitalization during the two years surveyed, and officials speculated that most of their dropouts were those who did not file any claims. Of the insured households in the Nidan cohort, 59 percent did not experience a hospitalization in the reported period. In view of the high financial exposure index ratio calculated for Nidan, we assumed that at least some dropouts were members who submitted an insurance claim yet were frustrated by the insufficient coverage. The fact that reimbursement in Nidan usually took two months (compared to one month or less in BAIF and UpLift) probably obliged some members to borrow the money, and the associated interest reduced the value of insurance. This suggests that severe and extended financial exposure of insured people could discourage affiliation in ways resembling those of people with no claims: the nonclaimants might wonder what benefit they get from paying a premium, and the severely exposed might wonder why they should insure if insurance benefits are "too little and too late."

■ **Bottom-line results.** Nevertheless, the successes of the microinsurance units are telling signs that resource-poor people are aware of health insurance, are willing to join voluntarily and pay for it even without premium subsidies, and seek a role through a process they trust in enhancing the transparency of operations and reducing administrative costs. In all three schemes, the low caps (at the low end of coverage in India) protected the insurance scheme rather than resource-poor insured people. Consequently, insurance with too low a cap was associated with inequity, when it should normally reduce inequity.

The three schemes chose different ways to ensure continuity of operations. BAIF ensured that its microinsurance unit will never pay out more than its premium income through its "relative benefit" plan. UpLift constituted a reserve fund and vested the authority to control expenses with members acting as a committee and using local information, notably through case-by-case benefit curtailment. Nidan was most at risk of discontinuity of insurance as it depended on the commercial underwriter's decisions to (dis)continue business with this group, on which Nidan had no say.

Finally, differences between the insured and uninsured may be influenced both by the practice of limiting affiliation only to people involved in the other activities of the "mother" organizations and by allowing those people the choice to opt out of (or not to join) the health insurance scheme. This may explain inconsistent socioeconomic differences between the insured and uninsured across the three schemes and the low renewal rates reported by two of them. UpLift directors suggested that most dropouts did not file any claims, while in Nidan, insured members who experienced high out-of-pocket spending (or high financial exposure) could also drop out.

FROM THIS STUDY we conclude that low caps and loss ratios are counterproductive in extending insurance coverage, financial protection, and high renewal rates among the poor in India. We also conclude that the microinsurance units, despite less funding and professional resources than commercial insurers enjoy, have provided no less, and maybe more, protection to their insured populations, through mobilization of context-relevant social processes.

This study was funded by the European Commission (Grant no. ASIE/2004/095-995) under the European Cross Cultural Program, conducted under the project Strengthening Micro Health Insurance Units for the Poor in India. It was implemented jointly by the University of Cologne, Erasmus University Rotterdam, and the Federation of Indian Chambers of Commerce and Industry in 2005–06. Additional funding to enlarge the sample size was provided by Deutsche Gesellschaft für Technische Zusammenarbeit. This funding support is gratefully acknowledged. The authors also are grateful to Olga van Putten-Rademaker for having classified self-reported illnesses into categories, and to Erika Binnendijk for research assistance.

NOTES

1. Dror DM, Soriano ES, Lorenzo ME, Sarol JN Jr, Azcuna RS, Koren R. Field based evidence of enhanced healthcare utilization among persons insured by micro health insurance units in Philippines. Health Policy. 2005;73(3):263–71.
2. Dror DM, Koren R, Steinberg DM. The impact of Filipino micro health-insurance units on income-related equality of access to healthcare. Health Policy. 2006;77(3):304–17.
3. Preker AS, Carrin G, Dror DM, Jakab M, Hsiao W, Arhin-Tenkorang D. Effectiveness of community health financing in meeting the cost of illness. Bull World Health Organ. 2002;80(2):143–50.
4. Ranson MK, Sinha T, Chatterjee M, Acharya A, Bhavsar A, Morris SS, et al. Making health insurance work for the poor: learning from the Self-Employed Women's Association's (SEWA) community-based health insurance scheme in India. Soc Sci Med. 2006;62(3):707–20.
5. Siegel PB, Alwang J, Canagarajah S. Viewing microinsurance as a social risk management instrument. Washington (DC): World Bank Social Protection Unit, Human Development Network; 2001. Social Protection Discussion Paper Series 0116.
6. ILO-STEP. The role of micro-insurance as a tool to face risks in the context of social protection. Geneva (Switzerland): ILO/STEP and GTZ; 2006.
7. Schmidt JO, Schramm B, Hohmann J, Holst J, Jowett M, Ramm G, et al. Linking up social protection systems in developing countries: overview of some experiences and approaches [Internet]. Eschborn (Germany): Deutsche Gesellschaft für Technische Zusammenarbeit; 2005 [cited 2009 Aug 25]. Available from: http://www2.gtz.de/dokumente/bib/06-1182.pdf
8. Tabor SR. Community-based health insurance and social protection policy. Washington (DC): World Bank; 2005. Social Protection Discussion Paper Series 0503.
9. International Social Security Association. Volume and cost of sickness benefits in kind and cash. Geneva (Switzerland): ISSA; 1961.
10. International Association of Insurance Supervisors and CGAP Working Group on Microinsurance. Issues in regulation and supervision of microinsurance. Basel (Switzerland): IAIS/CGAP; 2007.
11. Dror DM, Armstrong J. Do micro health insur-

ance units need capital or reinsurance? A simulated exercise to examine different alternatives. Geneva Papers on Risk and Insurance. 2006;31: 739–61.

12. Key-informant interviews with managers of the schemes.
13. The exchange rate (one U.S. dollar equals 44 Indian rupees) was valid at the time of the survey in 2005.
14. The following were capped at INR 5,000: cesarean section, paralysis of limbs, fracture, pneumonia, and critical surgery. The following were capped at INR 2,500: kidney stone operation, hernia, urinary infection, jaundice, and typhoid. The following was capped at INR 1,000: malaria.
15. Garand D. VimoSEWA India. Geneva (Switzerland): International Labor Organization; 2005. Case Study no. 16.
16. National Sample Survey Organisation. National Sample Survey (NSS) sixtieth round. New Delhi (India): Ministry of Statistics and Programme Implementation, Government of India; 2005. Report no. 505.
17. World Bank. Concentration curves. Washington (DC): World Bank; 2004. Quantitative Techniques for Health Equity Analysis, Technical Note no. 6.
18. World Bank. The concentration index. Washington (DC): World Bank; 2004. Quantitative Techniques for Health Equity Analysis, Technical Note no. 7.
19. The concentration index is twice the area between the concentration curve and the equality diagonal; values can vary between −1 and +1; negative values denote a pro-poor distribution and positive values, a pro-rich distribution.
20. Dror DM, Van Putten-Rademaker O, Koren R. Cost of illness: evidence from a study in five resource-poor locations in India. Indian J Med Res. 2008;127(4):347–61.
21. The income values observed in our study can be compared to Monthly per Capita Consumer Expenditure (MPCE) values published as part of the National Sample Survey's sixtieth round (2005). Accordingly, the MPCE in rural Bihar was INR 442 and in urban Bihar, INR 784. Compare this to our data, reflecting an aggregated rural-urban cohort that yielded INR 710. In Maharashtra the MPCE value was INR 569 (rural population) and INR 1,259 (urban population); in our study, the corresponding numbers were INR 1,208 for the rural cohort and INR 912 for the urban. (Exchange rate: 44 Indian rupees = one U.S. dollar.)
22. Bhat R, Jain N. Factoring affecting the demand for health insurance in a micro insurance scheme. Ahmadabad: Indian Institute of Management; 2006. Working Paper no. 2006-07-02.
23. National Sample Survey Organisation. Ministry of Statistics and Programme Implementation, Government of India. March 2006.
24. US$ equivalents are: INR 4,868 = $110.63; INR 4,515 = $102.61; INR 3,764 = $85.54; INR 8,204 = $186.45; INR 8,734 = $198.50; INR 5,472 = $124.36.
25. We examined the Gini coefficient by reference to total income per household, total income per houshold member, and cash income per household and per household member. The results were the same in all cases.
26. We calculated the financial exposure index (FEI) for the three microinsurance units and obtained the following average values: (1) FEI (BAIF) = 0.2547 × 8203.7/15621 = 0.134; (2) FEI (UpLift) = 0.172 × 8734.4/11054 = 0.136; and (3) FEI (Nidan) = (0.4296 × 5474.5/7817) × 2/3 + (0.1619 × 7028.99/7817) × 1/3 = 0.247. The estimate for Nidan is split into the values for Plans A and B.
27. In the case of Nidan, we weighted the financial exposure index according to the share of the membership in Plan A (with cap of INR 2,000) and Plan B (with cap of INR 6,000).
28. The financial exposure index values shown here could be somewhat biased downward (toward better protection), because the rules applied by UpLift and Nidan, to pay only 80 percent of eligible hospital bills, were ignored for the purpose of calculating the financial exposure index (because presumably they would not influence the amount payable above the cap). We also ignored the possibility that BAIF members would get less than full reimbursement when the cost of claims exceeded the premium income.
29. Nidan got its insurance through SEWA; a study done in 2003, using different methods to evaluate SEWA (and another scheme), concluded that these schemes provided only partial protection against catastrophic health expenditure. See Devadasan N, Criel B, Van Damme W, Ranson K, Van der Stuyft P. Indian community health insurance schemes provide partial protection against catastrophic health expenditure. BMC Health Serv Res. 2007 Mar 15;7:43.

Chapter 17

Can the Rural Poor in India Afford to Treat Non-communicable Diseases?*

Main Messages

- Data were sourced from two household surveys undertaken in 2009–2010 among 7,389 rural poor households (39,205 individuals) in Odisha and Bihar.
- Around 17% of the surveyed individuals in Odisha and 31% in Bihar reported an illness episode in the month preceding the survey.
- Non-communicable diseases (NCD) accounted for around 20% of the diseases in the month preceding the survey in Odisha and 30% in Bihar.

Focus Points

- Patients with NCD in rural poor settings in India paid considerably more than patients with CD, largely because of their preference for private practitioners.
- Patients with NCD have a higher incidence of hospitalization than CD patients.

---

*This chapter is reproduced from *Tropical Medicine & International Medicine* (2012), **17**(11), 1376–1385, Open Access, available at https://www.researchgate.net/publication/230796167_Can_the_rural_poor_in_India_afford_to_treat_non-communicable_diseases.

- The cost for NCD represented a larger portion of the patient's share in household income than CD.
- Patients with NCD have to often rely on informal intra-family cross-subsidization to meet their health care expenses.

Structured Abstract

Introduction

Over the years, there has been a significant increase in NCD in low-income countries, and this has been a concern since health care costs in these countries are paid mostly out-of-pocket. This study attempts to investigate the financial burden of NCD vs. communicable diseases (CD) among rural poor in two states of India (Odisha and Bihar), taking into account the prevalence of illness categories, and age and income of the ill persons.

Box 1: NCD and CD Statistics

- Nearly 80% of NCD deaths occurred in low- and middle-income countries (World Health Organization, 2011).
- Percentage of deaths due to NCD/CD
  Worldwide: nearly 60% of deaths worldwide were because of NCD, and around 23% because of CD (World Health Organization, 2008).
  India: nearly 50% of deaths in India were because of NCD, and around 28% because of CD (World Health Organization, 2004).
- NCD are responsible for the biggest part of disease burden as assessed by disability-adjusted life-years (DALYs) in 2004 (World Health Organization, 2008).
  Worldwide: 48%
  South-East Asian region: 44%.

Method

Data for this study were sourced from two household surveys undertaken in 2009–2010 among 7,389 rural poor households (39,205 individuals) in

Odisha and Bihar. Self-reported illnesses were classified as NCD, CD or 'other morbidities' (injuries, maternal, perinatal or nutritional conditions) following the WHO classification. For the purpose of the analysis, the member and non-member sub-cohorts were aggregated in each state as there was no significant difference in frequency of reported illness episodes.

Findings

NCD accounted for around 20% of the diseases in the month preceding the survey in Odisha and 30% in Bihar. Data revealed that women, older persons and less-poor households reported higher prevalence of NCD.

There was a significant difference in the health care expenses for the two diseases. Patients with NCD reported paying considerably more than patients with CD. One of the reasons for this is that patients with NCD sought care with private practitioners more frequently than patients with CD. The preference for private practitioners was a result of the shortage of qualified staff and supply in public health care facilities. Patients with NCD reported paying more for all types of outpatient care (consultations, medicines, tests), and medicines were the costliest component of outpatient care.

The findings suggest that patients with NCD are more likely to be hospitalized than the population with a CD. Although the cost of hospitalization was comparable for NCD and non-NCD cases, this higher incidence of hospitalization adds to the financial burden of patients with NCD.

The authors also examined the association between income proxy and reported prevalence of NCD and CD. It was observed that although the highest prevalence of NCD was among the less poor of the sampled rural poor, the cost for NCD represented a larger portion of the patient's share in household income than CD.

The analysis suggests that patients in Bihar (both CD and NCD) spent a much lower share of income on outpatient health care than in Odisha. The key reason for this was Bihar's higher average income, and lower mean outpatient costs.

Conclusion

Since the cost of NCD care represented a large part of the per person share of household income, patients with NCD have to often rely on informal intra-family cross-subsidization. The dependence on such informal sources is aggravated in NCD cases that are chronic, with recurring costs. Such arrangements work so long as the proportion of NCD cases in the overall household population remains relatively small.

However, this proportion is likely to increase with time because of expected decrease in household size[1] and increase in life expectancy. The capacity of households to continue funding NCD care of family members will consequently decrease, and may lead to lower drug and treatment compliance. This underscores the need to establish an alternative solution to finance NCD care for rural poor patients.

---

[1]Census of India (2001) Data Highlights. Government of India, Ministry of Home Affairs, New Delhi.

Can the rural poor in India afford to treat non-communicable diseases

Erika Binnendijk[1], **Ruth Koren**[2] **and David M. Dror**[3]

1 *Institute of Health Policy and Management, Erasmus University, Rotterdam, The Netherlands*
2 *Felsenstein Medical Research Center, Tel Aviv University Ramat Aviv, Tel Aviv, Israel*
3 *Micro Insurance Academy, New Delhi, India*

Abstract

OBJECTIVE Non-communicable diseases (NCD) are on the increase in low-income countries, where healthcare costs are paid mostly out-of-pocket. We investigate the financial burden of NCD *vs.* communicable diseases (CD) among rural poor in India and assess whether they can afford to treat NCD.

METHODS We used data from two household surveys undertaken in 2009–2010 among 7389 rural poor households (39 205 individuals) in Odisha and Bihar. All persons from the sampled households, irrespective of age and gender, were included in the analysis. We classify self-reported illnesses as NCD, CD or 'other morbidities' following the WHO classification.

RESULTS Non-communicable diseases accounted for around 20% of the diseases in the month preceding the survey in Odisha and 30% in Bihar. The most prevalent NCD, representing the highest share in outpatient costs, were musculoskeletal, digestive and cardiovascular diseases. Cardiovascular and digestive problems also generated the highest inpatient costs. Women, older persons and less-poor households reported higher prevalence of NCD. Outpatient costs (consultations, medicines, laboratory tests and imaging) represented a bigger share of income for NCD than for CD. Patients with NCD were more likely to report a hospitalisation.

CONCLUSION Patients with NCD in rural poor settings in India pay considerably more than patients with CD. For NCD cases that are chronic, with recurring costs, this would be aggravated. The cost of NCD care consumes a big part of the per person share of household income, obliging patients with NCD to rely on informal intra-family cross-subsidisation. An alternative solution to finance NCD care for rural poor patients is needed.

keywords India, non-communicable diseases, health financing, rural, low-income population

Introduction

Non-communicable diseases (NCD) are leading causes of death globally, but nearly 80% of NCD deaths occurred in low- and middle-income countries (World Health Organization, 2011). In 2004, nearly 60% of deaths worldwide were because of NCD, and around 23% because of communicable diseases (CD) (World Health Organization, 2008). In India, these percentages were 50% and 28%, respectively (World Health Organization, 2004). NCD are also responsible for the biggest part of disease burden as assessed by disability-adjusted life-years (DALYs),[1] both worldwide and in the south-east Asian region (48% and 44%, respectively, in 2004) (World Health Organization, 2008). NCD deaths are projected to increase by 15% globally between 2010 and 2020; in south-east Asia, this increase could even be more than 20% and is a major barrier to the development (World Health Organization, 2011).

In India, around 70% of total health expenditure is paid out-of-pocket (World Health Organization, 2011) and caused some 7% of rural households to drop below poverty line in 1 year (Berman *et al.* 2010). Any intervention aiming to reduce financial shocks because of illness needs information on prevalence and cost. As a higher burden of NCD is unavoidable, better insights are needed on the morbidity of NCD and the changing implications for out-of-pocket healthcare expenditures.

Most of the literature on NCD deals with reducing the impact of NCD by addressing a number of risk factors

[1]Quantification of the burden of disease which simultaneously considers both premature death (number of years of life lost due to premature death) as well as the non-fatal health consequences of disease and injury (number of years lived with a disability) (Murray 1994).

underlying most high-burden NCD (e.g. tobacco use, physical inactivity, unhealthy diet, alcohol abuse). The aim of this literature is to have countries address these risk factors in prevention programs and reduce the burden of these NCD. The burden is investigated mainly through mortality (premature death) and disability (DALY) because of NCD (Murray & Lopez 1997; Boutayeb & Boutayeb 2005; Lopez *et al.* 2006; Kinra *et al.* 2010; Beaglehole *et al.* 2011; Dans *et al.* 2011; World Health Organization, 2011). However, the information about the number of patients afflicted with NCD and the financial consequence of NCD is sorely rare. Some information is available about the prevalence of certain NCD but not all. The rare studies that deal with the financial burden, also deal with specific NCD. We found one study looking at cost implications of NCD for all India (Engelgau *et al.* 2012), based on data from 1995 to 1996 and 2004 of the National Sample Survey Organization that provides important insights. For example, in 2004, almost 50% of out-of-pocket health expenses were on NCD and medicines represented 46% of total out-of-pocket health spending (Engelgau *et al.* 2012). To the best of our knowledge, no study examined the financial implications of NCD amongst the most vulnerable segment of society in India: the rural poor.

The purpose of this article is to examine the financial implications of NCD relative to CD among rural poor communities in two states of India (Odisha and Bihar), taking into account the prevalence of illness categories, and age and income of the ill persons.

Data and methods

Setting and sampling

We used data from two household surveys conducted in rural areas of Odisha (Kalahandi, Khorda and Malkangiri districts, January 2009) and Bihar (Gaya district, May–June 2010). Average monthly per capita consumer expenditure for rural Odisha (INR559, PPP$35.5) is lowest of all states in India; average expenditure for rural Bihar (INR598, PPP$38.0) is fourth lowest (after Odisha, Chhattisgarh and Jharkhand) (National Sample Survey Organization, 2010). These studies formed part of a baseline study to initiate rural micro-health insurance programmes, and the locations were selected in agreement with implementing local non-government organizations (NGOs).[2]

We followed a two-stage sampling procedure in each state. In stage 1, 130 villages (27 in Kalahandi, 22 in Khorda, 31 in Malkangiri and 50 in Gaya) were selected randomly from lists that local NGOs provided where they organised self-help groups (SHGs)[3]; in Gaya, 50 additional villages were selected randomly from Census 2001 registry. In stage 2, households in each village were sampled randomly by applying the 'four winds' (or 'line sampling') technique (Som 1996). Only households where an adult was available at the time of the survey were sampled.[4] Households were sampled in two cohorts of equal size: member (if at least one person participated in an SHG linked to partner-NGOs) and non-member households. Sample size was 5383 households in Odisha (25 885 individuals) and 2006 households in Bihar (13 320 individuals). Hundred percentage of the sample was rural.

The survey questionnaire was translated from English into local languages (Oriya and Hindi), back translated for verification, and pre-tested in each state among 80 households. Surveyors fluent in local dialects conducted the interviews. In principle, one household member reported for all household members, but usually more persons were present to help. We obtained informed consent of the respondents and kept confidential participants' names in data recording and analysis. This research project met all the requirements of the funding agency (NWO-WOTRO) on ethical issues arising in social science research.

Data

The data collected included general demographics of household members (age, gender, education, economic activity), distance to their habitual primary care practitioner (min) and information on household expenditures. We obtained an income-proxy through questions on many items of household expenditure, following the method of the Indian National Sample Survey Organization (2008). Our 'income-proxy' is the monthly per capita consumer expenditure excluding healthcare costs, because we seek to identify patterns of financing healthcare (Flores *et al.* 2008; Wagstaff 2008).

[2]In Odisha the Madhyam Foundation [comprising 11 grassroots NGOs: Parivartan, PUSPAC, SOMKS, SDS, ODC (Malkangiri); Mahashakti Foundation, DAPTA, Lok Yojana, Sanginee (Kalahandi); MVPS, DSS (Khorda)] and in Bihar BASIX.

[3]SHGs represent a unique approach to financial intermediation in communities. The approach combines access to low-cost financial services with a process of self-management and development for the SHG members. SHGs are seen to confer many benefits, both economic and social.

[4]In rural India most of the time an adult is in the house or can be found near the house, and is willing to participate in an interview.

The household survey also included questions on illness episodes and illness-related outpatient expenditures of household members during 1 month preceding the survey, and hospitalisations (exceeding 24 h) with related costs during 1 year preceding the survey. Information about the episodes was queried through open questions on the illness or symptoms that caused the episode. Illnesses that were clearly different or occurred at different periods were treated as separate episodes. Information about per-episode outpatient expenditures was collected, including consultation fees of qualified allopathic practitioners, and expenditures for medicines, laboratory and imaging tests. The self-reported illnesses or symptoms were categorised, following the WHO classifications (World Health Organization, 2008), as specific categories of NCD, CD and 'other morbidities' (injuries, maternal, perinatal or nutritional conditions). Ailments that could not be well defined based on the reported symptoms were categorised as 'missing'. This classification of illnesses was carried out by two of the authors with some medical background, in consultation with a clinician who practiced in rural India.

Analysis

All persons from the sampled households, irrespective of age and gender, were included in the analysis. The significance of difference between means was tested by a two-tailed *t*-test and the significance of difference of frequencies was established by chi-square tests. We aggregated the member and non-member sub-cohorts in each state for the purpose of the analysis reported here as we found no significant difference in frequency of reported illness episodes.

We measured the inequality of reported illness episodes by income proxy, using concentration indices. An index of zero indicates there is no inequality, a negative (positive) index a disproportionate concentration of the health indicator among the poor (rich) (O'Donnell *et al.* 2008). We show two versions of the index: the index as described by O'Donnell *et al.* (2008) and a corrected index as suggested by Erreygers (2009). We used STATA version 11.1 (StataCorp, Texas, USA) for all the analyses.

All amounts, reported in Indian rupee (INR), were converted into international dollars (purchasing power parity, PPP$) using the exchange rate of PPP$1 = INR 16.692 for 2009 and 18.073 for 2010. The amounts from the National Sample Survey Organization report of 2009/2010 were converted using the average exchange rate for the 2 years (17.383). For the report of 2007/2008, this rate was 15.727 (15.323 + 16.13/2) (International Monetary Fund, 2012).

Findings

Socio-economic status of studied populations.
In both populations, the income proxy is on average around the poverty line: about PPP$1 per person per day in Odisha and PPP$1.5 in Bihar. Considering the relevant data from the Indian National Sample Survey Organization (NNSO), we found that our sampled populations were comparable to the rural averages of their states. Most people depend on hard physical labour for their income as daily wage labourers (e.g. in agriculture, load carrying, construction) or self-employment in agriculture (39.5% in Odisha and 45.3% in Bihar). A minority (12.8% in Odisha and 6.5% in Bihar) is employed in what can be considered sedentary work (salaried employee or self-employed in business/trade, mainly shopkeepers, teachers). In both locations, 46% of the adult population did not have any education. In Bihar, 41% of the adult population have finished class 6 and higher compared to 36% in Odisha. This information is shown in Table 1.

Around 17% of the surveyed individuals in Odisha and 31% in Bihar reported an illness episode in the month preceding the survey. Nearly 5.5% of the sampled population in Odisha and 2.5% in Bihar incurred a hospitalisation in the year preceding the survey. Respondents in Bihar reported that they needed 18 min on average to reach their preferred primary practitioner and in Odisha, 30 min.

Prevalence and classification of self-reported illness episodes.
In rural Odisha or Bihar, there are no official records about illness or treatment in the population. Our source of information on morbidity to classify illnesses as 'NCD', 'CD' or 'other morbidity' (Table 2) has therefore been the self-reported symptoms from our surveys.

Non-communicable diseases accounted for around 20% of all diseases in Odisha and 30% in Bihar. CD were responsible for most of the illness episodes. The three most prevalent categories of NCD in both locations were musculoskeletal, digestive and cardiovascular problems.

The population reporting NCD was significantly older than the population experiencing CD ($P < 0.001$, *t*-test, both locations). The average age of patients with NCD was 42.1 (±0.6) and 37.9 (±0.6) years old, while the average age of patients with CD was 27.2 (±0.4) and 21.1 (±0.4) years in Odisha and Bihar, respectively.

Women were more afflicted with an illness (χ^2, $P < 0.05$ in Odisha, $P < 0.001$ in Bihar). However, this effect was more pronounced for the prevalence of NCD than CD ($P < 0.001$, χ^2, both locations): in Odisha, of those who reported NCD last month, 59.0% were women and of

Table 1 Socio-economic and demographic status of studied populations

	Odisha (N = 25 885)	NSSO* Rural Odisha	Bihar (N = 13 320)	NSSO* Rural Bihar
Gender	% of sampled population			
Male	50.6		51.0	
Female	49.4		49.0	
Missing	0.05		0.0	
Age distribution				
Infant (under 5)	8.9	9.3	11.8	11.7
Child (5–14 years old)	22.7	21.9	28.5	28.8
Young adult (15–29 years old)	26.0	25.8	25.3	23.1
Adult (30–44 years old)	22.0	21.3	17.5	20.4
Midlife (45–59 years old)	13.0	14.2	9.5	10.6
Old age (over 60)	7.3	7.4	7.5	5.3
Missing	0.2	0.0	0.0	0.0
Education of adult population (15 years and older)†				
No education	45.7		45.8	
Class 1–5	17.0		12.2	
Class 6–10	29.3		32.6	
Class 11 and higher	6.5		8.3	
Missing	1.5		1.1	
Economic activity of adult population (15 years and older)†				
Daily wage labourer	20.7		32.7	
Self-employed in agriculture	18.2		12.2	
Self-employed in business/trade	9.4		3.6	
Regular salaried employee	3.2		2.8	
Domestic duties	32.2		28.1	
Other‡	14.6		19.7	
Missing	1.8		1.0	
Illness episode in month preceding survey	17.0		31.0	
Hospitalised (for more than 24 h) in year preceding survey	5.6		2.5	
	Mean (±SE)			
Distance to preferred primary care practitioner (in minutes)	29.95 (±0.18) (1.2% missing)		18.21 (±0.16) (0.0% missing)	
Income proxy per person per month (PPP$)	30.09 (±0.13) (4.7% missing)	35.54	43.84 (±0.28) (0.5% missing)	44.87

PPP, purchasing power parity.
*National statistics data from National Sample Survey Organization of India (NSSO). Information shown for rural Odisha is from 2007/2008 (reports 530 and 531) and for rural Bihar from 2009/2010 (reports 537 and 538), periods that correspond best to the time when our data were collected.
†Adult population: N = 17 716 in Odisha; N = 7954 in Bihar.
‡Other can mean going to school, being unemployed, disabled or pensioned.

those who reported CD last month 51.1% were women. In Bihar, respectively, 65.3% and 53.9% were women.

Outpatient health-seeking and expenses by illness types. We explored health-seeking behaviour and costs with three types of healthcare providers: government health facility, private general practitioner (GP) and private specialist (Table 3).

Patients with NCD accessed healthcare providers more frequently (except government facility in Odisha). This more frequent health seeking is most manifested in consultations with private specialists. Both in government facilities and at private GPs, patients with NCD paid about the same per visit as patients with CD, but private specialists were costlier per visit for patients with NCD.

Outpatient costs often include medicines, laboratory and imaging tests. The average costs for these services are shown in Table 4. Two main findings emerge clearly: outpatient costs were lower in Bihar than in Odisha and

Table 2 Classification of self-reported illness episodes

	% of illness episodes		% of NCD	
	Odisha (N = 4443)	Bihar (N = 4217)	Odisha (N = 917)	Bihar (N = 1253)
NCD	20.64	29.71		
(Malignant) Neoplasms			0.87	1.92
Diabetes mellitus			2.73	1.44
Endocrine disorders			0.22	0.32
Neuropsychiatric conditions			6.22	3.27
Sense organ diseases			0.11	1.2
Cardiovascular diseases			20.72	10.45
Respiratory diseases			5.67	4.39
Digestive diseases			23.45	35.12
Genitourinary diseases			2.07	2.47
Skin diseases			5.02	4.31
Musculoskeletal diseases			28.14	32.16
Congenital anomalies			0.44	0.00
Oral conditions			2.73	2.47
Rest			1.64	0.48
CD	73.73	51.93		
Other morbidities*	5.25	18.36		
Missing†	0.38	0.0		

NCD, non-communicable diseases; CD, communicable diseases.
*The group 'other morbidities' comprised of injuries, maternal, perinatal or nutritional conditions.
†Ailments that could not be well defined based on the reported symptoms were categorised as 'missing'.

patients with NCD had higher costs than patients with CD for all treatment categories. Aggregating all outpatient costs, patients with NCD reported about double the costs of patients with CD, in both locations. Medicines were the costliest item in all cases.

Income and the frequency of disease and its cost.
We examined the association between income proxy and reported prevalence of NCD and CD (Table 5). The positive concentration indices describing NCD show a significant 'pro-rich' distribution: NCD were reported more frequently by higher income segments of the study populations, more so than CD. This trend was consistent when calculated according to O'Donnell *et al.* (2008) and according to Erreygers (2009).

Having found that the prevalence of NCD was higher amongst the higher income segments of our sampled rural poor and that NCD were costlier than CD, we examined whether the two phenomena cancelled each other out. We therefore calculated outpatient costs (reported for last month) as percentage of income proxy (per person per month), both for NCD and CD cases. The percentage spent by NCD was significantly and materially higher than by CD, ($P < 0.001$, t-test, both locations). In Odisha, patients with CD spent on average 125.6% (±4.8%) of income proxy while patients with NCD spent on average 180.6% (±10.6%). In Bihar, these percentages were 21.1% (±1.5%) and 41.4% (±3.0%), respectively. Even though NCD were more prevalent among higher income segments, the treatment costs for NCD represented a bigger share of their income. It can be expected that in case of chronic NCD, these expenses will be incurred again in other months during the year.

The percentages above also indicate that patients in Bihar (both CD and NCD) spent a much lower share of income on outpatient healthcare than in Odisha. The difference across locations seems to be because of two reasons: in Bihar (i) average income was higher and (ii) mean outpatient costs were lower.

Inpatient treatment and expenditure.
We also examined the risk and cost of hospitalisations. Persons who reported an NCD (last month) were more likely to be hospitalised (last year) than the sampled population without NCD: in Odisha 15.5% *vs.* 5.2%, in Bihar 5.0% *vs.* 2.2% ($P < 0.001$, chi-square test). The average cost of hospitalisation was comparable: in Odisha PPP$312 (±53) for patients with NCD and PPP$197 (±9) for the sampled population without NCD; in Bihar PPP$425 (±81) and PPP$380 (±40), respectively.

Share of NCD categories in outpatient and inpatient expenditures.
Finally, we analysed which category of NCD was the costliest with respect to overall outpatient and inpatient expenditures (Figure 1). The relative share of costs is determined by the frequency of an NCD category and its severity in terms of aggregated cost.

The two NCD categories that contributed most to overall outpatient expenditures (both locations) were digestive and musculoskeletal problems, followed by cardiovascular and neuropsychiatric conditions. With respect to overall inpatient expenditures, digestive and cardiovascular diseases were amongst the three costliest. Neuropsychiatric, genitourinary and musculoskeletal problems were

Table 3 Frequency of access and costs of consultations

	% of ill cases where treatment was sought†		Average cost per visit (±SE) (PPP$)	
Treatment sought with	Odisha	Bihar	Odisha	Bihar
Government health facility				
NCD	68.9	10.0†††	1.43 (±0.40) (3.7% missing)	1.22 (±0.41) (0.0% missing)
CD	69.3	6.0	1.41 (±0.11) (4.8% missing)	0.86 (±0.23) (0.0% missing)
Private general practitioner				
NCD	15.9††	21.6†††	5.09 (±0.67) (1.5% missing)	6.19 (±0.51) (0.4% missing)
CD	11.6	13.6	5.19 (±0.50) (3.9% missing)	5.81 (±0.65) (0.0% missing)
Private specialist				
NCD	20.8†††	9.6†††	8.00 (±1.06)** (4.5% missing)	11.08 (±1.50)* (0.0% missing)
CD	6.8	3.8	4.66 (±0.56) (1.0% missing)	6.52 (±0.78) (0.0% missing)

NCD, non-communicable diseases; CD, communicable diseases; PPP, purchasing power parity.
†N = 917 NCD cases and 3276 CD cases in Odisha; N = 1253 NCD cases and 2190 CD cases in Bihar. Information on treatment was missing for 23 of the CD cases in Odisha (0.7%); no information was missing for the NCD cases in Odisha or CD and NCD cases in Bihar.
††Significance of difference in percentage of people that sought treatment with one of the listed providers out of the persons who reported either NCD or CD last month $P < 0.01$ (chi-square).
†††Significance of difference in percentage of people that sought treatment with one of the listed providers out of the persons who reported either NCD or CD last month $P < 0.001$ (chi-square).
*Significance of difference in cost between NCD and CD $P < 0.05$ (t-test).
**Significance of difference in cost between NCD and CD $P < 0.01$ (t-test).

also important contributors to the overall costs in both locations. The cost of malignancies in Odisha seems to be much higher than in Bihar but is probably due to a small number of outliers as only a modest percentage of hospitalisations was because of cancers (9% in Odisha, 6% in Bihar).

Discussion

The analysis of the financial burden of NCD on rural poor households in two states in India presented here differs from much of the literature on NCD in that it considers the information on prevalence and treatment cost of NCD, in general, and by the category of NCD, rather than deaths or DALYs associated with NCD. We found that, while CD represent the major share of self-reported illnesses, the prevalence of NCD is considerable, with about 20% of illness episodes in Odisha and 30% in Bihar. With increasing age (Lee & Mason 2011) and with a higher prevalence of NCD amongst the elderly, this percentage is likely to increase in the future.

Amongst the NCD, the three most prevalent in our study populations were musculoskeletal, digestive and cardiovascular diseases. These categories also represented the highest share of outpatient expenditures. Cardiovascular and digestive diseases generated the highest inpatient costs. The morbidity profile usually associated with NCD (cardiovascular problems, diabetes, cancers and chronic long conditions) (World Health Organization, 2011) is not replicated in our study. Instead, we see higher prevalence of NCD related to lifestyle, occupational and nutritional conditions of the rural poor which are exposed simultaneously to (i) very hard physical labour as daily wage labourers (e.g. in agriculture, load carrying, construction) or self-employment in agriculture (Table 1), (ii) unstable and irregular nutrition because of poverty that can cause cardiovascular diseases (Vorster & Kruger 2007; van Abeelen *et al.* 2012) and (iii) not very hygienic living conditions (Nath 2003; Khurana & Sen 2008; Asian Development Bank, 2009).

It is commonly claimed that poorer population segments are in worse health, also in low- and middle-income countries (Hosseinpoor *et al.* 2012). Our results showed, however, that self-reported illnesses, particularly NCD, are more frequent among the wealthier segments of the studied populations. This finding is in accordance

Table 4 Outpatient expenditures

	Average cost last month (±SE) (PPP$)	
	Odisha	Bihar
Consultations with qualified practitioners		
NCD	4.86 (±0.52)†††	3.30 (±0.30)†††
CD	2.31 (±0.13)	1.55 (±0.15)
Medicines		
NCD	45.24 (±2.52)†††	12.71 (±1.10)†††
CD	26.31 (±0.87)	6.52 (±0.68)
Lab tests		
NCD	2.56 (±0.38)††	0.76 (±0.19)†
CD	1.92 (±0.09)	0.34 (±0.05)
Imaging		
NCD	1.64 (±0.26)†††	0.94 (±0.16)†††
CD	0.37 (±0.06)	0.14 (±0.04)
Total outpatient expenditures		
NCD	53.49 (±2.86)††† (2.18% missing)	17.27 (±1.28)††† (0.9% missing)
CD	30.51 (±0.94) (2.0% missing)	8.45 (±0.75) (0.4% missing)

NCD, non-communicable diseases; CD, communicable diseases; PPP, purchasing power parity.
†Significance of difference in cost between NCD and CD $P < 0.05$ (*t*-test).
††Significance of difference in cost between NCD and CD $P < 0.01$ (*t*-test).
†††Significance of difference in cost between NCD and CD $P < 0.001$ (*t*-test).

Table 5 Association between income and prevalence of illness

	Concentration Index as described by O'Donnell *et al.* (2008) (±SE)		Concentration Index as described by Erreygers (2009) (±SE)	
	Odisha	Bihar	Odisha	Bihar
NCD	0.157 (±0.019)	0.115 (±0.016)	0.022 (±0.003)	0.044 (±0.007)
CD	0.022 (±0.010)	0.027 (±0.011)	0.011 (±0.005)	0.018 (±0.007)

NCD, non-communicable disease; CDs, communicable diseases.

with a previous report of positive association between household income and self-reported incidence among poor in India (Dror *et al.* 2009). Engelgau *et al.* (2012) also found that in India spending on NCD as share of income increases by income. As we investigate the lowest income segments only, it is possible that members of the poorest households cannot afford to stop daily activities for illnesses perceived as minor, and therefore they do not report them.

Analysis of the expenditure patterns of NCD revealed several important insights. First, patients with NCD sought care with private practitioners (GP or specialist) more frequently than patients with CD, even though these practitioners charge more than government facilities. In fact, patients with NCD even reported higher fees per visit with specialists than patients with CD. The public sector in India, especially the more peripheral facilities, commonly suffers from shortages in qualified staff and supply. The population therefore is sceptical about quality of public sector services (Berman 1998; Peters *et al.* 2002; Reddy *et al.* 2011). Viewed in combination with the possibility that patients with NCD consider their illness as requiring more serious diagnosis and treatment than CD, they might decide, despite their poverty, to prefer costlier private care.

Second, patients with NCD reported paying more for all types of outpatient care (consultations, medicines, tests) and medicines came out to be the costliest component of outpatient care. These findings are in line with those of Dror *et al.* (2008) that medicines were the largest component of healthcare costs for chronic care and of Engelgau *et al.* (2012) that patients with NCD had to bear higher costs for consultations and medicines than other patients.

Third, despite the higher prevalence of NCD among the less poor of our sampled rural poor, the cost for NCD represented a bigger portion of the patient's share in household income than CD. In this analysis, we looked at outpatient costs paid out-of-pocket during 1 month only. For chronic NCD [many of the illnesses categorised as NCD can be considered chronic (Beaglehole *et al.* 2011; Dans *et al.* 2011; World Health Organization, 2011)], clearly these costs can accumulate to a significant portion of the patient's share of income over the year. Such high costs we believe can only be met when considerable cross-subsidisation occurs within the household (other household members' share of income has to be used to pay the patient's treatment). When such informal cross-subsidisation is unavailable, access to care becomes unaffordable. This would presumably be more likely in small households composed of older persons only, or in poorer households. Indeed the higher reporting of NCD by households with more financial resources strengthens the impression that the diagnosis of and treatment for NCD strongly depends on intra-household cross-subsidisation.

Finally, patients with NCD were more likely to be hospitalised than the population without an NCD. And, even though the cost of a hospitalisation was comparable for NCD and non-NCD cases, this higher incidence of hospitalisations places an additional financial burden on patients with NCD.

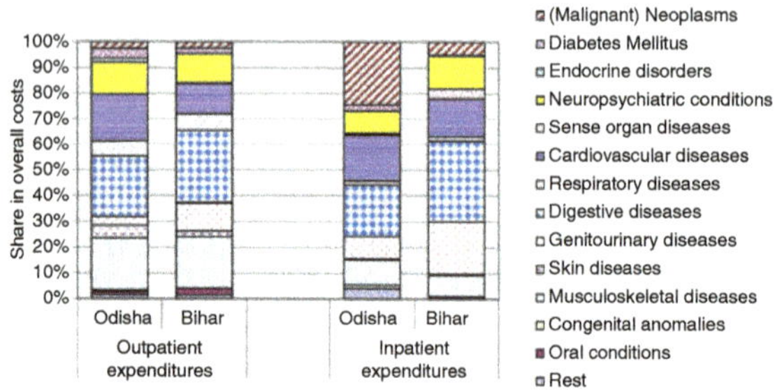

Figure 1 Share of non-communicable disease (NCD) categories in outpatient and inpatient expenditures.

At the time our surveys were conducted, the surveyed populations in Odisha and Bihar had practically no access to health insurance. The Government of India introduced hospitalisation insurance [Rashtriya Swasthya Bima Yojana (RSBY)] in 2008, which, however, was not implemented in the studied areas until much later (Ministry of Labour and Employment, India, 2012a). The information on enrolment, renewals and payment of claims is for the time being limited. Moreover, RSBY usually covers only the cost of care in an empanelled hospital. It has been shown here that most of the financial problems of patients with NCD arise from financing outpatient care. As this paper goes to print, the Government of India is piloting the expansion of RSBY to include outpatient care; however, it is unclear whether this pilot will be generalised, or which services would be included under RSBY in the future (Ministry of Labour and Employment, India, 2011, 2012b).

The big differences across the two locations included in this study do not change the general conclusion regarding the unaffordability of NCD care, or regarding the reliance of chronic NCD cases on intra-household subsidisation of their care costs. However, these big differences in reporting illnesses deserve some considerations. The higher income, better education and shorter travel time to primary care practitioners in Bihar, compared to Odisha (Table 1), may have contributed to the big difference in number of reported illness episodes; in Bihar, the sampled population had almost twice as many episodes compared to Odisha. On the other hand, the average treatment costs were higher in Odisha than in Bihar (Table 4) and several reasons could explain this: supply aspects (e.g. fewer providers), clinical aspects (e.g. morbidity that is more expensive to cure, or differences in seasonal morbidity).

This study offers a first estimation of the size of the problem of financing access to NCD-related care. On the basis of the results of this study, more qualitative questions could arise, such as, why is treatment sought with certain providers? Is there non-compliance of treatment and why (not)? These and similar questions could be addressed in a qualitative follow-up study.

A limitation of this study is that the data used for the analyses are self-reported. Reporting of the type, frequency, severity and cost can obviously suffer from recall bias and other biases, for example, underreporting of illnesses perceived as minor especially among the poorer households, or inaccurate reports by one household member of illnesses incurred by others.

Conclusion

Patients with NCD in rural poor settings in India pay considerably more for the treatment than patients with CD. This trend might be aggravated in the case of chronic NCD because of the expected recurrence of outpatient expenditures, which in this study were analysed only for 1 month. It is self-explanatory that chronicity is less likely with CD. This trend is likely to worsen over time because incidence, prevalence and chronicity are expected to increase with changes in lifestyle and extension of life-expectancy (Lopez *et al.* 2006; World Health Organization, 2008, 2011).

In the absence of any systemic solution (like insurance) to deal with the financing of access to care, we believe patients suffering from NCD rely on intra-household cross-subsidisation to pay for their care. This cross-subsidisation can work for as long as the proportion of NCD cases in the overall household population remains relatively small; but this proportion is likely to increase because of expected decrease in household size (Census of India, 2001) and increase in age. Consequently, the ability of households to continue funding family members requiring NCD care will decrease and could lead to lower drug and treatment compliance. This conclusion clearly points to the urgent need to develop suitable policy solutions which would allow rural poor populations to afford care for NCD even as NCD are expected to increase. Such policy choices would have to cover outpatient care in view of its major contribution to the financial burden of patients with NCD.

Acknowledgements

The authors gratefully acknowledge funding support from the Netherlands Organization for Scientific Research (NWO), under WOTRO Integrated Programme W01.65.309.00. Additional funding for the Odisha household survey was obtained from the German Federal Ministry for Economic Cooperation and Development. The authors gratefully acknowledge the logistical and research support from the Micro Insurance Academy (New Delhi) during data collection and field work. Thanks are extended to the NGOs that facilitated contacts with villages. The authors gratefully acknowledge useful suggestions on an early draft given by Dr. Richard Smith (formerly chief editor of BMJ) and Dr. Naomi Levitt (University of Cape Town). The authors affirm that their ability to complete the research as planned was not limited by any agreement with funding organizations and confirm that they had full control of all primary data. Partial and initial analysis of results was presented at ICDDR-B 13th Annual Scientific Conference-ASCON XIII (Dhaka, Bangladesh, 16 March 2011) and One Health Summit (Davos, Switzerland, 21 February 2012).

References

Asian Development Bank (2009) *India's Sanitation for All: How to Make it Happen.* Water for all No. 18. Asian Development Bank, Manila, Philippines.

Beaglehole R, Bonita R, Horton R *et al.* (2011) Priority actions for the non-communicable disease crisis. *Lancet* 377, 1438–1447.

Berman PA (1998) Rethinking health care systems: private health care provision in India. *World Development* 26, 1463–1479.

Berman PA, Ahuja R & Bhandari L (2010) The impoverishing effect of healthcare payments in India: new methodology and findings. *Economic and Political Weekly* 45, 65–71.

Boutayeb A & Boutayeb S (2005) The burden of non communicable diseases in developing countries. *International Journal for Equity in Health* 4, 2.

Census of India (2001) *Data Highlights*. Government of India, Ministry of Home Affairs, New Delhi.

Dans A, Ng N, Varghese C, Tai ES, Firestone R & Bonita R (2011) The rise of chronic non-communicable diseases in southeast Asia: time for action. *Lancet* 377, 680–689.

Dror DM, van Putten-Rademaker O & Koren R (2008) Cost of illness: evidence from a study in five resource-poor locations in India. *The Indian Journal of Medical Research* **127**, 347–361.

Dror DM, van Putten-Rademaker O & Koren R (2009) Incidence of illness among resource-poor households: evidence from five locations in India. *The Indian Journal of Medical Research* **130**, 146–154.

Engelgau M, Karan A & Mahal A (2012) The economic impact of non-communicable diseases on households in India. *Globalization and Health* **8**, 9.

Erreygers G (2009) Correcting the Concentration Index. *Journal of Health Economics* **28**, 504–515.

Flores G, Krishnakumar J, O'Donnell O & van Doorslaer E (2008) Coping with health-care costs: implications for the measurement of catastrophic expenditures and poverty. *Health Economics* **17**, 1393–1412.

Hosseinpoor AR, Bergen N, Mendis S *et al.* (2012) Socioeconomic inequality in the prevalence of noncommunicable diseases in low- and middle-income countries: results from the World Health Survey. *BMC Public Health* **12**, 474.

International Monetary Fund (2012) World economic outlook database. http://www.imf.org/external/pubs/ft/weo/2012/01/weodata/index.aspx [Retrieved 24 June 2012].

Khurana I & Sen R (2008) *Drinking Water Quality in Rural India: Issues and Approaches* Water Aid, London.

Kinra S, Bowen LJ, Lyngdoh T *et al.* (2010) Sociodemographic patterning of non-communicable disease risk factors in rural India: a cross sectional study. *BMJ (Clinical Research Ed.)* **341**, c4974.

Lee R & Mason A (2011) The price of maturity. *Finance & Development* **48**, 7–11.

Lopez AD, Mathers CD, Ezzati M, Jamison DT & Murray CJ (2006) Global and regional burden of disease and risk factors, 2001: systematic analysis of population health data. *Lancet* **367**, 1747–1757.

Ministry of Labour and Employment, India (2011) *Providing Outpatient Healthcare to Complement Rashtriya Swasthya Bima Yojana (RSBY), India's National Health Insurance Scheme*. Ministry of Labour and Employement, New Delhi, India.

Ministry of Labour and Employment, India (2012a) Rashtriya Swasthya Bima Yojana (RSBY). http://www.rsby.gov.in/index.aspx [Retrieved 22 June 2012].

Ministry of Labour and Employment, India (2012b) *RSBY Connect.* Issue number 2, March 2012. Ministry of Labour and Employement, New Delhi, India.

Murray CJ (1994) Quantifying the burden of disease: the technical basis for disability-adjusted life years. *Bulletin of the World Health Organization* **72**, 429–445.

Murray CJ & Lopez AD (1997) Global mortality, disability, and the contribution of risk factors: global Burden of Disease Study. *Lancet* **349**, 1436–1442.

Nath KJ (2003) Home hygiene and environmental sanitation: a country situation analysis for India. *International Journal of Environmental Health Research* **13**(Suppl. 1), S19–S28.

National Sample Survey Organization (2008) *Household Consumer Expenditure in India, 2006–07*. Report No. 527. National Sample Survey Organization, Ministry of Statistics and Programme Implementation, Government of India, New Delhi.

National Sample Survey Organization (2010) *Household Consumer Expenditure in India, 2007–08*. Report No. 530. National Sample Survey Organization, Ministry of Statistics and Programme Implementation, Government of India, New Delhi.

O'Donnell O, van Doorslaer E, Wagstaff A & Lindelow M (2008) *Analyzing Health Equity Using Household Survey Data*. World Bank, Washington, DC.

Peters DH, Yazbeck AS, Sharma RP, Ramana GNV, Pritchett LH & Wagstaff A (2002) *Better Health Systems for India's Poor: Findings, Analysis and Options*. World Bank, Washington, DC.

Reddy KS, Patel V, Jha P *et al.* (2011) Towards achievement of universal health care in India by 2020: a call to action. *Lancet* **377**, 760–768.

Som RK (1996) *Practical Sampling Techniques*, 2nd edn. Marcel Dekker, New York.

van Abeelen AF, Elias SG, Bossuyt PM *et al.* (2012) Cardiovascular consequences of famine in the young. *European Heart Journal* **33**, 538–545.

Vorster HH & Kruger A (2007) Poverty, malnutrition, underdevelopment and cardiovascular disease: a South African perspective. *Cardiovascular Journal of Africa* **18**, 321–324.

Wagstaff A (2008) *Measuring Financial Protection in Health*. Report No. 4554. World Bank, Washington, DC.

World Health Organization (2004) WHO global infobase. https://apps.who.int/infobase/Index.aspx [Retrieved 18 May 2011].

World Health Organization (2008) *The Global Burden of Disease: 2004 Update*. WHO, Geneva, Switzerland.

World Health Organization (2011) *Global Status Report on Noncommunicable Diseases 2010*. WHO, Geneva, Switzerland.

Corresponding Author David M. Dror, Micro Insurance Academy, 52B Okhla Industrial Estate Phase III, New Delhi 110020, India. Tel.: +91 99 5820 6633; Fax: +91 11 4379 9117; E-mail: daviddror@socialre.org

Chapter 18

"First We Go to the Small Doctor": First Contact for Curative Health Care Sought by Rural Communities in Andhra Pradesh and Orissa, India*

Main Messages

- Data for the study were sourced from a Household Survey (1,810 households in AP; 5,342 in Orissa), 48 Focus Group Discussions (19 in AP; 29 in Orissa), and 61 Key Informant Interviews with health care providers (22 in AP; 39 in Orissa).
- The villages were selected purposively, where local organizations were involved in the micro health insurance project.
- Evidence collected from health care seekers (demand side) was juxtaposed with evidence collected from providers (supply side) on first contact health care.

---

*This chapter is reproduced from *The Indian Journal of Medical Research* (2011), **134**, 627–638, Open Access, available at https://www.researchgate.net/publication/51924788_%27First_we_go_to_the_small_doctor%27_First_contact_for_curative_health_care_sought_by_rural_communities_in_Andhra_Pradesh_Orissa_India.

Focus Points

- Respondents named proximity as the most important reason for their choice of first contact provider being non-degree allopathic practitioners (NDAPs) or traditional healers.
- Around a quarter of the survey respondents in AP and roughly half that proportion in Orissa approached qualified allopathic doctors at first contact.
- Among those who approached a qualified doctor first, a majority gave the reason for their choice as quality of the doctor (56.0% AP; 58.2% Orissa), followed by proximity (38.9% AP; 35.8% Orissa).
- NDAPs help to fill a limited but essential gap in access to first contact curative health care in rural India.
- Two main problems raised during the FGDs: the money spent on transport to reach public facilities, and the money spent on medicines and tests (and sometimes for the consultation fee).

Structured Abstract

Introduction

Rural communities in India seek outpatient primary care from private providers as public facilities suffer from poor quality of care, poor availability of medicines, long distances, inconvenient opening hours, lengthy waiting, and staff absenteeism. In an attempt to increase access and quality of health care in rural areas, the Indian government launched its National Rural Health Mission (NRHM) in 2005. This study conducted in 2008–2009, sought to investigate the post NRHM status of curative health care seeking at first contact among rural communities in two States of India–Andhra Pradesh (AP) and Orissa.

Method

The cross-sectional study sourced data from a Household Survey (1,810 households in AP; 5,342 in Orissa), 48 Focus Group Discussions

(19 in AP; 29 in Orissa), and 61 Key Informant Interviews with health care providers (22 in AP; 39 in Orissa). Evidence collected from health care seekers (demand-side) was juxtaposed with evidence collected from providers (supply-side) on first contact health care, including the illnesses, patients' choices and providers' patient load, treatments, medicines, and referrals.

Findings

In the case of both states, FGD narratives suggested that the first response to an illness could be self-medication, with men more likely to buy an over-the-counter medicine and the women resorting to home remedies. Only when these were ineffective, they sought care from available providers.

The primary reason given by respondents for their choice of first contact provider being non-degree allopathic practitioners (NDAPs) or traditional healers was proximity to the provider. However, among those who approached a qualified doctor first, the majority said the reason was the doctor's quality, followed by proximity. There was no significant association between frequency of choice of traditional healer and literacy.

The authors also examined the association between the income of the population MPCE (monthly per capita expenditure) and choice of first contact provider. While this association was significant in Orissa, it was not so in AP. Orissa witnessed a significant decrease in the frequency of accessing traditional healers with income, and this was largely due to a lower frequency in the fifth income quintile. A positive association was seen between income quintiles and frequency of seeking care from qualified doctors.

The analysis of illnesses reported by people (juxtaposed against those reported by providers) suggested that NDAPs manage the most frequent illnesses. The role of NDAPs is therefore crucial in filling a limited but essential gap in access to first contact curative health care in rural India. In the FGDs, people referred to the NDAP as "choto doctor" (small doctor).

Box 1: Some Findings of FGDs

FGDs suggested that seeking first contact care from qualified doctors was related to

- economic status of the household as only better off households could afford the total higher costs (of transport, wage loss, fees, medicines, and tests) of approaching a qualified doctor;
- perceived severity of the health condition: if the condition was seen as beyond the scope of the village doctor (e.g. a snake bite or a heart problem), then people would bypass the village level and go straight to a doctor;
- proximity to the provider/facility: those communities that lived within easy walking distance of a health facility in Orissa were likely to go straight to that facility first.

In FGDs, people repeatedly complained about two problems:

- the money they had to spend on transport to reach public facilities — an amount that could exceed the cost of medicines;
- the money they had to spend out of pocket for medicines and tests, and sometimes for the doctors' consultation fee.

Conclusion

The authors conclude that there is a huge gap between the demand for primary level curative health care, and its availability through the government's three-tier system.

The policy recommendation is that primary curative health services need to cater to people's requirements in terms of being more mobile, proximate, and available for longer hours. It should also combine consultation and dispensing of medicines. The popularity of NDAPs in rural communities cannot be ignored as they help in filling a demand for primary curative care, with a new treatment-mix which the public system is not able to satisfy under existing operating conditions.

'First we go to the small doctor': First contact for curative health care sought by rural communities in Andhra Pradesh & Orissa, India

Meenakshi Gautham*, Erika Binnendijk*, Ruth Koren** & David. M. Dror*,†

*Erasmus University Rotterdam, (Institute of Health Policy & Management), Netherlands, **Tel Aviv University (Sackler School of Medicine), Israel & †Micro Insurance Academy, New Delhi, India

Received November 12, 2010

***Background & objectives*: Against the backdrop of insufficient public supply of primary care and reports of informal providers, the present study sought to collect descriptive evidence on 1st contact curative health care seeking choices among rural communities in two States of India - Andhra Pradesh (AP) and Orissa.**

***Methods*: The cross-sectional study design combined a Household Survey (1,810 households in AP; 5,342 in Orissa), 48 Focus Group Discussions (19 in AP; 29 in Orissa), and 61 Key Informant Interviews with healthcare providers (22 in AP; 39 in Orissa).**

***Results*: In AP, 69.5 per cent of respondents accessed non-degree allopathic practitioners (NDAPs) practicing in or near their village; in Orissa, 40.2 per cent chose first curative contact with NDAPs and 36.2 per cent with traditional healers. In AP, all NDAPs were private practitioners, in Orissa some pharmacists and nurses employed in health facilities, also practiced privately. Respondents explained their choice by proximity and providers' readiness to make house-calls when needed. Less than a quarter of respondents chose qualified doctors as their first point of call: mostly private practitioners in AP, and public practitioners in Orissa. Amongst those who chose a qualified practitioner, the most frequent reason was doctors' quality rather than proximity.**

***Interpretation & conclusions*: The results of this study show that most rural persons seek first level of curative healthcare close to home, and pay for a composite convenient service of consulting-cum-dispensing of medicines. NDAPs fill a huge demand for primary curative care which the public system does not satisfy, and are the *de facto* first level access in most cases.**

Key words First healthcare contact - health seeking - informal - non-degree allopathic providers - primary curative healthcare - rural - traditional healers

Primary curative outpatient healthcare is in great demand in India. According to National Health Accounts[1], 88 per cent of households' health expenditure is spent on curative services, of which 48 per cent is towards primary curative care, also defined as "ambulatory or outpatient treatment of illness"[2]. Dror *et al*[3] investigated the cost of illness among the poor in five locations in India and reported that 33 per cent of the costs were attributed to consultations and 49 per cent to payment for drugs.

National surveys suggest that the proportion of persons falling sick and seeking curative care in rural and urban India is comparable: the National Sample Survey (60th Round) reported 823/1000 ailments treated (in the 15 days preceding the survey) in rural vs. 893/1000 in urban areas[4]; this difference is offset by the higher proportion of rural population (more than 70%)[5], so in absolute numbers, rural treatment-seekers outnumber urban ones.

Despite a larger demand for healthcare among rural persons, the quality and quantity of healthcare supply is relatively lower in rural than in urban areas[6,7]. For instance, a survey of all healthcare providers in the State of Madhya Pradesh (population 60.4 million) enumerated 24,807 qualified doctors, of whom, 75.6 per cent worked in the private sector, mostly (80%) in urban areas[6].

Ambulatory outpatient care is supposed to be available in rural areas through the public delivery system at Primary Health Centres (PHCs). Each PHC serves on average 30,000 persons and is managed by a medical doctor. A PHC is linked to 6 sub-centres (SCs), each serving about 5,000 persons, and managed by an Auxiliary Nurse Midwife (ANM) who delivers family planning services, some maternity care and immunizations. Secondary level care is supposed to be delivered by Community Health Centres (CHCs), where four specialist doctors should offer specialized care to 120,000 persons[8]. A district hospital at the top provides tertiary referral care and supervision.

This basic 3-tier system has not changed since it was proposed by India's first Health Survey and Development Committee[9], but the Committee's recommended 'population norm' of one PHC per 10,000-20,000 population has never been achieved. With a current infrastructure of 23,458 PHCs and 4,276 CHCs, and with 18.8 per cent vacancies in PHC doctors' positions and 51.6 per cent vacancies in CHC specialists' positions[8], the system suffers from inadequate infrastructure and doctor shortages[10], while India's rural population has grown to more than 700 million[5]. There is low utilization of primary outpatient care in public facilities because of long distances, inconvenient opening hours, lengthy waiting, staff absenteeism, poor availability of medicines, and poor quality of care[11-13]. One analysis showed that public facilities were utilized by people in low income States more than by people in high- and middle-income States[14].

Evidence suggests that rural people seek outpatient primary care from private providers for many conditions, including newborn/child illnesses[15,16], malaria/febrile illnesses[17], TB[18] and women's health[19]. People's choice of provider may reflect provider proximity, cost, reputation, perceived 'recovery', lack of faith in the public sector, and lay notions of aetiology[13,20,21]. The private health sector in rural India includes a heterogeneous mix of providers; some are professionally trained, but the majority are unqualified. A survey done in 2007 enumerated only about 28 per cent qualified doctors[6]. Almost all the 89,090 unqualified providers practiced as private rural practitioners. Different types of practitioners and systems have existed in rural India. Studies from the 1960s and 1970s reported that traditional healers or indigenous medical practitioners used both modern and traditional medicines[22]. Later studies refer to "rural medical practitioners"[23] following mainly allopathic treatment practices. More recent studies have reported that in rural areas health-seekers approached traditional healers[17,21] and also qualified practitioners of AYUSH (Ayurveda, Unani, Siddha and Homeopathy systems)[6]. However, only a minority (14%) utilize the pure traditional cures[24].

The Indian government launched its National Rural Health Mission (NRHM) in 2005[25] to increase access and quality of healthcare in rural areas. The present study conducted in 2008-2009, sought to investigate the post NRHM status of curative health care seeking at first contact among rural communities. Evidence collected from health care seekers (demand side) was juxtaposed with evidence collected from providers (supply side) on first contact healthcare, including the illnesses, patients' choices and providers' patient load, treatments, medicines, and referrals. This study embraces a horizontal approach in investigating 1st contact curative care, regardless of the cause, and by all providers participating *de-facto* in the health system.

Material & Methods

This study was part of a larger baseline study to initiate rural micro health insurance programmes in two States – Andhra Pradesh (AP) and Orissa. Field work was conducted in AP during May-June 2008 and in Orissa during January-February 2009.

Quantitative methods

Household survey (HHS)

Sampling: In the two districts in AP there were 2031villages with a total population of 5,359,959 spread across 1,257,235 households[5]. In the three districts in Orissa (Kalahandi, Malkangiri and Khorda), there were 4436 villages, and a total population of 2,776,546 spread across 602,561households. For AP with a total of 1257,235 HHs and an assumed 10 per cent frequency of visiting qualified physicians (obtained by discussions with community leaders) the calculated sample size for an error of 2% and 99% confidence level was 1491 HHs. For Orissa, with a total of 602,561 HHs, the calculated sample size was 1489. The actual sample included 1,810 households in AP and 5,342 in Orissa.

The villages were selected purposively, where local organizations were involved in the micro health insurance project [Cooperative Development Foundation (CDF) in AP and the Madhyam Foundation in Orissa with its 11 affiliated NGOs]; 20 villages in AP (12 in Warangal and 8 in Karimnagar districts) and 80 villages in Orissa (27 in Kalahandi, 22 in Khorda, and 31 in Malkangiri districts). In every village, two cohorts were randomly sampled counting the same number of households: members of self-help groups (SHGs), and non-member households.

The SHGs were savings and borrowing societies that were already present at the two sites. The micro health insurance was intended only for existing SHG members, and we wanted to make sure that there was no difference in socio-economic status or education between the prospective insured and uninsured (to eliminate any confounding differences later on in our impact analysis).

Research tool and implementation: A structured questionnaire was developed in English, translated into Telugu and Oriya, and validated through back translation and cognitive pre-testing in 80 households each in AP and in Orissa, and modified as necessary. Project personnel trained local investigators to carry out the interviews. The questionnaire included close-ended questions on respondents' socio-demographic characteristics, healthcare utilization, providers approached first by household members for outpatient care when ill, and reasons for approaching these providers. In the Orissa survey, the inquiry was refined to confirm whether allopathic practitioners were degree vs. non-degree [which was inferred in AP by combining HHS and focus group discussion (FGD) data].

The method as adopted by the Indian National Sample Survey Organization (NSSO) was followed to obtain a proxy for income through questions on many items of household expenditures. Similar to NSSO, the monthly per capita expenditure (MPCE) served as proxy for income.

Qualitative methods

Focus group discussions (FGDs)

Sampling: A total of 19 FGDs (9 men's, 10 women's) in AP, and 29 FGDs (13 men's and 16 women's) were conducted in Orissa; 214 persons participated in FGDs in AP (96 men and 118 women), and 314 in Orissa (121 men, 193 women). Villages for FGDs were selected (5 in AP and 15 in Orissa) by location within districts, distance from towns and from medical facility (near, medium or far). Participants in FGDs were men and women aged 25 to 45 yr. Groups were gender- and income homogenous (proxy for income was land ownership). As far as possible, the same number of FGDs were conducted with males and females in each village.

Research tool and implementation: An FGD guide (pre-tested with 2 male and 2 female focus groups in each State) was developed and local persons (2 in AP, 4 in Orissa) were trained to facilitate discussions on morbidity and incidence, health seeking decisions, first providers approached, perceptions of how providers treated and what they charged. The facilitators were debriefed after every session. All FGDs were held in settings ensuring privacy and confidentiality to participants.

Key informant interviews (KII)

Sampling: KIIs were conducted with 9 village-based providers in AP and 20 in Orissa, plus solo general practitioners (GPs) and specialists in nearby towns, and hospital-based providers (13 in AP and 19 in Orissa). First popular providers were located and interviewed and then other providers were identified with their help.

Research tools and implementation: Semi-structured interview tools were developed per provider category (pre-tested with 4-6 providers in each State) to collect information on education and training of village providers, practice characteristics, services rendered, and types of patients. Interviews in health facilities or with GPs focused on listing services, staff, and basic information on patients.

Ethical compliance

This research project met all the requirements of the funding agency (NWO-WOTRO) on ethical issues arising in social science research. The research document for all the interventions (*e.g.* FGDs, HHS interviews, and KIIs) included an introductory section tantamount to a protocol of informed choice in which the researchers explained the purpose of the study, what would be done with the data, and sought and obtained verbal consent of participants to participate in the interviews and discussions, and to record the FGD meetings. Participants' names were kept confidential in data recording and analysis. All interviews were organized so as to ensure interviewees that confidentiality would be kept.

Statistical analysis: SPSS v.17 (*Source*: *www.ibm.com/software/analytics/spss*) was used to analyse HHS data. We organised the taped, transcribed and translated FGD data into matrices and explored similarities, differences, recurrent themes and categorizations within data driven sub themes, broadly covering perceptions of common diseases, hierarchy of care seeking, characteristics of and perceptions related to providers of first contact. KII data were entered in Excel, and simple frequencies for close-ended questions were calculated. Open-ended questions were entered verbatim and analyzed qualitatively to determine common characteristics, relationship with communities, and treatment patterns.

Table I. Profile of the study communities in Andhra Pradesh (AP) and Orissa

	AP (n=1810)	Orissa (n=5342)
Caste of household head:		
Scheduled Tribes	2.3	30.0**
Scheduled Castes	18.6	22.3*
Other Backward Castes	61.9	31.3**
Other Castes	17.1	16.5
Literacy of household head:		
Illiterate household heads	44.8	51.3**
Activity of household head:		
Casual wage labourer	42.1	30.8**
Self-employed in agriculture	26.2	38.7**
Self-employed in business/trade	15.7	16.1
Regular salaried employee	8.3	4.6**
Rest (non-income earning)	7.7	9.8*
Median MPCE (₹)	1289	504†

P *<0.01, **<0.001 (Chi squared) compated to AP; †<0.001 (ANOVA). Values are given in percentages. MPCE, monthly per capita expenditure

Results

The study populations in the two States reported significantly different household incomes. Median MPCE in AP was INR 1,289, more than twice that of Orissa (INR 504). The proportion of Scheduled Tribes (STs) was significantly (P<0.001) higher in Orissa than in AP, while the proportion of OBCs was higher (P<0.001) in AP. Illiteracy was higher (P<0.001) in Orissa (Table I). There were also differences in economic activity of household heads: in Orissa the largest group was that of self employed small farmers, while the largest group in AP was composed of casual wage labourers. No significant differences were found between SHG members and non-members. Women formed the majority of HHS respondents in both States: 72.3 per cent in AP and 67.7 per cent in Orissa. Other available household members if present, also contributed.

In AP as village sizes were bigger than in Orissa and there was sufficient representation of men and women from different socio-economic groups, four different FGDs were organized per village (2 men's and 2 women's) representing poor and better off households in each village. In most of the poorer groups, half or more of the participants were illiterate and a few only had completed 10 years of schooling. However, literacy differences were less pronounced in the women's groups where even the better off groups had more illiterate than literate members. Participants in the poorer groups were either landless and worked as "coolies"(daily wage farm labourers), or as other types of daily wage labourers (*e.g.* loaders), or had small farms less than 3 acres in size but also sometimes worked as "coolies" or ran small businesses (such as a small shop) to supplement their farm income. Participants in the better off groups usually owned medium sized (3-6 acres) farms and a few owned bigger ones (10-20 acres). These groups also had participants with less land but with bigger businesses (*e.g.* tailor) and some had salaried jobs (*e.g.* teacher, driver).

In Orissa, villages were smaller and communities more homogenous with respect to occupations and land ownership. Thus only two FGDs could be organized per village, one male and one female. In general, there were more illiterate participants here than in AP. While in each district 1-2 FGDs comprised landless daily wage labourers (*e.g.* farm labour/constructions workers/ small vendors), the majority were small farmers with 1-5 acres of land. As in AP the latter supplemented their income through daily wage activities, or through small businesses such as selling fruits, vegetables and also fish, and in those villages that were close to the capital city of Bhubaneswar, through salaried jobs (*e.g.* clerks and peons).

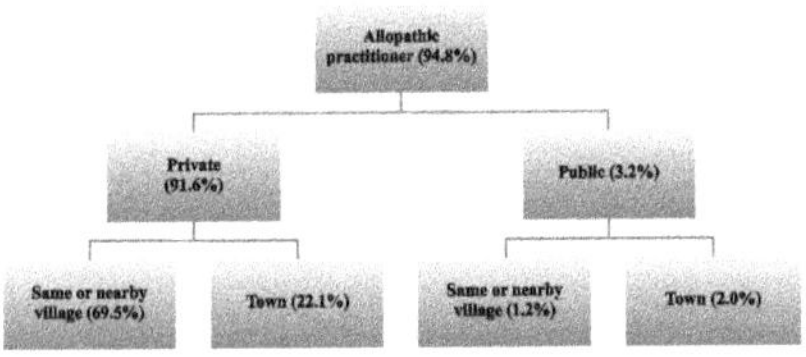

Fig. 1. First care seeking contact in Andhra Pradesh.

Providers of first health-seeking contact: In both States, FGD narratives suggested that the first response to an illness could be self medication, with men more likely to buy an over-the-counter paracetamol or other medicine and the women more likely to rely on home remedies. When these were not effective, they sought care from available providers. In AP, 94.8 per cent HHS respondents usually approached an allopathic practitioner first (Fig. 1); most (69.5%) approached private allopathic practitioners in the same village or nearby village and 22.1 per cent approached private practitioners in town. FGDs revealed that in villages, private 'allopathic' practitioners were informally trained and unlicensed, often called Registered Medical Practitioner (RMPs), a designation used in some States until the 1970s, and still included in some State Medical Councils[26], but currently synonymous with unregistered practitioners without formal qualifications in medicine. We refer to these as non-degree allopathic providers (NDAPs).

In Orissa 53.1 per cent of respondents had their first health-seeking contact was with an allopathic practitioner; of these 40.2 per cent approached NDAPs and 12.9 per cent consulted qualified physicians (Fig. 2). In the FGDs, people referred to the NDAP as "*choto doctor*" (small doctor). Triangulation of the HHS, FGDs and KIIs showed that in Orissa, some NDAPs (*e.g.* pharmacists, nurses and compounders) were employed in government health centres, and treated patients in villages for-a-fee. In Orissa, 32.6 per cent of HHS respondents usually approached such "public sector NDAPs" first, mostly in the same or nearby village (27.6%) (Fig. 2).

Around a quarter or less of respondents in both States approached qualified doctors in the first instance. In AP, these were doctors in private practice in nearby towns (22.1% - Fig. 1), whereas public practitioners were mentioned by only 3.2 per cent. In Orissa a smaller proportion of respondents (12.9%) approached qualified doctors first, and the majority of those (10.7%) went to public sector doctors (Fig. 2).

A substantial proportion of respondents in Orissa (36.2%) also approached other non-allopathic practitioners first: traditional healers. Fewer households approached other types of practitioners: only 0.2 per cent respondents in AP and 4.2 per cent in Orissa approached AYUSH practitioners, and 5 per cent in AP and 6.4 per cent in Orissa approached government health workers like ANMs, ASHAs (Accredited Social Health Activist) and AWWs (Aanganwadi Worker).

Association between income and choice of provider: In view of the diversity of first contact providers, association between income of the population (MPCE quintiles) and choice of first contact provider was examined, a significant association was seen in Orissa but not in AP (Table II). In Orissa, a significant decrease was observed in the frequency of accessing traditional

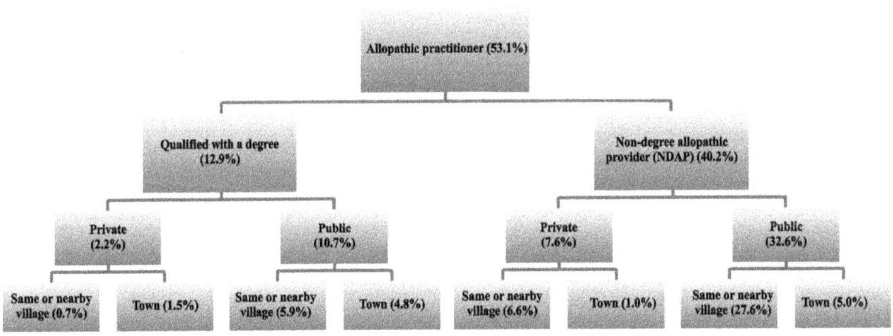

Fig. 2. First care seeking contact in Orissa (allopathic practitioner details).

Table II. Type of provider first approached by different MPCE quintiles in Andhra Pradesh (AP) and Orissa

State	Quintiles	NDAP (%)	Traditional healer	Qualified doctor (%)	AYUSH practitioner (%)	ANM/ ASHA/ AWW (%)	Any others (%)
AP	Quintile 1	67.3	N/A	26.5	0.3	4.5	1.4
	Quintile 2	69.5	N/A	25.1	0.0	4.2	1.1
	Quintile 3	69.3	N/A	22.5	0.0	5.9	2.3
	Quintile 4	71.3	N/A	21.7	0.3	6.2	.6
	Quintile 5	72.6	N/A	21.8	0.3	4.5	.8
	Significance	ns	ns	ns	ns	ns	ns
Orissa	Quintile 1	35.0	39.9%	7.4	3.1	14.6	N/A
	Quintile 2	37.1	44.8%	9.4	2.3	6.4	N/A
	Quintile 3	42.3	37.4%	12.4	3.1	4.8	N/A
	Quintile 4	40.2	34.1%	14.9	6.3	4.5	N/A
	Quintile 5	45.7	25.2%	20.6	5.8	2.8	N/A
	Significance	***	***	***	***	***	

***$P<0.001$ (Chi squared), Significance of difference between the different income quintiles; ns, not significant

N/A, not applicable; MPCE, monthly per capita expenditure; NDAP, non-degree allopathic practitioners; ANM, auxiliary nurse midwife; ASHA, accredited social health activist; AWW, Aanganwadi worker

healers with income, which was mainly due to a lower frequency in the fifth income quintile. A positive association was found between income quintiles and frequency of seeking care with qualified doctors. The lowest quintile reported 7.4 per cent and the highest 20.6 per cent. There was a small but significant increase in the frequency of choosing NDAPs with increasing income.

Reasons for choice of first contact provider: Respondents named proximity as the most important reason for their choice of first contact provider. It was the main reason for a majority of respondents that approached NDAPs and traditional healers (77.5% in AP and 58.9% in Orissa for NDAPs; 67.9% for traditional healers in Orissa; Table III). Fewer respondents named their reason as provider being 'best' (18.1% in AP and 32.7% in Orissa for NDAPs; 20.3% for traditional healers in Orissa). However, among those who approached a qualified doctor first, a majority said it was because that provider was 'best' (56.0% AP; 58.2% Orissa) followed by 'closest' (38.9% AP; 35.8% Orissa).

Provider profiles and people's perceptions

Traditional healers: Traditional healers provided a substantial proportion of health care at first contact in Orissa but not in AP. In Orissa, over one-third of the HHS respondents usually sought first consultation with traditional healers (Fig. 2) as they were their closest providers (Table III).

These practices could not be generalized across all study communities, since care seeking from traditional healers was expressed more by groups that were more remotely located and had fewer allopathic options in or around their villages, or among groups with greater economic impoverishment. These findings were in agreement with the HH survey results that showed an inverse relationship between income and care seeking from traditional healers. However, tribal populations (STs) chose traditional healers less frequently than SCs and OBCs (28.3 vs. 43.3% and 40.2% respectively, $P<0.001$). There was no significant association between frequency of choice of traditional healer and literacy.

Table III. Reasons why HHS respondents chose 1st contact health provider

	AP (%)			Orissa (%)		
	Closest	Best	Cheapest	Closest	Best	Cheapest
NDAPs	77.5	18.1	1.4	58.9	32.7	2.3
Traditional healer	NA	NA	NA	67.9	20.3	5.1
Qualified doctor	38.9	56.0	1.6	35.8	58.2	1.7
Overall	66.5	27.6	2.2	57.8	30.6	5.8

NDAP, non degree allopathic provider

Non-degree allopathic providers (NDAPs): NDAPs were sought by almost 70 per cent HHS respondents in AP and 40 per cent in Orissa. NDAPs in AP were private practitioners but in Orissa people also sought care from public sector NDAPs. Some employees in government health centres, especially the primary health centres (PHCs) including pharmacists, nurses, and even health attendants, acted as NDAPs in Orissa in three situations: firstly, when the health facility had no doctor and was managed entirely by non-doctor staff. Doctor shortages in Malkangiri (with large tracts of inaccessible areas) were particularly acute. Secondly, when a doctor was assigned, but absent from duty for any reason, some of the doctor's tasks were routinely performed by other health workers. Thirdly, when the doctor was present but patient load at the facility was high, other health workers (*e.g.* pharmacists, nurses, female/male health workers, health attendants) performed some of the doctor's tasks.

From the FGDs with men and women, and KIIs with 9 NDAPs, some common characteristics as well as differences were identified between private NDAPs in the two States. All were male. Their average age was 36 yr in AP (range of 24 to 50 yr) and 43 yr in Orissa (range of 28 to 60 yr). All had well-established independent practices with an average professional experience of 13.3 yr in AP and 20.5 yr in Orissa. The majority had completed 10 or more years of schooling. Most NDAPs acquired skills through informal apprenticeships, usually with other doctors both private and public. NDAPs in AP delivered mainly mobile services. All 9 possessed mobile phones and responded to emergency calls plus provided services within a radius of 0-5 km (1-5 villages) of where they lived; two who owned a scooter/motorcycle extended their catchment area to 20-25 km. Five NDAPs also had rudimentary clinics. Most, however, spent between 6 and 12 h daily circulating in villages and providing doorstep services. In Orissa, only half the NDAPs provided mobile healthcare in a larger radius of 5-20 km from their village; those who had a motorcycle travelled longer distances. The other half combined static and mobile services, during 1-4 h daily for rounds or to respond to calls, within a smaller radius of 2-5 km.

Most NDAPs in AP saw 20 or more patients daily (range from 10 to 70 patients); mobile providers had most patients. In Orissa, NDAPs saw a smaller average of 12 patients daily (range from 2 to 40 patients) and older practitioners had higher patient-loads. The providers were asked to estimate their catchment population (households they usually served). In AP, it ranged from 50 to 300 households, with an average of 100 households. In Orissa, it ranged from 40 to 1200 households with an average of 300 households.

NDAPs in both States treated the most commonly reported morbidities. We compared five most frequently treated conditions named by NDAPs with replies to the HHS question: "Did a person in the HH have an illness episode last month? What kind of illness was it?" The information from both sources tallied closely (Table IV). 'Fever' topped the list, followed by body pains and GI symptoms in AP, and malaria in Orissa.

NDAPs in both States used allopathic medicines to provide symptomatic relief. Typically, they dispensed medicines for 2-3 days (rarely up to a week), and if there was no improvement, they referred patients. NDAPs also referred in emergencies, sometimes providing first aid or accompanying patients to a qualified physician or hospital. In Orissa, NDAPs sometimes performed simple diagnostic tests (*e.g.* blood test for malaria).

Some NDAPs also prescribed drugs additional to those they dispensed. We listed 37 brand names of drugs named by NDAPs in AP and 49 in Orissa (Table V). The various drug types mentioned were classified by mode of action (following CIMS India Reference System)[27].

Table IV. Most common symptoms/illnesses reported by HHS respondents and private NDAPs in AP and Orissa

Symptoms	AP		Orissa	
	No. of providers reported these among top symptoms (KIIs)	Reported as illnesses in last month (HHS) (%)	No. of providers reported these among top symptoms (KIIs)	Reported as illnesses in last month (HHS) (%)
Fevers (including typhoid)	8/9	44.0	11/15	50.6
Malaria, dengue kala-azar, chikungunya	N/A	1.2	8/15	14.0
Body pain/joint pain	9/9	15.8	9/15	5.4
Gastrointestinal symptoms (GI)	9/9	8.5	14/15	8.3

Table V. Drugs named by private NDAPs in AP and Orissa

Drug class*	AP		Orissa	
	Number of names mentioned by providers	No. of NDAPs mentioned this drug class (KIIs)	Number of names mentioned by providers	No. of NDAPs mentioned this drug class (KIIs)
Analgesics and antipyretics, including antimalarials	3 brand names 2 generics	9/9	6 brand names 3 generic	14/15
Vitamins & haematopoietic	2 brand names	8/9	13 brand names 5 generics	13/15
Antibacterial (oral)	6 brand names 8 generics	8/9	11 brand names 5 generic	11/15
Non-steroidal anti inflammatory drugs	9 brand names 1 generic	9/9	3 brand names 1 generic	7/15

**Source*: Central Index of Medical Specialties (CIMS), India[27]

CIMS information revealed that 44 manufacturers produced the 37 AP brands and 48 produced the 49 Orissa brands. This suggests that NDAPs were familiar with multiple branded drugs with different names (different manufacturers) and that these brands were available over the counter in the retail market, from where NDAPs said they restocked their supplies weekly or fortnightly. NDAPs used mostly four classes of drugs: analgesics/antipyretics/antimalarial, vitamin and iron supplements, antibacterial and non steroidal anti inflammatory drugs (NSAIDs) (Table V). In Orissa, three providers also dispensed ayurvedic remedies. AP providers mentioned no indigenous medicines. Some NDAPs also gave nutritional advice on consumption of foods rich in vitamins and minerals such as leafy vegetables, eggs, milk and fruits.

NDAPs were asked to name five common conditions for which they referred patients, and where they referred to. Most NDAPs referred for gynaecological problems (*e.g.* pregnancy and institutional delivery), pains, chronic non-communicable conditions (*e.g.* heart problems, hypertension, diabetes, kidney related problems), acute fevers and gastrointestinal conditions, and in Orissa also for accidents and injuries including snakebites.

NDAPs usually referred to private doctors in AP, and to public facilities in Orissa. In Orissa, the public sector doctors (especially in peripheral facilities) confirmed that NDAPs referred cases for pregnancy, delivery and for serious conditions (*e.g.* malaria and pneumonia).

Yet we could not find any incentive for NDAPs to refer cases, either through training to improve recognition of referral conditions, or through financial incentives similar to those that government workers like ASHAs receive for each delivery they refer. In AP, NDAPs who referred to private doctors, received occasional gifts (like table calendars) but no financial incentives.

Qualified doctors: Around a quarter of HHS respondents in AP and roughly half that proportion in Orissa approached qualified allopathic doctors at first contact (Figs 1 & 2). The major difference was that doctors approached in AP were primarily town based private practitioners while in Orissa they were public servants employed at government PHCs and CHCs.

FGDs and KIIs confirmed these two different State scenarios. In AP, FGD participants, both men and women, named a number of private doctors and facilities that they approached in nearby towns, whereas in Orissa, when participants talked about care seeking from a qualified doctor, they usually referred to a government facility identifiable by its location and referred to as a "hospital" irrespective of whether it was a PHC or a CHC or a tertiary hospital.

However, whether public or private, people usually approached these qualified doctors as the second step in their care seeking pathway, if the first level intervention in the village did not succeed, or in multiple care-seeking at the same level (*e.g.* going from one specialist to another in AP). FGDs suggested that seeking first contact care from qualified doctors was related to *(i)* economic status of the household as only better off households could afford the total higher costs (of transport, wage loss, fees, medicines, and tests) of approaching a qualified doctor, *(ii)* perceived severity of the health condition: if the condition was seen as beyond the scope of the village doctor (*e.g.* a snake bite or a heart problem), then people would bypass the village level and go straight to a doctor, and *(iii)* proximity to the provider/facility: those communities that lived within easy walking distance of a health facility in Orissa were likely to go straight to that facility first.

In AP, people had access to many private doctors even at block level towns and semi urban areas, but not so at the village level. In Orissa, especially in the poorer districts of Kalahandi and Malkangiri, government PHCs and CHCs were the main source of care by qualified physicians (who were government employees), and these were located even in villages beyond the block towns. Although Orissa respondents accessed public facilities more than in AP, many of these facilities were understaffed, especially in Malkangiri and Kalahandi districts. Malkangiri's Chief Medical Officer informed that only 33 out of 100 sanctioned medical doctors were available in the district public health system.

The private sector provided rural AP communities with a multiplicity of options for care seeking from qualified physicians, and both men and women, even from poorer households appeared to prefer private to public because of better perceived care and treatment. For women, it was familiarity and faith in the doctor and the doctor's kindness that was important. More than one women's group close to a certain town (Narsampet) named the same doctors repeatedly as being among the nicer ones whom they approached both for general illnesses and for women's problems as well.

In AP, men, much more than women, had a tendency to analyse the mode of operation of private qualified doctors. They complained about the high costs, doctors' business orientation and malpractices but they still preferred to go to private doctors.

In AP, use of public primary facilities was limited to immunizations at the PHCs. Although intended for the poor and cheaper than private, public facilities were nonetheless not perceived as poor-friendly by poor consumers. In Orissa, public facilities were people's major and, in many places, only source of access to a qualified physician. Though doctor consultations were usually free of charge in PHCs and CHCs and even the sub-divisional hospitals, people said that doctors usually prescribed medicines and tests from outside private sources. In FGDs, people repeatedly complained about two problems: *(i)* the money they had to spend on transport to reach public facilities - an amount that could exceed the cost of medicines; and *(ii)* the money they had to spend out of pocket for medicines and tests, and at one district hospital (which allowed private practice by public doctors) also for the doctors' consultation fee.

Discussion

Through multifarious strategies and enhanced funding, the Government of India provides accessible, affordable and quality healthcare to rural persons. The National Rural Health Mission (NRHM) launched in 2005 for implementation up to 2012[25] is the most recent large-scale programme to strengthen the existing 3-tier public health delivery system. Our study demonstrated that the huge need for primary level curative healthcare was different from what the 3-tier system has been able to provide, and that this need was satisfied mainly outside the public system. For one, the data showed that the overwhelming reason given for the choice of first contact curative provider was proximity. From the FGDs it was known that the proximate providers were also available at all hours of the day and night, and responded to telephone calls.

The doctors at public, and even more at private health facilities, often required that patients undergo diagnostic tests and buy prescribed medicines, the combined cost of which was high, plus there were indirect costs of transportation and wage-loss. NDAPs were much closer to care-seekers in villages, made house calls when requested, charged lower fees and provided the all-in-one "quick-fix" service. Thus, more than 75 per cent of the population preferred to go to NDAPs and (in Orissa) also to traditional healers for first contact curative care. This evidence demonstrates that people seek a different type of primary curative care, which is not doctor-centric and is delivered not in a far away doctor's clinic, and for which clients are willing to pay.

The people did not choose their first contact provider by whether he was a "small doctor" or a "big doctor". Frequently, factors like distance and cost determined people's care-seeking preferences more than providers' skills or accreditation. This alternative treatment trail was mostly at odds with government policy, and people consulted professional doctors only when they, or their first contact NDAP, perceived a specific reason to do so.

Consistent with previous evidence[10,11], staff shortages and low utilization of the public sector were found. However, our findings do not uphold the assumption that the need among rural communities for proximate all-in-one primary curative healthcare would disappear even if all the PHCs and CHCs were to become fully staffed and well equipped. Thus, if the public system should deliver such care, health planners would need to revise the objectives and deliverables of the various tiers in the public system.

Our evidence on practice of NDAPs not only confirms previous reports about their widespread presence in rural areas[2,6], but also gives new details about the existence, in addition to private practitioners, of "public sector NDAPs".

Some scholars have explained the recourse to traditional healers (accessed by 36% of care-seekers in Orissa) by reference to illiteracy and tribal cultures[28]; in our examination, this explanation was not confirmed, as there was no significant difference in the rate of consulting traditional healers across literate or illiterate HH heads and, interestingly, tribal households approached traditional healers less than non tribal households. However, our data suggested that there was a negative association between income and frequency of traditional healer care seeking that was most apparent in the richest quintile in Orissa.

It was found that private qualified doctors practiced in AP even at block level, but almost none could be found in Orissa, especially in Kalahandi and Malkangiri (the poorer and more remote districts of Orissa). In these districts, the PHCs and CHCs, were understaffed. The reason why fewer private doctors practiced in Orissa was people's lower ability to pay, demonstrated by lower median MPCE (pattern confirmed by National Sample Survey 2005-06: ₹ 460.32 for Orissa and ₹ 704.17 in AP). Our findings provided additional evidence to support this conclusion, as the frequency of accessing qualified doctors increased significantly with income in Orissa.

Based on analysis of illnesses reported by people (juxtaposed against those reported by providers), it appears that NDAPs manage the most frequent illnesses, and thus fill a limited but essential gap in access to first contact curative healthcare in rural India. Similar to findings of others[23], NDAPs in our study were mostly male, with long-established practices of allopathy close to where they live, typically dispensing small doses of medicines when consulting patients, and charging a flat fee for both consultation and medicines. A new feature of NDAP services *i.e.* "on-call" services to respond to clients' needs for doorstep curative care as-and-when needed, anytime was also seen.

We found no signs of conflict of interests or "turf wars" between qualified doctors and NDAPs; on the contrary, we observed even some complementarity between the two categories of providers.

NDAPs referred complex cases to qualified doctors, often by accompanying the patients. This situation explains why, notwithstanding legal restrictions set out by the Indian Medical Council Act[29] on the practice of medicine, some experts in the Indian public health community suggest that the role of NDAPs should be reviewed[30]. Even certain government commissions made similar recommendations. *e.g.* the National Commission for Macroeconomics and Health[7], a Health Ministry Task Group on training and accreditation of rural practitioners[31], and the NRHM. Additionally, a Task Force on Medical Education recommended a 3- year programme to train community health practitioners[32], and the most recent official attempt is to design the curriculum for a Bachelor of Rural Health Care programme[33]. These programmes probably reflect the concern that the government should provide better than sub-optimal, first contact, primary curative care to rural populations.

NDAPs in our study treated with allopathic medicines and were familiar with not just one or two brand names of allopathic drugs, but with several, which they could access without any difficulties. This suggests that representatives and retailers of the pharmaceutical industry succeed in bringing drug related information (and drugs as well) to NDAPs in the same way as they reach qualified prescribers. As this study was not an empirical evaluation of the clinical quality of care of NDAPs, it is not possible to comment on the adequacy of use of the drugs they mentioned. However, the ease of access to drugs by persons lacking formal certification (like the NDAPs) and the absence of effective regulatory oversight of drug distribution in India raise some concern about practices of dispensing of medicines reported through this study.

The main study limitation was that due to resource constraints we could interview fewer first-contact providers than all those who were available. However, some of the providers most frequently approached as identified and located from people's descriptions in the FGDs were interviewed. Thus, these interviews provide a profile of providers that people accessed frequently in the study communities.

In conclusion, our study showed that the rural population in India indicates a need for "consult-cum-dispense" healthcare services for most common illnesses to be delivered most hours of the day and at doorstep (or at least served in or near their village). This treatment-trail for primary curative care has evolved unguided and unnoted by the formal system. The architecture of this treatment trail is crafted by the demand side, and has been solidified by the propagation of NDAPs practicing at village level. If the public sector should meet this health need, clearly the bottleneck would be not merely the insufficient number of doctors actually serving in PHCs and CHCs in rural areas. The policy conclusion is that services have to address the need expressed by people for more mobile, proximate - virtually doorstep - primary curative care that should combine consultation and dispensing of medicines, and would function many more hours. NDAPs fill a demand for primary curative care, with a new treatment-mix which the public system is not able to satisfy in rural India under existing operating conditions. The de-facto diffidence about *(i)* the need of rural populations for very different services than those planned under the existing 3-tier public system, and *(ii)* the important role of NDAPs in responding to the demand for these primary curative healthcare services, irrespective of policies or law, seems rather incongruous.

Acknowledgment

The authors acknowledge funding support from the Netherlands Organization for Scientific Research, under WOTRO Integrated Programme grant No. W01.65.309.00. Additional funding for the household survey in Orissa was obtained from the German Federal Ministry for Economic Cooperation and Development (through a contract between AWO International, Madhyam Foundation, Orissa and the Micro Insurance Academy, New Delhi). We benefited from logistical and research support from the Micro Insurance Academy, from Cooperative Development Foundation (CDF) in AP, and from Madhyam Foundation Bhubaneswar, Orissa and its 11 affiliated NGOs (Parivartan, PUSPAC, SOMKS, SDS, ODC, Mahashakti Foundation, DAPTA, Lok Yojana, Sanginee, MVPS, DSS). Authors thank all the respondents for their participation in the study.

References

1. MOHFW. *National Health Accounts 2001-02*. New Delhi: National Health Accounts Cell, Ministry of Health and Family Welfare, Government of India; 2005.
2. Berman PA. Rethinking health care systems: Private health care provision in India. *World Development* 1998; *26* : 1463-79.
3. Dror MD, van Putten-Radermaker O, Koren R. Cost of Illness: Evidence from a study in five resource-poor locations in India. *Indian J Med Res* 2008; *127* : 347-61.
4. NSSO. *Morbidity, health care and condition of the aged,* NSS 60th Round (January-June 2004). New Delhi: National Sample Survey Organisation, Ministry of Statistics and Programme Implementation, Government of India; 2006.
5. GOI. *Census of India*. Government of India. Available from: *http://censusindia.gov.in/2001*.
6. De Costa A, Diwan V. Where is the public health sector?' Public and private sector healthcare provision in Madhya Pradesh, India. *Health Policy* 2007; *84* : 269-76.
7. GOI. *Report of the National Commission on Macroeconomics and Health*. New Delhi: Ministry of Health and Family Welfare, Government of India; 2005.
8. GOI. Bulletin On Rural Health Statistics In India, Updated as on March 2008. New Delhi: Ministry of Health and Family Welfare, Government of India. Available from: *http://www.mohfw.nic.in/Bulletin* on RHS - March, 2008 - PDF version/, accessed on May 3, 2010.
9. Bhore J. *Report of the Health Survey and Development Committee*, vol, II: *Recommendations*. New Delhi: Government of India Press; 1946.
10. Satpathy S. Public health infrastructure in rural India : Challenges and opportunities. *Indian J Public Health* 2005; *49* : 57-62.
11. Dalal K, Dawad S. Non-utilization of public healthcare facilities: examining the reasons through a national study of women in India. *Rural Remote Health* 2009; *9* : 1178. (Online), 2009:1-10.
12. Kotwani A, Ewen M, Dey D, Iyer S, Lakshmi PK, Patel A, *et al*. Prices and availability of common medicines at six sites in India using a standard methodology. *Indian J Med Res* 2007; *125* : 645-54.
13. Ager A, Pepper K. Patterns of health service utilization and perceptions of needs and services in rural Orissa. *Health Policy Planning* 2005; *20* : 176-84.
14. Purohit B. Inter-State disparities in health care and financial burden on the poor in India. *J Health Social Policy* 2004; *18* : 37-60.
15. Kaushal M, Aggarwal R, Singal A, Shukla H, Kapoor SK, Paul VK. Breastfeeding practices and health-seeking behavior for neonatal sickness in a rural community. *J Trop Pediatr* 2005; *51* : 366-76.
16. Deshmukh P, Dongre AR, Sinha N, Garg BS. Acute childhood morbidities in rural Wardha: some epidemiological correlates and health care seeking. *Indian J Med Sci* 2009; *63* : 345-54.
17. Chaturvedi HK, Mahanta J, Pandey A. Treatment-seeking for febrile illness in north-east India: an epidemiological study in the malaria endemic zone. *Mal J* 2009; *8* : 301.
18. Fochsen G, Deshpande K, Diwan V, Mishra A, Diwan VK, Thorson A. Health care seeking among individuals with cough and tuberculosis: a population-based study from rural India. *Int J Tuberc Lung Dis* 2006; *10* : 995-1000.
19. Rani M, Bonu S. Rural Indian women's care-seeking behavior and choice of provider for gynecological symptoms. *Study Family Plann* 2003; *34* : 173-85.
20. Kamat VK. Reconsidering the popularity of primary health centers in India: A case study from rural Maharashtra. *Soc Sci Med* 1995; *41* : 87-98.

21. Dongre AR, Deshmukh PR , Garg BS. Perceptions and health care seeking about newborn danger signs among mothers in rural Wardha. *Indian J Pediatr* 2008; *75* : 325-9.
22. Bhatia JC, Vir D, Timmappaya A, Chuttani CS. Traditional healers and modern medicine. *Soc Sci Med* 1967; *9* : 15-21.
23. Rohde J, Vishwanathan H. The rural private practitioner. *Health Millions* 1994; *2* : 13-6.
24. Singh P, Yadav RJ, Pandey A. Utilization of indigenous systems of medicine & homoeopathy in India. *Indian J Med Res* 2005; *122* : 137-42.
25. GOI. *National Rural Health Mission: Meeting people's health needs in rural areas. Framework for Implementation 2005-2012*. New Delhi: Ministry of Health and Family Welfare, Government of India; 2005.
26. MPAct. The Madhya Pradesh Ayurvigyan Parishad Adhiniyam (Schedule), 1987, weblink: *http://www.mpmedicalcouncil.net/mpapa.html*, accessed on May 10, 2010. 1990.
27. CIMS India. Central Index of Medical Specialties, Druginfo, website: *http://cimsasia.com/index.aspx#*, accessed on May 10, 2010, 2010.
28. Vijayakumar KN, Gunasekaran K, Sahu SS, Jambulingam P. Knowledge, attitude and practice on malaria: A study in a tribal belt of Orissa state, India with reference to use of long lasting treated mosquito nets. *Acta Trop* 2009; *112* : 137-42.
29. IMC. *The Indian Medical Council Act, 1956*, Section 15 (2b). Delhi: Universal Law Publishing Co Pvt Ltd.;1956.
30. Yadav K, Jarhyan P, Gupta V , Pandav CS. Revitalizing rural health care delivery: Can rural health practitioners be the answer? *Indian J Community Med* 2009; *34* : 3-5.
31. GOI. *Recommendations of task-group set up to examine accreditation, training and integration of private rural medical practitioners, under National Rural Health Mission*. New Delhi: Ministry of Health and Family Welfare, Government of India; 2007.
32. GOI. *Task force on medical education for the National Rural Health Mission*. New Delhi: Ministry of Health and Family Welfare, Government of India. *http://www.mohfw.nic.in/NRHM/Documents/Task_Group_Medical_Education.pdf*, accessed on May 3, 2010.
33. Dhar A. Task Force to design curriculum for rural health cadre. The Hindu, July 19. New Delhi, *http://www.thehindu.com/news/national/article522247.ece*, accessed on July 20, 2010.

Reprint requests: Prof. Dr David Dror, Chairman, Micro Insurance Academy, 246 Sant Nagar, East of Kailash,
New Delhi 110 065, India
e-mail: daviddror@socialre.org

Part 4

Impact

Chapter 19

Field-based Evidence of Enhanced Health Care Utilization Among Persons Insured by MHI Units in Philippines*

Main Messages

- A cross-sectional research design was used. The household survey was carried out in six MIUs in the Philippines.
- A two-stage cluster sampling method was followed in selecting insureds and uninsureds. A total of 1,953 households, 890 insured households (4,639 individuals), and 1,063 uninsured households (5,550 individuals) were included in the study.
- Around 95% of the hospitalization cases among the surveyed households were physician-referrals rather than direct admissions.

Focus Points

- Persons insured by MIUs reported higher health care utilization than uninsured persons.

---

*This chapter is reproduced from *Health Policy* (2005), **73**, 263–271, available at https://www.researchgate.net/publication/7706876_Field_Based_Evidence_of_Enhanced_Healthcare_Utilization_Among_Persons_Insured_by_Micro_Health_Insurance_Units_in_Philippines.

- The proxy indicator for morbidity (which was the reported number of episodes of illness) was virtually the same among the insured and uninsured cohorts, countering an assumption of adverse selection.
- Increased health care utilization by the insured is not due to adverse selection.
- High referral-rate to hospitals suggests that excluding primary care from the benefit package may lead to underutilization of inpatient care.

Structured Abstract

Introduction

Underutilization of health care among poor communities has prompted policymakers to study initiatives that can improve health care utilization, and affiliation with MIUs is considered to be one such arrangement. In order to promote MIUs as a way to increase health care utilization of affiliated persons, evidence in support of this is needed. This chapter examines data collected from six MIUs in the Philippines; the data provide evidence that persons insured by MIUs reported increased utilization of inpatient care, which reflected referrals rather than self-hospitalization.

Method

A household survey was carried out in 2002 in six MIUs in the Philippine. A total of 1,953 households (890 insured households and 1,063 uninsured households) were included in the survey. Household heads were interviewed by following a structured questionnaire, and information recorded on the utilization of health services as recalled by the respondents and other household insureds.

A cross-sectional research design was used, where a two-stage cluster sampling method was adopted in the selection of insureds and uninsureds.

The χ^2 test was used to compare the proportions of qualitative variables and to assess the statistical significance of the differences between insureds and uninsureds at the $\alpha = 0.05$ level.

Findings

The two cohorts did not differ in demographic parameters and differed only marginally in income and education levels, both higher amongst the insured.

The findings suggest that persons insured by MIUs reported higher health care utilization than uninsured persons. This was manifest in terms of higher frequency of primary-care physician encounters, higher hospitalization rates, higher rates of professionally-attended deliveries, lower rates of delivery at home, a higher rate of diagnosed chronic diseases, and better drug compliance among chronically ill. Since most MIUs do not provide unlimited drugs, the difference in drug compliance can be attributed to better awareness among the insured.

Box 1: Utilization of Health Care by the Insured and Uninsured Cohorts

Primary care encounters

- Number of insured who were ill and sought physician's help was higher for insureds than for uninsureds (46.1% compared to 38.8%).

Hospitalizations

- Number of hospitalizations of insureds was higher than for uninsureds (6.3% compared to 4.2%).

Professional attendance during deliveries

- Rate of deliveries attended by a physician was higher for insureds than for uninsureds (54.5% compared to 44.0%).

Delivery at home

- The number of deliveries at home is higher among uninsureds than insureds (40.4% compared to 31.8%).

(*Continued*)

Box 1: (*Continued*)

Diagnosis of chronic diseases

- More chronic illnesses were diagnosed in the insured cohort than in the uninsured group (5.7% compared to 4.6%).

Drug-compliance

- Proportion of uninsured who did not comply with the drug regimen was higher compared to the proportion for the insured cohort (32.6% compared to 20.2%).

A large majority of the hospitalization cases (95%; 94% insured, 95.6% uninsured), were physician- referrals rather than direct admissions. Such high referral-rate to hospitals suggests that a policy-choice to exclude primary care from the benefit package may lead to underutilization of inpatient care due to underestimation by uninsured clients of their needs.

Another major insight is that increased utilization by the insured is not due to adverse selection, as suggested by two findings. Firstly, the proxy indicator for morbidity (the reported number of episodes of illness) among the insured and uninsured cohorts is virtually the same and does not support an assumption of adverse selection. Secondly, if adverse selection were prevalent, we could expect the insured cohort to report a higher number of deliveries during the 5 years preceding the survey compared to the uninsured, which was not the case. Instead, rates of deliveries were slightly higher among the uninsured. MIUs are therefore apparently not susceptible to adverse selection even though affiliation to MIUs is voluntary.

Conclusion

A comparison of the insured and uninsured cohort suggests that while the socio-economic differences between the two cohorts are small, insured persons reported higher health care utilization. We conclude that MIUs in the Philippines can alleviate underutilization of health care, and can contribute to the government's overall objective of enhancing access to health care. The analysis confirms that increased utilization by the insured cohort is not due to adverse selection.

Field based evidence of enhanced healthcare utilization among persons insured by micro health insurance units in Philippines

David M. Dror*, Elmer S. Soriano, Marilyn E. Lorenzo, Jesus N. Sarol Jr., Rosebelle S. Azcuna, Ruth Koren

Universite CB Lyon 1, Laboratoire d'Analyse de Systems de sante (LASS), Villeurbanne, Cedex, France

Abstract

Underutilization of healthcare is common among rural and low-income population segments in countries with lower income or inequitable income distribution.

Micro health insurance units (MIUs) are created by informal sector groups because people cannot access health insurance or are dissatisfied with the programmes they can access.

The policy choice to support MIUs relies on evidence that affiliation with these schemes increases healthcare utilization.

This article examines new evidence of the association between affiliation with MIUs and healthcare utilization. We analyzed field data collected in 6 MIUs in the Philippines in 2002 (through a household survey encompassing 890 insured- and 1063 uninsured households). The two cohorts did not differ in demographic parameters, and differed only marginally in income and education levels, both higher amongst the insured.

Insured persons reported higher hospitalization rates, higher rates of professionally-attended deliveries, lower rates of delivery at home, a higher frequency of primary-care physician encounters, a higher rate of diagnosed chronic diseases, and better drug compliance among chronically ill.

Increased utilization by the insured is not due to adverse selection, judging by two facts: morbidity of the two cohorts, as assessed by a proxy indicator (the reported number of episodes of illness) did not differ; and rates of deliveries were even slightly higher among the uninsured.

We conclude that MIUs in the Philippines can alleviate underutilization of heath care.

Keywords: Healthcare utilization; Community financing; Micro health insurance (MIUs); Insurance/health; Voluntary; Health services accessibility; Philippines

1. Introduction

One of the major objectives of the health system should be to provide adequate access to healthcare of all population segments. In countries with lower income or highly inequitable income distribution, this

* Corresponding author. Tel.: +41 78 790 6789; fax: +41 22 788 2288.

E-mail address: davidmdror@yahoo.com (D.M. Dror).

does not always happen; reports claim that low-income and rural populations exhibit very low healthcare utilization levels, e.g. [1] in India, [2] in the Philippines, and [3] in South Africa. In some countries, micro health insurance units (MIUs)[1] are created either because people cannot get health insurance through top-down programmes, or because they are dissatisfied with the programme(s) they can access. This situation has been reported from several countries [4–7], notably the Philippines [8]. At the same time, the effectiveness of MIUs is still debated [9,10], and [11]. The policy question that arises in this context is whether MIUs should be supported by public authorities, at least as an interim arrangement that offers a way to increase utilization of affiliated persons, through a mechanism that, at the same time, enlarges the flow of funds transiting a pooling arrangement. Such policy choice should, where possible, be based on evidence. This article examines the evidence in one country, the Philippines, by comparing utilization levels of MIU-members compared to uninsured persons living in the same regions.

1.1. Background on the situation in the Philippines

Between 30 and 40 million people out of the Philippines' 86.2 million population (July 2004 est.) [12] do not have health insurance. In 2000, per capita health expenditure was PPP$ 167, or 1.5% and 1.8% of GDP, respectively for public and private health expenditure [13]. Until 1991, the Department of Health operated a national health care system, but in 1991, responsibility for health care delivery was decentralized to the different levels of Local Government Units (LGUs) ([8], p. 331), which caused fragmentation of the system. In 1995, the government promulgated a framework law to achieve universal health insurance coverage, in a gradual process to be concluded by the year 2010 ([14], p. 208). In the meantime, multiple insurers sell health insurance in the Philippines: Private health insurers operate in the formal sector (mainly through large private employers or with wealthy self-employed); PhilHealth, the government health insurer, has a high market share in large urban centers and in the formal economy: in 2002, about half the Filipino population was covered [2,15,16], (and there is also a secondary market for complementary and supplementary health insurance that attracts mainly those benefiting from the PhilHealth package); some LGUs operate a substitutive local scheme; finally, some co-operatives and other groups have set up voluntary, community-based contributory health organizations, or MIUs, mainly in the informal economy or in rural areas ([8], p. 339).[2]

1.2. What are micro health insurance units?

Micro health insurance units (MIUs) are grassroots organizations whose purpose is to provide financial protection in case of illness. Four main types of MIUs can be identified: (i) schemes akin to cooperatives or mutual funds, which are often launched by members who are associated in other ways, e.g. through a trade organization, a micro finance institution, village committee, etc.; (ii) schemes started by a provider, where most or all services are provided by that same provider; (iii) schemes established by an external agent, e.g. a health NGO, a church, a development project etc.; (iv) schemes that are linked to a public authority or a commercial insurer, where a "super policy-holder" recruits the members of the group and facilitates the relationship between individuals and the insurer, e.g. by submitting pre-screened claims, collecting and distributing the benefits among the members, etc.

In this study, one MIU (Guimaras Health Insurance Program–GHIP) was set up by the public authority that also paid the contributions for older and poorer members; three MIUs were created by cooperatives for their members (*Davao City* MMG-CHP; *Quezon City*–Novaliches NOVADECI-NHCP; and the VALDECO-DPK). One MIU was started by an NGO (La *Union* OHPS, started by ORT international); and one was created by a group of health workers around a regional hospital (*Bayawan, Negros Oriental*: Peso for Health Program (PHP).

[1] Also known as community health financing schemes, mutual health organizations, community-based health organizations, etc.

[2] Community based health schemes may carry out several functions. We were interested in those that have a healthcare financing role. Other roles can include health care services providers; and administrative intermediaries with strong information, education, and communication activities.

2. Methods

2.1. MIUs included in this study

A household survey was carried out in 2002[3] in six MIUs in the Philippine.[4] We included sites from Northern Philippines, Metro Manila, Central Visayas and Mindanao. Our MIUs represent different occupational groups and organizational set-ups. Achieving this heterogeneity required accepting a purposive selection of MIUs. The six MIUs were selected out of a list of 19 schemes that were identified in a previous study (dating to 1999) as schemes that include a component of health financing ([8], p. 339).[5] Selection of MIUs for the current study was also influenced by the agreement of the schemes to cooperate with the research team.We interviewed household heads (by following a structured questionnaire), and noted information on utilization of health services as recalled by the respondents and other household insureds.

2.2. Sampling

A cross-sectional research design was used, where a two-stage cluster sampling method was employed in the selection of insureds and uninsureds. In each geographical area, the populations of insureds and uninsureds were separated. Within each category, the populations were further stratified according to distance from the residence (barangay, or Filipino for villages) to the point of service (the MIU), because healthcare utilization patterns depend also on this distance. Barangays located close-by (e.g. same location as the MIU) were classified as "inner barangays", and those further away from the MIU were classified as "outer barangays". In the list of insureds, two barangays (from the inner and outer groups) were selected with probabilities proportional to size, where size is the number of households. In Novaliches, Guimaras and Davao, where distances were small, four barangays were selected in a similar manner.

The second sampling stage consisted of selecting a random sample of approximately 160 households per area (40 insured households and 40 uninsured households, within inner and outer barangay for each selected MIU).

Data for all households was pooled together for the purpose of analysis. This approach gives equal weights to the different sites. The χ^2-test was used to compare the proportions of qualitative variables and to assess the statistical significance of the differences between insureds and uninsureds at the $\alpha = 0.05$ level.

The purpose has been to compare utilization levels of two groups: (i) a group of individuals who access benefits offered by an MIU; and (ii) a group of persons of the same community who are uninsured. We discovered that the distinction between insured and uninsured individuals is not easy to establish. For one, although the subscription unit is usually a household rather than an individual, there is no one-to-one match between the insurance of the household head and that of all other individuals belonging to the household. Some adult individuals may have a different or an additional health insurance contract, in which case the other insurance paid the cost of care reported by household heads.[6] Other individuals may have no insurance coverage at all. Secondly, MIU membership records are rarely matched with contribution payment records, and even less so with utilization records. Hence, it is probable that some individuals (mainly children) who are not formally insured nevertheless receive services from the MIU ("free riders") by virtue of the coverage of the household head. These caveats notwithstanding,

---

[3] This study was funded by a grant from the Ford Foundation (Manila office).

[4] The six are: (1) *Guimaras Island*: the Guimaras Health Insurance Program (GHIP); (2) *Davao City*: the Medical Missions Group Cooperators Health Program (MMG-CHP); (3) *Quezon City*: the Novaliches Development Cooperative, Inc. Health Care Program (NOVADECI-NHCP); (4) *San Fernando, La Union*: ORT Health Plus Scheme (OHPS); (5) *Bayawan, Negros Oriental*: Peso for Health Program (PHP); (6) *Valenzuela City*: the Valenzuela Development Cooperative Damayang Pangkalusugan (VALDECO-DPK).

[5] That earlier survey identified 66 community-based health care organizations (CBHCOs); 38 of the 66 community-based health care schemes were selected, using a five-point purposive sampling criteria that mostly ensured differentiation and sampling balance. Data sets from 35 of the 38 CBHCOs were accepted, and analyzed. Of these 35, 19 were in rural areas, 4 in urban areas, and 12 in mixed settings [8]. As mentioned, 19 of the 35 schemes had a health-financing component.

[6] However, the rate of enrolment in health insurance schemes other than MIUs was 28.9% among MIU-affiliated individuals and 29.5% among MIU-unaffiliated individuals. This insignificant difference cannot explain the difference in health services utilization between the two groups. Consequently, we can ignore this parameter.

the decision-rule we followed in this study has been to count as "insureds" all the households that were identified as members of MIUs (by lists provided by the MIUs or by spot-mapping carried out by our research teams), and to consider the rest of the households in the barangays as "uninsured" (non-MIUs households).

3. Results

The findings provided below are drawn from a comparison between insureds and uninsureds within the entire survey sample.[7]

3.1. Data yield

A total of 1953 households, 890 insured households and 1063 uninsured households were included in the study. These households included 4639 and 5550 individuals, respectively. The findings provided below are drawn from a comparison between insureds and uninsureds within the entire survey sample.

3.2. Demographics, socio-economic status and education

We looked at socio-economic parameters of insureds and uninsureds, because these parameters can influence healthcare utilization. The results are summarized below:

The gender ratio for both cohorts was 0.99 males for 1 female. The median age, 22 years, is the same for insureds and uninsureds. The majority of the population is within the age-range of economic activity, although the insureds' group includes slightly fewer young individuals aged below 15 years (32.7% among insureds compared to 35.4% among the uninsureds) and slightly more individuals that are over 60 years old (7% of the insureds, and 5.6% of the uninsureds). The marital status was also quite similar (57.6% of insured respondents were married, compared to 60.1% among the uninsured). Household size was also comparable: The average numbers of children and other dependents per household was 5.1 persons per household for both cohorts. The large similarity between the two cohorts indicated that differences in utilization could not be attributed to demographic parameters.

The differences in socio-economic parameters are slightly more pronounced. 34% of the sampled population (663 households, out of 1943) reported earning below PhP 5000 per month (=US$ 100). "Income" means income from all sources per household, including salary income and income from a microenterprise, where relevant. With an average household size of 5.1 persons, this is an income of less than PhP 1000 (=US$ 20) per person per month. This income group is smaller among insureds (29.2%) than among uninsureds (38.3%). At the upper end of the income distribution, more insureds (11.7%) than uninsureds (3.3%) earn a monthly income of PhP 35,000 or more (=US$ 700+), or US$ 136.72 per person per month. The highest income bracket is more than seven times richer than the poorest bracket. This would suggest that MIUs attract people with a wide income-range. However, the higher prevalence of lower income among the uninsured suggests that low income may be a limiting factor in the affiliation to insurance.

As the income levels reported above were derived from the structured questionnaires and not from independent sources, we validated the findings with 'ownership of assets' as proxy indicator.[8] The data confirms that more insured than uninsured own their house and lot; that on average, the insured own larger houses (31.4% own houses with 3+ bedrooms, compared to 24.6% among the uninsured); own a bit more appliances/durable goods (e.g., 62.1% of the insureds own a refrigerator, but only 49.2% of the uninsured).[9] In addition, we also looked at three other facilities: access to toilets, garbage disposal and water. On these three facilities there was no difference between insureds and uninsureds. In summary, the socio-economic differences between the two cohorts are small.

---

[7] Sample size is based on valid responses only. Therefore, sample size varies in different tables.

[8] Asset measurement is a recognized alternative to measure socio-economic status ([25] p. 11), ([26] p. 5), ([27] p. 13), ([28,29] p. 8).

[9] Incidentally, although there was no direct question on access to electricity, the information on ownership of appliances leaves no doubt that most households are connected to the electric grid It is noteworthy that some 85% of the population have TV and some 75% of the population have radios; this suggests that radio and TV are probably the best means to disseminate information to the entire population.

Table 1
Proxy indicators for overall healthcare utilization

Proxy indicator	Insureds	Uninsureds
Total sample (Households)	4639	5550
Frequency of episodes of illness in last 3 months	760 (16.4%)	882 (15.9%)
Total sample (Households)	4546	5543
Deliveries in the last 5 years (% of sample)	422 (9.3)%	618 (11.1)%

Finally, education is often viewed as a predictor of health [17,18] and income [17,19] and therefore, we collected information on educational levels of insured compared to the uninsured. Fewer insureds reported no education at all (4.2% compared to 6.4% among uninsured), and more insured individuals have completed college or post grad educational levels (25.3% compared to 18.9% among the uninsured). From the replies we gather that insured individuals are slightly better educated than the uninsured.

3.3. Risk profiles and healthcare needs

3.3.1. Smoking, alcohol consumption, obesity

It is common practice for health insurers to collect information to estimate the risk they underwrite. In this study we asked respondents [10] about their smoking, alcohol consumption and obesity status. The replies are as follows: while fewer insureds than uninsureds smoke, more insureds than uninsureds consume alcohol and are obese. These findings do not offer a consistent indicator of health outcomes, because whereas smoking is increasingly becoming recognized as risky behavior even among the poor, eating and drinking is considered in certain low-income societies as a sign of wealth and better life rather than a health risk [20].

3.3.2. Proxies for overall healthcare needs

In the absence of an independently validated source of information on overall morbidity within the target population, we recorded replies to a proxy indicator: the number of illness episodes in the household during the last 3 months preceding the survey. The reported frequency of such episodes was remarkably similar for insureds and uninsureds (Table 1). A second proxy indicator for the need for maternity services was the number of pregnancies in the 5 years preceding the survey. The data shows that the frequency of deliveries among the insureds was slightly lower than that reported by uninsureds.

3.4. Healthcare utilization

Access to healthcare is assessed here by six types of care: primary care encounters, hospitalizations, professional attendance during deliveries, delivery at home, diagnosis of chronic diseases, and drug-compliance among the chronically ill (Table 2).

The data reveals that, surprisingly, the majority of people who reported illness did not seek physician care. As can be seen in Table 2, only 46.1% of all insureds who were ill saw a physician (although they may have seen a nurse or another health worker). The number of uninsureds in the same situation was even lower, at 38.8%. The difference between the two groups is significant both statistically and materially, considering that the proxy indicator for morbidity was virtually the same for both groups (16.4% and 15.9% respectively, see Table 1).

The number of hospitalizations of insureds was higher than for uninsureds (6.3% compared to 4.2%), with very similar distribution between communicable and non-communicable diseases.

A similar pattern is observable regarding the rate of deliveries attended by a physician: 54.5% for insureds compared to 44.0% among uninsureds. The number of deliveries at home (least professional attendance) is commensurately higher among uninsureds, with 40.4% compared to 31.8% among insureds. It should be noted that the rates of professional attendance at delivery for both groups is still quite low.

More chronic illnesses were diagnosed in the insured cohort than in the uninsured group, 5.7% versus 4.6% (Table 2). The difference was more pronounced

[10] These questions were answered by only one respondent from each household, the household head or his/her spouse. Therefore, the replies provide only a partial picture of life style choices within the households.

Table 2
Access to healthcare

Visits to doctors in past 3 months	Insureds	Uninsureds	Significance
Sample (total)	4639	5550	
Care seeking individuals (% of total sample)	7.6%	6.2%	$P=0.0051$
Care-seekers in the last 3 months as % of all ill (see Table 1 for total number)	46.1%	38.8%	$P<0.0026$
Hospitalizations in past 2 years			
Sample	4639	5550	
Hospitalized	6.3%	4.23%	$P<0.0001$
Communicable diseases	3.0%	1.8%	$P<0.0001$
Non-communicable diseases	3.0%	2.2%	$P=0.0123$
Injury/accident	0.3%	0.23%	
Deliveries in past 5 years			
Sample (total sample)	4639	5550	
Deliveries attended by doctors among those who had episodes of pregnancy (see Table 1 for total number)	54.5%	44.0%	$P<0.0001$
Rate of deliveries at home among those who had episodes of pregnancy	31.76%	40.37%	$P<0.001$
Chronic illnesses			
Sample	4639	5550	
Diagnosed as chronically ill - total	5.65%	4.63%	$P=0.0051$
Diagnosed with diabetes and hypertension	3.0%	2.22%	$P=0.0210$
Drug compliance in chronically ill			
Sample	262	242	
Chronically ill not taking drugs	20.22%	32.64%	$P=0.0015$

when the comparison was limited to diabetes and hypertension (3.0% versus 2.2%). The difference between insureds and uninsureds in drug compliance (20.2% of the insured versus 32.6% of the uninsured do not comply with the drug regime) was perhaps more important.

4. Discussion

This study set out to collect information on levels of healthcare utilization as reported by persons insured by MIUs compared to a control group of uninsured persons.

For this comparison to be valid, we needed to ascertain that the two cohorts do not differ markedly from each other in demographic, socio-economic and education parameters, which are known to have an impact on healthcare utilization. We have found small differences: Slightly fewer insureds are married; they are slightly older; and there is a slightly higher prevalence of widowed/divorced/separated households amongst the insureds. However, the demographic disparities are minimal, and probably irrelevant in explaining differences in healthcare utilization. We also found that the insured cohort is slightly better educated, and slightly better-off than the uninsureds' cohort. Recalling the assertion of Dong et al. [21] that a higher socio-economic status positively influences willingness to pay, it is possible that these differences, small as they are, affect the decision to join a contribution-based health insurance scheme.

When comparing utilization levels, we must also ascertain that the two cohorts have a similar need for healthcare benefits. In this study, the morbidity was assessed by a proxy indicator: Frequency of episodes of illness in last 3 months (Table 1). The findings are remarkably similar for both cohorts. Therefore, one can probably dismiss 'differences in medical needs' as a confounding parameter in the comparison between the cohorts.

The evidence obtained in this survey clearly confirmed that persons insured by MIUs reported higher health care utilization than uninsured persons. This included a higher rate of access to physician-encounters among insureds, which however was still quite low in terms of the reported number of illnesses. Insureds reported higher hospitalization rates as well. We established from the replies to the questionnaire that about 95% of all cases of hospitalization were physician-referrals rather than direct admissions (94.0% for insureds, 95.6% for uninsureds). This high referral-rate to hospital suggests that general practitioners act as "gate-openers" rather than as gatekeepers. Hence, fewer primary care encounters among the uninsured cohort could explain, at least partly, why they also registered fewer hospitalizations. This insight suggests that a policy-choice to exclude primary care from the benefit package (which often happens, on the assumption that clients can pay for primary care out-of-pocket) may lead to underutilization of inpatient care due to underestimation by uninsured clients of their needs.[11] There is also a self-explanatory link between higher hospitalization rates among the insureds and the composition of the benefit package of the MIUs surveyed, all of which include hospitalizations.

We also looked at a proxy indicator for maternity needs, which was the total number of deliveries in the 5 years preceding the survey (Table 1). The rate of deliveries among the insured cohort was slightly lower than the rate recorded among the uninsured (9.3% compared to 11.1%). But the rate of deliveries attended by a doctor among those who had episodes of pregnancy was significantly higher among the insured cohort than among the uninsureds. At the same time, the rate of delivery at home was much higher among the uninsured.

The incidence of diagnosed hypertension and diabetes is 36% higher among the insured population than among the uninsured. One could argue that this difference could originate from the slightly higher age (7.0% insured over 60 years, compared to 5.6% among the uninsured) and prevalence of obesity among the insured population. Yet, these two chronic conditions are asymptomatic for a long time. Hence, a plausible explanation for the higher rate of diagnosis is the higher rate of primary-care physician encounters among the insured, which could provide the opportunity for screening.

Despite the small sample of chronically ill, one can observe a significantly higher rate of drug compliance among the insured. We are unable to establish the reason for this difference, other than to mention that most MIUs do not provide unlimited drugs. Hence, the difference may be due to better awareness (and the existence of "awareness groups" organized in some MIUs).

In summary, we observe an association between higher utilization and being insured by MIUs. Does this amount to the existence of a cause-effect relationship between higher utilization and being insured by the MIUs? For the cause-effect relation to be established unequivocally, one would need to carry out a longitudinal study, which would look at utilization levels before and after joining the insurance. However, this retrospective data is usually unavailable. This minor reserve notwithstanding, the association between higher utilization and being insured by MIUs is a significant finding, in particular against the backdrop of the reported underutilization of persons covered by the PhilHealth MSM program, which operated in comparable regions and constraints [22].[12]

One final point merits a short discussion: Affiliation to MIUs is voluntary. It is often assumed that voluntary affiliation to health insurance is attractive mainly to bad risks. Hence, individual/voluntary health insurance is assumed to be exposed to adverse selection [23,24]. We have no evidence to assume that this assertion applies to MIUs; quite the contrary, there is some indication for the opposite. For one, the proxy indicator for morbidity among the insured and uninsured cohorts is virtually the same (Table 1), and does not support an assumption of adverse selection. Secondly, if adverse selection were manifest, one could expect the insured cohort to report a higher number of deliveries during the 5 years preceding the survey compared to the uninsured. In reality, the opposite was registered. One explanation for this situation is the fact that MIUs operate substitutive rather than complementary and supplementary schemes, in a setting where group size is usually quite small (from 900 in Davao to 7000 in La Union), and where decisions to join are taken by households rather than single individuals, and in social settings where the group can influence members' conduct and therefore reduce deviant behavior. Thus, the MIUs are ap-

[11] It is recalled that the PhilHealth package does not include primary care, a fact that may explain why hospital care is reported to be underutilized among the PhilHealth insureds, notably the participants in the Indigent program [23].

[12] According to Almario and Weber [23], MSM to date covers only a small portion of the estimated poor population in the country (less than 10%).

parently not susceptible to the same market failures of voluntary health insurers in OECD countries.

This article examines evidence on the impact of being insured by MIUs in the Philippines on increasing healthcare utilization, in an environment where underutilization is otherwise prevalent. We have presented data upholding an association between insurance by MIUs and better healthcare utilization. Considering that the overall objective of the authorities in the Philippines, as in other countries, is to enhance access to healthcare and remedy underutilization, one can claim that grassroots initiatives such as the MIUs make a real contribution towards this goal.

Acknowledgements

We gratefully acknowledge a grant from the Ford Foundation (Manila office) to carry out the household survey in Philippines in 2002. We acknowledge the cost-sharing of the GTZ programme (German assistance to the Philippines health sector) in conducting the survey in Guimaras. The *Social Re* project (World Bank and ILO) provided project management and additional resources. Thanks to the ILO office in Manila for administrative backstopping. Acknowledgements and thanks to all.

References

[1] Purohit BC. Inter-state disparities in healthcare and financial burden on the poor in India. Journal of Health and Social Policy 2004;18:37–60.

[2] Schneider P, Racelis R. The impact of PhilHealth indigent insurance on utilization, cost, and finances in health facilities in the Philippines. In: The Partners for Health Reformplus Project. Bethesda, MD: ABT Associates Inc.; 2004.

[3] Pretorius CF, Greeff M. Health service utilization by pregnant women in the greater Mafikeng-Mmabatho District. Curationis 2004;27:72–81.

[4] Criel B, Waelkens MP. Declining subscriptions to the Maliando mutual health organisation in Guinea-Conakry (West Africa): what is going wrong? Social Science Medicine 2003;57:1205–19.

[5] Meesen B, Criel B, Kegels G. Formal pooling of health risks in sub-Saharan Africa: reflections on the obstacles encountered, International Social Security Review. Geneva: International Social Security Association 2002;55:71–93.

[6] Strand MA, Chen AI. Rural health care in North China in an era of rapid economic change. Acta Nutrimenta Sinica 2003;19:355–8.

[7] Wiesman D, Jütting J. The Emerging Movement of Community Based Health Insurance in Sub-Saharan Africa: Experiences and Lessons Learned. Afrika Spectrum 2000;35:9, http://www.wye.ic.ac.uk/AgEcon/ADU/eaaeannc/juetting.pdf.

[8] Flavier J, Soriano E, Nicolay A. Social health insurance in the Philippines: a review of the context. In: Dror D, Preker A, editors. Social Re-insurance: A New Approach to Sustaining Community Health Financing. Washington: The World Bank and International Labour Organ; 2002. pp. 329–351, Chapter 17.

[9] Dror D, Preker A, editors. Social Re-insurance: A New Approach to Sustaining Community Health Financing. Washington: The World Bank and International Labour Organisation; 2002.

[10] Preker AS, Carrin G, Dror D, Jakab M, Hsiao W, Arhin-Tenkorang D. Effectiveness of community health financing in meeting the cost of illness. Bulletin of World Health Organisation 2002;80:143–50.

[11] Bennett S. The role of community-based health insurance within the health care financing system: A framework for analysis. Health Policy and Planning 2004;19:147–58.

[12] CIA World Fact book–Philippines (2004) web edition, July 2004 update: http://www.cia.gov/cia/publications/factbook/geos/rp.html#People.

[13] UNDP Human Development Report 2003: Millennium Development Goals: A compact among nations to end human poverty, New York Oxford University Press for UNDP, Human Development Index, Tables 1 and 6, 2003, pp. 238 and 255.

[14] Arroyo GM. The Medium-Term Philippine Development Plan 2001–2004 with The State of the Nation Address of H.E. President Gloria Macapagal-Arroyo to the 12th Congress of the Philippines, Batasang Pambansa, Quezon City, July 23, 2001 Manila, National Economic and Development Authority, Chapter 11: Enhancing Health Care, Strategies, Health and Nutrition, Improving health care financing, 2001, p. 208, http://www.neda.gov.ph/mtpdp2001/PDF/MTPDP2001-2004-Final.pdf.

[15] PhilHealth Stats and Charts (2001–2002) Health Sector Reform Agenda: Table 1. Estimated National Health Insurance Program Membership By Sector/Philippines: Department of Health. http://www.doh.gov.ph/hsra2/hsra-statistics.htm.

[16] USAID/Philippines Management Sciences for Health–Health Sector Reform Technical Assistance Project. Accomplishments Health Insurance. Philippines: USAID/Philippines, 2002 August, http://www.usaid-ph.gov/health_msh.html.

[17] Abdullatif A. Partnership of the community in support of health for all. World Health Organization Eastern Mediterranean Region 2000;6:775–87, http://www.abc.com/.

[18] Scandlen G. Health Insurance: How Much Does It Matter? Brief analysis, No. 416. Dallas, National Center for Policy Analysis (NCPA), 2002, http://www.ncpa.org/pub/ba/ba416.

[19] McIntyre L, Petticrew M. Methods of health impact assessment: a literature review. Glasgow: University of Glasgow, MRC Social and Public Health Sciences Unit; 1999, 12 http://www.msoc-mrc.gla.ac.uk/Reports/PDFs/Occasional-Papers/OP-002.pdf.

[20] Pollak KI, Namenek, Brouwer RJ, Lyna P, Taiwo B, McBride CM. Weight and smoking cessation among low-income African Americans. American Journal of Preventive Medicine 2003;25(2):136–9.
[21] Dong H, Kouyate B, Snow R, Mugisha F, Sauerborn R. Gender's effect on willingness-to-pay for community-based insurance in Burkina Faso. Health Policy 2003;64:153–62.
[22] Almario ES, Weber A. Making PhilHealth Policies More Pro-Poor, Draft Policy Note dated 17 April 2002 (unpublished monograph).
[23] Pauly MV, Nichols L. The non-group health insurance market: Short on facts, long on opinions and policy disputes, Health Affairs, web exclusive, 2002. 10.1377/hltnaff.w2.325 http://content.healthaffairs.org/cgi/reprint/hlthaff.w2.325v1.
[24] Browne MJ. Evidence of adverse selection in the individual health insurance market. Journal of Risk and Insurance 1992:13–33.
[25] Gwatkin DR, Rustein S, Johnson K, Pande R, Wagstaff A. Socio-Economic Difference in Health Nutrition, and Population. In: HNP/Poverty Thematic Group of the World Bank. Washington DC: World Bank; 2000, http://www/worldbank.org/poverty/health/data/senegal/senegal.pdf.
[26] DSDS Ensuring Sustainable Livelihoods Challenges For Governments, Corporates and Civil Society At Rio + 10, New Delhi, Background paper prepared for the Delhi Sustainable Development Summit organized by the Tata Energy Research Institute, 8–11 February 2002. http://www.teriin.org/dsds/dsds2002/background.pdf.
[27] Gertler P, Levine DL, Moretti E. Microfinance Programs Help Families Insure Consumption Against Illness? Boston: Institute for Development Research; 2002. p. 13 http://www.bu.edu/econ/ied/seminars/pdf/levine9-30-02Microfinance.pdf.
[28] Micro Finance Consulting Group. Wealth Ranking for poverty assessment, Table 1: Wealth Ranking matrix: categories and examples of criteria, Section A: Rural. India: Micro-Finance Consulting Group, MCG (Chennai), 2002, http://www.mitrabharathi.com/wealthranking.htm.
[29] Lindelöw M, Wagstaff A. Health Facility Surveys: An Introduction. World Bank Policy Research Working Paper 2953. Washington: The World Bank, 2003, p. 8, http://econ.worldbank.org/files/23186_wps2953.pdf.

Chapter 20

Impact of Community-based Health Insurance in Rural India on Self-Medication and Financial Protection of the Insured*

Main Messages

- A baseline survey was conducted in March–May 2010 with a sample of 3,685 households; three years later, an endline survey was conducted when 3,307 households of the households included in the baseline were revisited.
- For each community-based health insurance (CBHI), data were sourced from MIS maintained by the Micro Insurance Academy (MIA).
- Impact of CBHI was quantified using both difference-in-difference (DiD) and conditional DiD.

Focus Points

- Post-intervention, self-medication was less practiced by insured households, and this was used as an indicator of improved access to health care.

*This chapter is reproduced from *Indian Journal of Medical Research* (2016), **143**, 809–820, Open Access, available at https://www.researchgate.net/publication/309121264_Impact_of_community-based_health_insurance_in_rural_India_on_self-medication_financial_protection_of_the_insured.

- The insured experienced a reduction in financial risks as suggested by reduced health-related borrowing.
- The probability of an insured household to benefit from quintile upgrade increased and the risk of quintile downgrade decreased after being insured for two years.
- Health insurance creates welfare gains in the form of better access to health care, reduced financial risks, and improved economic mobility.

Structured Abstract

Introduction

There exists a dearth of published research on the impact of health insurance on welfare gains of insured persons in the informal sector. This has prompted the authors to investigate the impact of CBHI on access to health care and financial protection within a large-scale randomized controlled field experiment in three rural locations in India.

Three CBHI schemes were implemented with technical assistance from the Micro Insurance Academy (MIA), in cooperation with local grassroots NGOs: BAIF Development Research Foundation, Shramik Bharti (both are located in Uttar Pradesh) and Nidan, located in Bihar.

Method

The analysis was based on data from two sources: household surveys and MIS maintained for each CBHI by the Micro Insurance Academy (MIA). First, a baseline survey was conducted in March-May 2010, with a sample of 3,685 households. Three years later an endline survey was conducted when 3,307 households of the households included in the baseline were revisited. The treatment group composed only of those that were "offered and joined", and the control, composed of all other persons that were not insured (including "offered not joined" and "not offered").

The study design was "staggered implementation" cluster randomized controlled trial with an enrollment of one-third of the treatment group in each of the years 2011, 2012 and 2013. Impact of CBHI was quantified using both difference-in-difference (DiD), and conditional-DiD.

Box 1: Outcome Variables of the Study

Self-medication (defined at an individual level)

- Is "1" if an individual resorted to self-medication for an illness at least once in the last 30 days prior to the survey.
- Is "0" otherwise.
- Results were expressed as the number of people who reported an illness and self-medication at least once, divided by the total number of people who reported an illness in the previous 30 days.

Borrowing-with-interest (defined at the household level)

- Is "1" if a household reported borrowing-with-interest at least once for illnesses not requiring hospitalization (acute or chronic) in the 30 days prior to the survey.
- Is "0" otherwise.

Household-level consumption expenditure for non-health items (defined at the household level)

- Mean/average household expenditure from all the sources excluding health-related expenditure per month (MPCE non-health).
- MPCE (non-health) quintiles and movement of HHs (upward/downward) across MPCE (non-health) quintiles over time.

Findings

The study revealed that being insured improved access to health care as there was a reduction in self-medication post-intervention (2013). There was, however, no change in the morbidity patterns of the insured population over the study period.

To measure the impact of CBHI on financial protection, two measures of financial protection were applied. First, the authors analyzed the proportion of households that borrowed with interest to pay health care costs (hardship financing), as this was a strong indicator of the risk of falling into poverty. It was observed that the insured experienced a reduction in financial risks as manifested by reduced health-related borrowing.

The second measure assessed the impact of insurance on economic mobility as measured by consumption spending on non-health items. This measures the capacity of a participant in a system to improve (or reduce) his/her economic status. The probability of an insured household to benefit from quintile upgrade increased and the risk of quintile downgrade decreased after being insured for two years.

The link between being insured and economic mobility could be a consequence of money saved during financing of ambulatory care or investments made by insured households in productive assets or education that could increase income. Further research can throw more light on the association between being insured and economic mobility.

Conclusion

The impact of CBHI in improving access to health care in rural India was evident with the insured population reducing its practice of self-medication. The change in the sampled population's insurance status brought about a positive attitude of seeking medical help. Furthermore, being insured provided more financial protection to the households.

Overall, the authors conclude that health insurance creates welfare gains in the form of better access to health care, reduced financial risks, and improved economic mobility. This has holistic ramifications for theoretical, ethical, policy, and practice considerations.

Impact of community-based health insurance in rural India on self-medication & financial protection of the insured

David M. Dror[1], Arpita Chakraborty[1,2], Atanu Majumdar[1], Pradeep Panda[1] & Ruth Koren[3]

[1]Micro Insurance Academy, New Delhi, India & Institute of Health Policy & Management, Erasmus University, Rotterdam, The Netherlands, [2]Public Health Foundation of India, Gurgaon, India & [3]Tel Aviv University, Rabin Medical Center, Petah Tikva, Israel

Received August 14, 2015

***Background & objectives*: The evidence-base of the impact of community-based health insurance (CBHI) on access to healthcare and financial protection in India is weak. We investigated the impact of CBHI in rural Uttar Pradesh and Bihar States of India on insured households' self-medication and financial position.**

***Methods*: Data originated from *(i)* household surveys, and *(ii)* the Management Information System of each CBHI. Study design was "staggered implementation" cluster randomized controlled trial with enrollment of one-third of the treatment group in each of the years 2011, 2012 and 2013. Around 40-50 per cent of the households that were offered to enroll joined. The benefits-packages covered outpatient care in all three locations and in-patient care in two locations. To overcome self-selection enrollment bias, we constructed comparable control and treatment groups using Kernel Propensity Score Matching (K-PSM). To quantify impact, both difference-in-difference (DiD), and conditional-DiD (combined K-PSM with DiD) were used to assess robustness of results.**

***Results*: Post-intervention (2013), self-medication was less practiced by insured HHs. Fewer insured households than uninsured households reported borrowing to finance care for non-hospitalization events. Being insured for two years also improved the HH's location along the income distribution, namely insured HHs were more likely to experience income quintile-upgrade in one location, and less likely to experience a quintile-downgrade in two locations.**

***Interpretation & conclusions*: The realized benefits of insurance included better access to healthcare, reduced financial risks and improved economic mobility, suggesting that in our context health insurance creates welfare gains. These findings have implications for theoretical, ethical, policy and practice considerations.**

Key words Community-based health insurance - financial protection - hardship financing - rural India - self-medication

There is little published research on the impact of health insurance on welfare gains of insured persons in the informal sector. A systematic review of health insurance offers inconclusive evidence of effective financial protection of insured poor[1]. Considering that commercial or social health insurance schemes are rare in rural India[2], it is necessary to explore the impact of health insurance on insured households (HHs) covered by mutual aid insurance, or community based health insurance (CBHI) operated among grassroots communities in India. The importance of awareness-raising in voluntary uptake of CBHI[3], the key parameters that determine uptake[4,5], the impact of thresholds and caps on the coverage level of CBHI[6], and the method through which members decide on benefits packages[7] are some important aspects of CBHI. However, much less is known on the impact of being insured under CBHI. The aim of this study was, therefore, to assess the impact of CBHI on access to healthcare and financial protection within a large-scale randomized controlled field experiment in three rural locations in India.

We hypothesize that CBHI improves insured HHs' *(i)* access to healthcare, by reducing self-medication; and *(ii)* financial protection, by reducing hardship financing and enhancing economic mobility. We consider reduction in self-medication, namely consumption of unprescribed medicines, as an indicator of improved access to healthcare because it is independent of requiring a uniform benefits package in all studied locations, and because self-medication is recognized globally as a major health risk that can lead to misdiagnosis, excessive or prolonged use of medicines, unsuitable dosage, drug interactions and polypharmacy[8-13].

Two measures of financial protection were applied: first, the proportion of HHs that borrowed with interest to pay healthcare costs, because borrowing-with-interest is a strong indicator of the risk of falling into indigent status[14-18] ; and second, the effect of insurance on economic mobility (*i.e.* the measurement of the capacity of a participant in a system to improve (or reduce) his/her economic status)[19] measured by consumption spending on non-health items.

Material & Methods

Three CBHI schemes were implemented in cooperation with local grassroots non-government organizations (NGOs): BAIF Development Research Foundation in Pratapgarh, Uttar Pradesh; *Shramik Bharti* in Kanpur-Dehat, Uttar Pradesh; and *Nidan*, in Vaishali, Bihar, with technical assistance by the Micro Insurance Academy (MIA), New Delhi (*https://www.microinsuranceacademy.org/project/uttar-pradesh-and-bihar-india/*).

This study was designed as a cluster randomized controlled trial (CRCT)[20] in which HHs were included in the sample if at least one female was affiliated in March 2010 to a Self-Help Group (SHG) operated in each of the three study locations by the grassroots NGOs. The three locations were divided into 48 equal-size clusters (a cluster was a group of geographically proximate villages). In each location, clusters were randomly assigned to one of three enrollment years (2011, 2012 and 2013) when one third of the HHs were offered to enroll in the CBHI (staggered implementation study-design). Under this study design, those HHs that were defined as control in early waves of the implementation were invited to join in later years.

Data for this analysis originated from two sources: *(i)* household surveys, conducted as part of the CRCT study design[20]; and *(ii)* the Management Information System maintained for each CBHI scheme by MIA (known as MIA-MIS) for operational details.

The ethics committee of the University of Cologne, Germany, a scientific partner in this project, approved both project design and research tools. The MIA Ethics Committee also approved the study.

Household information: A baseline survey was conducted in March-May 2010, with a sample of 3,685 HHs (21,373 individuals). The questionnaire queried socio-demographic characteristics, HH consumption expenditures for food and non-food items and financial issues. Information was collected on self-reported long-term and short-term health events, hospitalization, healthcare seeking (including self-medication), the associated costs, and how those costs were financed.

An endline survey was conducted in March-April 2013, when 3,307 HHs (18,322 individuals) of the HHs included in the baseline were revisited. Attrition rates during the follow up rounds were around 10 per cent.

Benefits packages: The groups of prospective insured persons were involved, together with representatives of the grassroots NGOs, in selecting benefits packages[7]. The benefits packages and premiums of the three CBHIs differed, and thus analysis of the data was done separately for each location.

Study cohorts and descriptive statistics: The unit of randomization for the CRCT experiment was the cluster. A HH was defined as insured if at least one female from the family was an active SHG member and enrolled in CBHI. Enrollment was voluntary. Each HH that was offered to enroll could do so, or not. A HH that joined could also enroll other members, in the year the principal member joined or in subsequent years. Not all HHs that were offered joined the CBHI, nor all individuals therein. A HH that chose not to enroll when offered could not do so later.

For the purpose of analyzing the impact of insurance only the insured HHs were included in the treatment group, but the insured group did not form a randomized sample of the target population because of the voluntary choice. In order to match appropriate control samples from the uninsured HHs and the uninsured individuals [irrespective of whether they were "offered and not joined" (ONJ) or "not offered" (NO)] to the treatment groups composed only of enrolled HHs ["offered and joined" (OJ)], we applied Kernel Propensity Score Matching (K-PSM)[21].

The details of the cohorts are shown in Table I. The descriptive statistics of the two sub-cohorts for the baseline and endline are shown in Table II (for HHs) and Table III (for individuals). In Table II, the monthly per capita consumption expenditure (MPCE) was calculated using the methods followed by the National Sample Survey Organization, India[22], and converted to purchasing power parity international dollar (PPP$).

Methods : The outcome variables (self-medication, borrowing-with-interest for healthcare, and non-health consumption expenditure) were defined in the following ways:

Self-medication was defined as 1 if an individual resorted to self-medication for an illness at least once in the last 30 days prior to the survey; 0 otherwise.The results were expressed as the number of people who reported an illness and self-medication at least once, divided by the total number of people who reported an illness in the previous 30 days.

Borrowing-with-interest was defined as 1 if a household reported borrowing-with-interest at least once for illnesses not requiring hospitalization (acute or chronic) in the 30 days prior to the survey; 0 otherwise.

Household-level consumption expenditure for non-health items was defined as mean/average household expenditure from all the sources excluding health-related expenditure per month (MPCE non-health). We also computed MPCE (non-health) quintiles and movement of HHs (upward/downward) across MPCE (non-health) quintiles over time. The outcome variable for this third indicator was computed by comparing the expenditure quintiles of the same households at two time-points (before and after intervention). Hence, DiD was not relevant and the temporal dimension was not included as an independent variable.

The extent of self-medication may vary by individual and episode. The decision to borrow was usually taken at the household level; and MPCE reflected the socio-economic status of a household and was estimated at household level in context. Therefore, the first indicator (self-medication) was defined at the individual level and the last two indicators (borrowing with interest and quintile shift) were defined at the household level.

Matching technique: As explained, the voluntary affiliation introduced selection bias to the treatment cohorts, both at inter- and at intra-household stage. K-PSM was used to construct comparable control and treatment groups to enable to attribute the changes in the outcome variables (self-medication and financial protection) from baseline and endline. The method was used to calculate the weighted averages of the observed characteristics of the uninsured groups to construct the counterfactual outcome[21]. Kernel propensity scores was estimated as a parametric logit model and the common support requirement of K-PSM was used to discard the unmatched observations from the analysis[23]. Finally, the balancing property of the K-PSM was satisfied using the Student's t-test, *i.e.* HHs/individuals with the same propensity score had the same distributions of all co-variates for each of the areas (Tables II, III).

Analysis of self-medication: To estimate the impact of insurance on self-medication of insured individuals, the conditional difference-in-difference (DiD) method was used[24]. This method combines K-PSM with DiD, so that at each period, a counterfactual outcome was estimated semi-parametrically for the insured cohort based on the observed covariates. Based on the conditionality of being enrolled in CBHI, the DiD estimator could be represented by the following specification:

$$DiD = E(SM_{T1} - SM_{T0} \mid INSUR=1, P(X)) - E(SM_{T1} - SM_{T0} \mid INSUR=0, P(X)) \quad \ldots\ldots\ldots\ldots\ldots\ldots (1)$$

Where, E was the expected value of the difference in self-medication (SM) between the post-intervention

Table I. Description of the cohorts by enrollment status

Year	Offered & joined	Offered & not joined	Not offered
2011	Year 1 HHs and joined CBHI (n=525)	Year 1 HHs and did not joined CBHI (n=810)	Years 2 and 3 HHs (n=2350)
2012	*(i)* Year 2 HHs and joined CBHI; *(ii)* HHs that renewed in Y2 (n=822)	*(i)* Year 2 HHs and did not join CBHI; *(ii)* HHs that dropped out in Y2 (n=862)	*(i)* Year 3 HHs *(ii)* HHs that did not join (but were offered) CBHI in Y1 (n=1634)
2013	*(i)* Year 3 HHs and joined CBHI; *(ii)* HHs that renewed in Y2 & again renewed in Y3; *(iii)* HHs that renewed in Y3 (from Y2) (n=728)	*(i)* Year 3 HHs and did not join CBHI; *(ii)* HHs that renewed in Y2 and dropped out in Y3; *(iii)* HHs that dropped out in Y3 (from Y2) (n=1025)	*(i)* HHs that did not join in Y1; *(ii)* HHs that did not join in Y2; *(iii)* HHs that dropped out in Y2 (from Y1) (n=1554)

CBHI, Community-Based Health Insurance; HHs, households.
Year represents implementation year.
Prior to enrollment each year, HHs in clusters assigned to one of the three years of this project were offered to join: 1335 HHs (in year 1) of the 3685 HHs of the total sample. 1244 HHs (in year 2) of the remaining 2350 HHs, and 1106 were assigned for year 3.
Y1, Y2 and Y3- year 1, 2 and 3 of implementation, respectively

(T1) and pre-intervention (T0) periods, subject to the probability of enrollment in CBHI (INSUR=1 means insured, 0 otherwise), which in turn depends on the set of observable covariates (X). The covariates (X) include age, years of education, number of (short-term and long-term) illnesses in the last one month, dummies for gender, marital status, employment status, caste of the household (1 if scheduled caste / scheduled tribe), household size, highest level of education in the household, MPCE (non-health) of the household and average travel time to the nearest health facility for outpatient (OP) care.

A DiD regression was performed for self-medication at the individual-level, using the following specification:

$$SM_{jt} = \alpha' INSUR_j + \beta' TIME_t + \gamma' INTR_{jt} + \delta' X_{jt0} + \varepsilon'_{jt} \text{ ...... (2)}$$

Where SM_{jt} signifies whether individual j at time t self-medicated or not (yes=1, no=0).

TIME signifies the dummy for time periods (0 and 1 for pre- and post-intervention periods, respectively); INTR was the interaction term between INSUR and TIME (INTR=INSUR× TIME). Vector X represents the set of observable variables for individual j mentioned above.

Standard errors were adjusted for clustering on the household level in the model mentioned in equation (2).

Analysis of borrowing for non-hospitalization events: Following a similar methodology, the conditional DiD method was used to analyze the impact of insurance on borrowing for non-hospitalization events. Non-hospitalization events were covered by all benefits packages, and therefore, the analysis was done in all locations.

The DiD equation for borrowing for non-hospitalization events can be expressed as:

$$DiD = E(BR_{T1} - BR_{T0} \mid INSUR=1, P(X)) - E(BR_{T1} - BR_{T0} \mid INSUR=0, P(X)) \text{.................(3)}$$

Where, E is the expected value of the difference in borrowing-with-interest between time period T1 and T0, subject to the probability of enrollment in CBHI (INSUR=1 means insured, 0 otherwise). The covariates (X) include dummies for caste of the household (1 if scheduled caste/scheduled tribe), MPCE (non-health), household size, highest level of education in the household, enrollment in *Rashtriya Swasthya Bima Yojna* (RSBY - the government's hospital insurance scheme for below-poverty-line persons) (1 if enrolled in RSBY), having a savings account (1 if at least one savings account holder in the family), average travel time for OP care and number of long-term and short-term illnesses of all members in the household in last one month.

The DiD regression, performed for borrowing at the household-level, can be expressed as:

$$BR_{it} = \alpha' INSUR_i + \beta' TIME_t + \gamma' INTR_{it} + \delta' X_{it0} + \varepsilon'_{it} \text{ ...... (4)}$$

Where BR_{jt} signifies whether household j at time t had borrowed or not (1 if yes, 0 if no).

Table II. Descriptive statistics for insured and uninsured households

Household indicators	2010				2013			
	Not-insured (NI)	Insured (I)	Difference		Not-insured (NI)	Insured (I)	Difference	
	Mean	Mean	(NI-I)	*P*-value	Mean	Mean	(NI-I)	*P* value
Pratapgarh								
Percentage of scheduled caste/scheduled tribe households	0.79 (0.01)	0.86 (0.03)	-0.07	0.035	0.78 (0.01)	0.84 (0.02)	-0.06	0.072
Household size	6.06 (0.08)	6.28 (0.2)	-0.22	0.329	5.66 (0.08)	6.03 (0.18)	-0.37	0.041
Highest level of education in the household	9 (0)	9 (0)	0	0.510	9 (0)	10 (0)	-1	0.001
Monthly per capita expenditure (in purchasing power parity – international dollar)	1161 (24)	1071 (36)	90	0.144	1633 (32)	1609 (48)	23	0.720
Average travel time to health facilities for out-patient services	19 (0)	20 (1)	-1	0.515	17 (0)	16 (1)	1	0.153
Average number of short-term and long-term illnesses (last 30 days)	2.44 (0.05)	2.79 (0.14)	-0.35	0.008	2.62 (0.06)	3.16 (0.12)	-0.54	<0.001
Kanpur Dehat								
Percentage of scheduled caste/scheduled tribe households	0.79 (0.01)	0.80 (0.04)	-0.01	0.770	0.80 (0.01)	0.77 (0.03)	0.03	0.336
Household size	6.06 (0.08)	5.75 (0.18)	0.31	0.192	5.53 (0.08)	5.75 (0.17)	-0.22	0.211
Highest level of education in the household	10 (0)	10 (0)	0	0.815	10 (0)	10 (0)	0	0.689
Monthly per capita expenditure (in purchasing power parity – international dollar)	1780 (49)	1816 (131)	-36	0.812	2242 (45)	2316 (91)	-74	0.445
Average travel time to health facilities for out-patient services	30 (1)	38 (3)	-8	0.029	22 (1)	24 (2)	-2	0.372
Average number of short-term and long-term illnesses (last 30 days)	2.16 (0.05)	2.08 (0.13)	0.08	0.610	3.22 (0.08)	3.32 (0.13)	-0.10	0.532
Vaishali								
Percentage of scheduled caste/scheduled tribe households	0.91 (0.01)	0.94 (0.02)	-0.03	0.193	0.92 (0.01)	0.92 (0.02)	0.00	0.945
Household size	5.30 (0.06)	5.57 (0.12)	-0.27	0.061	5.20 (0.07)	5.70 (0.12)	-0.50	<0.001
Highest level of education in the household	7 (0)	7 (0)	0	0.332	7 (0)	8 (0)	-1	<0.001
Monthly per capita expenditure (in purchasing power parity - international dollar)	1440 (32)	1371 (64)	69	0.354	1863 (37)	1819 (59)	-44	0.571
Average travel time to health facilities for out-patient services	17 (0)	17 (1)	0	0.625	16 (1)	15 (1)	1	0.252
Average number of short-term and long-term illnesses (last 30 days)	1.79 (0.04)	1.89 (0.09)	-0.1	0.269	2.76 (0.06)	3.16 (0.12)	-0.40	0.002

Figures in parentheses are standard error of mean
Student t test was used for comparison

Table III. Descriptive statistics for insured and uninsured individuals

Individual indicators	2010				2013			
	Not-insured (NI)	Insured (I)	Difference		Not-insured (NI)	Insured (I)	Difference	
	Mean	Mean	(NI-I)	*P* value	Mean	Mean	(NI-I)	*P* value
Pratapgarh								
Average age (yr)	24 (0)	26 (1)	-2	0.082	22.97 (0.25)	28.89 (0.73)	-5.92	<0.001
Proportion of females	0.51 (0.01)	0.56 (0.02)	-0.05	0.026	0.53 (0.01)	0.64 (0.02)	-0.11	<0.001
Proportion of married	0.44 (0.01)	0.51 (0.02)	-0.07	0.001	0.44 (0.01)	0.58 (0.02)	-0.14	<0.001
Proportion of self-help group members	0.29 (0.01)	0.47 (0.03)	-0.18	<0.001	0.23 (0.01)	0.55 (0.02)	-0.32	<0.001
Average years of education	4.46 (0.05)	4.10 (0.17)	0.36	0.057	4.67 (0.07)	4.55 (0.18)	0.12	0.533
Average number of acute and chronic illness	0.4 (0.01)	0.55 (0.03)	-0.15	<0.001	0.45 (0.01)	0.69 (0.02)	-0.24	<0.001
Kanpur Dehat								
Average age (yr)	24 (0)	28 (1)	-4	<0.001	23.59 (0.28)	29.45 (0.74)	-5.86	<0.001
Proportion of females	0.48 (0.01)	0.55 (0.03)	-0.07	0.008	0.49 (0.01)	0.54 (0.02)	-0.05	0.019
Proportion of married	0.44 (0.01)	0.58 (0.03)	-0.14	<0.001	0.44 (0.01)	0.63 (0.02)	-0.19	<0.001
Proportion of self-help group members	0.32 (0.01)	0.57 (0.04)	-0.25	<0.001	0.2 (0.01)	0.64 (0.03)	-0.44	<0.001
Average years of education	4.91 (0.06)	4.74 (0.24)	0.17	0.496	5.1 (0.07)	5.24 (0.19)	-0.14	0.466
Average number of acute and chronic illness	0.35 (0.01)	0.45 (0.03)	-0.10	0.004	0.56 (0.01)	0.75 (0.03)	-0.19	<0.001
Vaishali								
Average age (yr)	23 (0)	22 (1)	1	0.033	21.45 (0.26)	25.15 (0.63)	-3.7	<0.001
Proportion of females	0.51 (0.01)	0.57 (0.02)	-0.06	0.001	0.52 (0.01)	0.56 (0.02)	-0.04	0.019
Proportion of married	0.45 (0.01)	0.43 (0.02)	0.02	0.253	0.44 (0.01)	0.59 (0.02)	-0.15	<0.001
Proportion of self-help group members	0.34 (0.01)	0.48 (0.02)	-0.14	<0.001	0.22 (0.01)	0.6 (0.02)	-0.38	<0.001
Average years of education	3.16 (0.05)	3.17 (0.13)	-0.01	0.960	3.39 (0.05)	3.91 (0.16)	-0.52	0.002
Average number of acute and chronic illness	0.34 (0.01)	0.35 (0.02)	-0.01	0.597	0.51 (0.01)	0.71 (0.02)	-0.20	<0.001

Figures in parentheses are standard error of mean.
Student t test was used for comparison

Standard errors are adjusted for clustering on the cluster level in the model mentioned in equation (4).

Analysis of quintile movement of MPCE (non-health): To assess the association between affiliation in CBHI and the economic status of the household, we conducted a marginal effect estimate of logit regression of the direction of quintile shift, in which the household MPCE (non-health) was the dependent variable. The probability of quintile shift was:

$$(QSHIFT)_{ht} = \alpha' \, CBHI_{ht} + \beta' SD_{ht} + \gamma' HE_{ht} + \delta' FIN_{ht1} + \varepsilon_{ht}. \quad ....(5)$$

$QSHIFT_{ht}$ is 1 if the household h experienced an MPCE-non-health-quintile upgrade from pre (t-1) to post (t) invention phase, else 0, for the analysis of upward quintile movement. Similarly, for the analysis of downward quintile movement, $QSHIFT_{ht}$ is 1 if the household experienced a quintile downgrade in the post-intervention period. The vector CBHI comprised three dummy variables indicating whether the household has been insured for two years, one year or zero years (else uninsured). A household's economic status was assumed to depend on its socio-demographic status (SD), represented by the caste dummy, highest education level, and whether this was a joint family (joint=1, nuclear=0); recent health events in the family (HE) and existing financial profile (FIN) were looked at through proxies: enrollment in RSBY, having a savings account, having borrowed for non-health reason in the last 12 months, affiliation to another insurance (health, life or crop), and whether household members shared their income to meet day-to-day expenses. Standard errors were adjusted for clustering on the cluster level in the model mentioned in equation (5).

Results

Self-medication as an indicator of healthcare-seeking: In the context of measuring impact of CBHI, a reduction in self-medication among the insured could be viewed as evidence that easier/more affordable access to healthcare for insured persons rendered self-medication less necessary. We examined whether insured people were less inclined to resort to self-medication in non-hospitalization events. Prior to the intervention in 2010, self-medication was more prevalent among the treatment group than the uninsured group, and the difference was significant in Pratapgarh (Table IV). Post-intervention (2013), the DiD value was negative in Pratapgarh and Vaishali, suggesting that the insured group was less likely to self-medicate than the uninsured, but the difference was not significant. In Kanpur-Dehat, the DiD value was negative in 2013, after two years of being insured 16 per cent of the insured reported self-medication, compared to 30.2 per cent in 2010 before insurance cover; the uninsured group in the same location reported 19 per cent in 2013 and 27 per cent in 2010. The DiD regression results also confirmed the findings; the sign of the interaction terms was negative for all three locations.

Financial protection – Borrowing for non-hospitalization events: We examined the impact of being insured by CBHI on hardship financing associated with non-hospitalization events at least once in the 30 days preceding the survey (hospitalizations were not covered everywhere and prevalence rates were very low). Since the relevant unit for borrowing-with-interest was the HH, we compared borrowing of insured HHs (*i.e.* those with at least one person insured in CBHI) to uninsured HHs.

Table IV. Difference-in-difference (DiD) for self-medication among insured and uninsured groups

Group	Year	Pratapgarh	Kanpur Dehat	Vaishali
Not-insured	Pre (2010)	0.135	0.270	0.141
Insured		0.162	0.302	0.165
Not-insured	Post (2013)	0.150	0.191	0.193
Insured		0.157	0.160	0.177
Difference in pre (2010)		0.026 (0.086)	0.032 (0.147)	0.024 (0.175)
Difference in post (2013)		0.008 (0.679)	-0.031 (0.235)	-0.016 (0.481)
Difference-in-difference		-0.019 (0.444)	-0.063* (0.066)	-0.040 (0.161)

Figures in parentheses are P values (Student t test)

In 2010, *i.e.* prior to the intervention, a higher percentage of insured than uninsured HHs borrowed in Kanpur-Dehat and Vaishali, while in Pratapgarh the difference was minimal (Table V). In 2013, after the intervention, a substantially lower-percentage of insured HHs than uninsured HHs reported borrowing: 31.8, 27.7 and 42.5 per cent of insured HHs, compared to 46.1, 51.6 and 52.7 per cent of uninsured HHs, respectively in Pratapgarh, Kanpur-Dehat and Vaishali. Incidence of borrowing was seven percentage points lower among the insured than among the uninsured HHs in Kanpur Dehat, and the difference was significant (P<0.05). Overall, the DiD values were negative for all three locations, indicating that the insured HHs reported less borrowing than the uninsured HHs over time. The DiD was significant (P<0.05) for Kanpur-Dehat and Vaishali.

The interactions between time and treatment dummies were also negative for all three locations and significant for Kanpur-Dehat (P<0.05) and Vaishali (P<0.05). After being insured for two years (*i.e.* in 2013) HHs were less likely to borrow for healthcare costs than in 2010 (the time dummy was negative and significant for all the three locations). Scheduled caste/scheduled tribe HHs were more likely to borrow compared to HHs of a higher caste. Borrowing was positively related to MPCE (non-health) [probably reflecting the improved ability of HHs with higher MPCE (non-health) to obtain credit, but still rather low to require loans]. In Kanpur-Dehat and Vaishali, highest education level in the HH had a negative effect on borrowing. HHs with RSBY cover were more likely to borrow for non-hospitalization events in Pratapgarh and Vaishali. In these two locations, HHs with savings accounts were less likely to borrow than HHs without savings accounts.

Financial protection - Quintile movement of MPCE (non-health): Financial protection was reflected not only in absolute terms but also in the relative position of a household compared to others in the same community. Therefore, we measured the position of a household along the local income distribution in MPCE (non-health) as evidence of impact of health insurance on financial protection. HHs with two consecutive years of insurance by CBHI were 51.8 percentage point more likely to experience quintile upgrade compared to HHs that never joined CBHI in Vaishali (Table VI). In Pratapgarh, after one year of CBHI coverage, HHs were 28.2 percentage point more likely to have a quintile upgrade compared to the uninsured HHs. Among other explanatory variables, SC/ST HHs in Vaishali were more likely to have a quintile upgrade. In Kanpur-Dehat, quintile upgrade was positively associated with the highest education level in the household. On the other hand, having a savings account in Vaishali and past borrowing for non-health purposes were negatively related to quintile upgrade.

As expected, an opposite pattern was observed for downward shift. After two consecutive years of CBHI cover, insured HHs were less likely to experience a downward quintile shift in MPCE (non-health) compared to uninsured HHs; the effect was consistently negative for all three locations, and it was significant in Kanpur Dehat (P<0.05, Beta=-0.607) and in Vaishali (P<0.05, Beta=0.675). The SC/ST HHs had less probability of quintile downgrade compared to

Table V. Difference-in-difference (DiD) for borrowing for non-hospitalization events among insured and uninsured households

Group	Year	Pratapgarh	Kanpur Dehat	Vaishali
Uninsured	Pre (2010)	0.465	0.485	0.481
Insured		0.461	0.516	0.527
Uninsured	Post (2013)	0.334	0.348	0.469
Insured		0.318	0.277	0.425
Difference in pre (2010)		-0.004 (0.884)	0.031 (0.356)	0.046 (0.151)
Difference in post (2013)		-0.014 (0.611)	-0.071 (0.035)	-0.044 (0.154)
Difference-in-difference		-0.011 (0.794)	-0.102 (0.033)	-0.090 (0.043)

Figures in parentheses are P values

Table VI. Marginal effect estimations of shift in monthly per capita expenditure (Non-health) quintiles by households from 2010 to 2013

	Upward shift			Downward shift		
	Pratapgarh	Kanpur Dehat	Vaishali	Pratapgarh	Kanpur Dehat	Vaishali
Duration in community-based health insurance (CBHI)						
Completed two years in CBHI	0.0979	0.120	0.518**	-0.602*	-0.285	-0.675**
	(0.235)	(0.333)	(0.194)	(0.256)	(0.356)	(0.225)
Completed one year in CBHI	0.282	-0.289	-0.136	-0.0658	0.219	-0.0103
	(0.153)	(0.181)	(0.151)	(0.155)	(0.174)	(0.148)
Household socio-economic characteristics						
Scheduled caste/scheduled tribe households (base=Non-scheduled caste/	0.184	0.249	0.341*	-0.375**	-0.394*	-0.498**
scheduled tribe)	(0.129)	(0.158)	(0.135)	(0.132)	(0.165)	(0.142)
Highest level of education	-0.0107	0.0402	-0.00553	0.0114	-0.0176	0.00107
	(0.0176)	(0.0213)	(0.0161)	(0.0177)	(0.0212)	(0.0163)
Household health events						
No of illness in last one month	-0.00369	-0.000895	0.0292	-0.00858	0.0437	-0.0670
	(0.0413)	(0.0485)	(0.0514)	(0.0413)	(0.0480)	(0.0523)
No of hospitalization in last 12 months	-0.116	-0.126	0.0383	0.126	0.160	0.182
	(0.168)	(0.154)	(0.148)	(0.161)	(0.147)	(0.145)
Household financial profile						
Enrolled in *Rashtriya Swastya Bima Yojna* (base=Non-enrolled in	0.200	-0.231	-0.110	-0.228	0.0751	0.0598
Rashtriya Swastya Bima Yojna)	(0.164)	(0.179)	(0.128)	(0.172)	(0.175)	(0.129)
Holder of savings account (base=no savings a/c)	-0.182	-0.140	-0.256	0.0344	-0.0501	0.179
	(0.127)	(0.144)	(0.150)	(0.127)	(0.144)	(0.147)
Borrowed for non-health purposes in last 12 months	-0.484*	-0.0875	-0.327	0.381	0.0329	0.683**
	(0.239)	(0.262)	(0.204)	(0.259)	(0.269)	(0.230)
Has insurance other than community-based health insurance and	0.0926	-0.181	-0.0682	0.0697	0.208	0.00821
Rashtriya Swastya Bima Yojna (other health, crop, life)	(0.152)	(0.167)	(0.166)	(0.151)	(0.163)	(0.163)
Household shares money of all members	0.0510	-0.0921	0.170	0.0561	0.104	-0.0831
	(0.166)	(0.184)	(0.140)	(0.165)	(0.187)	(0.139)
Household is a joint family	0.0480	0.163	0.0433	0.0288	0.0613	-0.0700
	(0.128)	(0.142)	(0.131)	(0.128)	(0.143)	(0.132)
Constant	-0.174	-0.711*	-0.469	-0.884**	-0.679	-0.909**
	(0.296)	(0.356)	(0.247)	(0.313)	(0.361)	(0.267)
Observations	1167	932	1179	1,167	932	1,179

Figures in parentheses are standard error values; $P^{*}<0.05$; $^{**}<0.01$

upper-caste HHs in all three locations. Borrowing for non-health reasons was significantly associated with a household's downward quintile move in Vaishali.

Discussion

The study design of this staggered implementation model of CBHI, following the CRCT rules posited, "Enrolment decisions are intended to be made en-bloc: the members of each SHG must decide either to join the insurance scheme as a group, along with all the members of their households, or not enroll at all"[20]. In reality, this assumption could not be upheld, as this condition was in direct conflict with the voluntary nature of enrollment. This raised an ethical issue. In our experiment, the gap between the assumption embedded in the CRCT design and people's voluntary decision-pattern made it impossible to follow the clusters of treatment and control, because the "insured" cohort included many persons that did not join, rendering meaningless the comparison of the control (uninsured) cohort to the treatment (insured) group that also included many uninsured persons. Other analysts have already voiced similar critique of CRCT on the ground of study design considerations[25,26].

The key to identifying the impact of CBHI was the accurate identification of the treatment group so that it would be composed only of those that were "offered and joined" (OJ), and the control, composed of all other persons that were not insured [including "offered not joined" (ONJ) and "not offered" (NO)]. Moreover, this had to be done separately for each location, because the socio-demographic profiles and the specific benefits in each location[7] were different enough to render any aggregation of the data irrelevant. We solved the correction to the randomization of the treatment and control groups for the purpose of comparison of impact by applying K-PSM, as was previously shown by Gnawali *et al*[27]. Our analysis of impact of CBHI differed in the findings and conclusions from another study[28] that performed the analysis differently.

Impact of CBHI on self-medication: In our dataset, we observed a common denominator to the three study locations in that people self-medicated, which was at least in part independent of the composition of the benefits package. This could reflect people's behavioural choice to first self-medicate and consider approaching professional medical assistance only afterwards. In that framing, we examined self-medication in the light of a hypothesis that insured people would reduce that practice when insurance facilitated access to healthcare. We confirmed that the morbidity patterns of the insured population did not change over the study period (data not shown). Our findings indicated that the insured population reduced its self-medication, and as this effect increased with the length of the period of insurance, it appeared as an impact of insurance status. The more positive attitude toward seeking medical help went hand-in-hand with that change.

Impact of CBHI on financial protection: The enrolled members reported higher incidence of illness before enrollment/without CBHI and a slightly lower income, which suggested a higher propensity toward hardship financing. A drop in health-related borrowing of HHs was observed among the insured, which was not apparent among the uninsured. The probability of an insured HH to benefit from quintile upgrade increased, and the risk of quintile downgrade decreased after being insured for two years. The association between being insured and economic mobility could be a direct effect related to the money saved during financing of ambulatory care. It could also be something else: perhaps being protected by insurance increased the likelihood of a HH to invest in productive assets or education that could increase income. It could be possible that the association between insurance and quintile-shift was not a cause-effect relationship, and more research might reveal whether this was a reflection of lifestyle choices (*e.g.* new enterprises that improve financial status).

Our demonstration that CBHI reduces self-medication while providing financial protection has implications for theoretical, ethical, policy and practice considerations. From a theory perspective, our results suggest that the role of the insured population in selecting package design and pricing, and their ability to favour benefits that were likely to reduce hardship financing uphold the arguments of Dror and Firth[29] about demand. From an ethical perspective, the use of CRCT in our experiment implied withholding access of some people to benefits, and thus may not be the most suited research design. From a policy perspective, the assertion that being covered by CBHI (*i.e.* by voluntary, contributory, non-subsidized health insurance that was governed locally and designed by and for specific communities) had a positive impact on its members sets a rational foundation for policymakers to support the expansion of CBHI. From a practice perspective, the evidence on the positive impact of CBHI points to an option to improve healthcare-related financial protection and generate untapped contributions for health insurance, by catalyzing demand through CBHI.

Our study had certain limitations. The CRCT rules assumed that enrollment decisions would be *en-bloc* (which could be quasi-involuntary): all members of each SHG, along with all the members of their HHs, would have to join the insurance as a group, or not enroll at all. This assumption was inoperable, as many households in the control groups wanted to join instantly, and many in the treatment cohorts did not join. The process of randomization of CRCT thus did not work as planned. This introduced a limitation on impact evaluation. Similar observations have been made earlier[25,26]. As our intervention required that the insured group would be involved in the design and pricing of their benefits packages, it was foreseeable that each of the three CBHI schemes might choose a different benefits package. Such heterogeneity restricted the choice of indicators for the impact evaluation.

One of the expected outcomes of insurance is the reduction in out-of-pocket (OOP) spending for health. Measuring the impact of insurance was challenged by data that often ignored indirect costs and by the fact that such costs were usually not covered by CBHI. The estimate of reduced borrowing due to CBHI coverage faced a similar challenge. We could obtain information on borrowing with interest, but people failed to properly report the principal amount borrowed separately from the amount of interest paid, especially when amounts were small. This was overcome by choosing binary rather than continuous variables as indicators.

Choosing reduction in self-medication as an impact indicator has its limitation in that such reduction would not eliminate social and cultural aspects, and the information on the amount spent on self-medication was unreliable as consumption of home-made remedies or of previously purchased medicines was often ignored. Therefore, we chose incidence of self-medication as the indicator rather than its cost.

Finally, DiD is the conventional method to estimate the causal effects when a study involves control and treatment groups before and after an intervention. In a non-linear model in DiD, where the outcome variable is binary in nature, the DiD values may not be a full-proof estimator of the true interaction effect. However, DiD is based on certain assumptions (common trend, absence of serial correlation of the outcome variables) that have known limitations, which apply in this study as well. To reduce the limitation in the present analysis, the results obtained from the DiD analysis were cross-checked using logistic regressions.

***Conflicts of Interest*:** None.

References

1. Acharya A, Vellakkal S, Taylor F, Masset E, Satija A, Burke M, *et al.* The impact of health insurance schemes for the informal sector in low- and middle-income countries: A systematic review. *World Bank Res Obs* 2013; *28* : 236-26.
2. Insurance Regulatory and Development Authority (IRDA). *Annual report 2012-13*. New Delhi, India: IRDA; 2013.
3. Panda P, Chakraborty A, Dror DM. Building awareness to health insurance among the target population of community-based health insurance schemes in rural India. *Trop Med Int Health* 2015; *20* : 1093-107.
4. Dror DM, Hossain SAS, Majumdar A, Koehlmoos TLP, John D, Panda P. What factors affect voluntary uptake of community-based health insurance schemes in low- and middle-income countries? a systematic review and meta-analysis. *PLoS One* 2016; *11* : 1-31.
5. Panda P, Chakraborty A, Dror DM, Bedi AS. Enrolment in community-based health insurance schemes in rural Bihar and Uttar Pradesh, India. *Health Policy Plan* 2014; *29* : 960-74.
6. Binnendijk E, Koren R, Dror DM. A model to estimate the impact of thresholds and caps on coverage levels in community-based health insurance schemes in low-income countries. *Health* 2014; *6* : 822-35.
7. Dror DM, Panda P, May C, Majumdar A, Koren R. "One for all and all for one": consensus-building within communities in rural India on their health microinsurance package. *Risk Manag Health Policy* 2014; *7* : 139-53.
8. Hughes CM, McElnay JC, Fleming GF. Benefits and risks of self medication. *Drug Saf* 2001; *24* : 1027-37.
9. Ahmad A, Patel I, Mohanta G, Balkrishnan R. Evaluation of self medication practices in rural area of town sahaswan at northern India. *Ann Med Health Sci Res* 2014; *4* : S73-8.
10. Chang FR, Trivedi PK. Economics of self-medication: theory and evidence. *Health Econ* 2003; *12* : 721-39.
11. Khan H, Maheen S, Alamgeer GA, Mahmood A, Sarfraz RM, Ashraf Z, *et al.* Determinants of increasing trend of self-medication in a Pakistani community. *Trop J Pharm Res* 2014; *13* : 437-43.
12. Kotwani A, Wattal C, Joshi PC, Holloway K. Irrational use of antibiotics and role of the pharmacist: an insight from a qualitative study in New Delhi, India. *J Clin Pharm Ther* 2012; *37* : 308-12.
13. Ruiz ME. Risks of self-medication practices. *Curr Drug Saf* 2010; *5* : 315-23.
14. Babiarz P, Widdows R, Yilmazer T. Borrowing to cope with adverse health events: liquidity constraints, insurance coverage, and unsecured debt. *Health Econ* 2013; *22* : 1177-98.

15. Binnendijk E, Koren R, Dror DM. Can the rural poor in India afford to treat non-communicable diseases? *Trop Med Int Health* 2012; *17* :1376-85.

16. Binnendijk E, Koren R, Dror DM. Hardship financing of healthcare among rural poor in Orissa, India. *BMC Health Serv Res* 2012; *12* : 23.

17. Ir P, Jacobs B, Meessen B, Damme WV. Toward a typology of health-related informal credit: an exploration of borrowing practices for paying for health care by the poor in Cambodia. *BMC Health Serv Res* 2012; *12* : 383.

18. Pal R. Measuring incidence of catastrophic out-of-pocket health expenditure: with application to India. *Int J Health Care Finance Econ* 2012; *12* : 63-85.

19. Baulch B, Hoddinott J. Economic mobility and poverty dynamics in developing countries. *J Dev Stud* 2000; *36* : 1-24.

20. Doyle C, Panda P, de Poel EV, Radermacher R, Dror DM. Reconciling research and implementation in micro health insurance experiments in India: study protocol for a randomized controlled trial. *Trials* 2011; *12* : 224.

21. Heckman J, Ichimura H, Todd P. Matching as an econometric evaluation estimator. *Rev Econ Stud* 1998; *65* : 261-94.

22. National Sample Survey Organisation. *Key indicators of household consumption expenditure in India*, New Delhi, India: Ministry of Statistics and Programme Implementation; 2013.

23. Khandker SR, Koolwal GB, Samad HA. *Handbook on impact evaluation: quantitative methods and practices*. Washington DC: World Bank Publications; 2010.

24. Heckman J, Ichimura H, Smith J, Todd P. Characterizing selection bias using experimental data. *Econometrica* 1998; *66* : 1017-98.

25. Handley MA, Schillinger D, Shiboski S. Quasi-experimental designs in practice-based research settings: design and implementation considerations. *J Am Board Fam Med* 2011; *24* : 589-96.

26. Green D. Randomized controlled trials: panacea or mirage? poverty power; Available from: *https://oxfamblogs.org/fp2p/randomized-controlled-trials-panacea-or-mirage/*, accessed on October 7, 2015.

27. Gnawali DP, Pokhrel S, Sié A, Sanon M, De Allegri M, Souares A, *et al.* The effect of community-based health insurance on the utilization of modern health care services: evidence from Burkina Faso. *Health Policy* 2009; *90* : 214-22.

28. Raza WA, Poel EVD, Bedi AS, Rutten F. Impact of community-based health insurance on access and financial protection: evidence from three randomized control trials in rural India. *Health Econ* 2016; *25* : 675-87.

29. Dror DM, Firth LA. The demand for (micro) health insurance in the informal sector. *Geneva Pap Risk Insur - Issues Pract* 2014. Available from: *http://www.palgrave-journals.com/gpp/journal/vaop/ncurrent/full/gpp201424a.html*, accessed on September 11, 2014.

Reprint requests: Dr David M. Dror, Micro Insurance Academy, 86, 1st floor, Okhla Industrial Estate, Phase III, New Delhi 110 020, India
e-mail: david@mia.org.in, daviddror@socialre.org

Chapter 21

The Impact of Filipino Micro Health Insurance Units on Income-related Equality of Access to Health Care*

Main Messages

- Data are sourced through a household survey conducted in five MIUs in the Philippines; responses from 804 uninsured households and 740 insured households were used for the study.
- Concentration curves and indices are used as indicators of equality of access to health care relative to household income.
- A novel method "ranking of the ranks" was developed to rank households by income, ensuring that regional differences are neutralized.

Focus Points

- Rich uninsured households have a clear advantage in access to hospitalization and medical consultation compared to poor uninsured households.

---

*This chapter is reproduced from *Health Policy* (2006), **77**(3), 304–317, available at https://www.researchgate.net/publication/7581880_The_impact_of_Filipino_micro_health-insurance_units_on_income-related_equality_of_access_to_healthcare.

- In the insured cohort, there exists almost perfect equality of access to hospitalization and medical consultation between the richer and poorer households.
- Micro health insurance units (MIUs) systematically enhance income-related equality within the population-subgroups they reach.
- Affiliation with MIUs did not increase equality in access to professional attendance in deliveries.

Structured Abstract

Introduction

The key objective of this study is to assess the impact of being insured by MIUs on equality of access to health care among groups with inequitable income distribution. We measure equality by relating income with access to health care. The study examines five groups of households insured by MIUs in the Philippines.

Method

A household survey was conducted in five MIUs in the Philippines. A structured questionnaire was used to collect information on utilization of health services and income for each household in the five selected regions. After filtering out invalid and inconsistent replies, 804 uninsured households and 740 insured households were retained for the study. We used concentration curves (a type of Lorenz curve) and indices as indicators of equality of access to health care relative to household income. These indicators were generated for the insured and uninsured households (150 for each cohort in each region) based on ranking by household income.

Box 1: Interpreting Concentration Curves and Indices

Concentration curves

- The "equality diagonal" corresponds to equality of utilization of the health variable, regardless of income and unadjusted to need.

(*Continued*)

Box 1: (*Continued*)

- Real utilization levels are marked by a curve.
- The greater the distance of the concentration curve from the equality diagonal, below or above it, the greater the inequality.
- A trajectory of the curve below the equality diagonal indicates
  - disproportionately high utilization among the high-income group, and
  - disproportionately low utilization among low-income groups.
- A trajectory of the curve above the equality diagonal indicates
  - excessively low utilization by those with high-incomes, and
  - excessively high utilization by those with low-incomes.

Concentration indices

- Concentration index (CI) is defined as twice the area between the concentration curve and the equality diagonal.
- Values can vary between −1 and +1
  - If the curve is above the diagonal, values are negative.
  - If the curve is under the diagonal, values are positive.
  - If the curve follows exactly the equality diagonal, the value of the CI is 0.

Findings

The analysis revealed a significant effect of household income on access to hospitalization among the uninsured households, but such an effect did not exist among the insured households. Access to medical consultations was negatively correlated with household income among the uninsured and did not exhibit any relation to income among the insured. This implies that rich uninsured households have a clear advantage in accessing these types of health care services compared to poor uninsured households.

On comparing the concentration indices reflecting access to consultation with the indices reflecting equality of access to hospitalization among the uninsured, it appeared that access to consultations is less sensitive to household-income than the decision to hospitalize. This could be attributed to the lower cost involved in a consultation, or higher elasticity of demand for consultation compared to hospitalization.

For the insured cohort, the indices for the same benefits are very close to zero, implying almost perfect equality of access between the richer and poorer households. In other words, the marked differences in household income within each insured cohort notwithstanding, the increased access to health care was equally distributed.

This study also considered the income disparities at the level of each region, by calculating the respective Gini coefficients. The insured cohorts have slightly lower Gini coefficients than the uninsured cohorts. Further investigation revealed that the correlation between Gini coefficients and concentration indices for hospitalization among the uninsured cohorts was not significant. This suggested that the difference in Gini coefficients between insureds and uninsureds was too small to account for the large improvement in income-related equality of access to health care prevalent among the insureds.

Conclusion

There is ample evidence to conclude that MIUs in the Philippines improve income-related equality of access to two major health benefits: hospitalization and medical consultation. The analysis substantiates the claim that although MIUs operate on a small scale, they are capable of addressing income-related differences (within the insured cohorts) in accessing hospitalization (which can cause catastrophic costs) and consultation (which includes referral encounters that generate timely hospitalization). The findings call for appropriate government support for the operation of MIUs as successful suppliers of health insurance.

The impact of filipino micro health-insurance units on income-related equality of access to healthcare☆

David Mark Dror[a,*], Ruth Koren[b], David Mark Steinberg[c]

[a] *Erasmus University Rotterdam/MC, Institute for Health Policy and Management, Netherlands*
[b] *The Sackler Faculty of Medicine, Tel Aviv University, Tel Aviv, Israel*
[c] *Department of Statistics and Operations Research, Tel Aviv University, Tel Aviv, Israel*

Abstract

Background: This study aims to assess the impact of being insured by micro-health insurance units (MIUs) on equality of access to health care among groups with inequitable income distribution. We measure equality by relating income with access to healthcare. The analysis is based on a household survey conducted in five regions in the Philippines in 2002.
Methods: We generated concentration curves and indices (CI) for insured and uninsured households (150 for each cohort in each region). We also elaborated a method to retain the relative income rank of households when data were aggregated across regions, as the regions had quite different nominal income levels.
Results: We found a significant effect of household income on access to hospitalizations among the uninsured households (a positive CI), but no such effect among the insured households (CI close to zero). As regards professionally attended deliveries, an increased tendency of poorer households to deliver at home (CI slightly negative) and a lower rate of deliveries in hospital (CI slightly positive and statistically significant) were reported by both uninsured and insured households. Access to consultations was unrelated to income among the insured (CI close to 0), but negatively correlated with income among the uninsured (a positive and significant CI).
Conclusion: We conclude that MIUs in Philippines improve income-related equality of access to hospitalization and medical consultation in cases of illness. The findings of this study strengthen a claim for government support for the operation of MIUs as successful (albeit micro) suppliers of health insurance.

Keywords: Philippines; Micro-health insurance; Health insurance; Access to healthcare; Income-related equality of access

☆ An earlier version of this paper was presented at the Eighth International Conference on System Science in Health Care, University of Geneva (Switzerland), 1–3 September 2004.
* Corresponding author. Tel.: +41 78 790 6789; fax: +41 22 788 2288.
E-mail addresses: daviddror@socialre.org, d.dror@erasmusmc.nl (D.M. Dror), rkoren@post.tau.ac.il (R. Koren), dms@post.tau.ac.il (D.M. Steinberg).

1. Introduction

The objective of this article is to assess the effect of being insured by micro-health insurance units (MIUs) in the Philippines on equality of access to healthcare. In particular, we look at potential inequalities in access to health care related to income[1] [1–3]. We do not look at the related issue of (in)equity in health care access, which would require standardization of access for need. As we look at access to health care relative to income and not standardized for need, we will follow the usual terminology, and use the term (in)equality.

Unlike international or national comparisons of equality (or equity) that do not offer detailed insights on intra-country differences, or on differences within and across specific groups that are, or are not, covered by health insurance plans (e.g. [4–6]), this article looks at five MIUs which have been in operation for a few years within one and the same country, the Philippines. In this context, the term income-related equality encompasses several distinct meanings: (i) *intra-group equality*: this aspect refers to the impact of income disparity on access to healthcare within a group of persons who are all insured by the same MIU; (ii) *inter-group equality*: this aspect refers to a comparison of a group of persons insured by an MIU with a group of uninsured persons living in the same location in terms of the impact of income disparity on access to healthcare; (iii) *equality of affiliation to insurance*: this aspect looks at the rate of affiliation to insurance by household income; and (iv) *Income-related equality in financing*: this aspect looks at how the premiums charged by the MIUs relate to the members' household income (also known as income-rating). This article deals directly with points (i) and (ii), and indirectly with point (iii). It does not however deal with point (iv), which would require a discussion of wage and taxation policy, a topic well outside the scope of this paper.

Why focus on MIUs? MIUs are operated at the local level and through grassroots initiative. These schemes are often started because there are no alternative health insurance schemes, or as substitutes to other systems that fail to attract the population [7–9]. Recalling the claim of Ogawa et al. [10] that improved equality and solidarity are important predictors for the success of community-based schemes (a conclusion based on the experience of similar schemes founded in the 19th and 20th century in Japan and elsewhere), we seek to examine how MIUs, affiliating a wide range of income groups on a voluntary basis, perform on this count today.

Why look at the Philippines? Because income still plays a dominant role in access to healthcare in the Philippines, considering that national average out-of-pocket spending (OOPS) represented 60.9% of total health expenditure (2002 data) [11]. For people who are not covered by the national health insurance scheme (PhilHealth) – which reported affiliation of around 42% of the population, mostly civil servants and formal sector employees [12] – the rate of OOPS is presumably higher. Another reason to look at the Filipino MIUs is the finding, published recently [13] that average utilization levels of various health care benefits were significantly higher among the insured households compared to the uninsured groups in six locations where MIUs operated. This is all the more relevant if one bears in mind that the two cohorts were comparable in socio demographic parameters that are considered as affecting health care utilization (average age and gender distribution, distance from health facilities, morbidity patterns as assessed by illness-episodes in the 3 months preceding the study. We also compared household income of the two cohorts, on which the picture is however more complex[2]).

In this article, we look at five out of these six Filipino MIUs, and aim to provide new field evidence on the equality impact of being insured. We want to examine whether membership in the MIUs has been accompanied by equality of access with respect to income, alongside the increase in overall access.

If the link between insurance status and equality of access can be demonstrated, there could be policy

[1] Income is of course an important non-need factor. Other non-need factors, such as education or distance from facilities, are ignored here because it was shown that they are virtually identical for the population discussed here.

[2] When the entire sample is aggregated, average income of the insured and uninsured cohorts is similar, but when we look at each location separately we see inconsistent results. In two locations (La union and Guimaras), average income of the insured cohorts was lower than the uninsured; in two other locations (Novaliches and Davao) average income of the insured cohorts was higher; and in one location (Negros Oriental) income of the two cohorts was comparable. See data in Table 2.

implications: at the level of MIUs, the findings could help flag that all members enjoy equal access regardless of household income, an important achievement which in turn could encourage uninsured persons to join, and insured persons to retain membership. And at the government level, the findings could offer the evidence justifying adopting a policy of support of MIUs, in so far as the overriding objective of the government is to increase access of the population to affordable health insurance schemes that succeed to attract the population. The policy relevance exceeds the specific five MIUs studied here, because Filipino MIUs are under pressure from clients to demonstrate their capacity to enhance equality in access to health care more than other insurance carriers, notably the public services, which are perceived as having succeeded insufficiently on this count[3] [17]. This pressure is more consequential due to the fact that affiliation to MIUs is voluntary and can be terminated anytime, as well as due to people's tendency to compare themselves to their extended neighborhood rather than to people residing in a different province or another land. Hence, customers probably look not only at the cost/benefit ratio of the insurance (which may be difficult to measure) but also at how well they fared compared to their poorer and richer neighbors. This framework thus explains our research questions: First, what information on equality within the insured cohort is obtainable by relating income with access to healthcare within the membership of an MIU. Secondly, as affiliation is voluntary, and some neighbors (or households) are insured while others are not, it is relevant to look at how the insured compare to the uninsured in terms of equality of access. The analysis of these issues should strengthen the evidence-base on the performance of MIUs, and contribute to a better understanding of why people choose to be insured by MIUs.

[3] The MIUs studied here developed after the Philippines government introduced a major devolution of services in 1991, which included shifting management and delivery of health services from the National Department of Health to locally elected provincial, city and municipal governments. A recent study claimed that "subsequent to the introduction of devolution, quality and coverage of health services declined in some locations, particularly in rural and remote areas. It was found that in 1992–1997, system effects included a breakdown in management systems between levels of government, declining utilization particularly in the hospital sector, poor staff morale, a decline in maintenance of infrastructure and underfinancing of operational costs of services" [14]. In 1995 the Philippines Health Insurance Corporation was established (also known as PHIC and PhilHealth) [15], with the view to extending health insurance to the entire population by 2014. However, the government has never given PhilHealth monopoly status, and several other insurers are allowed to compete. Also, PhilHealth inducts low-income clients through a special "Indigents Program" only if the premium is subsidized by central and local government units. Many Provinces do not agree to pay this premium while also covering the cost of the Rural Health Units (where the indigents usually receive care). Hence, Rural Health Units are operating under capacity while many rural residents underutilize services [16]. Finally, while the Ministry of Health (chairing the Board of PhilHealth) probably expects PhilHealth to take the lead in implementing the government's policy of universal coverage, other agencies – and large segments of the population – may have different views on this question. Therefore, an unbiased evaluation of the performance of the MIUs is relevant for policy assessment.

2. Methods

2.1. The study

We carried out a household (HH) survey in 2002 in five MIUs in the Philippines (1. Quezon City: the Novaliches Development Cooperative, Inc. Health Care Program (NOVADECI-NHCP) [18]; 2. San Fernando, La Union: ORT Health Plus Scheme (OHPS) [19]; 3. Davao City: the Medical Missions Group Cooperators Health Program (MMG-CHP); 4. Guimaras Island: the Guimaras Health Insurance Program (GHIP); 5. Bayawan, Negros Oriental: Peso for Health Program (PHP)). These MIUs were selected out of a list of 19 schemes that had been identified in a previous study as including a component of health financing (out of a total of 66 community health schemes, most of which did not apply prepayment of a premium irrespective of individual levels of care-seeking) [20]. Selection of MIUs for the current study was also influenced by agreement of the schemes to cooperate with the research team.

We collected information on utilization of health services and income for each household (by following a structured questionnaire, described in Section 3). The focus on household was determined by the fact that the subscription unit for insurance in the MIUs is the household rather than the individual. Also, income is often derived from family micro-enterprises or other activity in the informal economy, and most expenses are made by households as one entity rather than by each

Table 1
Data yield

MIU		Uninsured HH		Insured HH	
		Number of HH	Persons/HH	Number of HH	Persons/HH
1	Novaliches	156	5.7	166	5.4
2	La Union	171	5.3	104	4.8
3	Davao	156	5.2	162	3.7
4	Guimaras	158	5.1	156	5.5
5	Negros Oriental	163	4.9	152	4.7
	Total	804		740	

individual separately. The household income recorded by interviewers is the sum of all income sources derived by all household members, including reported in-kind income.

2.2. *Data yield*

After filtering out invalid and inconsistent replies, 804 uninsured households and 740 insured households were retained. The breakdown of households by sites/MIUs is listed in Table 1. We calculated average household size in each locality, which incidentally was slightly lower in most cases than the national average of five persons per family (in 2000) as reported by the Philippines National Statistical Coordination Board (NSCB) [21].

2.3. *Sampling*

A cross-sectional research design and a two-stage sampling method were used in the selection of insured and uninsured households. The first stage consisted of selecting the five sites: we included MIUs from Northern Philippines (La Union OHPS), Metro Manila (Novaliches Health Care Program), Central Visayas (Guimaras Health Insurance Program and Negros Oriental Peso-for-Health), and Mindanao (Davao Medical Missions Health Program), representing different occupational groups and organizational set-ups. Achieving this heterogeneity with so few MIUs required accepting a purposive selection. In each geographical area, two barangays (Filipino villages) were selected with probabilities proportional to size (population sizes of insured and uninsured households per barangay were obtained for this purpose). The second sampling stage consisted of selecting a random sample of approximately 160 households per site (40 insured households and 40 uninsured households, from each selected barangay). A listing of insured and uninsured households was prepared for this purpose.

2.4. *Concentration curves and indices*

We used concentration curves (a type of Lorenz curve) and indices to examine income-related (in)equality. When applying this method to health variables, the cumulative proportion of the population is generally shown on the *X*-axis, ranked by reported total monthly household income, from lowest to highest; and the cumulative proportion of the health variable is shown on the *Y*-axis. The "equality diagonal" (the line running from the bottom-left to the top-right corner of the graph at 45°) corresponds to equality of utilization of the health variable, regardless of income and unadjusted to need. Real utilization levels are marked by a curve. The greater the distance of the concentration curve from the equality diagonal, below or above it, the greater the inequality. A trajectory of the curve below the equality diagonal indicates disproportionately high utilization among the high-income group (and disproportionately low utilization of low-income groups), and when the curve runs above the equality line it indicates excessively low utilization by those with high-incomes, and vice-versa for low-income households. The concentration index (CI) is defined as twice the area between the concentration curve and the equality diagonal; values can vary between −1 and +1. The values are negative when the curve is above the diagonal and positive when the curve is under the diagonal. If the curve follows exactly the equality diagonal, the value of the CI is 0 [1,22,23].

2.5. Ranking of households in the sample

When analyses were carried out separately for each region, ranking the insured and uninsured households by income was a straightforward exercise, because all households had the same reference nominal mean and median income level. Complications arose, however, when we wished to examine income-related equality on the entire sample. The different regions had different reference income levels, so that simple ranking of all households would have confounded income equality of access with regional differences in access. A ranking method was needed that would neutralize the regional differences. As we could not find a reference to a suitable ranking method, we developed a novel method, presented here for the first time. We converted each household's region-specific ordinal income rank to a common 0–1 scale and then ranked these income scores in aggregating data over regions. Mathematically, let $R_{i,j,k}$ ($k = 1, \ldots, n_{i,j}$) denote the income rank of the kth household in cohort j in locality i. The income rank score for that household was then defined as $R_{i,j,k}/(n_{i,j}+1)$. All households in cohort j were ranked for income by ranking the income rank scores. For example, all households that were in the 2nd quintile within their MIU were also ranked in the 2nd quintile when the whole population was aggregated, ignoring nominal differences in household income across regions. This '*ranking of the ranks*' retains the relative location of each household by reference to other households in the same region, and avoids the distortion in analyzing data in which one and the same HH could be ranked as belonging to different quintiles based on nominal income, once according to its ranking within a single MIU and once, differently, according to its location in the overall sample, thus invalidating conclusions about equality of access relative to the reference context. This method is based on an assumption that (above a poverty threshold) being poor and being rich are relative rather than absolute notions, which can best be understood vis-à-vis a reference group. For instance, the same nominal income (PhP 5000) will be perceived differently in reference to a median income of PhP 3300 (Guimaras uninsured cohort) or to a median income of PhP 25,300 (Novaliches insured cohort).

3. Results

3.1. Income information

The HH survey included a question about total monthly household income; the reported amount was noted. For each site, we tabulated the minimum and maximum values, and calculated median and mean values, as well as the Gini coefficient and its standard error (S.E.) for the insured and uninsured cohorts. With the view to providing an idea on possible selection bias in MIU membership and the success of MIUs in facilitating equality of affiliation to insurance, we also added the official poverty threshold numbers for that province (published by the Philippines Statistical Coordination Board) and the number of households below the poverty threshold for the insured and uninsured cohorts in each site. The data demonstrates that the success of the different MIUs in including the poorest HH is uneven,[4] and the overall social implication of equality of access is of course related to the number of very poor (and very rich) HH in the two cohorts. The data are compiled in Table 2.

The gap in monthly household income in each region can be inferred from the ratio of maximum to minimum household income. The gap is strikingly large for both cohorts. The great discrepancy between the mean and median income and the corresponding Gini coefficients attest to the inequality in income distribution at the level of communities where MIUs operate, with a few households with very high income, and a large number of poor households. As can be seen in Table 2, the Gini coefficients in Guimaras and Negros Oriental (the poorest locations in our sample) are higher than the national reference values provided by the NSCB in 2003 [24]: the Gini coefficient for the Philippines as a whole was 0.4814 in 2000 (a decrease of about 1.4% from 0.4881 in 1997).[5] Income

[4] The picture regarding the % of insured households with income below the poverty line is not consistent: in some MIUs (e.g. Novaliches, Davao) this % is lower in the insured cohort compared to the uninsured; whereas in other MIUs (e.g. La Union, Guimaras, Negros) this % is similar in both groups, or higher among the insured.

[5] In 3 out of 5 MIUs (La Union, Davao, Guimaras) the Gini is significantly lower among the insured compared to the uninsured. The larger homogeneity is however due to inconsistent reasons: in La Union, the lower Gini among the insured is associated with a lower median income, and reflects lower representation of richer house-

Table 2
Income information

		Minimum	Maximum	Mean	Median	Poverty threshold[a]	HH below poverty line (%)	Gini coefficient[b]	S.E.
Monthly income—uninsured households (columns 1–5 in PhP)									
1	Novaliches	400	187500	16255	9700	6546	26.8	0.47946	0.04459
2	La Union	208	170000	11096	6500	5467	41.5	0.54082	0.05929
3	Davao	500	128000	10832	6950	4142	23.7	0.48123	0.04344
4	Guimaras	250	141600	7394	3300	4463	62.7	0.61565	0.07935
5	Negros Oriental	50	73000	6043	3800	3725	49.1	0.49573	0.04666
Monthly income—insured households (columns 1–5 in PhP)									
1	Novaliches	1000	444000	34886	25300	6546	5.4	0.44186	0.04168
2	La Union	500	26733	6514	5000	5467	53.8	0.40716	0.01966
3	Davao	1500	71250	14800	12000	4142	6.2	0.37048	0.01717
4	Guimaras	242	30000	5110	3101	4463	62.8	0.51035	0.02704
5	Negros Oriental	250	92000	6878	4225	3725	44.1	0.52743	0.04941

[a] "Poverty threshold" is the amount of income an individual needed to meet food and non-food needs. The Philippines National Statistical Coordination Board estimated national annual per capita poverty threshold at PhP 11,605 in 2000 (with incidence in 28.4% of families). The poverty threshold varied between provinces and regions: in 2000, the annual provincial poverty threshold in the provinces in which the MIUs were located were: Novaliches (2nd District NCR): PhP 15,710 (incidence in 4.1% of families); La union (Region I): PhP 13,121 (incidence in 33.7% of families); Guimaras (Region VI) PhP 10,712 (incidence in 22.6% of families); Davao del Sur (Region IX): PhP 9,940 (incidence in 18.2% of families); and Negros Oriental (Region VII): PhP 8,940 (the lowest of all regions nationwide) (and incidence in 28.9% of families). The corresponding monthly poverty threshold for a household (of five members, the national average in 2000) was obtained by multiplying by five (persons) and dividing by 12 (months) [25].

[b] The Gini coefficient ranges from a minimum value of zero, when all individuals are equal (everyone has the same income), to a theoretical maximum of one in an infinite population in which perfect inequality is observed (one person has all the income, everyone else has nothing). The Gini coefficient is most easily calculated from unordered size data as the "relative mean difference", i.e. the mean of the difference between every possible pair of individuals, divided by the mean size μ, $G = \sum_{i=1}^{n}\sum_{j=1}^{n}|x_i - x_j|/2n^2\mu$. Alternatively, if the data is ordered by increasing size of individuals, G is given by $G = \sum_{i=1}^{n}(2i - n - 1)x_i^f/n^2\mu$. Source: [30].

distribution, and the corresponding Gini coefficient values, varied markedly by province, from 0.5355 (in Zamboanga del Norte province) to 0.2444 (in Sulu province). The top 10 provincial Gini values ranged from 0.5355 to 0.4734, and the lowest ten from 0.3601 to 0.2444 [24]. It is interesting to note that income distribution within our samples was not more homogeneous than that reported for the entire respective provinces. The data presented in Table 2 confirm that within each region, there are large income differences among the insured households and thus the accumulated data are relevant to examining the (in)equality impact of insurance status.

holds; in Davao, the lower Gini amongst the insured is associated with higher median income, and reflects lower representation of the poorest households. In Guimaras, the higher Gini among the uninsured is not associated with a change in median income, and reflects very few extremely rich HH. The data is thus inconclusive.

It is useful to remember that the level of disparity of income distribution of a province is not always associated with the level of its poverty incidence. For example, the 2nd District of National Capital Region (NCR) was ranked as the 10th least equal area in the country in terms of income distribution but had the lowest poverty incidence in the country. Zamboanga del Norte had the least equal income distribution in 2000, but ranked only 19th poorest province among 81 provinces/areas. Sulu was the poorest province, but a more equal income distribution was observed there [21].

3.2. Applicable benefit packages

One factor that could have considerable impact on utilization among the insured cohorts is their entitlement to benefits from the MIUs. In order to minimize or neutralize possible differences in entitlements, we looked at benefits that all MIUs include in their

Table 3
Income-related equality of access to hospitalization

MIU		Uninsured			Insured		
		CI	S.E.	*p*	CI	S.E.	*p*
1	Novaliches	0.16	0.107	NS	0.0395	0.088	NS
2	La Union	0.369	0.130	0.0044	−0.2757	0.118	0.02
3	Davao	0.239	0.104	0.021	0.0136	0.067	NS
4	Guimaras	0.0451	0.130	NS	0.033	0.149	NS
5	Negros Oriental	0.23	0.103	0.026	0.0926	0.104	NS
Aggregated curve		0.212	0.051	3.58E−05	0.0108	0.044	NS

Note: CI: concentration index; S.E.: standard error of concentration index; p = significance of the difference between CI and 0 calculated by a z-test.

respective benefit package. These include hospitalization, maternity and consultation (the precise qualifying conditions, maxima and user fees differ somewhat between the MIUs). On the other hand, the benefits regarding payment for medicines, lab procedures and medical imaging vary greatly, and therefore we refrained from using these benefits in the analysis.[6]

3.3. Utilization data

3.3.1. Hospitalization

3.3.1.1. Income-related equality of access within each MIU. The first health variable analyzed is the incidence of hospitalization; subjects were asked to report on hospitalization of a household member in the 2 years preceding the interview. Comparison was done by z-test for the aggregated CI. The analyzed results are presented in Table 3.

The results show that the incidence of hospitalization among the uninsured households is related to household income (less frequent among the poorer uninsured households compared to the richer ones). The concentration indices were positive for the uninsured households in all locations, and in three out of the five sites they were significantly different from zero. On the other hand, for the insured cohorts the CI were lower than those for the uninsured cohort in all cases, and not significantly larger than zero. Furthermore, in one MIU, La Union, the CI value obtained for the insured group was significantly lower than zero, indicating higher prevalence of hospitalization among the poorer households. One possible explanation for this higher prevalence might be higher morbidity among the lower-income insured families, another might be higher expressed need, etc. We do not have direct evidence supporting either explanation.

We looked also at the entire sample, by applying the 'ranking of the ranks' procedure. The results (see the last row of Table 3 and Fig. 1(f)) accentuate the conclusion described above: the concentration curve for the aggregated uninsured cohort lies below the equality diagonal, the concentration index is positive and highly significant. This signifies a disproportionate concentration of the access to hospitalization among the wealthier households. On the other hand, for the insured households, the concentration curve virtually overlaps the equality diagonal, the concentration index does not statistically differ from zero, and the meaning is that hospitalization is demonstrably more equally distributed among the insured households. The difference in CI between insureds and uninsureds is significant, with $p = 0.003$ (z-test).

3.3.1.2. Professional attendance at deliveries. The survey included a question on deliveries that had occurred in the household during the 5 years preceding the interview. We were interested in information on the level of professional attendance, but such a question could have been very vulnerable to recall-bias. As an alternative, households were asked to specify

[6] We are aware that inclusion of benefits such as medicines and tests might render MIU more attractive, and thus impact the composition of the insured population. However, this study set out to establish the degree of income-related equality of access among the insured, rather than attribute relative values to various causes that might explain this result.

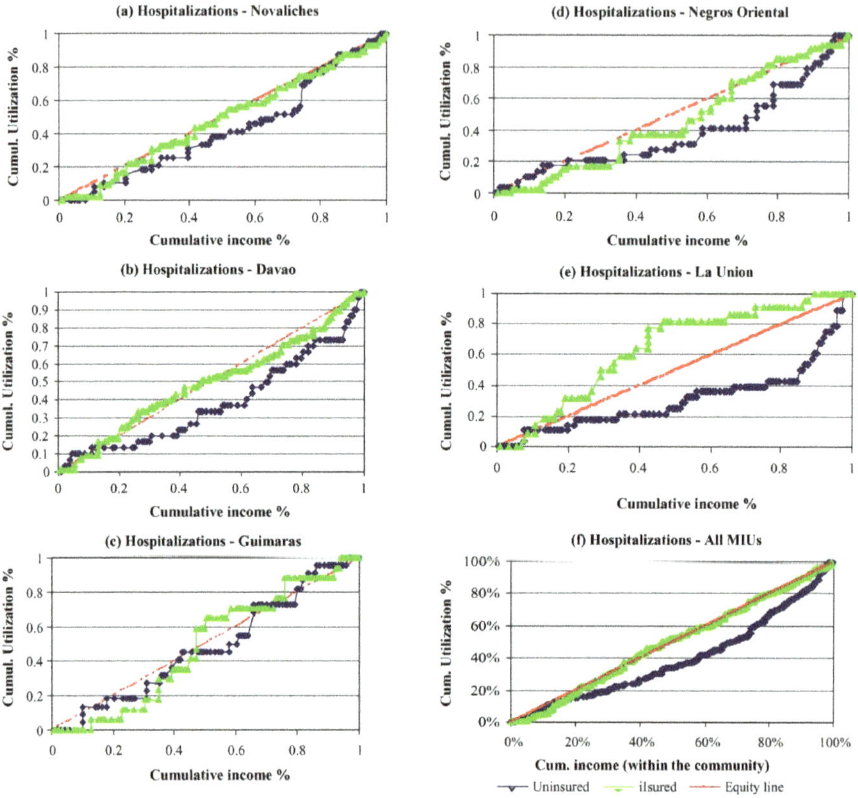

Fig. 1. Series 1 figures—income-related equality of access to hospitalization.

the location where each delivery had taken place: at home, in a clinic or in a hospital. We chose to ignore the deliveries in clinics, because levels of professional attendance vary widely (from presence of a midwife to physician attendance) and there was no reliable way of identifying the exact level of care given. On the other hand, deliveries at home and in hospital were distinct and coherent alternatives, which we retained as proxy indicators for level of professional attendance at deliveries.

We included in this analysis only households with one or more delivery within the specified time frame. The number of households reporting deliveries was too small for reliable statistical analysis within each region. We therefore aggregated the data for the entire sample. Households could have one or more delivery during the period, and these could occur in different locations (home or hospital). Therefore, we assigned each household a score (between 0 and 1), representing the proportion of deliveries in the specified location.

Table 4
Data yield for location of delivery

MIU		Uninsured				Insured			
		HH with[a] deliveries	Delivery in hospital	Delivery at home	Median income[b]	HH with[a] deliveries	Delivery in hospital	Delivery at home	Median income
1	Novaliches	70	30	28.1	8000	48	25.9	11.8	29500
2	La Union	62	41.5	15.5	6050	45	24.7	15.3	5867
3	Davao	54	35.1	8.8	6000	59	41.2	9.3	12165
4	Guimaras	47	16.5	27.2	2500	53	17	35	2600
5	Negros Oriental	51	13.6	37.4	3500	44	22	22	3920

[a] The number of deliveries includes, in addition to those counted "at home" and "in hospital", also deliveries in clinics (not shown in this table). The highest score can be 1 (the numbers in the table refer to households-with-deliveries rather than deliveries). Hence, the two columns do not add up to the total number of households-with-deliveries. Incidentally, most households that reported more than one delivery tended to choose the same location for all deliveries (this was true both for delivery at home, at hospital or in a clinic).

[b] Median income reported here is calculated only for households that reported at least one delivery in the period, and these values differ from median income for the entire population of each MIU which were reported in Table 2.

Table 5
Income-related equality in access to professional care for delivery

Location of delivery	Uninsured			Insured		
	CI	S.E.	p	CI	S.E.	p
At home	−0.1015	0.0377	0.0072	−0.0986	0.043	0.022
In hospital	0.1034	0.0323	0.0014	0.0777	0.0321	0.016

CI: concentration index, S.E.: standard error of concentration index. Significance of the difference between CI and 0 (calculated by a z-test).

Income ranks were computed within each region for each household with a delivery and were then aggregated across regions using our 'ranking of ranks' (see Section 2 for details). The income ranks and delivery location scores were then used to derive concentration indices and curves for assessing equality with respect to professional attendance at deliveries. The data are shown in Table 4, and the analysis is shown in Table 5 and Fig. 2(a) and (b).

Based on the data in Table 4, we know that 41.2% of uninsured households in the aggregated sample chose deliveries at home (compared to 37.5% among the insured households). Although the home delivery rates seem high, they are significantly lower than the 65.5% that was estimated by a World Bank study as the national rate [25]. The income-related concentration index for deliveries at home obtained in the said national survey was −0.199, indicating that

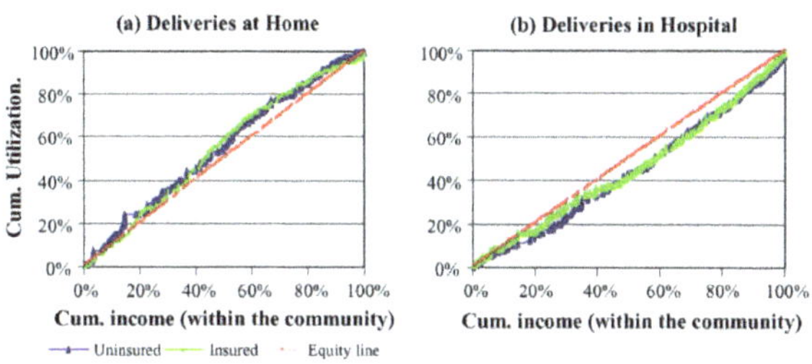

Fig. 2. Series 2 figures—income-related equality of access to delivery in hospital and at home.

Table 6
Income-related equality of access to consultation with a medical doctor

MIU		Uninsured			Insured		
		CI	S.E.	p	CI	S.E.	p
1	Novaliches	0.11	0.093	NS	0.0726	0.075	NS
2	La Union	0.1635	0.094	0.082	−0.127	0.071	0.072
3	Davao	0.2208	0.084	0.008	0.0245	0.063	NS
4	Guimaras	0.03105	0.083	NS	0.139	0.085	NS
5	Negros Oriental	0.0514	0.09	NS	−0.0583	0.089	NS
	Aggregated data	0.115	0.043	0.074[a]	0.0162	0.0344	NS

CI: concentration index; S.E.: standard error of concentration index; p = significance of the difference between CI and 0 (calculated by a z-test. NS: $p > 0.1$).

[a] We used the z-test to examine the significance of the difference of the CIs between the insured and uninsured cohorts significance; the result was marginally significant ($p = 0.072$).

income-related discrepancies in access reported in our study were less severe than in the country as a whole. These two indicators strengthen the impression that the sites that participated in this HH survey are not at the bottom of the pile on a national scale.

The concentration indices for delivery at home are negative and statistically significant. The concentration curve runs above the equality diagonal (see Fig. 2(a)), indicating disproportionate concentration of home deliveries among poorer households. As can be expected, for the complementary information on deliveries in hospital, the index is positive and the curve is below the equality line (see Fig. 2(b)). Interestingly, the difference between insureds and uninsureds is statistically insignificant, and the deviation from the equality line is small for both cohorts. This could reflect limitations of the benefit payable for delivery in hospital under the prevailing coverage, or distortions due to deliveries in clinics, which are not reflected here, or another parameter, such as preference among the poorer households for delivery at home with attending healthcare worker. This preference may not be solely related to the higher cost of hospital deliveries.

With a view to comparing the effect of household income on illness-related hospitalization versus delivery in hospital, we juxtaposed the absolute numbers of the concentration indices obtained for hospital delivery (0.1034 and 0.0777, respectively, for the uninsured and insured cohorts, Table 5) with those obtained for hospitalization in case of illness (0.212 and 0.0108, Table 3). Among uninsured households the CI are higher for illness-related hospitalization, and for the insured households the CI are higher for hospital deliveries. Being insured makes a large difference with respect to income-related equality of hospitalization, but only a small difference with respect to income-related equality of hospital births. We therefore conclude that the impact of household-income is much weaker in the case of deliveries than in the case of hospitalization. These findings also suggest that the choice of location of delivery (at home or in hospital) is probably influenced by other considerations that do not apply equally to hospitalization due to illness.

3.3.1.3. Consultation with a doctor. Access to consultation with a physician during the 2 years preceding the interview was noted, and the numbers analyzed by applying the same techniques. The results are presented in Table 6 and Fig. 3. The concentration indices for access to consultation are smaller for the insured cohorts than for the uninsured in four out of the five provinces; this is similar to what was observed in the case of hospitalization. The effect of insurance is even clearer in the aggregated data: the value of the

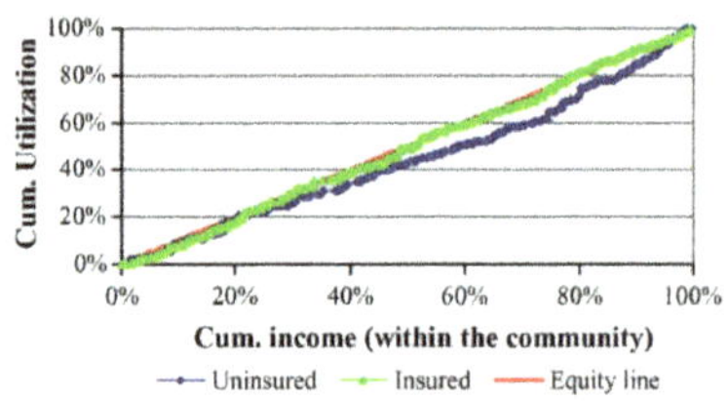

Fig. 3. Income-related equality of access to medical consultation.

concentration index for the uninsured cohort (0.115 and highly significant – see last line of Table 6) is reduced by more than seven-fold, and is statistically insignificant for the insured cohort. The significance of the difference between the two aggregated CI is $p = 0.07$ (z-test used).

We also compared the data on equality of access to medical consultation with the data on hospitalization (Tables 3 and 6). The concentration indices reflecting access to consultation of uninsured households tend to be smaller than the indices reflecting equality of access to hospitalization. This difference is marginally significant ($p = 0.085$ by unpaired t-test) and also apparent in the aggregated data. We interpret this result to imply that access to consultation is less sensitive to household-income than the decision to hospitalize. This finding may be due to the lower cost involved in a consultation, or higher elasticity of demand for consultation compared to hospitalization.

4. Discussion

The literature offers ample confirmation that a household's out-of-pocket spending for health care can reach catastrophic levels (defined as the proportion of households spending more than 20% of all expenditure) when a family member is seriously ill [26–28]. In countries with high OOPS such as the Philippines, the HH can reach ruinous levels not only in cases of a single disastrous disease in the family, but also when the aggregate OOPS of the family is high due to repeated episodes of less-severe illnesses. Therefore, there can be no doubt that income plays an important role in determining access to healthcare, particularly among economically weaker population segments. This study adds to the knowledge on equality of access to health care by examining five groups of households insured by MIUs. The interest in looking at the equality effect of these MIUs is nourished firstly by a quest to know whether the increase in utilization of insured households in these same MIUs, reported recently [13], is equally distributed or whether it just offers "more to those who have more already". Furthermore, this concern with intra-group equality of access is pertinent because it is one of the few ways to validate that MIUs have not introduced, perhaps inadvertently, concealed forms of income-related inequality through limitations or qualifying conditions in their benefit packages. Thirdly, this investigation offers health policy-makers the evidence on equality of access within MIUs, which they have not had so far, in order to accomplish their role. This role was eloquently asserted by Ekman [29] "Health policy-makers are faced with competing alternatives for systems of health care financing" ... and "need to be better informed as to both the costs and the benefits of implementing various financing options". For this reason we feel that the evidence submitted in this article is relevant to a wider audience than merely the specific MIUs, and can contribute to a broader assessment of the cost-benefit of these schemes. This is particularly valid for the Philippines, where on the one hand there is great regional variance in income and in access to healthcare, and on the other hand MIUs offer health insurance to some segments of the population.

In addition to assessment of equality among the insured households, we also checked inter-group equality, by comparing the insured cohorts in all locations with groups of uninsured households residing in the same communities.

Concentration indices and concentration curves are used in this study as indicators of equality of access to healthcare relative to HH income. These indicators were calculated for the insured and the uninsured groups based on ranking by household-income. In the absence of incontrovertible measurements of differences in the need for health services according to income level, it is difficult to normalize utilization for need. We pose no tacit assumption on the question whether need is identical for all income levels (but we observe that response to such need among the insured cohorts was shown to be unrelated to income, whereas the utilization among the uninsured cohorts was income-related). The ranking of each household within its reference income group was retained also for calculations that involved the entire sample population (using 'Ranking of the ranks'—see Section 2). The 'ranking of ranks' makes it possible to aggregate data from the five different MIUs, each with a different income level, without losing or distorting the main focus of this study.

The analysis confirms significant positive concentration indices in the uninsured cohort for access to hospitalization and to medical consultation, which means that rich uninsured households have a clear advantage in accessing these types of healthcare services compared to poor uninsured households.[7] On the other hand, in the insured cohort, the indices for the same benefits are very close to zero, which means almost perfect equality of access between the richer and poorer households. This finding allows us to conclude that in spite of the pronounced differences in HH income within each insured cohort, the increased access to health care was equally distributed. We also observed that the CI among the uninsured is significantly larger than the CI among the insured for hospitalization, and the difference is borderline significant for consultations. This finding suggests a cause-&-effect relationship between insurance status and equitable access at the level of the MIUs included in this study. One plausible explanation for this outcome is the strong impact of insurance as a mechanism that flattens differences between rich and poor, because once the premium is pre-paid the determination of rights to benefits is a function of need rather than of cost.

As stated earlier in this paper but in a different context, this study focuses directly on income-related equality of access, namely on the effect of household income on health care utilization. An assessment of equity would have required adjustment of utilization to needs. Recalling the analysis of incidence of episodes of illness, and a comparison of sociodemographic parameters reported by insured and uninsured cohorts in these MIUs [13], we assume that need is very similar among the insured and uninsured cohorts for hospitalization and consultation data. On maternity, the need is limited to those with pregnancy, and only those respondents were included in the analysis. One must nevertheless recognize that awareness to health needs may impact utilization, and that the parameters stated above are not directly associated with awareness to needs. Hence, one cannot exclude the possibility that households that are more aware of their healthcare needs might more likely become insured by MIUs. Hence, there is a possibility of an a priori confounding difference that could account to a small extent for the higher homogeneity in healthcare utilization within the insured groups. Yet, in the face of the finding that the concentration indices observed among the uninsured are positive, is it really reasonable to uphold a claim that this result stems from increased heath needs among the households with higher income? Such a deduction would run counter to many studies that have established an association between poverty and poor health, rather than an association between richness and illness, particularly for the kinds of services we observe here (which exclude comfort treatments and comfort drugs).

This study also looked at income disparities at the level of each region, by calculating the respective Gini coefficients. It is interesting to note that the Gini coefficients we calculated are within the range of the top 10 Gini coefficients per province published by the Philippines National Statistical Coordination Board [24]. However, the insured cohorts have slightly lower Gini coefficients than the uninsured cohorts. This finding also begs an explanation; one could hypothesize that as lower Gini coefficients mean smaller differences in absolute income, and as higher utilization was recorded with the insured, it could theoretically follow that similarly ranked insured households should have higher income than uninsured ones in the same community, which would explain, at least partly, the improved equality of utilization among the insured. If this were true, we would also expect smaller Gini coefficients among the uninsured cohorts to imply higher equality of utilization. However, a comparison of the data in Tables 2 and 3 reveals that the correlation between Gini coefficients and concentration indices for hospitalization among the uninsured cohorts was not significant, suggesting that the difference in Gini coefficients between insureds and uninsureds was too small to explain the large improvement in income-related equality of access to healthcare prevalent among the insureds.

5. Conclusions

This analysis strongly suggests that insurance status with MIUs improved the equality of access to two major health benefits: hospitalization and medical consultation. On the other hand, this study suggests that affiliation with MIUs did not increase equality in access to professional attendance in deliveries; the study did not have the necessary data to examine equality in drug utilization.

[7] These findings are consistent with some national data; for instance, the national concentration index for infants that were not vaccinated against measles is negative and highly significant (CI = −0.41471) or the concentration index for national death rate of children under 5 (CI = −0.19083[0]) [24].

This evidence substantiates the claim that even when health insurance is operated on a small scale by MIUs, it nevertheless remedies (within the insured cohorts) income-related differences in access to certain types of healthcare, notably hospitalization (which can cause catastrophic costs) and consultation (which includes the referral encounters that generate timely hospitalization); the comparison with unequal access recorded among the uninsured cohorts reinforces the conclusion that insurance by MIUs contributes to income-related equality. The inverse correlation between relative income and relative utilization found among the uninsured is absent in the insured cohorts. In no case were the insured cohorts worse off than the uninsured from the point of view of income-related equality, indicating that there is better income-related equality of access among MIU affiliates regardless of their income. We conclude that the information obtained in this HH survey confirms that MIUs systematically enhance equality within the population-subgroups they reach. This systematic gain in income-related equality seems inherent to the operation of health insurance.

This finding provides tangible proof not only that the condition of the poor who join these voluntary substitutive micro-health insurance units is improved compared to their condition when they are uninsured, but also that this improvement of access of low-income levels did not penalize other income levels. This finding can serve as a strong argument in the efforts of MIUs to draw new affiliates and to retain existing ones, because it shows that risk solidarity and self-help are affordable, functional and a "win-win" formula for all persons that participate. Finally, although this study does not aim to make recommendations at the national level, it nevertheless seems self-explanatory that policy-makers should probably be very interested in the results of this study, confirming that MIUs make a contribution to more equal access to healthcare. Considering that the government would probably incur lower cost in supporting MIUs than in operating health insurance, and considering the remarkable equality score of MIUs established in this study, policy-makers might wish to adopt a proactive policy of supporting the operation of MIUs, with the view to advancing the extension of health insurance coverage at attractive cost/benefit.

Acknowledgements

We gratefully acknowledge a grant from the Ford Foundation (Manila office) to carry out the HH survey in Philippines in 2002. We acknowledge the cost-sharing by the GTZ programme (German assistance to the Philippines health sector) of the HH survey in Guimaras. We recognize project management and additional resources provided by the *Social Re* project. Jesus Sarol, PhD, Marylin Lorenzo, DrPH, Elmer Soriano, MD and Rosebelle Azcuna, MSc directed the HH survey and collected the data. Ilana Galernter and Yulia Gavrilov provided assistance with the statistical analysis. Anonymous peer-reviewers provided useful comments. Thanks to all.

References

[1] Pan American Health Organization (PAHO). Measuring Health Inequalities: Gini Coefficient and Concentration Index. Epidemiology Bulletin 2001;22(1):3, http://www.paho.org/English/SHA/EB_v22n1.pdf.

[2] Macinko JA, Starfield B. Annotated Bibliography on Equity in Health 1980–2001. International Journal for Equity Health 2002;1:1, doi:10.1186/1475-9276-1-1, http://www.equityhealthj.com/content/1/1/1.

[3] Morris S, Sutton M, Gravelle H. Inequity and inequality in the use of health care in England: an empirical investigation. Social Science and Medicine 2005;60:1251–66.

[4] van Doorslaer E, Wagstaff A, van der Burg H, Christiansen T, De Graeve D, Duchesne I, et al. Equity in the delivery of health care in Europe and The US. Journal of Health Economic 2000;19(5):553–83.

[5] Navarro V, editor. The political economy of social inequalities: consequences for health and the quality of life. Amityville, NY: Baywood; 2001.

[6] Wagstaff A. Inequalities in health in developing countries: swimming against the tide? Policy Research Working Paper 2795. Washington, DC: World Bank; March 2002.

[7] Dau, R.K. Social security coverage through micro-insurance schemes in Tanzania, Paper presented at the session on "Extending social security coverage" at Meeting of Directors of Social Security Organizations in English-speaking Africa organized by the International Social Security Association, Banjul, The Gambia, 7–9 October 2003 (Doc. ISSA/AFRICA/RM/BANJUL/2003/2-TANZANIA). http://www.issa.int/pdf/banjul03/2dau.pdf #search='why do people join micro.

[8] Werner D. Communication as if People Mattered: Adapting Health Promotion and Social Action to the Global Imbalances of the 21st Century, internet source (PDF document, p. 7) last updated 23 February 2004. http://phmovement.org/pdf /background/phm-pha-background5.pdf.

[9] International Labour Office: Social security: Issues, challenges and prospects, Report VI to the 89th Session of the International Labour Conference, Geneva, June 2001. ISBN 92-2-111961-0, ISSN 0074-6681 http://www.ilo.org/public/english/standards/relm/ilc/ilc89/rep-vi.htm#The problem of non-coverage.

[10] Ogawa S, Hasegawa T, Carrin G, Kawabata K. Scaling up community health insurance: Japan's experience with the 19th century Jyorei scheme. Health Policy and Planning 2003;18(3):270–8.

[11] World Health Report; 2005. Annex 5, http://www.who.int/nha/country/whrannex/en/.

[12] For PhilHealth membership please see PhilHealth website: http://www.philhealth.gov.ph/membership.htm; For total population figure please see: http://www.odci.gov/cia/publications/factbook/geos/rp.html#People Both last browsed 21.5.2005.

[13] Dror DM, Soriano E, Sarol J, Azcuna R, Lorenzo M, Koren R. Field based evidence of enhanced healthcare utilization among persons insured by micro-health insurance units in Philippines. Health Policy 2005;73(3):263–71.

[14] Grundy J, Healy V, Gorgolon L, Sandig E. Overview of devolution of health services in the Philippines. Rural and Remote Health [electronic resource] 2003;3:220, http://rrh.deakin.edu.au.

[15] Public Act No. 7875, February 14, 1995. The National Health Insurance Act Of 1995. http://www.doh.gov.ph/ra/ra_7875.htm.

[16] Schneider P, Racelis R. The impact of PhilHealth indigent insurance on utilization, cost, and finances in health facilities in the Philippines. Bethesda, MD: The Partners for Health Reformplus Project, Abt Associates Inc.; 2004, http://www.phrplus.org/Pubs/Tech039_fin.pdf.

[17] "Rationale" section of the German Support To The Philippine Health Sector, Social Health Insurance Component. http://www.gtzshi-ph.org/shine.html.

[18] International Labour Office: The Novadeci Health Care Programme: Case Study. Geneva, September 2001. Social Security Department [http://www.ilo.org/public/english/protection/socsec/step/download/29p1.pdf].

[19] International Labour Office: ORT Health Plus Scheme in the Province of La Union, Philippines: A case study of a community based health micro-insurance scheme. Geneva, 2002. Social Security Policy and Development Branch. http://www.ilo.org/public/english/protection/socsec/step/download/26p1.pdf.

[20] Flavier J, Soriano E, Nicolay A. Social health insurance in the Philippines: a review of the context. In: Dror DM, Preker AS, editors. Social reinsurance: a new approach to sustainable community health financing. Washington: World Bank and ILO; 2002. p. 339.

[21] Philippines National Statistical Coordination Board. http://www.nscb.gov.ph/poverty/2000/00povth1.asp; http://www.nscb.gov.ph/poverty/2000/povertyprov.asp; http://www.nscb.gov.ph/poverty/2000/00povin1.asp.

[22] World Bank: Technical Note #7, The concentration index. In Quantitative Techniques for Health Equity Analysis; 2004. http://www.worldbank.org/poverty/health/wbact/health_eq_tn07.pdf.

[23] World Bank: Technical Note #6, Concentration curves. In Quantitative Techniques for Health Equity Analysis; 2004. http://www.worldbank.org/poverty/health/wbact/health_eq_tn06.pdf.

[24] Philippines National Statistical Coordination Board. http://www.nscb.gov.ph/poverty/2000/ot_gini.asp.

[25] Gwatkin D, Rustein S, Johnson K, Pande R, Wagstaff A. Socio-Economic Differences in health, nutrition and population in the Philippines + Tables in PovertyNet library. Washington: World Bank; May 2000. http://poverty.worldbank.org/library/view/4245/; http://siteresources.worldbank.org/INTPAH/Resources/Publications/Country-Reports/philippines.xls'.

[26] World Bank: Technical Note # 18: Catastrophic health care payments. In Quantitative Techniques for Health Equity Analysis; 2004. http://www.worldbank.org/poverty/health/wbact/health_eq_tn18.pdf.

[27] Wagstaff A, van Doorslaer E. Catastrophe and impoverishment in paying for health care, with applications to Vietnam 1993–1998. Health Economics 2003;12:921–33.

[28] Falkingham Jane. Poverty, out-of-pocket payments and access to health care: evidence from Tajikistan. Social Science and Medicine 2004;58:247–58.

[29] Ekman Björn. Community-based health insurance in low-income countries: a systematic review of the evidence. Health Policy and Planning 2004;19:249–70.

[30] Weisstein EW, Damgaard. CH. Gini Coefficient. In Math World A Wolfram Web Resource. http://mathworld.wolfram.com/GiniCoefficient.html.

Author Index

H

I

L

S

Subject Index

I

Q

R

S

Lightning Source UK Ltd.
Milton Keynes UK
UKHW022158231218
334474UK00002B/16/P

9 789813 238473